Fodor's 4th Edition
W9-CFS-545

South Florida

The Guide
for All Budgets

Completely
Updated

Where to Stay, Eat,
and Explore

On and Off
the Beaten Path

When to Go,
What to Pack

Maps, Travel Tips,
and Web Sites

Excerpted from *Fodor's Florida*

Fodor's Travel Publications • New York, Toronto, London, Sydney, Auckland
www.fodors.com

II

Fodor's South Florida

EDITORS: Shannon Kelly, Melissa Klurman

Editorial Contributors: Nancy Orr Athnos, Kathy Foster, Satu Hummasti, Lynne Helm, Jen Karetnick, Diane P. Marshall, Karen Schlesinger, Gretchen Schmidt, Chelle Koster Walton, Matthew Windsor

Editorial Production: Kristin Milavec

Maps: David Lindroth, *cartographer;* Rebecca Baer and Bob Blake, *map editors*

Design: Fabrizio La Rocca, *creative director;* Guido Caroti, *art director;* Jolie Novak, *senior picture editor;* Melanie Marin, *photo editor*

Cover Design: Pentagram

Production/Manufacturing: Colleen Ziemba

Cover Photo (South Beach, Miami): Jack Hollingsworth

Copyright

Fourth Edition

ISBN 1–4000–1052–7

ISSN 1526–2219

Important Tip

Although all prices, opening times, and other details in this book are based on information supplied to us at press time, changes occur all the time in the travel world, and Fodor's cannot accept responsibility for facts that become outdated or for inadvertent errors or omissions. So **always confirm information when it matters,** especially if you're making a detour to visit a specific place.

Special Sales

Fodor's Travel Publications are available at special discounts for bulk purchases for sales promotions or premiums. Special editions, including personalized covers, excerpts of existing guides, and corporate imprints, can be created in large quantities for special needs. For more information, contact your local bookseller or write to Special Markets, Fodor's Travel Publications, 1745 Broadway, New York, NY 10019. Inquiries from Canada should be directed to your local Canadian bookseller or sent to Random House of Canada, Ltd., Marketing Department, 2775 Matheson Boulevard East, Mississauga, Ontario L4W 4P7. Inquiries from the United Kingdom should be sent to Fodor's Travel Publications, 20 Vauxhall Bridge Road, London SW1V 2SA, England.

PRINTED IN THE UNITED STATES OF AMERICA

10 9 8 7 6 5 4 3 2 1

CONTENTS

1 **Destination: South Florida** *1*

2 **Miami and Miami Beach** *9*

3 **The Everglades** *85*

4 **Fort Lauderdale and Broward County** *110*

5 **Palm Beach and the Treasure Coast** *145*

6 **The Florida Keys** *197*

7 **Portraits of South Florida** *258*

Index *264*

Maps

ON THE ROAD WITH FODOR'S

A TRIP TAKES YOU OUT OF YOURSELF. Concerns of life at home completely disappear, driven away by more immediate thoughts—about, say, what marvels will beguile the next day, or where you'll have dinner. That's where Fodor's comes in. We make sure that you know all your options, so that you don't miss something that's around the next bend just because you didn't know it was there. Mindful that the best memories of your trip might have nothing to do with what you came to South Florida to see, we guide you to sights large and small all over the region. You might set out to laze on the beach, but back at home you find yourself unable to forget the sounds and smells of the vibrant Española Way market in Miami or celebrating the sunset in Key West. With Fodor's at your side, serendipitous discoveries are never far away.

About Our Writers

Our success in showing you every corner of Florida is a credit to our extraordinary writers. Although there's no substitute for travel advice from a good friend who knows your style, our contributors are the next best thing—the kind of people you would poll for travel advice if you knew them.

Nancy Orr Athnos, who updated Smart Travel Tips A to Z, has more than 20 years' experience in the publishing industry and spent 12 years at *Southern Living* magazine before starting her own freelance business in 1996. She stays busy writing for local and regional publications, as well as designing Web sites for small businesses.

Travel writer **Kathy Foster,** who has explored almost every spot from Miami to the Keys via bicycle, updated the Exploring, and Outdoor Activities and Sports, and A to Z sections in the Miami and Miami Beach chapter. When not biking, she's at work as an editor for the *Miami Herald*'s feature section.

Jen Karetnick, who updated the Fort Lauderdale and Miami dining sections, is a restaurant critic and columnist for the *Miami New Times* and *New Times Broward/Palm Beach* weekly newspapers.

She is the author of *Around Miami with Kids* (Fodor's) and the forthcoming cookbook *Miami Restaurant Recipes* (Tierra Publications).

Intrepid traveler and intrepid shopper **Diane Marshall** was formerly editor and publisher of the newsletter "The Savvy Shopper: The Traveler's Guide to Shopping Around the World." From her home in the Keys, she has written for numerous travel guides, newspapers, magazines, and on-line services.

Freelance writer **Karen Schlesinger** has been exploring South Florida shopping for more than a decade. She updated the Palm Beach and Miami shopping sections as well as the Fort Lauderdale chapter of this book. A local expert and regular contributor to newspapers, magazines, and books, Karen also has a Web site (theysay.cc)—a source for what's hip and haute in South Florida shopping and fashion. She lives in Ocean Ridge, Florida, with her husband and more than 200 pairs of shoes.

As a writer for travel and trade publications, longtime Miamian **Gretchen Schmidt** loves visiting exotic places. But she's always happy to return to South Florida's cacophony of languages, the perfume of gardenias and frangipani in the air, and the indescribable splendor of the full moon rising over Miami. She contributed to the Nightlife and the Arts section of the Miami chapter.

From her home of 20 years on Sanibel Island, **Chelle Koster Walton** has written and contributed to 10 guidebooks—two of which won Lowell Thomas Awards—and written magazine articles for *FamilyFun, Caribbean Travel & Life, National Geographic Traveler, Arthur Frommer's Budget Travel, Endless Vacation,* the *New York Post,* and other print and electronic media. Walton is cofounder of www.guidebookwriters.com and a member of the Society of American Travel Writers.

As an editor with Miami Lakes–based travel trade publication *Recommend,* **Matt Windsor** has had plenty of time to ponder the byzantine complexities of the South

Florida hotel scene and bring this knowledge to bear in updating the Lodging section of the Miami chapter. He didn't chafe at the idea of writing up the city's hotel day spas, either.

You can rest assured that you're in good hands—and that no property mentioned in the book has paid to be included. Each has been selected strictly on its merits, as the best of its type in its price range.

How to Use This Book

Up front is Smart Travel Tips A to Z, arranged alphabetically by topic and loaded with tips, Web sites, and contact information. Destination: South Florida helps get you in the mood for your trip. Subsequent chapters are arranged regionally. All city chapters begin with exploring information, with a section for each neighborhood (each recommending a good tour and listing sights alphabetically). All regional chapters are divided geographically; within each area, towns are covered in logical geographical order, and attractive stretches of road between them are indicated by the designation En Route. To help you decide what you'll have time to visit, all chapters begin with our writers' favorite itineraries. (Mix itineraries from several chapters, and you can put together a really exceptional trip.) The A to Z section that ends every chapter lists additional resources. At the end of the book you'll find Portraits of South Florida, including an in-depth look at Miami and a Books and Movies section that suggests enriching reading and viewing.

Icons and Symbols

★   Our special recommendations
✕   Restaurant
🏠   Lodging establishment
✕🏠   Lodging establishment whose restaurant warrants a special trip
⚑   Campgrounds
👶   Good for kids (rubber duckie)
☞   Sends you to another section of the guide for more information
✉   Address

☎   Telephone number
☺   Opening and closing times
💲   Admission prices (those we give apply to adults; substantially reduced fees are almost always available for children, students, and senior citizens)

Numbers in white and black circles ③ ❸ that appear on the maps, in the margins, and within the tours correspond to one another.

For hotels, you can assume that all rooms have private baths, phones, TVs, and air-conditioning unless otherwise noted and that all hotels operate on the European Plan (with no meals) if we don't specify another meal plan. We always list a property's facilities but not whether you'll be charged extra to use them, so when pricing accommodations, do ask what's included. For restaurants, it's always a good idea to book ahead; we mention reservations only when they're essential or are not accepted. All restaurants we list are open daily for lunch and dinner unless stated otherwise; dress is mentioned only when men are required to wear a jacket or a jacket and tie. Look for an overview of local dining-out habits in Smart Travel Tips A to Z and in the Pleasures and Pastimes section that follows each chapter introduction.

Don't Forget to Write

Your experiences—positive and negative—matter to us. If we have missed or misstated something, we want to hear about it. We follow up on all suggestions. Contact the South Florida editor at editors@fodors.com or c/o Fodor's at 1745 Broadway, New York, New York 10019. And have a fabulous trip!

Karen Cure

Karen Cure
Editorial Director

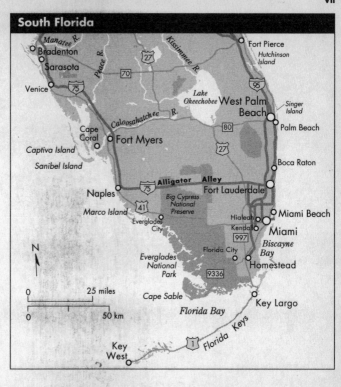

South Florida

Miami Metrorail

Florida

ALABAMA

Pensacola

Fort Walton Beach

Destin

De Funiak Springs

Mariana

Chattahoochee

Quincy

Panama City

Tallahassee

Apalachicola

Eastpoint

Gulf of Mexico

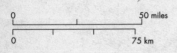

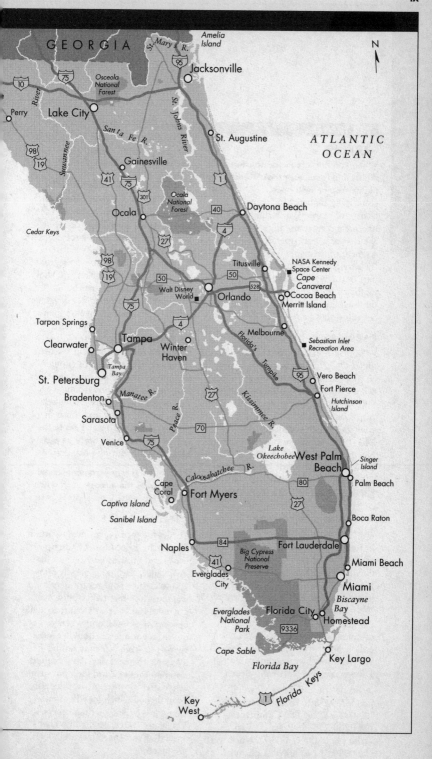

ESSENTIAL INFORMATION

AIR TRAVEL

BOOKING

When you book **look for nonstop flights** and **remember that "direct" flights stop at least once.** Try to avoid connecting flights, which require a change of plane. Two airlines may operate a connecting flight jointly, so ask if your airline operates every segment of the trip; you may find that the carrier you prefer flies you only part of the way. To find more booking tips and to check prices and make on-line flight reservations, log on to www.fodors.com.

CARRIERS

➤ MAJOR AIRLINES: **Air Canada** (☎ 888/247–2262, WEB www.aircanada. com). **American** (☎ 800/433–7300, WEB www.aa.com). **Continental** (☎ 800/525–0280, WEB www.continental. com). **Delta** (☎ 800/221–1212, WEB www.delta.com). **Midway** (☎ 800/ 446–4392, WEB www.midwayair.com). **Northwest** (☎ 800/225–2525, WEB www.nwa.com). **Spirit** (☎ 800/772– 7117, WEB www.spiritair.com). **TWA** (☎ 800/221–2000, WEB www.twa. com). **United** (☎ 800/241–6522, WEB www.ual.com). **US Airways** (☎ 800/ 428–4322, WEB www.usair.com).

➤ REGIONAL AIRLINES: **AirTran** (☎ 800/247–8726, WEB www.airtran.com) to Miami and Fort Lauderdale. **Jet Blue** (☎ 800/538–2583, WEB www. jetblue.com) to Fort Lauderdale and West Palm Beach. **Midwest Express** (☎ 800/452–2022, WEB www2. midwestexpress.com) to Fort Lauderdale. **Southwest** (☎ 800/435–9792, WEB www.southwesst.com) to Fort Lauderdale and West Palm Beach.

➤ FROM THE U.K.: **American** (☎ 0345/789–789). **British Airways** (☎ 0345/222–111). **Continental** (☎ 0800/776–464) via Newark. **Delta** (☎ 0800/414–767). **Northwest** (☎ 0990/561–000) via Detroit or Minneapolis. **TWA** (☎ 0800/222– 222) via St. Louis. **United** (☎ 0800/ 888–555). **Virgin Atlantic** (☎ 01293/ 747–747).

CHECK-IN AND BOARDING

Always **ask your carrier about its check-in policy.** Plan to arrive at the airport about 2 hours before your scheduled departure time for domestic flights and 2½ to 3 hours before international flights. Assuming that not everyone with a ticket will show up, airlines routinely overbook planes. When everyone does, airlines ask for volunteers to give up their seats. In return, these volunteers usually get a certificate for a free flight and are rebooked on the next flight out. If there are not enough volunteers, the airline must choose who will be denied boarding. The first to get bumped are passengers who checked in late and those flying on discounted tickets, so **get to the gate and check in as early as possible,** especially during peak periods.

Always **bring a government-issued photo I.D. to the airport;** even when it's not required, a passport is best.

CUTTING COSTS

The least expensive airfares to South Florida are priced for round-trip travel and must usually be purchased in advance. Airlines generally allow you to change your return date for a fee; most low-fare tickets, however, are nonrefundable. It's smart to **call a number of airlines,** and when you are quoted a good price, **book it on the spot**—the same fare may not be available the next day. Always **check different routings** and look into using alternative airports. Also, price off-peak flights, which may be significantly less expensive than others. Travel agents, especially low-fare specialists (☞ Discounts and Deals), are helpful.

Consolidators are another good source. They buy tickets for scheduled international flights at reduced rates from the airlines, then sell them at prices that beat the best fare available directly from the airlines. Sometimes you can even get your money back if you need to return the ticket. Carefully read the fine print detailing penalties for changes and cancellations, purchase the ticket with a credit card, and **confirm your consolidator reservation with the airline.**

When you **fly as a courier,** you trade your checked-luggage space for a ticket deeply subsidized by a courier service. There are restrictions on when you can book and how long you can stay. Some courier companies list with membership organizations, such as the Air Courier Association and the International Association of Air Travel Couriers; these require you to become a member before you can book a flight.

Many airlines, singly or in collaboration, offer discount air passes that allow foreigners to travel economically in a particular country or region. These visitor passes usually must be reserved and purchased before you leave home. Information about passes can be difficult to track down on airline Web sites, which tend to be geared to travelers departing from a given carrier's country rather than to those intending to visit that country. Try typing the name of the pass into a search engine, or search for "pass" within the carrier's Web site.

➤ CONSOLIDATORS: **Cheap Tickets** (☎ 888/922–8849, ⓦⒺⒷ www.cheaptickets. com). **Discount Airline Ticket Service** (☎ 800/576–1600). **Discount Travel Network** (☎ 800/409–6753, ⓦⒺⒷ www.bestfares.com).

➤ CHEAP RATES FROM THE U.K.: **Flight Express Travel** (✉ 77 New Bond St., London W1Y 9DB, U.K., ☎ 0171/409–3311). **Trailfinders** (✉ 42–50 Earls Court Rd., London W8 6FT, U.K., ☎ 0171/937–5400). **Travel Cuts** (✉ 295A Regent St., London W1R 7YA, U.K., ☎ 0171/ 637–3161).

➤ COURIER RESOURCES: **Air Courier Association** (☎ 800/282–1202, ⓦⒺⒷ

www.aircourier.org). **International Association of Air Travel Couriers** (☎ 352/475–1584, ⓦⒺⒷ www.courier. org).

ENJOYING THE FLIGHT

State your seat preference when purchasing your ticket, and then repeat it when you confirm and when you check in. For more legroom, you can request one of the few emergency-aisle seats at check-in, if you are capable of lifting at least 50 pounds— a Federal Aviation Administration requirement of passengers in these seats. Seats behind a bulkhead also offer more legroom, but they don't have under-seat storage. Don't sit in the row in front of the emergency aisle or in front of a bulkhead, where seats may not recline.

Ask the airline whether a snack or meal is served on the flight. If you have dietary concerns, **request special meals when booking.** These can be vegetarian, low-cholesterol, or kosher, for example. It's a good idea to pack some healthful snacks and a small (plastic) bottle of water in your carry-on bag. On long flights, try to maintain a normal routine, to help fight jet lag. At night, **get some sleep.** By day, **eat light meals, drink water** (not alcohol), and **move around the cabin** to stretch your legs. For additional jet-lag tips consult *Fodor's FYI: Travel Fit & Healthy* (available at bookstores everywhere).

Smoking policies vary from carrier to carrier. Many airlines prohibit smoking on all of their international flights; others allow smoking only on certain routes or certain departures. Ask your carrier about its policy.

FLYING TIMES

Approximate flying times to Miami are 3 hours from Chicago, 5 hours from Los Angeles, 6 hours from London, 3½ hours from Montréal, 3 hours from New York, and 3 hours from Toronto.

HOW TO COMPLAIN

If your baggage goes astray or your flight goes awry, complain right away. Most carriers require that you **file a claim immediately.** The Aviation Consumer Protection Division of the

Department of Transportation publishes *Fly-Rights*, which discusses airlines and consumer issues and is available on-line. At PassengerRights.com, a Web site, you can compose a letter of complaint and distribute it electronically.

➤ AIRLINE COMPLAINTS: **Aviation Consumer Protection Division** (✉ U.S. Department of Transportation, Room 4107, C-75, Washington, DC 20590, ☎ 202/366–2220, WEB www.dot.gov/airconsumer). **Federal Aviation Administration Consumer Hotline** (☎ 800/322–7873).

RECONFIRMING

Check the status of your flight before you leave for the airport. You can do this on your carrier's Web site, by linking to a flight-status checker (many Web booking services offer these), or by calling your carrier or travel agent.

AIRPORTS

If you're destined for the north side of Miami-Dade County (metro Miami), or are renting a car at the airport, **consider flying into Fort Lauderdale–Hollywood International**; it's much easier to use than Miami International, and often—if not always—cheaper. The airports are only 40 minutes apart by car.

➤ AIRPORT INFORMATION: **Fort Lauderdale–Hollywood International (FLL)** (☎ 954/359–1200). **Miami International Airport (MIA)** (☎ 305/876–7000). **Palm Beach International (PBI)** (☎ 561/471–7420).

BIKE TRAVEL

Many cities throughout South Florida do not offer safe biking paths such as sidewalks and specially marked bike lanes. However, plenty of wide open space and scenic trails twist through national and state parks.

Florida statutes require that bikers under 16 wear a helmet. Bicycle passengers under 4 years old must be in a sling or child seat. All bikes must have lamps or reflectors—white in the front, and red in the back, visible from 500 ft—between sunset and sunrise. *See* Outdoor Activities and Sports *in* regional chapters for more biking information.

BIKES IN FLIGHT

Most airlines accommodate bikes as luggage, provided they are dismantled and boxed; check with individual airlines about packing requirements. Airlines sell bike boxes, which are often free at bike shops, for about $15 (bike bags start at $100). International travelers often can substitute a bike for a piece of checked luggage at no charge; otherwise, the cost is about $100. Domestic and Canadian airlines charge $40–$80 each way.

BUSINESS HOURS

MUSEUMS AND SIGHTS

Many museums in South Florida are closed Mondays, but offer extended hours on another weekday and are usually open on weekends. Popular visitor attractions are usually open daily with the exception of Thanksgiving and Christmas Day.

PHARMACIES

Most pharmacies are open seven days a week, but some may close early on weekends. Many Wal-Mart stores and Walgreens pharmacies offer 24-hour pharmacy services.

BUS TRAVEL

Greyhound passes through practically every city in South Florida. For schedules and fares, **contact your local Greyhound Information Center.**

PAYING

Using a major credit card you can purchase Greyhound tickets on-line or from the designated 800 number. You can also purchase tickets using cash, travelers checks, or major credit cards at any Greyhound terminal where tickets are sold or through one of the many independent agents representing Greyhound. A complete state-by-state list of agents is available at the Greyhound Web site.

➤ BUS INFORMATION: **Greyhound Lines** (☎ 800/231–2222; or 800/229–9424 for credit card sales, WEB www.greyhound.com).

CAMERAS
AND PHOTOGRAPHY

The *Kodak Guide to Shooting Great Travel Pictures* (available at bookstores everywhere) is loaded with tips.

➤ PHOTO HELP: **Kodak Information Center** (☏ 800/242–2424, WEB www.kodak.com).

EQUIPMENT PRECAUTIONS

Don't pack film and equipment in checked luggage, where it is much more susceptible to damage. X-ray machines used to view checked luggage are becoming much more powerful and therefore are much more likely to ruin your film. Try to **ask for hand inspection of film,** which becomes clouded after repeated exposure to airport X-ray machines, and **keep videotapes and computer disks away from metal detectors.** Always **keep film, tape, and computer disks out of the sun.** Carry an extra supply of batteries, and **be prepared to turn on your camera, camcorder, or laptop** to prove to airport security personnel that the device is real.

CAR RENTAL

In-season rates in Miami begin at $36 a day and $170 a week for an economy car with air-conditioning, an automatic transmission, and unlimited mileage. Rates in Fort Lauderdale begin at $36 a day and $159 a week. This does not include tax on car rentals, which is 7%. Bear in mind that rates fluctuate tremendously—both above and below these quoted figures—depending on demand and the season. Rental cars are more expensive (and harder to find) during peak holidays and in season.

In the past, major rental agencies were located at the airport whereas cheaper firms weren't. Now, however, even the majors might be off airport property. It varies firm to firm and airport to airport. Speedy check-in and frequent shuttle buses make off-airport rentals almost as convenient as on-site service. However, it's wise to allow a little extra time for bus travel between the rental agency and the airport.

➤ MAJOR AGENCIES: **Alamo** (☏ 800/327–9633; WEB www.alamo.com). **Avis** (☏ 800/331–1212; 800/879–2847 in Canada; 02/9353–9000 in Australia; 09/526–2847 in New Zealand; 0870/606–0100 in the U.K.; WEB www.avis.com). **Budget** (☏ 800/527–0700; 0870/156–5656 in the U.K.; WEB www.budget.com). **Dollar** (☏ 800/800–4000; 0124/622–0111 in the U.K., where it's affiliated with Sixt; 02/9223–1444 in Australia; WEB www.dollar.com). **Hertz** (☏ 800/654–3131; 800/263–0600 in Canada; 020/8897–2072 in the U.K.; 02/9669–2444 in Australia; 09/256–8690 in New Zealand; WEB www.hertz.com). **National Car Rental** (☏ 800/227–7368; 020/8680–4800 in the U.K.; WEB www.nationalcar.com).

CUTTING COSTS

For a good deal, **book through a travel agent who will shop around.** Also, **price local car-rental companies**—whose prices may be lower still, although their service and maintenance may not be as good as those of major rental agencies—and **research rates on-line.** Remember to ask about required deposits, cancellation penalties, and drop-off charges if you're planning to pick up the car in one city and leave it in another. If you're traveling during a holiday period, also make sure that a confirmed reservation guarantees you a car.

➤ LOCAL AGENCIES: **Apex Rent A Car** (☏ 954/782–3400) in Fort Lauderdale. **Continental Florida Auto Rental** (☏ 954/764–1008 or 800/327–3791) in Fort Lauderdale. **Inter-American Car Rental** (☏ 305/871–3030 or 800/327–1278) in Fort Lauderdale, Miami, and Miami Beach. **Tropical Rent-A-Car** (☏ 305/294–8136) in Key West.

INSURANCE

When driving a rented car you are generally responsible for any damage to or loss of the vehicle. You may also be liable for any property damage or personal injury that you may cause while driving. Before you rent, see what coverage you already have under the terms of your personal auto-insurance policy and credit cards.

For about $15 to $20 a day, rental companies sell protection, known as a collision- or loss-damage waiver (CDW or LDW), that eliminates your liability for damage to the car; it's always optional and should never be automatically added to your bill. In most states you don't need a CDW if you have personal auto insurance or other liability insurance. However, **make sure you have enough coverage to pay for the car.** If you do not have auto insurance or an umbrella policy that covers damage to third parties, purchasing liability insurance and a CDW or LDW is highly recommended.

REQUIREMENTS AND RESTRICTIONS

In Florida you must be 21 to rent a car, and rates may be higher if you're under 25. Non-U.S. residents need a reservation voucher (for prepaid reservations that were made in the traveler's home country), a passport, a driver's license, and a travel policy that covers each driver, when picking up a car.

SURCHARGES

Before you pick up a car in one city and leave it in another, **ask about drop-off charges or one-way service fees,** which can be substantial. Note, too, that some rental agencies charge extra if you return the car before the time specified in your contract. To avoid a hefty refueling fee, **fill the tank just before you turn in the car,** but be aware that gas stations near the rental outlet may overcharge. It's almost never a deal to buy the tank of gas in the car when you rent it; the understanding is that you'll return it empty, but some fuel usually remains. Surcharges may apply if you're under 25. You'll pay extra for child seats (about $6 a day), which are compulsory for children under three, and for additional drivers (about $5 per day).

CAR TRAVEL

Two major interstates lead to South Florida. Interstate 95 begins in Maine, runs south through the Mid-Atlantic states, and enters Florida just north of Jacksonville. It continues south past Vero Beach, Palm Beach, and Fort Lauderdale, eventually ending in Miami.

Interstate 75 begins in Michigan at the Canadian border and runs south through Ohio, Kentucky, Tennessee, and Georgia, then moves south through the center of the state before veering west into Tampa. It follows the west coast south to Naples, then crosses the state through the northern section of the Everglades, and ends in Fort Lauderdale.

California and most southern states are connected to Florida by Interstate 10, which runs straight across the northern part of Florida to Jacksonville, where it connects with Interstate 95.

ROAD CONDITIONS

South Florida has its share of traffic problems. Downtown areas of Miami can be extremely congested during rush hours, usually 7 to 9 AM and 4 to 6 PM on weekdays. When you drive the interstate system try to **plan your trip so that you are not entering, leaving, or passing through a large city during rush hour,** when traffic can slow to 10 mph for 10 mi or more. In addition, snowbirds usually rent in South Florida for a month at a time, which means they all arrive on the first of the month and leave on the 31st. Believe it or not, from November to March, when the end and beginning of a month occur on a weekend, north–south routes like Interstate 75 and Interstate 95 almost come to a standstill during daylight hours. It's best to avoid traveling on these days if possible.

RULES OF THE ROAD

Speed limits are 55 mph on state highways, 30 mph within city limits and residential areas, and 55–70 mph on interstates and Florida's Turnpike. Be alert for signs announcing exceptions.

Always **strap children under age three into approved child-safety seats.** All passengers are required to wear seat belts. The driver will be held responsible for passengers under the age of 16 who are not wearing a seat belt. Florida's Alcohol/Controlled Substance DUI Law is one of the toughest in the United States. A blood alcohol level of .08 or higher can have serious repercussions even for the first-time offender.

Always **secure children under age five into an approved child-restraint device.**

SAFETY

Before setting off on any drive, **make sure you know where you're going** and carry a map. At the car-rental agency or at your hotel **ask if there are any areas that you should avoid.** Always **keep your doors locked,** and ask questions only at toll booths, gas stations, or other obviously safe locations. Also, **don't stop if your car is bumped from behind** or if you're asked for directions. One hesitates to foster rude behavior, but at least for now the roads are too risky to stop any place you're not familiar with (other than as traffic laws require). If you'll be renting a car and won't have a cellular phone with you, **ask the car-rental agency for a cellular phone.** Alamo, Avis, and Hertz are among the companies with in-car phones.

CHILDREN IN SOUTH FLORIDA

If you are renting a car, don't forget to **arrange for a car seat** when you reserve. For general advice about traveling with children, consult *Fodor's FYI: Travel with Your Baby* (available in bookstores everywhere).

Fodor's Around Miami with Kids available in bookstores everywhere, can help you plan your days together.

FLYING

If your children are two or older, **ask about children's airfares.** As a general rule, infants under two not occupying a seat fly at greatly reduced fares or even for free.

Experts agree that it's a good idea to use safety seats aloft for children weighing less than 40 pounds. Airlines set their own policies: U.S. carriers usually require that the child be ticketed, even if he or she is young enough to ride free, since the seats must be strapped into regular seats. Do **check your airline's policy about using safety seats during takeoff and landing.** Safety seats are not allowed everywhere in the plane, so get your seat assignments as early as possible.

When reserving, **request children's meals or a freestanding bassinet** (not available at all airlines) if you need them. But note that bulkhead seats, where you must sit to use the bassinet, may lack an overhead bin or storage space on the floor.

LODGING

Many South Florida hotels have organized children's programs. For instance, kids learn about the Keys' environment from marine-science counselors at Cheeca Lodge on Isla-madora. Sometimes kids' programs are complimentary; sometimes there's a charge. Not all accept children in diapers, and some offer programs when their central reservations services say they don't. Some programs are offered only during peak seasons or restrict hours in less-busy times. It always pays to **confirm details with the hotel in advance.** And **reserve space as soon as possible**; programs are often full by the morning or evening you need them.

Most hotels in South Florida allow children under a certain age to stay in their parents' room at no extra charge, but others charge for them as extra adults. Many bed-and-break-fasts and inns do not welcome young children; be sure to **find out the cutoff age for any applicable discounts or age restrictions.**

➤ BEST CHOICES: **Cheeca Lodge's Camp Cheeca** (✉ MM 82, OS, Box 527, Islamorada, FL 33036, ☎ 800/327–2888), ages 4–12. **Club Med's Sandpiper** (✉ 3500 S.E. Morningside Blvd., Port St. Lucie, FL 34952, ☎ 561/398–5100 or 800/258–2633), Baby Club ages 4–24 months, Mini Club ages 2–11. **Hawks Cay Resort's Island Adventure Club** (✉ MM 61, Duck Key, FL 33050, ☎ 800/432–2242), ages 5–12. **Hutchinson Island Marriott Resort's Pineapple Bunch Children's Camp** (✉ 555 N.E. Ocean Blvd., Hutchinson Island, Stuart, FL 34996, ☎ 561/225–3700), ages 4–12, plus a teen program. **Marriott's Harbor Beach Resort's Beachside Buddies** (✉ 3030 Holiday Dr., Fort Lauderdale, FL 33316, ☎ 954/525–4000 or 800/228–9290), ages 5–12. **Sonesta Beach Resort's Just Us Kids** (✉ 350 Ocean Dr., Key Biscayne, FL 33149, ☎ 305/361–2021 or 800/766–3782), ages 5–13. **Westin Beach Resort's Westin Kids Club** (✉ MM 96.9, BS, 97000 Overseas Hwy., Key

Largo, FL 33037, ☎ 305/852–5553 or 800/325–3535), ages 5–12.

SIGHTS AND ATTRACTIONS

Places that are especially appealing to children are indicated by a rubber-duckie icon (☺) in the margin.

TRANSPORTATION

Florida law requires that all children three years old or younger ride in a federally approved child safety seat when in any motor vehicle, regardless of the vehicle's registration state. Children four and five years of age must be restrained in either a child safety seat, booster seat, or safety belt.

CONSUMER PROTECTION

Whether you're shopping for gifts or purchasing travel services, **pay with a major credit card** whenever possible, so you can cancel payment or get reimbursed if there's a problem (and you can provide documentation). If you're doing business with a particular company for the first time, **contact your local Better Business Bureau and the attorney general's offices** in your state and (for U.S. businesses) the company's home state as well. Have any complaints been filed? Finally, if you're buying a package or tour, always **consider travel insurance** that includes default coverage (☞ Insurance).

➤ BBBs: **Council of Better Business Bureaus** (✉ 4200 Wilson Blvd., Suite 800, Arlington, VA 22203, ☎ 703/276–0100, FAX 703/525–8277, WEB www.bbb.org).

CRUISE TRAVEL

The port of Miami is the cruise capital of the world, with the world's largest year-round fleet. It also handles more megaships—vessels capable of transporting more than 2,000 people at a time—than any other port in the world. Port Everglades, located 23 mi north of Miami, is the world's second-busiest cruise-ship terminal. Seven-day eastern and western Caribbean cruises are the most popular type of cruise leaving from Miami-area ports. To learn how to plan, choose, and book a cruise-ship voyage, check out Cruise How-to's on www.fodors.com.

To learn how to plan, choose, and book a cruise-ship voyage, consult *Fodor's FYI: Plan & Enjoy Your Cruise* (available in bookstores everywhere).

➤ CRUISE LINES: **Royal Caribbean** (☎ 800/398–9819). **Celebrity Cruises** (☎ 800/437–3111). **Costa Cruises Lines** (☎ 800/462–6782). **Crystal Cruises** (☎ 800/446–6620). **Cunard Cruise Line** (☎ 800/728–6273). **Discovery Cruises** (☎ 800/866–8687). **Holland America Cruises** (☎ 877/932–4259). **Imperial Majesty Cruise Lines** (☎ 800/511–5737). **Norwegian Cruises** (☎ 800/327–7030 Ext. 111). **Princess** (☎ 800/774–6237). **Sea Escape Cruises** (☎ 800/327–2005). **SilverSea Cruises** (☎ 800/722–9955). **Windjammer** (☎ 800/327–2601).

DINING

The restaurants we list are the cream of the crop in each price category.

CATEGORY	COST*
$$$$	over $30
$$$	$20–$30
$$	$10–$20
$	under $10

*per person for a main course at dinner

One cautionary word: raw oysters have been identified as a problem for people with chronic illness of the liver, stomach, or blood, or who have immune disorders. Since 1993, all Florida restaurants serving raw oysters are required to post a notice in plain view of all patrons warning of the risks associated with consuming them.

The restaurants we list are the cream of the crop in each price category. Properties indicated by a ✕🏨 are lodging establishments whose restaurant warrants a special trip.

RESERVATIONS AND DRESS

Reservations are always a good idea; we mention them only when they're essential or not accepted. Book as far ahead as you can, and reconfirm as soon as you arrive. (Large parties should always call ahead to check the reservations policy.) We mention dress only when men are required to wear a jacket or a jacket and tie.

SPECIALTIES

A trip to South Florida is incomplete without a taste of Cuban food. The cuisine is heavy, with pork dishes like *lechon asado,* served in garlic-based sauces. The two most typical dishes are *arroz con frijoles* (the staple side dish of rice and black beans) and *arroz con pollo* (chicken in a sticky yellow rice). Though available elsewhere in South Florida, Key West is a mecca for lovers of key lime pie. Stands in Key West also serve up conch fritters. Stone crab claws, another South Florida delicacy, can be savored November through May.

WINE, BEER, AND SPIRITS

Beer and wine is usually available in South Florida's restaurants, whether you're dining first class or at a beachside bistro. A few chain restaurants in the major cities are microbreweries and have a variety of premise-made beers that change with the season. Liquor is generally available at fine-dining establishments only.

DISABILITIES
AND ACCESSIBILITY

Although there's no single organization that offers a completely comprehensive list of motels or inns that are equipped for travelers with disabilities, you can find helpful information and links at Florida Disabled Outdoor Association (FDOA) and Disability Travel and Recreation Resources. The Society for Accessible Travel and Hospitality is another good source.

Metro-Dade Disability Services publishes a free guidebook on the accessibility of Florida's hotels and motels, entitled *Directory of Services for the Physically Disabled in Dade County.*

➤ LOCAL RESOURCES: **Florida Disabled Outdoor Association (FDOA;** ☎ 850/668–7323, WEB www.nettally. com/fdoa). **Disability Travel and Recreation Resources** (WEB www. makoa.org/travel.htm). **Society for Accessible Travel and Hospitality** (☎ 212/447–7284, WEB www.sath. org). **Metro-Dade Disability Services** (✉ 1335 N.W. 14th St., Miami, FL 33125, ☎ 305/547–5445; 305/545– 3575 TDD).

Deaf Services Center (✉ 2182 Mc-Greggor Blvd., Fort Myers, FL 33901, ☎ 941/461–0334 or 813/ 939–9977 TDD). **Florida Relay Service** (☎ 800/955–8770).

LODGING

Despite the Americans with Disabilities Act, the definition of accessibility seems to differ from hotel to hotel. Some properties may be accessible by ADA standards for people with mobility problems but not for people with hearing or vision impairments, for example.

If you have mobility problems, ask for the lowest floor on which accessible services are offered. If you have a hearing impairment, check whether the hotel has devices to alert you visually to the ring of the telephone, knock at the door, and a fire/emergency alarm. Some hotels provide these devices without charge. Discuss your needs with hotel personnel if this equipment isn't available, so that a staff member can personally alert you in the event of an emergency.

If you're bringing a guide dog, get authorization ahead of time and write down the name of the person you spoke with.

RESERVATIONS

When discussing accessibility with an operator or reservations agent, **ask hard questions.** Are there any stairs, inside *or* out? Are there grab bars next to the toilet *and* in the shower/ tub? How wide is the doorway to the room? To the bathroom? For the most extensive facilities meeting the latest legal specifications, **opt for newer accommodations.** If you reserve through a toll-free number, consider also calling the hotel's local number to confirm the information from the central reservations office. Get confirmation in writing when you can.

➤ COMPLAINTS: **Aviation Consumer Protection Division** (☞ Air Travel) for airline-related problems. **Departmental Office of Civil Rights** (for general inquiries, ✉ U.S. Department of Transportation, S-30, 400 7th St. SW, Room 10215, Washington, DC 20590, ☎ 202/366–4648, FAX 202/ 366–3571, WEB www.dot.gov/ost/docr/

index.htm). **Disability Rights Section** (✉ NYAV, U.S. Department of Justice, Civil Rights Division, 950 Pennsylvania Ave. NW, Washington, DC 20530; ☎ ADA information line 202/514–0301; 800/514–0301; 202/514–0383 TTY; 800/514–0383 TTY, WEB www.usdoj.gov/crt/ada/adahom1.htm).

TRAVEL AGENCIES

In the United States, the Americans with Disabilities Act requires that travel firms serve the needs of all travelers. Some agencies specialize in working with people with disabilities.

➤ TRAVELERS WITH MOBILITY PROBLEMS: **Access Adventures** (✉ 206 Chestnut Ridge Rd., Scottsville, NY 14624, ☎ 716/889–9096, dltravel@prodigy.net), run by a former physical-rehabilitation counselor. **Accessible Vans of America** (✉ 9 Spielman Rd., Fairfield, NJ 07004, ☎ 877/282–8267; 888/282–8267 reservations, FAX 973/808–9713, WEB www.accessiblevans.com). **CareVacations** (✉ No. 5, 5110–50 Ave., Leduc, Alberta T9E 6V4, Canada, ☎ 780/986–6404 or 877/478–7827, FAX 780/986–8332, WEB www.carevacations.com), for group tours and cruise vacations. **Flying Wheels Travel** (✉ 143 W. Bridge St., Box 382, Owatonna, MN 55060, ☎ 507/451–5005, FAX 507/451–1685, WEB www.flyingwheelstravel.com).

➤ TRAVELERS WITH DEVELOPMENTAL DISABILITIES: **New Directions** (✉ 5276 Hollister Ave., Suite 207, Santa Barbara, CA 93111, ☎ 805/967–2841 or 888/967–2841, FAX 805/964–7344, WEB www.newdirectionstravel.com). **Sprout** (✉ 893 Amsterdam Ave., New York, NY 10025, ☎ 212/222–9575 or 888/222–9575, FAX 212/222–9768, WEB www.gosprout.org).

DISCOUNTS AND DEALS

Be a smart shopper and **compare all your options** before making decisions. A plane ticket bought with a promotional coupon from travel clubs, coupon books, and direct-mail offers or purchased on the Internet may not be cheaper than the least expensive fare from a discount ticket agency. And always keep in mind that what you get is just as important as what you save.

DISCOUNT RESERVATIONS

To save money, **look into discount reservations services** with Web sites and toll-free numbers, which use their buying power to get a better price on hotels, airline tickets, even car rentals. When booking a room, always **call the hotel's local toll-free number** (if one is available) rather than the central reservations number—you'll often get a better price. Always ask about special packages or corporate rates.

➤ AIRLINE TICKETS: ☎ 800/AIR–4LESS.

➤ HOTEL ROOMS: **Accommodations Express** (☎ 800/444–7666, WEB www.accommodationsexpress.com). **Central Reservation Service** (CRS; ☎ 800/548–3311, WEB www.roomconnection.net). **Hotel Reservations Network** (☎ 800/964–6835, WEB www.hoteldiscount.com). **Quikbook** (☎ 800/789–9887, WEB www.quikbook.com). **RMC Travel** (☎ 800/245–5738, WEB www.rmcwebtravel.com). **Steigenberger Reservation Service** (☎ 800/223–5652, WEB www.srs-worldhotels.com). **Turbotrip.com** (☎ 800/473–7829, WEB www.turbotrip.com).

PACKAGE DEALS

Don't confuse packages and guided tours. When you buy a package, you travel on your own, just as though you had planned the trip yourself. Fly/drive packages, which combine airfare and car rental, are often a good deal.

ECOTOURISM

South Florida's varied environment is one of its chief draws; it's also very fragile. If you're out in nature, follow the basic rules of environmental responsibility: **take nothing but pictures; leave nothing but footprints.** Most important, **be extremely careful around the tenuous dunes.** Picking the sea grasses that hold the dunes in place can carry stiff fines, as can walking or playing or digging in the dunes. An afternoon of roughhousing can completely destroy a dune that could take years for nature to rebuild. Ecotours (☞ Tours *in* each chapter's A to Z section) operate throughout the state and can help you see some of what makes Florida so distinct, usually in a way that makes the least impact possible.

GAY AND LESBIAN TRAVEL

Destinations in South Florida that have a reputation for being especially gay and lesbian friendly include South Beach and Key West.

For details about the gay and lesbian scene, consult *Fodor's Gay Guide to the USA* (available in bookstores everywhere).

➤ GAY- AND LESBIAN-FRIENDLY TRAVEL AGENCIES: **Different Roads Travel** (✉ 8383 Wilshire Blvd., Suite 902, Beverly Hills, CA 90211, ☎ 323/651–5557 or 800/429–8747, FAX 323/651–3678, lgernert@tzell.com). **Kennedy Travel** (✉ 314 Jericho Turnpike, Floral Park, NY 11001, ☎ 516/352–4888 or 800/237–7433, FAX 516/354–8849, WEB www.kennedytravel.com). **Now, Voyager** (✉ 4406 18th St., San Francisco, CA 94114, ☎ 415/626–1169 or 800/255–6951, FAX 415/626–8626, WEB www.nowvoyager.com). **Skylink Travel and Tour** (✉ 1006 Mendocino Ave., Santa Rosa, CA 95401, ☎ 707/546–9888 or 800/225–5759, FAX 707/546–9891), serving lesbian travelers.

GUIDEBOOKS

Plan well and you won't be sorry. Guidebooks are excellent tools—and you can take them with you. You may want to check out *Fodor's Miami* or study color-photo-illustrated *Fodor's Exploring Florida* and *Compass American Guide: Florida*, thorough on culture and history. *Fodor's Road Guide USA: Florida* has comprehensive restaurant, hotel, and attractions listings, and *Fodor's Around Miami with Kids* can help you plan your family days together.

HEALTH

If you are unaccustomed to strong subtropical sun, you run a risk of sunburn and heat prostration, even in winter. So hit the beach or play tennis, golf, or another outdoor sport before 10 or after 3. If you must be out **at midday, limit strenuous exercise, drink plenty of liquids, and wear a hat.** If you begin to feel faint, get out of the sun immediately and sip

water slowly. Even on overcast days, ultraviolet rays shine through the haze, so **use a sunscreen with an SPF of at least 15,** and have children wear a waterproof SPF 30 or better.

While you're frolicking on the beach, **steer clear of what look like blue bubbles on the sand.** These are Portuguese man-of-wars, and their tentacles can cause an allergic reaction. Also be careful of other large jellyfish, some of which can sting.

If you walk across a grassy area on the way to the beach, you'll probably encounter sand spurs. They are quite tiny, light brown, and remarkably prickly. You'll feel them before you see them; if you get stuck with one, just pull it out.

DIVERS' ALERT

Do not fly within 24 hours of scuba diving.

HOLIDAYS

Major national holidays include New Year's Day (Jan. 1); Martin Luther King, Jr., Day (3rd Mon. in Jan.); President's Day (3rd Mon. in Feb.); Memorial Day (last Mon. in May); Independence Day (July 4); Labor Day (1st Mon. in Sept.); Thanksgiving Day (4th Thurs. in Nov.); Christmas Eve and Christmas Day (Dec. 24 and 25); and New Year's Eve (Dec. 31).

INSURANCE

The most useful travel-insurance plan is a comprehensive policy that includes coverage for trip cancellation and interruption, default, trip delay, and medical expenses (with a waiver for preexisting conditions).

Without insurance you will lose all or most of your money if you cancel your trip, regardless of the reason. Default insurance covers you if your tour operator, airline, or cruise line goes out of business. Trip-delay covers expenses that arise because of bad weather or mechanical delays. Study the fine print when comparing policies.

U.K. residents can buy a travel-insurance policy valid for most vacations taken during the year in which it's purchased (but check preexisting-condition coverage).

Always **buy travel policies directly from the insurance company**; if you buy them from a cruise line, airline, or tour operator that goes out of business, you probably will not be covered for the agency or operator's default, a major risk. Before making any purchase, **review your existing health and home-owner's policies** to find what they cover away from home.

➤ TRAVEL INSURERS: In the U.S.: **Access America** (⊠ 6600 W. Broad St., Richmond, VA 23230, ☎ 800/284–8300, FAX 804/673–1491 or 800/346–9265, WEB www.accessamerica. com). **Travel Guard International** (⊠ 1145 Clark St., Stevens Point, WI 54481, ☎ 715/345–0505 or 800/826–1300, FAX 800/955–8785, WEB www.travelguard.com).

FOR INTERNATIONAL TRAVELERS

CAR RENTAL

When picking up a rental car, non-U.S. residents need a reservation voucher for any prepaid reservations that were made in the traveler's home country, a passport, a driver's license, and a travel policy that covers each driver.

CAR TRAVEL

At this writing, gas prices in South Florida are $1.40–$1.60 a gallon. Stations are plentiful. Most stay open late (24 hours along large highways and in big cities), except in rural areas, where Sunday hours are limited and where you may drive long stretches without a refueling opportunity. Highways are well paved. Interstate highways—limited-access, multilane highways whose numbers are prefixed by "I–"—are the fastest routes. Interstates with three-digit numbers encircle urban areas, which may have other limited-access expressways, freeways, and parkways as well. Tolls may be levied on limited-access highways. So-called U.S. highways and state highways are not necessarily limited-access but may have several lanes.

Along larger highways, roadside stops with rest rooms, fast-food restaurants, and sundries stores are well spaced. State police and tow trucks patrol major highways and lend assistance. If your car breaks down on an interstate, pull onto the shoulder and wait for help, or have your passengers wait while you walk to an emergency phone. If you carry a mobile phone, dial *55, noting your location on the small green roadside mileage markers.

Driving in the United States is on the right. Do **obey speed limits** posted along roads and highways. Watch for lower limits in small towns and on back roads. Florida law requires all passengers to wear seat belts. On weekdays between 6 and 10 AM and again between 4 and 7 PM expect heavy traffic. To encourage carpooling, some freeways have special lanes for so-called high-occupancy vehicles (HOV)—cars carrying more than one passenger.

Bookstores, gas stations, convenience stores, and rest stops sell maps (about $3) and multiregion road atlases (about $10).

CURRENCY

The dollar is the basic unit of U.S. currency. It has 100 cents. Coins include the copper penny (1¢); the silvery nickel (5¢), dime (10¢), quarter (25¢), and half-dollar (50¢); and the golden $1 coin, replacing a now-rare silver dollar. Bills are denominated $1, $5, $10, $20, $50, and $100, all green and identical in size; designs vary. The exchange rate at this writing is €1 to US$.94, £1 to US$1.46, C$1 to US$.65, A$1 to US$.57, and NZ$1 to US$.49.

ELECTRICITY

The U.S. standard is AC, 110 volts/60 cycles. Plugs have two flat pins set parallel to each other.

EMERGENCIES

For police, fire, or ambulance, **dial 911** (0 in rural areas).

INSURANCE

Britons and Australians need extra medical coverage when traveling overseas.

➤ INSURANCE INFORMATION: In the U.K.: **Association of British Insurers** (⊠ 51 Gresham St., London EC2V

7HQ, ☎ 020/7600–3333, FAX 020/
7696–8999, WEB www.abi.org.uk). In
Australia: **Insurance Council of Australia** (✉ Level 3, 56 Pitt St., Sydney,
NSW 2000, ☎ 02/9253–5100, FAX 02/
9253–5111, WEB www.ica.com.au). In
Canada: **RBC Insurance** (✉ 6880
Financial Dr., Mississauga, Ontario
L5N 7Y5, ☎ 905/816–2400 or 800/
668–4342, FAX 905/813–4704, WEB
www.rbcinsurance.com). In New
Zealand: **Insurance Council of New
Zealand** (✉ Level 7, 111–115 Customhouse Quay, Box 474, Wellington, ☎ 04/472–5230, FAX 04/473–
3011, WEB www.icnz.org.nz).

MAIL AND SHIPPING

You can buy stamps and aerograms
and send letters and parcels in post
offices. Stamp-dispensing machines
can occasionally be found in airports,
bus and train stations, office buildings, drugstores, and the like. You can
also deposit mail in the stout, dark
blue, steel bins at strategic locations
everywhere and in the mail chutes of
large buildings; pickup schedules are
posted.

For mail sent within the United
States, you need a 37¢ stamp for first-
class letters weighing up to 1 ounce
(23¢ for each additional ounce) and
23¢ for postcards. You pay 80¢ for 1-
ounce airmail letters and 70¢ for
airmail postcards to most other
countries; to Canada and Mexico,
you need a 60¢ stamp for a 1-ounce
letter and 50¢ for a postcard. An
aerogram—a single sheet of
lightweight blue paper that folds into
its own envelope, stamped for overseas airmail—costs 70¢.

To receive mail on the road, have it
sent c/o General Delivery at your
destination's main post office (use the
correct five-digit ZIP code). You must
pick up mail in person within 30
days and show a driver's license or
passport.

PASSPORTS AND VISAS

When traveling internationally, **carry
your passport** even if you don't need
one (it's always the best form of I.D.)
and **make two photocopies of the
data page** (one for someone at home
and another for you, carried sepa-
rately from your passport). If you lose

your passport, promptly call the
nearest embassy or consulate and the
local police.

Visitor visas are not necessary for
Canadian citizens, or for citizens of
Australia and the United Kingdom
who are staying fewer than 90 days.

➤ AUSTRALIAN CITIZENS: **Australian
State Passport Office** (☎ 131–232,
WEB www.passports.gov.au). **United
States Consulate General** (✉ MLC
Centre, 19–29 Martin Pl., 59th floor,
Sydney, NSW 2000, ☎ 02/9373–
9200, 1902/941–641 fee-based visa-
inquiry line, WEB www.usis-australia.
gov/index.html).

➤ CANADIAN CITIZENS: **Passport
Office** (to mail in applications: ✉
Department of Foreign Affairs and
International Trade, Ottawa, Ontario
K1A 0G3, ☎ 819/994–3500 or 800/
567–6868, WEB www.dfait-maeci.gc.
ca/passport).

➤ NEW ZEALAND CITIZENS: **New
Zealand Passport Office** (☎ 04/474–
8100 or 0800/22–5050, WEB www.
passports.govt.nz). **Embassy of the
United States** (✉ 29 Fitzherbert Terr.,
Thorndon, Wellington, ☎ 04/462–
6000, WEB usembassy.org.nz). **U.S.
Consulate General** (✉ Citibank Bldg.,
3rd floor, 23 Customs St. E, Auckland, ☎ 09/303–2724, WEB usembassy.
org.nz).

➤ U.K. CITIZENS: **London Passport
Office** (☎ 0870/521–0410, WEB www.
passport.gov.uk). **U.S. Consulate
General** (✉ Queen's House, 14
Queen St., Belfast, Northern Ireland
BT1 6EQ, ☎ 028/9032–8239, WEB
www.usembassy.org.uk). **U.S. Embassy** (enclose an SASE to ✉ Con-
sular Information Unit, 24 Grosvenor
Sq., London W1 1AE, for general
information; ✉ Visa Branch, 5 Upper
Grosvenor St., London W1A 2JB, to
submit an application via mail; ☎
09068/200–290 recorded visa information or 09055/444–546 operator
service, both with per-minute charges;
WEB www.usembassy.org.uk).

TELEPHONES

All U.S. telephone numbers consist of
a three-digit area code and a seven-
digit local number. Within most local
calling areas, you dial only the seven-
digit local number. Within the same area

code, dial "1" first. To call between area-code regions, dial "1" then all 10 digits; the same goes for calls to numbers prefixed by "800," "888," and "877"—all toll free. For calls to numbers preceded by "900" you must pay—usually dearly.

For international calls, dial "011" followed by the country code and the local number. For help, dial "0" and ask for an overseas operator. The country code is 61 for Australia, 64 for New Zealand, 44 for the United Kingdom. Calling Canada is the same as calling within the United States. Most local phone books list country codes and U.S. area codes. The country code for the United States is 1.

For operator assistance, dial "0." To obtain someone's phone number, call directory assistance, 555–1212 or occasionally 411 (free at public phones). To have the person you're calling foot the bill, phone collect; dial "0" instead of "1" before the 10-digit number.

At pay phones, instructions are usually posted. Usually you insert coins in a slot (10¢–50¢ for local calls) and wait for a steady tone before dialing. When you call long-distance, the operator tells you how much to insert; prepaid phone cards, widely available in various denominations, are easier. Call the number on the back, punch in the card's personal identification number when prompted, then dial your number.

LANGUAGE

Although English is spoken everywhere in South Florida, Spanish can be quite useful to know, especially in Miami-Dade county, where Hispanics make up more than half the population. A good percentage of Miami tourism comes from Latin America, so Spanish can be heard quite frequently in hotels, stores, and restaurants.

LODGING

South Florida has every conceivable type of lodging—from tree houses to penthouses, mansions for hire to hostels. Even with occupancy rates inching above 70%, there are almost always rooms available, except maybe at Christmas and other holidays. Affordable lodgings can be found in even the most glittery resort towns, typically motel rooms that may cost as little as $50–$60 a night; they may not be in the best part of town, mind you, but they won't be in the worst, either (perhaps along busy highways where you'll need the roar of the air-conditioning to drown out the traffic). Since beachfront properties tend to be more expensive, **look for properties a little off the beach.**

Children are welcome generally everywhere in South Florida. Pets are another matter, so **inquire ahead of time if you're bringing an animal with you.**

In the busy seasons—over Christmas and from late January through Easter, and during holiday weekends in summer—always **reserve ahead for the top properties.** Fall is the slowest season: rates are low and availability is high, but this is also the prime time for hurricanes. Key West is jam-packed for Fantasy Fest at Halloween. If you're not booking through a travel agent, call the visitor bureau or the chamber of commerce in the area where you're going to check whether any special event is scheduled for when you plan to arrive. If demand isn't especially high for the time you have in mind, you can often **save by showing up at a lodging in mid- to late afternoon**—desk clerks are typically willing to negotiate with travelers to fill those rooms late in the day. In addition, **check with chambers of commerce for discount coupons for selected properties.**

The lodgings we list are the cream of the crop in each price category. We always list the facilities that are available—but we don't specify whether they cost extra: when pricing accommodations, always ask what's included and what costs extra. Properties are assigned price categories based on the range from their least-expensive standard double room at high season (excluding holidays) to the most expensive. Properties marked ✕▥ are lodging establishments whose restaurants warrant a special trip.

CATEGORY	COST*
$$$$	over $220
$$$	$140–$220
$$	$80–$140
$	under $80

All prices are for a standard double room, excluding 6% sales tax (more in some counties) and 1%–4% tourist tax.

Assume that hotels operate on the **European Plan** (EP, with no meals), unless we specify that they use the **Continental Plan** (CP, with a Continental breakfast), **Breakfast Plan** (BP, with a full breakfast), **Modified American Plan** (MAP, with breakfast and dinner), or the **Full American Plan** (FAP, with all meals).

APARTMENT AND VILLA RENTALS

If you want a home base that's roomy enough for a family and comes with cooking facilities, **consider a furnished rental.** These can save you money, especially if you're traveling with a group. Home-exchange directories sometimes list rentals as well as exchanges.

➤ INTERNATIONAL AGENTS: **Hideaways International** (⊠ 767 Islington St., Portsmouth, NH 03801, ☎ 603/430–4433 or 800/843–4433, FAX 603/430–4444, WEB www.hideaways.com; membership $129). **Hometours International** (⊠ Box 11503, Knoxville, TN 37939, ☎ 865/690–8484 or 800/367–4668, WEB http://thor.he.net/~hometour/). **Interhome** (⊠ 1990 N.E. 163rd St., Suite 110, N. Miami Beach, FL 33162, ☎ 305/940–2299 or 800/882–6864, FAX 305/940–2911, WEB www.interhome.com). **Vacation Home Rentals Worldwide** (⊠ 235 Kensington Ave., Norwood, NJ 07648, ☎ 201/767–9393 or 800/633–3284, FAX 201/767–5510, WEB www.vhrww.com).

➤ LOCAL AGENTS: **Florida Sunbreak** (⊠ 828 Washington Ave., Miami Beach, FL 33139, ☎ 800/786–2732 or 305/532–1516). **Freewheeler Vacations** (⊠ Box 1634 [MM 86], Islamorada, FL 33036, ☎ 305/664–2075). **Marr Properties** (⊠ 101925 Overseas Hwy., Key Largo, FL 33037, ☎ 800/277–3728 or 305/451–4078).

BED-AND-BREAKFASTS

Small inns and guest houses are increasingly numerous in South Florida, but they vary tremendously, ranging from economical places that are plain but serve a good home-style breakfast to elegantly furnished Victorian houses with four-course gourmet morning meals and rates to match. Many offer a homelike setting. In fact, many are in private homes with owners who treat you almost like family, whereas others are more businesslike. It's a good idea to **make specific inquiries of B&Bs you're interested in.** The association listed below offers descriptions and suggestions for B&Bs throughout Florida. *Superior Small Lodging, a Guide to Fine Small Hotels,* is an excellent resource.

➤ BED-AND-BREAKFAST ASSOCIATION: **Florida Bed and Breakfast Inn** (⊠ Box 6187, Palm Harbor, FL 34684, ☎ 281/499–1374 or 800/524–1880, WEB www.florida-inns.com). *Superior Small Lodging, a Guide to Fine Small Hotels* (⊠ Daytona Beach Convention and Visitors Bureau, 126 E. Orange Ave., Daytona Beach, FL 32114, ☎ 356/255–0415 or 800/854–1234).

CAMPING

Camping is popular throughout South Florida. Camping on nondesignated beach sites is not allowed. For information on camping facilities, contact the national and state parks and forests you plan to visit and the Florida Department of Environmental Protection (☞ National Parks).

To find a commercial campground, **pick up a copy of the free annual "Official Florida Camping Directory,"** which lists 305 campgrounds, with more than 55,000 sites. It's available at Florida welcome centers, from the Florida Tourism Industry Marketing Corporation (☞ Visitor Information), and from the Florida Association of RV Parks & Campgrounds.

➤ CAMPING ASSOCIATION: **Florida Association of RV Parks & Campgrounds** (⊠ 1340 Vickers Dr., Tallahassee, FL 32303-3041, ☎ 850/562–7151, FAX 850/562–7179, WEB www.gocampingamerica.com).

CONDOS

➤ CONDO GUIDE: *The Condo Lux Vacationer's Guide to Condominium Rentals in the Southeast* (Vintage Books/Random House, New York; $9.95), by Jill Little.

HOME EXCHANGES

If you would like to exchange your home for someone else's, **join a home-exchange organization,** which will send you its updated listings of available exchanges for a year and will include your own listing in at least one of them. It's up to you to make specific arrangements.

➤ EXCHANGE CLUBS: **HomeLink International** (✉ Box 47747, Tampa, FL 33647, ☎ 813/975–9825 or 800/638–3841, FAX 813/910–8144, WEB www.homelink.org; $106 per year). **Intervac U.S.** (✉ Box 590504, San Francisco, CA 94159, ☎ 800/756–4663, FAX 415/435–7440, WEB www.intervacus.com; $93 yearly fee includes one catalog and on-line access).

HOSTELS

No matter what your age, you can **save on lodging costs by staying at hostels.** In some 4,500 locations in more than 70 countries around the world, Hostelling International (HI), the umbrella group for a number of national youth-hostel associations, offers single-sex, dorm-style beds and, at many hostels, rooms for couples and family accommodations. Membership in any HI national hostel association, open to travelers of all ages, allows you to stay in HI-affiliated hostels at member rates; one-year membership is about $25 for adults (C$35 for a two-year minimum membership in Canada, £13 in the U.K., A$52 in Australia, and NZ$40 in New Zealand); hostels run about $10–$30 per night. Members have priority if the hostel is full; they're also eligible for discounts around the world, even on rail and bus travel in some countries.

➤ ORGANIZATIONS: **Hostelling International–American Youth Hostels** (✉ 733 15th St. NW, Suite 840, Washington, DC 20005, ☎ 202/783–6161, FAX 202/783–6171, WEB www.hiayh.org). **Hostelling International–Canada** (✉ 400–205 Catherine St., Ottawa, Ontario K2P 1C3, ☎ 613/237–7884 or 800/663–5777, FAX 613/237–7868, WEB www.hihostels.ca). **Youth Hostel Association of England and Wales** (✉ Trevelyan House, Dimple Rd., Matlock, Derbyshire DE4 3YH, U.K., ☎ 0870/870–8808, FAX 0169/592–702, WEB www.yha.org.uk). **Youth Hostel Association Australia** (✉ 10 Mallett St., Camperdown, NSW 2050, ☎ 02/9565–1699, FAX 02/9565–1325, WEB www.yha.com.au). **Youth Hostels Association of New Zealand** (✉ Level 3, 193 Cashel St., Box 436, Christchurch, ☎ 03/379–9970, FAX 03/365–4476, WEB www.yha.org.nz).

HOTELS

Wherever you look in South Florida, it seems, you find lots of plain, inexpensive motels and luxurious resorts, independents alongside national chains, and an ever-growing number of modern properties as well as quite a few timeless classics. In fact, since South Florida has been a favored travel destination for some time, vintage hotels are everywhere, both grand edifices like the Breakers in Palm Beach, the Boca Raton Resort & Club in Boca Raton, the Biltmore in Coral Gables, and the Casa Marina in Key West, as well as smaller, historic places. All hotels listed have private bath unless otherwise noted.

➤ HOTEL AND MOTEL ASSOCIATION: **Florida Hotel & Motel Association** (✉ 200 W. College Ave., Box 1529, Tallahassee, FL 32301-1529, ☎ 850/224–2888).

➤ RESERVATION SERVICES: **Accommodations Express** (☎ 800/663–7666, WEB www.accommodationsexpress.com). **Florida Hotel Network** (☎ 800/538–3616, WEB www.floridahotels.com). **Florida Sunbreak** (✉ 828 Washington Ave., Miami Beach, FL 33139, ☎ 305/532–1516, WEB www.floridasunbreak.com).

➤ TOLL-FREE NUMBERS: **Baymont Inns** (☎ 800/428–3438, WEB www.baymontinns.com). **Best Western** (☎ 800/528–1234, WEB www.bestwestern.com). **Choice** (☎ 800/424–6423, WEB www.choicehotels.com). **Clarion** (☎ 800/424–6423, WEB www.

choicehotels.com). **Comfort Inn**
(☎ 800/424–6423, WEB www.
choicehotels.com). **Days Inn** (☎ 800/
325–2525, WEB www.daysinn.com).
Doubletree and Red Lion Hotels (☎
800/222–8733, WEB www.doubletree.
com). **Embassy Suites** (☎ 800/362–
2779, WEB www.embassysuites.com).
Fairfield Inn (☎ 800/228–2800, WEB
www.marriott.com). **Hilton** (☎ 800/
445–8667, WEB www.hilton.com).
Holiday Inn (☎ 800/465–4329,
WEB www.sixcontinentshotels.com).
Howard Johnson (☎ 800/654–4656,
WEB www.hojo.com). **Hyatt Hotels &
Resorts** (☎ 800/233–1234, WEB www.
hyatt.com). **La Quinta** (☎ 800/531–
5900, WEB www.laquinta.com). **Marriott** (☎ 800/228–9290, WEB www.
marriott.com). **Omni** (☎ 800/843–
6664, WEB www.omnihotels.com).
Quality Inn (☎ 800/228–5151,
WEB www.qualityinn.com). **Radisson**
(☎ 800/333–3333, WEB www.radisson.
com). **Ramada** (☎ 800/228–2828;
800/854–7854 international reservations, WEB www.ramada.com or
www.ramadahotels.com). **Renaissance Hotels & Resorts** (☎ 800/468–
3571, WEB www.renaissancehotels.
com). **Ritz-Carlton** (☎ 800/241–
3333, WEB www.ritzcarlton.com).
Sheraton (☎ 800/325–3535, WEB
www.starwood.com/sheraton). **Sleep
Inn** (☎ 800/753–3746, WEB www.
sleepinn.com). **Westin Hotels &
Resorts** (☎ 800/228–3000, WEB www.
starwood.com/westin). **Wyndham
Hotels & Resorts** (☎ 800/822–4200,
WEB www.wyndham.com).

VACATION OWNERSHIP RESORTS

Vacation ownership resorts sell hotel
rooms, condominium apartments,
and villas in weekly, monthly, or
quarterly increments. The weekly
arrangement is most popular; it's
often referred to as "interval ownership" or "time sharing." Of more
than 3,000 vacation ownership resorts around the world, some 500 are
in Florida. Nonowners can rent at
many of these resorts by contacting
the individual property or a real-
estate broker in the area.

MONEY MATTERS

Prices throughout this guide are given
for adults. Substantially reduced fees

are almost always available for children, students, and senior citizens.
For information on taxes, *see* Taxes.

ATMS

Automatic Teller Machines (ATMs)
are ubiquitous in South Florida. In
addition to banks, you will find them
at grocery store chains like Publix
and Winn-Dixie, in shopping malls
big and small, and, increasingly, at
gas stations.

CREDIT CARDS

Throughout this guide, the following
abbreviations are used: AE, American
Express; D, Discover; DC, Diners
Club; MC, MasterCard; and V, Visa.

➤ REPORTING LOST CARDS: **American
Express** (☎ 800/528–4800). **Diners
Club** (☎ 800/525–9135). **Discover**
(☎ 800/347–2683). **MasterCard**
(☎ 800/843–0777). **Visa** (☎ 800/
336–8472).

NATIONAL PARKS

Look into discount passes to save
money on park entrance fees. For
$50, the National Parks Pass admits
you (and any passengers in your
private vehicle) to all national parks,
monuments, and recreation areas, as
well as other sites run by the National
Park Service (NPS), for a year. (In
parks that charge per person, the pass
admits you, your spouse and children,
and your parents, when you arrive
together.) Camping and parking are
extra. The $15 Golden Eagle Pass, a
hologram you affix to your National
Parks Pass, functions as an upgrade,
granting entry to all sites run by the
NPS, the U.S. Fish and Wildlife Service, the U.S. Forest Service, and the
Bureau of Land Management (BLM).
The upgrade, which expires with the
parks pass, is sold by most national-
park, Fish-and-Wildlife, and BLM fee
stations. A percentage of the proceeds
from pass sales funds National Parks
projects.

Both the Golden Age Passport ($10),
for U.S. citizens or permanent residents who are 62 and older, and the
Golden Access Passport (free), for
those with disabilities, entitle holders
(and any passengers in their private
vehicles) to lifetime free entry to all
national parks, plus 50% off fees for

the use of many park facilities and services. (The discount doesn't always apply to companions.) To obtain them, you must show proof of age and of U.S. citizenship or permanent residency—such as a U.S. passport, driver's license, or birth certificate—and, if requesting Golden Access, proof of disability. The Golden Age and Golden Access passes, as well as the National Parks Pass, are available at any NPS-run site that charges an entrance fee. The National Parks Pass is also available by mail and via the Internet.

➤ PASSES BY MAIL: **National Park Service** (⊠ National Park Service/Department of Interior, 1849 C St. NW, Washington, DC 20240, ☎ 202/208–4747, WEB www.nps.gov). **National Parks Pass** (⊠ 27540 Ave. Mentry, Valencia, CA 91355, ☎ 888/GO–PARKS or 888/467–2757, WEB www.nationalparks.org).

PRIVATE PRESERVES

➤ FLORIDA SANCTUARY INFORMATION: **Audubon Florida** (⊠ 444 Birckell Ave., Suite 850, Miami, FL 33131, ☎ 305/371–6399, WEB www.audubonofflorida.org). **Nature Conservancy:** Blowing Rocks Preserve (⊠ 574 South Beach Rd., Hobe Sound, FL 33455, ☎ 561/744–6668). Offices: SE Division (⊠ 333 Fleming St., Key West, FL 33040, ☎ 305/745–8402; ⊠ Comeau Bldg., 319 Clematis St., Suite 611, West Palm Beach, FL 33401, ☎ 954/564–6144).

STATE PARKS

Florida's Department of Environmental Protection (DEP) is responsible for hundreds of historic buildings, landmarks, nature preserves, and parks. When requesting a free *Florida State Park Guide,* mention which parts of the state you plan to visit. For information on camping facilities at the state parks, ask for the free "Florida State Parks, Fees and Facilities" and "Florida State Parks Camping Reservation Procedures" brochures. Responding to cutbacks in its budget, the DEP established Friends of Florida State Parks, a citizen support organization open to all.

➤ STATE PARKS INFORMATION: **Florida Department of Environmental Protection** (⊠ Marjory Stoneman Douglas Bldg., MS 536, 3900 Commonwealth Blvd., Tallahassee, FL 32399-3000, ☎ 850/488–9872). **Friends of Florida State Parks** (☎ 850/488–8243).

OUTDOORS AND SPORTS

Recreational opportunities abound throughout South Florida. The Governor's Council on Physical Fitness and Sports puts on the Sunshine State Games each July in a different part of the state.

➤ GENERAL INFORMATION: **Florida Department of Environmental Protection** (⊠ Office of Greenways and Trails, MS 795, 3900 Commonwealth Blvd., Tallahassee, FL 32399-3000, ☎ 850/488–3701 or 877/822–5208) for information on bicycling, canoeing, kayaking, and hiking trails.

➤ MARINE CHARTS: **Teall's Guides** (⊠ 111 Saguaro La., Marathon, FL 33050, ☎ 305/743–3942, FAX 305/743–3943; $7.95 set, $3.60 each individual chart).

BIKING

Rails to Trails, a nationwide group that turns unused railroad rights-of-way into bicycle and walking paths, has made great inroads in Florida. In addition, just about every town in South Florida has its own set of bike paths and a bike rental outfit. For bike information, **check with Florida's Department of Transportation (DOT),** which publishes free bicycle trail guides, dispenses free touring information packets, and provides names of bike coordinators around the state.

➤ BICYCLE INFORMATION: **Rails to Trails** (☎ 850/942–2379). **DOT** state bicycle-pedestrian coordinator (⊠ 605 Suwannee St., MS 82, Tallahassee, FL 32399-0450, ☎ 850/487–1200).

CANOEING AND KAYAKING

You can canoe or kayak along creeks, rivers, and springs. Both the DEP (☞ General Information) and outfitter associations provide information on trails and their conditions, events, and contacts for trips and equipment rental.

➤ OUTFITTERS AND OUTFITTING ASSOCIATIONS: **Canoe Outpost System** (⊠ 2816 N.W. Rte. 661, Arcadia, FL 33821, ☎ 863/494–1215 or 800/

268–0083) comprises five outfitters. **Florida Professional Paddlesports Association** (⊠ Box 1764, Arcadia, FL 34265, ☎ no phone, WEB www. paddleflausa.com) has a state map available on-line and a directory of local resources.

FISHING

In Atlantic and gulf waters, fishing seasons and other regulations vary by location and species. You will need to **buy one license for freshwater fishing and another license for saltwater fishing.** Nonresident fees for a saltwater license are $31.50. Nonresidents can purchase freshwater licenses good for three days ($6.50), seven days ($16.50), or one year ($31.50). Typically, you'll pay a $1.50 surcharge at most any marina, bait shop, Kmart, Wal-Mart, or other license vendor.

➤ FISHING INFORMATION: **Florida Fish and Wildlife Conservation Commission** (⊠ 620 S. Meridian St., Tallahassee, FL 32399-1600, ☎ 850/488–1960) for the free *Florida Fishing Handbook* with license vendors, regional fishing guides, and educational bulletins.

HORSEBACK RIDING

Horseback riding is a popular sport outside of metropolitan areas. There are trails around the state and even beaches on which you can ride. Please refer to outdoor activities listed in individual chapters.

JOGGING, RUNNING, AND WALKING

Many towns have walking and running trails, and most of South Florida's beaches stretch on for miles, testing the limits of even the most stalwart runners and walkers. Local running clubs all over the state sponsor weekly public events. The Miami Runners Club has information about South Florida events. The Road Runners Club of America has chapters throughout the state.

➤ CLUBS AND EVENTS: **Miami Runners Club** (⊠ 8720 N. Kendall Dr., Suite 206, Miami, FL 33176, WEB www.miamirunnersclub.com). **Road Runners Club of America** (⊠ 23059 Redfish La., Cudjoe Key, FL 33042, ☎ 305/745–3027).

PARI-MUTUEL SPORTS

Jai-alai frontons and greyhound-racing tracks are in most major South Florida cities. Patrons can bet on the teams or dogs or on televised horse races.

➤ SCHEDULES: Department of Business & Professional Regulations **Division of Pari-Mutuel Wagering** (⊠ 1940 N. Monroe St., Tallahassee, FL 32399, ☎ 850/488–9130, FAX 850/488–0550).

TENNIS

Tennis is extremely popular in South Florida, and virtually every town has well-maintained public courts. In addition, many tennis tournaments are held in the state.

➤ TOURNAMENT AND EVENT SCHEDULES: **USA Tennis Florida** (⊠ 1 Deuce Court, Suite 100, Daytona Beach, FL 32124, ☎ 386/671–8949, FAX 386/671–8948, WEB www.usta-fl.com).

WILDERNESS AND RECREATION AREAS

South Florida is studded with trails, rivers, and parks that are ideal for hiking, bird-watching, canoeing, bicycling, and horseback riding. *Florida Trails: A Guide to Florida's Natural Habitats*, available from Florida Tourism Industry Marketing Corporation (☞ Visitor Information), has information for bicycling, canoeing, horseback riding, and walking trails; camping; snorkeling and scuba diving; and Florida ecosystems.

➤ PUBLICATIONS: *Florida Wildlife Viewing Guide,* available from Falcon Press (⊠ Box 1718, Helena, MT 59624, ☎ 800/582–2665); $10.95 plus $4 shipping, by Susan Cerulean and Ann Morrow, for marked wildlife-watching sites. *Recreation Guide to District Lands,* available from St. Johns River Water Management District (⊠ Box 1429, Palatka, FL 32178-1429, ☎ 386/329–4111); free for marine, wetland, and upland recreational areas.

PACKING

The Miami area is warm year-round and often extremely humid in summer months. Be prepared for sudden summer storms throughout South Florida in the summer months, but keep in mind that plastic raincoats are uncomfortable in the high humidity. Farther north, temperatures can get cool in winter months—be sure to take a heavy sweater. Even in the summer ocean breezes can be cool, so always **take a sweater or jacket** just in case.

Dress is casual throughout South Florida, with sundresses, jeans, or walking shorts appropriate during the day. A few restaurants request that men wear jackets and ties, but most do not. Be prepared for air-conditioning working in overdrive.

You can generally swim year-round in South Florida. Be sure to **take a sun hat and sunscreen** because the sun can be fierce, even in winter and even if it is chilly or overcast.

In your carry-on luggage, **pack an extra pair of eyeglasses or contact lenses and enough of any medication** you take to last the entire trip. You may also ask your doctor to write a spare prescription using the drug's generic name, since brand names may vary from country to country. In luggage to be checked, **never pack prescription drugs or valuables.** And don't forget to carry with you the addresses of offices that handle refunds of lost traveler's checks. Check *Fodor's How to Pack* (available in bookstores everywhere) for more tips.

To avoid customs and security delays, carry medications in their original packaging. Don't pack any sharp objects in your carry-on luggage, including knives of any size or material, scissors, manicure tools, and corkscrews, or anything else that might arouse suspicion.

CHECKING LUGGAGE

You are allowed one carry-on bag and one personal article, such as a purse or a laptop computer. Make sure that everything you carry aboard will fit under your seat or in the overhead bin. Get to the gate early, so you can board as soon as possible, before the overhead bins fill up.

If you are flying internationally, note that baggage allowances may be determined not by piece but by weight—generally 88 pounds (40 kilograms) in first class, 66 pounds (30 kilograms) in business class, and 44 pounds (20 kilograms) in economy.

Airline liability for baggage is limited to $2,500 per person on flights within the United States. On international flights it amounts to $9.07 per pound or $20 per kilogram for checked baggage (roughly $640 per 70-pound bag) and $400 per passenger for unchecked baggage. You can buy additional coverage at check-in for about $10 per $1,000 of coverage, but it excludes a rather extensive list of items, shown on your airline ticket.

Before departure, **itemize your bags' contents** and their worth, and label the bags with your name, address, and phone number. (If you use your home address, cover it so potential thieves can't see it readily.) Inside each bag, **pack a copy of your itinerary.** At check-in, **make sure that each bag is correctly tagged** with the destination airport's three-letter code. If your bags arrive damaged or fail to arrive at all, file a written report with the airline before leaving the airport.

SAFETY

Stepped-up policing of thieves who prey on tourists in rental cars has helped address what was a serious issue in the early '90s. Still, visitors should be especially wary when driving in strange neighborhoods and leaving the airport, especially in the Miami area. Don't assume that valuables are safe in your hotel room; use in-room safes or the hotel's safety deposit boxes. Try to use ATMs only during the day or in brightly lit, well-traveled locales.

BEACH SAFETY

Before swimming, **make sure there's no undertow.** Rip currents, caused when the tide rushes out through a narrow break in the water, can overpower even the strongest swimmer. If you do get caught in one, resist the urge to swim straight back to shore—you'll tire before you make it. Instead, stay calm. Swim parallel to the shore line until you are outside the current's pull, then work your way in to shore.

SENIOR-CITIZEN TRAVEL

Since Florida has a significant retired population, senior-citizen discounts are ubiquitous throughout the state. To qualify for age-related discounts, **mention your senior-citizen status up front** when booking hotel reservations (not when checking out) and before you're seated in restaurants (not when paying the bill). Be sure to have identification on hand. When renting a car, ask about promotional car-rental discounts, which can be cheaper than senior-citizen rates.

➤ EDUCATIONAL PROGRAMS: **Elderhostel** (✉ 11 Ave. de Lafayette, Boston, MA 02111-1746, ☎ 877/426–8056, FAX 877/426–2166, WEB www. elderhostel.org). **Interhostel** (✉ University of New Hampshire, 6 Garrison Ave., Durham, NH 03824, ☎ 603/862–1147 or 800/733–9753, FAX 603/862–1113, WEB www.learn. unh.edu).

STUDENTS IN SOUTH FLORIDA

Students flock to the beaches of South Florida during spring break, but there are also special tours for students year-round. Students presenting identification qualify for discounts at most movie theaters and art museums.

➤ I.D.s AND SERVICES: **STA Travel** (☎ 212/627–3111 or 800/781–4040, FAX 212/627–3387, WEB www.sta.com). **Travel Cuts** (✉ 187 College St., Toronto, Ontario M5T 1P7, Canada, ☎ 416/979–2406 or 888/838–2887, FAX 416/979–8167, WEB www.travelcuts. com).

TAXES

SALES TAX

Florida's sales tax is currently 7%, but local sales and tourist taxes can raise that number considerably, especially for certain items, such as lodging. Miami hoteliers, for example, collect roughly 12.5% for city and resort taxes. It's best to **ask about additional costs up front,** to avoid a rude awakening.

TELEPHONES

To make local calls within the 305 (Miami) calling area, **begin calls with the local area code,** dialing a total of 10 digits.

TIME

South Florida is in the Eastern Time Zone.

TIPPING

Whether they carry bags, open doors, deliver food, or clean rooms, hospitality employees work to receive a portion of your travel budget. In deciding how much to give, **base your tip on what the service is and how well it's performed.**

In transit, tip an airport valet $1–$3 per bag, a taxi driver 15%–20% of the fare.

For hotel staff, recommended amounts are $1–$3 per bag for a bellhop, $1–$2 per night per guest for chambermaids, $5–$10 for special concierge service, $1–$3 for a doorman who hails a cab or parks a car, 15% of the greens fee for a caddy, 15%–20% of the bill for a massage, and 15% of a room service bill (bear in mind that sometimes 15%–18% is automatically added to room service bills, so don't add it twice).

In a restaurant, give 15%–20% of your bill before tax to the server, 5%–10% to the maître d', 15% to a bartender, and 15% of the wine bill for a wine steward who makes a special effort in selecting and serving wine.

TOURS AND PACKAGES

Because everything is prearranged on a prepackaged tour or independent vacation, you spend less time planning—and often get it all at a good price.

BOOKING WITH AN AGENT

Travel agents are excellent resources. But it's a good idea to collect brochures from several agencies, as some agents' suggestions may be influenced by relationships with tour and package firms that reward them for volume sales. If you have a special interest, **find an agent with expertise in that area;** the American Society of Travel Agents (ASTA; ☞ Travel Agencies) has a database of specialists worldwide.

Make sure your travel agent knows the accommodations and other services of the place being recommended. Ask about the hotel's location, room size, beds, and whether it has a pool, room service, or programs for children, if you care about these. Has your agent been there in person or sent others whom you can contact?

Do some homework on your own, too: local tourism boards can provide information about lesser-known and small-niche operators, some of which may sell only direct.

BUYER BEWARE

Each year consumers are stranded or lose their money when tour operators—even large ones with excellent reputations—go out of business. So **check out the operator.** Ask several travel agents about its reputation, and try to **book with a company that has a consumer-protection program.** (Look for information in the company's brochure.) In the United States, members of the National Tour Association and the United States Tour Operators Association are required to set aside funds to cover your payments and travel arrangements in the event that the company defaults. It's also a good idea to choose a company that participates in the American Society of Travel Agents' Tour Operator Program (TOP); ASTA will act as mediator in any disputes between you and your tour operator.

Remember that the more your package or tour includes the better you can predict the ultimate cost of your vacation. Make sure you know exactly what is covered, and **beware of hidden costs.** Are taxes, tips, and transfers included? Entertainment and excursions? These can add up.

➤ TOUR-OPERATOR RECOMMENDATIONS: **American Society of Travel Agents** (☞ Travel Agencies). **National Tour Association** (NTA; ✉ 546 E. Main St., Lexington, KY 40508, ☎ 859/226–4444 or 800/682–8886, WEB www.ntaonline.com). **United States Tour Operators Association** (USTOA; ✉ 275 Madison Ave., Suite 2014, New York, NY 10016, ☎ 212/599–6599 or 800/468–7862, FAX 212/599–6744, WEB www.ustoa.com).

TRAIN TRAVEL

Amtrak provides north–south service on two routes to the major cities of West Palm Beach, Fort Lauderdale,

and Miami, with many stops in between on all routes.

➤ TRAIN INFORMATION: **Amtrak** (☎ 800/872–7245, WEB www.amtrak. com).

TRAVEL AGENCIES

A good travel agent puts your needs first. Look for an agency that has been in business at least five years, emphasizes customer service, and has someone on staff who specializes in your destination. In addition, **make sure the agency belongs to a professional trade organization.** The American Society of Travel Agents (ASTA)—the largest and most influential in the field with more than 24,000 members in some 140 countries—maintains and enforces a strict code of ethics and will step in to help mediate any agent-client disputes involving ASTA members if necessary. ASTA (whose motto is "Without a travel agent, you're on your own") also maintains a Web site that includes a directory of agents. (If a travel agency is also acting as your tour operator, *see* Buyer Beware *in* Tours and Packages.)

➤ LOCAL AGENT REFERRALS: **American Society of Travel Agents** (ASTA; ✉ 1101 King St., Suite 200, Alexandria, VA 22314, ☎ 800/965–2782 24-hr hot line, FAX 703/739–3268, WEB www.astanet.com). **Association of British Travel Agents** (✉ 68–71 Newman St., London W1T 3AH, ☎ 020/7637–2444, FAX 020/7637–0713, WEB www.abtanet.com). **Association of Canadian Travel Agents** (✉ 130 Albert St., Suite 1705, Ottawa, Ontario K1P 5G4, ☎ 613/237–3657, FAX 613/237–7052, WEB www.acta.net). **Australian Federation of Travel Agents** (✉ Level 3, 309 Pitt St., Sydney, NSW 2000, ☎ 02/9264–3299, FAX 02/9264–1085, WEB www. afta.com.au). **Travel Agents' Association of New Zealand** (✉ Level 5, Tourism and Travel House, 79 Boulcott St., Box 1888, Wellington 10033, ☎ 04/499–0104, FAX 04/499–0827, WEB www.taanz.org.nz).

VISITOR INFORMATION

For general information about South Florida's attractions, contact the office below; welcome centers are located on Interstate 75 and Interstate 95. For regional tourist bureaus and chambers of commerce see individual chapters.

➤ TOURIST INFORMATION: **Florida Tourism Industry Marketing Corporation** (⊠ Box 1100, 661 E. Jefferson St., Suite 300, Tallahassee, FL 32302, ☎ 850/488–5607, FAX 850/224–2938). In the U.K.: **ABC Florida** (⊠ Box 35, Abingdon, Oxon OX14 4TB, U.K., ☎ 0891/600–555, 50p per minute; send £2 for vacation pack).

WEB SITES

Do check out the World Wide Web when planning your trip. You'll find everything from weather forecasts to virtual tours of famous cities. Be sure to **visit Fodors.com** (www.fodors.com), a complete travel-planning site. You can research prices and book plane tickets, hotel rooms, rental cars, vacation packages, and more. In addition, you can post your pressing questions in the Travel Talk section. Other planning tools include a currency converter and weather reports, and there are loads of links to travel resources.

The state of Florida is very visitor-oriented and has created a terrific Web site—www.flausa.com—with superb links to help you find out all you want to know. It's a wonderful place to learn about everything from fancy resorts to camping trips to car routes to beach towns.

WHEN TO GO

South Florida is a region for all seasons, although most visitors prefer October–April.

Winter remains the height of the tourist season, when South Florida is crowded with "snowbirds" fleeing cold weather in the north. (It did snow in Miami once in the 1970s, but since then the average snowfall has been exactly 00.00 inches.) Hotels, bars, discos, restaurants, shops, and attractions are all crowded. Hollywood and Broadway celebrities appear in sophisticated supper clubs, and other performing artists hold the stage at ballets, operas, concerts, and theaters.

For the college crowd, spring vacation is still the time to congregate in South Florida. Fort Lauderdale, however, where city officials have refashioned the beachfront more as a family resort, no longer indulges young revelers, so it's much less popular with college students than it once was.

Summer in South Florida, as smart budget-minded visitors have discovered, is often hot and very humid, but along the coast, ocean breezes make the season quite bearable and many hotels lower their prices considerably.

CLIMATE

What follows are average daily maximum and minimum temperatures for major cities in South Florida.

KEY WEST (THE KEYS)

Jan.	76F	24C	May	85F	29C	Sept.	90F	32C
	65	18		74	23		77	25
Feb.	76F	24C	June	88F	31C	Oct.	83F	28C
	67	19		77	25		76	24
Mar.	79F	26C	July	90F	32C	Nov.	79F	26C
	68	20		79	26		70	21
Apr.	81F	27C	Aug.	90F	32C	Dec.	76F	24C
	72	22		79	26		67	19

MIAMI

Jan.	74F	23C	May	83F	28C	Sept.	86F	30C
	63	17		72	22		76	24
Feb.	76F	24C	June	85F	29C	Oct.	83F	28C
	63	17		76	24		72	22
Mar.	77F	25C	July	88F	31C	Nov.	79F	26C
	65	18		76	24		67	19
Apr.	79F	26C	Aug.	88F	31C	Dec.	76F	26C
	68	20		77	25		63	17

Smart Travel Tips A to Z

➤ FORECASTS: **Weather Channel Connection** (☎ 900/932–8437), 95¢ per minute from a Touch-Tone phone.

FESTIVALS AND SEASONAL EVENTS

➤ DEC.: In mid-December, the **Winterfest Boat Parade** lights up the Intracoastal Waterway in Fort Lauderdale (☎ 954/767–0686, WEB www. winterfestparade.com).

➤ LATE DEC.–EARLY JAN.: The **Orange Bowl and Junior Orange Bowl Festival,** in the Miami area, are best known for the downtown King Orange Jamboree Parade on December 31 and the Orange Bowl Football Classic at Pro Player Stadium but also include more than 20 youth-oriented events (☎ 305/371–4600).

➤ JAN.: Mid-month, **Art Deco Weekend** spotlights Miami Beach's historic district with an art deco street fair along Ocean Drive, a 1930s-style Moon Over Miami Ball, and live entertainment (☎ 305/672–2014).

The **Miami Jazz Festival** usually falls on the third weekend and takes place beneath the stars at the Bayfront Park Amphitheater (☎ 305/858–8545, WEB www.miamijazzfestival.com).

The **Everglades Seafood Festival,** a monthlong celebration of the ocean's bounty, features free entertainment with music, crafts, and seafood each weekend (☎ 941/695–4100).

Early in the month, **Polo Season** opens at the Palm Beach Polo and Country Club in West Palm Beach (☎ 561/793–1440).

➤ FEB.: The **Coconut Grove Art Festival,** midmonth, is the state's largest (☎ 305/447–0401).

The **Miami Film Festival,** sponsored by the Film Society of America, is 10 days of international, domestic, and local films (☎ 305/348–5555).

➤ MAR.: The self-proclaimed world's largest street party, **Calle Ocho** packs 1 million people onto Miami's Southwest Eighth Street for a frenetic day of live Latin music, ethnic food, and massive corporate product giveaways (☎ 305/644–8888).

Winter Park Sidewalk Arts Festival is one of the Southeast's most prestigious outdoor fine arts festivals and spotlights internationally known artists (☎ 407/672–6390, WEB www. wpsaf.org).

The **Lauderdale-by-the-Sea Craft Festival** features crafts vendors and live entertainment on the beachfront along Commercial Boulevard and A1A (☎ 954/472–3755); there's a second festival held in October.

➤ APR.: The **Delray Affair,** held the weekend following Easter, is Delray Beach's biggest event and includes arts, crafts, and food (☎ 561/279–1380, WEB www.delrayaffair.com).

➤ LATE APR.–EARLY MAY: The **Conch Republic Celebration** honors the founding fathers of the Conch Republic, "the small island nation of Key West" (☎ 305/296–0123).

➤ MAY: The **Air & Sea Show** draws more than 2 million people to the Fort Lauderdale beachfront for performances by big names in aviation, such as the navy's Blue Angels and the air force's Thunderbirds (☎ 954/ 527–5600 Ext. 88).

Nationally recognized Cajun and zydeco performers, the state's largest outdoor dance floor, and 25,000 pounds of crawfish attract both young and old to Fort Lauderdale's stadium for the **Cajun Zydeco Crawfish Festival** in mid-May (☎ 954/ 761–5934).

West Palm Beach celebrates everything under the sun during **Sunfest** (☎ 407/659–5992 or 800/786–3378).

➤ JUNE: The **Miami-Bahamas Goombay Festival,** in Miami's Coconut Grove, celebrates the city's Bahamian heritage the first weekend of the month (☎ 305/443–7928 or 305/ 372–9966) with food, crafts, and street music all day.

➤ JUNE–JULY: **Beethoven by the Beach,** in Fort Lauderdale, features Beethoven's symphonies, chamber pieces, and piano concertos performed by the Florida Philharmonic (☎ 954/561–2997).

➤ JULY: Cities all over the state celebrate Independence Day with outdoor events and spectacular fireworks displays. Fort Lauderdale gathers at the beach and Alexander Park for

Fourth Along the Coast (☎ 954/761–5813).

Summer Family Fun Film Fest, run by the Fort Lauderdale Film Festival, offers games for kids and family movies on Fort Lauderdale's South Beach beginning at sunset (☎ 800/245–4621).

➤ OCT.: The **Fort Lauderdale International Boat Show,** the world's largest show based on exhibit size, displays boats of every size, price, and description at the Bahia Mar marina and four other venues (☎ 954/764–7642).

The **Cedar Key Seafood Festival** is held on Main Street in Cedar Key (☎ 352/543–5600).

Fantasy Fest, in Key West, is a no-holds-barred Halloween costume party, parade, and town fair (☎ 305/296–1817, WEB www.fantasyfest.net).

➤ OCT.–NOV.: The **Fort Lauderdale International Film Festival** showcases three weeks of independent cinema from around the world beginning in late October (☎ 954/760–9898, WEB www.fliff.com).

➤ NOV.: The **Miami Book Fair International,** the largest book fair in the United States, is held on the Wolfson campus of Miami-Dade Community College (☎ 305/237–3032, WEB www.mdcc.edu/bookfair).

1 DESTINATION: SOUTH FLORIDA

The South Side of the Sunshine State

What's Where

Pleasures and Pastimes

Fodor's Choice

Great Itineraries

THE SOUTH SIDE
OF THE SUNSHINE STATE

F THE NICKNAME THE OCEAN STATE weren't being used by Rhode Island, Florida could easily adopt it. Luckily, its real nickname—the Sunshine State—is every bit as accurate. While much of the rest of the country endures Old Man Winter, South Florida maintains a pleasant, sub-tropical climate. The net result is that for more than a century, warm weather (and the bounty that flows from it) has drawn—and continues to draw—hordes of vacationers, snowbirds (winter residents), retirees, immigrants, and other new permanent denizens.

Fly into any South Florida airport during the Christmas season or spring break, and you'll have little doubt as to the economic importance of tourism. Examine the contents of travelers' suitcases—swimsuits, sunscreen, golf clubs, tennis rackets, credit cards—and there's even less doubt about their reasons for visiting: relaxation and recreation.

Of course, the most popular activities center on the coastline. South Florida has a surprising variety of beaches: from the people-watcher beaches to family beaches to secluded beaches. For those with sand aversion, there are the largely sandless, coral-reef-lined shore of Florida's Keys and the mangrove-studded margins in places like the Ten Thousand Islands and Biscayne National Park.

Florida's largest and most cosmopolitan city, Miami, hugs the state's southeastern coast. Whereas Miami Beach has its share of sun and sand, the metropolitan area is equally known for its international trade and international (most notably, Latin) flavor, as well as glitz and celebrity. It seems fitting in this varied state that just a stone's throw away from Miami is one of Florida's other distinctive treasures: the Everglades. This national park—comprising a quiet, slow-flowing river of grass—is home to unusual wildlife, including that quintessential Florida creature: the alligator.

In case you think that South Florida action is only on the coasts, travel inland; agriculture flourishes here—unfortunately, however, sometimes at the expense of the natural environment. Citrus fruits like oranges and grapefruit are as synonymous with Florida as pineapples are with Hawaii; but South Florida farms and ranches also produce sugarcane and cattle.

So how did the phenomenon that's South Florida come about? Almost from its beginnings as a flat, swampy plateau emerging from the ocean, it was home to all sorts of animals disinclined to the cold (at that time, glaciated) weather up north. It wasn't until 12,000–10,000 BC that humans (probably hunter/gatherers) arrived. These original Floridians began to farm and develop societies, and their descendants in South Florida would become the Seminole (south-central to southwest), Miccosukee (south), and Tequesta (southeast) tribes.

As in much of the Americas, the sovereignty of South Florida's native peoples did not last. By the 16th century, a succession of Spanish explorers, including Juan Ponce de León, Pánfilo de Narváez, Hernando de Soto, Tristán de Luna y Arellano, and Pedro Menéndez de Avilés, arrived with visions of wealth. They found little gold and often didn't stay long, but still managed to ravage, enslave, and spread disease among the native population.

After Florida became a U.S. territory in 1821, and then a state in 1845, an influx of whites from the north who were eager to farm and ranch created friction with native tribes, and a series of three wars, known as the Seminole Wars, ensued. Led by then-General (later president) Andrew Jackson, the Anglos ultimately drove many Native Americans off their lands and out.

The earliest European settlements in Florida were in the north—and in fact, the very first permanent settlement in what is now the United States was established in 1565 at St. Augustine. South Florida was not significantly settled by European descendants until after Florida became a state.

But by the late 19th century, a group of aggressive developers had begun to see Florida's potential as a tourist destination. South Florida owes much of the growth of its towns to developer Henry Morrison Flagler, whose Florida East Coast

Railway was extended to West Palm Beach in 1894, Miami in 1896, and eventually Key West in 1912.

Flagler also built opulent hotels that attracted Vanderbilts, DuPonts, Rockefellers, and their confrères. Other developers created their own legacies—Addison Mizner in Palm Beach and Boca Raton, Carl Fisher in Miami Beach, George Merrick in Coral Gables. These names live on today, in everything from island and street names to museums and shopping malls. Unfortunately, progress often meant draining swampland, paving or building over animal habitats, and straightening, damming, dredging, or building new waterways, thereby altering the natural environment forever.

The 20th century saw a succession of land booms and busts, as tourists repeatedly rediscovered the appeal of South Florida and its climate. The late '20s and early '30s depression hit tourism hard, as did a 1935 hurricane that cut off Key West from the mainland (except by boat). The '20s and '30s brought art deco to Miami Beach, whereas the '50s brought grand hotels, like Morris Lapidus's Fountainebleau and Eden Roc. But by the '70s and early '80s, Miami Beach and many other South Florida towns had become rundown geriatric centers (sometimes pejoratively referred to as "God's waiting room") or centers for spring-break debauchery.

By the late '80s, however, towns and cities were beginning to renew themselves. By the '90s, Miami Beach, its art-deco jewels preserved and restored, became hot again. Miami, with its ever-growing Latin population and flavor, finally began to embrace and even tout its multiculturalism. Fort Lauderdale and West Palm Beach spruced up and added new arts and entertainment attractions. Towns and resorts grew, attracting visitors and residents alike. And today, South Florida is once again basking in the sunshine.

WHAT'S WHERE

The Florida Keys

This slender necklace of landfalls off the southern tip of Florida is strung together by a 110-mi-long highway. The Keys have two faces: one a wilderness of flowering jungles and shimmering seas amid mangrove-fringed islands dangling toward the tropics, the other a traffic jam with a view of billboards, shopping centers, and trailer courts. Embrace the first; avoid the latter. Come here for beaches, deep-sea fishing, snorkeling and diving, and the balmy, semitropical weather.

No other place in America, much less Florida, resembles the Keys. The largest portion of the continental United States' only living coral reef is here. Protecting the reef and the fragile ecosystems it supports is a matter of critical concern. Appreciate the reef when you drive the Overseas Highway; it may not be with us forever.

The beauty of the Keys would be reason enough to visit. A bonus is the Keys lifestyle. This is where America goes Caribbean. Your wristwatch starts to chafe, and napping at midday feels obligatory (though not much else does). Welcome to the Land That Stress Forgot.

As you roll westward, leave the highway now and again to marvel at sun and sea or lay your head in places like **The Moorings** in Islamorada, as charming a lodging as you'll find, or the **Hawk's Cay Resort,** with its own movie-set appeal. The end of the road, literally, is Key West, a capital of High Quirk and, regrettably to admirers, no longer off the beaten track. No matter. If the crowds that gather daily at **Key West's Mallory Square** to watch the sunsets are bigger than ever, well, that just makes for a better street party afterward (and a party it is).

Following your own sun worship, repair to **Duval Street** for pure living theater. There is *nothing* you might not see here. On the way back to America proper, stop at **John Pennekamp Coral Reef State Park** on Key Largo. As you snorkel or scuba dive among the vivid coral reefs swarming with bewitchingly bright fish, time stands still, which might just make your vacation feel a little longer.

The Everglades

Created in 1947, **Everglades National Park,** in the southernmost extremity of the peninsula, preserves a portion of the slow-moving "River of Grass"—a 50-mi-wide stream flowing through marshy grassland en route to Florida Bay. **Biscayne National Park,** nearby, is the nation's largest marine park, with almost 96% of the park under water and containing spectacular living coral reefs.

To visit the Everglades is to see South Florida as it has been for a millennium, since long before the coastal swamps were drained and long before Miami rose a short heron's flight to the east. This wilderness of almost otherworldly beauty stands in perfect, fragile counterpoint to Miami's throbbing Latin energy, offering refuge not only to hundreds of species of plants and animals, but also to humans in need of communion with the natural world.

On guided day trips, by walkway or boat, you see things of ineffable beauty, like snowy egrets feeding among the mangrove trees, in zones where no discernible boundary exists between the sea and the land. You're likely to come upon alligators, too, key players in the delicate Everglades ecosystem—strikingly on display at attractions such as the **Everglades Gator Park.** (The vast majority of a gator's facial muscles are devoted to snapping its jaws shut. The opposing muscles, which open the jaws, are few and weak. In theory—mind you, in *theory*—a headlock applied to an alligator's jaws can keep them from opening. If a gator comes running at you with jaws wide open, run.)

To properly see the River of Grass preserved by the Everglades National Park, rent a canoe for a multiday paddle. Or climb into an airboat for a ride through similar terrain nearby. (Mosquito repellent is mandatory.) Or drive on down to **Smallwood's Store** in Chokoloskee Bay near Everglades City, built as a trading post in 1906 by an undauntable Everglades pioneer.

When the din of the cicadas palls, try snorkeling among the reefs or canoeing through the mangroves that edge the shore of Biscayne National Park. The northern extremity of Florida's living reef, with 180,000 acres of coral and cays in Biscayne Bay, is Florida at its wild, gorgeous best, and its beauty puts descriptions to shame.

Miami and Miami Beach

In the 1980s a stylized television cop show called *Miami Vice* brought notoriety to this southernmost of big Florida cities; **South Beach** put it on the map again in the 1990s with its revamping of the Art Deco District. Stomping ground for celebrities such as Madonna and Sylvester Stallone,

the city has gone from an enclave of retired northeasterners to an international crossroads with a Latin beat. Don't miss **Coconut Grove,** the South Florida mainland's oldest settlement. It's chic and casual, full of bistros, cafés, and galleries.

To get the most out of Miami and its neighbor, Miami Beach, it helps to be a bit of a hedonist. By day, many local pleasures revolve around water and sunshine, as at the **Venetian Pool,** perhaps the most whimsical municipal swimming hole anywhere, complete with gondola moorings and Italian architecture. You can also learn to enjoy life with a Latin rhythm.

Practical seminars are on view daily at Little Havana's **Domino Park,** on Southwest 15th Avenue, where Cuban-American retirees spend long afternoons indulging their passion. Forget about joining them, even if you think of yourself as a pretty good domino player—these guys will clean your clock. Instead, watch and wait for the subtropical sunset to turn the tempo way up: after nightfall, Miami is playland for party animals. Street musicians rule on **Calle Ocho** (Southwest 8th Street), not far from Domino Park. The area around the **Bayside Marketplace** offers live music and cuisines of the world until late, as well as till-you-drop shopping until 11 on weekends.

The pastels that brighten Miami's days give way to hot neon hues at bars like **The Clevelander.** Spend an hour strolling in superhip South Beach, home to hundreds of historic art deco buildings, where even the lifeguard stations have a retro look. If you know how to have fun, Miami is for you. If you're not sure how, well, *practice.* You've come to the right place.

Fort Lauderdale and Broward County

Fort Lauderdale has undergone a renaissance in the past decade. Once the premier spring-break spot to party hearty, the city has been transformed as officials have put the squeeze on student revelers and massively renovated the downtown beach areas. Students are still welcome in Fort Lauderdale, of course, but *Animal House* behavior is a thing of the past.

In fact, the **Fort Lauderdale beachfront** is looking better than ever. Yachts are spiffily tied up next to humbler craft at Pier

Sixty-Six and along the city's characteristic canals, which border the backyards along residential streets such as **Gordon Drive.** If you're yachtless, not to worry: grab a water taxi to tour the city's 300 miles of navigable waterways.

Downtown, along Las Olas Boulevard, musicians and crowds of strollers bring the night alive. At the Riverwalk, cafés and gazebos line the New River promenade. If you want to take a break from window shopping, play 18 holes on one of the area's championship links.

Palm Beach and the Treasure Coast

For more than a century, high society has made headlines along South Florida's Atlantic shore from Palm Beach to Boca Raton—part of the Gold Coast. Palm Beach was built by—and exclusively for—the very wealthy. The stage was set by Whitehall, now the **Henry Morrison Flagler Museum,** named after the Standard Oil cofounder and railroad baron, who spared no expense in its construction. During ensuing decades, Flagler's trains ferried other plutocrats, who created more trophy retreats, and today Rolls-Royces jostle Bentleys for parking spaces on **Worth Avenue.**

The coast north of Palm Beach County, called the Treasure Coast, comprises Martin, St. Lucie, and Indian River counties. Towns in these counties have their own affluent populations, but are dotted with nature preserves, fishing villages, and towns with active cultural scenes. Even in elegant communities such as Boca Raton, places like the **Gumbo Limbo Nature Center** let you get away from it all—and back to nature.

PLEASURES AND PASTIMES

Beaches

South Florida possesses many of the top beaches in the country, and no point in the state is more than 60 mi from salt water. From Miami Beach to Haulover Beach Park, a 300-ft-wide, man-made beach stretches a distance of 10 mi. Adding to South Florida's collection are Broward County's beachfront, which extends for miles

without interruption; the beaches along the Treasure Coast, sought out by nesting sea turtles; and the Florida Keys, which comprise about 2,000 mi of shoreline.

Canoeing

The Everglades has areas suitable for flat-water wilderness canoeing. The Loxahatchee River is another popular place to paddle. The Florida Department of Environmental Protection provides maps and brochures of canoe trails. Also contact individual national forests, parks, monuments, reserves, and seashores for information on their canoe trails. Local chambers of commerce have information on trails in county parks. The best time to canoe in South Florida is winter—the dry season—when you're less likely to get caught in a torrential downpour or become a snack for mosquitoes.

Dining

You can expect seafood to be a staple on nearly every South Florida menu, with greater variety on the coasts, and catfish, frogs' legs, and gator tail popular around inland lakes and at Miccosukee restaurants along the Tamiami Trail. South Florida has a diverse assortment of Latin American restaurants and it's also easy to find island specialties born of the Bahamas, Haiti, and Jamaica. A fusion of tropical, Continental, and nouvelle cuisine—some call it Floribbean—has gained widespread popularity. It draws on exotic fruits, spices, and fresh seafood. The influence of earlier Hispanic settlements remains in Key West. And every South Florida restaurant claims to make the best key lime pie. Traditional key lime pie is yellow, not green, with an old-fashioned graham cracker crust and meringue top. Some restaurants serve their key lime pie with a pastry crust; most substitute whipped cream for the more temperamental meringue. Each pie will be a little different. Try several. It is, after all, a vacation.

Fishing

Opportunities for saltwater fishing abound. Many seaside communities have fishing piers that charge admission to anglers (and usually a lower rate to spectators). These piers generally have a bait-and-tackle shop. It's easy to find a boat-charter service that will take you out into deep water. The Keys are dotted with charter services, and Key West has a big sportfishing fleet. Depending on your taste, budget, and needs, you can charter anything from an old wooden craft to a luxurious waterborne palace with state-of-the-art amenities.

In addition to the state's many natural freshwater rivers, South Florida has an extensive system of flood-control canals. In 1989 scientists found high mercury levels in largemouth bass and warmouth caught in parts of the Everglades and in Palm Beach, Broward, and Dade counties and warned against eating fish from those areas. Those warnings remain in effect.

Golf
Except in the heart of the Everglades, you'll never be far from a golf course. Palm Beach County is one of the Florida's leading golf locales. Many of the best courses allow you to play without being a member or hotel guest. You should reserve tee times in advance, especially in winter. Ask about golf reservations when you make your lodging reservations.

Scuba Diving and Snorkeling
South Florida and the Keys attracts huge numbers of the divers and snorkelers. The low-tech pleasures of snorkeling can be enjoyed throughout the Keys and elsewhere where shallow reefs hug the shore. In some locations you can swim near endangered manatees ("sea cows"), which migrate in from the sea to congregate around warm springs during the cool winter months.

FODOR'S CHOICE

Even with so many special places in South Florida, Fodor's writers and editors have their favorites. Here are a few that stand out.

Beaches
Bahia Honda State Park, Bahia Honda Key. The natural sandy beach here, unusual in the Keys, extends on both gulf and ocean sides, and activities in the park abound, from hawk-watching to hiking.

Bill Baggs Cape Florida State Recreation Area. Consistently voted one of South Florida's best beaches, this 414-acre park in Key Biscayne has a plethora of facilities, a historic lighthouse, and great views of the Miami skyline.

Fort Lauderdale Beach. The area along Route A1A between Las Olas and Sunrise boulevards is a hot spot again, thanks to a pedestrian-friendly promenade and the absence of spring breakers.

South Beach, Miami. At this beach, which is as much a social experience as a sun-worshipping spot, there are volleyball nets, *chickee* (palm frond–roofed) huts for shade, and the most vibrantly painted lifeguard stands you'll ever see. Separating the sand from the traffic of Ocean Drive is palm-fringed Lummus Park.

Spanish River Park, Boca Raton. Connected to a large park by pedestrian tunnels under Route A1A, this renourished beach is filled with native vegetation. The park has nature trails and plenty of picnic tables and grills.

Dining
Norman's, Coral Gables. Chef Norman Van Aken turns out artful masterpieces of New World cuisine, combining bold tastes from Latin, American, Caribbean, and Asian traditions. $$$$

Café des Artistes, Key West. A tropical version of French cuisine is served here in a series of intimate dining rooms filled with tropical art and on an outdoor patio. $$$–$$$$

Café L'Europe, Palm Beach. One of the area's most popular restaurants, noted for its European fine-dining experience and mood-setting atmosphere. $$$–$$$$

Mark's Las Olas, Fort Lauderdale. Chef–owner Mark Militello serves up dazzling Florida-style creations, adding flavors from the Mediterranean, Caribbean, and Southwest. $$–$$$$

Armadillo Café, Davie. The atmosphere is as creative and fun as the crowd-pleasing southwestern-style South Florida seafood. $$–$$$

Tom's Place, Boca Raton. Legendary barbecue ribs, friendly service, and moderate prices are mainstays at this local landmark. $–$$

Historic Sites
Henry Morrison Flagler Museum, Palm Beach. Whitehall, Flagler's mansion, is the backdrop for art and railway memorabilia.

Morikami Museum and Japanese Gardens, Delray Beach. The leading U.S. center for Japanese and American cultural exchange is in a model of a Japanese imperial villa.

Vizcaya Museum and Gardens, Coconut Grove. The Italian Renaissance–style villa anchoring the estate of industrialist James Deering contains Renaissance, Baroque, Rococo, and Neoclassical art and furniture.

Lodging

The Breakers, Palm Beach. The building, an opulent Italian Renaissance palace, is amazing as is the resort's ability to balance old-world luxury with modern conveniences. $$$$

Delano Hotel, Miami Beach. An air of surrealism surrounds this much-talked-about South Beach hotel, the hot spot for celebrities and other well-to-do visitors. $$$$

Little Palm Island, Florida Keys. On its own palm-fringed island 3 mi off the shores of Little Torch Key, this dazzling resort of thatch-roof villas on stilts provides a secluded, one-of-a-kind experience you could have only in the Keys. $$$$

The Moorings, Islamorada. Romantic cottages and houses are tucked into a tropical forest that opens onto a private beach at this onetime coconut plantation. $$$–$$$$

Banyan Marina Resort, Fort Lauderdale. For high-end amenities and a water view at bargain prices, this gem can't be beat. $–$$

Views

Everglades National Park from the tower on Shark Valley Loop. This 50-ft observation tower yields a splendid panorama of the River of Grass.

Ocean Drive in the Art Deco District, Miami Beach. This palm-lined beachfront is hopping around the clock.

GREAT ITINERARIES

South Florida is far more diverse than you might realize. It is full of natural wonders and cultural experiences from Latin-American rhythms to hip, movie-star chic.

Highlights of South Florida
5–8 days

The Florida Keys *2 or 3 days.* Key West, 100 mi by boat or bridge-laden highway from the mainland, has a classic island feel, with a laid-back culture and a quaint downtown dotted with famous watering holes. Clear waters make a snorkel or dive trip a must. It's also great fun to tour the island by moped, which you can rent at numerous spots downtown. On your way to Miami through the Middle and Upper Keys, make sure to leave time for a stop at Bahia Honda State Park, one of the loveliest spots in Florida. (☞ The Florida Keys *in* Chapter 6.)

Miami and Miami Beach *2 or 3 days.* Miami has its own spin on the urban experience, a cultural confluence of Latin vibes and subtropical hedonism mixed with an economic vibrancy based on its status as the U.S. gateway to Latin America; to envelop yourself in Latin culture, stop in the Calle Ocho district of Little Havana. Miami is considered hot by most anyone in this hemisphere who is chic or wants to be. You're as likely to see Madonna or Elton John in Miami Beach's South Beach as you are in Hollywood. The protected natural areas of the Everglades and Biscayne national park are only 45 mi southwest. (☞ Exploring Miami and Miami Beach *in* Chapter 2 and Everglades National Park *in* Chapter 3.)

Palm Beach *1 or 2 days.* If you feel at home at a polo match and don't shop at anyplace less upscale than Neiman-Marcus, Palm Beach is for you. It's the richest town, per capita, in Florida and one of the world's playgrounds for the extremely wealthy. And the rich don't choose shabby places. The sun-drenched beaches here are as impressive as the shopping and dining along Worth Avenue and the luxurious hotels, including the famous Breakers. (☞ Palm Beach *in* Chapter 5.)

Natural Wonders

2 to 4 days

Having no appreciable winter has done more for South Florida than make it a good place for golf courses. The constant spring-summer seasonal mix that has prevailed for 100 millennia or so has created beautiful forests and wetlands. If you have a map, a car, and several days, you can see a side of nature here you won't see elsewhere.

Biscayne National Park and Key Largo *1 or 2 days.* At Biscayne National Park, 30 minutes south of Miami, you can see living coral reefs by snorkeling, scuba diving, or taking a glass-bottom boat. Perhaps the best snorkeling and scuba diving, however, is another hour south at magnificent John Pennekamp Coral Reef State Park, near Key Largo, the northernmost of the Florida Keys. (☞ Biscayne National Park *in* Chapter 3 and The Upper Keys *in* Chapter 6.)

The Everglades *1 or 2 days.* For nature lovers, going to Florida and not seeing the Everglades would be like going to Arizona and not seeing the Grand Canyon. Miami is a great gateway to America's biggest protected wetland, and you can try anything from self-guided canoe tours (probably not a good idea for first-timers) to swamp buggy, airboat, and even airplane tours, offered by several parks and commercial operators on U.S. 41 west of Miami. (☞ Everglades National Park *in* Chapter 3.)

Great Beaches

Miami Area *1 or 2 days.* Beaches in the Miami area are not unlike some Los Angeles–area beaches, with lots of male and female would-be models rollerblading along walkways adjacent to the strand. In South Beach, a vibrant café and nightclub district faces the sand. Ten miles north at Haulover Beach you'll find Florida's only legal nude beach. (Signs mark the area.) Or try the sands at Key Biscayne's Bill Baggs Cape Florida State Recreation Area, a lovely park with a lighthouse and a great view of the Miami skyline. Along with their particular "scene," Miami's beaches offer surprisingly clear aqua water. (☞ South Beach/Miami Beach and Virginia Key and Key Biscayne *in* Chapter 2.)

2 MIAMI AND MIAMI BEACH

Miami is arguably the most exotic city that Americans can visit without a passport. On a typical evening in South Beach, for example, you witness the energy and passion of Rio, Monte Carlo, Havana, and Hemingway's Paris. Other neighborhoods also bring the world into clearer focus through diverse architecture, dining, and customs, and have sparked a renaissance for Miami and its sultry sister, Miami Beach, that's reminiscent of the cities' glory days in the 1920s.

Updated by
Kathy Foster,
Jen Karetnick,
Karen
Schlesinger,
Gretchen
Schmidt,
Matthew
Windsor

MIAMI IS DIFFERENT from any other city in America—or any city in Latin America, for that matter, even though it has a distinctly Latin flavor. Both logically and geologically, Miami shouldn't even be here. Resting on a paved swamp between the Everglades and the Atlantic Ocean, the city is subject to periodic flooding, riots, hurricanes, and the onslaught of swallow-size mosquitoes. Despite the downsides, however, Miami is a vibrant city that works and plays with vigor.

The Tequesta Indians called this area home long before Spain's gold-laden treasure ships sailed along the Gulf Stream a few miles offshore. Foreshadowing 20th-century corporations, they traded with mainland neighbors to the north and island brethren to the south. Today their descendants are the 150-plus U.S. and multinational companies whose Latin American headquarters are based in Greater Miami. For fans of international business and random statistics, Greater Miami is home to more than 40 foreign bank agencies, 11 Edge Act banks, 23 foreign trade offices, 31 binational chambers of commerce, and 53 foreign consulates.

The city has seen a decade of big changes. In the late 1980s Miami Beach was an ocean-side geriatric ward. Today's South Beach residents have the kind of hip that doesn't break. The average age dropped from the mid-sixties in 1980 to a youthful early forties today. Toned young men outnumber svelte young women two to one, and hormones are as plentiful as pierced tongues. At night the revitalized Lincoln Road Mall is in full swing with cafés, galleries, and theaters, but it is also suffering vacancies because of rapidly rising rents. The bloom may not be off the rose, but cash-crazy entrepreneurs hoping to strike it rich on Miami's popularity are finding the pie isn't large enough to feed their financial fantasies. Those who have seen how high rents can crush a dream are heading to North Beach and the southern neighborhoods of South Beach, whose derelict buildings are a flashback to the pre-renaissance days of the 1980s. Perhaps this is where the next revival will take place (file this under insider information).

As you plan your trip, know that winter *is* the best time to visit, but if money is an issue, come in the off-season—after Easter and before October. You'll find plenty to do, and room rates are considerably lower. Summer brings many European and Latin American vacationers, who find Miami congenial despite the heat, humidity, and intense afternoon thunderstorms.

Regardless of when you arrive, once you're here, you'll suspect that you've entered Cuban air space. No matter where you spin your radio dial, virtually every announcer punctuates each sentence with an emphatic "COO-BAH!" Look around, and you'll see Spanish on billboards, hear it on elevators, and pick it up on the streets. But Miami sways to more than just a Latin beat. *Newsweek* called the city "America's Casablanca," and it may be right. In addition to populations from Brazil, Colombia, El Salvador, Haiti, Jamaica, Nicaragua, Panama, Puerto Rico, Venezuela, and of course Cuba, there are also representatives from China, Germany, Greece, Iran, Israel, Italy, Lebanon, Malaysia, Russia, and Sweden—all speaking a veritable babel of tongues. Miami has accepted its montage of nationalities, and it now celebrates this cultural diversity through languages, festivals, world-beat music, and a wealth of exotic restaurants.

If you're concerned about Miami crime, you'll be glad to know that criminals are off the street—and seem to be running for public office. Forget about D.C. If you want weird politics, spread out a blanket and enjoy the show. Ex-mayor Xavier Suarez was removed from office in March 1998 after a judge threw out absentee ballots that included votes from dead people. The Miami City Commission chairman was also removed following a voter fraud conviction, and a state senator was reelected despite being under indictment for pocketing profits from sham home-health-care companies. Oddly enough, Miami-Dade County came out fairly unscathed in the 2000 Florida presidential race, perhaps overshadowed by the well-publicized ballot woes of Palm Beach County to the north.

Corrupt politicians aside, Miami has its share of the same crimes that plague any major city. However, you'll be happy to know that the widely publicized crimes against tourists of the early 1990s led to stepped-up and effective visitor-safety programs. Highway direction signs with red-sunburst logos are installed at ¼-mi intervals on major roads and lead directly to such tourist hot spots as Coconut Grove, Coral Gables, South Beach, and the Port of Miami. Patrol cars bearing the sunburst logo are driven by TOP (Tourist Oriented Police) Cops, who cruise heavily visited areas and add a sense of safety. Identification that made rental cars conspicuous to would-be criminals has been removed, and multilingual pamphlets on avoiding crime are widely distributed. The precautions have had a positive impact: since 1992 the number of tourist robberies in Greater Miami has decreased more than 80%.

What *is* on the increase is Miami's film profile. Arnold Schwarzenegger and Jamie Lee Curtis filmed *True Lies* here, Al Pacino and Johnny Depp dropped by to shoot scenes for *Donnie Brasco,* Jim Carrey rose to stardom through the Miami-based *Ace Ventura: Pet Detective,* Robin Williams and Nathan Lane used two deco buildings on Ocean Drive as their nightclub in *The Birdcage,* and Cameron Diaz discovered a new brand of hair gel in *There's Something About Mary.* All in all, it's a far cry from when Esther Williams used to perform water ballet in Coral Gables' Venetian Pool. Add to this mix daily fashion-magazine and TV shoots, and you'll see that Miami is made for the media.

You can easily have the kind of fun here that will drain your wallet. But look for less-flashy ways to explore Miami, too. Skip the chichi restaurant and go for an ethnic eatery. Tour Lincoln Road Mall, downtown Coral Gables, or Coconut Grove on foot. Or take South Beach's colorful Electrowave shuttle, Florida's first electric transportation system, which really works for getting around traffic-clogged South Beach. Nearly 10 million tourists arrive annually to see what's shaking in Miami-Dade County and discover a multicultural metropolis that invites the world to celebrate its diversity.

Pleasures and Pastimes

Beaches

Greater Miami has numerous free beaches to fit every style. A sandy, 300-ft-wide beach with several distinct sections extends for 10 mi from the foot of Miami Beach north to Haulover Beach Park. Amazingly, it's all man-made. Seriously eroded during the mid-1970s, the beach was restored in a $51.5 million project between 1977 and 1981 and remains an ongoing project for environmental engineers, who spiff up the sands every few years. Between 23rd and 44th streets, Miami Beach built boardwalks and protective walkways atop a dune landscaped with sea oats, sea grape, and other native plants whose roots keep the sand from blowing away. Farther north there's even a nude beach, and Key Biscayne adds more great strands to Miami's collection. Even if the Deco District didn't exist, the area's beaches would be enough to satisfy tourists.

Boating

It's not uncommon for traffic to jam at boat ramps, especially on weekend mornings, but the waters are worth the wait. If you have the opportunity to sail, do so. Blue skies, calm seas, and a view of the city skyline make for a pleasurable outing—especially at twilight, when the fabled "moon over Miami" casts a soft glow on the water. Key Biscayne's calm waves and strong breezes are perfect for sailing and windsurfing, and although Dinner Key and the Coconut Grove waterfront remain the center of sailing in Greater Miami, sailboat moorings and rentals sit along other parts of the bay and up the Miami River.

Miami's idle rich prefer attacking the water in sleek, fast, and nicotine-free cigarette boats, but there's plenty of less-powerful powerboating to enjoy as well. Greater Miami has numerous marinas, and dockmasters can provide information on any marine services you may need. Ask for *Teall's Tides and Guides, Miami-Dade County,* and other nautical publications.

Dining

Miami cuisine is what mouths were made for. The city serves up a veritable United Nations of dining experiences, including dishes native to Spain, Cuba, and Nicaragua as well as China, India, Thailand, Vietnam, and other Asian cultures. Chefs from the tropics combine fresh, natural foods—especially seafood—with classic island-style dishes, creating a new American cuisine that is sometimes called Floribbean. Another style finding its way around U.S. restaurants is the Miami-born New World cuisine. The title comes from chefs who realized their latest creations were based on ingredients found along the trade routes discovered by early explorers of the "New World."

Nightlife

Fast, hot, and as transient as the crowds who pass through their doors, Miami's nightspots are as sizzling as their New York and L.A. counterparts. The densest concentration of clubs is on South Beach along Washington Avenue, Lincoln Road Mall, and Ocean Drive. Other nightlife centers on Little Havana and Coconut Grove, and on the fringes of downtown Miami. Miami's nightspots offer jazz, reggae, salsa, various forms of rock, disco, and Top 40 sounds, most played at a body-thumping, ear-throbbing volume. Some clubs refuse entrance to anyone under 21, others to those under 25, so if that is a concern, call ahead. If you prefer to hear what people are saying, try the many lobby bars at South Beach's art deco hotels. Throughout Greater Miami, bars and cocktail lounges in larger, newer hotels operate nightly discos with live weekend entertainment. Many hotels extend their bars into open-air courtyards, where you can dine and dance under the stars throughout the year.

Spectator Sports

Greater Miami has franchises in basketball, football, and baseball. Fans still turn out en masse for the Dolphins, and—in the best fair-weather-fan tradition—show up for basketball's Heat and Sol and the 1997 World Series champion Marlins. Miami also hosts top-rated events in boat racing, auto racing, jai alai, golf, and tennis. Each winter, the FedEx Orange Bowl Football Classic highlights college football.

EXPLORING MIAMI AND MIAMI BEACH

Revised by
Kathy Foster

If you had arrived here 40 years ago with Fodor's guide in hand, chances are you'd be thumbing through listings looking for alligator wrestlers and u-pick citrus groves. Well, things have changed. While Disney sidetracked families in Orlando, Miami was developing a grown-up attitude courtesy of *Miami Vice,* European fashion photographers, and historic preservationists. Nowadays the wildest ride is the city itself.

Climb aboard and check out the different sides of Greater Miami. Miami, on the mainland, is South Florida's commercial hub, whereas its sultry sister, Miami Beach (America's Riviera), encompasses 17 islands in Biscayne Bay. Seducing winter refugees with its warm sunshine, sandy beaches, shady palms, and ever-rocking nightlife, this is what most people envision when planning a trip to what they think of as Miami. These same visitors fail to realize that there's more to Miami Beach than the bustle of South Beach and its Deco District. Indeed there are quieter areas to the north, with names like Sunny Isles, Surfside, and Bal Harbour.

During the day downtown Miami has become the lively hub of the mainland city, now more accessible thanks to the Metromover extension. Other major attractions include Coconut Grove, Coral Gables, Little Havana, and, of course, the South Beach/Art Deco District, but since these areas are spread out beyond the reach of public transportation, you'll have to drive. Rent a convertible if you can. There's nothing quite like wearing cool shades and feeling the wind in your hair as you drive across one of the causeways en route to Miami Beach.

To find your way around Greater Miami, it's important to know how the numbering system works. Miami is laid out on a grid with four quadrants—northeast, northwest, southeast, and southwest—which meet at Miami Avenue and Flagler Street. Miami Avenue separates east from west, and Flagler Street separates north from south. Avenues and courts run north–south; streets, terraces, and ways run east–west. Roads run diagonally, northwest–southeast. But other districts—Miami Beach, Coral Gables, and Hialeah—may or may not follow this system, and along the curve of Biscayne Bay, the symmetrical grid may shift diagonally. It's best to buy a detailed map, stick to the major roads, and ask directions early and often. However, make sure you're in a safe neighborhood or public place when you seek guidance; cabbies and cops are good resources.

Numbers in the text correspond to numbers in the margin and on the Miami Beach; Downtown Miami; Miami, Coral Gables, Coconut Grove, and Key Biscayne; and South Dade maps.

Great Itineraries

IF YOU HAVE 3 DAYS

To recuperate from your journey, grab your lotion and head to the ocean, more specifically **Ocean Drive** on **South Beach,** where you can catch some rays while relaxing on the white sands. Afterward, take a guided or self-guided tour of the **Art Deco District** to see what all the fuss is about. Keep the evening free to socialize at Ocean Drive cafés. The following day drive through **Little Havana** to witness the heartbeat of Miami's Cuban culture (and snag a stogie) on your way south to Coconut Grove's Vizcaya. Wrap up the evening a few blocks away in downtown **Coconut Grove,** enjoying its partylike atmosphere and many nightspots. On the last day head over to **Coral Gables** to take in the eye-popping display of 1920s Mediterranean revival architecture in the neighborhoods surrounding the city center and the majestic **Biltmore Hotel**; then take a dip in the fantastic thematic **Venetian Pool.** That night indulge in an evening of fine dining at your choice of gourmet restaurants in Coral Gables.

IF YOU HAVE 5 DAYS

Follow the suggested three-day itinerary, and on day four add a visit to the beaches of **Virginia Key** and **Key Biscayne,** where you can take a diving trip or fishing excursion, learn to windsurf, or do absolutely nothing but watch the water. On day five step back to the 1950s with a cruise up **Collins Avenue** to some of the monolithic hotels, such as the **Fontainebleau Hilton** and **Eden Roc**; continue north to the elegant shops of **Bal Harbour**; and return to **South Beach** for an evening of shopping, drinking, and outdoor dining at **Lincoln Road Mall.**

IF YOU HAVE 7 DAYS

A week gives you just enough time to experience fully the multicultural, cosmopolitan, tropical mélange that is Greater Miami and its beaches. On day six see where it all began. Use the Miami Metromover to ride above downtown Miami before touring the streets (if possible, on a tour with historian Dr. Paul George). Take time to visit the **Miami-Dade Cultural Center,** home of art and history museums. In the evening check out the shops and clubs at **Bayside Marketplace.** The final day can be used to visit **South Miami,** site of **Fairchild Tropical Garden** and the **Shops at Sunset Place.** Keep the evening free to revisit your favorite nightspots.

South Beach/Miami Beach

The hub of Miami Beach is South Beach (SoBe, to anyone but locals), and the hub of South Beach is the 1-square-mi Art Deco District, fronted on the east by Ocean Drive and on the west by Alton Road. The story of South Beach has become the story of Miami. In the early 1980s South Beach's vintage hotels were badly run down, catering mostly to infirm retirees. But a group of visionaries led by the late Barbara Baer Capitman, a spirited New York transplant, saw this collection of buildings as an architectural treasure to be salvaged from a sea of mindless urban renewal. It was, and is, a peerless grouping of art deco architecture from the 1920s to 1950s, whose forms and decorative details are drawn from nature, the streamlined shapes of modern transportation and industrial machinery, and human extravagance.

Investors started fixing up the interiors of these hotels and repainting their exteriors with a vibrant pastel palette—a look made famous by *Miami Vice.* International bistro operators sensed the potential for a new café society. Fashion photographers and the media took note, and celebrities like singer Gloria Estefan; the late designer Gianni Versace, whose fashions captured the feel of the awakening city; and record executive Chris Blackwell bought a piece of the action.

As a result, South Beach now holds the distinction of being the nation's first 20th-century district on the National Register of Historic Places, with more than 800 significant buildings making the roll. New high-rises and hotels spring up, areas like SoFi (south of Fifth) blossom, and clubs open (and close) with dizzying speed. Photographers pose beautiful models for shoots, tanned skaters zip past palm trees, and tourists flock to see the action.

Yet Miami Beach is more than just SoBe. (The northern edge of South Beach is generally considered to be around 24th–28th streets, whereas Miami Beach itself extends well north.) It also consists of a collection of quiet neighborhoods where Little Leaguers play ball, senior citizens stand at bus stops, and locals do their shopping away from the prying eyes of visitors. Surprisingly, Miami Beach is a great walking town in the middle of a great city.

Several things are plentiful in SoBe: pierced body parts, cell phones, and meter maids. Tickets are given freely when meters expire, and towing charges are high. Check the meter to see when parking fees are required; times vary by district. From midmorning on, parking is scarce along Ocean Drive. You'll do better on Collins or Washington avenues, the next two streets to the west. Fortunately, there are several surface parking lots south and west of the Jackie Gleason Theater, on 17th Street, and parking garages on Collins Avenue at 7th and 13th streets, on Washington Avenue at 12th Street, and west of Washington at 17th Street. Keep these sites in mind, especially at night, when cruising traffic makes it best to park your car and see SoBe on foot. Better yet, catch the colorful Electrowave shuttle buses that cover South Beach well into the wee hours—for 25¢, they're the best deal in town.

A Good Walk

The stretch of Ocean Drive from 1st to 23rd streets—primarily the 10-block stretch from 5th to 15th streets—has become the most talked-about beachfront in America. A bevy of art deco jewels hugs the drive, and across the street lies palm-fringed **Lummus Park** ①, the south end of which is a good starting point for a walk. Beginning early (at 8) gives you the pleasure of watching the awakening city without distraction. Sanitation men hose down dirty streets, merchants prepare window displays, bakers bake, and construction workers change the skyline one brick at a time. Cross to the west side of Ocean Drive, where there are many sidewalk cafés, and walk north, taking note of the Park Central Hotel, built in 1937 by deco architect Henry Hohauser.

At 10th Street recross Ocean Drive to the beach side and visit the **Art Deco District Welcome Center** ② in the 1950s-era Oceanfront Auditorium. Here you can rent tapes or hire a guide for a Deco District tour.

Look back across Ocean Drive and take a look at the wonderful flying-saucer architecture of the Clevelander, at No. 1020. On the next block you'll see the late Gianni Versace's Spanish Mediterranean **Casa Casuarina** ③, once known as Amsterdam Palace. Graceful fluted columns stand guard at art deco buildings the Leslie (No. 1244) and **The Carlyle** ④.

Walk two blocks west (away from the ocean) on 13th Street to Washington Avenue, where a mix of chic restaurants, avant-garde shops, delicatessens, produce markets, and nightclubs have spiced up a once-derelict neighborhood. Turn left on Washington and walk 2½ blocks south to **Wolfsonian–Florida International University** ⑤, which showcases artistic movements from 1885 to 1945.

Provided you haven't spent too long in the museum, return north on Washington Avenue past 14th Street, and turn left on **Espanola Way** ⑥, a narrow street of Mediterranean revival buildings, eclectic shops, and a weekend market. Continue west to Meridian Avenue and turn right. Three blocks north of Espanola Way is the redesigned **Lincoln Road Mall** ⑦, which is often paired with Ocean Drive as part of must-see South Beach.

The next main street north of Lincoln Road is 17th Street, and to the east is the Miami Beach Convention Center. Walk behind the massive building to the corner of Meridian Avenue and 19th Street to see the chilling **Holocaust Memorial** ⑧, a monumental record honoring the 6 million Jewish victims of the Holocaust.

Head east to the **Bass Museum of Art** ⑨, a Maya-inspired temple filled with European splendors. Return to Ocean Drive in time to pull up a chair at an outdoor café, order an espresso, and settle down for an evening of people-watching, SoBe's most popular pastime. If you've seen enough people, grab some late rays at one of the area's beaches, which offer different sands for different tans. You can go back to Lummus Park (*the* beach) or head north, where there's a boardwalk for walking but no allowance for skates and bicycles.

TIMING

To see only the art deco buildings on Ocean Drive, allow one hour minimum. Depending on your interests, schedule at least five hours and include a drink or meal at a café and browsing time in the shops on Ocean Drive, along Espanola Way, and at Lincoln Road Mall.

Start your walking tour as early in the day as possible. In winter the street becomes crowded as the day wears on, and in summer, afternoon heat and humidity can be unbearable, wilting even the hardiest soul. Finishing by midafternoon also enables you to hit the beach and cool your heels in the warm sand.

Sights to See

② **Art Deco District Welcome Center.** Run by the Miami Design Preservation League, the center provides information about the buildings in the district. A gift shop sells 1930s–1950s art deco memorabilia, posters, and books on Miami's history. Several tours—covering Lincoln Road, Espanola Way, North Beach, the entire Art Deco District—start here. You can rent audiotapes for a self-guided tour, join the regular Saturday-morning or Thursday-evening walking tours, or take a bicycle tour—all of the options provide detailed histories of the art deco hotels. Don't miss their special boat tours during Art Deco Weekend in early January. A second location (⊠ 520 Lincoln Rd., ☎ 305/672–2014), behind the Miami Beach Community Church, has art deco merchandise and furniture. ⊠ *1001 Ocean Dr., at Barbara Capitman Way (10th St.), South Beach,* ☎ *305/531–3484.* ⊡ *Tours $10–$15.* ☉ *Sun.–Thurs. 10–10, Fri.–Sat. 10 AM–midnight.*

Bal Harbour. This affluent community, known for its upscale shops, has a stretch of prime beach real estate, where wealthy condominium owners cluster during the winter. Look closely, and you may spy Bob Dole sunning himself outside his condo. ⊠ *Collins Ave. between 96th and 103rd Sts., Bal Harbour.*

⑨ **Bass Museum of Art.** A diverse collection of European art is the focus of this impressive museum in historic Collins Park, a short drive north of SoBe's key sights. Works on display include *The Holy Family,* a painting by Peter Paul Rubens; *The Tournament,* one of several 16th-century Flemish tapestries; and works by Albrecht Dürer and Henri de Toulouse-Lautrec. An $8 million, three-phase expansion by architect Arata Isozaki added another wing, cafeteria, and theater, doubling the museum's size to nearly 40,000 square ft. ⊠ *2121 Park Ave., South Beach,* ☎ *305/673–7530,* WEB *www.bassmuseum.org.* ⊡ *$5.* ☉ *Tues.–Sat. 10–5, except 2nd and 4th Thurs. of each month 1–9; Sun. 1–5.*

④ **The Carlyle.** Built in 1941, this empty deco building no longer functions as a hotel, but it's still popular as a movie location. Fans will recognize it and its neighbor, the Leslie, as the nightclub from *The Birdcage,* starring Robin Williams and Nathan Lane. ⊠ *1250 Ocean Dr., South Beach.*

③ **Casa Casuarina.** In the early 1980s, before South Beach became a hotbed of chicness, the late Italian designer Gianni Versace purchased this run-down Spanish Mediterranean residence, built before the arrival of deco. Today the home is an ornate three-story palazzo with a guest house and a copper-dome rooftop observatory and pool that were added at the expense of a 1950s hotel, the Revere. Its loss and the razing of the fabled deco Senator became a rallying point for preservationists. In July 1997 Versace was tragically shot and killed in front of his home. Like a tropical Ford's Theatre, this now attracts picture-taking tourists. Eerie. ⊠ *1114 Ocean Dr., South Beach.*

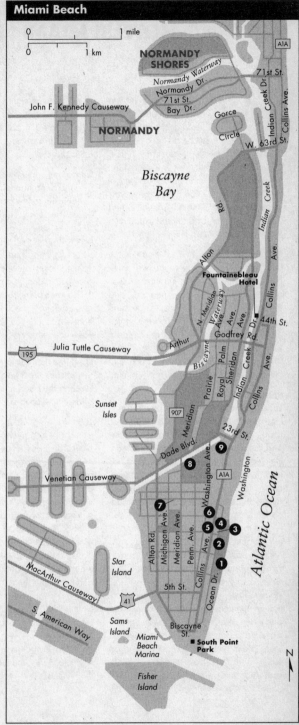

Miami Beach

ART DECO HOTELS: MIAMI NICE

WITH APOLOGIES TO the flamingo, Miami's most recognizable icons are now the art deco hotels of South Beach. Their story begins in the 1920s, when Miami Beach was a winter playground of the rich, and grand themed hotels ruled. By the late '20s, however, shipping problems and a hurricane turned the boom to bust, and another approach to attract vacationers was needed.

In the early 1930s it was the turn of the middle class, which was drawn south by a more affordable version of paradise. New hotels were needed, and the architectural motif of choice became what is called deco (for purists, moderne), based on a sleek and cheerful look with geometric designs and creative colors. It was introduced in Paris in the '20s and later crossed the Atlantic.

In South Beach, architects added other shapes brought to America by industrial designers: streamlined, aerodynamic forms based on trains, ocean liners, and automobiles. Using a steel-and-concrete box as a foundation, architects dipped into this new grab bag of styles to accessorize their hotels. Pylons, spheres, cylinders, and cubes thrust out from facades and roofs. "Eyebrows," small ledges topping window frames, popped out of buildings like concrete caps. To soften sharp edges, designers added wraparound windows and curved corners, many ornamented with racing stripes. To reflect the beach locale, nautical elements were added: portholes appeared in sets of three. Small images of seaweed, starfish, and rolling waves were plastered, painted, or etched on walls. Buildings looked ready to go to sea. Also taking advantage of the environment, sunlight, an abundant commodity, was brought indoors through glass blocks. But because there was no air-conditioning, coolness was achieved by planting shady palms and laying terrazzo tile.

Of course, everything has a life span, and the deco hotels were no exception. Eventually, bold colors and creative accents became cliché, and ensuing decades saw owners hide their hotels beneath coats of plain white or beige paint. Deco still had its proponents, inspiring later architects, most notably Morris Lapidus, to create larger-than-life 1950s deco hotels, such as the Fontainebleau and Eden Roc. But the days of small deco hotels had passed. By the 1970s they were no longer welcoming tourists . . . or welcoming to look at. Most had matured into flophouses or dirt-cheap homes for retirees. Various plans ranging from leveling the buildings to legalizing gambling were proposed—and defeated.

Then in the 1980s, an unusual confluence of people and events proved the area's salvation. The hyperactive cop show *Miami Vice,* set against the newly painted pastel facades of Ocean Drive, portrayed an exotic tropical appeal. European fashion photographers, restaurateurs, and entrepreneurs started using the area as a backdrop for models, cafés, and resurrected hotels. Above all, there was Barbara Baer Capitman, a senior citizen who reviewed South Beach's buildings and proposed them for the National Register of Historic Places. Thanks to her efforts and the ongoing drive of others to rescue, maintain, and improve these historic jewels, a new generation (yourself included) can experience the same tropical pleasures enjoyed by travelers of the 1930s.

★ ❻ **Espanola Way.** The Mediterranean revival buildings along this road were constructed in 1925 and frequented through the years by artists and writers. In the 1930s future bandleader Desi Arnaz strapped on a conga drum and started beating out a rumba rhythm at a nightclub that is now the Clay Hotel, a youth hostel. Since high rents have pushed some merchants out and vacant storefronts have resulted, try to visit this quaint avenue on a Sunday afternoon, when itinerant dealers and craftspeople set up shop to sell everything from garage-sale items to handcrafted bongo drums. Between Washington and Drexel avenues, the road has been narrowed to a single lane, and Miami Beach's trademark pink sidewalks have been widened to accommodate sidewalk cafés and shops selling imaginative clothing, jewelry, and art. ⊠ *Espanola Way, between 14th and 15th Sts. from Washington to Jefferson Aves., South Beach.*

★ **Fontainebleau Hilton Resort and Towers.** For a sense of what Miami was like during the Fabulous '50s, take a drive north to see the finest example of Miami Beach's grandiose architecture. By the 1950s smaller deco-era hotels were passé, and architects like Morris Lapidus got busy designing free-flowing hotels that affirmed the American attitude of "bigger is better." Even if you're not a guest, wander through the lobby and spectacular pool area just to feel the energy generated by an army of bellhops, clerks, concierges, and travelers. ⊠ *4441 Collins Ave., between 44th and 45th Sts., Miami Beach,* ☎ *305/538–2000,* WEB *www.fontainebleau.hilton.com.*

☁ **Haulover Beach Park.** At this county park, far from the action of SoBe, you can see the Miami of 30 years ago. Pack a picnic, use the barbecue grills, or grab a snack at the concession stand. If you're into fitness, you may like the tennis and volleyball courts or paths designed for exercise, walking, and bicycling. If you're into cleanliness, take advantage of the shower facilities. The beach is nice for those who want water without long marches across hot sand, and a popular clothing-optional section at the north end of the beach lures people who want to tan every nook and cranny. Other offerings are kite rentals, kayak rentals, charter fishing excursions, and a par-3, 9-hole golf course. ⊠ *10800 Collins Ave., Sunny Isles,* ☎ *305/947–3525,* WEB *co.miami-dade.fl.us/parks.* ⊠ *$4 per vehicle.* ☉ *Daily dawn–dusk.*

❽ **Holocaust Memorial.** The focus of the memorial is a 42-ft-high bronze arm rising from the ground, with sculptured people climbing the arm seeking escape. Don't stare from the street. Enter the courtyard to see the chilling memorial wall and hear the eerie songs that seem to give voice to the victims. ⊠ *1933–1945 Meridian Ave., South Beach,* ☎ *305/538–1663,* WEB *www.holocaustmmb.org.* ⊠ *Free.* ☉ *Daily 9–9.*

NEED A
BREAK?
   If your feet are still holding up, head to the **Delano Hotel** (⊠ 1685 Collins Ave., South Beach, ☎ 305/674–6400) for a drink. This surrealistic hotel, like a Calvin Klein ad come to life, delivers fabulousness every step of the way. It's popular among SoBe's fashion models and hepcats.

★ ☁ ❼ **Lincoln Road Mall.** The Morris Lapidus renovated Lincoln Road is fun, lively, and friendly for people old, young, gay, and straight—and their dogs. Folks skate, scoot, bike, or jog here, past the electronics stores at the Collins Avenue end toward the chichi boutiques and outdoor cafés heading west. The best times to hit the road are during Sunday-morning farmers markets and on weekend evenings, when cafés are bustling; art galleries, like Romero Britto's Britto Central, schedule openings; street performers take the stage; and bookstores, import shops, and clothing stores are open for late-night purchases. ⊠ *Lincoln Rd. between Collins Ave. and Alton Rd., South Beach.*

① Lummus Park. Once part of a turn-of-the-last-century plantation owned by brothers John and James Lummus, this palm-shaded oasis on the beach side of Ocean Drive attracts beach-going families with its children's play area. Senior citizens predominate early in the day. Volleyball, in-line skating along the wide and winding sidewalk, and a lot of posing go on here. Gays like the beach between 11th and 13th streets. The lush foliage is a pleasing, natural counterpoint to the ultrachic atmosphere just across the street, where endless sidewalk cafés make it easy to come ashore for everything from burgers to quiche. Like New York's Central Park, this is a natural venue for big-name public concerts by such performers as Luciano Pavarotti and past Art Deco Weekend stars Cab Calloway and Lionel Hampton. ⊠ *East of Ocean Dr. between 5th and 15th Sts., South Beach.*

North Beach. Families and those who like things quiet prefer this section of beach. Metered parking is ample right behind the dune and a block behind Collins Avenue along a pleasant, old shopping street. With high prices discouraging developers from SoBe, this area will no doubt see some redevelopment in years to come. However, without the cafés or 300-ft-wide beach to lure tourists, it may never match SoBe's appeal. ⊠ *Ocean Terr. between 73rd and 75th Sts., North Beach.*

OFF THE
BEATEN PATH

OLETA RIVER STATE RECREATION AREA – At nearly 1,000 acres, this is the largest urban park in Florida. It's backed by lush tropical growth rather than hotels and offers group and youth camping, 14 log cabins, kayak and canoe rentals, mountain-bike trails, and a fishing pier. Popular with outdoors enthusiasts, it also attracts dolphins, ospreys, and manatees, who arrive for the winter. ⊠ *3400 N.E. 163rd St., North Miami Beach,* ☎ *305/919–1846,* WEB *www.dep.state.fl.us/parks/district5/oletariver.* ⊠ *$4 per vehicle with up to 8 people, $1 for pedestrians.* ☉ *Daily 8–sunset.*

Sanford L. Ziff Jewish Museum of Florida. A permanent exhibit, *MOSAIC: Jewish Life in Florida,* depicts more than 235 years of the Florida Jewish experience through lectures, films, storytelling, walking tours, and special events. If you've never seen a crate of kosher citrus, drop in. From the photo of a party girl in a seashell dress to ark ornaments from a Florida synagogue to a snapshot of Miss Florida 1885 (Mena Williams), exhibits reflect all things Jewish. Even the building is the former Congregation Beth Jacob Synagogue. ⊠ *301 Washington Ave., South Beach,* ☎ *305/672–5044,* WEB *www.jewishmuseum.com.* ⊠ *$5.* ☉ *Tues.–Sun. 10–5.*

South Pointe Park. From the 50-yard Sunshine Pier, which adjoins the 1-mi-long jetty at the mouth of Government Cut, you can fish while watching huge ships pass. No bait or tackle is available in the park. Facilities include two observation towers, rest rooms, and volleyball courts. ⊠ *1 Washington Ave., South Beach.*

Surfside. *Parlez-vous français?* If you do, you'll feel quite comfortable in and around this community, a French Canadian enclave. Many folks have spent their winters along this stretch of beach (and elsewhere down to 72nd Street) for years. ⊠ *Collins Ave. between 88th and 96th Sts., Surfside.*

★ ⑤ Wolfsonian–Florida International University. An elegantly renovated 1927 storage facility is now both a research center and the site of the 70,000-plus-item collection of modern design and "propaganda arts" amassed by Miami native Mitchell Wolfson, Jr., a world traveler and connoisseur. Included in the museum's eclectic holdings, representing art moderne, art nouveau, arts and crafts, and other artistic movements, is a 1930s braille edition of Hitler's *Mein Kampf*. Exhibitions such as World's Fair designs and the architectural heritage of S. H. Kress add to the appeal. ⊠ *1001 Washington Ave., South Beach*, ☏ *305/531– 1001,* WEB *www.wolfsonian.fiu.edu.* ⊡ *$5.* ☉ *Mon.–Tues. and Fri.–Sat. 11–6, Thurs. 11–9, Sun. noon–5.*

Downtown Miami

Although steel-and-glass buildings have sprung up around downtown, the heart of the city hasn't changed much since the 1960s—except that it's a little seedier. By day there's plenty of activity downtown, as office workers and motorists crowd the area. Staid, suited lawyers and bankers share the sidewalks with Latino merchants wearing open-neck, intricately embroidered shirts called guayaberas. Fruit merchants sell their wares from pushcarts, young European travelers with backpacks stroll the streets, and foreign businesspeople haggle over prices in import-export shops, including more electronics and camera shops than you'd see in Tokyo. You hear Arabic, Chinese, Creole, French, German, Hebrew, Hindi, Japanese, Portuguese, Spanish, Yiddish, and even a little English now and then. But what's best in the heart of downtown Miami is its Latinization and the sheer energy of Latino shoppers.

At night, however, downtown is sorely neglected. Except for Bayside Marketplace and the AmericanAirlines Arena, the area is deserted, and arena patrons rarely linger. Travelers spend little time here since most tourist attractions are in other neighborhoods, but there is a movement afoot to bring a renaissance to downtown. A huge new performing-arts center within the next few years may revitalize the area yet.

Thanks to the Metromover, which has inner and outer loops through downtown plus north and south extensions, this is an excellent tour to take by rail, and it's only 25¢ to boot. Attractions are conveniently located within about two blocks of the nearest station. Parking downtown is no less convenient or more expensive than in any other city, but the best idea is to park near Bayside Marketplace or leave your car at an outlying Metrorail station and take the train downtown.

A Good Tour

A smart place to start is at the Bayfront Park Metromover stop. There's plenty of parking in lots in the median of Biscayne Boulevard and slightly more expensive covered parking at the Bayfront Marketplace. If you want, you can wait until you return to walk through the **Mildred and Claude Pepper Bayfront Park** ⑩, but look south of the park and you'll see the Hotel Inter-Continental Miami, which displays *The Spindle*, a huge sculpture by Henry Moore, in its lobby. A trip to **Brickell Village** ⑪, on the south side of the Brickell Avenue Bridge, makes a good detour. This burgeoning area, near the Fifth Street Station, has some rather popular restaurants, like Hardaway's Firehouse Four.

Now it's time to board the Metromover northbound and take in the fine view of Bayfront Park's greenery, the bay beyond, the stunning new AmericanAirlines Arena, the Port of Miami in the bay, and Miami Beach across the water. The next stop, College/Bayside, serves the downtown campus of **Miami-Dade Community College** ⑫, which has two fine galleries.

As the Metromover rounds the curve after the College/Bayside station, look northeast for a view of the vacant **Freedom Tower** ⑬, an important milepost in the history of Cuban immigration, now being renovated as a Cuban museum. You'll also catch a view of the *Miami Herald* building.

Survey the city as the train works its way toward Government Center station. Look off to your right (north) as you round the northwest corner of the loop to see the round, windowless, pink Miami Arena.

Now it's time to see the city on foot. Get off at Government Center, a large station with small shops, restaurants, and a hair salon, in case you're looking shaggy. It's also where the 21-mi elevated Metrorail commuter system connects with the Metromover, so this is a good place to start your tour if you're coming downtown by train. Walk out the east doors to Northwest 1st Street and head a block south to the **Miami-Dade Cultural Center** ⑭, which contains the city's main art museum, historical museum, and library and made an appearance in the movie *There's Something About Mary*.

After sopping up some culture, hoof it east down Flagler Street. On the corner is the **Dade County Courthouse** ⑮, whose pinnacle is accented by circling vultures. Now you're in the heart of downtown, where the smells range from pleasant (hot dog carts) to rancid (hot dog carts). If you cleaned up the streets and put a shine on the city, you'd see Miami circa 1950. Still thriving today, the downtown area is a far cry from what it was in 1896, when it was being carved out of pine woods and palmetto scrub to make room for Flagler's railroad. If you're in the market for jewelry, avoid the street peddlers and duck into the Seybold Building, at 36 Northeast 1st Street; it comprises 10 stories with 250 jewelers hawking watches, rings, bracelets, etc.

Just a few blocks from your starting point at the Bayfront Park Metromover station, stop in at the **Gusman Center for the Performing Arts** ⑯, a stunningly beautiful movie palace that now serves as downtown Miami's concert hall. If there's a show on—even a bad one—get tickets. It's worth it just to sit in here.

When you get back to your car and the entrance to the Bayfront Marketplace, you can opt to hit the road, go shopping, or grab a brew at a bay-front bar.

TIMING

To walk and ride to the various points of interest, allow two hours. If you want to spend additional time eating and shopping at Bayside, allow at least four hours. To include museum visits, allow six hours.

Sights to See

AmericanAirlines Arena. The stylish bay-front home of the NBA's Miami Heat and WNBA's Miami Sol includes Gloria Estefan's Bongos restaurant, shops, and a pedestrian bridge to Bayside Marketplace. ⊠ *Biscayne Blvd., between N.E. 8th and 9th Sts., Downtown,* ☎ *305/577–4328,* WEB *www.aaarena.com.*

☾ **American Police Hall of Fame and Museum.** This museum exhibits more than 11,000 law enforcement–related items, including weapons, a jail cell, and an electric chair, as well as a 400-ton marble memorial listing the names of police officers killed in the line of duty since 1960. ⊠ *3801 Biscayne Blvd., Buena Vista,* ☎ *305/573–0070,* WEB *www.aphf. org.* ⊡ *$12.* ☉ *Daily 10–5:30.*

⓫ **Brickell Village.** Brickell (rhymes with fickle) is an up-and-coming downtown area with new low-rise condos, a shopping area, Brickell Park, and good restaurants. **Hardaway's Firehouse Four** (⊠ 1000 S. Miami Ave.), underwritten by, you guessed it, NBA star Tim Hardaway, has a legendary happy hour and good burgers (including a tuna burger) in an old firehouse. **Perricone's Marketplace and Café** (⊠ 15 S.E. 10th St.) is the biggest and most popular of the area's many Italian restaurants, housed in a 120-year-old Vermont barn. The cooking is simple

Downtown Miami

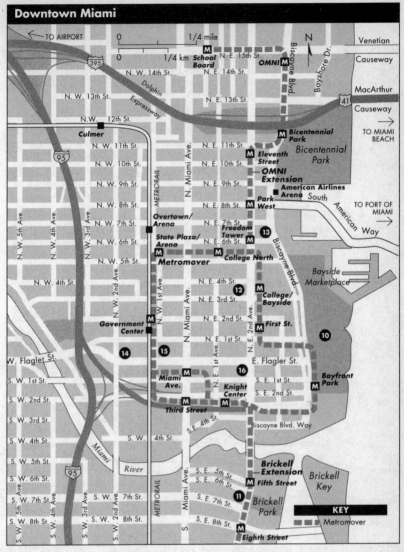

TO AIRPORT

0   1/4 mile

0   1/4 km

Venetian

Causeway

MacArthur

Causeway

TO MIAMI BEACH

TO PORT OF MIAMI

School Board

N. E. 15th St.

OMNI

Dolphin Expressway

N. W. 14th St.

N. E. 14th St.

Biscayne Blvd.

Bayshore Dr.

N. W. 13th St.

N. E. 13th St.

N. W. 12th St.

Culmer

N. W. 11th St.

N. E. 11th St.

Bicentennial Park

Eleventh Street

Bicentennial Park

N. W. 10th St.

N. E. 10th St.

OMNI Extension

N. W. 9th St.

N. E. 9th St.

METRORAIL

N. Miami Ave.

American Airlines Arena

South

N. W. 8th St.

N. E. 8th St.

Park West

American Way

Overtown/ Arena

N. W. 7th St.

N. E. 7th St.

Freedom Tower

13

State Plaza/ Arena

N. W. 6th St.

N. E. 6th St.

N. W. 5th St.

Metromover

College North

Bayside Marketplace

N. E. 4th St.

12

College/ Bayside

N. W. 4th St.

N. E. 3rd St.

10

N. E. 2nd St.

N. 1st Ave.

N. Miami Ave.

N. E. 1st Ave.

N. E. 2nd Ave.

First St.

Government Center

N. E. 1st St.

W. Flagler St.

14

15

E. Flagler St.

Bayfront Park

S. W. 1st St.

S. E. 1st St.

Miami Ave.

16

S. E. 2nd St.

S. W. 2nd St.

Knight Center

S. W. 3rd St.

Third Street

S. E. 4th St.

S. W. 4th St.

S. W. 4th St.

Biscayne Blvd. Way

S. W. 5th Ave.

S. W. 4th Ave.

S. W. 3rd Ave.

S. W. 2nd Ave.

S. W. 5th St.

S. E. 5th St.

Brickell Extension

Brickell Key

Miami River

METRORAIL

Miami Ave.

S. E. 6th St.

Fifth Street

S. W. 7th St.

S. E. 7th St.

11

Brickell Park

S. W. 8th St.

S. E. 8th St.

KEY

Metromover

Eighth Street

and good. Buy your wine from the on-premises deli and bring it to your table for a small corking fee. ⊠ *Between Miami River and S.W. 15 St., Brickell Village.*

⑮ **Dade County Courthouse.** Built in 1928, this was once the tallest building south of Washington, D.C. Unlike Capistrano, turkey vultures—not swallows—return to roost here in winter. ⊠ *73 W. Flagler St., Downtown,* ☎ *305/349–7000.*

⑬ **Freedom Tower.** In the 1960s this imposing Spanish baroque structure was the Cuban Refugee Center, processing more than 500,000 Cubans who entered the United States after fleeing Fidel Castro's regime. Built in 1925 for the *Miami Daily News,* it was inspired by the Giralda, an 800-year-old bell tower in Seville, Spain. Preservationists were pleased to see the tower's exterior restored in 1988, and a Cuban-American museum added in 2002. ⊠ *600 Biscayne Blvd., at N.E. 7th St., Downtown.*

★ ⑯ **Gusman Center for the Performing Arts.** Carry an extra pair of socks when you come here; the beauty of this former movie palace will knock yours clean off. Restored as a concert hall, it resembles a Moorish courtyard on the inside, with twinkling stars in the sky. You can catch performances by the Florida Philharmonic and movies of the Miami Film Festival. If the hall is closed, call the office and they may let you in. ⊠ *174 E. Flagler St., Downtown,* ☎ *305/372–0925.*

⑫ **Miami-Dade Community College.** The campus houses two fine galleries: the larger, third-floor **Centre Gallery** hosts various photography, painting, and sculpture exhibitions, and the fifth-floor **Frances Wolfson Art Gallery** houses smaller photo exhibits. ⊠ *300 N.E. 2nd Ave., Downtown,* ☎ *305/237–3278.* ⊡ *Free.* ☉ *Mon.–Wed., Fri. 10–4, Thurs. noon–6.*

★ ☖ ⑭ **Miami-Dade Cultural Center.** Containing three important cultural resources, this 3-acre complex is one of the focal points of downtown. From books to paintings to history, you'll find it all right here. The **Miami Art Museum** (☎ 305/375–3000, WEB www.miamiartmuseum.org) displays a permanent collection as well as putting on major touring exhibitions of work by international artists, focusing on work completed since 1945. Open Tuesday–Friday 10–5 and weekends noon–5, the museum charges $5 admission ($6 including the Historical Museum). At the **Historical Museum of Southern Florida** (☎ 305/375–1492, WEB www.historical-museum.org), you'll be treated to pure Floridiana, including an old Miami streetcar, cigar labels, and a railroad exhibit as well as a display on prehistoric Miami. Admission is $5 ($6 including the Miami Art Museum), and hours are Monday–Wednesday and Friday–Saturday 10–5, Thursday 10–9, and Sunday noon–5. The **Main Public Library** (☎ 305/375–2665), which is open Monday–Wednesday and Friday–Saturday 9–6, Thursday 9–9, and Sunday 1–5, contains nearly 4 million holdings and offers art exhibits in the auditorium and second-floor lobby. ⊠ *101 W. Flagler St., Downtown.*

⑩ **Mildred and Claude Pepper Bayfront Park.** This oasis among the skyscrapers borders the Bayfront Marketplace, making it a natural place for a pre- or post-shopping walk. An urban landfill in the 1920s, it became the site of a World War II memorial in 1943, which was revised in 1980 to include the names of victims of later wars. Japanese sculptor Isamu Noguchi redesigned the park before his death in 1989 to include two amphitheaters, a memorial to the *Challenger* astronauts, and a fountain honoring the late Florida congressman Claude Pepper and his wife. At the park's north end, the Friendship Torch was erected to honor JFK during his presidency and was dedicated in 1964. ⊠ *Biscayne Blvd. between 2nd and 3rd Sts., Downtown.*

Little Havana

More than 40 years ago the tidal wave of Cubans fleeing the Castro regime flooded into an older neighborhood west of downtown Miami. Don't expect a sparkling and lively reflection of 1950s Havana, however. What you will find are ramshackle motels and cluttered storefronts. With a million Cubans and other Latinos—who make up more than half the metropolitan population—dispersed throughout Greater Miami, Little Havana and neighboring East Little Havana remain magnets for Hispanics and Anglos alike, who come to experience the flavor of traditional Cuban culture. That culture, of course, functions in Spanish. Many Little Havana residents and shopkeepers speak little or no English.

A Good Tour

From downtown go west on Flagler Street across the Miami River to Teddy Roosevelt Avenue (Southwest 17th Avenue) and pause at **Plaza de la Cubanidad** ⑰, on the southwest corner. The plaza's monument is indicative of the prominent role of Cuban history and culture here.

Turn left at Douglas Road (Southwest 37th Avenue), drive south to **Calle Ocho** ⑱ (Southwest 8th Street), and turn left again. You are now on the main commercial thoroughfare of Little Havana. After you cross Unity Boulevard (Southwest 27th Avenue), Calle Ocho becomes a one-way street eastbound through the heart of Little Havana.

At Avenida Luis Muñoz Marín (Southwest 15th Avenue), stop at **Domino Park** ⑲, where elderly Cuban men pass the day with their black-and-white tiles. The **Brigade 2506 Memorial** ⑳, commemorating the victims of the unsuccessful 1961 Bay of Pigs invasion, stands at Memorial Boulevard (Southwest 13th Avenue). A block south are several other monuments relevant to Cuban history, including a bas-relief of and quotations by José Martí.

TIMING

If the history hidden in the monuments is your only interest, set aside one hour. Allow more time to stop along Calle Ocho for a strong cup of Cuban coffee or to shop for a cigar made of Honduran tobacco hand-rolled in the United States by Cubans.

Sights to See

⑳ **Brigade 2506 Memorial.** To honor those who died in the Bay of Pigs invasion, an eternal flame burns atop a simple stone monument with the inscription CUBA—A LOS MARTIRES DE LA BRIGADA DE ASALTO ABRIL 17 DE 1961. The monument also bears a shield with the Brigade 2506 emblem, a Cuban flag superimposed on a cross. ⊠ *S.W. 8th St. and S.W. 13th Ave., Little Havana.*

⑱ **Calle Ocho.** In Little Havana's commercial heart, experience such Cuban customs as hand-rolled cigars or sandwiches piled with meats and cheeses. Although it all deserves exploring, if time is limited, try the stretch from Southwest 14th to 11th avenues. ⊠ *S.W. 8th St., Little Havana.*

⑲ **Domino Park.** Officially known as Maximo Gomez Park, this is a major gathering place for elderly, guayabera-clad Cuban males, who, after 40 years, still pass the day playing dominoes while arguing anti-Castro politics. ⊠ *S.W. 8th St. and S.W. 15th Ave., Little Havana.* ☉ *Daily 9–6.*

OFF THE BEATEN PATH — **ELIÁN GONZÁLEZ'S HOUSE –** This humble two-bedroom home was where six-year-old González stayed for nearly six months after surviving a raft journey from Cuba that killed his mother. From this same house, he was

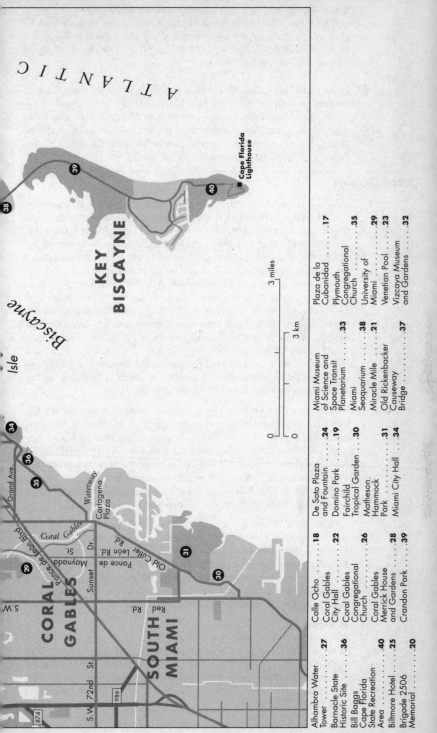

ATLANTIC

Isle Biscayne

KEY BISCAYNE

Cape Florida Lighthouse

3 miles

3 km

CORAL GABLES

SOUTH MIAMI

S.W. 72nd St.

Grand Ave.

Coral Gables Dr.

Ponce de León Blvd.

Red Rd.

Sunset Dr.

Maynada St.

Old Cutler Rd.

Waterway

Cartagena Plaza

removed by federal agents in a predawn raid that ultimately united him with his father, who took him home to Cuba. The Miami relatives have since moved, but bought the property to turn it into a shrine and museum. ⊠ *2319 N.W. 2nd St., at N.W. 23rd Ave., Little Havana.* ⊠ *Free.* ☉ *Sun. 10–6.*

⓱ **Plaza de la Cubanidad.** Redbrick sidewalks surround a fountain and monument with the words of José Martí, a leader in Cuba's struggle for independence from Spain and a hero to Cuban refugees and immigrants in Miami. The quotation, LAS PALMAS SON NOVIAS QUE ESPERAN (The palm trees are waiting brides), counsels hope and fortitude to the Cubans. ⊠ *W. Flagler St. and S.W. 17th Ave., Little Havana.*

Coral Gables

If not for George E. Merrick, Coral Gables would be just another suburb. Merrick envisioned an American Venice, with canals and gracious homes spreading across the community. In 1911 his minister father died, and Merrick inherited 1,600 acres of citrus and avocado groves; by 1921 he had upped that to 3,000 acres. Using this as a foundation, Merrick began designing a city based on centuries-old prototypes from Mediterranean countries. He planned lush landscaping, magnificent entrances, and broad boulevards named for Spanish explorers, cities, and provinces. His uncle, Denman Fink, helped Merrick crystallize his artistic vision, and he hired architects trained abroad to create themed neighborhood villages, such as Florida pioneer, Chinese, French city, Dutch South African, and French Normandy. The result was a planned community with Spanish Mediterranean architecture that justifiably calls itself the City Beautiful—a moniker it acquired by following the Garden City method of urban planning in the 1920s.

Unfortunately for Merrick, the devastating no-name hurricane of 1926 and the Great Depression prevented him from fulfilling many of his plans. He died at 54, working for the post office. His city languished until after World War II but then grew rapidly. Today Coral Gables has a population of about 41,000. In its bustling downtown, more than 140 multinational companies maintain headquarters or regional offices, and the University of Miami campus in the southern part of Coral Gables brings a youthful vibrancy: the median age of residents is 36.

Like much of Miami, Coral Gables has realized the aesthetic and economic importance of historic preservation and has passed a Mediterranean design ordinance, rewarding businesses for maintaining their building's architectural style. Even the street signs (ground-level markers that are hard to see in daylight, impossible at night) are preserved because of their historical value. They're worth the inconvenience, if only to honor the memory of Merrick.

A Good Tour

Heading south on downtown's Brickell Avenue, turn right onto Coral Way—also marked as Southwest 13th Street—and stay on Coral Way even as it turns into Southwest 3rd Avenue and Southwest 22nd Street. An arch of banyan trees prepares you for the grand entrance onto **Miracle Mile** ㉑, the heart of downtown Coral Gables. Park your car and take time to explore on foot.

When you've seen enough, continue driving west, passing the 1930s Miracle Theater on your left, which now serves as home of the Actors' Playhouse. Keep heading west, cross LeJeune Road, and bear right onto Coral Way, catching an eyeful of the ornate Spanish Renaissance **Coral Gables City Hall** ㉒.

Continue a few blocks until you see Toledo Street, and make a left. A few blocks up on your left, you'll see the gates surrounding the exotic and unusual Merrick-designed **Venetian Pool** ㉓, created from an old coral quarry. There's parking on your right. Immediately ahead of you is the Merrick-designed **De Soto Plaza and Fountain** ㉔.

As in many areas of Coral Gables, there's a traffic circle surrounding the fountain. Head to 12 o'clock (the opposite side of the fountain) and stay on De Soto for a magnificent vista and entrance to the, yes, Merrick-designed and reborn **Biltmore Hotel** ㉕. On your right, before you reach the hotel, you'll see the **Coral Gables Congregational Church** ㉖, one of the first churches in this planned community. After visiting the hotel, double back to the fountain, this time circling to 9 o'clock and Granada Boulevard. Several blocks away you'll arrive at the Granada Golf Course, where you turn left onto North Greenway. As you cruise up the street, notice the stand of banyan trees that separates the fairways. At the end of the course the road makes a horseshoe bend, but instead cross Alhambra to loop around the restored **Alhambra Water Tower** ㉗, a city landmark dating from 1924. By the way, it's Merrick designed.

Return to Alhambra and follow it straight to the next light (Coral Way), where you can turn left and ogle beautifully maintained Spanish homes from the 1920s. Although there's only a small sign to announce it, the **Coral Gables Merrick House and Gardens** ㉘, Merrick's boyhood home, is at Coral Way and Toledo Street. It's a charming glimpse into old-time Florida. Parking is behind the house.

Afterward, take a right on Coral Way, followed by a left on Granada, which winds south past Bird Road and eventually to Ponce de León Boulevard. Turn right and follow it to the entrance of the main campus of the **University of Miami** ㉙. Turn right at the first stoplight (Stanford Drive) to enter the campus, and park in the lot on your right designated for visitors to the Lowe Art Museum.

You may have noticed that this tour contains some backtracking. Unfortunately, no matter how you navigate Coral Gables, directions get confusing. This tour takes in the highlights first and lets you fill out the balance of your day as you see fit. Now bow to your partner, and bow to your corner, and promenade home.

TIMING

Strolling Miracle Mile should take slightly more than an hour—unless you plan to shop. In that case, allow four hours. Save time for a refreshing dip at the Venetian Pool, and plan to spend at least an hour getting acquainted with the Biltmore—longer if you'd like to order a drink and linger poolside. If you can pull yourself away from the lap of luxury, allow an hour to visit the University of Miami campus (if you're into college campuses).

Sights to See

㉗ **Alhambra Water Tower.** In 1924 this city landmark stored water and was clad in a decorative Moresque, lighthouselike exterior. After more than 50 years of disuse and neglect, the windmill-like tower was completely restored in 1993 with a copper-rib dome and multicolored frescoes. Pretty impressive when you consider its peers are merely steel containers. ⊠ *Alhambra Circle, Greenway Ct., and Ferdinand St., Coral Gables.*

㉕ **Biltmore Hotel.** Bouncing back from dark days as an army hospital, this 1926 hotel is now the jewel of Coral Gables. After extensive renovations it reopened in 1992 and hosted the Summit of the Americas in 1994. Its 16-story tower, like the Freedom Tower in downtown Miami, is a replica of Seville's Giralda Tower. To the west is the Biltmore Country Club, a richly ornamented beaux arts–style structure with a superb colonnade and courtyard; it was reincorporated into the hotel in 1989. Free tours are offered. ⊠ *1200 Anastasia Ave., Coral Gables,* ☎ *305/445–1926,* WEB *www.biltmorehotel.com.* ☉ *Tours Sun. 1:30, 2:30, and 3:30.*

㉒ **Coral Gables City Hall.** Far more attractive than today's modular city halls, this 1928 building has a three-tier tower topped with a clock and a 500-pound bell. A mural by Denman Fink (George Merrick's uncle and artistic adviser), inside the dome ceiling on the second floor, depicts the four seasons. (Although not as well known as Maxfield Parrish, Fink demonstrated a similar utopian vision.) Also on display are paintings, photos, and ads touting 1920s Coral Gables. ⊠ *405 Biltmore Way, Coral Gables,* ☎ *305/446–6800.* ☉ *Weekdays 8–5.*

NEED A
BREAK?
Whether you want to relax or grab an on-the-go snack, you can't miss with **Wrapido** (⊠ 2334 Ponce de León Blvd., Coral Gables, ☎ 305/ 443–1884). The funky, upbeat place shows signs of SoHo, and the healthful wraps, soups, and smoothies are made from scratch. Strawberry Fields, the restaurant's best-selling smoothie, is prepared with fresh bananas, strawberries, apple juice, and low-fat yogurt.

㉖ **Coral Gables Congregational Church.** The parish was organized in 1923, and with George Merrick as a charter member (and donor of the land), this small church became the first in the city. Rumor has it Merrick built it in honor of his father, a Congregational minister. The original interiors are still in magnificent condition. ⊠ *3010 De Soto Blvd., Coral Gables,* ☎ *305/448–7421.* ☉ *Weekdays 8:30–7, services Sun. 9:15 and 10:45.*

㉘ **Coral Gables Merrick House and Gardens.** In 1976 the city of Coral Gables acquired George Merrick's boyhood home. Restored to its 1920s appearance, it contains Merrick family furnishings and artwork. The lush and lazy tropical atmosphere suggests the inspiration for George's masterpiece: Coral Gables. ⊠ *907 Coral Way, Coral Gables,* ☎ *305/460–5361.* ☒ *House $5, grounds free.* ☉ *House Wed. and Sun. 1–4, grounds daily 8–sunset, also by appointment.*

㉔ **De Soto Plaza and Fountain.** Water flows from the mouths of four sculpted faces on a classical column on a pedestal in this Denman Fink– designed fountain from the early 1920s. The closed eyes of the face looking west symbolize the day's end. ⊠ *Granada Blvd. and Sevilla Ave., Coral Gables.*

㉑ **Miracle Mile.** This upscale yet neighborly stretch of retail stores is actually only ½ mi long. After years of neglect, it's been updated and upgraded, and now offers a delightful mix of owner-operated shops and chain stores, bridal shops, art galleries and bistros, and enough late-night hot spots to keep things hopping. ⊠ *Coral Way between S.W. 37th Ave. (Douglas Rd.) and S.W. 42nd Ave. (LeJeune Rd.), Coral Gables.*

㉙ **University of Miami.** With almost 14,000 full-time, part-time, and noncredit students, UM is the largest private research university in the Southeast. Walk around campus and visit the **Lowe Art Museum,** which has a permanent collection of 8,000 works that include Renaissance and baroque art, American paintings, Latin American art, and Navajo and Pueblo Indian textiles and baskets. The museum also hosts traveling exhibitions and the popular Beaux Arts Festival in January. ⊠ *1301 Stanford Dr., Coral Gables,* ☎ *305/284–3535 or 305/ 284–3536,* WEB *www.miami.edu.* 🖾 *$5.* ☉ *Tues.–Wed. and Fri.–Sat. 10–5, Thurs. noon–7, Sun. noon–5.*

★ ☾ ㉓ **Venetian Pool.** Sculpted from a rock quarry in 1923 and fed by artesian wells, this 825,000-gallon municipal pool remains quite popular because of its themed architecture—a fantasized version of a waterfront Italian village—created by Denman Fink. The pool has earned a place on the National Register of Historic Places and showcases a nice collection of vintage photos depicting 1920s beauty pageants and swank soirees held long ago. Paul Whiteman played here, Johnny Weissmuller and Esther Williams swam here, and you should, too (but no kids under three). A snack bar, lockers, and showers make this must-see user-friendly as well. ⊠ *2701 De Soto Blvd., Coral Gables,* ☎ *305/ 460–5356,* WEB *www.venetianpool.com.* 🖾 *$8, free parking across De Soto Blvd.* ☉ *Weekends 10–4:30; plus June–Aug., weekdays 11–7:30; Sept.–Oct. and Apr.–May, Tues.–Fri. 11–5:30; and Nov.–Mar., Tues.– Fri. 10–4:30.*

South Miami

South of Miami and Coral Gables is a city called South Miami, which is not to be confused with the region known as South Dade. A pioneer farm community, it grew into a suburb but retains its small-town charm. Fine old homes and stately trees line Sunset Drive, a city-designated Historic and Scenic Road to and through the town. The pace in this friendly suburb has picked up steam since the arrival of the Shops at Sunset Place, a retail complex larger than Coconut Grove's CocoWalk—big digs for a quiet town.

A Good Tour

Drive south from Sunset Drive on Red Road (watching for the plentiful orchid merchants) and turn left on scenic Old Cutler Road, which curves north along the uplands of southern Florida's coastal ridge toward the 83-acre **Fairchild Tropical Garden** ㉚. Just north of the gardens, Old Cutler Road traverses Dade County's lovely **Matheson Hammock Park** ㉛. From here you can follow the road back to U.S. 1, heading north to Miami.

TIMING

Most people should allow at least half a day to see these three natural attractions, but dedicated ornithologists and botanists will want to leave a full day. Driving from SoBe should take only 25 minutes—longer during afternoon rush hour.

Sights to See

★ ☾ ㉚ **Fairchild Tropical Garden.** Comprising 83 acres, this is the largest tropical botanical garden in the continental United States. Eleven lakes, a rain forest, and lots of palm trees, cycads, and flowers, including orchids, mountain roses, bellflowers, coral trees, and bougainvillea, make it a garden for the senses—and there's special assistance for the hearing impaired. Take the free guided tram tour, which leaves on the hour. Spicing up the social calendar are garden sales (don't miss the Ramble in November or the International Mango Festival in July), moonlight strolls, and symphony concerts. A combination bookstore–gift shop is a popular source for books on gardening and horticulture, ordered by botanists the world over. ⊠ *10901 Old Cutler Rd., Coral Gables,* ☎ *305/667–1651,* WEB *www.fairchildgarden.org.* 🖾 *$8.* ☉ *Daily 9:30–4:30.*

☾ ㉛ **Matheson Hammock Park.** In the 1930s the Civilian Conservation Corps developed this 100-acre tract of upland and mangrove swamp on land donated by a local pioneer, Commodore J. W. Matheson. The park, Miami-Dade County's oldest and most scenic, has a bathing beach and changing facilities. In 1997 the marina was expanded to include 243 slips, 71 dry-storage spaces, a bait-and-tackle shop, and a restaurant. Noticeably absent are fishing and diving charters, although there is a sailing school. ⊠ *9610 Old Cutler Rd., Coral Gables,* ☎ *305/665–5475,* WEB *www.co.miami-dade.fl.us/parks.* ⊡ *Parking for beach and marina $3.50 per car, $8 per car with trailer, $6 per bus and RV; limited free upland parking.* ☉ *Daily 6–sunset; pool lifeguards winter, daily 8:30–5; summer, weekends 8:30–6.*

OFF THE BEATEN PATH

PARROT JUNGLE – One of South Florida's original tourist attractions, Parrot Jungle opened in 1936 and is now the residence of more than 1,100 exotic birds (and a few orangutans), who look for handouts from visitors. The tone is kitschy (in the tradition of Florida favorites Silver Springs and Cypress Gardens) but oddly peaceful and exotic after you've experienced the urban jungle. Once you've photographed the postcard-perfect Caribbean flamingos and watched a trained-bird show, stroll among orchids and other flowering plants nestled in ferns, bald cypress, and massive live oaks. An imminent move (in January 2003) will take the birds to a new home on Watson Island (on Interstate 395) across from the Port of Miami, but this park will be preserved as some type of wildlife sanctuary. ⊠ *11000 S.W. 57th Ave., Pinecrest,* ☎ *305/666–7834,* WEB *www.parrotjungle.com.* ⊡ *$14.95.* ☉ *Daily 9:30–6, last admission 4:30; café daily 8–5.*

Coconut Grove

South Florida's oldest settlement, the Grove was inhabited as early as 1834 and established by 1873, two decades before Miami. Its early settlers included Bahamian blacks, "Conchs" (white Key Westers, many originally from the Bahamas), and New England intellectuals. They built a community that attracted artists, writers, and scientists to establish winter homes. By the end of World War I more people listed in *Who's Who* gave addresses in Coconut Grove than any other place in the country.

To this day Coconut Grove reflects its pioneers' eclectic origins. Posh estates mingle with rustic cottages, modest frame homes, and stark modern dwellings, often on the same block. To keep Coconut Grove a village in a jungle, residents lavish affection on exotic plantings while battling to protect remaining native vegetation.

The historic center of the Village of Coconut Grove went through a hippie period in the 1960s, a laid-back funkiness in the 1970s, and a teenybopper invasion in the early 1980s. Today the tone is upscale and urban, with a mix of galleries, boutiques, restaurants, bars, and sidewalk cafés. On weekends the Grove is jam-packed with both locals and tourists—especially teenagers—shopping at the Streets of Mayfair, CocoWalk, and small boutiques. Parking can be a problem, especially on weekend evenings, when police direct traffic and prohibit turns at some intersections to prevent gridlock. Be prepared to walk several blocks from the periphery into the heart of the Grove.

A Good Tour

From downtown Miami take Brickell Avenue south and follow the signs pointing to Vizcaya and Coconut Grove. If you're interested in seeing celeb estates, turn left at Southeast 32nd Road and follow the loop—Sylvester Stallone's former estate is the one with the huge gates on the right at the turn, and Madonna's past abode is the one at 3029 Brickell. Turn left back on South Miami Avenue.

Immediately on your left you'll see the entrance to the don't-miss **Vizcaya Museum and Gardens** ㉜, an estate with an Italian Renaissance–style villa. Less than 100 yards down the road on your right is the **Miami Museum of Science and Space Transit Planetarium** ㉝, a participatory museum with animated displays for all ages.

The road switches from four lanes to two and back again as you approach downtown Coconut Grove. With 28 waterfront acres of Australian pine, lush lawns, and walking and jogging paths, the bay-side David T. Kennedy Park makes a pleasant stop. If you're interested in the history of air travel, take a quick detour down Pan American Drive to see the 1930s art deco Pan Am terminal, which has been horribly renovated inside to become **Miami City Hall** ㉞. You'll also see the Coconut Grove Convention Center, where antiques, boat, and home shows are held, and Dinner Key Marina, where seabirds soar and sailboats ride at anchor.

South Miami Avenue, now known as South Bayshore Drive, heads directly into McFarlane Road, which takes a sharp right into the center of the action. If you can forsake instant gratification, turn left on Main Highway and drive less than ½ mi to Devon Road and the interesting **Plymouth Congregational Church** ㉟ and its gardens.

Return to Main Highway and travel northeast toward the historic Village of Coconut Grove. As you reenter the village center, note on your left the Coconut Grove Playhouse. On your right, beyond the benches and shelter, is the entrance to the **Barnacle State Historic Site** ㊱, a pioneer residence built by Commodore Ralph Munroe in 1891. After getting your fill of history, relax and spend the evening mingling with Coconut Grove's eccentrics.

TIMING

Plan on devoting from six to eight hours to enjoy Vizcaya, other bayfront sights, and the village's shops, restaurants, and nightlife.

Sights to See

㊱ **Barnacle State Historic Site.** The oldest Miami home still on its original foundation rests in the middle of 5 acres of native hardwood and landscaped lawns surrounded by flashy Coconut Grove. Built by Florida's first snowbird—New Yorker Commodore Ralph Munroe—the home has many original furnishings, a broad sloping roof, and deeply recessed verandas that channel sea breezes into the house. If your timing is right, you may catch one of the monthly Moonlight Concerts. ⊠ *3485 Main Hwy., Coconut Grove,* ☎ *305/448–9445,* WEB *www.barnacle.cjb.net.* ☞ *$1, concerts $5.* ⊙ *Fri.–Mon. 9–4; tours 10, 11:30, 1, and 2:30, but call ahead; group tours (10 or more) Tues.–Thurs. by reservation; concerts on evenings near the full moon, 6–9, call ahead for exact dates.*

㊴ **Miami City Hall.** Built in 1934 as the terminal for the Pan American Airways seaplane base at Dinner Key, the building retains its nautical-style art deco trim. Sadly, the interior is generic government, but a 1938 Pan Am menu on display (with filet mignon, *petit pois au beurre,* and Jenny Lind pudding) lets you know Miami officials appreciate from whence they came. ⊠ *3500 Pan American Dr., Coconut Grove,* ☎ *305/250–5400.* ⊙ *Weekdays 8–5.*

㊳ **Miami Museum of Science and Space Transit Planetarium.** This museum is chock-full of hands-on sound, gravity, and electricity displays for children and adults alike. A wildlife center houses native Florida snakes, turtles, tortoises, and birds of prey. Outstanding traveling exhibits appear throughout the year, and virtual-reality, life-science demonstrations, and Internet technology are on hand every day. An affiliation with the

Smithsonian Institution means top-notch exhibitions and development of a waterfront Science Center of the Americas a few years down the road. Stick around after dark on Friday and Saturday nights for the laser-light rock-and-roll shows presented in the planetarium. ⊠ *3280 S. Miami Ave., Coconut Grove,* ☎ *305/854–4247 museum; 305/854–2222 planetarium information,* WEB *www.miamisci.org.* ⊡ *Museum exhibits, planetarium shows, and wildlife center $8–10; laser show $6.* ☼ *Daily 10–6.*

㉟ Plymouth Congregational Church. Opened in 1917, this handsome coral-rock structure resembles a Mexican mission church. The front door, made of hand-carved walnut and oak with original wrought-iron fittings, came from an early-17th-century monastery in the Pyrenees. Also on the 11-acre grounds are the first schoolhouse in Miami-Dade County (one room), which was moved to this property, and the site of the original Coconut Grove water and electric works. ⊠ *3400 Devon Rd., Coconut Grove,* ☎ *305/444–6521.* ☼ *Weekdays 9–4:30, Sun. service at 10 AM.*

★ **㉜ Vizcaya Museum and Gardens.** Of the 10,000 people living in Miami between 1912 and 1916, about 1,000 of them were gainfully employed by Chicago industrialist James Deering to build this $20 million Italian Renaissance–style winter residence. Once comprising 180 acres, the grounds now cover a still-substantial 30-acre tract, including a native hammock and more than 10 acres of formal gardens and fountains overlooking Biscayne Bay. The house, open to the public, contains 70 rooms, 34 of which are filled with paintings, sculpture, antique furniture, and other decorative arts dating from the 15th through the 19th centuries and representing the Renaissance, baroque, rococo, and neoclassical styles. So unusual and impressive is Vizcaya, its guest list has included Ronald Reagan, Pope John Paul II, Queen Elizabeth II, Bill Clinton, and Boris Yeltsin. It's a shame the guided tour can be far less impressive and interesting than the home's guest list and surroundings. ⊠ *3251 S. Miami Ave., Coconut Grove,* ☎ *305/250–9133,* WEB *www.vizcayamuseum.com.* ⊡ *$10.* ☼ *Daily 9:30–4:30, garden 9:30–5:30.*

Virginia Key and Key Biscayne

Government Cut and the Port of Miami separate the city's dense urban fabric from two of its playground islands, Virginia Key and Key Biscayne. Parks occupy much of both keys, providing facilities for golf, tennis, softball, picnicking, and sunbathing, plus uninviting but ecologically valuable stretches of dense mangrove swamp. Key Biscayne's long and winding roads are great for rollerblading and bicycling, and its lush, lazy setting provides a respite from the buzz-saw tempo of SoBe.

A Good Tour

To reach Virginia Key and Key Biscayne take the Rickenbacker Causeway ($1 per car) across Biscayne Bay from the mainland at Brickell Avenue and Southwest 26th Road, about 2 mi south of downtown Miami. The causeway links several islands in the bay.

The William M. Powell Bridge rises 75 ft above the water to eliminate the need for a draw span. The panoramic view from the top encompasses the bay, keys, port, and downtown skyscrapers, with Miami Beach and the Atlantic Ocean in the distance. Just south of the Powell Bridge, a stub of the **Old Rickenbacker Causeway Bridge** ㊲, built in 1947, is now a fishing pier with a nice view.

Immediately after crossing the Rickenbacker Causeway onto Virginia Key, you'll see a long strip of bay front popular with windsurfers and jet skiers. Nearby rest rooms and a great view of the curving shoreline make this an ideal place to park and have your own tailgate party. Look for the gold dome of the **Miami Seaquarium** ㊳, one of the country's first marine attractions. Opposite the causeway from the Seaquarium, a road leads north to Virginia Key Beach and the adjacent Virginia Key Critical Wildlife Area, which is often closed to the public to protect nesting birds.

From Virginia Key the causeway crosses Bear Cut to the north end of Key Biscayne and becomes Crandon Boulevard. The boulevard bisects 1,211-acre **Crandon Park** ㊴, which has a popular Atlantic Ocean beach and nature center. On your right are entrances to the Crandon Park Golf Course and the Tennis Center at Crandon Park, home of the Ericsson Open (formerly known as the Lipton Championships). Keep your eyes open for pure Miami icons: coconut palms and iguana-crossing signs.

From the traffic circle at the south end of Crandon Park, Crandon Boulevard continues to the **Bill Baggs Cape Florida State Recreation Area** ㊵, a 460-acre park containing, among other things, the brick Cape Florida Lighthouse and light keeper's cottage.

Follow Crandon Boulevard back to Crandon Park through Key Biscayne's downtown village, where shops and a 10-acre village green cater mainly to local residents. On your way back to the mainland, pause as you approach the Powell Bridge to admire the Miami skyline. At night the brightly lighted NationsBank Tower looks like a clipper ship running under full sail before the breeze.

TIMING

Set aside the better part of a day for this tour, and double that if you're into beaches, fishing, and water sports.

Sights to See

★ ☕ ㊵ **Bill Baggs Cape Florida State Recreation Area.** Thanks to great beaches, blue-green waters, amenities, sunsets, and a lighthouse, this park at Key Biscayne's southern tip is well worth the drive. Since Hurricane Andrew, it has returned better than ever, with new boardwalks, 18 picnic shelters, and a café that serves beer, wine, and meals ranging from hot dogs to lobster. An additional 54 acres of wetlands were acquired in 1997, and a marina is on the drawing board. A stroll or ride along walking and bicycle paths and boardwalks provides wonderful views of Miami's dramatic skyline. Also on-site are bicycle and skate rentals, a playground, fishing piers, and kayak rental. Guided tours of the cultural complex and the **Cape Florida Lighthouse,** South Florida's oldest structure, are offered, but call for availability. The lighthouse was erected in 1845 to replace an earlier one destroyed in an 1836 Seminole attack, in which the keeper's helper was killed. ⊠ *1200 S. Crandon Blvd., Key Biscayne,* ☎ *305/361–5811 or 305/361–8779,* WEB *www.dep.state.fl.us/parks.* ⊡ *$4 per vehicle with up to 8 people; $1 per person on bicycle, bus, motorcycle, or foot.* ☉ *Daily 8–sunset, tours Thurs.–Mon. 10 and 1 (sign up ½ hr beforehand).*

㊴ **Crandon Park.** This laid-back park in northern Key Biscayne is popular with families, and many educated beach enthusiasts rate the 3½-mi county beach here among the top 10 beaches in North America. The sand is soft, there's a great view of the Atlantic, and parking is both inexpensive and plentiful. So large is this park that it includes a marina, a golf course, a tennis center, and ball fields. There is also a kids' section with a restored carousel (it's $1 for three rides), a playground, and a splash pool. At the north end of the beach is the free **Marjory Stoneman Douglas Biscayne Nature Center** (☎ 305/642–9600). Explore a variety of natural habitats by taking a tour that includes dragging nets through sea-grass beds to catch, study, and release such marine creatures as sea cucumbers, sea horses, crabs, and shrimp. Nature center hours vary, so call ahead. ☒ *4000 Crandon Blvd., Key Biscayne,* ☎ *305/361–5421,* WEB *www.co.miami-dade.fl.us/parks.* ☞ *Free; $4 per vehicle.* ☉ *Daily 8–sunset.*

👆 ㊳ **Miami Seaquarium.** This old-fashioned attraction has six daily shows featuring sea lions, dolphins, and Lolita, a killer whale. (Lolita's tank is small for seaquariums—just three times her length—and some wildlife advocates are trying to get her back to sea.) Exhibits include a shark pool, a 235,000-gallon tropical-reef aquarium, and manatees. Glass-bottom boats take tours of Biscayne Bay. Want to get your feet (and everything else) wet? The Water and Dolphin Exploration program (WADE) enables you to swim with dolphins during a two-hour session. Reservations are required. ☒ *4400 Rickenbacker Causeway, Virginia Key,* ☎ *305/361–5705,* WEB *www.miamiseaquarium.com.* ☞ *$24.45, WADE $125, parking $4.* ☉ *Daily 9:30–6, last admission 4:30; WADE Wed.–Sun. 8:30 and noon.*

㊲ **Old Rickenbacker Causeway Bridge.** Here you can watch boat traffic pass through the channel, pelicans and other seabirds soar and dive, and dolphins cavort in the bay. Park at its entrance, about a mile from the tollgate, and walk past anglers tending their lines to the gap where the center draw span across Biscayne Bay was removed. ☒ *Rickenbacker Causeway, south of Powell Bridge, east of Coconut Grove.*

DINING

Revised by Jen Karetnick

Restaurants listed here have passed the test of time, but you might double-check by phone before you set out for the evening. At many of the hottest spots, you'll need a reservation to avoid a long wait for a table. And when you get your check, note whether a gratuity is already included; most restaurants add 15% (ostensibly for the convenience of and protection from the many Latin-American and European tourists who are used to this practice in their homelands), but you can reduce or supplement it, depending on your opinion of the service.

CATEGORY	COST*
$$$$	over $30
$$$	$20–$30
$$	$10–$20
$	under $10

*per person for a main course at dinner

Coconut Grove

Contemporary

$$$$ ✕ **Aria.** As pretty as an operatic melody, this dining room in the Ritz-Carlton resort provides a high-end, global experience. Choose your view: the 126-seat restaurant has an exhibition kitchen, although an alfresco area offers views of landscaped gardens or breeze-brushed beaches. Then select your food, which may be even more difficult, given chef Jeff Vigila's artistry—items range from asparagus cappuccino with crab frittata and nutmeg foam to braised veal cheeks with langoustines, lentil ragout, and summer truffles. Aria is fortunate to have master sommelier Marita Leonard, whose palate is impeccable and whose wine list is impossible to resist. ☒ *455 Grand Bay Dr., Key Biscayne,* ☎ *305/365–4500. Reservations essential. AE, D, DC, MC, V.*

$$$–$$$$ ✕ **Mayfair Grill and Orchids Champagne and Wine Bar.** This long-running dining room in the Mayfair House Hotel can seem old-world, thanks to its muffled and carpeted elegance, but the cooking is more innova-

tive than the interior would suggest: Thai crab cakes with *panko* crumbs and a sesame-chili glaze; Colorado buffalo loin carpaccio splashed with white truffle oil; roulade of free-range chicken stuffed with spinach and goat cheese; and rack of lamb barbecued with notes of apple and ancho chile. There's also the outdoor courtyard at Orchids, the only champagne bar in town, where bubbly personalities can feel free to be themselves. ⊠ *3000 Florida Ave., Coconut Grove,* ☎ *305/441–0000. AE, D, DC, MC, V. No lunch.*

$$–$$$$ ✗ **Baleen.** Robbin Haas, culinary director of this resort restaurant, earned his New World stripes at a range of South Beach restaurants and was awarded the Best New Chef prize from *Food & Wine* magazine a few years ago for his efforts. Some of his signature dishes, like tangy Caesar salad or salmon tartare with Thai spices and citron caviar, have carried over from eatery to eatery, but others are reinvented: hummus-parsley-crusted salmon with tahini butter, for instance, or Roquefort-crusted filet mignon with red wine sauce. Main plates are à la carte, with steak house–type side dishes padding the bill. ⊠ *Grove Isle Hotel, 4 Grove Isle Dr., Grove Isle, Coconut Grove,* ☎ *305/858–8300. Reservations essential. AE, D, DC, MC, V.*

Indian

$–$$$ ✗ **Anokha.** "There is no doubt that all Indians love food," the menu says at Anokha, and there's also no doubt that all Miamians love *this* Indian food: shrimp cooked in pungent mustard sauce, fish soothed with an almond-cream curry, chicken wrapped in spinach and cilantro. The wait between starters and main courses can seem as long as a cab ride in Manhattan during rush hour. Don't fret—there's only one cook in the kitchen, and she's worth the delay. ⊠ *3195 Commodore Plaza, Coconut Grove,* ☎ *786/552–1030. AE, MC, V. Closed Mon.*

Coral Gables

Caribbean

$$–$$$$ ✗ **Ortanique on the Mile.** Named after an exotic citrus fruit, this restaurant screams "island"—or, more accurately, island resort—from the breezy interior decorated like a Jamaican terraced garden to the exquisite pan-Caribbean cuisine. Proprietor Delius Shirley and chef-proprietor Cindy Hutson offer such favorites as pumpkin soup; fried calamari salad; escovitched whole yellowtail snapper; or jerk pork loin. Dessert doesn't get better than drunken banana fritters, unless you accompany them with a press pot of Blue Mountain coffee, direct from Jamaica and practically vibrating with caffeine. ⊠ *278 Miracle Mile, Miracle Mile,* ☎ *305/446–7710. AE, DC, MC, V. No lunch weekends.*

Contemporary

$$$–$$$$ ✗ **Norman's.** This destination restaurant, which has won as many
★ awards as it has customers, turns out some of Miami's most imaginative cuisine. Chef Norman Van Aken created an international buzz by perfecting New World cuisine—a combination rooted in Latin, North American, Caribbean, and Asian influences. Bold tastes are delivered in every dish, from a simple black-and-white-bean soup with sour cream, chorizo, and tortillas to a rum-and-pepper-painted grouper on a mango-*habañero* sauce. The emphasis here is on service, and the ultragracious staff never seems harried, even when all seats are filled (usually every minute between opening and closing). ⊠ *21 Almeria Ave., CoralGables,* ☎ *305/446–6767. Reservations essential. AE, DC, MC, V. Closed Sun. No lunch.*

$$–$$$$ ✗ **Restaurant St. Michel.** The setting is utterly French, the little hotel it's in evokes the Mediterranean, and the cuisine is new American. Stuart Bornstein's window on Coral Gables is a lace-curtained café with

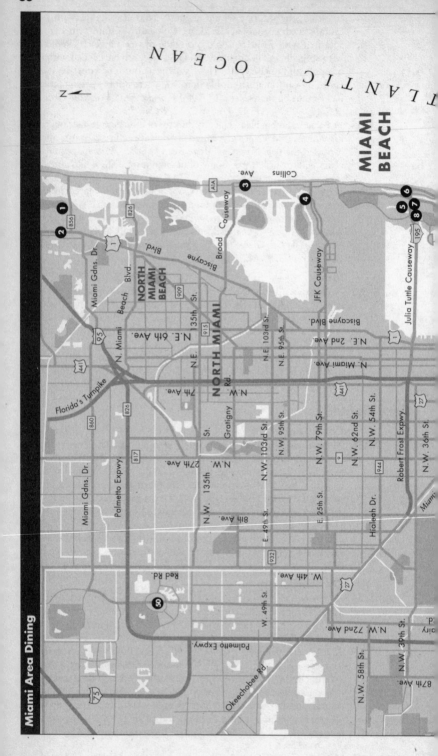

Miami Area Dining

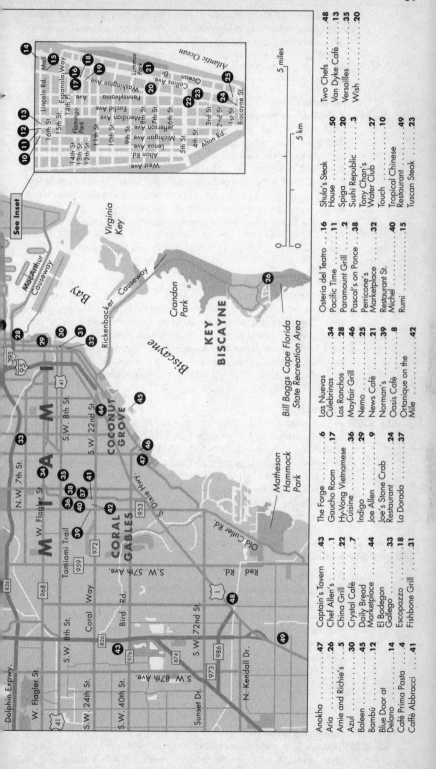

See Inset

Anokha	47	The Forge	43
Aria	26	Gaucho Room	17
Arnie and Richie's	5	Hy-Vong Vietnamese Cuisine	36
Azul	30	Indigo	29
Baleen	45	Joe Allen	9
Bambú	12	Joe's Stone Crab Restaurant	24
Blue Door at Delano	14	La Dorada	37
Café Prima Pasta	4		
Caffè Abbracci	41		
Captain's Tavern	43	Las Nuevas Culebrinas	34
Chef Allen's	1	Los Ranchos	28
China Grill	22	Mayfair Grill	46
Crystal Café	7	Nemo	25
Daily Bread Marketplace	44	News Café	21
El Gallego	33	Norman's	39
Escopazzo	18	Oasis Café	8
Fishbone Grill	31	Ortanique on the Mile	42

Osteria del Teatro	16	Shula's Steak House	48
Pacific Time	11	Spiga	20
Paramount Grill	2	Sushi Republic	3
Pascal's on Ponce	38	Tony Chan's Water Club	27
Perricone's Marketplace	32	Touch	10
Restaurant St. Michel	40	Tropical Chinese Restaurant	49
Rumi	15	Tuscan Steak	23
		Two Chefs	48
		Van Dyke Café	13
		Versailles	35
		Wish	20

Atlantic Ocean

Lummus Park

MIAMI

CORAL GABLES

COCONUT GROVE

KEY BISCAYNE

Virginia Key

Crandon Park

Biscayne Bay

MacArthur Causeway

Rickenbacker Causeway

Bill Baggs Cape Florida State Recreation Area

Matheson Hammock Park

Dolphin Expwy.

5 miles

5 km

sidewalk tables that would be at home across from a railroad station in Avignon or Bordeaux. Lighter dishes include moist couscous chicken and pasta primavera. Among the heartier entrées are a plum-, soy-, and lemon-glazed fillet of salmon; sesame-coated loin of tuna; and local yellowtail snapper. ⊠ *162 Alcazar Ave., Coral Gables,* ☎ *305/444–1666. AE, DC, MC, V.*

French

$$-$$$ ✕ **Pascal's on Ponce.** He's not a native son, but he might as well be. Chef-proprietor of Pascal's, Pascal Oudin, has been cooking here since the 1980s, when he opened Dominique's in the Alexander Hotel. His streamlined French cuisine disdains trends and discounts flash. Instead, you're supplied with substantive delicacies such as sautéed sea bass wrapped in a crispy potato crust with braised leeks or tenderloin of beef sautéed with snails and wild mushrooms. Service is proper, textures are perfect, and wines ideally complementary. The only dilemma is deciding between Oudin's own tarte tatin or a cheese course for dessert. ⊠ *2611 Ponce de León Blvd., Coral Gables,* ☎ *305/444–2024. Reservations essential. AE, D, DC, MC, V. No lunch weekends.*

Italian

$$-$$$ ✕ **Caffè Abbracci.** Long-running and much-beloved, this Italian restaurant is more like a club than an eatery. Start with some cold and hot antipasti, various carpaccios, porcini mushrooms, calamari, grilled goat cheese, shrimp, and mussels. Most pasta is made fresh, so consider sampling two or three, maybe with pesto sauce, Gorgonzola, and fresh tomatoes. Patrons tend to fare better when they're recognized, so go with a local or pretend you've been there before. ⊠ *318 Aragon Ave., Coral Gables,* ☎ *305/441–0700. Reservations essential. AE, DC, MC, V. No lunch weekends.*

Spanish

$$$-$$$$ ✕ **La Dorada.** This roomy two-story eatery sets the standard for fine Spanish cuisine in the city. Named after the royal sea bream, the restaurant brings in fresh fish daily from the Bay of Biscay, rather than Biscayne Bay. Preparations are both classic and excellent: scallops sautéed with grapes, monkfish stuffed with shrimp, whole fish baked in rock salt. Not a lot of English is spoken here, thanks to an all-Spanish staff, so service can be a little off. But they do make an effort to please, catering to those whims that get across language barriers. ⊠ *177 Giralda Ave., Coral Gables,* ☎ *305/446–2002. AE, MC, V.*

Downtown Miami

Chinese

$$ ✕ **Tony Chan's Water Club.** An outstanding Chinese restaurant, this dining room, just off the lobby of the Doubletree Grand Hotel, overlooks a bayside marina. On the menu of more than 200 appetizers and entrées are minced quail tossed with bamboo shoots and mushrooms wrapped in lettuce leaves. Indulge in a seafood spectacular of shrimp, conch, scallops, fish cakes, and crabmeat tossed with broccoli in a bird's nest, or go for pork chops sprinkled with green pepper in a black bean–garlic sauce. A lighter favorite is steamed sea bass with ginger and garlic. ⊠ *1717 N. Bayshore Dr., Downtown,* ☎ *305/374–8888. AE, D, DC, MC, V. No lunch weekends.*

Contemporary

$$-$$$$ ✕ **Azul.** This sumptuous restaurant has truly conquered the devil in the details. In addition to chef Michelle Bernstein's exotically rendered French-Caribbean cuisine, the thoughtful touches in service graciously anticipate your broader dining needs. Does your sleeveless blouse mean your shoulders are too cold to properly appreciate the poached eggs with lobster-knuckle hollandaise? Ask for one of the fashionable house pashminas. Forgot your reading glasses and can't decipher the hanger steak with foie gras sauce? Request a pair from the host. Want to see how the other half lives? Descend the interior staircase to Cafe Sambal, the all-day casual restaurant downstairs. ✉ *500 Brickell Key Dr., Mandarin Oriental Hotel, Brickell Key,* ☎ *305/913– 8288. Reservations essential. AE, MC, V. Closed Sat. lunch and Sun.*

$$–$$$ ✕ **Indigo.** When the Hotel Inter-Continental decided to redo its lobby restaurants, it didn't fool around. Now the entire lobby is one giant open-wall eatery where you can sup on the globally influenced cuisine. The menu's a trifle too cutesy for serious foodies, with categories like "salappzs and ladles" and "dare 2 share." Stone crab *croquetas* are on offer to start, and Moroccan *tagine* (stew) is available to share as an entrée. A great wine list and moderately priced brunches, lunch buffets, and happy-hour spreads suit the suits who work in nearby downtown. ✉ *100 Chopin Plaza, Downtown,* ☎ *305/854–9550. AE, D, DC, MC, V.*

Italian

$–$$ ✕ **Perricone's Marketplace and Café.** Brickell Avenue south of the Miami River is burgeoning with Italian restaurants. This is the biggest and most popular among them, housed in a 120-year-old barn from Vermont. The recipes were handed down from grandmother to mother to daughter, and the cooking is simple and good. Buy your wine from the on-premises deli and bring it to your table for a small corkage fee. Enjoy a glass with homemade minestrone; a generous antipasto; linguine with a sauté of jumbo shrimp, fresh asparagus, and chopped tomatoes; or gnocchi with four cheeses. The homemade tiramisu and fruit tart are top-notch. ✉ *15 S.E. 10th St., Brickell Village,* ☎ *305/374– 9449. AE, MC, V. Closed Sun. No lunch Sat.*

Latin

$–$$$ ✕ **Los Ranchos.** This steak-house chain sustains the tradition of Managua's original Los Ranchos by serving Argentine-style beef—lean, grass-fed tenderloin with *chimichurri* (a thick sauce of olive oil, vinegar, cayenne, and herbs). The Nicaraguan sauces include a tomato-based marinara and a fiery *cebollitas encurtidas* (with jalapeño and pickled onion). Specialties include spicy chorizo and *cuajada con maduro* (skim cheese with fried bananas). Don't look for veggies or brewed decaf—that's just not the Latin way—but there is live entertainment. ✉ *Bayside Marketplace, 401 Biscayne Blvd., Downtown,* ☎ *305/ 375–8188 or 305/375–0666;* ✉ *125 S.W. 107th Ave., Sweetwater,* ☎ *305/221–9367;* ✉ *2728 Ponce de León Blvd., Coral Gables,* ☎ *305/ 446–0050;* ✉ *The Falls, 8888 S.W. 136th St., Suite 303, Kendall, S. Miami,* ☎ *305/238–6867; AE, DC, MC, V.*

Middle-Eastern

$ ✕ **Daily Bread Marketplace.** Essentially a marketplace run by an Israeli family, the fare here actually comes under the heading pan–Middle Eastern. Falafel and gyro pita pockets, some of the most tempting in the county, counter Arabic meat pies and Greek spinach pies. Desserts are uniformly sticky with honey, drenched with butter, and encrusted with nuts—not a bad way to go out, whether you eat in at the self-service tables or take out. A new location on South Beach adds ethnic allure to the South of Fifth neighborhood. ✉ *2400 S.W. 27th St., Downtown,* ☎ *305/856–5893. AE, D, MC, V.*

Seafood

$–$$ ✕ **Fishbone Grill.** The artsy humor of this place is evident in the campy decor, but the fish here is artful. Start with cakelike jalapeño cornbread served alongside a small salad with homemade tomato-basil dressing. Then order your fish from a blackboard and have it grilled, blackened, sautéed, baked, Française-style, or Asian. Pizzas are available, too, as is a mean cioppino, the San Francisco–style tomato-based fish stew. Fishbone serves beer and wine only and justifiably prides itself on a reasonably priced, varied selection. Watch for winemakers' dinners, when superb vintages are paired with the chef's whims. ⊠ *650 S. Miami Ave., Downtown,* ☎ *305/530–1915. AE, MC, V. No dinner Sun.*

Spanish
$ ✕ **El Bodegon Gallego.** Ridiculously cheap and relentlessly craving-in-ducing, this shabby little Spanish-only storefront serves tasty tapas and hefty main courses. Although the menu may escape those who speak only English, sign language will get you an absurdly large order of chick-peas sautéed with chorizo or a lusty seafood soup or yellow rice with chicken and shrimp. Consider the wrought iron on the windows not as an indication of how bad the neighborhood is, but of how good the creamy desserts flavored with alcohol are—most customers will will-ingly put themselves behind bars just for a single spoonful. ⊠ *3174 N.W. 7th Ave., Downtown,* ☎ *305/649–0801. No credit cards.*

Little Havana

Cuban
$–$$$ ✕ **Versailles.** Cubans meet to dine on Calle Ocho in what is quite pos-sibly the most ornate budget restaurant you'll ever see, all mirrors and candelabras. And the royal treatment is not limited to the decor in this veritable institution. The food is terrific, especially such classics as ropa vieja, *arroz con pollo* (chicken and rice), *palomilla* (thin, boneless) steak, *sopa de platanos* (plantain soup), ham shank, and roast pork. To com-plete the experience, have the town's strongest Cuban coffee and ter-rific flan or sweet *tres leches* (literally, "three milks," a creamy Latin dessert) to finish. ⊠ *3555 S.W. 8th St., Little Havana,* ☎ *305/444–0240. AE, D, DC, MC, V.*

Spanish
$–$$ ✕ **Las Neuvas Culebrinas.** A Spanish *tapacería* (house of little plates) is a place to live each meal as if it were your last, though you may wait for it as long as some inmates do for an appeal. Tapas are not small at all; some are entrée size, such as a succulent mix of garbanzos with ham, sausage, red peppers, and oil, or the Spanish tortilla, a giant Fris-bee-shape omelet. Indulge in a tender fillet of crocodile, fresh fish, grilled pork, or the kicker, goat in Coca-Cola sauce. For dessert there's *crema Catalana,* caramelized table-side with a blowtorch. ⊠ *4700 W. Fla-gler St., Little Havana,* ☎ *305/445–2337. AE, MC, V.*

Vietnamese
$–$$ ✕ **Hy-Vong Vietnamese Cuisine.** This plain little restaurant is an
★   anomaly on Calle Ocho, and also a novelty—come before 7 PM to avoid a wait. Spring springs forth in spring rolls of ground pork, cellophane noodles, and black mushrooms wrapped in homemade rice paper. Folks'll mill about on the sidewalk for hours to sample the whole fish panfried with *nuoc man* (a garlic-lime fish sauce), not to mention the thinly sliced pork barbecued with sesame seeds, almonds, and peanuts. Beer-savvy proprietor Kathy Manning serves a half-dozen top brews (Double Grimbergen, Moretti, and Spaten, among them) to further in-oculate the experience from the ordinary. ⊠ *3458 S.W. 8th St., Little Havana,* ☎ *305/446–3674. AE, D, MC, V. Closed Mon. No lunch.*

Miami Beach North of South Beach

Contemporary

$$–$$$ ✕ **Crystal Café.** As cozy as Grandma's dining room, this New Continental restaurant takes the classics and lightens 'em up. Beef Stroganoff and chicken *paprikash* (chicken and onions browned in bacon drippings, then braised with stock and paprika) are two such updated stars; and osso buco literally falls off the bone. More contemporary items include chicken Kiev, stuffed with goat cheese and topped with a tricolor salad, and pan-seared duck breast with raspberry sauce. Klime Kovaceski, the multiple Golden Spoon award–winning Macedonian chef-proprietor, takes pride in serving more food than you can possibly manage, including home-baked rhubarb pie. ✉ *726 41st St., Miami Beach,* ☎ *305/673–8266. AE, D, DC, MC, V. Closed Mon. No lunch.*

Continental

$$$–$$$$ ✕ **The Forge.** Often compared to a museum, this landmark bills itself as "the Versailles of steak." Each intimate dining salon has historical artifacts, including a chandelier that hung in James Madison's White House. The wine cellar contains 380,000 bottles—including more than 500 dating from 1822 (and costing as much as $35,000). In addition to steak, specialties include Norwegian salmon with spinach vinaigrette and free-range duck roasted with black currants. For dessert try the blacksmith pie. This place is a hot party spot on Wednesday night, and the adjoining club, Café Nostalgia, is very popular with the "I remember Cuba" crowd. ✉ *432 Arthur Godfrey Rd., Miami Beach,* ☎ *305/538–8533. Reservations essential. AE, DC, MC, V. No lunch.*

Delicatessens

$–$$ ✕ **Arnie and Richie's.** Take a deep whiff when you walk in, and you'll know what you're in for: onion rolls, smoked whitefish salad, half-sour pickles, herring in sour cream sauce, chopped liver, corned beef, pastrami. Deli doesn't get more delicious than in this family-run operation. Casual to the extreme, most customers are regulars and seat themselves at tables that have baskets of plastic knives and forks; if you request a menu, it's a clear sign you're a newcomer. Service can be brusque, but it sure is quick. ✉ *525 41st St., Miami Beach,* ☎ *305/531–7691. AE, MC, V.*

Italian

$–$$$ ✕ **Café Prima Pasta.** One of Miami's many signatures is this exemplary Argentine-Italian spot, which rules the emerging North Beach neighborhood. Service can be erratic, but you forget it all on delivery of fresh-made bread with a bowl of spiced olive oil. Tender carpaccio and plentiful antipasti are a delight to share, but the real treat here is the hand-rolled pasta, which can range from crab-stuffed ravioli to simple fettuccine with seafood. If overexposed tiramisu hasn't made an enemy of you yet, try this legendary one to add espresso notes to your unavoidable garlic breath. ✉ *414 71st St., North Beach, Miami Beach,* ☎ *305/867–0106. MC, V.*

Japanese

$–$$ ✕ **Sushi Republic.** A long and narrow storefront with sponge-painted walls, this eatery prides itself on welcoming customers, so don't be surprised when the sushi chefs say, "Hi!" when you walk in. Nor should you expect anything but the freshest sashimi, which is elegantly presented and perfectly succulent. As far as cooked fare goes, the Republic is more like a democracy—everything is even and consistent. *Shumai,* soft shrimp dumplings with *ponzu* (soy, rice vinegar, sake, seaweed, and dried bonito flakes) dipping sauce; whole fried soft-shell crab; and salmon teriyaki are particularly noteworthy. ✉ *9583 Harding Ave., Surfside,* ☎ *305/867–8036. AE, D, DC, MC, V. Closed Mon. No lunch Sun.*

Mediterranean

$–$$ ✗ **Oasis Café.** The emphasis in Mediterranean cuisine is on health, and Oasis, a coolly tiled spot with breezy decor, makes sure you don't keel over at the tables—the chefs here stuff grape leaves, not arteries. In other words, natural-food enthusiasts feel right at home, with delicacies such as eggplant salads, hummus, grilled sesame tofu, and sautéed garlic spinach for starters, and for entrées, pan-seared turkey chop, roasted vegetable lasagna, grilled fresh fish on focaccia, or penne with turkey, tomato, saffron, and pine nuts. The homemade rum cake is a superb way to drink dessert. ✉ *976 41st St., Miami Beach,* ☎ *305/674–7676. AE, D, DC, MC, V.*

North Miami Beach and North Dade

Contemporary

$$$–$$$$ ✗ **Chef Allen's.** Chef Allen Susser presents his global cuisine in this art
★ gallery of a dining room. At the 25-ft-wide picture window, you can watch him create contemporary American masterpieces from a menu that changes nightly. After a salad of baby greens and warm wild mushrooms or a rock-shrimp hash with roasted corn, consider swordfish with conch-citrus couscous, macadamia nuts, and lemon or grilled lamb chops with eggplant timbale and a three-nut salsa. It's hard to resist finishing off your meal with a soufflé; order it early to eliminate a mouthwatering wait at the end of your meal. ✉ *19088 N.E. 29th Ave., Aventura,* ☎ *305/935–2900. Reservations required. AE, DC, MC, V.*

$–$$$ ✗ **Paramount Grill.** This handsomely appointed, bistro-style eatery is a treat, even if its location in the second story of a major shopping mall seems like a trick. Creative innovations may include pizza topped with smoked salmon and citrus cream cheese; rock shrimp cakes with lemon aioli; Caribe-crusted skirt steak; or key lime chicken with yuca fries—at about half the dough you'd spend elsewhere. Sit under the flickering gaslights, lean against a redbrick column, and raise a toast to mall eateries, after all. ✉ *19501 Biscayne Blvd., Aventura,* ☎ *305/466–1466. AE, MC, V.*

Steak

$$$–$$$$ ✗ **Shula's Steak House.** Prime rib, fish, steaks, and 3-pound lobsters are almost an afterthought to the *objets de sport* in this NFL shrine in the Don Shula's Hotel. Dine in a manly wood-lined room with a fireplace, surrounded by memorabilia of retired coach Don Shula's perfect 1972 season with the Miami Dolphins. Polish off the 48-ounce porterhouse steak and achieve a sort of immortality—your name on a plaque and an autographed picture of Shula to take home. Also for fans, there's Shula's Steak 2, a sports-celebrity hangout in the resort's hotel section, as well as a branch at the Alexander Hotel in Miami Beach. ✉ *7601 N.W. 154th St., Miami Lakes,* ☎ *305/820–8102. AE, DC, MC, V.*

South Beach

American

$$ ✗ **Joe Allen.** Hidden away in an exploding neighborhood of condos, town houses, and stores, this casual upscale eatery is a hangout for locals who crave a good martini along with a terrific burger. The eclectic crowd includes kids and grandparents, and the menu has everything from pizzas to calves' liver to steaks. Start with an innovative salad, such as arugula with pear, prosciutto, and a Gorgonzola dressing, or roast beef salad on greens with Parmesan. Desserts are home style as well, including banana cream pie and ice cream and cookie sandwiches. ⊠ *1787 Purdy Ave., South Beach,* ☏ *305/531–7007. MC, V.*

Café

$$ ✕ **News Café.** An Ocean Drive landmark, this 24-hour café attracts
★ a crowd with snacks, light meals, and drinks, and the people parade on the sidewalk out front. Most prefer sitting outside, where they can feel the salt breeze and gawk at the human scenery. Offering a little of this and a little of that—bagels, pâtés, chocolate fondue, sandwiches, and a terrific wine list—this joint has something for all appetites. Although service can be indifferent to the point of laissez-faire, the café remains a scene. ⊠ *800 Ocean Dr., South Beach,* ☏ *305/538–6397. Reservations not accepted. AE, DC, MC, V.*

$–$$ ✕ **Van Dyke Café.** Just as its parent, News Café, draws the fashion crowd, this offshoot attracts the artsy crowd. Indeed this place seems even livelier than its Ocean Drive counterpart, with pedestrians passing by on the Lincoln Road Mall and live jazz playing upstairs every evening—or, more to the point, every early morning. The kitchen serves dishes from mammoth omelets with home fries to soups and grilled dolphin sandwiches to basil-grilled lamb and pasta dishes, though it's best to stick to basics. There's an enticing list of cocktails such as Bellinis and Kir Royales. ⊠ *846 Lincoln Rd., South Beach,* ☏ *305/534–3600. AE, DC, MC, V.*

Contemporary

$$$–$$$$ ✕ **Blue Door at the Delano.** In a hotel where style reigns supreme, this
★ restaurant provides both glamour and tantalizing cuisine. Acclaimed consulting chef Claude Troisgros and executive chef Elizabeth Barlow combine the flavors of classic French cuisine with South American influences to create dishes such as the Big Ravioli, filled with crab-and-scallop mousseline, and osso buco in Thai curry sauce with caramelized pineapple and bananas. Equally pleasing is dining with the crème de la crème of Miami (and New York, and Paris) society. ⊠ *1685 Collins Ave., South Beach,* ☏ *305/674–6400. Reservations essential. AE, D, DC, MC, V.*

$$$–$$$$ ✕ **Rumi.** Rumi is what happens when club kids and party organizers like Alan Roth and Sean Saladino grow up: they open a sophisticated dinner lounge named for a mystical poet. Co-chefs J. D. Harris and Scott Fredel contribute to the sensual, heavy-lidded environment with culinary delights such as Florida pompano with truffled Peruvian potatoes or Sonoma duck breast with orange crepes. After 11 or so, the two-story storefront turns into a club, complete with velvet rope and mandatory champagne purchases if you intend on sitting at a table. ⊠ *330 Lincoln Rd., South Beach,* ☏ *305/672–4353. Reservations essential. AE, MC, V. No lunch.*

$$–$$$$ ✕ **Nemo.** The open-air setting, bright colors, copper fixtures, and
★ tree-shaded courtyard lend casual comfort; but its setting is not the main reason why Nemo receives the raves it does. The menu, which blends Caribbean, Asian, Mediterranean, and Middle Eastern influences, promises an explosion of cultures in each bite. And it delivers. Popular appetizers include garlic-cured salmon rolls with Tabiko caviar and wasabi mayo, and crispy prawns with spicy salsa. Main courses might include wok-charred salmon or grilled Indian-spice pork chop. Hedy Goldsmith's funky pastries are exquisitely sinful. Look also for the sibling sushi bar called Shoji Sushi next door. ⊠ *100 Collins Ave., South Beach,* ☏ *305/532–4550. AE, MC, V.*

$$–$$$$ ✕ **Wish.** If what you wish for is stupendous cuisine served in a designer-deco environment, consider your wish granted. Fashion designer Todd Oldham redesigned the former Tiffany Hotel, the art deco gem that houses this fresh, youthful restaurant. His whimsical, colorful design

(you'll marvel at the creative use of dozens of hanging light fixtures) provides an apt setting for chef E. Michael Redit's French-Brazilian cuisine. His sensibility results in dishes like seared scallops over *brandade* (cod puree) and brandied onions or rare tuna with charred watermelon and avocado Hollandaise, and they make as much of a statement as the room. ⊠ *801 Collins Ave., South Beach,* ☎ *305/674–9474. AE, D, DC, MC, V.*

Italian

$$-$$$$ ✕ **Escopazzo.** A romantic storefront takes you away, like Calgon, from the din of bustling Washington Avenue. The northern Italian menu offers some of the area's best—and most expensive—Italian food. But innovative treatments of standard ingredients make it worth the outlay of cash. Sea bass gets "scales" of crusty potato, goat cheese and arugula are mixed into a risotto, and various soufflés hide vegetables and mixed seafood. Service can be slow as a speedboat in a manatee zone; pass the time by taking a tour of the 1,000-bottle wine cellar. ⊠ *1311 Washington Ave., South Beach,* ☎ *305/674–9450. AE, DC, MC, V. No lunch.*

$$-$$$$ ✕ **Tuscan Steak.** Dark wood and mirrors define this masculine, chic,
★   expensive place, where food is served family style. Tuscan can be busy as a subway stop, and still the staff will be gracious and giving. The chefs take their cues from the Tuscan countryside, where pasta is rich with truffles and main plates are simply but deliciously grilled. Sip a deep red Barolo with any of the house specialties: three-mushroom risotto with white truffle oil, gnocchi with Gorgonzola cream, Florentine T-bone with roasted garlic puree, whole yellowtail snapper with braised garlic, or the filet mignon with a Gorgonzola crust. ⊠ *431 Washington Ave., South Beach,* ☎ *305/534–2233. AE, DC, MC, V.*

$$-$$$ ✕ **Osteria del Teatro.** Thanks to word of mouth, this northern Italian
★   restaurant is constantly full. Orchids grace the tables in the intimate gray-on-gray room with a low, laced-canvas ceiling, deco lamps, and the most refined clink and clatter along Washington Avenue. Regulars know not to order off the printed menu, however. A tremendous array of daily specials offers the best options here. A representative appetizer is poached asparagus served over polenta triangles with a Gorgonzola sauce. Stuffed pastas, including spinach crepes overflowing with ricotta, can seem heavy but taste light; fish dishes yield a rosemary-marinated tuna in a pink peppercorn–citrus sauce. ⊠ *1443 Washington Ave., South Beach,* ☎ *305/538–7850. Reservations essential. AE, DC, MC, V. Closed Sun. No lunch.*

$-$$ ✕ **Spiga.** When you need a break from Miami's abundant exotic fare, savor the modestly priced Italian standards served with flair in this small, pretty place. Homemade is the hallmark here, where pastas and breads are fresh daily. Carpaccio *di salmone* (thinly sliced salmon with mixed greens) is a typical appetizer, and the *zuppa di pesce* (fish stew) is unparalleled. Entrées include ravioli *di vitello ai funghi shitaki* (homemade ravioli stuffed with veal and sautéed with shiitake mushrooms). The cozy restaurant has become a neighborhood favorite, where customers sometimes bring in CDs for personalized enjoyment. ⊠ *1228 Collins Ave., South Beach,* ☎ *305/534–0079. AE, D, DC, MC, V.*

Pan-Asian

$$$-$$$$ ✕ **Bambú.** Cameron Diaz may be an in-name owner only, but do anticipate glam surroundings and customers who are (or think they are) equal to her status. Bambú's muted khaki colors, woven raffia drapes, bars formed from river rocks and coconut wood, and spectacular 14-ft granite waterfall provide some Zen for the world-weary. But the real beauty here lies in executive chef Rob Boone's fare: tuna hand rolls with avocado, cilantro, and pickled eggplant; soy-lacquered cod with tempura chrysanthemum leaves; and Kobe beef with tiny Asian vegetables and lotus root. ⊠ *1661 Meridian Ave., South Beach,* ☎ *305/531–4800. Reservations essential. AE, MC, V. No lunch.*

$$$–$$$$ ✕ **China Grill.** This crowded, noisy, ever-vaunted celebrity haunt turns out not Chinese food but rather "world cuisine" in large portions meant for sharing. Crispy duck with scallion pancakes and caramelized black-vinegar sauce is a nice surprise, as is pork and beans with green apple and balsamic mojo (a garlicky Cuban marinade). Mechanical service delivers the acceptable broccoli rabe dumpling starter, the wild mushroom pasta entrée, or the flash-fried crispy spinach that shatters like a good martini glass thrown into a fireplace. Unless you're frequent diner Boris Becker or George Clooney, don't expect your drinks to arrive before your food. ⊠ *404 Washington Ave., South Beach,* ☎ *305/534–2211. Reservations essential. AE, DC, MC, V. No lunch Sat.*

$$$–$$$$ ✕ **Pacific Time.** Packed nearly every night, chef-proprietor Jonathan
★ Eismann's superb eatery has a high blue ceiling, banquettes, plank floors, and an open kitchen. The brilliant American-Asian cuisine includes such entrées as cedar-roasted salmon, rosemary-roasted chicken, and dry-aged Colorado beef grilled with shiitake mushrooms. The cuttlefish appetizer and the Florida pompano entrée are masterpieces. Desserts include a fresh pear-pecan spring roll. ⊠ *915 Lincoln Rd., South Beach,* ☎ *305/534–5979. Reservations essential. AE, DC, MC, V.*

Seafood

$$–$$$$ ✕ **Joe's Stone Crab Restaurant.** Joe's stubbornly operates by its own rules: be prepared to wait up to an hour in line just to register your name for a table, and resign yourself to waiting up to another *three* hours before you finally sit down to eat. The centerpiece of the ample à la carte menu is, of course, stone crab, with a piquant mustard sauce. Side orders include creamed garlic spinach, french-fried onions, fried green tomatoes, and hash browns. Desserts include a justifiably famous key lime pie. If you can't stand loitering hungrily, come for lunch or go next door for Joe's takeout. ⊠ *11 Washington Ave., South Beach,* ☎ *305/673–0365; 305/673–4611 for takeout; 800/780–2722 for overnight shipping. Reservations not accepted. AE, D, DC, MC, V. Closed May–Oct. 15. No lunch Sun.–Mon.*

Steak

$$$–$$$$ ✕ **Gaucho Room.** Granted, you may never bite down on a more succulent steak than in this Argentine-cowboy-themed room, but don't you dare call this a steak house. The chef cut his culinary teeth on fusion cuisine, and the results are seen in pulled duck empanada with smoked chili sauce or Chilean sea bass with ginger-*boniato* (sweet potato) puree. Which is not to say that you shouldn't order the supple *churrasco* (a whole skirt steak that is marinated, grilled, and then sliced table-side). Service may be the finest and most solicitous in South Beach—a compliment indeed. ⊠ *Loew's Hotel, 1601 Collins Ave., South Beach,* ☎ *305/604–5290. Reservations essential. AE, D, DC, MC, V. No lunch. Closed Mon.*

South Miami

Contemporary

$$–$$$$ ✕ **Two Chefs.** Meet the two chefs—Jan Jorgensen and Soren Bredahl—both Danes, who've been cooking together for decades. This restaurant, decorated like a Williams-Sonoma catalog, has an ever-changing menu, but scan for seared foie gras with gnocchi, an unusually textured combination that includes reduced boysenberries. The chefs pride themselves on the unexpected and think nothing of pairing goat meat with lobster or composing an escargot potpie. ⊠ *8287 S. Dixie*

Hwy., South Miami, ☎ *305/663–2100. AE, D, DC, MC, V. Closed Sun.*

Seafood

$$–$$$$ ✕ **Captain's Tavern.** This beloved family fish house has an unusually interesting menu fortified with Caribbean and South American influences. The paneled walls may be hokey, but the food can take your mind off the surroundings. Beyond good versions of the typical fare— conch chowder and conch fritters—you'll find Portuguese fish stew, fish with various tropical fruits, a delightful black bean soup, and oysters in cream sauce with fresh rosemary, not to mention decadent desserts. ⊠ *7495 S.E. 98th St., South Miami,* ☎ *305/661–4237. AE, MC, V.*

West Miami

Chinese

$–$$$ ✕ **Tropical Chinese Restaurant.** This big, lacquer-free room feels as open and busy as a railway station. You'll find unfamiliar items on the menu—early spring leaves of snow pea pods, for example, which are sublimely tender and flavorful. The extensive menu is filled with tofu combinations, poultry, beef, and pork, as well as tender seafood. An exuberant dim sum lunch—brunch on the weekends—allows you to choose an assortment of small dishes from wheeled carts. In the open kitchen, 10 chefs prepare everything as if for dignitaries. ⊠ *7991 S.W. 40th St. (Bird Rd.), Westchester,* ☎ *305/262–7576 or 305/262–1552. AE, DC, MC, V.*

LODGING

Revised by
Matt Windsor

Although some hotels (especially on the mainland) have adopted steady year-round rates, many adjust their rates to reflect seasonal demand. The peak occurs in winter, with a dip in summer (prices are often more negotiable than rate cards let on). You'll find the best values between Easter and Memorial Day (which is actually a delightful time in Miami but a difficult time for many people to travel) and in September and October (the height of hurricane season). Keep in mind that Miami hoteliers collect roughly 12.5%—ouch—for city and resort taxes; parking fees can run up to $16 per evening; and tips for bellhops, valet parkers, concierges, and housekeepers add to the expense. Some hotels actually tack on an automatic 15% gratuity. All told, you can easily spend 25% more than your room rate to sleep in Miami.

CATEGORY	COST*
$$$$	over $220
$$$	$140–$220
$$	$80–$140
$	under $80

All prices are for a standard double room, excluding 6% sales tax (more in some counties) and 1%–4% tourist tax.

Coconut Grove

$$$–$$$$ 🏨 **Wyndham Grand Bay.** Combining the classical elegance of Greece,
★   a stepped facade that looks vaguely Aztec, a hint of the South, and a brush of the tropical, the Grand Bay is like no other in South Florida. Guest rooms are filled with superb touches, such as antique sideboards that store away house phones and televisions. But what sets the hotel apart are the atypically spacious suite terraces—perfect for private dinners—with sweeping views of Biscayne Bay. Bice, a trendy Italian

restaurant on the premises, is extremely popular. ⊠ *2669 S. Bayshore Dr., Coconut Grove 33133,* ☎ *305/858–9600 or 800/327–2788,* FAX *305/859–2026,* WEB *www.wyndham.com/CoconutGrove. 125 rooms, 52 suites. Restaurant, pool, health club, hair salon, hot tub, massage, sauna, bar, concierge, parking (fee). AE, DC, MC, V.*

$$–$$$$ 🏨 **Mayfair House.** This European-style luxury hotel sits within the Streets of Mayfair, an exclusive open-air shopping mall in the heart of the Grove. The feel of the neighborhood runs through the hotel, and is mirrored in the Tiffany windows, polished mahogany and marble accents, imported ceramics and crystal, and an impressive glass elevator. The individually furnished suites have terraces facing the street, screened by vegetation and wood latticework. Each room has a small Japanese hot tub on the balcony or a Roman tub inside, and 10 have antique pianos. Although the rooftop pool area is peaceful, the miniature lap seems out of place. ⊠ *3000 Florida Ave., Coconut Grove 33133,* ☎ *305/441–0000 or 800/433–4555,* FAX *305/447–9173,* WEB *www.mayfairhousehotel. com. 179 suites. Restaurant, snack bar, pool, hot tub, bar, laundry service, concierge, business services, parking (fee). AE, D, DC, MC, V.*

Coral Gables

$$$–$$$$ 🏨 **Biltmore Hotel.** Miami's grand boom-time hotel recaptures a bygone
★ era, with its semicircular drive and formal facade, grand swimming pool flanked by a colonnaded walkway, and period furnishings and artwork indoors. Now owned by the city of Coral Gables, the 1926 hotel rises like a sienna-color wedding cake in the heart of a residential district. The vaulted lobby has hand-painted rafters on a twinkling sky-blue background. Large guest rooms are done in a restrained Moorish style, and for slightly more than the average rate ($2,550) you can book the Everglades (a.k.a. Al Capone) Suite—Bill Clinton's favorite room when he was in town. ⊠ *1200 Anastasia Ave., Coral Gables 33134,* ☎ *305/ 445–1926 or 800/727–1926,* FAX *305/913–3159,* WEB *www.biltmorehotel. com. 237 rooms, 38 suites. Restaurant, café, 18-hole golf course, 10 tennis courts, pool, health club, sauna, spa, bar, lobby lounge, meeting room. AE, D, DC, MC, V.*

$$ 🏨 **Hotel Place St. Michel.** Art nouveau chandeliers suspended from
★ vaulted ceilings light the public areas of this intimate boutique hotel within easy walking distance of Miracle Mile. Built in 1926, the historic inn is kept filled with the scent of fresh flowers, circulated by paddle fans. Each guest room has its own dimensions, personality, and antiques imported from England, Scotland, and France, although plusher beds would be a welcome improvement. Dinner at the superb Restaurant St. Michel is a must, but there is also a more casual bar/dining area behind the lobby, better suited for quiet breakfasts or late-night aperitifs. ⊠ *162 Alcazar Ave., Coral Gables 33134,* ☎ *305/444–1666 or 800/848–4683,* FAX *305/529–0074,* WEB *www.hotelplacestmichel.com. 24 rooms, 3 suites. Restaurant, bar, laundry service, parking (fee). AE, DC, MC, V. CP.*

Downtown Miami

$$$$ 🏨 **Mandarin Oriental Miami.** Though it's a favorite of Wall Street ty-
★ coons and Latin American CEOs doing business with the Brickell Avenue banks, anyone who can afford to stay here won't regret it. The location is excellent, at the tip of Brickell Key in Biscayne Bay; rooms facing west have a panoramic view of the dazzling downtown skyline; those facing east overlook Miami Beach and the blue Atlantic beyond. The Mandarin is fanatically picky about details, from the Bulova alarm clocks and hand-painted room numbers on rice paper to the recessed data ports on room desks that eliminate laptop cord clutter. ⊠ *500*

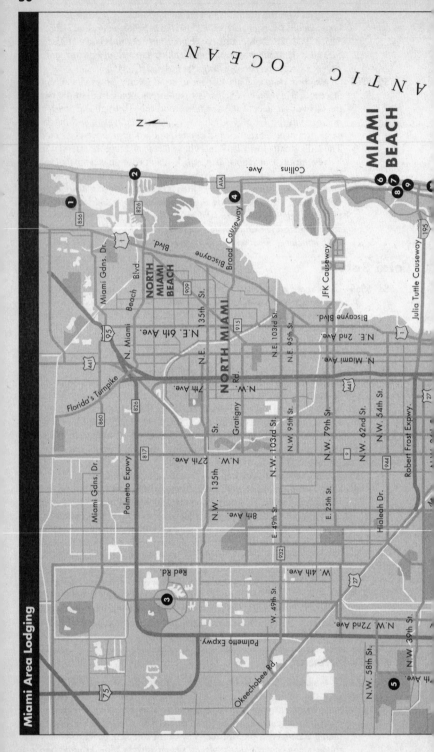

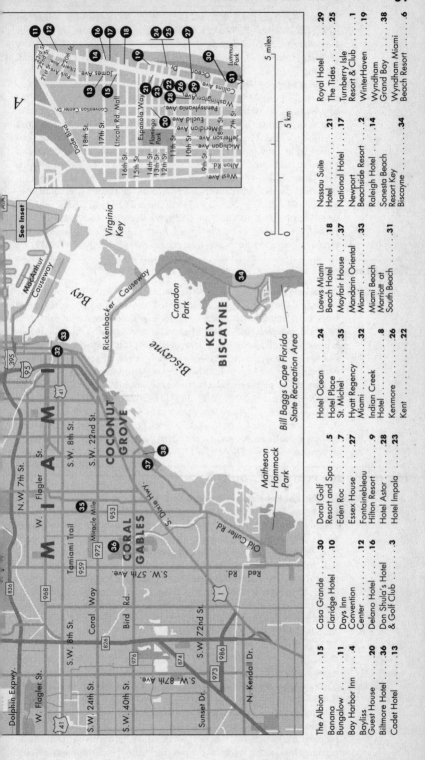

51

The Albion **15**
Banana
Bungalow **11**
Bay Harbor Inn **4**
Bayliss
Guest House **20**
Biltmore Hotel **36**
Cadet Hotel **13**

Casa Grande **30**
Claridge Hotel **10**
Days Inn
Convention
Center **12**
Delano Hotel **16**
Don Shula's Hotel
& Golf Club **3**

Doral Golf
Resort and Spa **5**
Eden Roc **7**
Essex House **27**
Fontainebleau
Hilton Miami **9**
Hotel Astor **28**
Hotel Impala **23**

Hotel Ocean **24**
Hotel Place
St. Michel **35**
Hyatt Regency
Miami **32**
Indian Creek
Hotel **8**
Kenmore **26**
Kent **22**

Loews Miami
Beach Hotel **18**
Mayfair House **37**
Mandarin Oriental
Miami **33**
Miami Beach
Marriott at
South Beach **31**

Nassau Suite
Hotel **21**
National Hotel **17**
Newport
Beachside Resort . . **2**
Raleigh Hotel **14**
Sonesta Beach
Resort Key
Biscayne **34**

Royal Hotel **29**
The Tides **25**
Turnberry Isle
Resort & Club **1**
WinterHaven **19**
Wyndham
Grand Bay **38**
Wyndham Miami
Beach Resort **6**

Brickell Key Dr., Brickell Key 33131, ☎ *305/913–8288 or 866/888–6780,* FAX *305/913–8300,* WEB *www.mandarinoriental.com. 329 rooms. Restaurant, in-room data ports, in-room safes, pool, spa, 2 bars, dry cleaning, laundry service, concierge, business services, meeting rooms, parking (fee). AE, D, DC, MC, V.*

$$$ 🏨 **Hyatt Regency Miami.** The Hyatt is well positioned to enjoy the fruits of Miami's late-'90s renaissance—the Miami Avenue Bridge, the Port of Miami, and AmericanAirlines Arena seemed to sprout up around it. If your vacation is based on boats, basketball, or business, you can't do much better. The distinctive public spaces are more colorful than businesslike, and guest rooms are done in an unusual combination of avocado, beige, and blond. Rooms also yield views of the river or port. The James L. Knight International Center is accessible without stepping outside, as is the downtown Metromover and its Metrorail connection. ⊠ *400 S.E. 2nd Ave., Downtown 33131,* ☎ *305/358–1234 or 800/233–1234,* FAX *305/358–0529,* WEB *www.miami.hyatt.com. 612 rooms, 51 suites. Restaurant, pool, health club, 2 bars, laundry service, concierge, business services, parking (fee). AE, D, DC, MC, V.*

Key Biscayne

$$$–$$$$ 🏨 **Sonesta Beach Resort Key Biscayne.** Architecturally dull but still one of Miami's best, this beautifully located resort has stunning sea views from east-facing units. Rooms are done in sand tones with fabrics in emerald, purple, gold, and ruby. Villas are actually three-bedroom homes with full kitchens and screened pools. The 750-ft beach, one of Florida's most gorgeous, its Olympic pool, variety of activities, and kids' program make it a good family getaway. Museum-quality modern art by prominent painters and sculptors graces public areas. ⊠ *350 Ocean Dr., Key Biscayne 33149,* ☎ *305/361–2021 or 800/766–3782,* FAX *305/361–3096,* WEB *www.sonesta.com. 284 rooms, 15 suites, 3 villas. 3 restaurants, snack bar, 9 tennis courts, pool, massage, steam room, aerobics, health club, beach, windsurfing, parasailing, 3 bars, children's programs (ages 5–13). AE, D, DC, MC, V.*

Miami Beach North of South Beach

$$$$ 🏨 **Eden Roc Renaissance Resort & Spa.** This grand 1950s hotel designed by Morris Lapidus has always been overshadowed by its next-door neighbor and archrival, the larger, older Fontainebleau. But it shouldn't be. The free-flowing lines of the deco architecture impart a modern, elegant feel to the public areas, especially the terribly hip lobby bar, with its low-slung, meandering couches. South Florida's only indoor rock-climbing wall is found at the popular 55,000-square-ft Spa of Eden; and former Dolphins coach Jimmy Johnson's beachside sports bar caters to those who prefer lifting weights 16 ounces at a time. Rooms blend a touch of the '50s with informal elegance. ⊠ *4525 Collins Ave., Mid-Beach 33140,* ☎ *305/531–0000 or 800/327–8337,* FAX *305/674–5555,* WEB *www.renaissancehotels.com. 349 rooms. 2 restaurants, 2 pools, gym, spa, basketball, racquetball, squash, sports bar, meeting rooms. AE, MC, V.*

$$$–$$$$ 🏨 **Wyndham Miami Beach Resort.** Of the great Miami Beach hotels,
★ this 18-story modern glass tower is a standout, as is its polished staff offering exceptional service, from helping you find the best shopping to bringing you an icy drink on the beach. The bright rooms have a tropical blue color scheme and are filled with attentive details: mini-refrigerators, three layers of drapes (including blackout curtains), big closets, and bathrooms with high-end toiletries and a magnifying mirror. Two presidential suites were designed in consultation with the Secret Service, and a rooftop meeting room offers views of bay and

ocean. ✉ *4833 Collins Ave., Mid-Beach 33140,* ☎ *305/532–3600 or 800/203–8368,* FAX *305/534–7409,* WEB *www.wyndham.com. 378 rooms, 46 suites. 2 restaurants, tennis court, pool, gym, massage, beach, 2 bars, meeting room. AE, D, DC, MC, V.*

$$–$$$$ ⊡ **Fontainebleau Hilton Resort.** This big, busy, and ornate grande
★ dame has completed an overhaul of its original building, but even more grandiose plans are in the works, with the ongoing construction of a new hotel/condominium complex that will remove several tennis courts but add a spa. All public areas and guest rooms have been renovated, but rooms still vary wildly, ranging from 1950s to very contemporary furnishings. Adults enjoy free admission to the hotel's *Club Tropigala* Vegas-style floor show. The most popular spot for kids is Cookie's World, a water playground with multiple slides and jets emerging from a giant purple octopus. ✉ *4441 Collins Ave., Mid-Beach 33140,* ☎ *305/538– 2000 or 800/548–8886,* FAX *305/673–5351,* WEB *www.hilton.com. 1,146 rooms, 60 suites. 12 restaurants, 4 tennis courts, 3 pools, health club, sauna, spa, beach, windsurfing, boating, jet skiing, parasailing, volleyball, 4 bars, nightclub, children's programs (ages 5–14), playground, convention center, some pets allowed (fee). AE, D, DC, MC, V.*

$$$ ⊡ **Claridge Hotel.** A cool Mediterranean breeze in a somewhat stagnant corner of Miami Beach, the Claridge is the city's most impressive hotel renovation. The exterior has been restored to the canary-yellow glory of the 1928 original; inside, rich Venetian frescoed walls are hung with Peruvian oil paintings, the floors are fashioned from volcanic ash, and the whole is supported by majestic volcanic stone columns. A Moroccan terrace overlooks the soaring inner atrium, which has a splash Jacuzzi at the far end. Rooms are a mix of Asian and European influences, with straw mats laid over wood floors, and ornate wood furniture. ✉ *3500 Collins Ave., Mid-Beach 33140,* ☎ *305/604–8485 or 888/422–9111,* FAX *305/674–0881,* WEB *www.claridgefl.com. 52 rooms and suites. Restaurant, in-room data ports, in-room safes, hot tub, concierge, business services, parking (fee). AE, D, DC, MC, V.*

$$–$$$ ⊡ **Indian Creek Hotel.** Not as grand as the North Beach behemoths or
★ as hectic as the Ocean Drive offerings, this 1936 Pueblo deco jewel may just be Miami's most charming and sincere lodge. Owner Marc Levin rescued the inn and filled its rooms with art deco furniture. To keep things fresh, the garden rooms recently underwent further redecorating. Suites have VCR/CD players and modem capabilities. The dining room offers an eclectic and appetizing menu, which you can also enjoy outdoors by the lush pool and garden. Stay a while, and manager Zammy Migdal and his staff will have you feeling like family. ✉ *2727 Indian Creek Dr., Mid-Beach 33140,* ☎ *305/531–2727 or 800/491–2772,* FAX *305/531–5651,* WEB *www.indiancreekhotelmb.com. 55 rooms, 6 suites. Restaurant, refrigerators, pool, meeting room. AE, D, DC, MC, V.*

North Miami, North Miami Beach, and North Dade

$$$–$$$$ ⊡ **Turnberry Isle Resort & Club.** Finest of the grand resorts, even more
★ so with the addition of a stellar spa, Turnberry is a tapestry of islands and waterways on 300 superbly landscaped acres by the bay. You'll stay at the 1920s Addison Mizner–designed Country Club Hotel on the Intracoastal Waterway where oversize rooms in light woods and earth tones have large curving terraces and hot tubs. The marina has moorings for 117 boats, and there are not one but two Robert Trent Jones golf courses. The oceanfront Ocean Club has a new playground for kids, but no longer offers accommodations. ✉ *19999 W. Country Club Dr., Aventura 33180,* ☎ *305/932–6200 or 800/327–7028,* FAX *305/ 933–6560,* WEB *www.turnberryisle.com. 354 rooms, 41 suites. 4 restaurants, in-room safes, minibars, 2 18-hole golf courses, 19 tennis courts,*

2 pools, health club, spa, steam room, beach, docks, windsurfing, boating, racquetball, 5 bars, helipad. AE, D, DC, MC, V.

$$-$$$ 🏨 **Bay Harbor Inn.** The inn's not on the ocean, but the tranquil Indian Creek flowing outside is sure to soothe. One of the most pleasing touches is your own front porch, where you can sit with a book or a drink and a view of Bal Harbour, a five-minute walk away. Rooms have queen- and king-size beds and baths are large. The hotel staff is composed largely of hotel students from Johnson & Wales University, so the service is enthusiastic but not flawlessly professional. ⊠ *9660 E. Bay Harbor Dr., Bal Harbour Miami Beach 33154,* ☎ *305/868–4141,* FAX *305/867–9094,* WEB *www.bayharborinn.com. 22 rooms, 23 suites. Restaurant, pool, gym, bar, meeting room. AE, MC, V. CP.*

$$-$$$ 🏨 **Don Shula's Hotel & Golf Club.** This low-rise resort is part of Miami Lakes, a planned town about 14 mi northwest of downtown. The well-maintained golf club, opened in 1962, has a championship course, a lighted executive course, and a golf school. All club rooms are English traditional in style, rich in leather and dark wood, and have balconies. The hotel, on the other hand, has a typical Florida-tropics look—light pastels and furniture of wicker and light wood. In both locations the best rooms are near the lobby for convenient access. Sixteen two-bedroom suites are geared for extended stays, with refrigerator, microwave, and VCR. ⊠ *6842 Main St., Miami Lakes 33014,* ☎ *305/821–1150 or 800/247–4852,* FAX *305/820–8071,* WEB *www.donshula.com. 205 rooms, 16 suites. 2 restaurants, 2 18-hole golf courses, 9 tennis courts, 2 pools, aerobics, health club, sauna, steam room, basketball, racquetball, volleyball, 2 bars. AE, DC, MC, V.*

$$-$$$ 🏨 **Newport Beachside Resort.** Built before the present crop of luxury
★ towers sprang up, Newport is still one of the nicest hotels in Sunny Isles. The combination time-share and hotel is a good, clean, safe place to enjoy the beach and outdoor activities. The pool area, with its wading pool and standard pool, is perfectly suited for enjoying the sun, not to mention the ocean and fishing pier—the only remaining hotel fishing pier in Miami. Back inside, the lobby is large and bright, and so are the rooms, after a remodeling that replaced all remaining standard rooms with one-bedroom suites. ⊠ *16701 Collins Ave., Sunny Isles 33160,* ☎ *305/949–1300 or 800/327–5476,* FAX *305/947–5873,* WEB *www.newportbeachsideresort.com. 290 suites. 4 restaurants, microwaves, refrigerators, pool, gym, beach, bar, nightclub, shops, concierge, meeting rooms, parking (fee). AE, D, DC, MC, V.*

South Beach

$$$$ 🏨 **Casa Grande.** A luxe and spicy Eastern-tinged flavor sets this hotel
★ apart from the typical icy-cool minimalism found on Ocean Drive. Luxurious Balinese-inspired suites are done in teak and mahogany, with dhurrie rugs, Indonesian fabrics and artifacts, two-poster beds with ziggurat turns, full electric kitchens with utensils, and large baths—practically unheard of in the Art Deco District. Insulated windows keep the noise of the Ocean Drive revelers at bay. Book well in advance for stays during peak periods. ⊠ *834 Ocean Dr., South Beach 33139,* ☎ *305/672–7003,* FAX *305/673–3669,* WEB *www.casagrandehotel.com. 34 suites. Café, in-room safes, in-room VCRs, kitchenettes, refrigerators, beach, shops, laundry service, concierge, business services, travel services. AE, D, DC, MC, V.*

$$$$ 🏨 **Delano Hotel.** You'll marvel at the lobby hung with massive white,
★ billowing drapes and yet try to act casual while watching for celebrities such as Ben Affleck, George Clooney, and Spike Lee, all of whom stop by when in town. Fashion models and men of independent means gather beneath cabanas, pose by the infinity pool, and sniff the heady

aromas from the Blue Door restaurant. There are comprehensive business services and a rooftop bathhouse and solarium. Although the standard rooms are of average size, their stark whiteness makes them appear larger. The real appeal here is the *Alice in Wonderland*–like surrealism. ✉ *1685 Collins Ave., South Beach 33139,* ☎ *305/672–2000 or 800/555–5001,* FAX *305/532–0099. 184 rooms, 24 suites. Restaurant, pool, health club, spa, beach, bar, lobby lounge, laundry service, concierge, business services. AE, D, DC, MC, V.*

$$$$
★
🏨 Hotel Impala. It's all very European here at the Impala, from the mineral water and orchids to the Mediterranean-style armoires, Italian fixtures, and triple-sheeted white-on-white modified Eastlake sleigh beds. Everything from wastebaskets to towels to toilet paper is of extraordinary quality. The building is a stunning tropical Mediterranean Revival and is a block from the beach. Iron, mahogany, and stone on the inside are in sync with the sporty white-trim ocher exterior and quiet courtyard. Rooms are elegant and comfortable and complete with a TV/VCR/stereo and a stock of CDs and videos. The hotel does not admit children under 16. ✉ *1228 Collins Ave., South Beach 33139,* ☎ *305/673–2021 or 800/ 646–7252,* FAX *305/673–5984,* WEB *www.hotelimpalamiamibeach.com. 14 rooms, 3 suites. Restaurant, in-room data ports, in-room VCRs, bar, laundry service, concierge. AE, D, DC, MC, V. CP.*

$$$$
🏨 National Hotel. The most spectacular part of this resurrected 1939 shorefront hotel is its tropical pool—it's also Miami Beach's longest (205 ft). In daylight it's a perfect backdrop for the film crews that often work here. With curtains closed, poolside rooms could be generic Holiday Inn, displaying little of the creativity of other recently arrived hotels. Rooms in the main building are far more appealing, however. Applause is in order for preserved pieces, such as the original chandelier and furniture in the dining room. Another notable highlight is the clubby 1930s-style Press Room cigar bar and meeting room, off the lobby. ✉ *1677 Collins Ave., South Beach 33139,* ☎ *305/532–2311 or 800/327–8370,* FAX *305/534–1426,* WEB *www.nationalhotel.com. 115 rooms, 5 suites. Restaurant, in-room data ports, in-room safes, minibars, pool, gym, beach, bar, laundry service, concierge, meeting room, parking (fee); no-smoking floor. AE, DC, MC, V.*

$$$$
🏨 Raleigh Hotel. Hidden behind a thick veil of greenery, this hotel was among the first Art Deco District hotels to be renovated, and it has retained Victorian accents (hallway chandeliers and in-room oil paintings) to soften the 20th-century edges. Standard rooms are spacious, and the suites more so. The fleur-de-lis pool is the focal point year-round, especially on December 31, when synchronized swimmers dive in at the stroke of midnight. Other pluses: the lobby coffee bar, a romantic restaurant (Tiger Oak Room), and the old-fashioned Martini Bar. ✉ *1775 Collins Ave., South Beach 33139,* ☎ *305/534–6300 or 800/848– 1775,* FAX *305/538–8140,* WEB *www.raleighhotel.com. 111 rooms, 18 suites. Restaurant, in-room data ports, in-room safes, refrigerators, in-room VCRs, pool, gym, massage, beach, bar, laundry service, concierge, business services, meeting room, parking (fee). AE, D, DC, MC, V.*

$$$$
★
🏨 The Tides. Miami hotels like white, and this one is no exception. However, hotelier and music magnate Chris Blackwell has put a creative twist on what can often be a sterile design motif by introducing hospitality-inspiring elements from the small—spyglasses in each room (since they all have big windows and face the ocean), a blackboard for messages to housekeeping, newspapers on request—to the large—every room has a king-size bed, capacious closets, and generous baths, the result of turning 115 rooms into 45 suites. At the Olympic-size (the only one on Ocean Drive) mezzanine pool, women can go topless. ✉ *1220 Ocean Dr., South Beach 33139,* ☎ *305/604–5000 or 800/688– 7678,* FAX *305/604–5180,* WEB *www.islandoutpost.com. 45 suites. 2*

restaurants, in-room data ports, in-room safes, minibars, pool, gym, beach, baby-sitting, dry cleaning, concierge, business services, meeting room, travel services. AE, D, DC, MC, V.

$$$–$$$$ 🏨 **The Albion.** Avant-garde Boston architect Carlos Zapata updated this stylish 1939 nautical-deco building by Igor Polevitzky, and the place is full of his distinctive touches. The two-story lobby sweeps into a secluded courtyard and is framed by an indoor waterfall. A crowd of hip but friendly types make up the clientele; they like to gather at the mezzanine-level pool, which has portholes that allow courtyard strollers an underwater view of the swimmers. As with other Rubell properties (the Beach House and the Greenview), guest rooms are minimalist in design, though filled with upscale touches. ⊠ *1650 James Ave., South Beach 33139,* ☎ *305/913–1000 or 888/665–0008,* FAX *305/674–0507,* WEB *www.rubellhotels.com. 85 rooms, 9 suites. 2 restaurants, in-room data ports, minibars, pool, gym, bar, laundry service, concierge, meeting room. AE, D, DC, MC, V.*

$$$–$$$$ 🏨 **Essex House.** A favorite with Europeans, Essex House moved into the upscale category over the past few years with a major renovation and amenities like the Il Paradiso day spa, where you can reverse the damage of a day at the beach with a combination of massages, facials, and peeling treatments. The large suites, reached by crossing a tropical courtyard, are well worth the price: each has a wet bar, king-size bed, pull-out sofa, 100-square-ft bathroom, refrigerator, and hot tub. Rooms are no slouches, either. Club chairs, custom carpet and lighting, mahogany entertainment units and matching desks, and marble tubs. ⊠ *1001 Collins Ave., South Beach 33139,* ☎ *305/534–2700 or 800/553–7739,* FAX *305/532–3827,* WEB *www.essexhotel.com. 59 rooms, 20 suites. In-room data ports, in-room safes, in-room VCRs, pool, spa, bar, dry cleaning, laundry service, parking (fee). AE, D, MC, V.*

$$$–$$$$ 🏨 **Hotel Astor.** The Astor stands apart from the crowd by double-insulating walls against noise and offering such quiet luxuries as thick
★   towels, down pillows, paddle fans, and a seductive pool. Guest rooms are built to recall deco ocean liner staterooms, complete with faux-portholes, and are furnished with custom-milled French furniture, Roman shades, and sleek sound and video systems. A tasteful, muted color scheme and the most comfortable king beds imaginable make for eminently restful nights, and excellent service eliminates any worries about practical matters. The Astor Place restaurant is exceptional for its cuisine, service, and space. ⊠ *956 Washington Ave., South Beach 33139,* ☎ *305/531–8081 or 800/270–4981,* FAX *305/531–3193,* WEB *www.hotelastor.com. 40 rooms. Restaurant, room service, in-room data ports, in-room safes, minibars, pool, massage, bar, laundry service, concierge, business services, parking (fee). AE, DC, MC, V.*

$$$–$$$$ 🏨 **Hotel Ocean.** If the street signs didn't read Ocean Drive, you might suspect you were whiling away the day on the Riviera at this hotel formerly known as the Ocean Front Hotel. The tropical French feel is evident when you enter the shaded, bougainvillea-draped courtyard and see diners enjoying a complimentary breakfast in the hotel's brasserie. The two buildings connected by this courtyard contain a few surprises: soft beds; authentic 1930s art deco pieces; large foldout couches; clean, spacious baths; and soundproof windows ensure that rooms (which average 425 square ft each) are comfortable and quiet. ⊠ *1230–38 Ocean Dr., South Beach 33139,* ☎ *305/672–2579 or 800/ 783–1725,* FAX *305/672–7665,* WEB *www.hotelocean.com. 4 rooms, 23 suites. Restaurant, in-room data ports, in-room safes, in-room VCRs, minibars, bar, concierge. AE, D, DC, MC, V.*

$$$–$$$$ 🏨 **Loews Miami Beach Hotel.** Unlike other neighborhood properties,
★   this 18-story, 800-room gem was built from the blueprints up. Not only did Loews manage to snag 99 ft of beach, but it also took over the

vacant St. Moritz next door and restored it to its original 1939 art deco splendor, adding another 100 rooms to the complex. The resort has kids' programs, a health spa, 85,000 square ft of meeting space, and an enormous ocean-view grand ballroom. Dining, too, is a pleasure, courtesy of the Argentinian-inspired Gaucho Room, Preston's South Beach Coffee Bar, and Hemisphere Lounge. ⊠ *1601 Collins Ave., South Beach 33139,* ☎ *305/604–1601,* FAX *305/531–8677,* WEB *www.loewshotels.com. 740 rooms, 50 suites. 4 restaurants, pool, spa, beach, 2 bars, lobby lounge, children's programs (ages 4–12), meeting room. AE, D, DC, MC, V.*

$$$–$$$$ 🖬 **Miami Beach Marriott at South Beach.** Continuing the trend started by Loews, Marriott's move into South Beach was late and big, with nouveau art deco flourishes meant to conceal a pragmatic beach resort designed to yield as many ocean-view rooms as possible. The rooms are larger than most on the beach, with a liberal helping of very un-Marriott-like tropical color that proves the mega-brand really is trying to fit in. A minispa, quiet beach, and reliable service make this a safe bet for business types or families who want to experience South Beach while keeping the wildest partying at a distance. ⊠ *161 Ocean Drive., South Beach 33139,* ☎ *305/536–7700 or 800/228–9290,* FAX *305/536–9900,* WEB *www.miamibeachmarriott.com. 236 rooms, 7 suites. Restaurant, in-room data ports, in-room safes, pool, spa, beach, 2 bars, laundry service, concierge, business services, meeting rooms, parking (fee). AE, D, DC, MC, V.*

$$$–$$$$ 🖬 **WinterHaven.** "Bright" and "airy" are not words usually associated
★ with South Beach hotels, but this artfully restored classic is both—in spades. WinterHaven is a riot of color, from the garnet and aquamarine lobby to the ginger and cream upholstery in guest rooms. Here, black and white photos of South Beach's former self hang over the custom-designed deco furniture that—surprise—doesn't strive to be a conversation piece. The two-story lobby and split-level mezzanine regularly play host to parties and fashion shoots, but if you take your complimentary breakfast up to the rooftop sundeck, you'll have a bird's-eye view of South Beach at dawn. ⊠ *1400 Ocean Dr., South Beach 33139,* ☎ *305/531–5571 or 800/395– 2322,* FAX *305/538–6387,* WEB *www.winterhavenhotelsobe.com. 71 rooms. In-room data ports, in-room safes, bar, concierge, parking (fee). AE, D, DC, MC, V. CP.*

$$$ 🖬 **Kent.** There are toys in the Day-Glo colored lobby, beanbag chairs in the rooms, and chrome ceiling fans throughout at this wackiest of the South Beach Island Outpost offerings (the Tides, the Marlin, and the Cavalier are the others). Sure, the rooms are on the small side, and there isn't much of a view, but the vibe, the pumped-up staff, and those great prices make the Kent hard to beat if you're in the mood for a good time. ⊠ *1131 Collins Ave., South Beach 33139,* ☎ *305/604–5000 or 800/688–7678,* FAX *305/531–0720,* WEB *www.islandoutpost.com. 52 rooms, 2 suites. In-room safes, minibars, in-room VCRs, business services, meeting room, travel services. AE, D, DC, MC, V.*

$$–$$$ 🖬 **Nassau Suite Hotel.** For a boutique hotel one block from the beach, this airy retreat almost qualifies as a steal (by South Beach standards). The original 1937 floor plan of 50 rooms gave way to 22 spacious and smart-looking suites with king beds, fully equipped kitchens, hardwood floors, white wood blinds, and free local calls. The Nassau is in the heart of the action yet quiet enough to give you the rest you need. Note: this three-floor hotel has no elevator and no bellhop. There's also very limited parking. ⊠ *1414 Collins Ave., South Beach 33139,* ☎ *305/534–2354 or 866/859–4177,* FAX *305/534–3133,* WEB *www.nassausuite.com. 22 suites. In-room data ports, kitchenettes, concierge. AE, D, DC, MC, V.*

$$–$$$ 🖬 **Royal Hotel.** *Austin Powers* meets *2001* in this avant-garde hotel that
★ doesn't take itself too seriously. Each room really only has two pieces of furniture: a "digital chaise longue" and a bed, both molded white

plastic contortions from designer Jordan Mozer. The bed's projecting wings hold a phone and alarm clock. The headboard arcs back like a car spoiler, and doubles as a minibar, filled to your taste. The chaise longue holds a TV/Web TV and keyboard for surfing the Net. A wild shag carpet and rainbow-paisley bathrobes remind you you're here to have fun— *yeah, baby.* ✉ *758 Washington Ave., South Beach 33139,* ☎ *305/673– 9009 or 888/394–6835,* FAX *305/673–9244,* WEB *www.royalhotelsouthbeach. com. 38 rooms, 4 suites. Restaurant, in-room data ports, laundry service, business services, meeting room. AE, D, DC, MC, V.*

$$ 🏨 **Cadet Hotel.** Clark Gable stayed in Room 225 when he came to Miami for Army Air Corps training in the 1940s. Although this Lincoln Road district lodging doesn't have the glamour to attract stars today, it's still a clean, friendly, and perfectly placed little hotel. Just a few minutes' walk from the convention center and two blocks from the ocean, it's about half the cost of an Ocean Drive hotel. Bright without glitz, rooms have ordinary furniture, which is mixed but not necessarily matched— nor is it crummy. A complimentary breakfast is served in the lobby or on the terrace. ✉ *1701 James Ave., South Beach 33139,* ☎ *305/672– 6688 or 800/432–2338,* FAX *305/532–1676,* WEB *www.cadethotel.com. 44 rooms. Refrigerators. AE, D, DC, MC, V. CP.*

$$ 🏨 **Days Inn Convention Center.** Nothing flashy and nothing trashy, this link in a well-known chain is a fairly decent one. The lobby is bright and floral, with a fountain and gift shop. Rooms are standard hotel issue and include in-room safes and cable TV; deluxe rooms throw in impressive views of the ocean. If you're more concerned about your wallet than your image, this is a good bet. Keep in mind that if you want something with character, you can find that elsewhere at these rates. Here you'll find the basic franchise dependables literally seconds from the beach and the Miami Beach Cultural Center. ✉ *100 21st St., South Beach 33139,* ☎ *305/538–6631 or 800/451–3345,* FAX *305/674–0954,* WEB *www.daysinnsouthbeach.com. 172 rooms. Restaurant, refrigerators, pool, beach, bar, laundry service, parking (fee). AE, D, DC, MC, V.*

$$ 🏨 **Kenmore.** Utilitarian comfort is the theme at this place, which preserves the essence of 1930s art deco. The glass-block facade of the lobby invites you to a no-nonsense lodging experience, extending to clean but smallish tropical-theme rooms with twin or king-size beds. On a very active street, the surprising privacy of the Kenmore is a strong selling point. A quiet pool (and courtyard bar) hidden behind a low wall allows you to tan without being the subject of voyeurs. You're only a short walk from the clubs and shops of South Beach—and you get a free breakfast, to boot. ✉ *1020–1050 Washington Ave., South Beach 33139,* ☎ *305/532–1930 or 888/424–1930,* FAX *305/972–4666,* WEB *www. parkwashingtonresort.com. 60 rooms. Restaurant, refrigerators, pool, bar. AE, MC, V. CP.*

$–$$ 🏨 **Bayliss Guest House.** At the Bayliss, rooms are abnormally large and surprisingly inexpensive. Not only are the bedrooms large, but so are the kitchen, the sitting room, and bath. There are also kitchenless standard rooms available. An easy three blocks west of the ocean, the Bayliss is in a residential neighborhood that's comfortably close to— but far enough away from—the din of the Art Deco District. Can't do much better than this, if you don't mind carrying your own bags. There's very limited parking. ✉ *500–504 14th St., South Beach 33139,* ☎ *305/531–3488,* FAX *305/531–4440. 12 rooms, 7 suites. Some kitchens, refrigerators, laundry facilities. AE, D, DC, MC, V.*

$ 🏨 **Banana Bungalow.** This may seem like a university dormitory—indeed, some rooms have dorm-style bunk beds for about $15 a night— but the cleanliness, friendliness, and abundance of activities make this spot worth checking into, especially for hard-core student travelers.

The Bungalow's social center is the large pool area, which has outdoor grills, and is surrounded by a patio bar, game room, and café. Some may be put off by the smell of the brackish canal nearby, but for others it's a small price to pay for a small price to stay. ⊠ *2360 Collins Ave., South Beach 33139,* ☎ *305/538–1951 or 800/746–7835,* ℻ *305/531–3217,* WEB *www.bananabungalow.com. 60 private rooms, 25 dorm-style rooms, all with bath. Café, pool, billiards, bar, recreation room, video game room, laundry service. MC, V. CP.*

West Dade

$$$$ 🖬 **Doral Golf Resort and Spa.** This 650-acre golf-and-tennis resort has eight beautifully renovated, low-slung lodges that nestle beside its six golf courses. Rooms, decorated in understated tropical hues, open onto the green or the lush foliage of the garden, and have private balconies and terraces. Plantation shutters keep out the strong sun but invite in the Caribbean breezes. At the expansive spa, massages from head to foot, European facials, aroma scrubs and wraps, stress reduction, hypnotherapy, and several dozen other indulgences rejuvenate the mind, body, and soul. The Blue Lagoon, an extravagant water park, and friendly golf instruction keep the kids busy. ⊠ *4400 N.W. 87th Ave., Miami West 33178,* ☎ *305/592–2000 or 800/713–6725,* ℻ *305/591–4682,* WEB *www.doralresort.com. 693 rooms, 48 suites. 5 restaurants, 5 18-hole golf courses, 11 tennis courts, pro shop, pool, health club, spa, fishing, basketball, volleyball, 3 bars, concierge, business services. AE, D, DC, MC, V.*

NIGHTLIFE AND THE ARTS

Revised by
Gretchen
Schmidt

For information on what's happening around town, Greater Miami's English-language daily newspaper, the *Miami Herald,* publishes reliable reviews and comprehensive listings in its "Weekend" section on Friday and in the "IN South Florida" section on Sunday. They also publish a free tabloid, *Street,* with entertainment listings. Call ahead to confirm details. *El Nuevo Herald* is the paper's Spanish version.

If you read Spanish, check *Diario Las Américas,* the area's largest independent Spanish-language paper, for information on the Spanish theater and a smattering of general performing-arts news.

The best, most complete source is the *New Times,* a free weekly distributed throughout Miami-Dade County each Thursday. A good source of information on the performing arts and nightspots is the calendar in *Miami Today,* a free weekly newspaper available each Thursday in downtown Miami, Coconut Grove, and Coral Gables. Various tabloids reporting on Deco District entertainment and the Miami social scene come and go. *Wire* reports on the gay community.

The free *Greater Miami Calendar of Events* is published twice a year by the Miami-Dade County Cultural Affairs Council (⊠ 111 N.W. 1st St., Suite 625, Downtown 33128, ☎ 305/375–4634).

The **Greater Miami Convention & Visitors Bureau** (☎ 305/539–3000 or 800/283–2707, WEB www.tropiculture.com) publishes a comprehensive list of dance venues, theaters, and museums, as well as a seasonal guide to cultural events.

The Arts

Greater Miami's cultural renaissance is a work in progress. The basics are in place: solid cultural institutions such as the Florida Grand Opera, the New World Symphony, the Miami City Ballet, the Concert Association of South Florida, the Fort Lauderdale–based Florida Philharmonic; a plethora of multicultural arts groups and festivals year-round; and burgeoning arts districts in South Beach, Coral Gables, and the Design District north of downtown, to name a few. Ground has been broken on a monumental Performing Arts Center downtown that will help the city take a quantum leap onto the cultural scene when it's completed in 2004.

In addition to established music groups, several churches and synagogues run classical-music series with international performers. In theater, Miami offers English-speaking audiences an assortment of professional, collegiate, and amateur productions of musicals, comedy, and drama. Spanish theater also is active.

The not-for-profit **Concert Association of Florida** (⌂ 555 17th St., South Beach, ☎ 305/532–3491), led by Judith Drucker, presents classical arts, music, and dance in venues throughout Miami-Dade and Broward counties. On its roster have been some of the greatest names in the worlds of music and dance—Itzhak Perlman, Isaac Stern, Baryshnikov, Pavarotti, and the Russian National Ballet.

To order tickets for performing-arts events by telephone, call **Ticket-Master** (☎ 305/358–5885).

Arts Venues

What was once a 1920s movie theater has become the 465-seat **Colony Theater** (⌂ 1040 Lincoln Rd., South Beach, ☎ 305/674–1026). The city-owned performing-arts center spotlights dance, drama, music, and experimental cinema.

If you have the opportunity to attend a concert, ballet, or touring stage production at the **Gusman Center for the Performing Arts** (⌂ 174 E. Flagler St., Downtown, Miami 33131, ☎ 305/374–2444 for administration; 305/372–0925 for box office), do so. Originally a movie palace, this 1,700-plus-seat theater is as far from a mall multiplex as you can get. The stunningly beautiful hall resembles a Moorish courtyard, with twinkling stars and rolling clouds skirting across the ceiling and Roman statues guarding the wings.

Not to be confused with the ornate Gusman theater, **Gusman Concert Hall** (⌂ 1314 Miller Dr., Coral Gables, ☎ 305/284–2438) is a 600-seat facility on the University of Miami campus. Presenting primarily recitals and concerts by students, it has good acoustics and plenty of room, but parking is a problem when school is in session.

Acoustics and visibility are perfect for all 2,700 seats in the **Jackie Gleason Theater of the Performing Arts** (TOPA, ⌂ 1700 Washington Ave., South Beach, ☎ 305/673–7300). A pleasant walk from the heart of SoBe, TOPA hosts the Broadway Series, with five or six major productions annually; guest artists, such as David Copperfield, Stomp, and Shirley MacLaine; and classical-music concerts.

Midway between Coral Gables and downtown Miami, the **Miami-Dade County Auditorium** (⌂ 2901 W. Flagler St., Little Havana, Miami 33135, ☎ 305/545–3395) satisfies patrons with nearly 2,500 comfortable seats, good sight lines, and acceptable acoustics. Opera, concerts, and touring musicals are usually on the schedule, and past performers have included David Helfgott and Celia Cruz.

Dance

The **Miami City Ballet** (⌂ 2200 Liberty Ave., South Beach, ☎ 305/929–7000) has risen rapidly to international prominence since its arrival in

1985. Under the direction of Edward Villella (a principal dancer with the New York City Ballet under George Balanchine), Florida's first major, fully professional resident ballet company has become a world-class ensemble. The company re-creates the Balanchine repertoire and introduces works of its own during its September–March season. Villella also hosts children's works-in-progress programs. Performances are held at the Jackie Gleason Theater of the Performing Arts; the Broward Center for the Performing Arts; Bailey Concert Hall, also in Broward County; the Raymond F. Kravis Center for the Performing Arts; and the Naples Philharmonic Center for the Arts.

Film

Several theaters and events cater specifically to fans of fine film. In December, Florida International University sponsors the **Jewish Film Festival** (☎ 305/576–4030 Ext. 14), which presents screenings of new work as well as workshops and panel discussions with filmmakers in several Miami Beach locations. Screenings of new films from all over the world—including some made here—are part of the **FIU–Miami Film Festival** (✉ 444 Brickell Ave., Suite 229, Miami, ☎ 305/377–3456, WEB www.miamifilmfestival.com). Each year more than 45,000 people descend on the eye-popping Gusman Center for the Performing Arts to watch about 25 movies over 10 days in February. Two more venues—South Beach's Colony Theater and Regal Cinema—have been added, and the number of movies is expected to double.

In April the **Miami Gay and Lesbian Film Festival** (☎ 305/534–9924) presents screenings at the Colony Theater on Lincoln Road and at other nearby venues. In March, the **Miami Latin Film Festival** (☎ 305/279–1809, WEB www.hispanicfilm.com) actually presents French, Italian, and Portuguese movies along with exhibitions of Spanish and Latin American movies. Each May, South Beach hosts the **Brazilian Film Festival** (☎ 305/899–8998, WEB www.brazilianfilmfestival.com), which unveils on a huge outdoor movie screen built on the beach especially for the occasion.

Music

From October to May, **Friends of Chamber Music** (✉ 169 E. Flagler St., Suite 1619, Downtown, ☎ 305/372–2975) presents a series of chamber concerts by internationally known guest ensembles, such as the Emerson and Guarneri quartets. Concerts are held at the Gusman Concert Hall at the University of Miami, with tickets averaging about $20.

Although Greater Miami has no resident symphony orchestra, the **New World Symphony** (✉ 555 Lincoln Rd., South Beach, Miami Beach, ☎ 305/673–3331 or 305/673–3330), known as "America's training orchestra" because its musicians are recent graduates of the best music schools, helps fill the void. Under the direction of conductor Michael Tilson Thomas, the New World has become a widely acclaimed, artistically dazzling group that tours extensively. In a season that runs October–May, performances take place in its home venue, the acoustically perfect Lincoln Theater on Lincoln Road Mall. The symphony's concerts are broadcast live via speaker (and sometimes video) over the Lincoln Road Mall. Guest conductors have included Leonard Bernstein and Georg Solti.

Opera

South Florida's leading company, the **Florida Grand Opera** (✉ 1200 Coral Way, Miami, ☎ 305/854–1643) presents five operas each year in the Miami-Dade County Auditorium, featuring the Florida Philharmonic Orchestra (Stewart Robinson, musical director) from Fort Lauderdale. The series brings such luminaries as Placido Domingo and

Luciano Pavarotti (Pavarotti made his American debut with the company in 1965 in *Lucia di Lammermoor*). Operas are sung in the original language, with English subtitles projected above the stage.

Theater

Actor's Playhouse at the Miracle Theater (✉ 280 Miracle Mile, Coral Gables, ☎ 305/444–9293), a professional Equity company, presents musicals, comedies, and dramas year-round in Coral Gables' very hip, newly renovated, 600-seat Miracle Theater. Performances of musical theater for younger audiences take place in the 300-seat Children's Balcony Theatre.

Built in 1926 as a movie theater, the **Coconut Grove Playhouse** (✉ 3500 Main Hwy., Coconut Grove, ☎ 305/442–4000 or 305/442–2662) is now a serious regional theater owned by the state of Florida. The Spanish rococo Grove stages tried-and-true Broadway plays and musicals, many with Broadway actors, as well as experimental productions in its main theater and cabaret-style/black box Encore Room.

The critically acclaimed **GableStage** (☎ 305/446–1116) presents classic and contemporary theater. They're scheduled to move from their Biltmore Hotel location; call for their new location.

Lyric Theater. Once one of the major centers of entertainment for the African-American community, the Lyric showcased more than 150 performers, including Aretha Franklin, Count Basie, Sam Cooke, B. B. King, Ella Fitzgerald, and the Ink Spots. This newly restored theater is now the anchor site of the Historic Overtown Folklife Village. ✉ *819 N.W. 2nd Ave., Overtown,* ☎ *305/358–1146.*

New Theatre. The company has relocated to a 104-seat theater, where it mounts contemporary and classical plays, with an emphasis on new works and imaginative staging. ✉ *4120 Laguna St., Coral Gables,* ☎ *305/443–5909,* WEB *www.new-theatre.org.*

Productions at the University of Miami's **Jerry Herman Ring Theater** (✉ 1380 Miller Dr., Coral Gables, ☎ 305/284–3355) are often as ambitious as those by its professional counterparts (Broadway legend Jerry Herman is the drama school's most successful alumnus).

SPANISH THEATER

Spanish theater prospers, although many companies have short lives. About 20 Spanish companies perform light comedy, puppetry, vaudeville, and political satire. To find them, read the Spanish newspapers. When you call, be prepared for a conversation in Spanish—few box office personnel speak English.

Teatro Avante. This is the city's most successful crossover theater, programming works that cater to the tastes of its middle-aged Cuban-American audiences and providing subtitles on an overhead screen for the benefit of non-Spanish-speakers. Each summer Teatro Avante sponsors the Hispanic Theatre Festival, during which international theater artists converge on Miami, often presenting the most provocative stagings around, all in Spanish, English, and Portuguese and attracting a multicultural audience to various venues in the Greater Miami area. ✉ *235 Alcazar Ave., Coral Gables, Coral Gables,* ☎ *305/445–8877,* WEB *www.teatroavante.com.*

The 255-seat **Teatro de Bellas Artes** (✉ 2173 S.W. 8th St., Little Havana, ☎ 305/325–0515), on Calle Ocho, presents Spanish plays and musicals staged throughout the year. Midnight musical follies and female impersonators round out the showbiz lineup.

Nightlife

Bars and Lounges

COCONUT GROVE

Drinking cold beer and gorilla-size margaritas in the middle of the Grove at Cocowalk is part of the fun at touristy **Fat Tuesday** (⊠ 3015 Grand Ave., Coconut Grove, ☎ 305/441–2992). The bar offers up drinks called 190 Octane (190-proof alcohol), Swampwater (also 190 proof), and Grapeshot (a meager 151-proof rum and bourbon concoction). At the Streets of Mayfair, the **Iguana Cantina and Babalu Bar** (⊠ 3390 Mary St., Coconut Grove, ☎ 305/443–3300) serves up salsa, merengue, and Latin music on weekends. The waterfront **Monty's in the Grove** (⊠ 2550 S. Bayshore Dr., at Aviation Ave., Coconut Grove, ☎ 305/858–1431) has lots of Caribbean flair, thanks to live calypso and island music. It's very kid-friendly on weekend days, when Mom and Dad can kick back and enjoy a beer and the raw bar while the youngsters dance to live music. Evenings bring a DJ and reggae music.

CORAL GABLES

What fueled the Gables' nightlife renaissance? Some think it was **The Globe** (⊠ 377 Alhambra Circle, ☎ 305/445–3555). Crowds of twentysomethings spill out onto the street for live jazz on weekends. Two Irishmen missed the Emerald Isle so they opened **John Martin's Restaurant and Irish Pub** (⊠ 253 Miracle Mile, ☎ 305/445–3777). It serves up fish-and-chips, bangers and mash, shepherd's pie, and all the accoutrements of a Dublin pub—plus the requisite pints of Guinness, Harp, Bass, and other ales. In a building that dates from 1926, **Stuart's Bar-Lounge** (⊠ 162 Alcazar Ave., ☎ 305/444–1666), inside the charming Hotel Place St. Michel, is favored by locals. The style is created by beveled mirrors, mahogany paneling, French posters, pictures of old Coral Gables, and art nouveau lighting.

MIAMI

Tobacco Road (⊠ 626 S. Miami Ave., Miami, ☎ 305/374–1198), opened in 1912, holds Miami's oldest liquor license: Number 0001! Upstairs, in space occupied by a speakeasy during Prohibition, local and national blues bands perform nightly, accompanied by single-malt Scotch and bourbon.

MIAMI BEACH

At **The Clevelander** (⊠ 1020 Ocean Dr., ☎ 305/531–3485), a giant pool-bar area attracts a young crowd of revelers for happy-hour drink specials and live music. The Rose Bar at the **Delano** (⊠ 1685 Collins Ave., ☎ 305/672–2000) is dramatic and chic, with long gauzy curtains and huge pillars creating private conversation nooks around the outdoor infinity pool. Inside, the cool chic lounge area creates a glamorous space for the modelesque crowd. **Lola** (⊠ 247 23rd St., ☎ 305/695–8697) attracts savvy locals and celebs who want to keep a low profile. Offering more character than chic, the **Marlin** (⊠ 1200 Collins, ☎ 305/673–8770) sports a colorful Austin Powers look—fuchsia and orange pillows and cushions and mirrors everywhere. Deejays spin different music every night for the 25-to-40 crowd. At the upscale **Mynt Ultra Lounge** (⊠ 1901 Collins Ave., South Beach, ☎ 786/276–6132), the name is meant to be taken literally—not only are the walls bathed in soft green shades, but an aromatherapy system pumps out different fresh scents, including mint. For South Beach fabulousness, the glass-topped bar at **The Tides** (⊠ 1220 Ocean Dr., ☎ 305/604–5000) is the place to go for martinis and piano jazz. At the top of the 21-story tower that makes up part of the long-awaited Shore Club, the **Tower Bar** (⊠ 1901 Collins Ave., South Beach, ☎ 305/695–3100), with its solid teak floors, white leather cushioned banquettes, and green silk walls, is a sophisticated place to unwind with a vintage tequila.

Dance Clubs

MIAMI

Want 24-hour partying? **Club Space** (✉ 142 N.E. 11th St., Downtown, ☎ 305/375–0001), created from four warehouses downtown, has three dance rooms, an outdoor patio, a New York industrial look, and a 24-hour liquor license. It's open on weekends only, and you'll need to look good to be allowed past the velvet ropes.

KEY BISCAYNE

Madfish House (✉ 3301 Rickenbacker Causeway, Key Biscayne, ☎ 305/365–9391) has reggae 'til the wee hours on Friday, and salsa on Saturday. The view of the skyline along the waterfront is spectacular.

MIAMI BEACH

South Beach is headquarters for nightclubs that start late and stay open until the early morning. The clientele includes freak-show rejects, sullen male models, and sultry women.

The **Bermuda Bar & Grille** (✉ 3509 N.E. 163rd St., ☎ 305/945–0196) is way north of SoBe, but worth the drive if you want to hang with the locals. Rock radio stations do remote broadcasts, and hard liquor and bottled beer are favored over silly drinks with umbrellas. The music is as loud as the space is large—two floors and seven bars—and hours run 4 PM–6 AM. Male bartenders wear knee-length kilts, and female bartenders are in matching minis. The vibe and crowd, though, are stylish, and there's a big tropical-forest scene, booths you can hide in, and pool tables to dive into. The joint is closed from Sunday through Tuesday.

One of several high-profile venues to hit South Beach, **Billboardlive** (✉ 1501 Collins Ave., South Beach, ☎ 305/538–2251) is four dazzling floors of fun with a performance stage, restaurants, bars, dance floors, private rooms, and a skybox. Expect to find world-class DJs here, too. **Crobar** (✉ 1445 Washington Ave., ☎ 305/531–5027), an import from Chicago, is the latest hot spot—the exterior is the historic Cameo Theater, and the interior is a *Blade Runner*-esque blend of high-tech marvels with some performance art thrown in. It's dazzling and lots of fun. **Honey** (✉ 645 Washington Ave., Miami Beach, ☎ 305/604–8222) has soft lighting, cozy couches and chaise longues, and vibey music that goes down as smoothly as their trademark honey-dipped apples. **Level** (✉ 1235 Washington Ave., ☎ 305/532–1525) has an impressive four dance floors, and—as its name suggests—lots of levels to search out fun.

Nikki Beach Club and Barefoot Beach Club (✉ 1 Ocean Dr., ☎ 305/538–1231) has seven bars in a beautiful beachfront location—complete with teepee cabanas—and includes Pearl Restaurant and Champagne Bar, fast becoming a celeb hangout. Popular with casually chic twenty- and thirtysomethings, **Opium Garden** (✉ 136 Collins Ave., at First St., South Beach, ☎ 305/674–8360) has a lush waterfall, an Asian temple motif with lots of candles, dragons, and tapestries, and a restaurant next door.

Blues

CORAL GABLES

Satchmo Blues Bar & Grill (✉ 60 Merrick Way, ☎ 305/774–1883) turns out live blues and jazz—including top-notch local and national talent—every night, with Cajun treats on the side.

Jazz

MIAMI BEACH

Jazid (✉ 1342 Washington Ave., at 13th St., South Beach, ☎ 305/673–9372), a stylishly redecorated standout on the strip, is sultry and candlelighted; the music is jazz, with blues and R&B. More restaurant than jazz club, **Van Dyke Café** (⊠ 846 Lincoln Rd., ☎ 305/534–3600) serves music on the second floor seven nights a week. Its location on the Lincoln Road Mall makes it a great spot to take a break during an evening shopping excursion.

Nightclub

MIAMI BEACH

You can dine as you watch the show at the Fontainebleau Hilton's **Club Tropigala** (⊠ 4441 Collins Ave., ☎ 305/672–7469), which tries to blend modern Vegas with 1950s Havana. The four-tier round room is decorated with orchids, banana leaves, and philodendrons to create an indoor tropical jungle. Some of the performances are stellar, with a Latin flavor—Ricky Martin, Julio Iglesias, and Jose Feliciano have made appearances here. Hotel guests are comped, but others pay a $20 cover. Reservations are suggested.

OUTDOOR ACTIVITIES AND SPORTS

Revised by
Kathy Foster

In addition to contacting the addresses below directly, you can get tickets to major events from **TicketMaster** (☎ 305/358–5885).

Auto Racing

Hialeah Speedway holds stock-car races on a ⅓-mi asphalt oval in a 5,000-seat stadium. Don't be fooled: the enthusiasm of the local drivers makes this as exciting as Winston Cup races. Five divisions of cars run weekly. The Marion Edwards Jr. Memorial Race, for late-model cars, is held in December. The speedway is on U.S. 27, ¼ mi east of the Palmetto Expressway (Route 826). ⊠ *3300 W. Okeechobee Rd., Hialeah,* ☎ *305/821–6644.* 🎟 *$10, special events $15.* ☺ *Sat., gates open at 5 PM, races 7–11. Closed mid-Dec.–late Jan.*

For Winston Cup events, head south to the **Homestead-Miami Speedway,** which brought the NASCAR Winston Cup Series to South Florida for the first time with the 1999 Penzoil 400. The Winston Cup race highlights the annual speedway schedule and is held on the second Sunday in November in conjunction with the Miami 300, part of the NASCAR Busch series. The racing facility, built in 1995, is also home to the Infiniti Grand Prix of Miami (March 2003), and Indy car racing. Other major races include the Grand Am Sports Car Event in spring and a NASCAR Craftsmen Truck Series in fall. From Miami take Florida's Turnpike (Route 821) south to Exit 6, at S.W. 137th Avenue. ⊠ *1 Speedway Blvd., Homestead,* ☎ *305/230–7223.* ☺ *Weekdays 9–5.* 🎟 *Prices vary according to event.*

Baseball

Although the **Florida Marlins** team that won the 1997 World Series was split up soon afterward, games are still as exciting as baseball can be. Home games are played at Pro Player Stadium, which is 16 mi northwest of downtown. ⊠ *2267 N.W. 199th St., Lake Lucerne,* ☎ *305/626–7400 or 305/626–7426,* 🖳 *www.marlins.mlb.com or www.pro-player-stadium.com.* 🎟 *$4–$55, parking $9.*

Basketball

The **Miami Heat** are four-time defending NBA Atlantic Division champs (1996–97 through 1999–2000). They play their games at the 19,600-seat, waterfront AmericanAirlines Arena, which has a bay-front patio, a special-effects scoreboard, indoor fireworks, and restaurants. Home games are held November–April. ⊠ *AmericanAirlines Arena, 601 Biscayne Blvd., Downtown, Miami,* ☎ *786/777–4328; 800/462–2849 ticket hot line,* 🖳 *www.nba.com/heat.* 🎟 *$10–$180.*

The **Miami Sol**, a WNBA team, is coached by Ron Rothstein, the first head coach for the Miami Heat. The team plays a 32-game season from June through August at the bay-front AmericanAirlines Arena. ⊠ *601 Biscayne Blvd., Downtown, Miami,* ☎ *786/777–4765.* ⊡ *$8–$50.*

Biking

Perfect weather and flat terrain make Miami-Dade County a popular place for cyclists. A free color-coded map that points out streets best suited for bicycles, and information about bike rack–equipped buses is available from bike shops and also from the **Miami-Dade County Bicycle Coordinator** (⊠ Metropolitan Planning Organization, 111 N.W. 1st St., Suite 910, Miami 33128, ☎ 305/375–1647), whose purpose is to share with you the glories of bicycling in South Florida. Information on dozens of monthly group rides is available from the **Everglades Bicycle Club** (☎ 305/598–3998). For a free map of the 10 mi of traffic-free bike trails on Key Biscayne, stop by **Mangrove Cycles** (⊠ 260 Crandon Blvd., Key Biscayne, ☎ 305/361–5555), which rents bikes for $7 for two hours or $10 per day. On Miami Beach, the proximity of the **Miami Beach Bicycle Center** (MBBC; ⊠ 601 5th St., South Beach, Miami Beach, ☎ 305/674–0150) to Ocean Drive and the ocean itself makes it worth the $20 per day (or $5 per hour). Tours of the Deco District are held monthly.

Boating

The popular full-service **Crandon Park Marina** (⊠ 4000 Crandon Blvd., Key Biscayne, ☎ 305/361–1281; ☉ office daily 8–6) is a one-stop shop for all things ocean-y. You can embark on deep-sea-fishing or scuba-diving excursions, dine at a marina restaurant, or rent powerboats through **Club Nautico** (⊠ 5420 Crandon Blvd., Key Biscayne, ☎ 305/361–9217; ⊠ 2560 Bayshore Dr., Coconut Grove, ☎ 305/858–6258), a national powerboat rental company. Half- to full-day rentals range from $229 to $699, or you can buy a membership, which costs a bundle at first but saves around 60% on future rentals.

Whether you're looking to be on the water for a few hours or a few days, **Cruzan Yacht Charters** is a good choice for renting manned or unmanned sailboats and motor yachts. If you plan to captain the boat yourself, expect a three- to four-hour checkout cruise and at least a $400 daily rate (three-day minimum). ⊠ *3375 Pan American Dr., Coconut Grove,* ☎ *305/858–2822 or 800/628–0785.*

Named for an island where early settlers had picnics, **Dinner Key Marina** is Greater Miami's largest, with nearly 600 moorings at nine piers. There is space for transients and a boat ramp. ⊠ *3400 Pan American Dr., Coconut Grove,* ☎ *305/579–6980.* ☉ *Daily 7 AM–11 PM.*

Haulover Marine Center is low on glamour but high on service. It offers a bait-and-tackle shop, marine gas station, and boat launch. ⊠ *15000 Collins Ave., Sunny Isles, Miami Beach,* ☎ *305/945–3934.* ☉ *Bait shop and gas station open 24 hrs.*

Although **Matheson Hammock Park** has no charter services, it does have 252 slips and boat ramps. It also has **Castle Harbor** (☎ 305/665–4994), which rents sailboats for those with U.S. Sailing certification and holds classes for those without. When you're ready to rent, take your pick of boats ranging from 23 ft to 41 ft. ⊠ *9610 Old Cutler Rd., Coral Gables,* ☎ *305/665–5475.* ☉ *Daily 6–sunset.*

Near the Art Deco District, **Miami Beach Marina** has about every marine facility imaginable—restaurants, charters, boat and vehicle rentals, a complete marine-hardware store, a dive shop, excursion vendors, a large grocery store, a fuel dock, concierge services, and 400 slips accommodating vessels up to 190 ft. There's also a U.S. Customs clearing station. One charter outfit here is the family-owned **Florida Yacht Charters** (☎ 305/532–8600 or 800/537–0050). After completing the requisite checkout cruise and paperwork, you can take off for the Keys or the Bahamas on a catamaran, sailboat, or motor yacht. Charts, lessons, and captains are available if needed. ⊠ *300 Alton Rd., South Beach, Miami Beach,* ☎ *305/673–6000 for marina.* ☉ *Daily 7–6.*

Dog Racing

Flagler Greyhound Track has dog races during its June–November season and a poker room that's open when the track is running. Closed-circuit TV brings harness-racing action here as well. The track is five minutes east of Miami International Airport, off Dolphin Expressway (Route 836) and Douglas Road (N.W. 37th Avenue). ⊠ *401 N.W. 38th Ct., Little Havana, Miami,* ☎ *305/649–3000.* ☒ *Free for grandstand and clubhouse; parking free–$3.* ☉ *Racing Mon.–Sun. 8:05 PM; Tues., Thurs., and Sat. 1:05 PM.*

Fishing

Before there was fashion, there was fishing. Deep-sea fishing is still a major draw in Miami, and anglers drop a line for sailfish, kingfish, dolphin, snapper, wahoo, grouper, and tuna. Small charter boats cost $450–$500 for a half day and provide everything but food and drinks. If you're on a budget, you might be better off paying around $30 for passage on a larger fishing boat—rarely are they filled to capacity. Most charters have a 50/50 plan, which allows you to take (or sell) half your catch while they do the same. Just don't let anyone sell you an individual fishing license; a blanket license for the boat should cover all passengers.

Crandon Park Marina has earned an international reputation for its knowledgeable charter-boat captains and good catches. Heading out to the edge of the Gulf Stream (about 3 to 4 mi), you're sure to wind up with something on your line (sailfish are catch-and-release). ⊠ *4000 Crandon Blvd., Key Biscayne,* ☎ *305/361–1281.* ☒ *6-passenger boats $750 full day, $500 half day (5 hrs).*

Haulover Beach Park. Plenty of ocean-fishing charters depart from Haulover Beach Park, including **Blue Waters Sportfishing Charters** (☎ 305/944–4531, ☒ 6-passenger boats, $750 full day, $450 half day), the **Kelley Fleet** (☎ 305/945–3801, ☒ 65- or 85-ft party boats, $29 per person), *Therapy IV* (☎ 305/945–1578, ☒ 6-passenger boat, $90 per person), and about 10 others. ⊠ *Haulover Beach Park, 10800 Collins Ave., Sunny Isles, Miami Beach,* ☎ *305/947–3525.* ☒ *$4 per car.* ☉ *Daily sunrise–sunset.*

Among the charter services at **Miami Beach Marina** is the two-boat **Reward Fleet** (☎ 305/372–9470). Rates run $30 per person, including bait, rod, reel, and tackle. ⊠ *MacArthur Causeway, 300 Alton Rd., South Beach, Miami Beach,* ☎ *305/673–6000.*

Football

Consistently ranked as one of the top teams in the NFL, the **Miami Dolphins** (☎ 305/620–2578) has one of the largest average attendance figures in the league. Fans may be secretly hoping to see a repeat of the 1972 perfect season, when the team, led by legendary coach Don Shula, compiled a 17–0 record (a perfect record that has yet to be broken by another team). From September through January, on home game days, the Metro Miami-Dade Transit Agency runs buses to **Pro Player Stadium**, 16 mi northwest of downtown. ⊠ *2267 N.W. 199th St., Downtown, Miami,* ☎ *305/626–7426.* ☒ *$20–$140, parking $20.*

Also worth checking out is the **University of Miami Hurricanes** (☎ 305/284–2263 or 800/462–2637) football team. A powerhouse within the Big East Conference, the team is regularly a Top-10 contender, with four national football championships since 1983. During the September–November season, the home-team advantage is measured in decibels, as about 45,000 fans literally rock the stadium when the team is on a roll. They play their home games at downtown's venerable **Orange Bowl Stadium**. ⊠ *1145 N.W. 11th St., Downtown,* ☎ *305/575–5240.* ⊠ *$20–$40, parking $8–$20.*

Golf

Greater Miami has more than 30 private and public courses. Fees at most courses are higher on weekends and in season, but you can save money by playing weekdays and after 1 PM or 3 PM (call to find out when afternoon or twilight rates go into effect). That said, costs are reasonable to play in such an appealing setting as Miami.

To get the **"Golfer's Guide for South Florida,"** which includes information on most courses in Miami and surrounding areas, call ☎ 800/864–6101. The cost is $3.

The 18-hole, par-71 championship **Biltmore Golf Course,** known for its scenic layout, has been restored to its original Donald Ross design, circa 1925. Greens fees range from $29 to $55 in season, and the gorgeous hotel makes a great backdrop. ⊠ *1210 Anastasia Ave., Coral Gables,* ☎ *305/460–5364.* ⊠ *Optional cart $21.*

The **California Golf Club** has an 18-hole, par-72 course, with a tight front 9 and three of the area's toughest finishing holes. A round of 18 holes will set you back between $35 and $50, cart included. ⊠ *20898 San Simeon Way, North Miami Beach,* ☎ *305/651–3590.*

Overlooking the bay, the **Crandon Golf Course,** formerly the Links at Key Biscayne, is a top-rated 18-hole, par-72 public course in a beautiful tropical locale. Expect to pay around $126 for a round in winter, $50 in summer, cart included. After 3, the winter rate drops to $36, cart included. The Royal Caribbean Classic is held here. ⊠ *6700 Crandon Blvd., Key Biscayne,* ☎ *305/361–9129.*

Don Shula's Hotel & Golf Club has one of the longest championship courses in Miami (7,055 yards, par 72), a lighted par-3 course, and a golf school, and it hosts more than 100 tournaments a year. Weekdays you can play the championship course for $90, $125 on weekends; golf carts are included. The lighted par-3 course is $12 weekdays, $15 weekends, and $15 for an optional cart. ⊠ *7601 Miami Lakes Dr., Miami Lakes,* ☎ *305/820–8106.*

Among its six courses and many annual tournaments, the **Doral Golf Resort and Spa** is best known for the par-72 Blue Monster course and the annual Genuity Classic, with $2 million in prize money. Fees range from $190 to $250—halfprice after 3, carts included. ⊠ *4400 N.W. 87th Ave., Miami West,* ☎ *305/592–2000 or 800/713–6725.*

For a casual family outing or for beginners, the 9-hole, par-3 **Haulover Golf Course** is right on the Intracoastal Waterway at the north end of Miami Beach. The longest hole on this walking course is 120 yards; greens fees are only $6, less weekdays for senior citizens. ⊠ *10800 Collins Ave., Sunny Isles,* ☎ *305/940–6719.*

Normandy Shores Golf Course (⊠ 2401 Biarritz Dr., Miami Beach, ☎ 305/868–6502) is good for seniors, with some modest slopes and average distances. The **Turnberry Isle Resort & Club** (⊠ 19999 W. Country Club Dr., Aventura, ☎ 305/933–6929) has 36 holes designed by

Robert Trent Jones. The South Course's 18th hole is a killer, and greens fees range from $107 to $147, but since it's private, you won't be able to play unless you're a hotel guest.

Horse Racing

The **Calder Race Course,** opened in 1971, is Florida's largest glass-enclosed, air-conditioned sports facility. It often has an unusually extended season, from late May to early January, though it's a good idea to call the track for specific starting and wrap-up dates, since Calder and Gulfstream Park rotate their race dates. Each year between November and early January, Calder holds the Tropical Park Derby for three-year-olds. The track is on the Miami-Dade–Broward County line near Interstate 95 and the Hallandale Beach Boulevard exit, ¾ mi from Pro Player Stadium. ✉ *21001 N.W. 27th Ave., Lake Lucerne, Miami,* ☎ *305/625–1311.* ✆ *$2, clubhouse $4, parking $1–$5.* ⊙ *Gates open at 11, racing 12:30–5.*

Gulfstream Park, just north of the Miami-Dade County line, usually has the January through March race dates; it hosted the 1999 Breeder's Cup; the track's premiere race is the Florida Derby. ✉ *21301 Biscayne Blvd. (U.S. 1), between Ives Dairy Rd. and Hallandale Beach Blvd., Hallandale,* ☎ *954/454–7000.* ✆ *$3, clubhouse $5, parking free.* ⊙ *Wed.–Mon. post time 1 PM.*

Jai Alai

Built in 1926, the **Miami Jai Alai Fronton,** a mile east of the airport, is America's oldest fronton. It presents 13 games (14 on Friday and Saturday) daily except Tuesday—some singles, some doubles. This game, invented in the Basque region of northern Spain, is the world's fastest. Jai alai balls, called pelotas, have been clocked at speeds exceeding 170 mph. The game is played in a 176-ft-long court, and players literally climb the walls to catch the ball in a cesta (a woven basket), which has an attached glove. You can place your wager on the team you think will win or on the order in which you think the teams will finish. ✉ *3500 N.W. 37th Ave., Downtown, Miami,* ☎ *305/633–6400.* ✆ *$1, reserved seats $2, Courtview Club $5.* ⊙ *Mon., Wed.–Sat, noon–5; also Wed., Fri., Sat., 7–midnight; Sun. 1–6.*

Jogging

There are numerous places to run in Miami, but these recommended jogging routes are considered among the most scenic and the safest: in Coconut Grove, along the pedestrian-bicycle path on South Bayshore Drive, cutting over the causeway to Key Biscayne for a longer run; from the south shore of the Miami River, downtown, south along the sidewalks of Brickell Avenue to Bayshore Drive, where you can run alongside the bay; in Miami Beach, along Bay Road (parallel to Alton Road) or on the sidewalk skirting the Atlantic Ocean, opposite the cafés of Ocean Drive; and in Coral Gables, around the Riviera Country Club golf course, just south of the Biltmore Country Club. **Foot Works** (✉ 5724 Sunset Dr., South Miami, ☎ 305/667–9322), a running-shoe store that sponsors races and organizes marathon training, is a great source of information. The **Miami Runners Club** (✉ 8720 N. Kendall Dr., Suite 206, Miami, ☎ 305/227–1500) has information on running-related matters, such as routes and races.

Scuba Diving and Snorkeling

Diving and snorkeling on the offshore coral wrecks and reefs can be comparable to the Caribbean, especially on a calm day. Chances are excellent you'll come face to face with a flood of tropical fish. One option is to find Fowey, Triumph, Long, and Emerald reefs in 10- to 15-ft dives that are perfect for snorkelers and beginning divers. On the edge of the continental shelf a little more than 3 mi out, these reefs are just ¼ mi away from depths greater than 100 ft. Another option is to paddle around the tangled prop roots of the mangrove trees that line the coast, peering at the fish, crabs, and other creatures hiding there.

Perhaps the most unusual diving options in Greater Miami are the artificial reefs. Since 1981, **Miami-Dade County's Department of Environmental Resources Management (DERM)** (✉ 1920 Meridian Ave., South Beach, Miami Beach, ☎ 305/672–1270) has sunk tons of limestone boulders and a water tower, army tanks, a 727 jet, and almost 200 boats of all descriptions to create a "wreckreational" habitat where you can swim with yellow tang, barracudas, nurse sharks, snapper, eels, and grouper. Most dive shops sell a book listing the location of these wrecks.

Bubbles Dive Center (✉ 2671 S.W. 27th Ave., at Unity Blvd., Downtown, Miami, ☎ 305/856–0565), an all-purpose dive shop with PADI affiliation, runs night and wreck dives right in the center of it all. Its boat, *Divers Dream,* berths at the Miami Beach Marina on Alton Road. **Divers Paradise of Key Biscayne** (✉ 4000 Crandon Blvd., Key Biscayne, ☎ 305/361–3483), next to the full-service Crandon Park Marina, has a complete dive shop and diving-charter service. On offer are equipment rental and scuba instruction with PADI affiliation. The PADI-affiliated **Diving Locker** (✉ 223 Sunny Isles Blvd., Sunny Isles, Miami Beach, ☎ 305/947–6025) sells, services, and repairs scuba equipment, plus it has three-day and three-week international certification courses as well as more advanced certifications. The three-day accelerated course for beginners is $350. Wreck and reef sites are reached aboard fast and comfortable six-passenger dive boats.

Tennis

Greater Miami has more than a dozen tennis centers open to the public, and countywide nearly 500 public courts are open to visitors. Nonresidents are charged an hourly fee. If you're on a tight schedule, try calling in advance, as some courts take reservations on weekdays.

Biltmore Tennis Center has 10 hard courts and a view of the beautiful Biltmore Hotel. ✉ *1150 Anastasia Ave., Coral Gables,* ☎ *305/460–5360.* ▣ *Day rate $4.50 per person per hr, night rate $5.50.* ◷ *Weekdays 7 AM–10 PM, weekends 7–8.*

Very popular with locals, **Flamingo Tennis Center** has 19 clay courts smack dab in the middle of Miami Beach. You can't get much closer to the action. ✉ *1000 12th St., South Beach,* ☎ *305/673–7761.* ▣ *Day rate $2.67 per person per hr, night rate $3.20.* ◷ *Weekdays 8 AM–9 PM, weekends 8–8.*

North Shore Tennis Center, within Miami Beach's North Shore Park, has nine lighted courts, six clay courts, and three hard courts. Two additional hard courts are for daytime use only. ✉ *350 73rd St., at Harding Ave., near Isle of Normandy, Miami Beach,* ☎ *305/993–2022.* ▣ *Day rate $2.66 per person per hr, night rate $3.20.* ◷ *Weekdays 8 AM–9 PM, weekends 8–7.*

Thirty-acre **Tennis Center at Crandon Park** is one of America's best. Included are 2 grass, 8 clay, and 17 hard courts. Reservations are required for night play. The only time courts are closed to the public is during the **Nasdaq 100 Open** (formerly the Ericsson Open) (☎ 305/442–3367), held for 11 days each spring. Top players such as Pete Sampras, Andre Agassi, Gustavo Kuerten, Venus and Sabrina Williams, and Martina Hingis compete in a 14,000-seat stadium for more than $6 million in prize money. ✉ *7300 Crandon Blvd., Key Biscayne,*

☎ 305/365–2300. ⊠ *Laykold courts: day rate $3 per person per hr, night rate $5; clay and grass courts $6 per person per hr day rate; courts are closed at night.* ◷ *Daily 8 AM–9 PM.*

Windsurfing

Windsurfing is more popular than ever in Miami. The safest and most popular windsurfing area is at **Hobie Beach,** sometimes called Windsurfer Beach, just off the Rickenbacker Causeway on your way to Key Biscayne. In Miami Beach, the best spots are at **1st Street** (just north of the Government Cut jetty) and at **21st Street**; you can also windsurf on the beach at 3rd, 10th, and 14th streets.

Sailboards Miami (⊠ 1 Rickenbacker Causeway, Key Biscayne, ☎ 305/361–7245), ⅓ mi past the causeway tollbooth, rents equipment and claims to teach more windsurfers each year than anyone in the United States. Rentals average $20 for one hour, $38 for two hours, and $150 for 10 hours. They promise to teach anyone to windsurf within two hours.

SHOPPING

Revised by Karen Schlesinger

In Greater Miami you're never more than 15 minutes from a major shopping area and the familiar *ka-ching* of a cash register. Miami-Dade County has more than a dozen major malls, an international free-trade zone, and hundreds of miles of commercial streets lined with stores and small shopping centers. Latin neighborhoods contain a wealth of Latin merchants and merchandise, including children's *vestidos de fiesta* (party dresses) and men's guayaberas (a pleated, embroidered tropical shirt), conveying the feel of a South American *mercado* (market).

Malls

Aventura Mall (⊠ 19501 Biscayne Blvd. Aventura) has more than 250 upscale shops anchored by Macy's, Lord & Taylor, JCPenney, Sears, Burdines, and Bloomingdale's, along with a 24-screen theater with stadium seating and a Cheesecake Factory. In a tropical garden setting, **Bal Harbour Shops** (⊠ 9700 Collins Ave., Bal Harbour) is a swank collection of 100 shops, boutiques, and department stores, such as Chanel, Gucci, Cartier, Fendi, Hermès, Neiman Marcus, and Saks Fifth Avenue. If it's luxe, it's here. **Bayside Marketplace** (⊠ 401 Biscayne Blvd., Downtown), the 16-acre shopping complex on Biscayne Bay, has more than 150 specialty shops, entertainment, tour-boat docks, a food court, and a Hard Rock Cafe. It's open late (until 10 during the week, 11 on Friday and Saturday), but its restaurants stay open even later. It's a great place to browse, buy, or simply relax by the bay with a tropical drink.

The heartbeat of Coconut Grove, **CocoWalk** (⊠ 3015 Grand Ave., Coconut Grove) has three floors of nearly 40 specialty shops (Victoria's Secret, the Gap, Banana Republic, among others) that stay open almost as late as the popular restaurants and clubs. Kiosks with cigars, beads, incense, herbs, and other small items are scattered around the ground level, and the restaurants and nightlife (e.g., Hooters, Fat Tuesday, an AMC theater) are upstairs. If you're ready for an evening of people-watching, this is the place.

The oldest retail mall in the county, **Dadeland Mall** (⊠ 7535 N. Kendall Dr., Kendall) is always upgrading. It sits at the south side of town close to the Dadeland North and Dadeland South Metrorail stations. Retailers include Saks Fifth Avenue, JCPenney, Lord & Taylor, more than 175 specialty stores, 17 restaurants, and the largest Burdines, Limited, and Limited Express in Florida. The $250 million **Dolphin Mall** (⊠ 11401 N.W. 12th St., at State Rd. 836 and Florida's Turnpike, West Dade

Miami), 5 mi west of the airport, has plenty of outlet and discount shopping, including a Marshall's Megastore, Oshman's Super Sports USA, and Saks Off Fifth outlet, plus a 28-screen cinemaplex and 850-seat food court. **The Falls** (✉ 8888 S.W. 136th St., at U.S. 1, South Miami), which derives its name from the several waterfalls inside, is the most upscale mall on the south side of the city. It contains a Macy's and Bloomingdale's as well as another 100 specialty stores, restaurants, and a 12-theater multiplex.

As its name suggests, **Loehmann's Fashion Island** (✉ 18701 Biscayne Blvd., Aventura) is dominated by Loehmann's, the nationwide retailer of off-price designer fashions for women and men. Fashion-conscious shoppers can also shop other specialty boutiques and browse a Barnes & Noble bookstore.

With a huge banyan tree to welcome visitors, **Shops at Sunset Place** (✉ 5701 Sunset Dr., at U.S. 1 and Red Rd., South Miami) is even larger than CocoWalk. The three-story, family-oriented center has upped the ante for shopping/entertainment complexes with a 24-screen cinemaplex, IMAX theater, Virgin Megastore, NikeTown, A/X Armani Exchange, and GameWorks (a Spielberg-movie-inspired virtual-reality attraction wrapped into a restaurant). **Streets of Mayfair** (✉ 2911 Grand Ave., Coconut Grove) is an open-air promenade of shops that bustles both day and night. Thanks to its Coconut Grove locale, along with the News Café, the Limited, Borders Books Music Cafe, and a few dozen other shops and restaurants, this is a safe bet. Entertainment is provided by an improv comedy club and the nightclubs Iguana Cantina and Martini Bar.

Outdoor Markets

Coconut Grove Farmers Market (✉ Grand Ave., 1 block west of MacDonald Ave. [S.W. 32nd Ave.], Coconut Grove), open Saturday 8–2, originated in 1977 and still specializes in organically grown local produce. The **Española Way Market** (✉ Española Way, Miami Beach), open Sunday noon–9, has been a city favorite since its debut in 1995. Scattered among the handcrafted items and flea market merchandise, musicians beat out Latin rhythms on bongos, conga drums, steel drums, and guitars. Food vendors sell inexpensive Latin snacks and drinks. Each Saturday morning from 8 to 1, mid-January to late March, some 25 produce and plant vendors sell herbs, fruits, fresh-squeezed juices, chutneys, cakes, and muffins at the **Farmers Market at Merrick Park** (✉ LeJeune Rd. [S.W. 42nd Ave.] and Biltmore Way, Coral Gables). Regular features include gardening workshops, children's activities, and cooking demonstrations offered by Coral Gables' master chefs. More than 500 vendors sell a range of goods at the **Flagler Dog Track** (✉ 401 N.W. 38th Ct., Miami Beach), every weekend 9–4. The **Lincoln Road Farmers Market** (✉ Lincoln Rd. between Meridian and Euclid Aves., Miami Beach), open Sunday 9–5:30, brings about 15 local produce vendors coupled with plant workshops and children's activities. From 10 to 5 on the second and fourth Sundays of each month, locals set up the **Outdoor Antique and Collectibles Market** (✉ Lincoln and Alton Rds., Miami Beach). Meandering through the market is a great way to while away a Sunday afternoon. The eclectic goods should satisfy postimpressionists, deco-holics, Edwardians, Bauhausers, and Gothic, atomic, and '50s junkies.

Shopping Districts

The shopping is great on a two-block stretch of **Collins Avenue** (✉ between 6th and 8th Aves., Miami Beach). Club Monaco, Polo Sport, Nicole Miller, Nike, Kenneth Cole, Guess, Armani Exchange, and Banana Republic are among the high-profile tenants, and a parking garage is just a block away. The busy **Lincoln Road Mall** is just a few blocks from the beach and convention center, making it popular with locals and tourists. There's an energy to shopping here, especially on weekends when the pedestrian mall is filled with locals. You'll find a Victoria's Secret, Pottery Barn, Gap, and Williams-Sonoma, as well as many smaller emporiums with unique personalities. Creative merchandise, galleries, and a Sunday-morning antiques market can be found among the art galleries and cool cafés. An 18-screen movie theater anchors the west end of the street.

There are 500 garment manufacturers in Miami and Hialeah, and many sell their clothing locally in the **Miami Fashion District** (⊠ 5th Ave. east of I–95, between 25th and 29th Sts., Miami Beach), making Greater Miami the fashion marketplace for the southeastern United States, the Caribbean, and Latin America. Most of the more than 30 factory outlets and discount fashion stores are open Monday–Saturday 9–5. Don't expect to find a flood of shoppers here; the surrounding neighborhood keeps many tourists away. The **Miami Design District** (⊠ between N.E. 36th and N.E. 41st Sts. and between N.E. 2nd Ave. and N. Miami Ave., Design District, Miami) contains some 225 designer showrooms and galleries specializing in interior furnishings, decorative arts, antiques, and a rich mix of exclusive and unusual merchandise. **Miracle Mile** (⊠ Coral Way between 37th and 42nd Aves., Coral Gables) consists of some 160 shops along a wide, tree-lined boulevard. Shops range from posh bridal boutiques to bargain basements, from beauty salons to chain restaurants. As you go west, the quality improves.

Specialty Stores

ANTIQUES

Alhambra Antiques Center (⊠ 2850 Salzedo, Coral Gables, ☎ 305/446–1688) is a collection of four antiques dealers that sell high-quality decorative pieces from Europe. **Architectural Antiques** (⊠ 2500 S.W. 28th La., Coconut Grove, ☎ 305/285–1330) carries large and eclectic items—railroad crossing signs, statues, English roadsters—in a store so cluttered that shopping here becomes an adventure promising hidden treasures for the determined.

Leah's Gallery (⊠ 191 N.E. 40th St., Design District, ☎ 305/573–9700) is four floors of wonderful finds, including 19th-century statuary and sculpture, park benches, mannequins, stained-glass doors and panels, and a gigantic carved-wood Victorian birdcage.

BOOKS

Like others in the superstore chain, **Barnes & Noble** (⊠ 152 Miracle Mile, Coral Gables, ☎ 305/446–4152) manages to preserve the essence of a neighborhood bookstore by encouraging customers to pick a book off the shelf and lounge on a couch without being hassled. A well-stocked magazine and national/international news rack and an espresso bar–café complete the effect. Greater Miami's best English-language bookstore, **Books & Books, Inc.** (⊠ 265 Aragon Ave., Coral Gables, ☎ 305/442–4408; ⊠ 933 Lincoln Rd., Miami Beach, ☎ 305/532–3222) specializes in books on the arts, architecture, Florida, and contemporary and classical literature. At the newer Coral Gables location, you can lounge at the café, browse the photography gallery, or sit in the courtyard and flip through magazines. Both locations host poetry readings, book signings, and author readings. If being in the Grove prompts you to don a beret, grow a goatee, and sift through a volume of Kerouac, head to **Borders** (⊠ 3390 Mary St., at Grand Ave., Coconut Grove, ☎ 305/447–1655; ⊠ 9205 S. Dixie Hwy., Pinecrest, ☎ 305/665–8800; ⊠ 19925 Biscayne Blvd., Aventura, ☎ 305/935–0027) at the Streets of Mayfair. Its 100,000 book titles, 70,000 CDs, 10,000 video titles, and more than 2,000 periodicals and newspapers in 10 languages from 15 countries make it seem like the southern branch of the Library of Congress.

CHILDREN'S BOOKS AND TOYS

Afro-In Books and Things (⊠ 5575 N.W. 7th Ave., Miami, ☎ 305/756–6107) presents books by African-American writers for children and teen readers—it even has an impressive section of books for adults. **F.A.O. Schwarz** (⊠ 9700 Collins Ave., Bal Harbour Shops, Bal Harbour, ☎ 305/865–2361; ⊠ 19501 Biscayne Blvd., Aventura Mall, Aventura, ☎ 305/692–9200; ⊠ 5701 Sunset Dr., Shops at Sunset Place, South Miami, ☎ 305/668–2300), the ultimate toy store, has three area locations. **La Canastilla Cubana** (⊠ 1300 W. 49th St., Hialeah, ☎ 305/557–5505) carries children's books and toys and specializes in elegant furnishings and designer clothing for new arrivals. The store's Spanish name means "stork's basket."

CIGARS

Although Tampa is Florida's true cigar capital, Miami's Latin population is giving it a run for its money. Smoking anything even remotely affiliated with a legendary Cuban has boosted the popularity of Miami cigar stores and the small shops where you can buy cigars straight from the press.

Bill's Pipe & Tobacco (⊠ 2309 Ponce de León Blvd., Coral Gables, ☎ 305/444–1764) has everything for the pipe and cigar smoker, including a wide selection of pipes and pipe tobacco, cigars, accessories, and gifts. With soft terra-cotta and ocher tones suggestive of an Italian villa, **Condal & Peñamil** (⊠ 741 Lincoln Rd., Miami Beach, ☎ 305/604–9690) is Miami's most beautiful cigar bar. In addition to carrying the traditional ashtrays, cutters, and humidors, C&P has a "cigar cave" with a private salon, enabling you to complement your smoke with a coffee or cocktail.

In the heart of Little Havana, **El Credito Cigars** (⊠ 1106 S.W. 8th St., Little Havana, ☎ 305/858–4162) seems to have been transported from the Cuban capital lock, stock, and stogie. Rows of workers at wooden benches rip through giant tobacco leaves, cut them with rounded blades, wrap them tightly, and press them in vises. Dedicated smokers like Robert DeNiro, Gregory Hines, and George Hamilton have found their way here to pick up a $90 bundle or peruse the *gigantes, supremos,* panatelas, and Churchills available in natural or maduro wrappers. **Macabi Cigars** (⊠ 3473 S.W. 8th St., Miami, ☎ 305/446–2606) carries cigars, cigars, and more cigars, including premium and house brands. Humidors and other accessories make great gifts.

CLOTHING FOR MEN AND WOMEN

BASE (⊠ 939 Lincoln Rd., Miami Beach, ☎ 305/531–4982) has good karma and great eclectic island wear for men and women. Stop here and you may run into the often present designer. For fashions by Barbara Bui, Catherine Malandrino, and Mint mixed in with up and coming designer clothing and accessories, **Chroma** (⊠ 920 Lincoln Rd., Miami Beach, ☎ 305/695–8808) is where local fashionistas go. **Koko & Palenki** (⊠ 3015 Grand Ave., Coconut Grove, ☎ 305/444–1772), in CocoWalk, is where Grovers go for a well-edited selection of shoes and accessories by Casadei, Charles David, Stuart Weitzman, Via Spiga, and others.

In the Shore Club Hotel, **Scoop** (⊠ 1901 Collins Avenue, Miami Beach, ☎ 305/695–3297) is a small but spaciously arranged store carrying all the latest fashion requirements by Helmut Lang, Marc Jacobs, Earl, and Seven.

Seize sur Vingt (⊠ 203 11th St., Miami Beach, ☎ 305/695–1779) is known for its gorgeous custom-tailored and ready-to-wear men's clothes. The house specialty is the modern dress shirt, made from your choice of exquisite Egyptian cotton patterns. **Vintage Soul** (⊠ 1235 Alton Rd., Miami Beach, ☎ 305/538–2644) is a shabby-chic style house filled with rooms of vintage clothing and charming home furnishings.

ESSENTIALS

Wall-to-wall merchandise is found at the **Compass Market** (⊠ 860 Ocean Dr., Miami Beach, ☎ 305/673–2906), a cute and cozy basement shop that carries all the staples you'll need, especially if you're staying in an efficiency. The market stocks sandals, souvenirs, cigars, deli items, umbrellas, newspapers, and produce. If the heat of Miami gets you hot and bothered, try **Condom USA** (⊠ 3066 Grand Ave., Coconut Grove, ☎ 305/445–7729) on for size. Sexually oriented games and condoms are sold by the gross. If you're easily offended, stay away. If you're easily aroused, stay the night.

JEWELRY

Beverlee Kagan (⊠ 5831 Sunset Dr., South Miami, ☎ 305/663–1937) specializes in vintage and antique jewelry, including art deco–era bangles, bracelets, and cuff links. Easily overlooked in the quick pace of downtown, the 10-story **Seybold Building** (⊠ 36 N.E. 1st St., Downtown, ☎ 305/374–7922) is filled from bottom to top with more than 250 independent jewelry companies. Diamonds, bracelets, necklaces, and rings are sold in a crowded, lively spot. Word is that competition makes prices flexible; it's closed Sunday.

SOUVENIRS AND GIFT ITEMS

Art Deco District Welcome Center (⊠ 1001 Ocean Dr., South Beach, ☎ 305/531–3484) hawks the finest in Miami-inspired kitsch, from flamingo salt-and-pepper shakers to alligator-shape ashtrays, along with books and posters celebrating the Art Deco District and its revival.

Gotta Have It! Collectibles (⊠ 4231 S.W. 71st Ave., Miami Beach, ☎ 305/446–5757) will make fans of any kind break out in a cold sweat. Autographed sports jerseys, canceled checks from the estate of Marilyn Monroe, fabulously framed album jackets signed by all four Beatles, and an elaborate autographed montage of all the *Wizard of Oz* stars are among this intriguing shop's museum-quality collectibles.

The **Indies Company** (⊠ 101 W. Flagler St., Downtown, ☎ 305/375–1492), the Historical Museum of Southern Florida's gift shop, offers interesting artifacts reflecting Miami's history, including some inexpensive reproductions. The collection of books on Miami and South Florida is impressive.

SIDE TRIP

South Dade

Although the population of these suburbs southwest of Dade County's urban core was largely dislocated by Hurricane Andrew in 1992, little damage is evident today. Indeed, FEMA grants and major replanting have made the area better than ever. All attractions—many of which are especially interesting for kids—have reopened, and a complete exploration of them would probably take two days. Keep an eye open for hand-painted signs announcing agricultural attractions, such as orchid farms, fruit stands, u-pick farms, and horseback riding.

76

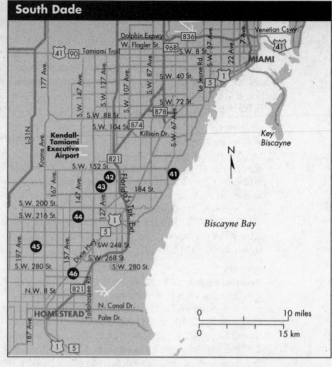

South Dade

🌵 **46** **Coral Castle of Florida.** The castle was born when 26-year-old Edward Leedskalnin, a Latvian immigrant, was left at the altar by his 16-year-old fiancée. She went on with her life, while he went off the deep end and began carving a castle out of coral rock. It's hard to believe that Eddie, only 5 ft tall and 100 pounds, could maneuver tons of coral rock single-handedly. Built between 1920 and 1940, the 3-acre castle is one of South Florida's original tourist attractions. There is a 9-ton gate a child could open, an accurate working sundial, and a telescope of coral rock aimed at the North Star. ☒ *28655 S. Dixie Hwy.,* ☎ *305/ 248–6345,* WEB *www.coralcastle.com.* ☜ *$9.75.* ☉ *Daily 7 AM–9 PM.*

41 **Deering Estate at Cutler.** In 1913 Charles Deering, brother of James Deering, who built Vizcaya in Coconut Grove, bought this property for a winter residence. Nine years later he built the Mediterranean revival stone house that stands here today. This site is fascinating on several levels: historical, archaeological, and natural. Far more austere than its ornate cousin Vizcaya, the stone house has wrought-iron gates, copper doors, and a unique stone ceiling. Next door, the Richmond Cottage—fully restored after being destroyed by 1992's Hurricane Andrew—was the first inn to be built between Coconut Grove and Key West (1900), and is a fine example of South Florida frame vernacular architecture. Take a naturalist-guided tour to learn more about the area's archaeology: scientists discovered human remains here and carbon-dated them to 10,000 years ago; they may belong to Paleo-Indians. A fossil pit contains the bones of dog-size horses, tapirs, jaguars, peccaries, sloths, and bison. Coastal tropical hardwood hammocks, rare orchids and trees, plus a range of wildlife, such as gray foxes, bobcats, limpkins, peregrine falcons, and cormorants, populates the property. A huge environmental education and visitor center presents programs for children and adults. Nature tours and canoe trips to nearby Chicken Key are available. ☒ *16701 S.W. 72nd Ave.,* ☎ *305/235–1668,* WEB *www.co. miami-dade.fl.us/parks.* ☜ *$6.* ☉ *Daily 10–5.*

Gold Coast Railroad Museum. Historic railroad cars on display here include a 1949 *Silver Crescent* dome car and the *Ferdinand Magellan*, the only Pullman car constructed specifically for U.S. presidents. It was used by Franklin Delano Roosevelt, Harry Truman, Dwight Eisenhower, and Ronald Reagan. On weekends, a train ride is included in the price of admission to the museum, which is next to the zoo. ⊠ *12450 Coral Reef Dr. (S.W. 152nd St.),* ☎ *305/253–0063,* WEB *www.goldcoast-railroad.org.* ▨ *$5.* ◷ *Weekdays 11–3, weekends 11–4.*

Metrozoo. One of the few zoos in the United States in a subtropical environment, the first-class, 290-acre Metrozoo is state of the art. Inside the cageless zoo, some 800 animals roam on islands surrounded by moats. Take the monorail to see major attractions, including the Tiger Temple, where white tigers roam, and the African Plains exhibit, where giraffes, ostriches, and zebras graze in a simulated habitat. There are also koalas, Komodo dragons, and other animals whose names begin with a *K*. The children's petting zoo has a meerkat exhibit, and Dr. Wilde's World is an interactive facility with changing exhibits. Kids can touch Florida animals such as alligators and possums at the Ecology Theater. ⊠ *12400 S.W. 152nd St.,* ☎ *305/251–0401.* ▨ *$8.95, 45-min tram tour $2.* ◷ *Daily 9:30–5:30, last admission at 4.*

Monkey Jungle. Still a kitschy attraction for adults, more than 300 monkeys representing 25 species—including orangutans from Borneo and Sumatra and golden lion tamarins from Brazil—roam free here. Exhibits include Lemurs of Madagascar, Parrots of the Amazon, and the Cameroon Jungle. Perhaps the most fun is feeding monkeys who scurry across the fences overhead, hauling up peanuts you place in a metal cup. ⊠ *14805 Hainlin Mill Dr. (S.W. 216th St.),* ☎ *305/235–1611,* WEB *www. monkeyjungle.com.* ▨ *$15.95.* ◷ *Daily 9:30–5, last admission at 4.*

Redland Fruit & Spice Park. The 35 acres here have been a Dade County treasure since 1944, when it was opened as a 20-acre showcase of tropical fruits and vegetables. Plants are grouped by country of origin and include more than 500 economically important varieties of exotic fruits, herbs, spices, nuts, and poisonous plants from around the world. A sampling reveals 85 types of bananas, 40 varieties of grapes, and 100 kinds of citrus fruits. The park store offers many varieties of tropical-fruit products, jellies, seeds, aromatic teas, and reference books. ⊠ *24801 Redland Rd. (S.W. 187th Ave.),* ☎ *305/247–5727.* ▨ *$3.50.* ◷ *Daily 10–5, tours daily at 11, 1:15, and 2:30.*

MIAMI AND MIAMI BEACH A TO Z

Revised by
Kathy Foster

To research prices, get advice from other travelers, and book travel arrangements, visit www.fodors.com.

ADDRESSES

Greater Miami is made up of more than 30 municipalities, and tourist favorites Miami and Miami Beach are only two of the cities that make up what is actually Miami-Dade County. Within Greater Miami, addresses fall into four quadrants: NW, NE, SW, and SE. The north–south dividing line is Flagler Street, and the east–west dividing line is Miami Avenue. Numbering starts from these axes and gets higher the farther away an address is from them. Avenues run north–south and streets east–west. Some municipalities have their own street naming and numbering systems, including Miami Beach, Coral Gables, Coconut Grove, and Key Biscayne, so a map is a good idea. In South Beach, all north–south roads are named and the main drags are Ocean Drive, Collins, and Washington avenues, and Alton Road. Streets are numbered and run east–west; 1st Street is at the beach's southernmost point and numbers get higher as you head north.

AIR TRAVEL TO AND FROM MIAMI

CARRIERS

In addition to the multitude of airlines that fly into Miami International Airport (MIA) (*see* Air Travel *in* Smart Travel Tips A to Z), there's also Pan Am Air Bridge—starting over where the original Pan Am began—with seaplane flights. Departing from Watson Island, the 30- to 60-minute rides to Bimini and Paradise Island in the Bahamas are exciting, anachronistic, and somewhat cramped. Still, if you've got an extra $200–$300, a round-trip could be quite fun. Chalk's Ocean Airways offers daily seaplane service from Watson Island in Miami and Fort Lauderdale International Airport to Bimini and Paradise Island.

AIRPORTS AND TRANSFERS

Miami International Airport, 6 mi west of downtown Miami, is the only airport in Greater Miami that provides scheduled service. More than 1,400 daily flights make MIA the ninth-busiest passenger airport in the world. Approximately 34 million people pass through annually, more than half of them international travelers. Altogether, more than 100 airlines serve nearly 150 cities and five continents with nonstop or one-stop service from here, making it the nation's number one airport for international passengers, more than any other airport in the Western Hemisphere.

Anticipating continued growth, the airport has begun a more than $5 billion expansion program that is expected to be completed by 2005. Passengers will mainly notice rebuilt and expanded gate and public areas, which should reduce congestion.

A greatly underused convenience for passengers who have to get from one concourse to another in this long, horseshoe-shape terminal is the amazingly convenient moving walkway on the skywalk level (third floor), with access points at every concourse. MIA, the first to offer duty-free shops, now boasts 14, carrying liquors, perfumes, electronics, and various designer goods.

Heightened security at MIA has meant that it's suggested you check in two hours before departure for a domestic flight, three hours for an international flight. Services for international travelers include 24-hour multilingual information and paging phones and currency conversion booths throughout the terminal. There is an information booth with a multilingual staff across from the 24-hour currency exchange at the entrance of Concourse E on the upper level.

The county's Metrobus still costs $1.25, although equipment has improved. From Concourse E on the ground level, you can take Bus 7 to downtown (weekdays 5:30 AM–9 PM every 40 minutes; weekends 6:30 AM–7:30 PM every 40 minutes), Bus 37 south to Coral Gables and South Miami (6 AM–10 PM every 30 minutes) or north to Hialeah (5:30 AM–11:30 PM every 30 minutes), Bus J south to Coral Gables (6 AM–12:30 AM every 30 minutes) or east to Miami Beach (4:30 AM–11:30 PM every 30 minutes), and Bus 42 to Coconut Grove (5:30 AM–7:20 PM hourly). Some routes change to 60-minute schedules after 7 PM and on weekends, so be prepared to wait or call the information line for exact times.

Miami has more than 100 limousine services, although they're frequently in and out of business. If you rely on the Yellow Pages, look for a company with a street address, not just a phone number. Offering 24-hour service, Club Limousine Service has shuttle vans and minibuses as well as limos. One of the oldest companies in town is Vintage Rolls Royce Limousines of Coral Gables, which operates a 24-hour reservation service and provides chauffeurs for privately owned, collectible Rolls-Royces from the 1940s.

Except for the flat-fare trips described below, cabs cost $3.25 for the first mile, $2 a mile after that, plus a $1 toll for trips originating at MIA or the Port of Miami. Approximate fares from MIA include $17 to Coral Gables or downtown Miami, $31 to Key Biscayne. In addition, Miami's regulatory commission has established flat rates for five zones of the city, four of which are listed here: $24 to between 63rd Street and the foot of Miami Beach (including South Beach); $41 to Golden Beach and Sunny Isles, north of Haulover Beach Park; $34 to between Surfside and Haulover Beach Park; and $29 to between 63rd and 87th streets. These fares are per trip, not per passenger, and include tolls and $1 airport surcharge but not tip. The fare between MIA and the Port of Miami is a flat fare of $18.

For taxi service to destinations in the immediate vicinity, ask a uniformed county taxi dispatcher to call an ARTS (Airport Region Taxi Service) cab for you. These special blue cabs offer a short-haul flat fare in two zones. An inner-zone ride is $7; the outer-zone fare is $10. The area of service is north to 36th Street, west to the Palmetto Expressway (77th Avenue), south to Northwest 7th Street, and east to Douglas Road (37th Avenue). Maps are posted in cab windows on both sides.

SuperShuttle vans transport passengers between MIA and local hotels, the Port of Miami, and even individual residences on a 24-hour basis. At MIA the vans pick up at the ground level of each concourse (look for clerks with yellow shirts, who will flag one down). The company's service area extends from Palm Beach to Monroe County (including the Lower Keys). Drivers provide narration en route. Service from MIA is available around the clock on demand; for the return it's best to make reservations 24 hours in advance, although the firm will try to arrange pickups within Miami-Dade County on as little as four hours' notice. The cost from MIA to downtown hotels runs $9–$10; to the beaches it can be $11–$19 per passenger, depending on how far north you go. Additional members of a party pay a lower rate for many destinations, and children under three ride free with their parents. There's a pet transport fee of $5 for a cat, $8 for a dog under 50 pounds in kennels.
➤ AIRPORT INFORMATION: **Miami International Airport** (MIA, ☎ 305/876–7000). **Miami International Airport Hotel** (✉ Concourse E, upper level, ☎ 305/871–4100).
➤ TAXIS AND SHUTTLES: **Club Limousine Service** (✉ 12050 N.E. 14th Ave., Miami 33161, ☎ 305/893–9850 or 800/824–4820; 800/325–9834 in Florida). **Metrobus** (☎ 305/770–3131). **SuperShuttle** (☎ 305/871–2000 from MIA; 954/764–1700 from Broward [Fort Lauderdale]; 800/874–8885 from elsewhere). **Vintage Rolls Royce Limousines** (✉ 7242 S.W. 42nd Terr., South Miami 33155, ☎ 305/662–5763 or 800/888–7657).

BIKE TRAVEL

Cruise America offers Hondas and Suzukis with daily/weekly rentals starting at $109/$545. You must be 21 with a credit card, valid driver's license, and motorcycle endorsement.

Great weather and flat terrain make Miami perfect for cycling enthusiasts, but as a general method of transportation, it shouldn't be your first choice given traffic and limited bike paths. You can opt for Miami-Dade Transit's "Bike and Ride" program, which lets permitted cyclists take single-seat two-wheelers on Metrorail and select bus routes. **Miami-Dade Bicycle/Pedestrian Coordinator** has details on permits, bike maps, and lockers, and is open weekdays 8–5.
➤ BIKE RENTALS: **Cruise America** (✉ 5801 N.W. 151st St., Miami Lakes, Miami, ☎ 800/327–7799 or 305/828–1198). **Miami-Dade Bicycle/Pedestrian Coordinator** (☎ 305/375–4507).

BOAT AND FERRY TRAVEL

If you enter the United States in a private vessel along the Atlantic Coast south of Sebastian Inlet, you must call the **U.S. Customs Service.** Customs clears most boats of less than 5 tons by phone, but you may be directed to a marina for inspection.

The Port of Miami, in downtown Miami near Bayside Marketplace and the MacArthur Causeway, justifiably bills itself as the cruise capital of the world. Home to 18 ships and the largest year-round cruise fleet in the world, the port accommodates more than 3 million passengers a year. It has 12 air-conditioned terminals, duty-free shopping, and limousine service. Taxicabs are available at all terminals, and Avis is at the port, although other rental companies offer shuttle service to off-site locations. Parking is $10 per day and short-term parking is a flat rate of $4. From here, 2-, 3-, 4-, 5-, and 7-day cruises depart for the Bahamas and Eastern and Western Caribbean, with longer sailings to the Far East, Europe, and South America.

➤ BOAT INFORMATION: **Port of Miami** (✉ 1015 North American Way, Miami, ☎ 305/347–4860 or 305/371–7678). **U.S. Customs Service** (☎ 800/432–1216 for small vessel arrival near Miami; 305/536–5263 for Port of Miami office).

➤ CRUISE LINES: **Carnival Cruise Lines** (☎ 800/327–9501). **Celebrity Cruises** (☎ 800/437–3111). **Norwegian Cruise Lines** (☎ 800/327–7030). **Royal Caribbean International** (☎ 800/255–4373).

BUS TRAVEL TO AND FROM MIAMI AND MIAMI BEACH

Regularly scheduled, interstate **Greyhound** buses stop at five terminals in Greater Miami; the airport terminal is 24-hour.

➤ BUS INFORMATION: **Greyhound** (☎ 800/231–2222; Homestead, ✉ 5 N.E. 3rd Rd., ☎ 305/247–2040; Miami Bayside/Downtown, ✉ 100 N.W. 6th St., Overtown, ☎ 305/374–6160; Miami South, ✉ 20505 S. Dixie Hwy., Cutler Ridge, ☎ 305/296–9072; Miami West/Airport, ✉ 4111 N.W. 27th St., ☎ 305/871–1810; North Miami, ✉ 16560 N.E. 6th Ave., ☎ 305/945–0801).

BUS TRAVEL WITHIN MIAMI AND MIAMI BEACH

Metrobus stops are marked by blue-and-green signs with a bus logo and route information. The frequency of service varies widely, so call in advance to obtain specific schedules. The fare is $1.25 (exact change), transfers 25¢; 60¢ with 10¢ transfers for people with disabilities, senior citizens (65 and older), and students. Some express routes carry surcharges of $1.50. Reduced-fare tokens, sold 10 for $10, are available from Metropass outlets. All trains and stations are accessible to persons with disabilities; lift-equipped buses for people with disabilities are available on more than 50 routes, including one from the airport that links up with many routes in Miami Beach as well as Coconut Grove, Coral Gables, Hialeah, and Kendall. Miami Beach has a tourism hot line with information on accessibility, sign language interpreters, rental cars, and area recreational activities for the disabled.

The best thing to arrive in Miami Beach since sand, the Electro-Wave is a fleet of *free* electric trolleys running every few minutes up and down Washington Avenue between 5th and 17th streets. New service continues south of 5th Street, west to Alton Road, and over by the Miami Beach Marina. Considering the great lengths between South Beach attractions, it'll save a lot of shoe leather. Trolleys operate Monday– Wednesday 8 AM–2 AM, Thursday–Saturday 8 AM–4 AM, and Sunday and holidays 10 AM–2 AM.

FARES AND SCHEDULES
➤ Bus Information: **Electro-Wave** (☎ 305/843–9283). **Special Transportation Services** (☎ 305/263–5400).

CAR RENTAL

The following agencies have booths near the baggage-claim area on MIA's lower level: Avis, Budget, Dollar, Globetrotters, Hertz, National, and Royal. Avis and Budget also have offices at the Port of Miami.

If money is no object, check out Excellence Luxury Car Rental. As the name implies, you can rent some wheels (a Ferrari, perhaps?) to cruise SoBe and pretend you're Don Johnson. If you can't find the excellent car you want, you can rent a Dodge Viper, BMW, Hummer, Jag, Porsche, or Rolls from Exotic Toys. Airport pickup is provided.
➤ Local Agencies: **Alamo** (☎ 800/468–2583). **Avis** (☎ 800/331–1212). **Budget** (☎ 800/527–0700). **Dollar** (☎ 800/800–4000). **Excellence Luxury Car Rental** (☎ 305/526–0000). **Exotic Toys Car Rental** (☎ 305/888–8448). **Hertz** (☎ 800/654–3131). **Globetrotters** (☎ 800/899–3204). **National** (☎ 800/227–7368). **Royal** (☎ 800/314–8616).

CAR TRAVEL

The main highways into Greater Miami from the north are Florida's Turnpike (a toll road) and Interstate 95. From the northwest take Interstate 75 or U.S. 27 into town. From the Everglades, to the west, use the Tamiami Trail (U.S. 41), and from the south use U.S. 1 and the Homestead Extension of Florida's Turnpike.

In general, Miami traffic is the same as in any other big city, with the same rush hours and the same likelihood that parking garages will be full at peak times. Many drivers who aren't locals and don't know their way around might turn and stop suddenly, or drop off passengers where they shouldn't. Some drivers are short-tempered and will assault those who cut them off or honk their horn.

Motorists need to be careful, even when their driving behavior is beyond censure, however, especially in rental cars. Despite the removal of identifying marks, cars piled with luggage or otherwise showing signs that a tourist is at the wheel remain prime targets for thieves. Your best bet is to "follow the sun"; major (and safer) travel routes are marked by huge sunburst logos, which connect to tourist hot spots like the Deco District. Stick with these, and you should get where you need to go fairly easily and quickly. The city has also initiated a TOP (Tourist Oriented Police) Cops program to assist tourists with directions and safety. For more safety advice on driving in Miami, *see* Car Travel *in* Smart Travel Tips A to Z.

EMERGENCIES

Dial 911 for police or ambulance. You can dial free from pay phones.

Randle Eastern Ambulance Service Inc. operates at all hours, although in an emergency they'll direct you to call 911. Dade County Medical Association is open weekdays 9–5 for medical referral. East Coast District Dental Society is open weekdays 9–4:30 for dental referral. After hours stay on the line and a recording will direct you to a dentist. Services include general dentistry, endodontics, periodontics, and oral surgery.
➤ Doctors and Dentists: **Dade County Medical Association** (✉ 1501 N.W. North River Dr., Miami, ☎ 305/324–8717). **East Coast District Dental Society** (✉ 420 S. Dixie Hwy., Suite 2E, Coral Gables, ☎ 305/667–3647).
➤ Hot Lines: **Randle Eastern Ambulance Service Inc.** (✉ 7255 N.W. 19th St., Suite C, Miami 33126, ☎ 305/718–6400).

➤ LATE-NIGHT PHARMACIES: **Eckerd Drug** (✉ 9031 S.W. 107th Ave., Kendall, Miami, ☎ 305/274–6776). **Walgreens** (✉ 4895 E. Palm Ave., Hialeah, ☎ 305/231–7454; ✉ 2750 W. 68th St., Hialeah, ☎ 305/828–0268; ✉ 12295 Biscayne Blvd., North Miami, ☎ 305/893–6860; ✉ 5731 Bird Rd., Miami, ☎ 305/666–0757; ✉ 1845 Alton Rd., South Beach, ☎ 305/531–8868; ✉ 791 N.E. 167th St., North Miami Beach, ☎ 305/652–7332).

TAXIS

One cab "company" stands out immeasurably above the rest. It's actually a consortium of drivers who have banded together to provide good service, in marked contrast to some Miami cabbies, who are rude, unhelpful, unfamiliar with the city, or dishonest, taking advantage of visitors who don't know the area. To plug into this consortium—they don't have a name, simply a number—call the dispatch service, although they can be hard to understand over the phone. If you have to use another company, try to be familiar with your route and destination. For information call the Metro-Dade Passenger Transportation Regulatory Service, also known as the Hack Bureau. It takes complaints and monitors all for-hire vehicles.

Starting in 1998, fares were set at $3.25 per first mile and $2 every mile thereafter, with no additional charge for up to five passengers, luggage, and tolls. Taxis can be hailed on the street, although you may not always find one when you need one—it's better to call for a dispatch taxi or have a hotel doorman hail one for you. Some companies with dispatch service are Central Taxicab Service, Diamond Cab Company, Metro Taxicab Company, Miami-Dade Yellow Cab, Society Cab Company, Super Yellow Cab Company, Tropical Taxicab Company, and Yellow Cab Company. Many now accept credit cards; inquire when you call.
➤ TAXI COMPANIES: **Dispatch service** (☎ 305/888–4444). **Central Taxicab Service** (☎ 305/532–5555). **Diamond Cab Company** (☎ 305/545–5555). **Metro-Dade Passenger Transportation Regulatory Service** (☎ 305/375–2460). **Metro Taxicab Company** (☎ 305/888–8888). **Miami-Dade Yellow Cab** (☎ 305/633–0503). **Society Cab Company** (☎ 305/757–5523). **Super Yellow Cab Company** (☎ 305/888–7777). **Tropical Taxicab Company** (☎ 305/945–1025). **Yellow Cab Company** (☎ 305/444–4444).

TOURS

Coconut Grove Rickshaw centers its operations at CocoWalk. Two-person rickshaws scurry along Main Highway in Coconut Grove's Village Center, nightly 7 PM–midnight. You can take a 10-minute ride through Coconut Grove or a 20-minute lovers' moonlight ride to Biscayne Bay; prices start at $5 per person, and you can pick them up curb-side.

BOAT TOURS

Island Queen, Island Lady, and *Pink Lady* are 150-passenger double-decker tour boats docked at Bayside Marketplace. They go on daily 90-minute narrated tours of the Port of Miami and Millionaires' Row, costing $14. Refreshments are available.

For something a little more private and luxe, *RA Charters* sails out of the Dinner Key Marina in Coconut Grove. Full- and half-day charters include snorkeling and even sailing lessons on the 40-ft sloop, with extended trips to the Florida Keys and Bahamas. For a romantic night, have Captain Masoud pack some delicious fare and sail sunset to moonlight while you enjoy Biscayne Bay's spectacular skyline view of Miami. Prices range from $300 to $400 for a half day to $600–$700 for a full day, depending on the number of people aboard and refreshments provided.

➤ FEES AND SCHEDULES: *Island Queen, Island Lady,* and *Pink Lady* (✉ 401 Biscayne Blvd., Bayside Marketplace, ☎ 305/379–5119). *RA Charters* (☎ 305/854–7341 or 305/666–7979).

PRIVATE GUIDES

Professor Paul George, a history professor at Miami-Dade Community College and past president of the Florida Historical Society, leads walking tours as well as boat tours and tours that make use of the Metrorail and Metromover. Choose from tours covering downtown, historic neighborhoods, cemeteries, Coconut Grove, and the Miami River. They start Saturday at 10 and Sunday at 11 at various locations, depending on the tour, and generally last about 2½ hours. Call for each weekend's schedule and for additional tours by appointment. The fee is $15.
➤ CONTACTS: **Professor Paul George** (✉ 1345 S.W. 14th St., Little Havana, ☎ 305/858–6021).

WALKING TOURS

The Art Deco District Tour, operated by the Miami Design Preservation League, is a 90-minute guided walking tour that departs from the league's welcome center at the Oceanfront Auditorium. It costs $10 (tax-deductible) and starts at 10:30 AM Saturday and 6:30 PM Thursday. Private group tours can be arranged with advance notice. You can go at your own pace with the league's self-guided $5 audio tour, which takes roughly an hour and a half and is available in English, Spanish, French, and German.
➤ FEES AND SCHEDULES: **Art Deco District Tour** (✉ 1001 Ocean Dr., Bin L, South Beach 33139, ☎ 305/672–2014).

TRAIN TRAVEL

Amtrak provides service from 500 destinations to the Greater Miami area, including three trains daily from New York City. North–south service stops in the major Florida cities of Jacksonville, Orlando, Tampa, West Palm Beach, and Fort Lauderdale. For extended trips, or if you're visiting other areas in Florida, come via Auto Train from Lorton, Virginia, just outside of Washington, D.C., to Sanford, Florida, just outside of Orlando.

Tri-Rail, South Florida's commuter train system, offers daily service connecting Miami-Dade with Broward and Palm Beach counties via Metrorail (transfer at the TriRail/Metrorail Station at the Hialeah station, at 79th Street and East 11th Avenue). They also offer shuttle service to and from MIA from their airport station at 3797 Northwest 21st Street. Tri-Rail stops at 18 stations along a 71-mi route. Fares are established by zones, with prices ranging from $3.50 to $9.25 for a round-trip ticket.

Elevated Metrorail trains run from downtown Miami north to Hialeah and south along U.S. 1 to Dadeland, daily 5:30 AM–midnight. Trains run every six minutes during peak hours, every 15 minutes during weekday midhours, and every 30 minutes after 8 PM and on weekends. The fare is $1.25. Transfers, which cost 25¢, must be bought at the first station entered. Parking at train stations costs $2.

Metromover has two loops that circle downtown Miami, linking major hotels, office buildings, and shopping areas. The system spans 4½ mi, including the 1½-mi Omni Extension, with six stations to the north, and the 1-mi Brickell Extension, with six stations to the south. Quite convenient and amazingly cheap, it beats walking all around downtown. Service runs daily, every 90 seconds during rush hour and every three minutes off-peak, 6 AM–midnight along the inner loop and 6 AM–10:30 PM on the Omni and Brickell extensions. The fare is 25¢. Transfers to Metrorail are $1.

➤ TRAIN INFORMATION: **Amtrak** (✉ 8303 N.W. 37th Ave., Hialeah, ☎ 800/872–7245). **Metromover** (☎ 305/770–3131). **Metrorail** (☎ 305/770–3131). **Tri-Rail** (✉ 1 River Plaza, 305 S. Andrews Ave., Suite 200, Fort Lauderdale, ☎ 800/874–7245).

TRANSPORTATION AROUND MIAMI AND MIAMI BEACH

Greater Miami resembles Los Angeles in its urban sprawl and traffic. You'll need a car to visit many attractions and points of interest. Some are accessible via the public transportation system, run by a department of the county government—the Metro-Dade Transit Agency, which consists of 650 Metrobuses on 70 routes, the 21-mi Metrorail elevated rapid-transit system, and the Metromover, an elevated light-rail system. Free maps and schedules are available.

➤ INFORMATION: **Miami-Dade Transit** (✉ Government Center Station, 111 N.W. 1st St., Downtown 33128, ☎ 305/654–6586 for Maps by Mail; 305/770–3131 for route information weekdays 6 AM–10 PM and weekends 9–5).

VISITOR INFORMATION

Florida Gold Coast Chamber of Commerce serves the beach communities of Bal Harbour, Bay Harbor Islands, Golden Beach, North Bay Village, Sunny Isles Beach, and Surfside.

➤ TOURIST INFORMATION: **Greater Miami Convention & Visitors Bureau** (✉ 701 Brickell Ave., Suite 2700, Downtown 33131, ☎ 305/539–3063 or 800/283–2707, WEB www.tropicoolmiami.com). Satellite tourist information centers are at **Bayside Marketplace** (✉ 401 Biscayne Blvd., Bayside Marketplace, Miami 33132, ☎ 305/539–2980) and **Tropical Everglades Visitor Information Center** (✉ 160 U.S. 1, Florida City 33034, ☎ 305/245–9180 or 800/388–9669, FAX 305/247–4335). **Coconut Grove Chamber of Commerce** (✉ 2820 McFarlane Rd., Coconut Grove 33133, ☎ 305/444–7270, FAX 305/444–2498). **Coral Gables Chamber of Commerce** (✉ 50 Aragon Ave., Coral Gables 33134, ☎ 305/446–1657, FAX 305/446–9900). **Florida Gold Coast Chamber of Commerce** (✉ 1100 Kane Concourse, Suite 210, Bay Harbor Islands 33154, ☎ 305/866–6020). **Greater Miami Chamber of Commerce** (✉ 1601 Biscayne Blvd., Miami 33132, ☎ 305/350–7700, FAX 305/374–6902). **Greater North Miami Chamber of Commerce** (✉ 13100 W. Dixie Hwy., North Miami 33181, ☎ 305/891–7811, FAX 305/893–8522). **Greater South Dade/South Miami Chamber of Commerce** (✉ 6410 S.W. 80th St., South Miami 33143-4602, ☎ 305/661–1621, FAX 305/666–0508). **Key Biscayne Chamber of Commerce** (✉ Key Biscayne Bank Bldg., 87 W. McIntyre St., Key Biscayne 33149, ☎ 305/361–5207). **Miami Beach Chamber of Commerce** (✉ 1920 Meridian Ave., South Beach, Miami Beach 33139, ☎ 305/672–1270, FAX 305/538–4336). **Surfside Tourist Board** (✉ 9301 Collins Ave., Surfside 33154, ☎ 305/864–0722 or 800/327–4557, FAX 305/861–1302).

3 THE EVERGLADES

South Florida's wide, slow-moving "River of Grass"—the largest roadless expanse in the United States—is home to Everglades National Park and spectacular plant and animal life found no place else in the country. Nearby Biscayne National Park protects living coral reefs, mangroves, undeveloped islands, a shallow bay, and all the wild things that come with them. Both areas, within minutes of Miami's metropolis, maintain a fragile balance between humans and nature.

Updated by
Diane P.
Marshall

T HE ONLY METROPOLITAN AREA in the United States with two national parks and a national preserve in its backyard is Miami. Everglades National Park, created in 1947, was meant to preserve the slow-moving "River of Grass"—a freshwater river 50 mi wide but only 6 inches deep, flowing from Lake Okeechobee through marshy grassland into Florida Bay. Along the Tamiami Trail (U.S. 41), marshes of cattails extend as far as the eye can see, interspersed only with hammocks (rich-soil areas) or tree islands of bald cypress and mahogany, while overhead southern bald eagles make circles in the sky. An assembly of trees and flowers, including ferns, orchids, and bromeliads, shares the brackish waters with otters, turtles, marsh rabbits, and occasionally that gentle giant, the West Indian manatee. Not so gentle, though, is the saw grass. Deceptively graceful, these tall, willowy sedges have small sharp teeth on the edges of their leaves.

Biscayne National Park, established as a national monument in 1968 and 12 years later expanded and designated a national park, is the nation's largest marine park and the largest national park within the continental United States with living coral reefs. A small portion of the park's almost 274 square mi consists of mainland coast and outlying islands, but 96% is underwater, much of it in Biscayne Bay. The islands contain lush, heavily wooded forests with an abundance of ferns and native palm trees. Of particular interest are the mangroves and their tangled masses of stiltlike roots and stems that thicken the shorelines. These "walking trees," as locals sometimes call them, have striking curved prop roots, which arch down from the trunk, and aerial roots that drop from branches. These trees draw freshwater from saltwater and create a coastal nursery capable of sustaining all types of marine life.

Congress established Big Cypress National Preserve in 1974 after buying up one of the least-developed watershed areas in South Florida to protect the watershed of Everglades National Park. The preserve, on the northern edge of Everglades National Park, entails extensive tracts of prairie, marsh, pinelands, forested swamps, and sloughs. Although preservation and recreation are the preserve's mainstay, hunting, off-road vehicle use, oil and gas exploration, and grazing are allowed.

Unfortunately, Miami's backyard is threatened by suburban sprawl, agriculture, and business development. What results is competition among environmental, agricultural, and developmental interests. The biggest issue is water. Originally, alternating floods and dry periods maintained a wildlife habitat and regulated the water flowing into Florida Bay. The brackish seasonal flux sustained a remarkably vigorous bay, including the most productive shrimp beds in American waters, with thriving mangrove thickets and coral reefs at its Atlantic edge. The system nurtured sea life and attracted anglers and divers. Starting in the 1930s, however, a giant flood-control system began diverting water to canals running to the gulf and the ocean. As you travel Florida's north–south routes, you cross this network of canals symbolized by a smiling alligator representing the South Florida Water Management District, ironically known as "Protector of the Everglades" (ironic because most people feel it's done more for the developers than the environment).

The unfortunate side effect of flood control has been devastation of the wilderness. Park visitors decry diminished bird counts (a 90% reduction over 50 years); the black bear has been eliminated; and the Florida panther is nearing extinction. Meanwhile, the loss of freshwater has made

Florida Bay saltier, devastating breeding grounds and creating dead zones where pea-green algae has replaced sea grasses and sponges.

Even as the ecosystem fades, new policies, still largely on paper, hold promise. More than a score of government agencies and a host of conservation groups and industries have worked out restoration plans. The future of the natural system will be determined in the next decade.

Pleasures and Pastimes

Biking and Hiking

In the Everglades there are several nice places to ride and hike. The Shark Valley Loop Road (15 mi round-trip) makes a good bike trip. Lists at the visitor centers describe others. Inquire about insect and weather conditions before you go and plan accordingly, stocking up on insect repellent, sunscreen, and water, as necessary.

Boating and Canoeing

One of the best ways to experience the Everglades is by boat, and almost all of Biscayne National Park is accessible only by water. Boat rentals are available in both parks. Rentals are generally for half day (four hours) and full day (eight hours).

In the Everglades the 99-mi inland Wilderness Trail between Flamingo and Everglades City is open to motorboats as well as canoes, although powerboats may have trouble navigating the route above Whitewater Bay. Flat-water canoeing is best in winter, when temperatures are moderate, rainfall is minimal, and mosquitoes are tolerable. You don't need a permit for day trips, but tell someone where you're going and when you expect to return. Getting lost is easy, and spending the night without proper gear can be unpleasant, if not dangerous.

On the Gulf Coast you can explore the nooks, crannies, and mangrove islands of Chokoloskee Bay, as well as many rivers near Everglades City. The Turner River Canoe Trail, a good day trip, passes through mangrove, dwarf cypress, coastal prairie, and freshwater slough ecosystems of Everglades National Park and Big Cypress National Preserve.

Dining

With a few exceptions, dining centers on low-key mom-and-pop places that serve hearty home-style food and small eateries specializing in local fare: seafood, conch, alligator, turtle, and frogs' legs. Native American restaurants add another dimension, serving local favorites as well as catfish, Indian fry bread (a flour-and-water dough), pumpkin bread, Indian burgers (ground beef browned, rolled in fry-bread dough, and deep-fried), and tacos (fry bread with chili, lettuce, tomato, and shredded cheddar cheese on top). Restaurants in Everglades City appear to operate with a "captive audience" philosophy: prices run high, service is mediocre, and food preparation is uninspired. The closest good restaurants are in Naples, 35 mi northwest.

Although both Everglades and Biscayne national parks and Big Cypress National Preserve are wilderness areas, there are restaurants within a short drive. Most are between Miami and Shark Valley along the Tamiami Trail (U.S. 41), in the Homestead–Florida City area, in Everglades City, and in the Florida Keys along the Overseas Highway (U.S. 1). The only food service in the preserve or in either of the parks is at Flamingo, in the Everglades, but many independent restaurants will pack picnics. You can also find fast-food establishments on the Tamiami Trail east of Krome Avenue and west of Everglades City in Naples, and along U.S. 1 in Homestead–Florida City.

CATEGORY	COST*
$$$$	over $30
$$$	$20–$30
$$	$10–$20
$	under $10

per person for a main course at dinner

Fishing

Largemouth bass are plentiful in freshwater ponds, and snapper, red-fish, and sea trout are caught in Florida Bay. The mangrove shallows of the 10,000 Islands, along the gulf, yield tarpon and snook. White-water Bay is also a favorite spot. **Note:** the state has issued health advisories for sea bass, largemouth bass, and other freshwater fish, especially those caught in the canals along the Tamiami Trail, because of their high mercury content. Signs are posted throughout the park, and consumption should be limited.

Lodging

All prices are for a standard double room, excluding 6% sales tax (more in some counties) and 1%–4% tourist tax.

CATEGORY	COST
$$$$	over $220
$$$	$140–$220
$$	$80–$140
$	under $80

Exploring the Everglades

The southern tip of the Florida peninsula is largely taken up by Everglades National Park, but land access to it is primarily by two roads. The main park road traverses the southern Everglades from the gateway towns of Homestead and Florida City to the outpost of Flamingo, on Florida Bay. In the northern Everglades you can take the Tamiami Trail (U.S. 41) from the Greater Miami area in the east to the western park entrance in Everglades City. In far southeastern Florida, Biscayne National Park lies almost completely offshore. As a result, most sports and recreational opportunities in both national parks are based on water, the study of nature, or both, so even on land, be prepared to get a bit damp on the region's marshy trails.

Although relatively compact compared with the national parks of the West, these parks still require a bit of time to see. The narrow, two-lane roads through the Everglades make for long travel, whereas it's the necessity of sightseeing by boat that takes time at Biscayne.

Numbers in the text correspond to numbers in the margin and on the Everglades and Biscayne National Parks map.

Great Itineraries

IF YOU HAVE 1 DAY

You'll have to make a choice—the Everglades, Big Cypress, or Biscayne. If you want interpretive trails and lots of exhibits, go with the Everglades. If you're interested in boating or underwater flora and fauna, Biscayne is your best bet. For quiet, wilderness canoeing, and nature, don't miss Big Cypress. Whichever you choose, you'll experience a little of what's left of the "real" Florida.

For a day in Everglades National Park, begin in **Florida City** ⑭, the southern/western gateway to the park. Head to the **Ernest F. Coe Visitor Center** ① for an overview of the park and its ecosystems, and continue to the **Royal Palm Visitor Center** ② for a look at several unique plant systems. Then go to **Flamingo** ③, where you can rent a boat or take a tour of Florida Bay.

If Biscayne is your preference, begin at **Convoy Point** ⑮ for an orientation before forsaking dry land. Sign up for a snorkel or dive trip or an outing on a glass-bottom boat, kayak, or canoe.

To spend a day in Big Cypress National Preserve, begin at the **Oasis Visitor Center** ⑨ to pick up information about canoe and walking trails and learn about the park's ecosystem. Then head to **Everglades City** ⑫, where you can rent a canoe for a tour of the Turner River.

IF YOU HAVE 3 DAYS

With three days you can explore both the northern and southern Everglades as well as Biscayne National Park. Start in the north by driving west along the Tamiami Trail, stopping at **Everglades Safari Park** ④ for an airboat ride; at **Shark Valley** ⑥ for a tram tour, walk, or bicycle trip; at the **Miccosukee Indian Village** ⑦ for lunch; at the **Big Cypress Gallery** ⑧ to see Clyde Butcher's photographs; and then at the **Ochopee post office** ⑩, before ending in ⊞ **Everglades City** ⑫, home of Everglades National Park's Gulf Coast Visitor Center. From here you can visit historic Smallwood's Store on Chokoloskee Island and watch the sunset. Day two is for exploring the south. Return east on the Tamiami Trail to **Homestead** ⑬, pausing at Everglades Air Tours to take a sightseeing trip before following the one-day Everglades itinerary above and overnighting in ⊞ **Florida City** ⑭. Biscayne National Park is the subject of day three. If you plan to scuba or take the glass-bottom boat, get an early start. You can explore the visitor center at **Convoy Point** ⑮ when you return and finish your day checking out sights in Florida City and Homestead. Snorkel trips leave later, giving you time to see Florida City and Homestead, have lunch, and learn about the park's ecosystem at the visitor center first. Be warned that, although you can fly and then scuba dive, you *can't* dive and then fly within 24 hours. So if you're flying out, reverse the days' sequence accordingly.

IF YOU HAVE 5 DAYS

Follow day one above, spending the night in ⊞ **Everglades City** ⑫. Begin the second day with a canoe, kayak, or boat tour of the 10,000 Islands, then make arrangements to rent a canoe for the next day's trip to Big Cypress National Preserve's Turner River. In the late afternoon take a walk on the half-mile boardwalk at **Fakahatchee Strand Preserve State Park** ⑪ to see rare epiphytic orchids or on a 2½-mi trail at the Big Cypress National Preserve. On day three, drive to the Big Cypress Oasis Visitor Center to put in for the canoe tour. If it's December to April, you can join a ranger-led canoe tour. Drive east to Coopertown and take a nighttime ride with Ray Cramer's Everglades Airboat Tours. Spend the night in ⊞ **Florida City** ⑭. Day four is spent at Biscayne National Park, then sightseeing in **Homestead** ⑬ and **Florida City** ⑭ as suggested above. On day five, augment your picnic lunch with goodies from the remarkable fruit stand Robert Is Here, before heading to the southern portion of Everglades National Park, as described above.

When to Tour the Everglades

Winter is the best time to visit Everglades National Park and Big Cypress National Preserve. Temperatures and mosquito activity are low to moderate, low water levels concentrate the resident wildlife around sloughs that retain water all year, and migratory birds swell the avian population. Winter is also the busiest time in the park. Make reservations and expect crowds at Flamingo, the main visitor center (known officially as the Ernest F. Coe Visitor Center), and Royal Palm.

In spring the weather turns hot and rainy, and tours and facilities are less crowded. Migratory birds depart, and you must look harder to see wildlife. Be careful with campfires and matches; this is when the wild-fire-prone saw-grass prairies and pinelands are most vulnerable.

Summer brings intense sun and billowing clouds unleashing torrents of rain almost every afternoon. Start your outdoor activities early to avoid the rain and the sun's strongest rays, and use sunscreen. Water levels rise and wildlife disperses. Mosquitoes hatch, swarm, and de-scend on you in voracious clouds. (Carrying mosquito repellent is a good idea at any time of year, but it's a necessity in summer.) Euro-peans constitute 80% of the summer visitors.

Even if you're not lodging in Everglades National Park, try to stay until dusk, when dozens of bird species feed around the ponds and trails. While shining a flashlight over the water in marshy areas, look for two yellowish-red reflections above the surface—telltale alligator signs.

EVERGLADES NATIONAL PARK

11 mi southwest of Homestead, 45 mi southwest of Miami International Airport.

The best way to experience the real Everglades is to get your feet wet either by taking a walk in the muck, affectionately called a "slough slog," or by paddling a canoe into the River of Grass to stay in a back-country campsite. Most day-trippers don't want to do that, however. Luckily, there are several ways to see the wonders of the park with dry feet. Take a boat tour in Everglades City or Flamingo, ride the tram at Shark Valley, or walk the boardwalks along the main park road. And there's more to see than natural beauty. Miccosukee Indians operate a scope of attractions and restaurants worthy of a stop.

Admission to Everglades National Park is valid at all entrances for seven days. Coverage below begins in the southern Everglades, followed by the northern Everglades, starting in the east and ending in Everglades City.

The Main Park Road

The main park road (Route 9336) travels from the main visitor center to Flamingo, across a section of the park's eight distinct ecosystems: hardwood hammock, freshwater prairie, pinelands, freshwater slough, cypress, coastal prairie, mangrove, and marine-estuarine. Highlights of the trip include a dwarf cypress forest, the ecotone (transition zone) between saw grass and mangrove forest, and a wealth of wading birds at Mrazek and Coot Bay ponds. Boardwalks, looped trails, several short spurs, and observation platforms allow you to stay dry.

★ ☙ ❶ **Ernest F. Coe Visitor Center.** At park headquarters, the visitor center has numerous interactive exhibits and films. Stand in a simulated blind and peer through a spyglass to watch birds in the wild; although it's actually a film, the quality is so good you'll think you're outside. Move on to a bank of telephones to hear differing viewpoints on the Great Water Debate. There's a 15-minute film on the park, two movies on hurricanes, and a 45-minute wildlife film for children. Computer mon-itors present a schedule of daily ranger-led activities parkwide as well as information on canoe rentals and boat tours. In the Everglades Dis-covery Shop you can browse through lots of neat nature, science, and kids' stuff and pick up the insect repellent you forgot. The center pro-vides information on the entire park. ⊠ *11 mi southwest of Home-stead on Rte. 9336,* ☎ *305/242-7700.* ☞ *Park $10 per car, $5 per pedestrian or bicyclist, $5 per motorcycle.* ☉ *Daily 8–5.*

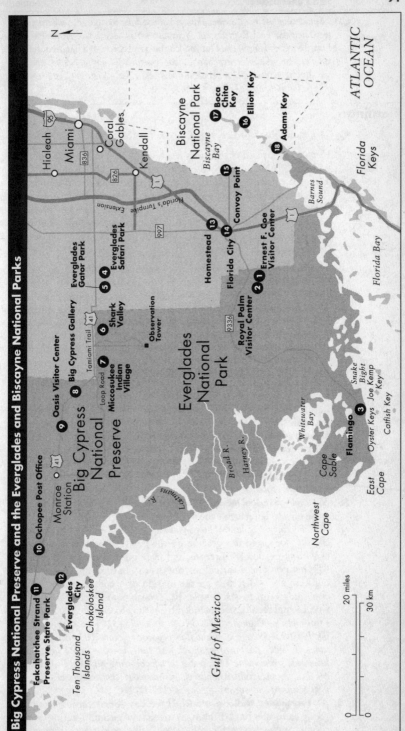

Big Cypress National Preserve and the Everglades and Biscayne National Parks

❷   **Royal Palm Visitor Center.** This is a must for anyone who wants to experience the real Everglades. You can stroll along the Anhinga Trail boardwalk or follow the Gumbo Limbo Trail through a hardwood hammock. The visitor center has an interpretive display, a bookstore, and vending machines. ⊠ *4 mi west of Ernest F. Coe Visitor Center on Rte. 9336,* ☎ *305/242–7700.* ☉ *Daily 8–5.*

Flamingo

❸   *38 mi southwest of Ernest F. Coe Visitor Center.*

Here at the far end of the main road, you'll find a cluster of buildings where a former town of the same name was established in 1893. Today, it contains a visitor center, lodge, restaurant and lounge, gift shop, marina, and bicycle rentals, plus an adjacent campground. Tour boats narrated by interpretive guides, fishing expeditions of Florida Bay, and canoe and kayak trips all leave from here. Nearby is Eco Pond, one of the most popular wildlife observation areas. Some facilities, like the restaurant, are seasonal.

The **Flamingo Visitor Center** provides an interactive display and has natural-history exhibits in the small Florida Bay Flamingo Museum. Check the schedule for ranger-led activities, such as naturalist discussions, evening programs in the campground amphitheater, and hikes along area trails. ☎ *941/695–2945.* ☉ *Dec.–Apr., daily 7:30–5; May–Nov., hrs vary.*

Dining and Lodging

$–$$ ✕ **Flamingo Restaurant and Buttonwood Patio Cafe.** The grand view, convivial lounge, and casual style are great reasons to visit here. Big picture windows on the visitor center's second floor overlook Florida Bay, revealing eagles, gulls, pelicans, and vultures. Dine at low tide to see birds flock to the sandbar just offshore. The restaurant menu has seafood and local dishes such as coconut fried shrimp and chicken breast with a mango salsa. Downstairs, the Buttonwood Patio Cafe is open for pizza, sandwiches, and salads. ⊠ *Flamingo Lodge, 1 Flamingo Lodge Hwy.,* ☎ *941/695–3101. AE, D, DC, MC, V. Restaurant closed May–Oct. Café closed Apr. and Oct.*

$$ 🏨 **Flamingo Lodge, Marina & Outpost Resort.** This simple low-rise motel is the only lodging inside the park. Accommodations are basic but well kept, and an amiable staff helps you adjust to bellowing alligators, roaming raccoons, and ibis grazing on the lawn. Rooms have contemporary furniture, floral bedspreads, and art prints of birds. They face Florida Bay, but don't necessarily look out over it. Bathrooms are small. Cottages, in a wooded area on the margin of a coastal prairie, can accommodate up to six people. Reservations are essential in winter; Continental breakfast is included from May to October. ⊠ *1 Flamingo Lodge Hwy., Flamingo, 33034,* ☎ *941/695–3101 or 800/600–3813,* FAX *941/695–3921,* WEB *www.flamingolodge.com. 102 rooms, 24 cottages, 1 suite. Restaurant, snack bar, fans, in-room data ports, some kitchens, some cable TVs, pool, beach, boating, fishing, bicycles, hiking, bar, shops, laundry facilities, business services, meeting rooms, some pets allowed; no-smoking rooms. AE, D, DC, MC, V.*

$ ⚠ **Everglades National Park.** Three developed campgrounds and group campsites have drinking water, a sewage dump station, and rest rooms. Some also have picnic tables, grills, cold-water showers, and tent and trailer pads. Long Pine Key has 108 drive-up sites; Flamingo has 234 drive-up sites, 64 walk-in sites, 20 on the water, and cold showers; and Chekika, which was closed at press time following hurricane damage, has 20 sites, warm showers, and a sulfur spring where you can swim, although it's not advised. Pets are welcome in the park, but definitely should not be allowed to swim in areas where there are alligators. From late November through April, sites at Long Pine Key and Flamingo are available through a reservation system, but the rest of the year all sites are first-come, first-served. In addition, deep in the park are 48 backcountry sites, many inland with some on the beach. Three are accessible by land, the others by canoe; 16 have *chickees* (raised wooden platforms with thatched roofs). Most have chemical toilets. Several are within an easy day's canoeing of Flamingo; five are near Everglades City. You'll need to carry your food, water, and supplies in; carry out all trash. You'll also need a site-specific permit, available on a first-come, first-served basis from the Flamingo or Gulf Coast Visitor Center. Developed sites are free June–August and $14 per night the rest of the year. Groups pay $28, and backcountry sites cost $10 or more, depending on group size. ☎ *305/242–7700; 800/365–2267 for campsite reservations. 471 sites. Picnic area, some pets allowed. D, MC, V.*

Outdoor Activities and Sports

BIKING

Flamingo Lodge, Marina & Outpost Resort (☎ 941/695–3101) rents bikes for $14 a day, $8 per half day. Snake Bight Trail and the park's main road are good places to ride to see wildlife.

BOATING

The marina at **Flamingo Lodge, Marina & Outpost Resort** (☎ 941/695–3101) rents 16-ft power skiffs for $90 per day, $65 per half day, and $22 per hour; four Carolina skiffs for $155 per day and $100 per half day; as well as fully furnished and outfitted houseboats that sleep up to eight. From November to April, rates (two-day minimum) run $475 without air-conditioning for two days, $575 with air-conditioning for two days. Off-season (summer) rates are lower. Several private boats are also available for charter. There are two ramps, one for Florida Bay, the other for Whitewater Bay and the backcountry. The hoist across the plug dam separating Florida Bay from the Buttonwood Canal can take boats from 16 ft to 26 ft long. A small store sells food, camping supplies, bait and tackle, propane, and fuel. A concessionaire rents rods, reels, binoculars, and coolers by the half and full day.

CANOEING AND KAYAKING

The Everglades has six well-marked canoe trails in the Flamingo area, including the south end of the 99-mi Wilderness Trail from Everglades City to Flamingo. **Flamingo Lodge, Marina & Outpost Resort** (☎ 941/695–3101) rents canoes in two sizes: small (up to two paddlers) and family size (up to four). Small canoes rent for $32 per day, $22 per half day, and $8 per hour; family-size run $40, $30, and $12, respectively. Single-person kayaks cost $43 per day, $27 per half day, and $11 per hour; doubles rent for $54, $38, and $16, respectively. Overnight rentals are also available.

FISHING

Flamingo Lodge, Marina & Outpost Resort (☎ 941/695–3101) helps arrange charter fishing trips for two to four people. The cost is $350 a day for up to two people, $25 each additional person.

Tamiami Trail

141 mi from Miami to Fort Myers.

In 1915, when officials decided to build an east–west highway linking Miami to Fort Myers and continuing north to Tampa, someone suggested calling it the Tamiami Trail. In 1928 the road became a reality, cutting through the Everglades and altering the natural flow of water and the lives of the Miccosukee Indians who eked out a living fishing, hunting, and frogging here.

Today the highway's traffic screams through Everglades National Park, Big Cypress National Preserve, and Fakahatchee Strand Preserve State Park. The landscape is surprisingly varied, changing from hardwood hammocks to pinelands, then abruptly to tall cypress trees dripping with Spanish moss and back to coastal prairie. Those who slow down to take in the scenery are rewarded with glimpses of alligators sunning themselves along the banks of roadside canals and in the shallow waters, and hundreds of waterbirds, especially in the dry winter season. The man-made landscape has chickee huts, Native American villages, and airboats parked at roadside enterprises.

Businesses along the trail give their addresses either based on their distance from Krome Avenue, Florida's Turnpike, and Miami on the east coast or Fort Myers and Naples on the west coast or by mile marker. Between Miami and Fort Myers, the road goes by several names, including Tamiami Trail, U.S. 41, and, at the Miami end, Southwest 8th Street.

❹ Everglades Safari Park. A perennial favorite with tour bus operators, this has an arena that seats up to 300 people to watch an educational alligator show and wrestling demonstration. Before and after the show, you can get a closer look at the alligators, walk through a small wildlife museum, or climb aboard an airboat for a 30-minute ride through the River of Grass (included in admission). There's also a restaurant, a gift shop, and an observation platform that looks out over the Glades. ✉ *26700 Tamiami Trail, 9 mi west of Krome Ave.,* ☎ *305/226–6923 or 305/223–3804.* ☞ *$15.* ⊙ *Daily 8:30–5.*

❺ Everglades Gator Park. After visiting here you can tell your friends you came face-to-face with—and even touched—an alligator, albeit a baby one. Then you can squirm in a "reptilium" of venomous and nonpoisonous native snakes or learn about Native Americans of the Everglades through a reproduction of a Miccosukee village. The park also has wildlife shows with native and exotic animals, 45-minute airboat tours, fishing charters, and RV campsites, as well as a gift shop and restaurant. The last airboat ride departs 45 minutes before sunset. ✉ *24050 Tamiami Trail, 12 mi west of Florida's Turnpike,* ☎ *305/559–2255 or 800/559–2205.* ☞ *Free, tours $14.* ⊙ *Daily 9–sunset.*

❻ Shark Valley. It takes a bit of nerve to walk the paved 15-mi loop here because alligators lie on the road and alongside it, basking in the sun—most, however, do move quickly out of the way. Less fearless, or energetic, types can ride a bicycle or take a tram tour. Stop at the halfway point to climb the concrete observation tower's ramp, which spirals skyward 50 ft. From there everything as far as the eye can see is the vast River of Grass. You can observe all kinds of waterbirds as well as alligators at water holes. Just behind the bike-rental area, a short boardwalk trail meanders through the saw grass. A small visitor center has rotating exhibits, a bookstore, and park rangers ready to answer questions. Shark Valley is the national park's north entrance; however, no roads here lead to other parts of the park. ✉ *23½ mi west of Florida's Turnpike,* ☎ *305/221–8776.* ☞ *Park $8 per car; $4 per pedestrian, bicyclist, or motorcyclist.* ⊙ *Visitor center daily 8:30–5:30.*

❼ Miccosukee Indian Village. For more than 25 years, the cultural center here has showcased Miccosukee foods, crafts, skills, and lifestyle. It also presents educational alligator shows and crafts demonstrations. Narrated 30-minute airboat rides take you into the heart of the wilderness in which these Native Americans escaped after the Third Seminole War and Indian Removal Act during the mid-1800s. There's also a restaurant and gift shop. The Everglades Music & Craft Festival falls on a July weekend, and the weeklong Indian Arts Festival is in late December. ⊠ *West of Shark Valley entrance, 25 mi west of Florida's Turnpike,* ☎ *305/223–8380.* ⌨ *$5, rides $10.* ☉ *Daily 9–5.*

⑧ Big Cypress Gallery. Clyde Butcher does for the River of Grass and Big Cypress Swamp what Ansel Adams did for the West, and you can check out his stunning photographs at his gallery in the Big Cypress National Preserve. Working with large-format black-and-white film, Butcher captures every blade of grass, barb of feather, and flicker of light. Special exhibits, lectures, tours, photo expeditions, and slide presentations are given throughout the year. ⊠ *52388 Tamiami Trail, 37 mi west of Miami, 45 mi east of Naples,* ☎ *941/695–2428.* ⌨ *Free.* ☉ *Apr.–Nov., Wed.–Sat. 10–5, Dec.–Mar., Wed.–Mon. 10–5.*

⑩ Ochopee Post Office. This tiny building is the smallest post office in North America. Buy a picture postcard of the little one-room shack and mail it to a friend, thereby helping to keep this picturesque spot in business. ⊠ *75 mi west of Miami, Ochopee,* ☎ *941/695–4131.* ☉ *Weekdays 9:30–noon and 1–4:30, Sat. 9:30–11:30.*

⑪ Fakahatchee Strand Preserve State Park. The ½-mi boardwalk here gives you an opportunity to see rare plants, bald cypress, and North America's largest stand of native royal palms and largest concentration and variety of epiphytic orchids. From November to April the park's rookery, accessed down a short road 2 mi east of the boardwalk, is a birder's paradise beginning an hour before sunset. The sight of 5,000 to 7,000 wading birds returning to roost for the night is spectacular. You can launch a kayak or watch from the shore. ⊠ *Boardwalk on north side of Tamiami Trail 7 mi west of Rte. 29; rookery on south side of Tamiami Trail 5 mi west of Rte. 29; ranger station ¼ mi north of Tamiami Trail on Rte. 29, Box 548, Copeland 34137,* ☎ *941/695–4593,* WEB *www.dep.state.fl.us/parks.* ⌨ *Free.* ☉ *Daily 8–sunset.*

Dining and Lodging

$$ ✕ **Joanie's Blue Crab Café.** Movie set designers could not have created
★ a more quintessential 1950s-style swamp café than this landmark restaurant near the Ochopee post office. The decor consists of wood-plank floors, open rafters hung with cobwebs, stuffed owls, postcards from around the globe, and kitschy gator art. Joanie, the chief cook and bottle washer, came here in 1987. The staff picks fresh blue crabs—up to 372 pounds in a weekend—that they catch each day to go into sandwiches and soups. Chill out with a beer or glass of wine on the screened deck. It's open daily 9 AM to 5 PM. ⊠ *39395 Tamiami Trail, 50 mi west of Florida's Turnpike, Ochopee,* ☎ *941/695–2682. D, MC, V.*

$–$$ ✕ **Coopertown Restaurant.** For more than a half century this rustic eatery just into the Everglades west of Miami has been full of Old Florida style—not to mention alligator skulls, stuffed alligator heads, and gator accessories. House specialties are frogs' legs and alligator tail prepared breaded or deep-fried, and they're available for breakfast, lunch, or dinner. You can also order more conventional selections, such as catfish, shrimp, or sandwiches. ⊠ *22700 S.W. 8th St., Miami,* ☎ *305/226–6048. MC, V.*

$–$$ ✕ **Miccosukee Restaurant.** Murals depict Native American women cooking and men engaged in a powwow in this Native American restaurant at the Miccosukee Indian Village. Favorites are catfish and frogs' legs breaded and deep-fried, Indian fry bread, pumpkin bread, and Indian burgers and tacos. Breakfast and lunch are served daily. ⊠ *25 mi west of Florida's Turnpike,* ☎ *305/223–8380 Ext. 2374. MC, V.*

$–$$ ✕ **Pit Bar-B-Q.** On a day with a breeze, you can smell this rustic roadside eatery's barbecue and blackjack-oak smoke long before you can see it. Order at the counter, pick up your food when called, and eat at one of the indoor or outdoor picnic tables. Specialties include barbecued chicken and ribs with a tangy sauce, french fries, coleslaw, and a fried biscuit as well as catfish and frogs' legs deep-fried in vegetable oil. ⊠ *16400 Tamiami Trail, Miami,* ☎ *305/226–2272. AE, D, MC, V.*

$$–$$$ 🏨 **Miccosukee Resort & Convention Center.** Big-name entertainers and major sporting events draw crowds to this resort at the crossroads of Tamiami Trail and Krome Avenue. Like an oasis on the horizon, it's the only facility for miles and it's situated to attract the attention of travelers going to the Everglades, driving across the state, or looking for casino action. Most units have a view of Everglades saw grass and wildlife. In addition to an enormous children's play area and a teen center, there are tours to Everglades National Park and the Miccosukee Indian Village, shuttles to area malls, and a gaming complex. ⊠ *500 S.W. 177th Ave., Miami 33194,* ☎ *305/925–2555 or 877/242–6464. 256 rooms, 46 suites. 3 restaurants, snack bar, in-room data ports, in-room safes, some in-room hot tubs, minibars, cable TV with movies and video games, indoor pool, health club, hair salon, hot tub, sauna, spa, lounge, showroom, video game room, shops, playground, laundry services, Internet, business services, convention center, meeting rooms, airport shuttle, travel services; no-smoking rooms. AE, D, DC, MC, V.*

$ 🛶 **Everglades Gator Park.** Popular with the RV set, the park has full hookups for as many as 80 vehicles, in addition to airboats, Everglades attractions, and a small store. You can rent a campsite by the night ($25), week ($100), or month ($350), or store your RV in the short-term area. ⊠ *24050 S.W. 8th St., Miami,* ☎ *305/559–2255 or 800/559–2205;* ⊠ *mailing address: 13800 S.W. 8th St., Box 107, Miami 33184. 80 sites. Restaurant, lake, fishing. AE, D, DC, MC, V.*

Outdoor Activities and Sports

Shark Valley Tram Tours (⊠ Shark Valley, ☎ 305/221–8455) rents bikes daily 8:30–4 (last rental at 3) for $4.75 per hour.

Shopping

The shopping alone should lure you to the **Miccosukee Indian Village** (⊠ 25 mi west of Florida's Turnpike, just west of Shark Valley entrance, ☎ 305/223–8380). Wares include well-made Native American crafts such as beadwork, moccasins, dolls, pottery, baskets, and patchwork fabric and clothes. There are also some fun, kitschy Florida souvenirs.

Everglades City

⑫ *35 mi southeast of Naples, 83 mi west of Miami.*

Ignore the Circle K and BNP gas stations on the main road into town, and the setting is perfect Old Florida. No high-rises mar the landscape at this western gateway to Everglades National Park, just off the Tamiami Trail. It was developed in the late 19th century by Barron Collier, a wealthy advertising man. When Collier built a company town to house workers for his numerous projects, including construction of the Tamiami Trail, the town grew and prospered until the Depression and World War II, and in 1953 it changed its name to Everglades City. Today it draws visitors to the park for canoeing, fishing, and bird-watching excursions. (Airboat tours, though popular with visitors, are banned within the preserve and park because of the environmental damage they cause to the mangroves. They are not recommended even outside the park in this area because operators feed wildlife dog biscuits and marshmallows to attract the alligators to the boats.) The annual Seafood Festival, held the first weekend of February, attracts 60,000–75,000 visitors to eat seafood, hear nonstop music, and buy crafts.

Dining choices are limited to a few basic eateries. For fine food drive west to Naples. In the past year, several dockside fish markets opened small restaurants inside and outside along the docks. It's best to avoid most of these because of poor food-handling practices.

Gulf Coast Visitor Center. There's no better place to find information about the park's watery western side than this visitor center. Except during the off-season, it's filled with canoeists checking in for trips to the 10,000 Islands and 99-mi Wilderness Waterway Trail, visitors viewing interpretive exhibits about local flora and fauna while they wait for the departure of a naturalist-led boat trip, rangers answering questions, and backcountry campers purchasing permits. There are no roads from here to other sections of the park. ⊠ *Rte. 29,* ☎ *941/695–3311.* 🎫 *Park free.* ☉ *Mid-Nov.–mid-Apr., daily 7:30–5; mid-Apr.–mid-Nov., daily 8:30–4:30.*

Museum of the Everglades. Through artifacts and photographs, you can meet the Native Americans, pioneers, businessmen, and fishermen who played a role in the development of southwest Florida at this museum that chronicles the 2,000-year history of human habitation in the southwestern Everglades. It's in the only remaining unaltered structure original to the town of Everglades, where it opened in 1927 as the town's laundry. In addition to the permanent displays, there are traveling exhibits, lectures, and works by local artists. The building is on the National Register of Historic Places. ⊠ *105 W. Broadway,* ☎ *941/695–0008.* 🎫 *$2.* ☉ *Tues.–Sat. 10–4.*

OFF THE BEATEN PATH

SMALLWOOD'S STORE – Ted Smallwood pioneered this last American frontier in 1906 and built a 3,000-square-ft pine trading post raised on pilings in Chokoloskee Bay. Smallwood's granddaughter Lynn McMillin reopened it in 1989, after it had been closed several years, and installed a small gift shop and museum chock-full of original goods from the store; historic photographs; Native American clothing, furs, and hides; and area memorabilia. In March an annual festival celebrates the nearly 100-year relationship the store has had with local Native Americans. ⊠ *360 Mamie St., Chokoloskee Island,* ☎ *941/695–2989.* 🎫 *$2.50.* ☉ *Dec.–Apr., daily 10–5; May–Nov., daily 11–5.*

Dining and Lodging

$$–$$$ ✕ **Rod and Gun Club.** The striking polished woodwork in this historic building dates from the 1920s, when wealthy hunters, anglers, and yachting parties from around the world came for the winter season. The main dining room primarily holds the overflow from the popular enormous screened porch that overlooks the river. Slow service is a problem; the quality of food is not. Fresh seafood dominates a menu that includes stone crab claws in season, a turf-and-surf combo of steak and shrimp, a swamp-and-turf combo of frogs' legs and steak, and several seafood and pasta pairings. You can come by boat or land. ⊠ *200 Riverside Dr.,* ☎ *941/695–2101. No credit cards.*

$$ ✕ **Everglades Fish Company.** Every day during stone crab season (October–May) locals, and a growing number of visitors, stop by this fish market to buy the fresh, succulent claws. Pick up a hammer for an extra dollar and take them to your hotel room or the nearby city park for a picnic. There's no debate that these are the best in town. They also ship, but the cost is outrageous. It's much more affordable to have them pack some in a travel cooler to take home. When crab season is over, raw fish and raw and cooked shrimp are for sale. ⊠ *208 Camellia St.,* ☎ *941/695–3241 or 888/695–2208. MC, V.*

$$ ✕ **Everglades Seafood Depot.** This 1928 Spanish-style stucco structure on Lake Placid has had many lives. It began as the old Everglades depot,

was part of the University of Miami, appeared in the film *Winds Across the Everglades*, and has housed several restaurants. Today's menu has well-prepared seafood—from shrimp and grouper to frogs' legs and alligator. The staff is slow, but eager to please. For big appetites there are generously portioned entrées of steak and fish specials that include soup or salad, potato or rice, and warm, fresh-baked biscuits. ⊠ *102 Collier Ave.,* ☎ *941/695–0075. AE, D, MC, V.*

\$\$ ✕ **Oar House Restaurant.** Locals line up outside on Friday nights for \$12.95 prime rib in this wood-paneled eatery whose picnic table–style booths and mishmash of kitschy fishing and Glades decor give it the ambience of a diner. The menu has a blend of simple seafood and such local specialties as frogs' legs, turtle, conch, and gator. To its credit, the service is friendly, prices are very reasonable, the food is fried in canola and corn oils, and most dishes can be grilled or broiled, if you prefer. It's popular for country-style breakfasts. ⊠ *305 Collier Ave.,* ☎ *941/695–3535. AE, D, MC, V.*

\$\$ 🏨 **Ivey House.** A remodeled 1928 boardinghouse originally for workers building the Tamiami Trail, the Ivey House today fits many budgets. One part is a friendly B&B bargain with shared baths. The inn, connected by a ramp, has rooms with private baths. Most inn rooms surround the screen-enclosed pool and courtyard. The layout is designed to promote camaraderie, but there are secluded patios with chairs and tables for private moments. The Ivey House is run by the owners of Everglades Rentals & Eco Adventures, so you can stay here before or after the ecotours and save 20% on canoe and kayak rentals. ⊠ *107 Camellia St., 34139,* ☎ *941/695–3299,* ℻ *941/695–4155,* 🌐 *www.iveyhouse.com. 27 rooms, 17 with bath, 1 2-bedroom cottage. Restaurant, in-room data ports, some refrigerators, some cable TVs, wading pool, boating, bicycles, library, shop, laundry facilities, no smoking. MC, V.*

\$\$ 🏨 **On the Banks of the Everglades.** The owners drew upon the building's former use as a bank built in 1923 to develop this pleasant B&B lodge. Spacious rooms, suites, and efficiencies have queen- or king-size beds and stylish coordinating linens, wall coverings, and draperies. Suites and efficiencies have private baths and kitchens (the staff does the dishes). A complimentary full breakfast, including freshly baked breads and muffins, is served in the bank's vault and outside deck. Free tennis rackets are provided for use on the public courts next door. ⊠ *201 W. Broadway, Box 570, 34139,* ☎ *941/695–3151 or 888/431–1977,* ℻ *941/695–3335,* 🌐 *www.banksoftheeverglades.com. 9 units, 6 with bath. Some kitchens, some kitchenettes, cable TV, bicycles, library, shop; no room phones, no smoking. AE, D, MC, V. Closed Dec. 23–25.*

\$ 🏨 **Outdoor Resorts.** This clean, amenity-rich RV resort, set on the water's edge of secluded Chokoloskee Island, has sunny sites with concrete pads. Tropical vegetation adds shade and color. All sites have a view. Some are along the shore; others have dockage. Retirees escape the icy northern winters for outdoor fun here with boat rentals, tennis and shuffleboard, and a marina and bait shop. A recreation hall and health spa help while the hours away on rainy days. There's a motel with two double-bed efficiency rooms for those who come without an RV. ⊠ *Rte. 29, 6 mi south of Tamiami Trail, Box 429, Chokoloskee Island, 34138,* ☎ *941/695–3788. 283 sites. 3 pools, shop, laundry facilities. MC, V.*

Outdoor Activities and Sports

BIKING

Everglades Rentals & Eco Adventures (⊠ Ivey House, 107 Camellia St., ☎ 941/695–4666), formerly North American Canoe Tours, rents bikes for \$3 per hour (free for Ivey House guests).

BOATING

Glades Haven Marina (⊠ 801 S. Copeland Ave., ☎ 941/695–2579) can put you on the water to explore the 10,000 Islands in everything from 16-ft Carolina skiffs and pontoon boats to 19-ft sailfish. Rates start at $110 a day, with multiday discounts and a half-day option. They also rent kayaks and canoes.

CANOEING AND KAYAKING

Everglades National Park Boat Tours (⊠ Gulf Coast Visitor Center, ☎ 941/695–2591; 800/445–7724 in FL) rents 17-ft Grumman canoes for day and overnight use. Rates are $24 per day. Car shuttle service is provided for canoeists paddling the Wilderness Trail, and travelers with disabilities can be accommodated. **Everglades Rentals & Eco Adventures** (⊠ Ivey House, 107 Camellia St., ☎ 941/695–4666) is an established source for canoes, sea kayaks, and guided Everglades trips (November–April). Canoes cost from $32 the first day, $25 for each day thereafter, and kayaks are from $35 per day. Half-day rentals are available.

GATEWAY TOWNS

The farm towns of Homestead and Florida City, flanked by Everglades National Park on the west and Biscayne National Park to the east, provide the closest visitor facilities to the parks. (The area's better restaurants are in Homestead, but the best lodgings are in Florida City.) The towns date from early in the 20th century, when Henry Flagler extended his railroad to Key West but soon decided that farming would do more for rail revenues than ferrying passengers.

Homestead

⑬ *30 mi southwest of Miami.*

When Hurricane Andrew tore across South Florida in 1992, with winds approaching 200 mph, it ripped apart lives and the small community of Homestead. The city rebuilt itself, redefining its role as the "Gateway to the Keys" and attracting hotel chains, a shopping center, sports complex, and residential development. The historic downtown area has become a preservation-driven Main Street city. Krome Avenue (Route 997), which cuts through the city's heart, is lined with restaurants and antiques shops.

West of north–south Krome Avenue, miles of fields grow fresh fruits and vegetables. Some are harvested commercially. Others have U-PICK signs, inviting you to harvest your own. Stands that sell farm-fresh produce and nurseries that grow and sell orchids and tropical plants abound.

In addition to its agricultural legacy, the town has an eclectic flavor, attributable to its population mix: descendants of pioneer Crackers, Hispanic growers, and farmworkers as well as latter-day northern retirees. Until Hurricane Andrew, the military had a huge presence at Homestead Air Force Base. The economy still suffers from its loss.

Homestead Bayfront Park. With a saltwater atoll pool that's flushed by tidal action, the park, adjacent to Biscayne National Park, is popular among local families as well as anglers and boaters. Highlights include a playground, ramps for people with disabilities (including a ramp that leads into the swimming area), and a picnic pavilion with grills, showers, and rest rooms. ⊠ *9698 S.W. 328th St.,* ☎ *305/230–*

3034. ◨ *$4 per passenger vehicle, $8 per vehicle with boat, $8 per RV.* ☉ *Sunrise–sunset.*

Dining and Lodging

$–$$ ✕ **El Toro Taco.** This family-run area institution has a rustic atmosphere,
★   good Mexican food in generous servings, homemade tortilla chips
(sometimes a little greasy), and friendly service. Selections range from
tasty favorites like fajitas, enchiladas, tamales, and burritos to more
traditional Mexican dishes like *mole de pollo,* which combines unsweet-
ened chocolate and Mexican spices with chicken. Desserts include *tres
leches* (a cake soaked in a syrup of three types of milk—evaporated,
sweetened condensed, and heavy cream) and flan. You can order spicing from mild to tongue-challenging. The restaurant is also open for
breakfast. ⊠ *1 S. Krome Ave.,* ☎ *305/245–8182. D, MC, V. BYOB.*

$ ✕ **Tiffany's.** A large banyan tree shades this casual restaurant deco-
rated in frilly nouveau Victorian style, with teaberry-color tablecloths
and floral place mats. The room is quaint but noisy. The lunch menu
includes crabmeat au gratin, asparagus rolled in ham with hollandaise
sauce, shrimp- and egg-salad sandwiches on fresh-baked croissants, and
the most popular dish, quiche made daily. Among the homemade
desserts, choose from a very tall carrot cake, strawberry whipped-cream
cake, and a harvest pie that has layers of apples, cranberries, walnuts,
raisins, and a caramel topping. Sunday brunch is served, too. ⊠ *22
N.E. 15th St.,* ☎ *305/246–0022. MC, V. Closed Mon. No dinner.*

$$ ⊞ **Redland Hotel.** When it opened in 1904, the inn was the town's first
hotel. It later became the first mercantile store, the first U.S. Post Of-
fice, the first library, and the first boardinghouse. Today, each room
has a different layout and furnishings and some have access to a shared
balcony, perfect for gatherings. The style is Victorian, with lots of pas-
tels and reproduction antique furniture. There are good restaurants and
antiques shops nearby. However, the pub and dining room are fast be-
coming popular with locals. The neighborhood is slowly being re-
stored and gentrified. ⊠ *5 S. Flagler Ave., 33030,* ☎ *305/246–1904,*
WEB *www.redlandhotel.com. 13 units. Restaurant, room service, fans,
in-room data ports, cable TV, in-room VCRs, pub, meeting rooms; no-
smoking rooms. AE, D, DC, MC, V.*

Outdoor Activities and Sports

AUTO RACING

The **Miami-Dade Homestead Motorsports Complex** (⊠ 1 Speedway Blvd.,
33035, ☎ 305/230–7223) is a state-of-the-art facility with two tracks:
a 2.21-mi continuous road course and a 1.5-mi oval. There's a sched-
ule of year-round manufacturer and race-team testing, club racing, and
other national events.

BOATING

Boaters give high ratings to the facilities at **Homestead Bayfront Park.**
The 174-slip marina has a ramp, dock, bait-and-tackle shop, fuel sta-
tion, ice, dry storage, and boat hoist, which can handle vessels up to
25 ft long with lifting rings. The park also has a tidal swimming area.
⊠ *9698 S.W. 328th St.,* ☎ *305/230–3033.* ◨ *$4 per passenger vehi-
cle, $8 per vehicle with boat, $8 per RV, $10 hoist.* ☉ *Sunrise–sunset.*

Shopping

In addition to Homestead Boulevard (U.S. 1) and Campbell Drive
(Southwest 312th Street and Northeast 8th Street), **Krome Avenue** is
popular for shopping. In the heart of old Homestead, it has a brick
sidewalk and many antiques stores.

Florida City

🅐 *2 mi southwest of Homestead.*

Florida's Turnpike ends in this southernmost town on the peninsula, spilling thousands onto U.S. 1 and eventually west to Everglades National Park, east to Biscayne National Park, or south to the Florida Keys. As the last civilization before 18 mi of mangroves and water, this stretch of U.S. 1 is lined with fast-food eateries, service stations, hotels, bars, dive shops, and restaurants.

Like Homestead, Florida City has roots planted in agriculture, as shown by the hundreds of acres of farmland west of Krome Avenue and a huge farmers' market that processes produce to be shipped around the country.

Dining and Lodging

$$–$$$ ✕ **Mutineer Restaurant.** This roadside steak and seafood restaurant with an indoor-outdoor fish and duck pond was built in 1980, back when Florida City was barely on the map. Etched glass divides the bilevel dining rooms, where striped-velvet chairs, stained glass, and a few portholes set the scene; in the lounge are an aquarium and nautical antiques. The big menu offers 18 seafood entrées plus another half dozen daily seafood specials, as well as game, ribs, and steaks. There's live music Friday and Saturday evenings. ✉ *11 S.E. 1st Ave. (U.S. 1 and Palm Dr.),* ☎ *305/245–3377. AE, D, DC, MC, V.*

$$ ✕ **Richard Accursio's Capri Restaurant and King Richard's Room.** Lo-
★ cals have been dining here—one of the oldest family-run restaurants in Miami-Dade County—since 1958. Outside it's a nondescript building with a big parking lot. The interior has dark-wood paneling and heavy wooden furniture. The tasty fare ranges from pizza with light, crunchy crusts and ample toppings to mild, meaty conch chowder. Mussels come in garlic or marinara sauce, and the yellowtail snapper *française* is a worthy selection. Early-bird entrées are offered 4:30–6:30 for $10.95, including soup or salad and potato or spaghetti. ✉ *935 N. Krome Ave.,* ☎ *305/247–1544. AE, MC, V. Closed Sun.*

$–$$ ✕ **Farmers' Market Restaurant.** Although it's in the farmers' market and serves fresh vegetables, this restaurant's specialty is seafood. A family of fishermen runs the place, so fish and shellfish are only hours from the sea. Catering to the fishing and farming crowd, it opens at 5:30 AM, serving pancakes, jumbo eggs, and fluffy omelets with home fries or grits. The lunch and dinner menus have shrimp, fish, steaks, and conch baskets, as well as burgers, salads, and sandwiches. Normally the fish comes fried, but you can ask for it broiled or grilled. ✉ *300 N. Krome Ave.,* ☎ *305/242–0008. No credit cards.*

$$ 🏨 **Best Western Gateway to the Keys.** If you want easy access to Everglades and Biscayne national parks as well as the Florida Keys, you'll be well situated at this two-story motel. All rooms are decorated in tropical colors and have coffeemakers. Standard rooms have two queen-size beds or one king-size bed. More expensive rooms also have a wet bar, refrigerator, and microwave. ✉ *411 S. Krome Ave., 33034,* ☎ *305/ 246–5100,* 🄵🄰🄇 *305/242–0056. 114 units. In-room data ports, some microwaves, some refrigerators, cable TV, pool, hot tub, laundry service, meeting rooms, no smoking. AE, D, DC, MC, V. CP.*

$$ 🏨 **Hampton Inn.** Racing fans can hear the engines roar from this two-story motel next to an outlet mall and within 15 minutes of the raceway and Everglades and Biscayne national parks. Carpeted rooms are bright and clean and have upholstered chairs, coffeemaker, and an iron and ironing board. Included free are a Continental breakfast and local calls. ✉ *124 E. Palm Dr., 33034,* ☎ *305/247–8833 or 800/426–7866,*

FAX 305/247–6456. *123 units. Some refrigerators, cable TV with movies, pool, laundry service; no-smoking rooms. AE, D, DC, MC, V.*

Shopping

Prime Outlets at Florida City (⊠ 250 E. Palm Dr.) has more than 50 discount stores plus a small food court. **Robert Is Here** (⊠ 19200 Palm Dr. [S.W. 344th St.], ☎ 305/246–1592), a remarkable fruit stand, sells vegetables, fresh-fruit milk shakes, 10 flavors of honey, more than 100 flavors of jams and jellies, fresh juices, salad dressings, and some 40 kinds of tropical fruits, including carambola, litchi, egg fruit, monstera, sapodilla, soursop, sugar apple, and tamarind. The stand started in 1960, when six-year-old Robert sat at this spot selling his father's bumper crop of cucumbers. Now Robert ships around the world, and everything is first quality. Seconds are given to needy area families. The stand opens at 8 and never closes earlier than 7.

BISCAYNE NATIONAL PARK

Occupying 180,000 acres along the southern portion of Biscayne Bay, south of Miami and north of the Florida Keys, this national park is 96% underwater, and its altitude ranges from 4 ft above sea level to 10 fathoms, or 60 ft, below. Contained within it are four distinct zones, which from shore to sea are mangrove forest along the coast, Biscayne Bay, the undeveloped upper Florida Keys, and coral reefs.

Mangroves line the mainland shore much as they do elsewhere in South Florida. Biscayne Bay functions as a lobster sanctuary and a nursery for fish, sponges, and crabs. Manatees and sea turtles frequent its warm, shallow waters. Lamentably, the bay is under assault from forces similar to those in Florida Bay.

To the east, about 8 mi off the coast, lie 44 tiny keys, stretching 18 nautical mi north–south and accessible only by boat. There is no commercial transportation between the mainland and the islands, and only a handful can be visited: Elliott, Boca Chita, Adams, and Sands keys. The rest are either wildlife refuges or too small, or have rocky shores or waters too shallow for boats. It's best to explore the Keys between December and April, when the mosquito population is relatively quiescent. Bring repellent just in case. Diving is best in the summer, when calmer wind and smaller seas result in clearer waters.

Another 3 mi east of the Keys, in the ocean, lies the park's main attraction—the northernmost section of Florida's living tropical coral reefs. Some are the size of a student's desk, others as large as a football field. You can take a glass-bottom boat ride to see this underwater wonderland, but you really have to snorkel or scuba dive to appreciate it fully. A diverse population of colorful fish—angelfish, gobies, grunts, parrot fish, pork fish, wrasses, and many more—flits through the reefs. Shipwrecks from the 18th century are evidence of the area's international maritime heritage. A Native American midden (shell mound) dating from AD 1000 and Boca Chita Key, listed on the National Register of Historic Places for its 10 historic structures, illustrate the park's rich cultural heritage.

More than 170 species of birds have been seen around the park. Although all the Keys offer excellent birding opportunities, Jones Lagoon, south of Adams Key, between Old Rhodes Key and Totten Key, is one of the best. It's approachable only by nonmotorized craft.

Convoy Point

⑮ *9 mi east of Florida City, 30 mi south of downtown Miami.*

Dante Fascell Visitor Center. Reminiscent of area pioneer homes, this wooden building with a metal roof has a wide veranda from which you can look out across mangroves and Biscayne Bay and see the Miami skyline. Inside is a museum, where hands-on and historical exhibits and videos explore the park's four ecosystems. Among the facilities are a 50-seat auditorium, the park's canoe and tour concessionaire, rest rooms with showers, a ranger information area, and gift shop. The latter also sells packaged sandwiches and snacks. A short trail and boardwalk lead to a jetty and launch ramp. This is the only area of the park accessible without a boat. ☒ *9700 S.W. 328th St., Homestead,* ☎ *305/230–7275,* WEB *www.nps.gov/bisc.* ☒ *Free.* ☉ *Daily 8:30–5.*

Outdoor Activities and Sports

CANOEING

Biscayne National Underwater Park, Inc. (☒ Convoy Point Visitor Center, Box 1270, Homestead 33090, ☎ 305/230–1100), the park's official concessionaire, has half a dozen canoes and kayaks for rent on a first-come, first-served basis. Canoe prices are $8 an hour, kayaks $16 an hour. Half-day rates are also available.

SCUBA DIVING AND SNORKELING

Biscayne National Underwater Park, Inc. (☒ Convoy Point Visitor Center, Box 1270, Homestead 33090, ☎ 305/230–1100) rents equipment and conducts snorkel and dive trips aboard the 45-ft *Boca Chita.* Three-hour snorkel trips ($29.95) leave twice a day on weekdays, once a day on weekends and include mask, fins, snorkel, vest, and instruction. About half the time is spent on the reef and wrecks. Two-tank scuba trips to shallow reefs depart at 8:30 AM or 1 PM on Friday–Saturday, with a wall dive for advanced divers on Sunday at the same times and cost $45, tanks and weights included. Additional trips are offered in winter. Complete gear rental and instruction are available. Even with a reservation (recommended), you should arrive one hour before departure to sign up for gear.

Elliott Key

⑯ *9 mi east of Convoy Point.*

This key, accessible only by boat (on your own or by special arrangement with the concessionaire), has a rebuilt boardwalk made from recycled plastic and two nature trails with tropical plant life. Take an informal, ranger-led nature walk or walk its 7-mi length on your own along a rough path through a hammock. Videos shown at the ranger station describe the island. Facilities include rest rooms, picnic tables, fresh drinking water, showers (cold), grills, and a campground. Pets are allowed on the island but not on trails.

A 30-ft-wide sandy beach about a mile north of the harbor on the west (bay) side of the key is the only one in the national park. Boaters like to anchor off it to swim. For day use only, it has picnic areas and a short trail that follows the shore and cuts through the hammock.

Boca Chita Key

⑰ *10 mi northeast of Convoy Point.*

This island was once owned by Mark C. Honeywell, former president of Minneapolis's Honeywell Company. A half-mile hiking trail curves around the south side of the island. Climb the 65-ft ornamental light-house for a panoramic view of Miami and surrounding waters. There is no fresh water, but grills, picnic tables, campsites, and saltwater rest rooms are available. Access is by private boat only. No pets are allowed.

Adams Key

⑱ *9 mi southeast of Convoy Point.*

This small key, a stone's throw off the western tip of Elliott Key, is open for day use and has picnic areas, rest rooms, dockage, and a short trail that runs along the shore and through a hardwood hammock. Access is by private boat.

Lodging

$ ⚠ Biscayne National Park. Although Elliott Key's campsites are listed as primitive, there are rest-room facilities nearby. Just bring plenty of insect repellent. Boca Chita Key has a grassy, waterside campground with grills, picnic tables, and toilets, but no running water. There is no regular ferry service or boat rental. However, the park concessionaire's snorkel boat provides drop-off and pick-up service to campers ($24.95 round-trip). Reservations are required. ✉ *9700 S.W. 328th St., Home-stead 33090,* ☎ *305/230–7275,* WEB *www.nps.gov/bisc. Elliott Key 40 sites, Boca Chica Key 39 sites. No credit cards.*

BIG CYPRESS NATIONAL PRESERVE

Through the 1950s and early 1960s, the world's largest cypress-logging industry prospered in the Big Cypress Swamp. The industry died out in the 1960s, and the government began buying parcels. Today, 729,000 acres, or nearly half of the swamp, has become this national preserve.

The word "big" in its name refers not to the size of the trees, but to the swamp, which juts down into the north side of Everglades National Park like a piece in a jigsaw puzzle. Its size and strategic location make it an important link in the region's hydrological system, in which rain-water first flows through the preserve, then south into the park, and eventually into Florida Bay.

Its variegated pattern of wet prairies, ponds, marshes, sloughs, and strands provides a sanctuary for a variety of wildlife, and because of a politically dictated policy of balanced land use—"use without abuse"—the watery wilderness is devoted to research and recreation as well as preservation. The preserve allows—in limited areas—hunting, off-road vehicle (airboat, swamp buggy) use by permit, and cattle grazing.

Compared with Everglades National Park, the preserve is less developed and has fewer visitors. That makes it ideal for naturalists, birders, and hikers who prefer to see more wildlife than humans. Roadside picnic areas are located off the Tamiami Trail.

There are two types of trails—walking and canoeing; neither is interpretive. Both trail types are easily accessed from the Tamiami Trail near the preserve's visitor center. Equipment can be rented from outfitters in Everglades City, 24 mi west, and Naples, 40 mi west.

Projects on the drawing board for completion in the next few years include several boardwalks and interpretive trails through the preserve.

Oasis Visitor Center

24 mi east of Everglades City, 50 mi west of Miami, 20 mi west of Shark Valley.

9 **Oasis Visitor Center.** The center is a welcome respite along the Tamiami Trail, so slow down. If you speed past on the way between Miami
and Naples, you'll miss out on an opportunity to learn about the surrounding Big Cypress National Preserve. Inside are a small exhibit area,
an information center, a bookshop, a theater that shows a 15-minute
film on the preserve and Big Cypress Swamp, and rest rooms. It also
has myriad seasonal ranger-led and self-guided activities, such as camp-
fire talks, bike hikes, slough slogs, and canoe excursions. The 8-mi Turner
River Canoe Trail begins here and crosses through Everglades National
Park before ending in Chokoloskee Bay, near Everglades City. Hikers
can join the Florida National Scenic Trail, which runs north–south
through the preserve for 31 mi. Two 5-mi trails, Concho Billy and Fire
Prairie, can be accessed a few miles east off Turner River Road. Turner
River Road and Birdon Road form a 17-mi gravel loop drive that is
excellent for birding. All of the trails can be very wet and possibly im-
passable during the rainy season. Rangers at the visitor center provide
road-condition information. Five primitive campsites are available on
a first-come, first-served basis. ✉ *24 mi east of Everglades City, 50 mi
west of Miami, 20 mi west of Shark Valley,* ☎ *941/695–4111.* ☞ *Free.*
☺ *Daily 8:30–4:30.*

Lodging

$ ⛺ **Big Cypress National Preserve.** There are four no-fee primitive
campgrounds within the preserve along the Tamiami Trail and Loop
Road. A fifth site, Monument Lake Campground, has rest rooms, an
amphitheater, and activities and seasonal programs (December–mid-
April). The fee is $14 a night for tents and RVs at Monument Lake.
Dona Drive Campground has a dump station ($4) and potable water.
✉ *Tamiami Trail (Hwy. 41), between Miami and Naples (HCR 61, Box
110, Ochopee, FL 34141),* ☎ *941/695–4111,* WEB *www.nps.gov/bicy.*
No credit cards.

THE EVERGLADES A TO Z

*To research prices, get advice from other travelers, and book travel ar-
rangements, visit www.fodors.com.*

AIRPORTS

Miami International Airport (MIA) is 34 mi from Homestead and 83
mi from Flamingo in Everglades National Park.

Airporter runs shuttle buses three times daily that stop at the Hampton Inn in Florida City on their way between MIA and the Florida Keys.
Shuttle service, which takes about an hour, runs 6:10–5:20 from Florida
City, 7:30–6 from the airport. Reserve in advance. Pickups can be arranged for all baggage-claim areas. The cost is $25 one-way.

Greyhound Lines buses from MIA to the Keys make a stop in Homestead four times a day. Buses leave from Concourse E, lower level, and
cost from $8.50 one-way, from $16.50 round-trip.

SuperShuttle operates 11-passenger air-conditioned vans to Homestead. Service from MIA is available around the clock; booths are outside most luggage areas on the lower level. For the return to MIA, reserve
24 hours in advance. The one-way cost is $43 per person for the first
person, $14 for each additional person at the same address.
➤ AIRPORT INFORMATION: **Miami International Airport** (☎ 305/876–
7000). **Airporter** (☎ 800/830–3413). **Greyhound Lines** (☎ 800/231–
2222; Homestead: ✉ 5 N.E. 3rd Rd., ☎ 305/247–2040). **SuperShuttle** (☎ 305/871–2000 or 800/874–8885).

BOAT TRAVEL

If you're entering the United States by pleasure boat, you must phone U.S. Customs either from a marine phone or upon first arriving ashore.

Bring aboard the proper NOAA nautical charts before you cast off to explore park waters. The charts run $17 at many marine stores in South Florida, at the Convoy Point Visitor Center in Biscayne National Park, and at Flamingo Marina in the Everglades.

The annual *Waterway Guide* (southern regional edition) is widely used by boaters. Bookstores all over South Florida sell it, or you can order it directly from the publisher for $39.95 plus $5 shipping and handling.

➤ BOAT INFORMATION: **U.S. Customs** (☎ 800/432–1216). *Waterway Guide* (✉ Primedia Business, Book Department, Box 12901, Overland Park, KS 66282-2901, ☎ 800/233–3359).

BUS TRAVEL

The Dade-Monroe Express provides daily bus service from the Florida City Wal-Mart Supercenter to Mile Marker 98 in Key Largo. The bus makes several stops in Florida City, then heads for the islands for daily round-trips on the hour from 6 AM to 10 PM. The cost is $1.50 each way.

➤ BUS INFORMATION: **Dade-Monroe Express** (☎ 305/770–3131).

CAR RENTAL

Agencies in the area include A&A Auto Rental, Budget, and Enterprise Rent-a-Car.

➤ LOCAL AGENCIES: **A&A Auto Rental** (✉ 30005 S. Dixie Hwy., Homestead 33030, ☎ 305/246–0974). **Budget** (✉ 29949 S. Dixie Hwy., Homestead 33030, ☎ 305/248–4524 or 800/527–0700). **Enterprise Rent-a-Car** (✉ 29130 S. Dixie Hwy., Homestead 33030, ☎ 305/246–2056 or 800/736–8222).

CAR TRAVEL

From Miami the main highways to the area are U.S. 1, the Homestead Extension of Florida's Turnpike, and Krome Avenue (Route 997 [old U.S. 27]).

To reach Everglades National Park's Ernest F. Coe Visitor Center and Flamingo, head west on Route 9336 in Florida City and follow signs. From Homestead the Ernest F. Coe Visitor Center is 11 mi; Flamingo is 49 mi. The north entrance of Everglades National Park at Shark Valley is reached by taking the Tamiami Trail about 20 mi west of Krome Avenue. To reach the west entrance of Everglades National Park at the Gulf Coast Visitor Center in Everglades City, take Route 29 south from the Tamiami Trail. To reach Biscayne National Park from Homestead, take U.S. 1 or Krome Avenue to Lucy Street (Southeast 8th Street) and turn east. Lucy Street becomes North Canal Drive (Southwest 328th Street). Follow signs for about 8 mi to the park headquarters.

EMERGENCIES

Dial 911 for police, fire, or ambulance. In the national parks, rangers answer police, fire, and medical emergencies. The Florida Fish and Wildlife Conservation Commission, a division of the Florida Department of Natural Resources, maintains a 24-hour telephone service for reporting boating emergencies and natural-resource violations. The Miami Beach Coast Guard Base responds to local marine emergencies and reports of navigation hazards. The base broadcasts on VHF-FM Channel 16. The National Weather Service supplies local forecasts.

> CONTACTS: **Hospital emergency line** (☎ 305/596–6556). **Home-stead Hospital** (✉ 160 N.W. 13th St., Homestead, ☎ 305/248–3232; 305/596–6557 physician referral). **Florida Fish and Wildlife Conservation Commission** (☎ 305/956–2500). **Miami Beach Coast Guard Base** (✉ 100 MacArthur Causeway, Miami Beach, ☎ 305/535–4300 or 305/535–4314). **National Parks–Biscayne unit** (☎ 305/247–7272). **National Parks–Everglades unit** (☎ 305/247–7272). **National Weather Service** (☎ 305/229–4522).

ENGLISH-LANGUAGE MEDIA

NEWSPAPERS AND MAGAZINES

The *South Dade News Leader* is published thrice weekly.

TELEVISION AND RADIO

WRLN (National Public Radio) 91.3, 92.1, or 93.5, depending on your location; WLVE (easy listening) 93.9; WFLC (pop) 97.3.

TAXIS

South Dade Taxi has cabs that service the area.
> TAXI INFORMATION: **South Dade Taxi** (☎ 305/256–4444).

TOURS

The National Park Service organizes a range of free programs, typically focusing on native wildlife, plants, and park history. At Biscayne National Park, for example, rangers give informal tours of Elliott and Boca Chita keys, which you can arrange in advance, depending on ranger availability. Contact the respective visitor center for details.

10,000 Islands Aero-Tours operates scenic, low-level flight tours of the 10,000 Islands, Big Cypress National Preserve, Everglades National Park, and the Gulf of Mexico in a Cessna 170. On the 20- to 60-minute flights you can see saw-grass prairies, Native American shell mounds, alligators, and wading birds. Prices start at $30. For an all-day outing, opt for flights across the gulf to the Florida Keys in a float plane.

Wooten's Everglades Airboat Tours runs airboat and swamp-buggy tours ($17) through the Everglades. (Swamp buggies are giant tractor-like vehicles with oversize rubber wheels.) Tours last approximately 30 minutes.

Southwest of Florida City near the entrance to Everglades National Park, Everglades Alligator Farm runs a 4-mi, 30-minute tour of the River of Grass with departures 20 minutes after the hour. The tour ($14.50) includes a free hourly alligator, snake, or wildlife show, or you can take in the show only ($9).

From the Shark Valley area, Buffalo Tiger's Florida Everglades Airboat Ride is led by a former chairman of the Miccosukee tribe. The 35- to 40-minute trip includes a stop at an old Native American camp. Tours cost $10 and operate 10–5 daily, except Friday. Reservations are not required. Coopertown Airboat Ride operates the oldest airboat rides in the Everglades (since 1945). The 30- to 40-minute tour ($14) visits two hammocks and alligator holes. Everglades Gator Park offers 45-minute narrated airboat tours ($14). Everglades Safari Park runs 40-minute airboat rides for $15. The price includes a show and gator tour. The Miccosukee Indian Village 30-minute narrated airboat ride stops off at a 100-year-old family camp in the Everglades to hear tales and allow passengers to walk around and explore ($10) in addition to its other attractions.

When the namesake owner sold Ray Cramer's Everglades Airboat Tours, Inc. to longtime friend Bill Barlow, with whom he had fished, frogged, and hunted in the Everglades since 1949, Bill didn't change anything but the number of trips he offered a day. His two-hour personalized excursions, on airboats accommodating only 6 to 12 passengers, venture 40 mi into the River of Grass. Daytime trips are exciting, but the tour that departs an hour before sundown lets you see birds and fish in daylight and alligators, raccoons, and other nocturnal animals when night falls. The cost is $40 per person. Half-day trips for two to five people cost $275 for the group.

Tours at Biscayne National Park are run by people-friendly Biscayne National Underwater Park, Inc. Daily trips (at 10, with a second trip at 1 during high season, depending on demand) explore the park's living coral reefs 10 mi offshore on *Reef Rover IV,* a 53-ft glass-bottom boat that carries up to 48 passengers. On days when the weather is unsuitable for reef viewing, an alternative three-hour, ranger-led interpretive tour visits Boca Chita Key. Reservations are recommended. The cost is $19.95, and you should arrive at least one hour before departure.

If you're in Everglades National Park, you can climb aboard a six-passenger boat for the four-hour narrated Dolphin Cruise ($39) through the shallow waters of the backcountry. Flamingo Lodge, Marina & Outpost Resort Boat Tours is the official concession authorized to operate sightseeing tours through Everglades National Park. The two-hour backcountry cruise ($16) is the most popular. The boat winds under a heavy canopy of mangroves, revealing abundant wildlife—from alligators, crocodiles, and turtles to herons, hawks, and egrets. A quieter option is the Sailboat Cruise ($18) into Florida Bay that runs mid-December to spring. The 90-minute Florida Bay cruise ($10) ventures into the bay to explore shallow nursery areas and encounter plentiful bird life and often dolphins, sea turtles, and sharks. On the west side, Everglades National Park Boat Tours is the official park concession authorized to operate 1½-hour tours ($16) through the 10,000 Islands region and mangrove wilderness. Boats can accommodate large numbers and wheelchairs (not electric), and one large boat has drink concessions. The 2½-hour Mangrove Wilderness tour ($25) ventures into the shallow waters of the mangrove community, where birds nest and fish have their nurseries, but only when the tide is high enough.

Everglades Rentals & Eco Adventures leads one-day to nine-night Everglades tours November–April. Highlights include bird and gator sightings, mangrove forests, no-man's-land beaches, relics of the hideouts of infamous and just plain reclusive characters, and spectacular sunsets. Included in the cost of extended tours ($250–$1,125) are canoes or kayaks, all necessary equipment, a guide, meals, and lodging for the first night at the Ivey House. There is a four-person minimum. Day trips with a naturalist by kayak, canoe, or powerboat cost $40–$95.

Starting at the Shark Valley visitor center, Shark Valley Tram Tours follows a 15-mi loop road into the interior, stopping at a 50-ft observation tower especially good for viewing gators. Two-hour narrated tours cost $11 and depart hourly 9–4, December to April, the rest of the year they run from 9:30 to 3. Reservations are recommended December–April.

➤ Tours Information: **Biscayne National Underwater Park, Inc.** (✉ Convoy Point, east end of North Canal Dr. [S.W. 328th St.], Box 1270, Homestead 33090, ☎ 305/230–1100). **Buffalo Tiger's Florida Everglades Airboat Ride** (✉ 12 mi west of Krome Ave., 20 mi west of Miami city limits on Tamiami Trail, ☎ 305/559–5250). **Coopertown Airboat Ride** (✉ 5 mi west of Krome Ave. on Tamiami Trail, ☎ 305/226–6048). **Everglades Alligator Farm** (✉ 40351 S.W. 192nd Ave., ☎ 305/247–2628 or 800/644–9711). **Everglades Gator Park** (✉ 12 mi west of Florida's Turnpike on Tamiami Trail, ☎ 305/559–2255 or 800/

559–2205). **Everglades National Park Boat Tours** (✉ Gulf Coast Visitor Center, Everglades City, ☎ 941/695–2591; 800/445–7724 in FL). **Everglades Rentals & Eco Adventures** (✉ Ivey House, 107 Camellia St., Box 5038, Everglades City 34139, ☎ 941/695–3299). **Everglades Safari Park** (✉ 26700 Tamiami Trail, 9 mi west of Krome Ave., ☎ 305/226–6923 or 305/223–3804). **Flamingo Lodge, Marina & Outpost Resort Boat Tours** (✉ 1 Flamingo Lodge Hwy., Flamingo, ☎ 941/695–3101 Ext. 286 or 180). **Miccosukee Indian Village** (✉ 25 mi west of Florida's Turnpike on Tamiami Trail, ☎ 305/223–8380). **Ray Cramer's Everglades Airboat Tours, Inc.** (✉ Coopertown, ☎ 305/852–5339 or 305/221–9888; ✉ mailing address: Box 940082, Miami 33194). **Shark Valley Tram Tours** (✉ Box 1739, Tamiami Station, Miami 33144, ☎ 305/221–8455). **10,000 Islands Aero-Tours** (✉ Everglades Airport, 650 Everglades City Airpark Rd., Box 482, Everglades City 34139, ☎ 941/695–3296). **Wooten's Everglades Airboat Tours** (✉ Wooten's Alligator Farm, 1½ mi east of Rte. 29 on Tamiami Trail, ☎ 941/695–2781 or 800/282–2781).

VISITOR INFORMATION

➤ TOURIST INFORMATION: **Big Cypress National Preserve** (✉ HCR61, Box 11, Ochopee 34141, ☎ 941/695–4111). **Biscayne National Park** Dante Fascell Visitor Center (✉ 9700 S.W. 328th St., Box 1369, Homestead 33090-1369, ☎ 305/230–7275). **Everglades City Chamber of Commerce** (✉ Rte. 29 and Tamiami Trail, Box 130, Everglades City 34139, ☎ 941/695–3941). **Everglades National Park** Ernest F. Coe Visitor Center (✉ 40001 Rte. 9336, Homestead 33034-6733, ☎ 305/242–7700). **Flamingo Visitor Center** (✉ 1 Flamingo Lodge Hwy., Flamingo 33034-6798, ☎ 941/695–2945). **Gulf Coast Visitor Center** (✉ Rte. 29, Everglades City 34139, ☎ 941/695–3311). **Greater Homestead–Florida City Chamber of Commerce** (✉ 43 N. Krome Ave., Homestead 33030, ☎ 305/247–2332). **Tropical Everglades Visitor Association** (✉ 160 U.S. 1, Florida City 33034, ☎ 305/245–9180 or 800/388–9669).

4 FORT LAUDERDALE AND BROWARD COUNTY

From Hollywood north to Fort Lauderdale and beyond, the county's famous beaches are just one of the attractions. Downtowns are being spruced up, and Fort Lauderdale's Arts and Science District draws the culturally minded.

Updated
by Karen
Schlesinger

A COLLEGE STUDENT FROM THE 1960S returning to Fort Lauderdale for a vacation today wouldn't recognize the place. Back then, the Fort Lauderdale beachfront was lined with bars, T-shirt shops, souvenir stores, and fast-food stands, and the downtown area consisted of a single office tower and some government buildings. Now, following an enormous renovation program, the beach is home to up-scale shops and restaurants, including the popular Beach Place retail and dining complex, and downtown growth continues at a rapid pace. The entertainment areas, Las Olas Riverfront and Himmarshee, are thriving; several office towers and luxury apartment buildings have been built; and a major airport expansion and renovation continues.

In the years following World War II, sleepy Fort Lauderdale—with miles of inland waterways—promoted itself as the "Venice of America" and the nation's yachting capital. But in 1960 the film *Where the Boys Are* changed everything. The movie described how college students—upward of 20,000—were beginning to swarm to the city for spring break. By 1985 the 20,000 had mushroomed to 350,000. Hotel owners complained of 12 students to a room, the beachfront was littered with tacky bars, and drug trafficking and petty theft were major problems. So city leaders put in place policies and restrictions designed to encourage students to go elsewhere. They did, and no one seems to miss them.

A major beneficiary is Las Olas Boulevard, whose emergence has been credited with creating a new identity for Fort Lauderdale. It was already famous for its trendy shops, but now the sidewalks aren't rolled up when the sun goes down. Dozens of restaurants have sprung up, and on weekend evenings strollers tour the boulevard, taking in the food, the jazz bands, and the scene. On-street parking on weekends has slowed traffic, and the street has a village atmosphere.

Farther west, along New River, is evidence of Fort Lauderdale's cultural renaissance: the arts and entertainment district and its crown jewel, the Broward Center for the Performing Arts. Still farther west is the county's major-league sports venue, the arena for the National Hockey League's Florida Panthers, in Sunrise.

Of course, what makes Fort Lauderdale and Broward County a major draw for visitors is the beaches. Fort Lauderdale's 2-mi stretch of unobstructed beachfront has been enhanced even further with a sparkling promenade designed for the pleasure of pedestrians rather than cars.

Tying this all together is a transportation system that is relatively hassle free, unusual in congested South Florida. An expressway system connects the city and suburbs and even provides a direct route to the Fort Lauderdale–Hollywood International Airport and Port Everglades. For a slower and more scenic ride to really see this canal-laced city, cruise aboard the water taxi.

None of this was envisioned by Napoleon Bonaparte Broward, Florida's governor from 1905 to 1909, for whom the county was named. His drainage schemes opened much of the marshy Everglades region for farming, ranching, and settling (in retrospect, an environmental disaster). Fort Lauderdale's first known white settler, Charles Lewis, established a plantation along the New River in 1793. But it was for Major William Lauderdale, who built a fort at the river's mouth in 1838 during the Seminole Indian wars, that the city was named.

Incorporated in 1911 with just 175 residents, Fort Lauderdale grew rapidly during the Florida boom of the 1920s. Today its population is 150,000, and its suburbs keep growing—1.6 million live in the county.

New homes, offices, and shopping centers have filled in the gaps between older communities along the coastal ridge. Now they're marching west along Interstate 75, Interstate 595, and State Road 869 (the Sawgrass Expressway). Broward County is blessed with near-ideal weather, with some 3,000 hours of sunshine a year. The average temperature is 66°F–77°F in winter, 84°F in summer. Once a home for retirees, the county today attracts younger, working-age families, many living in such new communities as Weston, southwest of Fort Lauderdale. With a revitalized downtown, many young professionals also are buying aging beachside condominiums as they come on the market, and remodeling them. The area has always been a sane and pleasant place to live. Now it's also becoming one of Florida's most diverse and dynamic places to vacation.

Pleasures and Pastimes

Beaches

The character of the communities behind the miles of Broward County beachfront can change dramatically. For example, in Hallandale the beach is backed by towering condominiums; in Hollywood, by motels and the Broadwalk; and just north of there—blessedly—there's nothing at all.

Dining

Food critics in dining and travel magazines agree that the Greater Fort Lauderdale area offers some of the finest and most varied dining of any U.S. city its size. You can choose from the cuisines of Asia, Europe, or Central and South America—and, of course, good ol' America—and enjoy more than just the food. The ambience, wine, service, and decor can be as varied as the language spoken, and as memorable, too.

CATEGORY	COST*
$$$$	over $30
$$$	$20–$30
$$	$10–$20
$	under $10

*per person for a main course at dinner

Fishing

Four main types of fishing are available in Broward County: bottom or drift-boat fishing from party boats, deep-sea fishing for large sport fish on charters, angling for freshwater game fish, and dropping a line off a pier. For bottom fishing, party boats typically charge between $20 and $22 per person for up to four hours, including rod, reel, and bait. For charters, a half day for as many as six people runs up to $325, six-hour charters up to $495, and full-day charters (eight hours) up to $595. Skipper and crew plus bait and tackle are included. Split parties can be arranged at a cost of about $85 per person for a full day.

Several Broward towns—Dania Beach, Lauderdale-by-the-Sea, Pompano Beach, and Deerfield Beach—have fishing piers that draw anglers for pompano, amberjack, bluefish, snapper, blue runners, snook, mackerel, and Florida lobster.

Golf

More than 50 courses green the landscape in Greater Fort Lauderdale, including famous championship links. Most area courses are inland, in the suburbs west of the city, and there are some great bargains. Off-season (May–October) greens fees start at $15; peak-season (November–April) charges run from $35 to more than $100. Fees can be trimmed by working through Next Day Golf, a local service, and many hotels offer golf packages.

Lodging

All prices are for a standard double room, excluding 6% sales tax (more in some counties) and 1%–4% tourist tax.

CATEGORY	COST
$$$$	over $220
$$$	$140–$220
$$	$80–$140
$	under $80

Scuba Diving

There's good diving within 20 minutes of shore. Among the most popular of the county's 80 dive sites is the 2-mi-wide, 23-mi-long Fort Lauderdale Reef, the product of Florida's most successful artificial reef–building program. More than a dozen houseboats, ships, and oil platforms have been sunk in depths of 10 to 150 ft to provide a habitat for fish and other marine life, as well as to help stabilize beaches. The most famous sunken ship is the 200-ft German freighter *Mercedes,* which was blown onto Palm Beach socialite Mollie Wilmot's pool terrace in a violent Thanksgiving storm in 1984; the ship is now underwater a mile off Fort Lauderdale beach.

Exploring Fort Lauderdale and Broward County

Although most activity centers on Fort Lauderdale, there's plenty to see in other parts of Broward County, to the north, south, and, increasingly, west.

The metro area is laid out in a basic grid system, and only the hundreds of canals and waterways interrupt the straight-line path of the streets and roads. Nomenclature is important here. Streets, roads, courts, and drives run east–west. Avenues, terraces, and ways run north–south. Boulevards can run any which way. Las Olas Boulevard is one of the most important east–west thoroughfares, whereas Route A1A—referred to as Atlantic Boulevard and Ocean Boulevard along some stretches—runs along the north–south oceanfront. These names can be confusing to visitors, as there are separate streets called Atlantic and Ocean in Hollywood and Pompano Beach.

The boulevards, those that are paved and those made of water, give Fort Lauderdale its distinct character. Honeycombed with more than 260 mi of navigable waterways, the city is home port for about 44,000 privately owned boats. You won't see the gondolas you'd find in Venice, but you will see just about every other type of craft imaginable docked beside the thousands of homes and businesses that each have a little piece of waterfront. Visitors can tour the canals via the city's water-taxi system, made up of small motor launches that provide transportation and quick, narrated tours. Larger, multideck touring vessels and motorboat rentals for self-guided tours are other options. The Intracoastal Waterway, a massive canal that parallels Route A1A, is the nautical equivalent of an interstate highway. It runs north–south through the metro area and provides easy access to neighboring beach communities; Deerfield Beach and Pompano Beach lie to the north and Dania and Hollywood lie to the south. All are within a 15-mi radius of the city center.

Great Itineraries

Since most Broward County sights are relatively close to one another, it's easy to pack a lot into very little time, but you will probably need a car. You can catch a lot of the history, the museums, and the shops and bistros in Fort Lauderdale's downtown area and along Las Olas Boulevard, and then if you feel like hitting the beach, just take a 10-minute drive east to the intersection of Las Olas and A1A and you're there. Many of the neighboring suburbs, with attractions of their own, are just north or south of Fort Lauderdale. As a result, you can hit most of the high points in three days, and with seven to 10 days, you can see virtually all of Broward's mainstream charms.

Numbers in the text correspond to numbers in the margin and on the Broward County and Fort Lauderdale maps.

IF YOU HAVE 3 DAYS

With a bigger concentration of hotels, restaurants, and sights to see than its suburban neighbors, ⊞ **Fort Lauderdale** ①–⑪ makes a logical base of operations for any visit. On your first day there see the downtown area, especially Las Olas Boulevard between Southeast Third and Southeast 15th avenues. After enjoying lunch at a sidewalk café, head for the nearby Arts and Science District and the downtown **Riverwalk** ⑤, which you can see at a leisurely pace in half a day. On your second day spend at least some time at the **Fort Lauderdale beachfront** ⑨, shopping when the hot sun drives you off the sand. Tour the canals on the third day, either on a rented boat from one of the various marinas along Route A1A, or via the water taxi or a sightseeing boat, both of which can be boarded all along the Intracoastal Waterway.

IF YOU HAVE 5 DAYS

With additional time you can see more of the beach and the arts district and still work in some outdoor sports—and you'll be more able to rearrange your plans, depending on the weather. On the first day visit the Arts and Science District and the downtown **Riverwalk** ⑤. Set aside the next day for an offshore adventure, perhaps a deep-sea fishing charter or a dive trip to the Fort Lauderdale Reef. On the third day shop, dine, and relax along the **Fort Lauderdale beachfront** ⑨, and at the end of the day, sneak a peek at the Hillsboro Light, at **Lighthouse Point** ⑱. Another good day can be spent at the **Hugh Taylor Birch State Recreation Area** ⑩. Enjoy your fifth day in ⊞ **Hollywood** ⑳, perhaps combining time on the Broadwalk with a visit to the Anne Kolb Nature Center, at West Lake Park.

IF YOU HAVE 7 DAYS

With a full week you have time for a wider variety of attractions, fitting in beach time around other activities. In fact, enjoy any of the county's public beach areas on your first day. The second day can be spent in another favorite pastime—shopping, either at chic shops or at one of the malls. On the next day tour the canals on a sightseeing boat or water taxi. Then shop and dine along Las Olas Boulevard. The fourth day might be devoted to the many museums in downtown Fort Lauderdale and the fifth to an airboat ride at **Sawgrass Recreation Park** ⑭, at the edge of the Everglades. Fort Lauderdale offers plenty of facilities for outdoor recreation; spend the sixth day fishing and picnicking on one of the area's many piers or playing a round at a top golf course. Set aside the seventh day for ⊞ **Hollywood** ⑳, where you can stroll along the scenic Broadwalk or walk through the aviary at Flamingo Gardens, in **Davie** ㉒, before relaxing in peaceful Hollywood North Beach Park.

When to Tour Fort Lauderdale and Broward County

Tourists visit the area all year long, choosing to come in winter or summer, depending on interests, hobbies, and the climate where they live. The winter season, roughly Thanksgiving through March, still sees the biggest influx of visitors and "snowbirds"—seasonal residents who show up when the snow starts to fly up north. Concert, art, and show seasons are at their height then, and restaurants and highways all show the stress of crowds, Americans, Canadians, and Europeans alike.

Summer has its own fans. Waits at even the most popular restaurants are likely to be reasonable or even nonexistent, but although few services close in the summer, some may establish slightly shorter hours than during the peak season. Summer is the rainy season; the tropics-style rain arrives about midafternoon and is usually gone in an hour, but the heat and humidity do not quickly subside and summer seems to linger at a slow and sticky pace.

For golfers, almost anytime is great for playing. As everywhere else, waits for tee times are longer on weekends year-round.

Remember that sun can cause scorching burns all year long, especially at midday, marking the tourist from the experienced resident or vacationer. And if you jump in the water to cool off when the sun is the strongest, the sun reflecting off the water can substantially increase your chance of burning. You might want to plan your beach time for morning and late afternoon and go sightseeing or shopping in between.

FORT LAUDERDALE

Like some southeast Florida neighbors, Fort Lauderdale has been revitalizing itself for several years. What's unusual in a state where gaudy tourist zones stand aloof from workaday downtowns is that the city exhibits consistency at both ends of the 2-mi Las Olas corridor. The sparkling look results from a decision to thoroughly improve both beachfront and downtown, as opposed to focusing design attention in town and letting the beach fall prey to development solely by T-shirt retailers. Matching the downtown's innovative arts district, cafés, and boutiques is an equally inventive beach area with its own share of cafés and shops facing an undeveloped shoreline.

Downtown

The jewel of the downtown area along the New River is the arts and entertainment district. You can see Broadway shows, the Florida Philharmonic, the Florida Grand Opera, and the Miami City Ballet at the riverfront Broward Center for the Performing Arts. Clustered within a five-minute walk are the Museum of Discovery and Science, the expanding Fort Lauderdale Historical Museum, and the Museum of Art. Restaurants, sidewalk cafés, bars, and blues, folk, jazz, reggae, and rock clubs flourish. Las Olas Riverfront is a multistory entertainment, dining, and retail complex along several waterfront blocks once owned by pioneers William and Mary Brickell.

Tying this district together is the Riverwalk, which extends 2 mi along the New River's north and south banks. Tropical gardens with benches and interpretive displays fringe the walk on one side, boat landings on the other. East along Riverwalk is Stranahan House, and a block away Las Olas attractions begin. Tropical landscaping and trees separate the traffic lanes in some blocks, setting off fine shops, restaurants, and popular nightspots. From here it's five minutes by car or 30 minutes by water taxi back to the beach.

A Good Tour

Start on Southeast 6th Avenue at Las Olas Boulevard, where you'll find **Stranahan House** ①, a turn-of-the-last-century structure that's now a museum. Between Southeast 6th and 15th avenues, Las Olas has Spanish colonial buildings housing fashion boutiques, jewelry shops, and art galleries. If you drive east, you'll cross into the Isles, Fort Lauderdale's most prestigious neighborhood, where homes line canals with large yachts beside the seawalls.

Return west on Las Olas to Andrews Avenue, turn right, and park in one of the municipal garages so you can walk around downtown Fort Lauderdale. First stop is the **Museum of Art** ②, which has a major collection of works from the CoBrA (Copenhagen, Brussels, and Amsterdam) movement. Walk one block north to the **Broward County Main Library** ③ to see works from Broward County's Public Art and Design Program.

Go west on Southeast 2nd Street to Southwest 2nd Avenue, turn left, and stop at the **Old Fort Lauderdale Museum of History** ④, which surveys the city's not-so-recent history. Just to the south is the palm-lined **Riverwalk** ⑤, a good place for a leisurely stroll. Head north toward a cluster of facilities collectively known as the Arts and Science District. The district contains the outdoor Esplanade, whose exhibits include a hands-on display of the science and history of navigation, and the major science attraction, the **Museum of Discovery and Science/Blockbuster IMAX Theater** ⑥. The adjacent Broward Center for the Performing Arts, a massive glass-and-concrete structure by the river, is home to Broadway touring shows, Florida Grand Opera, Florida Philharmonic, and Miami City Ballet.

Finally, go west along Las Olas Boulevard to Southwest 7th Avenue and the entrance to **Sailboat Bend** ⑦. You can return to the start of the tour by traveling east along Las Olas Boulevard.

TIMING

Depending on how long you like to linger in museums and how many hours you want to spend in the quaint shops on Las Olas Boulevard, you can spend anywhere from half a day to an entire day on this tour.

Sights to See

❸ **Broward County Main Library.** This distinctive building of Florida limestone with a stepped glass facade was designed by Marcel Breuer to complement the environment. Works are on display here from Broward County's Public Art and Design Program encompassing paintings, sculpture, photographs, and weavings by nationally renowned and Florida artists. A community technology center has personal computers for public use and assistant/adaptive devices for people with special learning and physical disabilities. Productions from theater to poetry readings are presented in a 300-seat auditorium. ⊠ *100 S. Andrews Ave.,* ☎ *954/357–7444; 954/357–7457 for self-guided Art in Public Places walking tour brochure,* WEB *www.broward.org/library.* ⊠ *Free.* ☉ *Mon.–Thurs. 9–9, Fri.–Sat. 9–5, Sun. noon–5:30.*

NEED A BREAK?

Don't miss **La Charcuterie** (⊠ 100 S. Andrews Ave., ☎ 954/357–7444), a cozy cafeteria set amid the books on the second floor of the Broward County Main Library. There are wonderful homemade breakfast treats such as muffins, scones, and coffee cakes, and an extensive lunch menu with soup, salad, and entrées. Open weekdays from 8 to 2:30, it caters to the library's bookworms and downtown's worker bees.

★ ❷ **Museum of Art.** In an Edward Larrabee Barnes–designed building that's considered an architectural masterpiece, this museum has Florida's largest art exhibition space. The impressive permanent collection features 20th-century European and American art, including works by Picasso, Calder, Dalí, Mapplethorpe, Warhol, and Stella, as well as a notable collection of works by celebrated Ashcan School artist William Glackens. When it opened in 1986, the museum launched a revitalization of

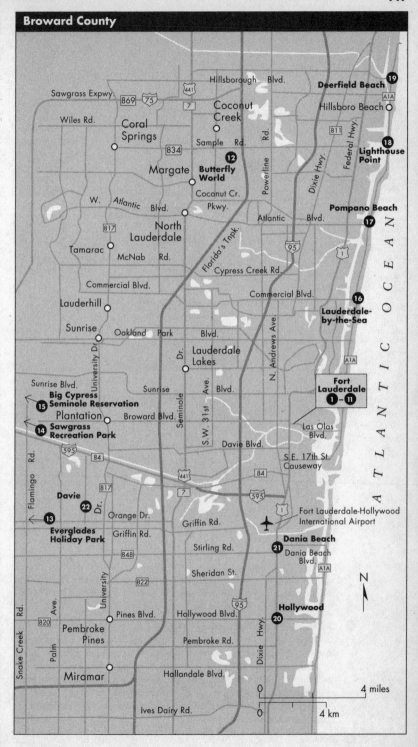

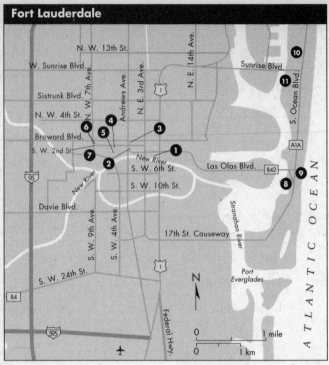

the downtown district and nearby Riverwalk area. ⊠ *1 E. Las Olas Blvd.,* ☎ *954/763–6464,* WEB *www.museumofart.org.* ⊠ *$10.* ☉ *Tues.– Sat. 10–5, Sun. noon–5.*

★ ☺ **⑥ Museum of Discovery and Science/Blockbuster IMAX Theater.** The aim here is to show children—*and* adults—the wonders of science in an entertaining fashion. And as soon as you see the 52-ft-tall Great Gravity Clock in the courtyard entrance, you'll know you're in for a cool experience. Inside, exhibits include Choose Health, about making healthful lifestyle choices; Kidscience, which encourages youngsters to explore the world around them; and Gizmo City, a look at how gadgets work. Florida Ecoscapes has a living coral reef as well as live bees, bats, frogs, turtles, and alligators. An IMAX theater, part of the complex, shows changing films (some 3-D) on a five-story screen. ⊠ *401 S.W. 2nd St.,* ☎ *954/467–6637 for museum; 954/463–4629 for IMAX,* WEB *www.mods.org.* ⊠ *Museum $13, includes one IMAX show.* ☉ *Mon.–Sat. 10–5, Sun. noon–6.*

④ Old Fort Lauderdale Museum of History. The museum surveys city history from the Seminole era to more recent times. In recent years the museum has expanded into several adjacent historic buildings, including the King-Cromartie House, the Historical Society's research center, and the New River Inn, the home of the museum. The research facility archives original manuscripts, maps, and more than 250,000 photos. ⊠ *231 S.W. 2nd Ave.,* ☎ *954/463–4431,* WEB *www.oldfortlauderdale.org.* ⊠ *$5.* ☉ *Tues.–Sun. noon–5.*

★ **⑤ Riverwalk.** This lovely, paved promenade on the north bank of the New River is great for entertainment as well as views. On the first Sunday of every month a jazz brunch attracts visitors. The walk has been extended 2 mi on both sides of the beautiful urban stream, connecting the facilities of the Arts and Science District.

CRUISING FOR A TAXI

SHOUT "TAXI! TAXI!" IN FORT LAUDERDALE, and your ship may have just come in.

Actually, it's a water taxi–boat, a floating "cab" that you can hail from one of the many docks along the Intracoastal Waterway.

The venture was started by longtime resident Bob Bekoff, who decided to combine the need for transportation with one of the area's most appealing features: its miles of waterways that make the city known as the Venice of America. The water taxis may not have crooning gondoliers like their Italian counterparts, but they do provide a delightful and surprisingly efficient way to get from one place to another.

For a day of sightseeing, the taxi will pick you up at one of a number of hotels along the waterway, and you can stop off at attractions like the Performing Arts Center or Beach Place. For lunch, you can enjoy a restaurant on Las Olas Boulevard or Las Olas Riverfront. In the evening, it's a great way to go bar hopping (no worry about a designated driver) or a fun way to go out to dinner.

Water Taxi and Broward County Mass Transit have partnered to create Water Buses. These environmentally friendly electric ferries can carry 70 passengers. Ride either the water taxi or water bus unlimited from 6:30 AM to 12:30 AM for $5 (one-way adult fare is $4). The best way to use the water taxi or bus is by calling 954/467-6677 about 20 minutes ahead of your desired pickup or check out the schedule at www.watertaxi.com.

— Alan Macher

❼ Sailboat Bend. Between Las Olas and the river, as well as just across the river, lies a neighborhood with much of the character of Old Town in Key West and historic Coconut Grove in Miami. No shops or services are located here.

❶ Stranahan House. The oldest residence in the city was once the home of pioneer businessman Frank Stranahan. Stranahan arrived in 1892 and, with his wife, Ivy, befriended the Seminole Indians, traded with them, and taught them "new ways." In 1901 he built a store and later made it his home. Now it's a museum with many of his original furnishings on display. ⊠ 335 S.E. 6th Ave. (at Las Olas Blvd.), ☎ 954/524-4736, WEB www.stranahanhouse.com. ☜ $5. ◷ Wed.–Sat. 10–3, Sun. 1–3.

Along the Beach

Fort Lauderdale's beachfront offers the best of all possible worlds, with easy access not only to strands of white sand, but also to restaurants and shops. For 2 mi heading north, beginning at the Bahia Mar yacht basin, along Route A1A you'll have clear views, typically across rows of colorful beach umbrellas, to the sea and ships passing in and out of nearby Port Everglades. If you're on the beach, you can look back on an exceptionally graceful promenade.

Pedestrians rank ahead of cars in Fort Lauderdale. Broad walkways line both sides of the beach road, and traffic has been trimmed to two gently curving northbound lanes, where in-line skaters dance alongside slow-moving cars. On the beach side, a low masonry wall, which serves as an extended bench, extends the promenade. At night the wall is wrapped in ribbons of fiber-optic color. The most crowded portion of beach is between Las Olas and Sunrise boulevards. The tackiness of this onetime strip—famous for the springtime madness spawned by the film *Where the Boys Are*—is now but a memory.

North of the redesigned beachfront is another 2 mi of open and natural coastal landscape. Much of the way parallels the Hugh Taylor Birch State Recreation Area, which preserves a patch of primeval Florida.

A Good Tour

Go east on Southeast 17th Street across the Brooks Memorial Causeway over the Intracoastal Waterway and bear left onto Seabreeze Boulevard (Route A1A). You will pass through a neighborhood of older homes set in lush vegetation before emerging at the south end of Fort Lauderdale's beachfront strip. On your left is the Radisson Bahia Mar Beach Resort, where novelist John McDonald's fictional hero from his series of mystery novels, Travis McGee, is honored with a plaque at marina slip F-18, where he docked his houseboat. Three blocks north, visit the **International Swimming Hall of Fame Museum and Aquatic Complex** ⑧. As you approach Las Olas Boulevard, you will see the lyrical styling that has given a distinctly European flavor to the **Fort Lauderdale beachfront** ⑨. Plan to break for lunch and perhaps a bit of shopping at Beach Place, the 100,000-square-ft entertainment, retail, and dining complex just north of Las Olas.

Turn left off Route A1A at Sunrise Boulevard, then right into **Hugh Taylor Birch State Recreation Area** ⑩, where many outdoor activities can be enjoyed amid vivid flora and fauna. Cross Sunrise Boulevard and visit the **Bonnet House** ⑪ to marvel at both the mansion and the surrounding subtropical 35-acre estate.

TIMING·

The beach is all about recreation and leisure. To enjoy it as it's meant to be, allow at least a day to loll about.

Sights to See

★ ⑪ **Bonnet House.** A 35-acre oasis in the heart of the beach area, this subtropical estate is a tribute to the history of Old South Florida. The charming mansion was the winter residence of Frederic and Evelyn Bartlett, artists whose personal touches and small surprises are evident throughout. Whether you're interested in architecture, artwork, or the natural environment, this is a special place. ⊠ *900 N. Birch Rd.,* ☎ *954/ 563–5393,* WEB *www.bonnethouse.com.* ⊡ *$9.* ☉ *Wed.–Fri. 10–3, weekends noon–4.*

★ ⑨ **Fort Lauderdale Beachfront.** A wave theme unifies the setting—from the low, white wave-shape wall between the beach and beachfront promenade to the widened and bricked inner promenade in front of shops, restaurants, and hotels. Alone among Florida's major beachfront communities, Fort Lauderdale's beach remains open and uncluttered. More than ever, the boulevard is worth promenading.

⑩ **Hugh Taylor Birch State Recreation Area.** Amid the tropical greenery of this 180-acre park you can stroll along a nature trail, visit the Birch House Museum, picnic, play volleyball, pitch horseshoes, and paddle a rented canoe. Since parking is limited on A1A, you can park here and take a walkway underpass to the beach (between 9 and 5). ⊠ *3109 E. Sunrise Blvd.,* ☎ *954/564–4521,* WEB *www.abfla.com/parks.* ⊡ *$3.25 per vehicle with up to 8 people.* ☉ *Daily 8–sunset; ranger-guided nature walks Fri. at 10:30.*

⑧ **International Swimming Hall of Fame Museum and Aquatic Complex.**
This monument to underwater accomplishments has two 10-lane, 50-m pools that are open daily to the public, when not hosting international aquatic competitions. The exhibition building features photos, medals, and other souvenirs from major swimming events around the world, as well as a theater that shows films of onetime swimming and film stars Johnny Weissmuller and Esther Williams. ✉ *1 Hall of Fame Dr. (1 block south of Las Olas at A1A),* ☎ *954/462–6536 for museum; 954/468–1580 for pool,* WEB *www.ishof.org.* ✉ *Museum $3, pool $3.* ☉ *Mid-Jan.–late-Dec.: museum and pro shop daily 9–7; pool weekdays 8–4 and 6–8, weekends 8–4.*

Dining

American

$$–$$$$ ✕ **Burt & Jack's.** At the far end of Port Everglades, this local favorite has been operated by veteran restaurateur Jack Jackson and actor Burt Reynolds since 1984. Behind the heavy mission doors and bougainvillea, you can dine on Maine lobster, steaks, and chops after choosing from the raw ingredients presented by the waitstaff before your order is taken. The two-story gallery of haciendalike dining rooms surrounded by glass are ideal for watching the cruise ships steam out. ✉ *Berth 23, Port Everglades,* ☎ *954/522–2878 or 954/525–5225. AE, D, DC, MC, V. No lunch.*

$$–$$$$ ✕ **Shula's on the Beach.** It's only fitting that Don Shula, former Miami Dolphins head coach, should have a South Florida steak house. The good news for steak—and sports—fans is that the staff here turns out winners. The meat is cut thick and is grilled over a superhot fire for quick charring. This is a pure steak house, so don't look for many other menu choices. Appetizers are adequate although unexciting; you'll probably want to go straight to the porterhouse. Outside tables give you sand and ocean; inside ones have access to sports memorabilia and large-screen TVs so you can watch your favorite game. ✉ *Sheraton Yankee Trader, 321 N. Fort Lauderdale Beach Blvd.,* ☎ *954/355–4000. AE, D, DC, MC, V.*

$$ ✕ **Tropical Acres.** This popular family-owned restaurant has been serving up sizzling steaks from a fireplace grill since 1949—a millennium by South Florida standards. There are more than 40 other entrée items to choose from, including excellent seafood dishes. Scrod is the best choice for fish. The waitstaff has been here for many years, and it shows in its friendly service. Locals and visitors are drawn to some of the best early-bird specials around. The wine list is slim, but the prices are moderate. ✉ *2500 Griffin Rd.,* ☎ *954/989–2500. AE, DC, MC, V.*

$–$$ ✕ **Floridian.** This Las Olas landmark has been around for as long as anyone can remember, and it still serves up one of the best breakfasts in the downtown area. People flock here on weekend mornings for oversize omelets, sausage, bacon, and biscuits. Servers can be a bit brusque, but it's all part of the atmosphere. Open 24 hours every day of the year—even during hurricanes—the restaurant also serves sandwiches and hot platters for lunch and dinner. ✉ *1410 E. Las Olas Blvd.,* ☎ *954/463–4041. No credit cards accepted.*

Asian

$–$$ ✕ **Siam Cuisine.** Locals say this restaurant, tucked away in a small storefront in Wilton Manors, serves up the best Thai in the Fort Lauderdale area, and they may be right. The waitstaff is attentive and efficient, and the family-run kitchen consistently turns out appealing and flavorful delights. Thai curry dishes with chicken or shrimp are favorites, along with appetizers of steamed dumplings. Another specialty is roast duck. ✉ *2010 Wilton Dr.,* ☎ *954/564–3411. AE, MC, V.*

Contemporary

$$–$$$$ ✕ **By Word of Mouth.** This unassuming but outstanding restaurant never
★   advertises, hence its name. But word has gotten around, because lo-
        cals consistently put it at the top of "reader's choice" restaurant polls.
        There is no menu. Patrons are shown the day's specials and then make
        their choice. There's usually a good selection of fish, fowl, beef, pasta,
        and vegetarian entrées. A salad is served with each dinner entrée.
        There's also a good selection of appetizers and desserts. ✉ *3200 N.E.*
        12th Ave., ☎ *954/564–3663. AE, MC, V.*

$$–$$$$ ✕ **Mark's Las Olas.** Mark Militello, a star among South Florida chefs,
★   is in command at this popular restaurant, where metallic finishes
        bounce the hubbub around the room. Militello's loyal following is en-
        chanted with his Florida-style cuisine, which blends flavors from
        Caribbean, southwestern, and Mediterranean traditions. Entrées change
        daily, but typical choices include brilliantly prepared gulf shrimp, dol-
        phinfish, and yellowtail snapper, often paired with combinations of
        callaloo (a West Indian spinach), chayote, ginger, jicama, and plantain.
        ✉ *1032 E. Las Olas Blvd.,* ☎ *954/463–1000. AE, D, DC, MC, V. Reser-*
        vations required. No lunch weekends.

Continental

$$$–$$$$ ✕ **Grill Room on Las Olas.** With all of the trendy eateries sprouting up
        along Las Olas Boulevard, you may be ready to take a break and try
        some of the excellent Continental cuisine served up at this historic River-
        side Hotel. The room is accented in the grand style of a colonial British
        officers club, and the menu has traditional favorites such as grilled steaks
        and chateaubriand and rack of lamb—both prepared for two. Many
        dishes are prepared table-side, including a grand Caesar salad. An ex-
        tensive wine list is available. The adjacent Golden Lyon Bar has the
        feeling of a pub somewhere in India. ✉ *Riverside Hotel, 620 E. Las*
        Olas Blvd., ☎ *954/467–2555. AE, MC, V.*

French

$$–$$$$ ✕ **La Coquille.** Although this French restaurant sits at the edge of busy
        Sunrise Boulevard, it seems worlds away thanks to an art deco look.
        Service comes with a delightful French accent. The cuisine is equally
        authentic: Dubonnet and vermouth cassis aperitifs are a prelude to seared
        sea scallops with spring vegetables, honey-glazed duckling with lin-
        gonberry sauce and wild rice, sweetbreads in a morel and truffle sauce,
        or veal with shallots and sweet bell peppers. Chef-owner Jean Bert al-
        ways offers a soufflé among the desserts, and a multicourse dinner spe-
        cial most nights. ✉ *1619 E. Sunrise Blvd.,* ☎ *954/467–3030. AE, D,*
        MC, V. Closed Mon. No lunch Sat.–Thurs.

$$$ ✕ **Left Bank.** Just off busy Las Olas Boulevard, this quiet oasis has been
        drawing a loyal following for more than two decades. Now chef-owner
        Andrew Fox has lightened the decor—light beige walls decorated with
        paintings to create a Renoir-like appearance—and also the menu. Some
        of the low-fat choices include seared rare tuna with mushrooms, Cajun-
        spiced mahimahi, and grilled salmon with rum and vanilla sauce. Two
        menus are offered, one à la carte, and another providing a complete din-
        ner with three choices of appetizers, four entrées, and dessert. ✉ *214*
        S.E. 6th Ave., ☎ *954/462–5376. AE, D, DC, MC, V.*

$$–$$$ ✕ **French Quarter.** This 1920 building, formerly a Red Cross head-
        quarters, sits on a quiet street just off bustling Las Olas Boulevard. The
        French-style architecture has a touch of New Orleans, and the food
        captures both creole and traditional French elements. Among the fa-
        vorites are shrimp *maison* (large shrimp sautéed with carrots and
        mushrooms in beurre blanc), bouillabaisse, crab cakes, and escargot
        appetizers. French baking, including delicious bread, is done on-site,
        and a prix-fixe three-course pretheater dinner is served until 6:30. ✉

215 S.E. 8th Ave., ☎ *954/463–8000. AE, D, DC, MC, V. Closed Sun. No lunch Sat.*

Italian

$$–$$$$ ✕ **Louie, Louie.** Some of the best pasta dishes on Las Olas are served at this friendly, tavern-style establishment. The menu is varied: you can order individual pizza, sandwiches, or complete dinners. Fresh fish specials are offered daily. Sea bass, for example, is cooked to perfection. Prices are reasonable, and while waiting for a table you can sample one of the large selection of beers on tap. ⊠ *1103 E. Las Olas Blvd.,* ☎ *954/524–5200. AE, MC, V.*

$$–$$$ ✕ **Primavera.** Creative Italian food is the specialty at this lovely find in the middle of an ordinary shopping plaza. Elegant floral arrangements enhance the fine dining experience. In addition to interesting pasta and risotto entrées, there is a wide variety of creative fish, poultry, veal, and beef dinners. One of chef-owner Giacomo Dresseno's favorites is veal chop Boscaiola (with shallots, wild mushrooms, and bordelaise sauce). Primavera is renowned for its spectacular assortment of both appetizers and desserts as well as live entertainment nightly. ⊠ *830 E. Oakland Park Blvd.,* ☎ *954/564–6363. AE, D, DC, MC, V. No lunch.*

$$ ✕ **Casa D'Angelo.** Owner-chef Angelo Elia has re-created his former Café D'Angelo into a gem of a Tuscan-style restaurant. Almost everything is created from scratch, and the oak oven turns out some marvelous seafood and beef dishes. The *pappardelle* (wide, rippled noodles) with porcini mushrooms takes pasta to a new level. Another favorite from the pasta menu is linguine with arugula, shrimp, and scallops. Be sure to ask about the oven-roasted fish of the day. ⊠ *1201 N. Federal Hwy.,* ☎ *954/564–1234. AE, D, DC, MC, V. No lunch.*

Mexican

$$–$$$$ ✕ **Eduardo de San Angel.** Forget tacos and burritos, which aren't even available here, and try the classic dishes served in true Mexican style. Authentic chilies, spices, and herbs enhance an array of seafood, meat, and poultry dishes. Typical specialties are beef tenderloin tips sautéed with Portobello mushrooms and onions in a chipotle chili sauce, and a marvelous mesquite-grilled red snapper flavored with jalapeños and mango salsa. The gourmet dishes are matched by a sophisticated setting. ⊠ *2822 E. Commercial Blvd.,* ☎ *954/772–4731. AE, D, DC, MC, V. Closed Sun.*

Seafood

$$$–$$$$ ✕ **Blue Moon Fish Company.** Virtually every table has a lovely water
★ view over the Intracoastal Waterway. But the real magic is in the kitchen, where chefs Baron Skorish and Bryce Statham create some of the region's best seafood dishes. Favorites include pan-seared snapper with asparagus, sea bass fillet crusted with macadamia nuts, and rare-charred tuna. Appetizers include choices from the raw bar, a sushi sampler, tasty crab and crawfish cakes, and charred Portobello mushrooms. ⊠ *4405 W. Tradewinds Ave.,* ☎ *954/267–9888. AE, D, DC, MC, V.*

$$–$$$ ✕ **15th Street Fisheries.** An impressive view of the Intracoastal Waterway is only the beginning at this two-story seafood spot. A variety of satisfying dishes include a cold seafood salad and a spicy conch chowder for starters. Homemade breads, a specialty, are accompanied by a cold onion spread. More than 65 entrées range from the traditional, such as grilled mahimahi, to the exotic, such as alligator; downstairs supplies a more casual atmosphere. The fresh key lime pie has an Oreo crust. ⊠ *1900 S.E. 15th St.,* ☎ *954/763–2777. AE, D, DC, MC, V.*

$–$$$ ✕ **Rustic Inn Crabhouse.** Wayne McDonald started with a cozy one-room roadhouse in 1955, when this stretch was a remote service road just west of the little airport. Now, the plain, rustic place is huge. Steamed crabs seasoned with garlic and herbs, spices, and oil are opened with mallets on tables covered with newspapers; peel-and-eat shrimp are served either with garlic and butter or spiced and steamed with Old Bay seasoning. The big menu includes other seafood items as well. Pies and cheesecakes are offered for dessert. ⊠ *4331 Ravenswood Rd.,* ☎ *954/584–1637. AE, D, DC, MC, V.*

Southwestern

$$–$$$ ✕ **Canyon.** Adventurous southwestern cuisine helps you escape the or-
★ dinary at this small but very popular spot. Take, for example, the os-
trich skewers, smoked salmon tostada, Brie and wild-mushroom quesadilla, and marvelous Chilean sea bass. Free-range chicken and brook trout are served with a tempting crabmeat salsa. Many guests like to start off with Canyon's famous prickly-pear margaritas, or choose from a well-rounded wine list or selection of beers, including many microbrews. ⊠ *1818 E. Sunrise Blvd.,* ☎ *954/765–1950. AE, MC, V. No lunch.*

Lodging

On the Beach

$$$–$$$$ 🏨 **Marriott's Harbor Beach Resort.** If you look down from the upper
stories (14 in all) at night, this 16-acre property south of the big pub-
lic beach shimmers like a jewel. Spacious guest rooms have rich trop-
ical colors, lively floral art prints, and warm woods. Part of the hotel's big budget renovation is the addition of a state-of-the-art European spa. No other hotel on the beach gives you so many activity options. ⊠ *3030 Holiday Dr., 33316,* ☎ *954/525–4000 or 800/222–6543,* 𝔽𝔸𝕏 *954/766–6152,* 𝚆𝙴𝙱 *www.marriottharborbeach.com. 602 rooms, 35 suites. 3 restaurants, in-room data ports, room TVs with movies and video games, 5 tennis courts, 2 pools, gym, spa, beach, snorkeling, boat-ing, parasailing, volleyball, 2 bars, children's programs (ages 5–12). AE, D, DC, MC, V.*

$$–$$$ 🏨 **Lago Mar Resort & Club.** The sprawling Lago Mar has been owned
★ by the Banks family since the early 1950s and, after a round of reno-
vations in recent years, is now a premiere oceanfront resort. Most ac-
commodations are suites, making it an ideal choice for family vacations. Suite highlights include a king-size bed, pull-out sofa, and full kitchen. Allamanda trellises and bougainvillea plantings edge the swimming la-
goon, and guests have direct access to a large private beach in an ex-
clusive neighborhood. ⊠ *1700 S. Ocean La., 33316,* ☎ *954/523–6511 or 800/524–6627,* 𝔽𝔸𝕏 *954/524–6627,* 𝚆𝙴𝙱 *www.lagomar.com. 52 rooms, 143 1-bedroom suites, 17 2-bedroom suites. 4 restaurants, miniature golf, tennis court, 2 pools, shuffleboard, volleyball, playground. AE, DC, MC, V.*

$$–$$$ 🏨 **The Pillars Hotel at New River Sound.** Described as Fort Laud-
erdale's "small secret" by locals in the know, this property is one block in from the beach on the Intracoastal. Its design recalls the colorful ar-
chitecture of British colonial plantations found in the Caribbean in the 18th century. Most rooms have views of the Intracoastal Waterway or poolside, with French doors opening to individual patios or balconies. Rooms have rattan and mahogany headboards, antique reproduction desks and nightstands, and lush draperies. Suites include wet bars with refrigerators and microwaves. ⊠ *111 N. Birch Rd., 33304,* ☎ *954/467–9639,* 𝔽𝔸𝕏 *954/763–2845,* 𝚆𝙴𝙱 *www.pillarshotel.com. 19 rooms, 4 suites. Room service, in-room data ports, minibars, in-room VCRs, pool, concierge; no-smoking rooms. AE, D, DC, MC, V.*

$ 🏨 **Nina Lee/Imperial House.** The Nina Lee and the adjacent Imperial
House operate as one property. The Nina Lee offers homey, clean, and comfortably sized efficiencies with gas kitchens, large closets, and

tub-showers. The pool is set in a garden, and the entire property is just removed enough from the beach causeway to be quiet. The Imperial House has apartment-style accommodations consisting of a living room, kitchen, and bedroom. Guests may use the facilities at the nearby beach-front Sheraton Yankee Clipper hotel. ⊠ *3048 Harbor Dr., 33316,* ☎ *954/524–1568,* FAX *954/763–2931. 26 units. Pool. AE, D, DC, MC, V.*

Downtown and Beach Causeways

$$$–$$$$ 🏨 **Hyatt Regency Pier Sixty-Six.** The trademark of this high-rise re-sort on the Intracoastal Waterway is its rooftop Pier Top Lounge that revolves every 66 minutes. The 17-story tower dominates a 22-acre spread that includes the Spa 66, a full-service European-style spa. Each room has a balcony with views of the 142-slip marina, the ocean, the pool, or Intracoastal Waterway. For panoramic views of the city book a tower or lanai room. Lush landscaping, and convenience to the beach, shopping, and restaurants add to this resort's appeal. Hail the water bus at the resort's dock for a three-minute trip to the beach. ⊠ *2301 S.E. 17th St. Causeway, 33316,* ☎ *954/525–6666 or 800/327–3796,* FAX *954/728–3551,* WEB *www.pier66.com. 380 rooms, 8 suites. 6 restaurants, 2 tennis courts, 2 pools, gym, hot tub, spa, snorkeling, boating, marina, parasailing, waterskiing, fishing, 3 bars. AE, D, DC, MC, V.*

$$–$$$ 🏨 **Riverside Hotel.** On Las Olas Boulevard, just steps from boutiques, restaurants, and art galleries, this charming hotel was built in 1936. Old Fort Lauderdale photos grace the hallways, and rooms are out-fitted distinctively, with antique oak furnishings, framed French prints, and European-style baths. You can enjoy afternoon tea in the lobby, and fine dining at Indigo, which has Southeast Asian cooking, or the elegant Grill Room. ⊠ *620 E. Las Olas Blvd., 33301,* ☎ *954/467–0671 or 800/325–3280,* FAX *954/462–2148,* WEB *www.riversidehotel.com. 207 rooms, 10 suites. 2 restaurants, pool, dock, 2 bars; no-smoking rooms. AE, DC, MC, V.*

$$–$$$ 🏨 **Schubert Hotel.** This fully restored 1950s art deco property in Vic-toria Park is a small luxury boutique hotel tucked into a tropical land-scape. Rooms are oversize with marble and granite baths, and most have kitchenettes and either a king-size bed or two double-size beds. A café serves breakfast and lunch overlooking the pool and has a wine bar—a perfect place to unwind. The property feels secluded, yet is a short walk from the beach, shopping, and restaurants. ⊠ *855 N.E. 20th Ave., 33304,* ☎ *954/763–7434 or 866/338–7666,* FAX *954/763–4132,* WEB *www.schuberthotel.com. 30 rooms. Café, grill, room service, pool, spa, shuffleboard, bar, business services. AE, DC, MC, V.*

$–$$ 🏨 **Banyan Marina Resort.** These outstanding waterfront apartments,
★   on a residential island just off Las Olas Boulevard, are set amid imag-inative landscaping that includes a walkway through the upper branches of a banyan tree. With leather sofas, springy carpets, high-quality art, French doors, and jalousies for sweeping the breeze in, the luxurious units are as comfortable as any first-class hotel—but for half the price. Apartments and efficiencies include a full kitchen and dining area. All units enjoy the property's beautiful gardens, dockage for eight yachts, and exemplary housekeeping. ⊠ *111 Isle of Venice, 33301,* ☎ *954/524–4430 or 800/524–4431,* FAX *954/764–4870,* WEB *www.banyanmarina. com. 3 rooms, 1 efficiency, 4 1-bedroom apartments, 2 2-bedroom apartments. Dining room, pool, dock. MC, V.*

Nightlife and the Arts

For the most complete weekly listing of events, read the **"Showtime!"** entertainment insert and events calendar in the Friday *South Florida Sun-Sentinel.* **"Weekend,"** in the Friday Broward edition of the *Miami*

Herald, also carries listings of area happenings. The weekly **City Link** is principally an entertainment and dining paper with an "underground" look. **New Times** is a free alternative news weekly that circulates a Broward–Palm Beach County edition. **East Sider** is another free weekly entertainment guide. A 24-hour **Arts & Entertainment Hotline** (☎ 954/357–5700) provides updates on art, attractions, children's events, dance, festivals, films, literature, museums, music, opera, and theater.

Tickets are sold at individual box offices and through **Ticketmaster** (☎ 954/523–3309); there is a service charge.

The Arts

Broward Center for the Performing Arts (✉ 201 S.W. 5th Ave., ☎ 954/462–0222) is the waterfront centerpiece of Fort Lauderdale's cultural arts district. More than 500 events a year are scheduled at the 2,700-seat architectural masterpiece, including Broadway musicals, plays, dance, symphony and opera, rock, film, lectures, comedy, and children's theater.

Nightlife

BARS AND LOUNGES

Café Iguana (✉ Beach Place, 17 S. Fort Lauderdale Beach Blvd., ☎ 954/763–7222) has a nightly DJ to keep the dance floor hopping, and you can dance all night long every night of the week. **Chili Pepper** (✉ 200 W. Broward Blvd., ☎ 954/525–0094) brings hot current rock bands to the stage of this warehouse-size, open-air venue. **Howl at the Moon** (✉ Beach Place, 17 S. Fort Lauderdale Beach Blvd., ☎ 954/522–5054) has dueling piano players and sing-alongs nightly. **Maguire's Hill 16** (✉ 535 N. Andrews Ave., ☎ 954/764–4453) highlights excellent bands in a classic Irish pub setting. **Murphy's Law Irish Pub** (✉ Las Olas Riverfront, 300 S.W. 1st Ave., ☎ 954/525–0044) is where the weekend house band gets the customers dancing on top of the bar. **O'Hara's Jazz Café** (✉ 722 E. Las Olas Blvd., ☎ 954/524–1764) belts out the live jazz, blues, R&B, and funk nightly. Its packed crowd spills onto this prettiest of downtown streets. **Rush Street** (✉ 220 S.W. 2nd St., ☎ 954/522–6900) is where hipsters line up around the corner to gain access to one of the best martini bars in Broward County. **Side Bar** (✉ 210 S.W. 2nd St., ☎ 954/524–1818) has a contemporary industrial setting with a polished professional crowd. **Tarpon Bend**'s (✉ 200 S.W. 2nd St., ☎ 954/523–3233) specialties—food, fishing gear and bait, and live bands playing current covers—draw a casual, beer-drinking crowd. **Tavern 213** (✉ 213 S.W. 2nd St., ☎ 954/463–6213) is a small, no-frills club, where cover bands do classic rock nightly. **Voodoo Lounge** (✉ 111 S.W. 2nd Ave., ☎ 954/522–0733) plays the latest in club music inside the nightclub and high hip-hop on the elegant outside deck. The scene here doesn't start until after midnight.

Outdoor Activities and Sports

Baseball

From mid-February to the end of March, the **Baltimore Orioles** (✉ Fort Lauderdale Stadium, 5301 N.W. 12th Ave., ☎ 954/776–1921) are in spring training.

Biking

Some of the most popular routes are Route A1A and Bayview Drive, especially early in the morning before traffic builds, and a 7-mi bike path that parallels State Road 84 and the New River and leads to Markham Park, which has mountain-bike trails. Most area bike shops also have cycling maps.

When you pack your MCI Calling Card, it's like packing your loved ones along too.

Your MCI Calling Card is the easy way to stay in touch when you travel. Use it to call to and from over 125 countries. Plus, every time you call, you can earn frequent flier miles. So wherever your travels take you, call home with your MCI Calling Card. It's even easy to get one. Just visit **www.mci.com/worldphone** or **www.mci.com/partners**.

EASY TO CALL WORLDWIDE

1. Just enter the WorldPhone® access number of the country you're calling from.
2. Enter or give the operator your MCI Calling Card number.
3. Enter or give the number you're calling.

Aruba ⁜	800-888-8	Barbados ⁜	1-800-888-8000
Bahamas ⁜	1-800-888-8000	Bermuda ⁜	1-800-888-8000
		British Virgin Islands ⁜	1-800-888-8000
		Canada	1-800-888-8000
		Mexico	01-800-021-8000
		Puerto Rico	1-800-888-8000
		United States	1-800-888-8000
		U.S. Virgin Islands	1-800-888-8000

⁜ Limited availability.

EARN FREQUENT FLIER MILES

Find America *with a Compass*

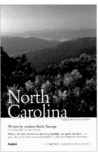

Written by local authors and illustrated throughout
with spectacular color images, Compass American
Guides reveal the character and culture of more than
40 of America's most fascinating destinations. Perfect
for residents who want to explore their own backyards
and for visitors who want an insider's perspective
on the history, heritage, and all there is to see and do.

Fishing

If you're interested in a saltwater charter, check out the **Radisson Bahia Mar Beach Resort** (✉ 801 Seabreeze Blvd., ☎ 954/627–6357). Both sportfishing and drift-fishing bookings can be arranged.

Scuba Diving and Snorkeling

Lauderdale Diver (✉ 1334 S.E. 17th St. Causeway, ☎ 954/467–2822 or 800/654–2073), which is PADI affiliated, arranges dive charters throughout the county. Dive trips typically last four hours. Nonpackage reef trips are open to divers for $42; scuba gear is extra.

Pro Dive (✉ 515 Seabreeze Blvd., ☎ 954/761–3413 or 800/772–3483), a PADI five-star facility, is the area's oldest diving operation and offers packages with Radisson Bahia Mar Beach Resort, from where its 60-ft boat departs. Snorkelers can go out for $27 on a two-hour snorkeling trip, which includes equipment. Scuba divers pay $39 using their own gear or $79 with all rentals included.

Tennis

With 21 courts, 18 of them lighted clay courts, the **Jimmy Evert Tennis Center at Holiday Park** is Fort Lauderdale's largest public tennis facility. Chris Evert, one of the game's greatest players, learned the sport here under the watchful eye of her father, Jimmy, who retired after 37 years as the center's tennis professional. ✉ 701 N.E. 12th Ave., ☎ 954/828–5378. 🎫 $4.50 per person per hr. ☉ Weekdays 8 AM–9 PM, weekends 8–6.

Shopping

Malls

Just north of Las Olas Boulevard on Route A1A is the happening **Beach Place** (✉ 17 S. Fort Lauderdale Beach Blvd. [A1A]). Here you can browse through such shops as the Gap, Bath & Body Works, and Banana Republic; have lunch or dinner at an array of restaurants, from casual Caribbean to elegant American; or carouse at a selection of nightspots—all open late. By and large, eateries on the lower level are more upscale, whereas on the upper level the prices are lower and the ocean view is better.

With a convenient in-town location just west of the Intracoastal Waterway, the split-level **Galleria Mall** (✉ 2414 E. Sunrise Blvd.) contains more than 1 million square ft of space. It's anchored by Neiman-Marcus, Lord & Taylor, Dillards, Burdines, and Saks Fifth Avenue and features 150 specialty stores with an emphasis on fashion.

The **Swap Shop** (✉ 3291 W. Sunrise Blvd.) is the South's largest flea market with 2,000 vendors open every day. While exploring this 80-acre indoor/outdoor entertainment and shopping complex, enjoy the giant carousel, the drive-in movies, or the free daily circus.

Shopping Districts

When you're downtown, check out the **Las Olas Riverfront** (✉ 1 block west of Andrews Ave. on the New River), a shopping, dining, and entertainment complex. **Vogue Italia** (✉ Las Olas Riverfront, 300 S.W. 1st Ave., ☎ 954/527–4568) is packed with trendy fashions by D&G, Ferre, Versus, Moschino, Iceberg, and more at wholesale prices.

If only for a stroll and some window-shopping, don't miss **Las Olas Boulevard** (✉ 1 block off New River east of Andrews Ave.). The city's best boutiques plus top restaurants and art galleries line a beautifully landscaped street. **Atlantic Yard** (✉ 2424 E. Las Olas Blvd., ☎ 954/779–1191) has everything for the avant gardener from unique and unusual gardening goods to stylish teak furniture collections. **Casa**

Chameleon (⊠ 619 E. Las Olas Blvd., ☎ 954/763–2543) carries a romantic selection of decorative items, including fine gifts, antiques, linens, and beautiful things to top your table. **Kilwin's of Las Olas** (⊠ 809 E. Las Olas Blvd., ☎ 954/523–8338) lures pedestrians with the sweet smell of waffle cones to this old-fashioned confectionery where they hand-paddle fudge and scoop homemade ice cream. **Lily Pulitzer by Lauderdale Lifestyle** (⊠ 819 E. Las Olas Blvd., ☎ 954/524–5459) specializes in the South Florida dress requisite—clothing and accessories in Lily Pulitzer's signature tropical colors and prints. **Pino Formica** (⊠ 825 E. Las Olas Blvd., ☎ 954/522–2479) focuses on sleek shoes, handbags, and belts by Furla, Fendi, Prada, and other Italian labels. **Seldom Seen** (⊠ 817 E. Las Olas Blvd., ☎ 954/764–5590) is a gallery of contemporary and folk art, including furniture, jewelry, ceramics, sculpture, and blown glass with a whimsical touch. **Zola Keller** (⊠ 818 E. Las Olas Blvd., ☎ 954/462–3222) caters to those looking for special occasion dresses—cocktail dresses, evening gowns, and even Miss Florida and Mrs. America's pageant dresses.

Side Trips

The Western Suburbs and Beyond

West of Fort Lauderdale is an ever-growing mass of suburbs flowing one into the other. They're home to most of the city's golf courses as well as some attractions and large malls. As you head farther west, the terrain becomes more Evergladeslike, and you'll occasionally see an alligator sunning itself on a canal bank. No matter how dedicated developers are to building over this natural resource, the Everglades keeps trying to assert itself. Waterbirds, fish, and other creatures are found in canals and lakes, even man-made ones, throughout the western areas.

⑫ As many as 80 butterfly species from South and Central America, the Philippines, Malaysia, Taiwan, and other Asian nations are typically found within **Butterfly World,** a 3-acre site inside Tradewinds Park. A screened aviary called North American Butterflies is reserved for native species. The Tropical Rain Forest Aviary is a 30-ft-high construction, with observation decks, waterfalls, ponds, and tunnels where thousands of colorful butterflies flit and fly about. ⊠ 3600 W. Sample Rd., Coconut Creek, ☎ 954/977–4400, WEB www.butterflyworld. com. 💲 $13.95. ☉ Mon.–Sat. 9–5, Sun. 1–5.

⑬ The 30-acre **Everglades Holiday Park** provides a good glimpse of the Everglades. Here you can take an airboat tour, look at an 18th-century-style Native American village, or watch an alligator-wrestling show. A souvenir shop, TJ's Grill, a convenience store, and a campground with RV hookups and tent sites are all here as well. ⊠ 21940 Griffin Rd., ☎ 954/434–8111, WEB www.evergladesholidaypark.com. 💲 Free, airboat tour $15.50. ☉ Daily 9–5.

⑭ To understand and enjoy the Everglades, take an airboat ride at **Sawgrass Recreation Park.** You'll see all sorts of plants and wildlife, such as birds, alligators, turtles, snakes, and fish. Included in the entrance fee along with the airboat ride is admission to an Everglades nature exhibit, a native Seminole village, and exhibits about alligators, other reptiles, and birds of prey. A souvenir and gift shop, food service, and an RV park with hookups are also at the park. ⊠ U.S. 27 north of I–595, ☎ 954/426–2474, WEB www.evergladestours.com. 💲 $15.65. ☉ Weekdays 7–6, weekends 6–6, airboat rides daily 9–5.

⑮ Some distance from Fort Lauderdale's tranquil beaches, but worth the one-hour drive, is the **Big Cypress Seminole Reservation** and its two

🔄 very different attractions. At the **Billie Swamp Safari,** you can experience the majesty of the Everglades firsthand. Daily tours of the wetlands and hammocks, where wildlife abound, yield sightings of deer, water buffalo, bison, wild hogs, hawks, eagles, alligators, and even the rare Florida panther. Tours are provided aboard swamp buggies—customized motor vehicles specially designed to provide you with an elevated view of the frontier. ⊠ *19 mi north of I–75 Exit 14,* ☎ *863/ 983–6101 or 800/949–6101,* WEB *www.seminoletribe.com.* ⊇ *Free, swamp buggy ecotour/alligator and snake education show/airboat ride package $38.* ⊙ *Daily 8–5.*

Not far away from the Billie Swamp Safari is the **Ah-Tha-Thi-Ki Museum,** whose name means "a place to learn, a place to remember." It is just that. The museum honors the culture and tradition of the Seminoles through artifacts and reenactments of rituals and ceremonies. The site includes a living Seminole village, nature trails, and a boardwalk through a cypress swamp. ⊠ *17 mi north of I–75 Exit 14,* ☎ *863/902– 1113,* WEB *www.seminoletribe.com.* ⊇ *$6.* ⊙ *Tues.–Sun. 9–5.*

DINING AND LODGING

$–$$$ ✕ **Wolfgang Puck Café.** Just in case you were lacking an excuse, here's another reason to go the mall. Amid your shopping bags, you'll be treated to excellent service and quality dishes. Wolfgang Puck's plate-size pizzas are crispy and have tasty toppings, including spicy shrimp with peppers, vegetable combinations, and smoked salmon. One of the unusual but flavorful pasta dishes is roasted pumpkin ravioli. All-American entrées include rosemary chicken and a very good meat loaf with garlic mashed potatoes. ⊠ *Sawgrass Mills, 2610 Sawgrass Mills Circle, Sunrise,* ☎ *954/846–8668. AE, D, MC, V.*

$$–$$$ 🏨 **Marriott Coral Springs.** The resort is adjacent to the Tournament Players Club golf course in Heron Bay, home of the Honda Golf Classic. Its location near the Sawgrass Expressway also makes it convenient to area attractions. Spacious rooms are furnished with oak and cherrywood and have data ports for those with laptops in tow. The property also has a conference center, an outdoor terrace, and a game room. ⊠ *11775 Heron Bay Blvd., 33076,* ☎ *954/753–5598,* FAX *954/ 753–2888,* WEB *www.radisson.com. 218 rooms, 6 suites. Restaurant, 18-hole golf course, pro shop, pool, gym, sauna, bar. AE, D, MC, V.*

$$–$$$ 🏨 **Wyndham Bonaventure Resort & Spa.** This resort draws convention crowds with its luxurious amenities, which include a full service spa and affiliation with two championship golf courses. Spacious guest rooms and suites are done in tropical colors with rattan seating and most overlook a golf course. Oversize baths have dressing areas. The resort offers separate spa and golf packages. Golf and tennis facilities adjacent to the hotel are independent of the resort. ⊠ *250 Racquet Club Rd., Westin 33326,* ☎ *954/389–3300,* FAX *954/384–1416,* WEB *www.wyndham.com. 400 rooms, 96 suites. 2 restaurants, 2 18-hole golf courses, 16 tennis courts, 5 pools, gym, hair salon, spa, 2 bars, convention center. AE, D, DC, MC, V.*

NIGHTLIFE AND THE ARTS

Sunrise Musical Theatre (⊠ 5555 N.W. 95th Ave., Sunrise, ☎ 954/741– 7300) is a 4,000-seat theater presenting everything from ballet to top-name pop, rock, and country artists.

OUTDOOR ACTIVITIES AND SPORTS

Fishing. The marina at **Everglades Holiday Park** (⊠ 21940 Griffin Rd., ☎ 954/434–8111) caters to freshwater fishing. For $67.50 for five hours, you can rent a 14-ft johnboat (with a 9.9-horsepower Yamaha outboard) that carries up to four people. A rod and reel rent for $9 a day with a refundable $20 deposit; bait is extra. For two people, a fishing guide for a half day (four hours) is $170; for a full day (eight hours), $220. A third person adds $35 for a half day, $70 for a full day. You can also buy a freshwater fishing license (mandatory) here; a seven-day nonresident license is $17. Freshwater fishing with a guide out of **Sawgrass Recreation Park** (⊠ U.S. 27 and I–75, ☎ 954/426–2474) costs $175 for two people for a half day, $225 for a full day. Independent boat rentals, resident and nonresident fishing licenses, and live bait are available.

Golf. Next Day Golf (☎ 954/772–2582) provides access at no extra fee to private courses normally limited to members—a big advantage for golfers during the summer months, but still limited availability during the busy winter months. They also offer last-minute discount tee times (call 12 hours in advance).

Bonaventure Country Club (⊠ 200 Bonaventure Blvd., ☎ 954/389–2100) has 36 holes. **Broken Woods Country Club** (⊠ 9001 W. Sample Rd., Coral Springs, ☎ 954/752–2140) has 18 holes. **Colony West Country Club** (⊠ 6800 N.W. 88th Ave. [Pine Island Rd.], Tamarac, ☎ 954/726–8430) offers play on 36 holes. **Ft. Lauderdale Country Club** (⊠ 418 E. Country Club Circle, Fort Lauderdale, ☎ 954/587–4700) is a premier green in Fort Lauderdale. Just west of Florida's Turnpike, the **Inverrary Country Club** (⊠ 3840 Inverrary Blvd., Lauderhill, ☎ 954/733–7550) has three 18-hole courses. **Jacaranda Golf Club** (⊠ 9200 W. Broward Blvd., Plantation, ☎ 954/472–5836) has 18 holes to play.

Ice Hockey. National Car Rental Center is the home of the National Hockey League's **Florida Panthers** (⊠ 2555 N.W. 137th Way [Panther Pkwy.], Sunrise, ☎ 954/835–8326).

SHOPPING

Broward's shopping extravaganza, **Fashion Mall at Plantation** (⊠ 321 N. University Dr., north of Broward Blvd., Plantation) is a jewel of a mall. The three-level complex includes Macy's and Lord & Taylor; a Sheraton Suites Hotel; and more than 100 specialty shops. In addition to a diverse food court, the Brasserie Max restaurant offers gourmet dining.

Travel industry surveys reveal that shopping is vacationers' number one activity. With 26 million visitors annually, **Sawgrass Mills** (⊠ 12801 W. Sunrise Blvd., at Flamingo Rd., Sunrise), 10 mi west of downtown Fort Lauderdale, proves the point, ranking as the second-biggest tourist attraction in Florida, behind Disney. This so-called world's most popular retail outlet mall is one of the first places visitors ask about. The complex itself is alligator shape, and walking every nook and cranny is about 2 mi. There are 11,000 self-parking spaces, valet parking, and two information centers to meet your needs. The more than 400 shops—many of them manufacturer's outlets, retail outlets, and name-brand discounters—include Neiman Marcus, Calvin Klein, Ann Taylor, Levi's, Donna Karan, Saks Fifth Avenue, Kenneth Cole, and Ron Jon Surf Shop. At the Oasis, restaurants such as Hard Rock Cafe, Legal Sea Foods, Wolfgang Puck Cafe, Rainforest Cafe and others are joined by entertainment venues Regal 23 Cinemas and GameWorks.

NORTH ON SCENIC A1A

North of Fort Lauderdale's Birch Recreation Area, Route A1A edges back from the beach through the section known as the Galt Ocean Mile, and a succession of ocean-side communities lines up against the sea. Traffic can line up, too, as it passes through a changing pattern of beach-blocking high-rises and modest family vacation towns and back again.

Here and there a scenic lighthouse or park punctuates the landscape, and other attractions and recreational opportunities are found inland.

Lauderdale-by-the-Sea

⑯ *5 mi north of Fort Lauderdale.*

Tucked just north of Fort Lauderdale's northern boundary, this low-rise family resort town bans construction of more than three stories. You can drive along lawn-divided El Mar Drive, lined with garden-style motels a block east of Route A1A. However, you don't actually need a car in Lauderdale-by-the-Sea—it's only 3 mi long and restaurants and shops are in close proximity to hotels and the beach.

Where Commercial Boulevard meets the ocean, you can walk out onto **Anglin's Fishing Pier,** stretching 875 ft into the Atlantic. Here you can fish, stop in at any of the popular restaurants clustered around the seafront plaza, or just soak up the scene.

Dining and Lodging

$$–$$$$ ✕ **Sea Watch.** After more than 25 years this nautical-theme restaurant right on Lauderdale-by-the-Sea's beach stays packed during lunch and dinner. The menu has all the right appetizers: oysters Rockefeller, gulf shrimp, clams casino, and Bahamian conch fritters, plus entrée daily specials such as oat-crusted sautéed yellowtail snapper with roasted red bell pepper sauce and basil, or a charbroiled dolphinfish fillet marinated with soy sauce, garlic, black pepper, and lemon juice. Desserts include a cappuccino brownie and strawberries Romanoff. ⊠ *6002 N. Ocean Blvd. (Rte. A1A), Fort Lauderdale,* ☎ *954/781–2200. AE, MC, V.*

$–$$$ ✕ **Aruba Beach Café.** This is your best bet at the pier. A big beachside barn of a place—very casual, always crowded, always fun—it serves large portions of Caribbean conch chowder, Cuban black-bean soup, fresh tropical salads, burgers, sandwiches, and seafood. A reggae/jazz band performs Friday and Sunday 2 to 7. ⊠ *1 E. Commercial Blvd.,* ☎ *954/776–0001. AE, D, DC, MC, V.*

$$–$$$ 🏨 **A Little Inn by the Sea.** French, German, and English are spoken at this inn, which caters to an international clientele. Innkeeper Uli Brandt and his family maintain tropical charm and a bed-and-breakfast-style inn. A complimentary breakfast is set up each morning in the lobby. All rooms have bamboo and rattan furniture. Adding to the flavor are fountains and classical background music at breakfast. The inn is directly on the ocean with a beautiful beach, and rooms have nice views from private balconies. ⊠ *4546 El Mar Dr., 33308,* ☎ *954/772–2450 or 800/492–0311,* ℻ *954/938–9354,* ⅦⅢ *www.alittleinn.com. 10 rooms, 7 suites, 12 efficiencies. Pool, beach, bicycles. AE, D, DC, MC, V.*

$$ 🏨 **Tropic Seas Resort Motel.** It's only a block off A1A, but it's a million-dollar location—directly on the beach and two blocks from municipal tennis courts. Built in the 1950s, units are plain but clean and comfortable, with tropical rattan furniture and ceiling fans. Muffins and coffee are served daily. ⊠ *4616 El Mar Dr., 33308,* ☎ *954/772–2555 or 800/ 952–9581,* ℻ *954/771–5711,* ⅦⅢ *www.tropicseasresort.com. 16 rooms, 6 efficiencies, 7 apartments. Pool, beach. AE, D, DC, MC, V.*

$–$$ 🏨 **Blue Seas Courtyard.** Innkeeper Cristie Furth, with her husband, Marc, runs this small one- and two-story motel—in a quiet resort area across from the beach. Lattice fencing, fountains, and gardens of cactus and impatiens provide privacy around the brick patio and pool. Guest quarters have a Mexican hacienda look with hand-painted/stenciled decor, and have kitchens, terra-cotta tiles, and bright artwork. Unfortunately, it can be quite difficult to get through to the Furths by phone. ⊠ *4525 El Mar Dr., 33308,* ☎ *954/772–3336,* ℻ *954/772–*

6337, WEB *www.blueseascourtyard.com. 12 units. Pool, laundry facilities. MC, V.*

Outdoor Activities and Sports
Anglin's Fishing Pier (☎ 954/491–9403) is open for fishing 24 hours a day. Fishing costs $4, tackle rental is an additional $5 (plus $10 deposit), and bait averages $2.

Pompano Beach

⑰ *3 mi north of Lauderdale-by-the-Sea.*

As Route A1A enters this town directly north of Lauderdale-by-the-Sea, the high-rise procession begins again. Sportfishing is big in Pompano Beach, as its name implies, but there's more to beachside attractions than the popular Fisherman's Wharf. Behind a low coral-rock wall, Alsdorf Park extends north and south of the wharf along the road and beach.

Dining and Lodging

$$$–$$$$ ✕ **Cafe Maxx.** New-wave epicurean dining had its South Florida start
★   here in the early 1980s, and Cafe Maxx remains popular among regional food lovers. Chef Oliver Saucy's menu changes nightly but always showcases foods from the tropics such as jumbo stone crab claws with honey-lime mustard sauce and black-bean and banana-pepper chili with Florida avocado. Appetizer favorites include duck and smoked mozzarella ravioli with brown butter, basil, and sun-dried tomatoes. Desserts such as praline macadamia mousse over chocolate cake with butterscotch sauce stay the tropical course. More than 200 wines are offered by the bottle, another 20 by the glass. ⊠ *2601 E. Atlantic Blvd.,* ☎ *954/782–0606. AE, D, DC, MC, V. No lunch.*

$$–$$$ 🏠 **Best Western Beachcomber.** This property's beach location is central to most Broward County attractions and a mile from the Pompano Pier. Ocean views are everywhere, from the oversize guest-room balconies to the dining rooms. Although there are also villas and penthouse suites atop the eight-story structure, standard rooms are spacious. The multilingual staff is attentive to guest requests. ⊠ *1200 S. Ocean Blvd.,* *33062,* ☎ *954/941–7830 or 800/231–2423,* FAX *954/942–7680,* WEB *www.beachcomberhotel.com. 134 rooms, 9 villas, 4 suites. Restaurant, 2 pools, beach, shuffleboard, volleyball, bar. AE, D, DC, MC, V.*

$$–$$$ 🏠 **Fairfield Palm-Aire Resort & Spa.** This time-share resort has studios, one-bedroom, two-bedroom, and four-bedroom apartments that are individually owned, but share the same decor. Some units have whirlpool tubs and washers and dryers, and kitchens range from partial to full, depending on the unit. Housekeeping is provided on a weekly basis, but is available more often, for a charge. The spa and fitness complex has sauna, steam room, cardiovascular machines, weight equipment, fitness classes, and body treatments. Five championship golf courses at the Palm-Aire Country Club are just a chip away. Lunch and drinks are available at the Tiki Hut. ⊠ *2601 Palm-Aire Dr. N, 33069,* ☎ *954/972–3300,* FAX *954/968–2711,* WEB *www.efairfield.com. 298 units. 37 tennis courts, 3 pools, gym, hot tub, spa. AE, D, DC, MC, V.*

Outdoor Activities and Sports
FISHING
Pompano Pier (☎ 954/943–1488) extends 1,080 ft into the Atlantic. Admission is $2.65; rod-and-reel rental is $5, plus $5 deposit.

For drift fishing try **Fish City Pride** (⊠ Fish City Marina, 2621 N. Riverside Dr., ☎ 954/781–1211). Morning, afternoon, and evening trips cost $28 and include fishing gear and bait. You can arrange for a saltwater charter boat through the **Hillsboro Inlet Marina** (⊠ 2629 N. Riverside

Dr., ☎ 954/943–8222). The 10-boat fleet offers half-day charters for $395, including gear, for up to six people.

GOLF

Crystal Lake South Course (✉ 3800 Crystal Lake Dr., ☎ 954/943–2902) has 18 holes. **Palm-Aire Country Club** (✉ 3701 Oaks Clubhouse Dr., ☎ 954/978–1737; 954/975–6244 for tee line) has five golf courses, including a course with an extra three holes.

HORSE RACING

Pompano Harness Track, Florida's only harness track, has world-class trotters and pacers during its October–August meet. The Top o' the Park restaurant overlooks the finish line. The track also has a poker room and afternoon and evening simulcast betting. ✉ *1800 S.W. 3rd St.,* ☎ *954/972–2000.* ✄ *Grandstand free, clubhouse $2.* ⊙ *Racing Mon., Wed., Fri., and Sat. 7:30.*

ICE-SKATING

Visitors from the North who miss ice and cold can skate at the **Ice-breakers Arena** during morning, afternoon, or evening sessions. ✉ *4601 N. Federal Hwy.,* ☎ *954/943–1437.* ✄ *Sessions $6, skate rental $2.* ⊙ *Weekdays 9:20 AM–11:50 AM and Fri. 8:30 PM–11 PM, Sat. 1:50 PM–3:50 PM and 8–9:30.*

Shopping

Bargain hunters head to the **Festival Flea Market Mall** (✉ 2900 W. Sample Rd.), where more than 800 stores, booths, and kiosks sell new brand name merchandise at a discount. Shopping diversions include an arcade, beauty salon, farmers' market, and food court. The **Pompano Square Mall** (✉ 2001 N. Federal Hwy., at Copans Rd.) is a comfortably sized city mall with 60 shops, three department stores, and a few places for food.

Lighthouse Point

⓲ *2 mi north of Pompano Beach.*

The big attraction here is the view across Hillsboro Inlet to **Hillsboro Light,** the brightest lighthouse in the Southeast. Mariners have used this landmark for decades. From the ocean you can see the light almost halfway to the Bahamas. Although the lighthouse is on private property and is inaccessible to the public, it's well worth a peek.

Dining

$$–$$$ ✕ **Cap's Place.** On an island that was once a bootlegger's haunt, this
★ seafood restaurant is reached by launch and has served such luminaries as Winston Churchill, FDR, and John F. Kennedy. Cap was Captain Theodore Knight, born in 1871, who, with partner-in-crime Al Hasis, floated a derelict barge to the area in the 1920s. Today the rustic restaurant, built on the barge, is run by descendants of Hasis. Baked wahoo steaks are lightly glazed and meaty, the long-cut french fries arouse gluttony, hot and flaky rolls are baked fresh several times a night, and tangy lime pie is a great finishing touch. ✉ *Cap's Dock, 2765 N.E. 28th Ct.,* ☎ *954/941–0418. AE, MC, V. No lunch.*

En Route To the north, Route A1A traverses the so-called Hillsboro Mile (actually more than 2 mi), a millionaire's row of some of the most beautiful and expensive homes in Broward County. The road runs along a narrow strip of land between the Intracoastal Waterway and the ocean, with bougainvillea and oleanders edging the way and yachts docked along both banks. In winter the traffic often creeps at a snail's pace, as vacationers and retirees gawk at the views.

Deerfield Beach

⑲   *3½ mi north of Lighthouse Point.*

☙   The name **Quiet Waters Park** belies what's in store for kids here. Splash Adventure is a high-tech water-play system with slides and tunnels, among other activities. There's also cable waterskiing and boat rental on the park's lake. ✉ *401 S. Powerline Rd.,* ☎ *954/360–1315.* ▣ *$1 weekends, free weekdays; Splash Adventure $3.* ◷ *Daily 8–6. Splash Adventure closed Oct.–mid-Feb.*

Deerfield Island Park, which can be reached only by boat, is a paradise of coastal hammock islands. Officially designated an urban wilderness area along the Intracoastal Waterway, it contains a mangrove swamp that provides a critical habitat for gopher tortoises, gray foxes, raccoons, and armadillos. Boat shuttles run on the hour Wednesday 10–noon and Sunday 10–3; space is limited, so call for reservations. Call also for special events. ✉ *1720 Deerfield Island Park,* ☎ *954/360–1320.* ▣ *Free.*

Dining and Lodging

$$–$$$$ ✕ **Brooks.** This is one of the area's better restaurants, thanks to a French
★   perfectionist at the helm, Bernard Perron. Meals are served in a series of rooms filled with replicas of old masters, cut glass, antiques, and tapestrylike floral wallpaper. Fresh ingredients go into distinctly Floridian cuisine. Main courses include red snapper in papillote, broiled fillet of pompano with seasoned root vegetables, and a sweet lemongrass linguine with bok choy and julienned crisp vegetables. ✉ *500 S. Federal Hwy.,* ☎ *954/427–9302. AE, D, MC, V.*

$$ ✕ **Whale's Rib.** If you're looking for a casual, almost funky, nautical
★   setting near the beach, look no farther. For more than 20 years the Williams family has been serving up fish specials along with whale fries—thinly sliced potatoes that look like hot potato chips. Those with smaller appetites can choose from a good selection of salads and fish sandwiches. Other favorites are specials from the raw bar, Ipswich clams, and a popular fish dip for starters. ✉ *2031 N.E. 2nd St.,* ☎ *954/421–8880. AE, MC, V.*

$$–$$$$ ▥ **Ocean Terrace Suites.** This four-story motel is in one of the quieter sections of north Broward, just south of the Palm Beach county line, across the narrow shore road from the beach. Large units—efficiencies and one- and three-bedroom apartments—all have big balconies overlooking the sea. Colors vary from shore-washed to bright; pink and green pastels tint the bedrooms. The updated furniture is rattan, and units are clean and neat. ✉ *2080 E. Hillsboro Blvd., 33441,* ☎ *954/427–8400,* ℻ *954/427–0555,* ▥ *www.ocean-terracesuites.com. 32 units. Kitchens, pool, laundry. AE, D, DC, MC, V.*

$$–$$$ ▥ **Royal Flamingo Villas.** A small community of houselike villas built in the 1970s reaches from the Intracoastal Waterway to the ocean. The roomy and comfortable one- and two-bedroom villas are condominiums and are individually owned and decorated. All are so quiet that you hear only the soft click of the ceiling fans. If you don't need lavish public facilities, this is your upscale choice at a reasonable price. ✉ *1225 Hillsboro Mile (Rte. A1A), Hillsboro Beach 33062,* ☎ *954/427–0660 or 800/241–2477,* ℻ *954/427–6110,* ▥ *www.royalflamingovillas. com. 40 villas. Pool, beach, dock, boating, shuffleboard, laundry facilities. D, MC, V.*

$–$$ ▥ **Carriage House Resort Motel.** This clean and tidy motel sits one block from the ocean. The white, two-story colonial-style motel with black shutters is actually two buildings connected by a second-story sundeck. Steady improvements have been made to the facility, including the addition of Bahama beds that feel and look like sofas. Kitchenettes are equipped with good-quality utensils. Rooms are self-contained and quiet and have walk-in closets and room safes. ✉ *250 S. Ocean Blvd., 33441,* ☎ *954/427–7670,* FAX *954/428–4790,* WEB *www.carriagehouseresort. com. 6 rooms, 14 efficiencies, 10 1-bedroom apartments. Pool, shuffle-board, laundry facilities. AE, D, DC, MC, V.*

Outdoor Activities and Sports

FISHING

The **Cove Marina** (✉ Hillsboro Blvd. and the Intracoastal Waterway, ☎ 954/360–9343) is home to a deep-sea charter fleet. During the winter season there are excellent runs of sailfish, kingfish, dolphinfish, and tuna. A half-day charter costs about $425 for six people. Enter the marina through the Cove Shopping Center.

GOLF

Off Hillsboro Boulevard west of Interstate 95, **Deer Creek Golf Club** (✉ 2801 Country Club Blvd., ☎ 954/421–5550) has 18 holes.

SCUBA DIVING

One of the area's most popular dive boats, the 48-ft *Lady Go-Diver* (✉ Cove Marina, Hillsboro Blvd. and the Intracoastal Waterway, ☎ 954/ 260–7856) has morning and afternoon dives, plus evening dives on weekends. Snorkelers and certified divers can explore the marine life of nearby reefs and shipwrecks. The cost is $42.50 and riders are welcome for $25.

SOUTH BROWARD

From Hollywood's Broadwalk, a 27-ft-wide thoroughfare paralleling 2 mi of palm-fringed beach, to the western reaches of Old West–flavored Davie, this region has a personality all its own. South Broward's roots are in early Florida settlements. Thus far it has avoided some of the glitz and glamour of its neighbors to the north and south, and folks here like it that way. Still, there's plenty to see and do—excellent restaurants in every price range, world-class pari-mutuels, and a new focus on the arts.

Hollywood

 7 mi south of Fort Lauderdale.

Hollywood is a city undergoing a revival. New shops, restaurants, and art galleries open at a persistent clip. The city spiffed up its Broadwalk, a wide pedestrian walkway along the beach, where rollerbladers are as common as visitors from the North. Trendy sidewalk cafés have opened, vying for space with mom-and-pop T-shirt shops. Downtown, along Harrison Street and Hollywood Boulevard, jazz clubs and still more fashionable restaurants are drawing young professionals to the scene. Design studios and art galleries are also abundant along these two streets.

In 1921 Joseph W. Young, a California real-estate developer, began developing the community of Hollywood from the woody flatlands. It quickly became a major tourist magnet, home to casino gambling and everything else that made Florida hot. Reminders of the glory days of the Young era remain in places like Young Circle (the junction of U.S. 1 and Hollywood Boulevard) and the stately old homes that line east Hollywood streets.

The **Art and Culture Center of Hollywood** is a visual and performing-arts center with an art reference library, outdoor sculpture garden, arts school, and museum store. It's just east of Young Circle. ✉ *1650 Har-*

rison St., ☎ *954/921–3274.* 🖃 *$5.* ◷ *Tues.–Wed. and Fri.–Sat. 10–4, Thurs. 10–8, and Sun. 1–4.*

With the Intracoastal Waterway to its west and the beach and ocean to the east, the 2.2-mi paved promenade known as the **Broadwalk** has been popular with pedestrians and cyclists since 1924. Expect to hear French spoken along this scenic stretch, especially during the winter; Hollywood Beach has been a favorite winter getaway for Québecois ever since Joseph Young hired French-Canadians to work here in the 1920s.

Hollywood North Beach Park is at the north end of the Broadwalk. No high-rises overpower the scene, nothing hip or chic, just a laid-back, old-fashioned place for enjoying the sun, sand, and sea. ⊠ *Rte. A1A and Sheridan St.,* ☎ *954/926–2444.* 🖃 *Free; parking $4 until 2, $2 after.* ◷ *Daily 8–6.*

☺ Comprising 1,500 acres at the Intracoastal Waterway, **West Lake Park** is one of Florida's largest urban nature facilities, providing a wide range of recreational activities. You can rent a canoe, kayak, or boat with an electric motor (no fossil fuels are allowed in the park) or take the 40-minute environmental boat tour. Extensive boardwalks traverse a mangrove community, where endangered and threatened species abound. A 65-ft observation tower allows views of the entire park. More than $1 million in exhibits are on display at the **Anne Kolb Nature Center,** named after the late county commissioner who was a leading environmental advocate. A great place to take youngsters, the center's exhibit hall features 27 interactive displays, an ecology room, and a trilevel aquarium. ⊠ *1200 Sheridan St.,* ☎ *954/926–2410.* 🖃 *Weekends $1, weekdays free; exhibit hall $2.* ◷ *Daily 8–6.*

☺ At the edge of Hollywood lies **Seminole Native Village,** a reservation where you can pet a cougar, hold a baby alligator, and watch other wildlife demonstrations. The Seminole also sell their arts and crafts here. Across the street from the Seminole Native Village, **Hollywood Seminole Gaming** (⊠ 4150 N. State Rd. 7, ☎ 954/961–3220) is open 24/7 and has high-stakes bingo, low-stakes poker, and more than 1,000 gaming machines. ⊠ *3551 N. State Rd. 7,* ☎ *954/961–4519.* 🖃 *Self-guided tour $5, guided tour including alligator wrestling and snake demonstrations $10.* ◷ *Daily 9–5.*

In addition to displaying a collection of artifacts from the Seminoles and other tribes, Joe Dan and Virginia Osceola sell contemporary Native American arts and crafts at the **Anhinga Indian Trading Post.** It's ½ mi south from the Seminole Native Village, although that technically puts it over the Fort Lauderdale border. ⊠ *5791 S. State Rd. 7, Fort Lauderdale,* ☎ *954/581–0416.* ◷ *Daily 9–5.*

Dining and Lodging

$$–$$$$ ✗ **Giorgio's Grill.** Good food and service are hallmarks of this large, 400-seat restaurant overlooking the Intracoastal Waterway. Seafood is a specialty on the self-described "Mediterranean-inspired" menu, but you'll also find a nice selection of pasta and meat dishes. A great water view and friendly staff add to the experience. A surprisingly extensive wine list is reasonably priced. ⊠ *606 N. Ocean Dr.,* ☎ *954/929–7030. AE, D, DC, MC, V.*

$$–$$$$ ✗ **Martha's.** You have two choices of dining locations here, both of which have impressive views of the Intracoastal Waterway. Martha's Tropical Grille, on the upper deck, is more informal. Martha's Supper Club, on the lower level, is dressier, and piano music accompanies dinner. Both floors offer similar menus, however—chiefly Florida seafood: flaky dolphinfish in a court bouillon; shrimp dipped in a piña colada

batter, rolled in coconut, and panfried with orange mustard sauce; and snapper prepared 17 ways. Complimentary dock space is provided if you're arriving by boat. ⊠ *6024 N. Ocean Dr.,* ☎ *954/923–5444. Reservations recommended. AE, D, DC, MC, V.*

$$–$$$ ✕ **Las Brisas.** Right next to the beach, this cozy bistro offers seating inside or out, and the food is Argentine with an Italian flair. A small pot sits on each table filled with *chimichurri*—a paste made of oregano, parsley, olive oil, salt, garlic, and crushed pepper—for spreading on steaks. Grilled or deep-fried fish is a favorite, as are pork chops, chicken, and pasta entrées. Desserts include a rum cake, a flan like *mamacita* used to make, and a *dulce con leche* (a sweet milk pudding). The wine list is predominantly South American. ⊠ *600 N. Surf Rd.,* ☎ *954/923–1500. AE, D, DC, MC, V. No lunch.*

$$–$$$ ✕ **Sushi Blues Café.** First-class Japanese food is served up in a cubicle setting that's so jammed you'll wonder where this hip group disappears to by day. Japanese chefs prepare conventional and macrobiotic-influenced dishes that range from a variety of sushi and rolls (California, tuna, and the Yozo roll, with snapper, flying-fish eggs, asparagus, and Japanese mayonnaise) to steamed veggies with tofu and steamed snapper with miso sauce. The Sushi Blues Band performs on Friday and Saturday; guest musicians often sit in. ⊠ *1836 S. Young Circle,* ☎ *954/929–9560. AE, MC, V. No lunch.*

$–$$ ✕ **Le Tub.** Formerly a Sunoco gas station, this place is now a quirky waterside saloon with a seeming affection for claw-foot bathtubs. Hand-painted tubs are everywhere—under ficus, sea grape, and palm trees. The eatery is highly favored by locals for affordable food: mostly shrimp, burgers, and barbecue. ⊠ *1100 N. Ocean Dr.,* ☎ *954/921–9425. No credit cards.*

$$$–$$$$ 🏨 **The Westin Diplomat Resort & Spa.** The new Diplomat, opened in
★ 2002 on the site of the original 1950s hotel of the same name, is a grand 39-story, dual-tower property. The hotel has a lobby/atrium area with ceilings soaring to 60 ft in height. A signature of the resort is its 120-ft bridged pool, extending from the lobby to the beachfront. A Mediterranean-inspired spa offers complete fitness facilities and more than 20 luxury treatments. The Diplomat's country club is across the Intracoastal and has 60 rooms, golf, tennis, and a spa. You'll have use of facilities at both properties and shuttle service is provided. ⊠ *1995 E. Hallandale Beach Blvd., 33309,* ☎ *954/457–2000 or 800/327–1212,* 🌐 *www.diplomatresort.com. 900 rooms, 100 1- or 2-bedroom suites. 3 restaurants, in-room data ports, minibars, 18-hole golf course, 10 tennis courts, 3 pools, health club, 2 spas, marina, 2 bars, business services, convention center. AE, DC, MC, V.*

$$–$$$ 🏨 **Greenbriar Beach Club.** In a neighborhood of Hollywood Beach known for its flowered streets, this oceanfront all-suites hotel retains its 1950s style outside, but inside the rooms have been renovated and include full kitchens. The staff is multilingual, and the TVs even have four Spanish and two French channels. On a 200-ft stretch of beach, the hotel bills itself as "Florida's best-kept secret," and it just could be. ⊠ *1900 S. Surf Rd., 33019,* ☎ *954/922–2606 or 800/861–4873,* 📠 *954/923–0897,* 🌐 *www.greenbriarbc.com. 47 suites. Pool, beach, volleyball, laundry facilities. AE, D, MC, V.*

$$ 🏨 **Manta Ray Inn.** Canadians Donna and Dwayne Boucher run this im-
★ maculate and affordable two-story inn nestled in a quiet setting on a sandy beach perfect for a low-key getaway. Dating from the 1940s, the inn offers casual, comfortable beachfront accommodations. Kitchens are equipped with pots, pans, and mini-appliances that make housekeeping convenient. Apartments have full closets and shower stalls, and two-bedroom units also have tub-showers. ⊠ *1715 S. Surf Rd., 33019,* ☎ *954/*

921–9666 or 800/255–0595, FAX *954/929–8220,* WEB *www.mantarayinn. com. 12 units. Beach. AE, D, MC, V.*

$–$$ 🏨 **Driftwood on the Ocean.** This attractive late-1950s-era resort motel faces the beach at the secluded south end of Surf Road. The setting is what draws guests, but attention to maintenance and frequent refurbishing are what make it a value. Accommodations range from a studio to a deluxe two-bedroom, two-bath suite. Most units have a kitchen; all have balconies or terraces. ⊠ *2101 S. Surf Rd., 33019,* ☎ *954/923–9528 or 800/ 944–3148,* FAX *954/922–1062,* WEB *www.driftwoodontheocean.com. 7 rooms, 9 2-bedroom apartments, 13 1-bedroom apartments, 20 efficiencies. Pool, beach, bicycles, shuffleboard, laundry facilities. AE, D, MC, V.*

$–$$ 🏨 **Sea Downs.** This three-story lodging directly on the Broadwalk is a good choice for efficiency or apartment living (one-bedroom apartments can be joined to make two-bedroom units). All but two units have ocean views. Kitchens are fully equipped, and most units have tub-showers and closets. Housekeeping is provided once a week. In between, fresh towels are provided daily and sheets upon request, but you must make your own bed. ⊠ *2900 N. Surf Rd., 33019-3704,* ☎ *954/923–4968,* FAX *954/923–8747,* WEB *www.seadowns.com. 6 efficiencies, 8 1-bedroom apartments. In-room data ports, pool, laundry facilities. No credit cards.*

Nightlife and the Arts

THE ARTS

Harrison Street Art and Design District in downtown Hollywood is home to galleries that carry original artwork (eclectic paintings, sculpture, photography, and mixed media), Costa Rican collectibles, and African artifacts. Friday nights the artists' studios, galleries, and shops stay open late while crowds meander along Hollywood Boulevard and Harrison Street. **Indaba** (⊠ 2029 Harrison St., ☎ 954/920–2029) celebrates African art with an extensive collection of masks, statues, cloth, baskets, and furniture. **Mosaica** (⊠ 2020 Hollywood Blvd., ☎ 954/923– 7006) design studio is where unique mosaic tile tables, mirrors, and art are displayed in a beautiful gallery setting. The colorful home furnishings gallery **Alliage** (⊠ 2035 Harrison St., ☎ 954/922–7017) has tables, wall consoles, and sculptures handcrafted from brushed aluminum and sand-blasted glass.

NIGHTLIFE

Although downtown Hollywood has a small town feel, it has an assortment of coffee bars, Internet cafés, sports bars, martini lounges, and dance clubs. The downtown area is known for its live jazz and blues venues. **O'Hara's Hollywood** (⊠ 1903 Hollywood Blvd., ☎ 954/ 925–2555) highlights top local talents with live jazz and blues six nights a week. For New Orleans–style jazz, head to **Ellington's** (⊠ 2009 Harrison St., ☎ 954/920–9322). Sushi café and wine bar **Sushi Blues** (⊠ 1836 Young Circle, ☎ 954/929–9560) serves up live blues Friday and Saturday nights starting at 9. **Warehaus 57** (⊠ 1904 Hollywood Blvd., ☎ 954/926–6633) is where aspiring novelists and poets share their words with the café's crowd. The late-night coffee bar **Now Art Café** (⊠ 1820 Young Circle, ☎ 954/922–0506) hosts art exhibits and live one-man bands.

Outdoor Activities and Sports

BIKING

The 2-mi **Broadwalk,** which has its own bike path, is popular with cyclists.

DOG RACING

Hollywood Greyhound Track has live dog-racing action during its December–May season and simulcasting every day. The Dog House is its new sports bar and grill with TVs. ✉ *831 N. Federal Hwy., Hallandale,* ☎ *954/924–3200.* ⊞ *Grandstand $1, clubhouse $2, parking free.* ⊘ *Racing nightly at 7:30 and Tues., Thurs., and Sat. at 12:30 PM.*

Sea Leg's III (✉ 5400 N. Ocean Dr., ☎ 954/923–2109) runs drift-fishing trips from 8 AM to 12:30 PM and 1:30 to 6 and bottom-fishing trips from 7 PM to midnight. Trips cost $30 to $35, and include fishing gear.

The **Diplomat Country Club & Spa** (✉ 501 Diplomat Pkwy., Hallandale, ☎ 954/457–2000), with 18 holes and a spa, is southwest of the resort. The course at **Emerald Hills** (✉ 4100 N. Hills Dr., ☎ 954/961–4000) has 18 holes.

Gulfstream Park Race Track is the winter home of some of the nation's top thoroughbreds, trainers, and jockeys. In addition to races, there are family days with attractions for kids and scheduled concerts with name performers. The season is capped by the $1 million Florida Derby, which features Kentucky Derby hopefuls. Racing is held January through April. ✉ *901 S. Federal Hwy., Hallandale,* ☎ *954/454–7000 or 800/771–TURF.* ⊞ *Grandstand $3, clubhouse $5.* ⊘ *Racing Wed.–Mon. at 1 and nightly simulcasting.*

Dania Beach

㉑ *3 mi north of Hollywood, 4 mi south of Fort Lauderdale.*

This town at the south edge of Fort Lauderdale is probably best known for its antiques dealers, but there are other attractions as well.

★ ☾ The **South Florida Museum of Natural History** has an extensive prehistoric collection, including the Bambiraptor feinbergi, better known as "Bambi"—the missing link in the dinosaur–bird evolution. This hidden treasure of a museum also has a wide-ranging permanent collection ranging from pre-Columbian art and Greco-Roman materials to artifacts from early Florida. Also on display are a 3-ton quartz crystal and dioramas on Tequesta life and shipwreck artifacts. Monthly lectures, conferences, field trips, and a summer archaeological camp are offered. ✉ *481 S. Federal Hwy.,* ☎ *954/925–7770,* ᵂᴱᴮ *www.sfmuseumnh.org.* ⊞ *$9.95.* ⊘ *Tues.–Fri. 10–4, Sat. 10–6, Sun. noon–6.*

The **John U. Lloyd Beach State Recreation Area** is a pleasant plot of land with a pine-shaded beach, a jetty pier where you can fish, a marina, nature trails, and canoeing on Whiskey Creek. This is a great spot to watch cruise ships entering and departing Port Everglades, to the west across the waterway. ✉ *6503 N. Ocean Dr.,* ☎ *954/923–2833.* ⊞ *$4 per vehicle with up to 8 people.* ⊘ *Daily 8–sunset.*

★ **IGFA Fishing Hall of Fame and Museum** is a shrine to the sport of fishing. Near the Fort Lauderdale airport at Interstate 95 and Griffin Road, the center is the creation of the International Game Fishing Association. In addition to checking out the World Fishing Hall of Fame, a marina, and an extensive museum and research library, you can visit seven galleries with virtual-reality fishing and other interactive displays. And in the Catch Gallery, you can cast off via virtual reality and try to reel in a marlin, sailfish, trout, tarpon, or bass. ✉ *300 Gulfstream Way, Dania Beach,* ☎ *954/922–4212,* ᵂᴱᴮ *www.igfa.org.* ⊞ *$4.99.* ⊘ *Daily 10–6.*

Outdoor Activities and Sports

FISHING

The 920-ft **Dania Pier** (☎ 954/927–0640) is open around the clock. Fishing is $3 (including parking), tackle rental is $6, bait is about $3, and spectators pay $1.

JAI ALAI

Dania Jai-Alai Palace has one of the fastest ball games on the planet, scheduled year-round. Added features include simulcast wagering from other tracks, and a poker room. ⊠ *301 E. Dania Beach Blvd.,* ☎ *954/ 920–1511.* ☜ *$1.50; reserved seats $2–$7.* ☉ *Games Tues. and Sat. at noon, Sun. at 1, nightly Tues.–Sat. at 7:15.*

ROLLER COASTER

Dania Beach Hurricane roller coaster isn't the highest, fastest, or longest coaster in the world, but it's near the top in all those categories, and it is the tallest wooden roller coaster south of Atlanta. This is a retro-feeling ride—a wooden coaster that creaks like an old staircase while you travel its 3,200 ft of track and plummet from a height of 100 ft at speeds of up to 55 mph. ⊠ *1760 N.W. 1st St.,* ☎ *954/921–7433.* ☜ *$5.89.* ☉ *Sun.–Thurs. 10 AM–11:30 PM, Fri. and Sat. 10 AM–2 AM.*

MINIATURE GOLF

Boomers! has action games for kids of all ages—go-kart and naskart racing, miniature golf, batting cages, bumper boats, lasertron, and a skycoaster. ⊠ *1801 N.W. 1st St.,* ☎ *954/921–1411.* ☉ *Sun.–Thurs. 10 AM–2 AM, Fri. and Sat. 10 AM–6 AM.*

Shopping

More than 250 antiques dealers in **Dania Antique Row** buy and sell items from antique furniture to vintage knickknacks. This two-square-block area is on Federal Highway (U.S. 1), ½ mi south of the Fort Lauderdale airport and ½ mi north of Hollywood. Take the Stirling Road or Griffin Road East exit off Interstate 95.

Davie

㉒ *4 mi west of Dania.*

This town's horse farms and estates are the closest thing to the Old West in South Florida. Folks in Western wear ride their fine horses through downtown—where they have the same right of way as motorists—and order up takeout at "ride-through" windows. With 70,000 residents, the town has doubled in size in 15 years, and gated communities are now found alongside ranches. A monthly rodeo is Davie's most famous activity.

☾ Gators, crocodiles, river otters, and birds of prey can be seen at **Flamingo Gardens and Wray Botanical Collection,** as can a 25,000-square-ft walk-through aviary, a plant house, and an Everglades museum in the pioneer Wray Home. A half-hour guided tram ride winds through a citrus grove and wetlands area. ⊠ *3750 S. Flamingo Rd.,* ☎ *954/473–2955,* WEB *www.flamingogardens.org.* ☜ *$12, tram ride $3.* ☉ *Daily 9:30– 5:30; closed Mon. June–Sept.*

☾ At the **Young at Art Children's Museum,** kids can work with paint, graphics, sculpture, and crafts according to themes that change three times a year. Then they take their masterpieces home with them. ⊠ *11584 W. State Rd. 84, in the Plaza,* ☎ *954/424–0085,* WEB *www.youngatartmuseum. org.* ☜ *$4.* ☉ *Mon.–Sat. 10–5, Sun. noon–5.*

Dining

$$–$$$ ✕ **Armadillo Cafe.** Chefs Eve Montella and Kevin McCarthy have cre-
★ ated a restaurant whose southwestern theme, regional decor, and inspired food have made it a destination for visitors from around the world
for more than a decade. Seafood is the mainstay of the menu, but other
specialties include grilled tenderloin of ostrich with sun-dried cherry
sauce and steaks with pasilla chili sauce. An extensively researched wine
list offers cult and niche vintages. ✉ *3400 S. University,* ☎ *954/423–
9954. AE, D, DC, MC, V.*

Nightlife and the Arts

THE ARTS

Bailey Concert Hall (✉ Central Campus of Broward Community College, 3501 S.W. Davie Rd., ☎ 954/475–6884) is a popular place for
classical music concerts, dance, drama, and other performing-arts activities, especially October–April.

NIGHTLIFE

Davie Junction (✉ 6311 S.W. 45th St., ☎ 954/581–1132), South
Florida's hottest location for country music, is in the heart of Broward's
horse country. Local and national performers perform regularly and
dance lessons are available. It's open for dinner and dancing until 4
AM Tuesday through Saturday.

Uncle Funny's Comedy Club (✉ 9160 State Rd. 84, Pine Island Plaza,
☎ 954/474–5653) showcases national and local comics Wednesday
through Friday and Sunday at 8:30, Friday and Saturday at 11, plus
Saturday at 7 and 9.

Outdoor Activities and Sports

BIKING

Bicycle and in-line skating enthusiasts can ride at the **Brian Piccolo Skate
Park and Velodrome** (✉ 9501 Sheridan St., Cooper City, ☎ 954/437–
2626), south of Davie. Hours are geared to after-school and weekend
skating.

RODEO

The local **Davie Rodeo** (✉ 4271 Davie Rd., ☎ 954/384–7075) is held
on the Bergeron Rodeo Grounds the fourth weekend of every month.
Saturday night bull riding starts at 8 PM. Special national rodeos come
to town some weekends.

FORT LAUDERDALE AND BROWARD COUNTY A TO Z

*To research prices, get advice from other travelers, and book travel ar-
rangements, visit www.fodors.com.*

AIR TRAVEL

CARRIERS

More than 40 scheduled airlines, commuters and charters operate in
and out of Fort Lauderdale–Hollywood International Airport.

➤ MAJOR AIRLINE CONTACTS: **Air Canada** (☎ 800/689–2247). **Air Jamaica** (☎ 800/523–5585). **Air Tran** (☎ 800/247–8726). **America West**
(☎ 800/235–9292). **American** (☎ 800/433–7300). **Continental** (☎ 800/
525–0280). **Delta** (☎ 800/221–1212). **JetBlue** (☎ 800/538–2583).
MetroJet (☎ 888/638–7653). **Midway** (☎ 800/446–4392). **Northwest**
(☎ 800/225–2525). **Southwest** (☎ 800/435–9792). **Spirit** (☎ 800/772–
7117). **TWA** (☎ 800/221–2000). **United** (☎ 800/241–6522). **US Airways** (☎ 800/428–4322).

AIRPORTS

Fort Lauderdale–Hollywood International Airport, 4 mi south of downtown Fort Lauderdale and just off U.S. 1, is one of Florida's busiest, serving more than 16 million passengers a year. A major airport expansion added a new terminal, parking, and access roads.

Broward County Mass Transit operates bus route No. 1 between the airport and its main terminal at Broward Boulevard and Northwest 1st Avenue, in the center of Fort Lauderdale. Service from the airport is every 20 minutes and begins daily at 5:40 AM; the last bus leaves the airport at 11:15 PM. The fare is $1 (50¢ for senior citizens). Airport Express provides limousine service to all parts of Broward County. Fares to most Fort Lauderdale beach hotels are in the $8–$12 range.
➤ AIRPORT INFORMATION: **Fort Lauderdale–Hollywood International Airport** (☎ 954/359–6100). **Airport Express** (☎ 954/561–8888). **Broward County Mass Transit** (☎ 954/357–8400).

BOAT AND FERRY TRAVEL

Water Taxi provides service along the Intracoastal Waterway in Fort Lauderdale between the 17th Street Causeway and Oakland Park Boulevard daily from 6 AM until midnight.
➤ BOAT AND FERRY INFORMATION: **Water Taxi** (☎ 954/467–6677).

BUS TRAVEL

Greyhound Lines buses stop in Fort Lauderdale.

Broward County Mass Transit bus service covers the entire county and ventures into Dade and Palm Beach counties. The fare is $1; unlimited daily, weekly, and monthly passes are available. Route service starts at 5 AM and continues to 11:30 PM, except on Sunday. Call for route information.

TMAX Express is free and covers both the downtown loop and the beach area. The Courthouse Route runs every 10 minutes weekdays from 7:30 until 6. The Las Olas & Beach Route runs every half hour Friday to Saturday 5:45 PM–1:45 AM.

CUTTING COSTS

Broward County Mass Transit offers special seven-day tourist passes that cost $9 and are good for unlimited use on all county buses. These are available at some hotels, at Broward County libraries, and at the main bus terminal.
➤ BUS INFORMATION: **Broward County Mass Transit** (Main Bus Terminal: ✉ Broward Blvd. at N.W. 1st Ave., Fort Lauderdale, ☎ 954/357–8400). **Greyhound Lines** (Fort Lauderdale: ✉ 515 N.E. 3rd St., ☎ 800/231–2222 or 954/764–6551). **TMAX** (☎ 954/761–3543).

CAR RENTAL

Agencies in the airport include Avis, Budget, Dollar, and National. Other car rental companies offer shuttle services to nearby rental centers.
➤ LOCAL AGENCIES: **Alamo** (☎ 954/525–4713). **Avis** (☎ 954/359–3255). **Budget** (☎ 954/359–4700). **Dollar** (☎ 954/359–7800). **Enterprise** (☎ 954/760–9888). **Hertz** (☎ 954/764–1199). **National** (☎ 954/359–8303).

CAR TRAVEL

Access to Broward County from north or south is via Florida's Turnpike, Interstate 95, U.S. 1, or U.S. 441. Interstate 75 (Alligator Alley) connects Broward with Florida's west coast and runs parallel to State Road 84 within the county.

Except during rush hour, Broward County is a fairly easy place in which to drive. East–west Interstate 595 runs from westernmost Broward County and links Interstate 75 with Interstate 95 and U.S. 1, providing handy access to the airport. The scenic but slow Route A1A generally parallels the beach. Another road less traveled is the Sawgrass Expressway (also known as State Road 869 north of I–595 and I–75 south), a toll road that's a handy link to Sawgrass Mills shopping and the ice-hockey arena, both in Sunrise.

EMERGENCIES

Dial 911 for police or ambulance.

➤ 24-Hour Pharmacies: **Eckerd Drug** (⊠ 1701 E. Commercial Blvd., Fort Lauderdale, ☎ 954/771–0660; ⊠ 154 N. University Dr., Pembroke Pines, ☎ 954/432–5510). **Walgreens** (⊠ 2855 Stirling Rd., Fort Lauderdale, ☎ 954/981–1104; ⊠ 601 E. Commercial Blvd., Oakland Park, ☎ 954/772–4206; ⊠ 289 S. Federal Hwy., Deerfield Beach, ☎ 954/481–2993; ⊠ 3015 S. University Dr., Davie, ☎ 954/475–9375; ⊠ 9005 Pines Blvd., Hollywood, ☎ 954/392–4749).

MEDIA

NEWSPAPERS AND MAGAZINES

The *South Florida Sun-Sentinel* and its affiliated magazine *City & Shore* cover South Florida news and events with a focus on Greater Fort Lauderdale.

RADIO

FM: 91.3 WLRN, public radio; 93.9 WLVE, jazz; 97.3 WFLC, adult contemporary; 98.7 WKGR, rock; 99.9 WKIS, country; 100.7 WHYI, Top 40; 101.5 WLIF, adult contemporary; 102.7 WMXJ, oldies; 105.9 WBGG, classic rock. AM: 560 WQAM, sports; 610 WIOD, news.

TAXIS

It's difficult to hail a cab on the street. Sometimes you can pick one up at a major hotel. Otherwise, phone ahead. Fares are not cheap; meters run at a rate of $2.75 for the first mile and $2 for each additional mile; waiting time is 25¢ per minute. The major company serving the area is Yellow Cab.

➤ Taxi Information: **Yellow Cab** (☎ 954/565–5400).

TOURS

Carrie B., a 300-passenger day cruiser, gives 90-minute tours up the New River and Intracoastal Waterway. Cruises depart at 11, 1, and 3 each day and cost $11.95.

Jungle Queen III and *Jungle Queen IV* are 175-passenger and 527-passenger tour boats that take day and night cruises up the New River through the heart of Fort Lauderdale. The sightseeing cruises at 10 and 2 cost $12.95, and the evening dinner cruise costs $27.95. You can also take a daylong trip to Miami's Bayside Marketplace ($15.95), on Biscayne Bay, for shopping and sightseeing on Wednesday and Saturday, departing at 9:15. Call in advance for availability.

Professional Diving Charters operates the 60-ft glass-bottom boat *Pro Diver II*. On Tuesday through Saturday mornings and Sunday afternoon, two-hour sightseeing trips costing $20 take in offshore reefs; snorkeling can be arranged at $27 per person.

➤ Tours Information: *Carrie B.* (⊠ Riverwalk at S.E. 5th Ave., Fort Lauderdale, ☎ 954/768–9920). *Jungle Queen III* and *Jungle Queen IV* (⊠ Radisson Bahia Mar Beach Resort, 801 Seabreeze Blvd., Fort Lauderdale, ☎ 954/462–5596). **Professional Diving Charters** (⊠ 515 Seabreeze Blvd., Fort Lauderdale, ☎ 954/761–3413).

TRAIN TRAVEL

Amtrak provides daily service to the Fort Lauderdale station as well as other Broward County stops at Hollywood and Deerfield Beach.

Tri-Rail operates train service daily 4 AM–11 PM (more limited on weekends) through Broward, Miami-Dade, and Palm Beach counties. There are six Broward stations west of Interstate 95: Hillsboro Boulevard in Deerfield Beach, Pompano Beach, Cypress Creek, Fort Lauderdale, Fort Lauderdale Airport, Sheridan Street in Hollywood, and Hollywood Boulevard.

➤ TRAIN INFORMATION: **Amtrak** (Fort Lauderdale: ✉ 200 S.W. 21st Terr., ☎ 800/872–7245 or 954/587–1287). **Tri-Rail** (☎ 800/874–7245).

VISITOR INFORMATION

➤ TOURIST INFORMATION: **Chamber of Commerce of Greater Fort Lauderdale** (✉ 512 N.E. 3rd Ave., Fort Lauderdale 33301, ☎ 954/462–6000, WEB www.ftlchamber.com). **Davie/Cooper City Chamber of Commerce** (✉ 4185 S.W. 64th Ave., Davie 33314, ☎ 954/581–0790, WEB www.davie-coopercity.org). **Greater Deerfield Beach Chamber of Commerce** (✉ 1601 E. Hillsboro Blvd., Deerfield Beach 33441, ☎ 954/427–1050, WEB www.deerfieldchamber.com). **Greater Fort Lauderdale Convention & Visitors Bureau** (✉ 1850 Eller Dr., Suite 303, Fort Lauderdale 33316, ☎ 954/765–4466, WEB www.broward.org). **Hollywood Chamber of Commerce** (✉ 330 N. Federal Hwy., Hollywood 33020, ☎ 954/923–4000, WEB www.hollywoodchamber.org). **Lauderdale-by-the-Sea Chamber of Commerce** (✉ 4201 N. Ocean Dr., Lauderdale-by-the-Sea 33308, ☎ 954/776–1000, WEB www.lbts.com). **Pompano Beach Chamber of Commerce** (✉ 2200 E. Atlantic Blvd., Pompano Beach 33062, ☎ 954/941–2940, WEB www.pompanobeachchamber.com).

5 PALM BEACH AND THE TREASURE COAST

Golden beaches dotted with luxuriant palms and other tropical foliage stretching mile after mile unify this part of Florida's eclectic central east coast, anchored by Palm Beach, Florida's haute playground for relaxation, exploration, shopping, and dining. To the north, you'll encounter the Treasure Coast, a mix of rustic and sometimes upscale beach towns interspersed with nature preserves. South of Palm Beach, along what's known as the Palm Beaches, you'll find other intriguing communities, among them fashionable Delray Beach and Boca Raton.

Revised by
Lynne Helm

MUCH LIKE A KALEIDOSCOPE, this multifaceted section of Atlantic coast resists categorization for good reason. The territory from Palm Beach south to Boca Raton glitters as the northern portion of the Gold Coast, extending south past Fort Lauderdale to Miami. North of Palm Beach you'll uncover the comparatively undeveloped Treasure Coast—liberally sprinkled with coastal gems—where towns and wide spots in the road await your discovery. Altogether, you'll find delightful disparity from the unrivaled old-money allure of Palm Beach, pulsing faster with plenty of surviving post–dot-com wealth, to the low-key ambiance of Hutchinson Island, Manalapan, or the seaside trailer park simplicity of Briny Breezes. Seductive as the beach scene interspersed by eclectic dining options can be, you should also take advantage of flourishing commitments to historic preservation and the arts, with town after town boasting intriguing museums, galleries, theaters, and gardens.

Long reigning as the epicenter of where the crème de la crème go to shake off winter's chill, Palm Beach has evolved into a year-round hotbed of platinum-grade consumption. Rare is the visitor to this region who can resist popping over for a peek, if for no reason other than to gawk. Yes, other Florida gems such as Jupiter Island consistently rank higher on per capita wealth meters of financial intelligence sources such as *Worth* magazine. But there's no competing with the historic social supremacy of Palm Beach, long a winter address for heirs of icons named Rockefeller, Vanderbilt, Colgate, Post, Kellogg, and Kennedy. Yet even newer power brokers with names like Kravis, Peltz, and Trump are made to understand that strict laws govern everything from building to landscaping, and not so much as a pool awning gets added without a town council nod. If Palm Beach were to fly a flag, it's been observed there might be three interlocking Cs, standing not only for Cartier, Chanel, and Calvin Klein, but also for clean, civil, and capricious. Only three bridges allow access to the island and huge tour buses are a no-no. Yet when a freighter once ran aground near a Palm Beach socialite's pool, she was quick to lament not having "enough Bloody Mary mix for all these sailors."

To learn who's who and what's what in Palm Beach, it helps to pick up a copy of the *Palm Beach Daily News*—locals call it the Shiny Sheet because its high-quality paper avoids smudging society hands or the Porthault linens—for, as it is said, to be mentioned in the Shiny Sheet is to be Palm Beach.

All this fabled ambience started with Henry Morrison Flagler, Florida's premier developer and cofounder, along with John D. Rockefeller, of Standard Oil. No sooner did Flagler bring the railroad to Florida in the 1890s, than he erected the famed Royal Poinciana and Breakers hotels. Rail access sent real estate prices soaring, and ever since, princely sums have been forked over for personal stationery engraved with the 33480 zip code of Palm Beach. To service Palm Beach with servants and other workers, Flagler also developed an off-island community a mile or so west. West Palm Beach now bustles with its own affluent identity even if there's still no competing with Florida's toniest island resort.

With Palm Beach proper representing only 1% of Palm Beach County's land, remaining territory is given over to West Palm and other classic Florida coastal towns, along with—to the west—citrus farms, the Arthur R. Marshall–Loxahatchee National Wildlife Refuge, and Lake Okeechobee, a world-class bass-fishing hot spot and Florida's largest lake.

Well worth exploring are the Treasure Coast territory, covering northernmost Palm Beach County, plus Martin, St. Lucie, and Indian River counties. Despite a growing number of malls and beachfront condominiums, much shoreline remains blissfully undeveloped. Inland you'll find cattle ranching in tracts of pine and palmetto scrub along with sugar and citrus production. Shrimp farming is taking on fresh appeal with new techniques for acclimatizing shrimp from saltwater—land near seawater is costly—to freshwater, all the better to serve demand from restaurants popping up all over the region.

Along the coast, the broad tidal lagoon called the Indian River separates barrier islands from the mainland. It shelters boaters on the Intracoastal Waterway, functions as a nursery for saltwater game fish, and helps guard orange and grapefruit trees from frost. Sea turtles come ashore at night from late April to September to lay eggs on its beaches.

Pleasures and Pastimes

Beaches
Logically from a tourism marketing standpoint, many towns along this idyllic stretch officially embrace the word *beach,* and why not? Here you find miles of golden strands—some relatively quiet, others buzzing—blessed with shades of blue-green waters you won't encounter farther north. Among the least crowded are those at Hobe Sound National Wildlife Refuge and Fort Pierce Inlet State Recreation Area. To see and be seen, head for Boca Raton's three beaches or Delray Beach's broad stretch of sand.

Dining
Not surprisingly, numerous elegant establishments offer upscale Continental and contemporary cuisine, but the area also teems with casual waterfront spots serving up affordable burgers and fresh seafood feasts. Grouper, fried or blackened, is especially big here, along with the ubiquitous shrimp. An hour west from the coast, around Lake Okeechobee, you can dine on catfish, panfried to perfection and so fresh it seems barely out of the water. Early-bird menus, a Florida hallmark, typically entice the budget-minded with several dinner entrées at reduced prices when ordered during certain hours, usually before 5 or 6 PM.

CATEGORY	COST*
$$$$	over $30
$$$	$20–$30
$$	$10–$20
$	under $10

per person for a main course at dinner

Fishing
Except for ice fishing, you'll find within a 50-mi radius of Palm Beach virtually every form of hook-and-line activity going on any season you please. Charter boats for deep-sea fishing abound from Boca Raton to Sebastian Inlet. West of Vero Beach, there's great marsh fishing for catfish and perch. Lake Okeechobee is the place for bass fishing.

Golf
For golfers, the Treasure Coast and the Palm Beaches are nirvana, starting with the Professional Golfing Association (PGA) headquarters at the PGA National Resort & Spa in Palm Beach Gardens, with five courses. If you're not yet ready to go pro, the Academy at PGA National Resort & Spa can help you improve with its golf school packages. In all, more than 150 public, private, and semiprivate golf courses dot Palm Beach County, and challenging courses also await along the Treasure Coast.

Lodging

All prices are for a standard double room, excluding 6% sales tax (more in some counties) and 1%–4% tourist tax.

CATEGORY	COST*
$$$$	over $220
$$$	$140–$220
$$	$80–$140
$	under $80

Shopping

There's no shortage of baubles to ogle on Palm Beach's Worth Avenue, known locally as The Avenue and often compared to Beverly Hills' Rodeo Drive, even though such California comparisons displease many old-line Palm Beachers. There's also plenty of reasonably priced shopping at the Mall at Wellington Green, Town Center, and The Gardens. For open-air shopping, dining, and entertainment, CityPlace and Mizner Park are great choices. Both have upscale national retailers mixed with unique independent boutiques and art galleries. You can browse more art galleries and antiques shops all along this stretch, especially in Vero Beach and Delray Beach.

Exploring Palm Beach and the Treasure Coast

Palm Beach, with Gatsby-era architecture, stone and stucco estates, extravagant landscaping, and highbrow shops, can reign as the focal point for your sojourn any time of year. From Palm Beach, you can head off in any of three directions: south along the scenic Gold Coast toward Boca Raton along an especially scenic route known as A1A, back to the mainland and north to the barrier-island treasures of the Treasure Coast, or west for more rustic inland delights.

Great Itineraries

Tucked into an island 14 mi long and about ½ mi wide, Palm Beach can be covered in a day or two. In several days, you can explore everything from galleries to subtropical wildlife preserves, and with a week on tap, it's possible to expand horizons from Sebastian all the way south to Boca Raton. Or you could do as so many others do—laze around, soak up sunshine amid the tropical atmosphere, and venture out mostly for mealtime pleasures.

Numbers in the text correspond to numbers in the margin and on the Gold Coast and Treasure Coast and the Palm Beach and West Palm Beach maps.

IF YOU HAVE 3 DAYS

When time is tight, make ▣ **Palm Beach** ①–⑪ your base. On the first day, start downtown on **Worth Avenue** ⑦ to window-shop and gallery browse. After a *très* chic bistro lunch, head for that other must-see on even the shortest itinerary: the **Henry Morrison Flagler Museum** ②. Your second day is for the beach. Two good options are Lantana Public Beach or Oceanfront Park in **Boynton Beach** ㉕. Budget your last day for exploring attractions that pique your interest such as the Morikami Museum and Japanese Gardens in nearby **Delray Beach** ㉗, tantamount to day-tripping to Japan, or Lion Country Safari in ▣ **West Palm Beach** ⑫–㉒, yielding tastes of Africa.

IF YOU HAVE 5 DAYS

Five days allow you more contemplation at the galleries and museums, more leisure at the beaches, with time for more serendipitous exploring. Stay in ▣ **Palm Beach** ①–⑪ for two nights. The first day visit the **Henry Morrison Flagler Museum** ② and the luxury hotel known as **The**

Breakers ④, another Flagler legacy. Then head to **Worth Avenue** ⑦ for lunch and afternoon shopping, even if it's only the window variety. On the second day, drive over to ⊞ **West Palm Beach** ⑫–㉒ and the **Norton Museum of Art** ⑬, to view an extensive collection of 19th-century French Impressionists. On day three, choose between an overnight visit to ⊞ **Lake Okeechobee,** the world's bass-fishing capital, or staying in Palm Beach another night and driving a half hour or so to explore the Arthur R. Marshall–Loxahatchee National Wildlife Refuge. Or head for the **National Croquet Center** ⑱, where you can bring your own mallets or rent from the pro shop. Head south to ⊞ **Boca Raton** ㉘ on the fourth day, and check into a hotel near the beach before spending the afternoon wandering through Mizner Park's shops. On your fifth day, meander through Mizner Park's Boca Raton Museum of Art in the morning and get some sun at South Beach Park after lunch.

IF YOU HAVE 7 DAYS

With an entire week, you can get a more comprehensive look at the Gold and Treasure coasts, with time to fit in sailing, a polo match, deep-sea fishing, or jet skiing. Stay two nights in ⊞ **Palm Beach** ①–⑪, spending your first day taking in stellar sights, mentioned above. On day two, rent a bicycle and follow the bike path along Lake Worth, providing great glimpses at backyards of many Palm Beach mansions. During the fall, you'll encounter gardeners busy clipping hedges and trimming palm fronds in preparation for the winter social season. Drive north on day three, going first to the mainland and then across Jerry Thomas Bridge to Singer Island and John D. MacArthur Beach State Park. Spend the third night farther north, on ⊞ **Hutchinson Island** ㉞, and relax the next morning on the beach at your hotel. On your way back south, explore **Stuart** ㉝ and its intriguing historic downtown area, and pause at the Arthur R. Marshall–Loxahatchee National Wildlife Refuge before ending up in ⊞ **Boca Raton** ㉘, for three nights at a hotel near the beach. Split day five between shopping at Mizner Park and sunning at South Beach Park. Day six is for cultural attractions: the Boca Raton Museum of Art followed by the galleries and the Morikami in **Delray Beach** ㉗. With time to spare on your last day, check out one of Boca Raton's other two beaches, Spanish River and Red Reef parks.

When to Tour Palm Beach and the Treasure Coast

You'll find the weather optimum November through May, but the trade-off is that roadways and facilities are more crowded and prices higher. In summer, to spend much time outside, it helps to have a tolerance for heat, humidity, and afternoon downpours. No matter when you visit, bring insect repellent for outdoor activities.

PALM BEACH

78 mi north of Miami.

Setting the tone in this town of unparalleled Florida opulence is the ornate architectural work of Addison Mizner, who began designing homes and public buildings here in the 1920s and whose Moorish-Gothic style has influenced virtually all community landmarks. Thanks to Mizner and his lasting influence, Palm Beach remains a magnetic backdrop for the playground of the rich, famous, and discerning.

Exploring Palm Beach

For a taste of what it's like to jockey for position in this status-conscious town, stake out a parking place on Worth Avenue, and squeeze in among the Mercedes and Bentleys. Actually, the easiest, most affordable way to reach Worth Avenue is by foot, since there's little on-street parking and space is at a premium at nearby lots. Away from downtown, along County Road and Ocean Boulevard (the shore road, also designated as Route A1A), are Palm Beach's other defining landmarks: residences that are nothing short of palatial, topped by the seemingly de rigueur barrel-tile roofs and often fronted by 20-ft thick-hedgerows. The low wall that separates the dune-top shore road from the sea hides eroded shoreline in many places. Here and there, where the strand deepens, homes are built directly on the beach.

A Good Tour

Start on the island's north end with a quick drive through the bit of sandstone and limestone intrigue called the **Canyon of Palm Beach** ① on Lake Way Road. Drive south, across Royal Poinciana Way, to the **Henry Morrison Flagler Museum** ②, a 73-room palace Flagler built for his third wife. From here, backtrack to Royal Poinciana Way, turn right, and follow the road until it ends at North County Road and the Spanish-style **Palm Beach Post Office** ③. Here County Road changes from north to south designations. Head southbound and look for the long, stately driveway on the left that leads to **The Breakers** ④, built by Flagler in the style of an Italian Renaissance palace. There's free parking out front. Continue south on South County Road about ¼ mi farther to **Bethesda-by-the-Sea** ⑤, a Spanish Gothic Episcopal church. Keep driving south on South County Road until you reach Royal Palm Way; turn right, then right again on Cocoanut Row. Within a few blocks you'll see the gardens of the **Society of the Four Arts** ⑥ that locals call one of the island's best secrets, offering hours of family fun, pleasure, and enlightenment.

Head south on Cocoanut Row until you reach famed **Worth Avenue** ⑦, where you can park, stroll, and ogle designer goods. Then drive south on South County Road to peek at magnificent estates, including **El Solano** ⑧, designed by Addison Mizner, and the fabled **Mar-a-Lago** ⑨, now owned by Donald Trump and operating as a private club. At this point, if you want some sun and fresh air, continue south on South County Road until you reach **Phipps Ocean Park** ⑩ and its stretch of beach, or head back toward town along South Ocean Boulevard to the popular **Mid-Town Beach** ⑪.

TIMING

You'll need half a day, minimum, for these sights. A few destinations are closed Sunday or Monday. In winter, often heavy traffic gets worse as the day wears on, so plan most exploring for the morning.

Sights to See

⑤ **Bethesda-by-the-Sea.** This Spanish Gothic Episcopal church with stained-glass windows was built in 1925 by the first Protestant congregation in southeast Florida. Guided tours follow some services, and there's a book shop. Adjacent are the formal, ornamental **Cluett Memorial Gardens.** ⊠ *141 S. County Rd.,* ☎ *561/655–4554,* WEB *www.bbts.org.* ☉ *Church and gardens daily 8–5; services Sept.–May, Sun. at 8, 9, and 11, Tues. at 8, Wed. at 12:05, Fri. at 12:05; June–Aug., Sun. at 8 and 10. Call to confirm.*

★ ④ **The Breakers.** Originally built by Henry Flagler in 1895 and rebuilt by his descendants after a 1925 fire, this luxury hotel resembling an Italian Renaissance palace helped launch Florida tourism with its new opulence attracting influential, wealthy northerners. Park free out front and head for the lobby to gaze at painted arched ceilings hung with crystal chandeliers, the ornate Florentine Dining Room with its 15th-century Flemish tapestries, and other public spaces. ⊠ *1 S. County Rd.,* ☎ *561/655–6611,* WEB *www.thebreakers.com.*

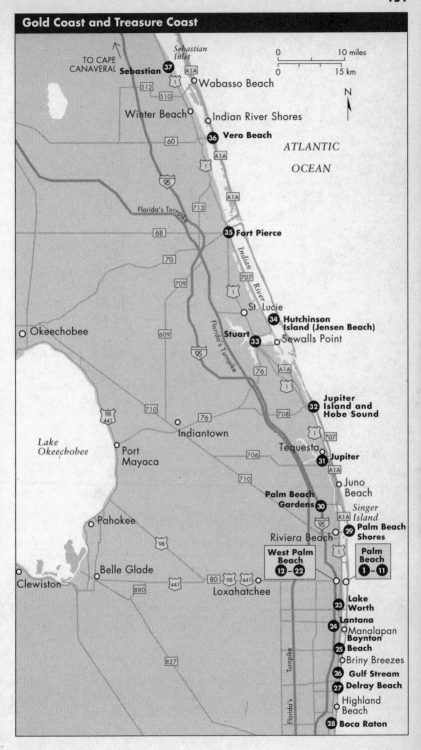

Palm Beach and West Palm Beach

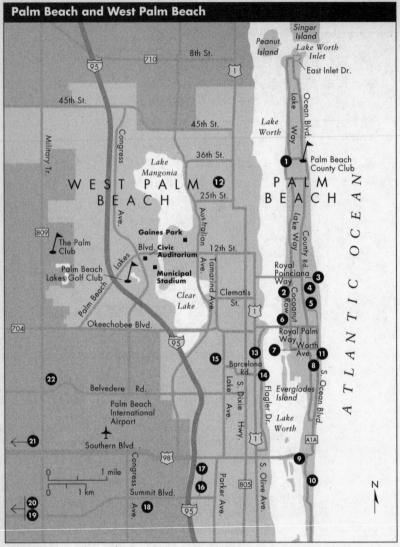

❶ Canyon of Palm Beach. A road runs through a ridge of reddish-brown sandstone and oolite limestone, providing a brief sense of the desert Southwest. It's the remains of an ancient coral reef, and 15-ft-high canyon walls line both sides of the road. ✉ *Lake Way Rd.*

❽ El Solano. No Palm Beach mansion better represents the town's luminous legacy than the Spanish-style home built by Addison Mizner as his personal residence in 1925. Mizner then sold El Solano to Harold Vanderbilt, and the property was long a favorite among socialites for parties and photo shoots. Vanderbilt, like many of the socially attuned, would open his home to social peers to accommodate good, often charitable causes. This is typical in South Florida, and most everywhere. El Solano was a favorite in those days. Beatle John Lennon and Yoko Ono bought it less than a year before Lennon's death, and it's now owned by a banker and not open to the public. ✉ *721 S. County Rd.*

★ ❷ Henry Morrison Flagler Museum. The opulence of Florida's Gilded Age lives on at Whitehall, the palatial 73-room mansion Henry Flagler commissioned in 1901 for his third wife, Mary Lily Kenan. Architects John Carrère and Thomas Hastings were instructed to create the finest home imaginable, and they outdid themselves. Whitehall, now a museum, rivals the grandeur of European palaces and has an entrance hall with baroque ceiling similar to Louis XIV's Versailles. To create the museum, Flagler's granddaughter, Jean Flagler Matthews, in 1960 bought back the property, which had been operating as the Whitehall Hotel from 1929 to 1959. You'll see many original furnishings, an art collection, a 1,200-pipe organ, and Florida East Coast Railway exhibits, along with Flagler's personal rail car, the *Rambler,* awaiting behind the building. Tours takes about an hour and are offered at frequent intervals. ✉ *1 Whitehall Way,* ☏ *561/655–2833,* WEB *www.flagler.org.* ☑ *$8.* ☉ *Tues.–Sat. 10–5, Sun. noon–5.*

❾ Mar-a-Lago. Breakfast food heiress Marjorie Meriweather Post commissioned a Hollywood set designer to create Ocean Boulevard's famed Mar-a-Lago, with Italianate towers silhouetted against the sky. Owner Donald Trump has turned it into a private membership club. ✉ *1100 S. Ocean Blvd.*

⓫ Mid-Town Beach. Just east of Worth Avenue, this small beach is convenient, but be warned that parking is scarce, with the only meters along Ocean Boulevard—ergo, the only easy public parking access—between Worth Avenue and Royal Palm Way. ✉ *400 S. Ocean Blvd.,* ☏ *no phone.* ☑ *Parking 25¢ for 15 mins.* ☉ *Daily 8–8.*

❸ Palm Beach Post Office. Spanish-style architecture defines the exterior of this 1932 National Historic Site building. Inside, murals depict Seminole Indians in the Everglades and stately royal and coconut palms. ✉ *95 N. County Rd.,* ☏ *800/275–8777.*

❿ Phipps Ocean Park. In addition to the shoreline, picnic tables, and grills, this park has a Palm Beach County landmark in the **Little Red School-house.** Dating from 1886, it served as the first schoolhouse in what was then Dade County. Tours are offered weekday mornings. No alcoholic beverages are permitted in the park. ✉ *2145 S. Ocean Blvd.,* ☏ *561/832–0731.* ☑ *Free.* ☉ *Daily sunrise–sunset.*

★ ❻ Society of the Four Arts. Feel like unwinding amid Blackberry Lilies and Japanese Sago Palms, Confederate Jasmine, Weeping Juniper, and Fairy Carpet Begonias? Despite widespread misconceptions of members-only exclusivity, this privately endowed institution—founded in 1936 to encourage appreciation of art, music, drama, and literature—is funded for public enjoyment. A gallery building—designed by Addison Mizner, of course—artfully melds an exhibition hall, library, 13 distinct gardens, and the Philip Hulitar Sculpture Garden. Open from about Thanksgiving to Easter, its programs are extensive and there's ample free parking. ⊠ *Four Arts Plaza,* ☎ *561/655–7226,* WEB *www. fourarts.org.* ⊡ *$4.* ☉ *Galleries Dec.–mid-Apr., Mon.–Sat. 10–5, Sun. 2–5; library, children's library, and gardens Nov.–May, weekdays 10– 5, Sat. 9–1.*

★ **❼** **Worth Avenue.** Called The Avenue by Palm Beachers, this ¼-mi-long street is synonymous with exclusive shopping. Nostalgia lovers recall an era when faces or names served as charge cards, purchases were delivered home before customers returned from lunch, and bills were sent directly to private accountants. Times have changed, but a stroll amid the Moorish architecture of its shops offers a tantalizing taste of the island's ongoing commitment to elegant consumerism. ⊠ *Between Cocoanut Row and S. Ocean Blvd.*

Dining and Lodging

$$$–$$$$ ✕ **Bice Ristorante.** A favorite of Palm Beach society, the Italian atmosphere in this historic Addison Mizner villa is so complete that you may be surprised when you're greeted in English. Bougainvillea-laden trellises set the scene at the main entrance on Peruvian Way. Weather permitting, many patrons prefer the outside patio dining. The aroma of basil, chives, and oregano fills the air as waiters bring out home-baked focaccia to accompany northern Italian favorites entrées from an extensive menu, including a delectable line-up of pastas, veal chops, and a walnut-crusted rack of lamb served with Brussels sprouts and avocado. ⊠ *313¼ Worth Ave.,* ☎ *561/835–1600. AE, DC, MC, V.*

$$$–$$$$ ✕ **Café L'Europe.** One of the most enduring, elegant Palm Beach en-
★   claves, this Continental restaurant is consistently ranked as one of the best by dining critics. To remain at the pinnacle, owners Norbert and Lidia Goldner practice hands-on management and it shows in the attentive service and consistency of excellence here. Best-sellers include traditional favorites like rack of lamb and Dover sole, along with creations such as crispy sweetbreads with poached pear and mustard sauce. Apart from the caviar bar, appetizers include fresh hearts of palm. The signature dessert is a delectable old-fashioned apple pancake with a seasonal fruit compote. ⊠ *331 S. County Rd.,* ☎ *561/655–4020. Reservations essential. Jacket required. AE, DC, MC, V. No lunch Sun.– Mon.*

$$$–$$$$ ✕ **Chez Jean-Pierre.** With walls adorned with Dali- and Picasso-like
★   art, this is where the Palm Beach Old Guard likes to let down its guard, all the while partaking of sumptuous French cuisine and an impressive wine list. Forget caloric or cholesterol concerns, and indulge in scrambled eggs with caviar or homemade duck foie gras, along with desserts like hazelnut soufflé or profiteroles au chocolat. Attentive waiters are friendly and detail-oriented. ⊠ *132 N. County Rd.,* ☎ *561/ 833–1171. Reservations essential. AE, DC, MC, V. No lunch.*

$$$–$$$$ ✕ **Echo.** Palm Beach's window on Asia has a sleek sushi bar and floor-to-ceiling glass doors separating the interior from a popular terrace dining. Chinese, Japanese, Thai, and Vietnamese selections are neatly categorized: Wind (small plates starting your journey), Water (beverages, sushi), Fire (from grill, wok, fry pan), and Earth (land and sea) to Flavor (desserts, sweets). Pick from dim sum to sashimi, pad Thai to Peking duck, steamed sea bass to lobster lo mein. ⊠ *230 Sunrise Ave.,* ☎ *561/802–4222. Reservations essential. AE, D, MC, V. Closed Mon. No lunch.*

$$$–$$$$ ✕ **Leopard Supper Club and Lounge.** Let's hope the sleek leopard
★ never changes its spots, set off by black and red lacquer trim, mark-
ing this elegant, intimate enclave in the Chesterfield Hotel. Choose a
cozy banquette by the wall or a table near the open kitchen. Daily spe-
cialties depend on the season. You might start with sweet corn and crab
chowder with Peruvian purple potato or a jumbo crab cake, moving
on to an arugula or spinach salad followed by a prime strip steak or
a glazed rack of lamb. The Leopard is superb for lunch and breakfast,
too. ✉ *363 Cocoanut Row,* ☎ *561/659–5800. AE, DC, MC, V.*

$$$–$$$$ ✕ **Maison Janeiro.** Versace dinnerware and Riedel crystal on black linens
★ provide for spectacularly elegant contemporary French dining. Appe-
tizers include lobster and crayfish cakes with a champagne lobster sauce
and goat cheese baked with tomatoes in a pastry shell. Entrées, pre-
sented under silver domes, range from bouillabaisse to grilled Chilean
sea bass with red mullet caviar, boneless rack of lamb in puff pastry,
and a beef fillet with green peppercorn sauce. For a grand finale try
the chocolate soufflé topped with edible gold leaf. ✉ *191 Bradley Pl.,*
☎ *561/659–5223. Reservations essential. Jacket required. AE, DC, MC,
V. No lunch.*

$$–$$$$ ✕ **Amici.** A celebrity-magnet bistro atmosphere with an open view to
the kitchen in back has proved a crowd-pleaser with the Palm Beach
crowd. The northern Italian menu highlights house specialties such as
rigatoni with spicy tomato sauce and roasted eggplant, potato gnocchi, grilled veal chops, risottos, and pizzas from a wood-burning oven.
There are nightly pasta and fresh-fish specials as well. To avoid the
crowds, stop by for a late lunch. ✉ *228 S. County Rd.,* ☎ *561/832–
0201. Reservations essential. AE, DC, MC, V. No lunch Sun.*

$$–$$$ ✕ **Chuck & Harold's.** This combo power-lunch bar, sidewalk café, and
nocturnal jazz hot spot attracts both locals and tourists hungry to peo-
ple-watch for breakfast, lunch, and dinner. For optimum viewing, take
a seat in the outdoor café next to begonia pots mounted on the sidewalk rail. Options stretch from local clams from Sebastian or conch
chowder to terrific hamburgers, grilled steaks, and key lime pie, with
plenty more in between. There's nightly entertainment, with the likes
of the Fabulous Baker Boys playing here at intervals. ✉ *207 Royal Poinciana Way,* ☎ *561/659–1440. AE, DC, MC, V.*

$$–$$$ ✕ **Ta-boó.** Ruling on Worth Avenue for more than 60 years, there's no
★ arguing the staying power of this peach stucco landmark with green
shutters. Table seating counts here, with the best by the windows at
the front of the bar or near the fireplace. Appetizers range from na-
chos with chili to Beluga caviar, and entrées include Black Angus dry-
aged beef or roast duck, along with main-course salads, pizzas, and
burgers, plus desserts like apple crisp and coconut lust (a pielike fantasy with walnut cookie crust, coconut cream filling, and whipped cream
topping). Drop in late night during the winter season and you'll probably spot a celebrity or two. ✉ *221 Worth Ave.,* ☎ *561/835–3500.
AE, DC, MC, V.*

$–$$ ✕ **TooJay's.** New York deli food served in a bright California-style set-
ting—what could be more Florida? The menu here—there are several
TooJay's in the Sunshine State—includes matzo-ball soup, a salami-
on-rye layered with onions, Muenster cheese, coleslaw, and Russian
dressing, and a killer cake with five kinds of chocolate topped with
whipped cream. During the autumn Jewish holidays, look for carrot
tzimmes (a sweet vegetable compote), brisket, and roast chicken. Wise-
cracking waitresses keep things moving. ✉ *313 Royal Poinciana Way,*
☎ *561/659–7232. AE, DC, MC, V. Beer and wine only.*

$$$$ ⊞ **The Breakers.** Dating from 1896, and on the National Register of
★ Historic Places, this opulent Italian Renaissance–style resort sprawls

over 140 oceanfront acres. Cupids frolic at the main Florentine fountain, and majestic frescoes grace ceilings leading to restaurants. A $120 million guest room renovation also brought the addition of a spa and beach club, a new golf and tennis clubhouse, and upgrades at the historic Ocean Course. Elegance thus enhanced, a relaxed atmosphere replaces old-world formality, with jackets and ties no longer *required* after 7 PM. ☒ *1 S. County Rd., 33480,* ☎ *561/655–6611 or 888/273–2537,* FAX *561/659–8403,* WEB *www.thebreakers.com. 569 rooms, 49 suites. 5 restaurants, room service, in-room data ports, room TVs with movies and video games, 36-hole golf course, putting green, 10 tennis courts, 5 pools, health club, sauna, spa, beach, boating, croquet, shuffleboard, 4 bars, shops, baby-sitting, children's programs (ages 3– 12), concierge, business services. AE, D, DC, MC, V.*

$$$$ 🏨 **The Colony.** What distinguishes this legendary pale yellow Georgian-style hotel only steps from Worth Avenue is an attentive staff: youthful yet experienced, buzzing with competence and a desire to please. Cool and classical guest rooms, with small baths, have fluted blond cabinetry and matching curtains and bedcovers in floral pastels. ☒ *155 Hammon Ave., 33480,* ☎ *561/655–5430 or 800/521–5525,* FAX *561/ 832–7318,* WEB *www.thecolonypalmbeach.com. 68 rooms, 19 suites and apartments, 7 villas. Restaurant, pool, spa, bicycles, bar, concierge, meeting rooms. AE, DC, MC, V.*

$$$$ 🏨 **Four Seasons Resort Palm Beach.** Relaxed elegance are the watch-
★ words at this four-story resort on 6 acres with a delightful beach at the south end of town. Fanlight windows, marble, chintz, and palms create a serene, hospitable atmosphere. Rooms are spacious, with a separate seating area and private balcony, many with ocean views. On weekends, piano music accompanies cocktails in the Living Room lounge. Jazz groups perform on some weekends in season. The restaurant is worth staying in for; children are amply provided for. ☒ *2800 S. Ocean Blvd., 33480,* ☎ *561/582–2800 or 800/432–2335,* FAX *561/547– 1557,* WEB *www.fourseasons.com/palmbeach. 200 rooms, 10 suites. 3 restaurants, room service, in-room data ports, in-room safes, minibars, golf privileges, 3 tennis courts, pool, health club, hair salon, hot tub, sauna, spa, steam room, beach, boating, fishing, bicycles, 2 bars, shop, baby-sitting, children's programs (ages 3–12), dry cleaning, concierge, business services, meeting rooms, no-smoking rooms. AE, D, DC, MC, V.*

$$$–$$$$ 🏨 **Brazilian Court.** Steps from Worth Avenue shopping, the yellow stucco
★ Spanish-style facade and red-tile roof here underscore this boutique hotel's Roaring '20s origins. Rooms and spacious suites—all with rich marble baths and kitchenettes—are in warm tropical hues and look out onto gardens. Outside are stone fountains and enchanting flower-filled courtyards. Chancellor's restaurant offers a choice of service in the elegant dining room, the courtyard, poolside, or on your private terrace. ☒ *301 Australian Ave., 33480,* ☎ *561/655–7740; 800/228– 6852 in Canada;* FAX *561/655–0801,* WEB *www.braziliancourt.com. 63 rooms, 40 suites. Restaurant, room service, in-room data ports, kitch-enettes, refrigerators, some in-room VCRs, pool, gym, hair salon, spa, bicycles, bar, library, laundry facilities, concierge, meeting rooms, some pets allowed (fee); no-smoking rooms. AE, D, DC, MC, V.*

$$–$$$$ 🏨 **Palm Beach Historic Inn.** Downtown, tucked between Town Hall and a seaside residential block, touches here include a deluxe Continental breakfast served in bed or in the courtyard and tea and cookies delivered to your room upon your arrival. Guest rooms tend toward the frilly with lace, ribbons, and scalloped edges. Most are furnished with Victorian antiques and reproductions and chiffon draped above the bed. ☒ *365 S. County Rd., 33480,* ☎ *561/832–4009,* FAX *561/832–6255,*

WEB *www.palmbeachhistoricinn.com. 9 rooms, 4 suites. Refrigerators, some in-room VCRs, library. AE, D, DC, MC, V. CP.*

$–$$$$ ⊞ **The Chesterfield.** Two blocks north of Worth Avenue, you'll find this
★ elegant four-story, white stucco, European-style luxury hotel with inviting rooms ranging from small to spacious. All are richly decorated with plush upholstered chairs, antique desks, paintings, and marble baths. Settle on a leather couch near the cozy library's fireplace with an international newspaper or a book selected from floor-to-ceiling shelves. A quiet courtyard surrounds a large pool. The Leopard restaurant is exceptional. Ongoing but unobtrusive renovation and redecoration keeps this hotel in tip-top shape. ⊠ *363 Cocoanut Row, 33480,* ☎ *561/659–5800 or 800/243–7871,* FAX *561/659–6707,* WEB *www.redcarnationhotels. com. 44 rooms, 11 suites. Restaurant, room service, some refrigerators, some in-room VCRs, pool, bar, library, concierge, Internet, business services, meeting rooms. AE, D, DC, MC, V.*

$$$ ⊞ **Plaza Inn.** This three-story hotel, deco-designed from the 1930s with
★ a vibrant pink exterior, operates bed-and-breakfast style. Its Stray Fox Pub Piano Bar, palm- and ficus-lined pool, and courtyard gardens have the intimate charm of a trysting place. Courteous staff and a location in the heart of Palm Beach are pluses. Uncluttered rooms are individually decorated and have phones and refrigerators, a welcome change from other B&Bs. ⊠ *215 Brazilian Ave., 33480,* ☎ *561/832–8666 or 800/233–2632,* FAX *561/835–8776,* WEB *www.plazainnpalmbeach.com. 48 rooms, 5 suites. In-room data ports, refrigerators, pool, hot tub, bar, concierge, some pets allowed. AE, MC, V. BP.*

$$–$$$ ⊞ **Palm Beach Hawaiian Ocean Inn.** Families seeking down-to-earth prices gravitate to this casual, two-story resort on the beach. Don't—repeat don't—count on anything fancy, but large, adequately furnished rooms and suites face tropical gardens, and a few look out to the ocean. Beach frontage is the draw here. A wide wooden sundeck surrounds the free-form pool, and both look on to the ocean. The informal restaurant and outdoor bar also overlook the water. ⊠ *3550 S. Ocean Blvd., 33480,* ☎ FAX *561/582–5631,* WEB *www.palmbeachhawaiian.com. 50 rooms, 8 suites. Restaurant, room service, refrigerators, pool, beach, bar. D, MC, V.*

Nightlife and the Arts

The Arts

The **Royal Poinciana Playhouse** (⊠ 70 Royal Poinciana Plaza, ☎ 561/659–3310) presents more than a half dozen productions each year between December and April. **Society of the Four Arts** (⊠ Four Arts Plaza, ☎ 561/655–7226) has concerts, lectures, and films December–March. Movie tickets can be purchased at time of showing; other tickets may be obtained a week in advance.

Nightlife

For cabaret-style ambiance, the **Royal Room at the Colony** (⊠ 155 Hammon Ave., ☎ 561/655–5430) seats just 68 and has dimmed chandeliers, crimson velvet curtains, a dressy-dress code, and a lineup of nationally known jazz and cabaret acts. Dinner and show are $69; show only is $40. Young professionals gather at the **Leopard Lounge** (⊠ 363 Cocoanut Row, ☎ 561/659–6767) in the Chesterfield Hotel for piano music during cocktail hour, and later to dance until the wee hours. As the weekend dinner crowd thins out, late-night revelers fill up **Ta-boó** (⊠ 221 Worth Ave., ☎ 561/835–3500), where a DJ keeps everyone moving.

Outdoor Activities and Sports

Biking

Bicycling is a pivotal way for getting a closer look at Palm Beach. Only 14 miles long, a half mile wide, flat as the top of a billiard table, and just as green, it's a perfect biking locale. The palm-fringed **Palm Beach Bicycle Trail** (⊠ parallel to Lake Way) skirts backyards of many palatial mansions and the edge of Lake Worth. The trail starts at the Society of the Four Arts, heading north—just follow the signs. A block from the bike trail, the **Palm Beach Bicycle Trail Shop** (⊠ 223 Sunrise Ave., ☎ 561/659–4583) rents by the hour or day.

Dog Racing

Since 1932 the hounds have raced year-round at the 4,300-seat **Palm Beach Kennel Club.** Enjoy simulcasts of jai alai and horse racing, as well as wagering on live and televised sports. ⊠ *1111 N. Congress Ave.,* ☎ *561/683–2222.* ☑ *50¢, terrace level $1, parking free.* ☉ *Racing Mon., Wed., Fri., Sat. at 12:40, Wed.–Sat. also at 7:30, Sun. at 1; simulcasts Thurs.–Tues. at 12:30, Mon., Wed., Fri. at 7:35.*

Golf

Breakers Hotel Golf Club (⊠ 1 S. County Rd., ☎ 561/655–6611 or 800/833–3141) has 36 holes. The **Palm Beach Golf Club** (⊠ 2345 S. Ocean Blvd., ☎ 561/547–0598) has 18 holes, including four on the Atlantic and three on the inland waterway.

Shopping

One of the world's showcases for high-quality shopping, **Worth Avenue** runs ¼ mi east–west across Palm Beach, from the beach to Lake Worth. The street has more than 250 shops, and many upscale stores (Gucci, Hermès, Pucci, Saks Fifth Avenue, and Tourneau) are represented, their merchandise appealing to the discerning tastes of the Palm Beach clientele. The six blocks of **South County Road** north of Worth Avenue have interesting (and somewhat less expensive) stores. For specialty items (out-of-town newspapers, health foods, and books), try the shops along the north side of **Royal Poinciana Way.** Most stores are closed on the weekend and many go on hiatus during the summer months.

Go visit the girls of **At Home . . . with Nancy and Beth** (⊠ Paramount, 139 N. County Rd., ☎ 561/659–0550) for a handpicked selection of vintage housewares, decorative items, memorabilia, and original retro fashions. **Calypso** (⊠ 247-B Worth Ave., ☎ 561/832–5006), tucked into Via Encantada, is where owner Christiane Celle—known for handcrafted fragrances—has curated a lively collection of resort wear for the whole family. **Chris Kellogg** (⊠ Gucci Courtyard, 256 Worth Ave., ☎ 561/820–2407) stocks the Palm Beach uniform of linen button-down shirts and cotton toile print pants. An institution on the island, **Church Mouse** (⊠ 374 S. County Rd., ☎ 561/659–2154) thrift store is where many high-end resale boutique owners first grab their merchandise. **Déjà Vu** (⊠ Via Testa, 219 Royal Poinciana Way, ☎ 561/833–6624) could be the resale house of Chanel, it has so many gently used, top-quality pieces. There is no digging through piles here; clothes are in impeccable condition and very organized. **Designers to You** (⊠ 307 Royal Poinciana Way, ☎ 561/833–3363) is where you can find discount special occasion clothing by Carolina Herrera, Cerutti, Halston, and other couture designers. Skirt suits and dresses are organized by price on racks. **Giorgio's** (⊠ 230 Worth Ave., ☎ 561/655–2446) is over-the-top indulgence with 50 colors of silk and cashmere sweaters and 22 colors of ostrich and alligator adorning everything from bags to bicycles. Giorgio's also has men's and women's boutiques in the Breakers. Collector, trader, and expert **Otten von Emmerich** (⊠ Via Flora, 240 Worth Ave., ☎ 561/659–0071) offers a museumlike historical presentation of antique and pre-owned Louis Vuitton and Hermès and maritime art. **Tracey Tooker Hats** (⊠ Via Bice, 313½ Worth Ave., ☎ 561/835–1663) custom-made creations are appointed with bone buttons, real and faux fur, double grosgrain silk bows, satin linings, ostrich feathers, and silk flowers. Holding court for more than 60 years, **Van Cleef & Arpels** (⊠ 249 Worth Ave., ☎ 561/655–6767) is where legendary members of Palm Beach society shop for tiaras and formal jewels.

WEST PALM BEACH

2 mi west of Palm Beach.

Long considered Palm Beach's less-privileged relative, sprawling West Palm has evolved into an economically vibrant destination of its own, ranking as the cultural, entertainment, and business center of the entire county and territory to the north. Sparkling buildings like the mammoth Palm Beach County Judicial Center and Courthouse and the State Administrative Building underscore the breadth of the city's governmental and corporate activity, and facilities such as the glittering Kravis Center for the Performing Arts attest to the strength of the arts and entertainment community. In 2002, Kravis Center officials, intent on driving home commitment to quality, created quite a stir by declaring an unprecedented ticket refund to the tune of $60,000 for a sold-out performance that it categorized as substandard.

Downtown

The heart of revived West Palm Beach is a small, attractive downtown area, spurred on by active historic preservation. Along beautifully landscaped Clematis Street, you'll find boutiques and restaurants in charmingly restored buildings and an increasingly exuberant nightlife. In fact, downtown rocks on Thursdays from 5:30 PM on with Clematis by Night, a celebration of music, dance, art, and food at Centennial Square. Even on downtown's fringes, you'll encounter sights of cultural interest. There's a free downtown shuttle by day and free on-street parking at night and on weekends.

A Good Tour

From a geographical perspective, the best place to start is at the north end of the city with a walk through the **Old Northwood Historic District** ⑫, on the National Register of Historic Places. Drive south on U.S. 1, take a left onto 12th Street, and then a right onto South Olive Avenue to view the exceptional art collection at the **Norton Museum of Art** ⑬. From here, it is just a few blocks south to the peaceful **Ann Norton Sculpture Gardens** ⑭. Finally, drive west across Barcelona Road to the **Robert and Mary Montgomery Armory Arts Center** ⑮ to check out the current exhibit.

TIMING

Late morning is ideal for starting this tour, so you can walk through the historic neighborhood before having lunch on Clematis Street. In the afternoon you'll need about three hours at the various arts-oriented sights. Being out during daytime business hours is pivotal for this tour.

Sights to See

⑭ **Ann Norton Sculpture Gardens.** This monument to the late American sculptor Ann Weaver Norton, second wife of Norton Museum founder Ralph H. Norton, consists of charming 3-acre grounds displaying seven granite figures and six brick megaliths. The plantings were designed by Norton, an environmentalist, to attract native bird life. ⊠ *253 Barcelona Rd., ☏ 561/832–5328. ☑ $5. ☉ Wed.–Sun. 11–4 (call ahead; schedule is not always observed) or by appointment.*

★ ⓱ **Norton Museum of Art.** Constructed in 1941 by steel magnate Ralph H. Norton, this museum has an extensive permanent collection of 19th- and 20th-century American and European paintings, including works by Picasso, Monet, Matisse, Pollack, and O'Keeffe, with an emphasis on 19th-century French Impressionists. There's a sublime outdoor covered loggia, Chinese bronze and jade sculptures, and a library. Galleries, including the Great Hall of the Museum, also showcase traveling exhibits. ⊠ *1451 S. Olive Ave., ☏ 561/832–5194,* WEB *www. museum@norton.org. ☑ $6. ☉ Tues.–Sat. 10–5, Sun. 1–5.*

⓬ **Old Northwood Historic District.** This 1920s-era neighborhood, on the National Register of Historic Places, hosts special events and free Sunday walking tours. ⊠ *West of Flagler Dr. between 26th and 35th Sts.*

⓯ **Robert and Mary Montgomery Armory Arts Center.** Built by the WPA in 1939, the facility is now a visual-arts center hosting rotating exhibitions and art classes throughout the year. ⊠ *1703 S. Lake Ave., ☏ 561/ 832–1776. ☑ Free. ☉ Weekdays 9–5:30, Sat. 9:30–2:30, Sun. 10–2.*

Away from Downtown

West Palm Beach's outskirts, flat stretches lined with fast-food outlets and car dealerships, may not inspire but are worth driving through to reach attractions scattered around the city's southern and western reaches. Several are especially rewarding for children and other animal and nature lovers.

A Good Tour

Head south from downtown and turn right on Southern Boulevard, left onto Parker Avenue, and right onto Summit Boulevard to reach the **Palm Beach Zoo at Dreher Park** ⓰. In the same area (just turn right onto Dreher Trail) and also appealing to kids, the **South Florida Science Museum** ⓱, with its Aldrin Aquarium and McGinty Aquarium, is full of hands-on exhibits. If a quick game of croquet intrigues you, head to the **National Croquet Center** ⓲, less than 2 mi from the museum, by turning right onto Summit Boulevard from Dreher Trail North and proceeding to Florida Mango Road, where you will again turn right.

Backtrack to Summit Boulevard and go west to the 150-acre **Pine Jog Environmental Education Center** ⓳. For more natural adventure, head farther west on Summit until you reach Forest Hills Boulevard, where you turn right to reach the **Okeeheelee Nature Center** ⓴ and its miles of wooded trails.

Now retrace your route to Summit Boulevard, drive east until you reach Military Trail, and take a left. Drive north to Southern Boulevard and turn west to reach **Lion Country Safari** ㉑, a 500-acre cageless zoo. For the last stop on this tour, backtrack to Military Trail and travel north to the gardens of the **Mounts Botanical Gardens** ㉒.

TIMING

Tailor your time based on specific interests, since you could easily spend most of a day at any of these attractions. Gird yourself for heavy rush hour traffic, and remember that sightseeing in the morning (not *too* early, to avoid rush hour) will be less congested.

Sights to See

☺ ㉑ **Lion Country Safari.** Drive your own vehicle (with windows closed) on 8 mi of paved roads through a 500-acre cageless zoo with 1,000 free-roaming animals. Lions, elephants, white rhinos, giraffes, zebras, antelopes, chimpanzees, and ostriches are among the wild things in residence. Exhibits include the Kalahari, designed after a South African bush plateau and containing water buffalo and Nilgai (the largest type of Asian antelope), and the Gir Forest, modeled after a game forest in India and showcasing a pride of lions. A walk-through park area has bird feeding and a petting zoo, or you can take a pontoon boat tour. There's also paddle-boating, miniature golf, and picnic tables. No convertibles or pets are allowed. ⊠ *Southern Blvd. W,* ☎ *561/793–1084,* WEB *www.lioncountrysafari.com.* ▨ *$16.95, van rental $8 per 1½ hrs.* ⊘ *Daily 9:30–5:30, last vehicle in by 4:30.*

㉒ **Mounts Botanical Gardens.** Take advantage of balmy weather by walking among the tropical and subtropical plants here. Free tours are given. ⊠ *531 N. Military Trail,* ☎ *561/233–1749.* ▨ *Free.* ⊘ *Mon.–Sat. 8:30–4:30, Sun. 1–5; tours Sat. 11, Sun. 2:30.*

★ ⑱ **National Croquet Center.** The world's largest croquet complex, the 10-acre center is also the headquarters for the U.S. Croquet Association. Vast expanses of manicured lawn are the stage for fierce competitions—in no way resembling the casual backyard games where kids play with wide wire wickets. There's also a clubhouse with a pro shop and Café Croquet, with verandas for dining and viewing, and a museum hall. Half-day and full-day reservations for play on a dozen lawns can be booked. From January through April, you can get a court for two hours, including 30 minutes with a pro to teach you golf croquet at $50 for two, $80 for four. Courts can be reserved up to seven days in advance. ⊠ *700 Florida Mango Rd. (at Summit Blvd.),* ☎ *561/478–2300,* WEB *www.croquetnational.com.* ⊘ *Court times daily 9–5.* ▨ *$15 per player per 2-hr period.*

⑳ **Okeeheelee Nature Center.** Here you can explore 5 mi of trails through 90 acres of native pine-flat woods and wetlands. A spacious visitor center/gift shop features hands-on exhibits. ⊠ *7715 Forest Hill Blvd.,* ☎ *561/233–1400.* ▨ *Free.* ⊘ *Visitor center Tues.–Fri. 1–4:45, Sat. 8:15–4:45; trails open daily sunrise–sunset.*

☺ ⑯ **Palm Beach Zoo at Dreher Park.** This wild kingdom is a 23-acre complex with more than 400 animals representing more than 125 species, from Florida panthers to the giant Aldabra tortoise and the first outdoor exhibit of Goeldi's monkeys in the nation. The Tropics of America exhibit has 6 acres of rain forest plus Mayan ruins, an Amazon river village, and an aviary. Also notable are a nature trail, an Australian Outback exhibit, and a children's petting zoo. ⊠ *1301 Summit Blvd.,* ☎ *561/533–0887 or 561/547–9453,* WEB *www.palmbeachzoo.com.* ▨ *$6.* ⊘ *Daily 9–5, until 7 on spring and summer weekends.*

☺ ⑲ **Pine Jog Environmental Education Center.** The draw here is 150 acres of mostly undisturbed Florida pine-flat woods with one self-guided ½-mi trail. Formal landscaping around five one-story buildings includes native plants, and dioramas and displays illustrate ecosystems. School groups use the trails during the week but the public is also welcome. Call for an event schedule. ⊠ *6301 Summit Blvd.,* ☎ *561/686–6600.* ▨ *Free.* ⊘ *Weekdays 9–5.*

☺ ⑰ **South Florida Science Museum.** Here at the museum, which includes the Aldrin Planetarium and McGinty Aquarium, you'll find hands-on exhibits with touch tanks, laser shows featuring the likes of Pink Floyd and

Led Zeppelin, and a chance to observe the heavens Friday nights through the most powerful telescope in South Florida (weather permitting). ⊠ *4801 Dreher Trail N,* ☎ *561/832–1988,* WEB *www.sfsm.org.* ⚏ *$6, planetarium $2 extra, laser show $4 extra for matinee, $6.50 for evening.* ⊙ *Mon.–Thurs. 10–5, Fri. 10–10, Sat. 10–6, Sun. noon–6.*

Dining and Lodging

$$–$$$$ ✕ **Raindancer Steak House.** Since 1975, steak lovers have headed for this dark, cozy establishment to indulge in thick and juicy filet mignons, 24-ounce porterhouse cuts, sizzling sirloins for two, New York strips prepared au poivre, and grilled lean flanks. If beef isn't your choice, there are also lamb chops, chicken breasts, lobster, shrimp, scallops, and more on the menu. ⊠ *2300 Palm Beach Lakes Blvd.,* ☎ *561/684–2811. AE, MC, V. No lunch.*

$$–$$$ ✕ **Café Protégé.** At this 150-seat restaurant of the Florida Culinary Institute, you can sample superb Continental cuisine at less than astronomical prices. Menus change frequently, and there's a $12 chef's buffet lunch. You can watch students slicing, dicing, and sautéing in the observation kitchen. ⊠ *2400 Metrocentre Blvd.,* ☎ *561/687–2433. AE, MC, V. No lunch weekends; no dinner Sun.–Mon.*

$$ ✕ **Pescatore Seafood and Oyster Bar.** After wandering around Clematis Street, slip through the French doors of this trendy spot for a light lunch, afternoon snack, or leisurely dinner. Fresh oysters and clams star, but you'll also find grilled fish and shrimp, steamed Maine lobster, assorted pasta dishes, and a grilled Black Angus burger. ⊠ *200 Clematis St.,* ☎ *561/837–6633. AE, DC, MC, V.*

$–$$ ✕ **Aleyda's Tex-Mex Restaurant.** This casual, family-friendly eatery consistently scores high on local popularity polls. Fajitas, the house specialty, are brought to the table sizzling in the pan, along with such classic Mexican offerings as enchiladas, chili con queso, and quesadillas. The bartenders claim to make the best margaritas in town. ⊠ *1890 Okeechobee Blvd.,* ☎ *561/688–9033. AE, DC, MC, V. No lunch weekends.*

$$–$$$ ⊡ **Hibiscus House.** Hosts Raleigh Hill and Colin Rayner work diligently
★ to promote not only their delightful B&B, but also their neighborhood, Old Northwood, which is now listed on the National Register of Historic Places thanks to their efforts. Filling their Cape Cod–style property are antiques Hill has collected, including a 150-year-old four-square piano, a green cane planter chair, and Louis XV pieces in the living room. Individually decorated guest rooms are done in a mix of antiques and reproductions, and the tropical pool-patio area is delightful. ⊠ *501 30th St., 33407,* ☎ *561/863–5633 or 800/203–4927,* WEB *www.hibiscushouse.com. 8 rooms. Pool. AE, DC, MC, V. BP.*

$$–$$$ ⊡ **Hotel Biba.** In the El Cid historic district, this 1940s motel has gotten a fun, stylish revamp from Barbara Hulanicki, designer of the 1960s Biba fashion line. Each guest room has a vibrant mélange of colors along with handcrafted mirrors, mosaic bathroom floors, and custom mahogany furnishings. Luxury touches include Egyptian cotton sheets, down pillows and duvets, and lavender-scented closets. The hotel is about a mile from Clematis Street nightlife. ⊠ *320 Belvedere Rd., 33405,* ☎ *561/832–0094,* WEB *www.hotelbiba.com. 43 rooms. In-room data ports, pool, bar. AE, DC, MC, V.*

$–$$ ⊡ **Royal Palm House Bed & Breakfast.** In the Old Northwood Historic District, this charming two-story frame house was built in 1925. Three guest rooms and a suite are in the main house and close by is a one-bedroom cottage with a kitchenette. All are individually decorated in a tasteful, uncluttered fashion with pretty garden views. Rates include morning breakfast and cocktail-hour wine and cordials. A pool surrounded by a exotic plants and a butterfly garden offers a relaxation haven. ✉ *3215 Spruce Ave., 33407,* ☎ *561/863–9836 or 800/ 655–3196,* FAX *561/848–7350,* WEB *www.royalpalmhouse.com. 3 rooms, 1 suite, 1 cottage. Pool. AE, MC, V. BP.*

$–$$ 🏠 **Tropical Gardens Bed & Breakfast.** This cozy, informal cottage house painted in a sunny yellow with white trim in the historic Old Northwood area has several room options ranging from the twin-bedded Canary Room to the deluxe Carriage House, in a separate building with French doors leading out to the pool. The tropical colors and relaxed attitude make this B&B feel as though it were in Key West. Included in the complimentary Continental breakfast are delicious homemade bread and scones. ✉ *419 32nd St., 33407,* ☎ *561/848–4064 or 800/736–4064,* WEB *www.tropicalgardensbandb.com. 4 rooms. Pool, bicycles; no smoking. AE, D, MC, V. CP.*

Nightlife and the Arts

The Arts

Starring amid the treasury of local arts attractions is the **Raymond F. Kravis Center for the Performing Arts** (✉ 701 Okeechobee Blvd., ☎ 561/832–7469), a 2,200-seat glass, copper, and marble showcase perched on what passes for high ground near the railroad tracks in West Palm Beach. Its 250-seat Rinker Playhouse has children's programming, family productions, and other events. A packed year-round schedule unfolds here with drama, dance, and music—from gospel and bluegrass to jazz and classical, including performances of the Palm Beach Pops, New World Symphony, and Miami City Ballet.

Palm Beach Opera (✉ 415 S. Olive Ave., ☎ 561/833–7888) stages four productions each winter at the Kravis Center with English translations projected above the stage and tickets from $20 to $125. The **Carefree Theatre** (✉ 2000 S. Dixie Hwy., ☎ 561/833–7305) is Palm Beach County's premier showcase of foreign and art films.

Nightlife

Palm Beach Casino Line. Take to the high seas on a five-hour getaway aboard the *Palm Beach Princess,* sailing twice daily from the Port of Palm Beach. You'll find a 15,000-square-ft casino, assorted lounges, a sports booking bar with nine televisions, a gift shop, entertainment, and more, along with a prime rib buffet in the evening. Sailings are at 11 AM and 6:30 PM daily, and you'll need to allow time for preboarding procedures. Fares are $40 per person weekdays, $45 on weekends. ✉ *777 E. Port Rd.,* ☎ *561/845–2101 or 800/841–7447.*

CityPlace comes alive at **Blue Martini** (✉ 550 S. Rosemary Ave., ☎ 561/ 835–8601), a bar with eclectic music that attracts a spirited and diverse crowd. It's nothing short of **Bliss** (✉ 313 Clematis St., ☎ 561/ 833–1444), where DJs spin high-energy dance tunes for an energetic young crowd. Tuesday is college night.

You'll find full-size palm trees and trellises bright with bougainvillea blooms plus a light and laser sound system and a 7,500-square-ft dance floor at the Caribbean-theme **Monkeyclub** (✉ 219 Clematis St., ☎ 561/833–6500), where the music is 1970s, '80s, and '90s. The **Respectable Street Café** (✉ 518 Clematis St., ☎ 561/832–9999) explodes in high energy like an indoor Woodstock. This hip, dimly lit alterna-lounge features underground sound, new wave, and retro. Call for schedules and special concerts. **Underground Coffeeworks** (✉ 105 S. Narcissus Ave., ☎ 561/835–4792), a retro '60s spot, has mellow live music and a good selection of coffees Tuesday–Saturday. Cover charges vary, depending on performers.

Outdoor Activities and Sports

If you yearn for drag racing action, the **Moroso Motorsports Park** (⊠ 17047 Beeline Hwy., Palm Beach Gardens, ☎ 561/622–1400) awaits with swap meets and diversified events all year long on a 2.25-mi-long strip. Spectator admission is $12 on Saturday, $15 on Sunday, and there's a $20 two-day pass.

Picturesque **Binks Forest Golf Club** (⊠ 400 Binks Forest Dr., Wellington, ☎ 561/795–0595) has an 18-hole layout. The plush **Emerald Dunes** (⊠ 2100 Emerald Dunes Dr., ☎ 561/684–4653) offers 18 holes of golf. **Palm Beach Polo and Country Club** (⊠ 13198 Forest Hill Blvd., Wellington, ☎ 561/798–7000) features 45 holes with an excellent overall layout. The **West Palm Beach Country Club** (⊠ 7001 Parker Ave., ☎ 561/582–2019) has 18 holes with no water hazards, unusual for Florida.

Shopping

If you are looking for a mix of food, art, performance, landscaping, and retailing, then head to renewed downtown West Palm around **Clematis Street.** Water-view parks with attractive plantings and lighting—including fountains where kids can cool off—add to the pleasure of browsing, window-shopping, and resting at an outdoor café. Hip national retailers such as the Gap, Banana Republic, Ann Taylor Loft, and Chico's blend in with stores that carry the gamut from fabric to tattoos.

The 55-acre, $550 million **CityPlace** (⊠ 700 S. Rosemary Ave., ☎ 561/366–1000) attracts people of all ages to enjoy the restaurants, cafés, and outdoor bars; a 20-screen Muvico; the Harriet Himmel Gilman Theater; and a 36,000-gallon dancing water and light show. This family-friendly dining, shopping, and entertainment complex has plenty to see and do. Among CityPlace's 78 stores are popular national retailers Macy's, FAO Schwarz, and Restoration Hardware and several boutiques unique to Florida. Inside **Dolly Duz** (☎ 561/514–0991), spaciously organized shoes and handbags by Vaneli, Donald Pliner, and Stuart Weitzman line the room's edges, and interior cabinets highlight vintage shoes—for display only—from the owner's personal collection. Behind the punchy, brightly colored clothing in the front window of **C. Orrico** (☎ 561/832–9203) are family fashions and accessories by Lily Pulitzer and girlie casual gear by Three Dots and Trina Turk. **Rhythm Clothiers** (☎ 561/833–7677) attracts fashion-forward types with a stock of men's and women's clothing by Dolce & Gabbana, Beth Bowley, Diesel, Miss Sixty, and Samsonite. With shelves piled high with men's shirts and armoires overflowing with ladies' knits, **Stuart Norman** (☎ 561/835–9335) shows how dressed-up casual is done in South Florida.

The free downtown trolley runs a continuous loop linking Clematis Street and CityPlace, so you won't miss a shop.

Lake Okeechobee
40 mi west of West Palm Beach.

Rimming the western edges of Palm Beach and Martin counties, the United States' second-largest freshwater lake is girdled by 120 mi of road, yet remains shielded from sight for almost its entire circumference. Lake Okeechobee—the Seminole's Big Water and the heart of the great Everglades watershed—measures 730 square mi, roughly 33 mi north–south and 30 mi east–west, with an average natural depth of only 10 ft (flood control brings the figure up to 12 ft and deeper). Six major lock systems and 32 separate water-control structures manage the water.

Encircling the lake is a 30-ft-high grassy levee—locals call it "the wall"—and the Lake Okeechobee Scenic Trail, a segment of the Florida National Scenic Trail, providing a challenge for even the most experienced hikers and mountain bicyclists. This primitive and intriguing 110-mi trail encircles the lake atop the 35-ft Herbert Hoover Dike. Inside the wall, on the lake itself, you'll spot happy anglers from all over, hooked themselves on some of the best bass fishing in North America.

Small towns dot the lakeshore in this still largely agricultural area. To the southeast is Belle Glade—motto: HER SOIL IS HER FORTUNE—playing a role as the eastern hub of the 700,000-acre Everglades Agricultural Area, the crescent of farmlands south and east of the lake. To the southwest lies Clewiston, bragging itself up as "the sweetest town in America" thanks to presence of "Big Sugar," more formally known as the United States Sugar Corporation. At the lake's north end, around Okeechobee, citrus production has outgrown cattle ranching as the principal economy, although still-important dairying diminishes as the state acquires more acreage in efforts to reduce water pollution. Set back from the lake, Indiantown is the western hub of Martin County, noteworthy for citrus production, cattle ranching, and timbering. The town reached its apex in 1927, when the Seaboard Airline Railroad briefly established its southern headquarters and a model town here.

Municipal Complex. Grouped together here in Belle Glade are the public library and the **Lawrence E. Will Museum**, both with materials on town history. On the front lawn is a Ferenc Verga sculpture of a family fleeing a wall of water rising from the lake during the catastrophic hurricane of 1928. More than 2,000 people perished and 15,000 families were left homeless by torrential flooding. ✉ *530 Main St., Belle Glade,* ☎ *561/996–3453.* 🎫 *Free.* ☉ *Mon.–Wed. 10–8, Thurs.–Sat. 10–5.*

Clewiston Museum. Detailing city history, the museum has stories not only of Big Sugar and the Herbert Hoover Dike construction, but also of a ramie crop grown here to make rayon, of World War II RAF pilots training at the Clewiston airfield, and of a German POW camp. ✉ *112 S. Commercio St., Clewiston,* ☎ *863/983–2870.* 🎫 *Free.* ☉ *Tues.–Fri. 10–4.*

Barley Barber Swamp. The Florida Power and Light Company's Martin Power Plant maintains this 400-acre freshwater cypress swamp preserve. A 5,800-ft-long boardwalk provides a good view of what near-coastal Florida was largely like before vast water-control efforts began in the 19th century. Dozens of birds, reptiles, and mammals inhabit these wetlands and lowlands, with an outstanding reserve of bald cypress trees, swamp growth, and slow-flowing coffee-color water. Reservations are required at least one week in advance for tours, conducted weekdays, October to May. Terrorist attacks on the United States forced closing of the swamp for the 2002 winter season because of power plant security reasons. Reopening to the public is expected by 2003. Call for schedules on manatee walks in January and February and turtle walks in June and July. ✉ *Rte. 710, Indiantown,* ☎ *800/552–8440.* 🎫 *Free.* ☉ *Tours Fri.–Wed. 8:30 and 12:30.*

DINING AND LODGING

$–$$ ✗ **Colonial Dining Room.** The Clewiston Inn's restaurant has ladder-back chairs, chandeliers, fanlight windows, good food, and an attitude that's anything but fancy. The southern regional and Continental dishes—chicken, pork, steak, and the ubiquitous catfish—are mighty tasty. ✉ *108 Royal Palm Ave., at U.S. 27, Clewiston,* ☎ *863/983–8151. MC, V.*

$–$$ ✕ **Lightsey's.** The pick of the lake, this lodgelike restaurant at the Okee-Tantie Recreation Area started closer to town as a fish company with four tables in a corner. Now folks come out here. You can get most items fried, steamed, broiled, or grilled. The freshest are the catfish, cooter (freshwater turtle), frogs' legs, and gator. ⊠ *10430 Rte. 78W, Okeechobee,* ☎ *863/763–4276. MC, V. Beer and wine only.*

$$ 🏨 **Clewiston Inn.** A classic antebellum-style country hotel in the heart of town, this inn was built in 1938. The cypress-panel lobby, wood-burning fireplace, colonial dining room, and Everglades lounge with a wraparound Everglades mural are standouts. Pleasant rooms with reproduction furniture are an excellent value, and rates include a full breakfast cooked to order. There's a pool across the street in the park. ⊠ *108 Royal Palm Ave., at U.S. 27, Clewiston 33440,* ☎ *863/983–8151 or 800/749–4466,* FAX *863/983–4602,* WEB *www.clewistoninn.com. 48 rooms, 5 suites. Restaurant, 6 tennis courts, bar. AE, MC, V. BP.*

$–$$ 🏨 **Seminole Country Inn.** Once the Seaboard Airline Railroad's south-
★ ern headquarters, this two-story, Mediterranean revival inn with its cy-press ceilings and pine hardwood floors was restored by Holman Wall. It's now run by the late Indiantown patriarch's daughter, Jonnie Wall Williams, a fifth-generation native. Carpeted rooms are done in coun-try ruffles and prints, with comfy beds. Rocking chairs await on the porch, and there's Indiantown memorabilia in the lobby, a sitting area on the second floor, and good local art throughout. ⊠ *15885 S.W. Warfield Blvd., Indiantown 34956,* ☎ *561/597–3777 or 888/394–3777,* WEB *www.seminoleinn.com. 28 rooms. 2 restaurants, pool, horseback riding. AE, D, MC, V. CP.*

$ ⛺ **Belle Glade Marina Campground.** A few miles north of downtown Belle Glade, just offshore in Lake Okeechobee, is Torry Island. Camp-sites have water and electrical hookups; some have sewer hookups and docking facilities. ⊠ *Torry Island 33493,* ☎ *561/996–6322. 370 campsites. Picnic area, dock, boating, fishing, horseshoes, shuffle-board. MC, V.*

$ 🏨 **Okeechobee Inn.** Rooms in this simple, two-story L-shape motel, 2 mi west of Belle Glade, are done in green floral prints. Large win-dows let in plenty of light, and balconies overlook the pool. Fishing and boat ramps are a mile away. ⊠ *265 N. U.S. 27, South Bay 33493,* ☎ *561/996–6517. 115 rooms. Pool, playground. MC, V.*

$ ⛺ **Okee-Tantie Recreation Area.** In addition to recreational facilities, the park has RV sites, tent sites, picnic spots, rest rooms, and show-ers, and a shop for sandwiches and groceries. Lightsey's restaurant over-looks the marina. ⊠ *10430 Rte. 78W, Okeechobee 34974,* ☎ *863/ 763–2622. 215 RV sites, 38 tent sites. Restaurant, grocery, picnic area, dock, boating, fishing, playground. MC, V.*

$ 🏨 **Pier II Resort.** This modern two-story motel on the rim canal has a five-story observation tower for peeking over the lake's levee. Large, clean, motel-plain rooms are nicely maintained. Out back are a 600-ft fishing pier and the Oyster Bar, one of the lake area's best hangouts for shooting pool or watching TV, attracting a mix of locals and out-of-towners. ⊠ *2200 S.E. U.S. 441, Okeechobee 34974,* ☎ *863/763–8003 or 800/874–3744,* FAX *863/763–2245. 89 rooms. Fishing, bar. AE, D, DC, MC, V.*

OUTDOOR ACTIVITIES AND SPORTS

Fishing. J-Mark Fish Camp (⊠ Torry Island, ☎ 561/996–5357) pro-vides fully equipped bass boats, airboat rides, fishing guides, tackle, bait, and licenses. Since the **Okee-Tantie Recreation Area** (⊠ 10430 Rte. 78W, Okeechobee, ☎ 863/763–2622) has direct lake access, it's a popular fishing outpost. There are two public boat ramps, fish-clean-ing stations, a marina, picnic areas and a restaurant, a playground, rest rooms, showers, and a **bait shop** (☏ 863/763–9645) that stocks groceries. In addition to operating the bridge to Torry Island (among Florida's last remaining swing bridges—it's cranked open and closed by hand, swinging at right angles to the road), brothers Charles and Gordon Corbin run **Slim's Fish Camp** (⊠ Torry Island, ☏ 561/996–3844). Here you'll find a complete tackle shop, guides, camping facilities, bass boats, and even the name of a taxidermist to mount your trophy.

Golf. Belle Glade Municipal Country Club (⊠ Torry Island Rd., Belle Glade, ☏ 561/996–6605) has an 18-hole golf course and restaurant open to the public.

SOUTH TO BOCA RATON

Strung together by Route A1A, the towns between Palm Beach and Boca Raton are notable for their variety. Although the aura of Palm Beach has rubbed off here and there, you'll also find pockets of modesty such as Briny Breezes with its oceanside trailers. In one town, you'll find a cluster of sophisticated art galleries and fancy dining, whereas the very next town will yield mostly hamburger joints and mom-and-pop stores stocking the basics.

Lake Worth

㉓ *2 mi south of West Palm Beach.*

For years, tourists looked here mainly for inexpensive lodging and easy access to Palm Beach, since a bridge leads from the mainland to a barrier island that is home to Lake Worth's beach. Now Lake Worth boasts several blocks of restaurants and art galleries, making this a worthy destination on its own.

Lake Worth Municipal Park. Also known as Casino Park, this has a beach, Olympic-size swimming pool, fishing pier, picnic areas, shuffleboard, restaurants, and shops. ⊠ *Rte. A1A at end of Lake Worth Bridge,* ☏ *561/533–7367.* 🎫 *Pool $3, parking 25¢ for 15 mins.* ☉ *Daily 9–4:45.*

Dining and Lodging

$$–$$$$ ✕ **Paradiso.** The aroma of garlic prevails as you step into this noisy, popular Italian eatery with a mural depicting the Italian countryside. Numerous pasta offerings are served as appetizers or entrées. Other delicious options include veal scallopini with prosciutto, chicken breast stuffed with goat cheese, and risotto specials. ⊠ *625 Lucerne Ave.,* ☏ *561/547–2500. AE, MC, V. No lunch Sun.*

$–$$ ✕ **John G's.** Count on a line here until closing at 3 PM. The menu is as big as the crowd: grand fruit platters, sandwich-board superstars, grilled burgers, seafood, and eggs every which way, including a United Nations of omelets. Breakfast is served until 11. ⊠ *Lake Worth Casino,* ☏ *561/ 585–9860. Reservations not accepted. No credit cards. No dinner.*

$$–$$$ 🏠 **Mango Inn.** It's only a 10-minute walk to the beach from this white frame B&B built as a private house in 1915. All rooms are individually decorated and some rooms have four-poster beds. The two first-floor rooms have elegant French doors opening out onto a patio and overlook the pool. A poolside cottage has two bedrooms, two bathrooms, and houselike amenities. You can have your complimentary breakfast in the dining room, on the veranda overlooking the heated pool, or in the peaceful courtyard. ⊠ *128 N. Lakeside Dr., 33460,* ☏ *561/533– 6900, 888/626–4619,* 🖷 *561/533–6992,* 🌐 *www.mangoinn.com. 7 rooms, 1 cottage. Some refrigerators, pool; no phones in some rooms, no TV in some rooms, no kids, no smoking. AE, MC, V. BP.*

$–$$$ ☒ **Sabal Palm House.** Built in 1936, this historic two-story frame en-
clave is a short walk from the Intracoastal Waterway and a golf course.
Three rooms and a suite are in the main house with three more rooms
across a brick courtyard in the carriage house. Each room is inspired
by a different artist—including Renoir, Dalí, Norman Rockwell, and
Chagall—and all have oak floors, antique furnishings, and private
balconies. Two units have Jacuzzis. There's an inviting parlor, and a
gourmet breakfast is served indoors or in the courtyard, under the palms.
☒ *109 N. Golfview Rd., 33460,* ☎ *561/582–1090,* FAX *561/582–0933,*
WEB *www.sabalpalmhouse.com. 6 rooms, 1 suite. No kids under 14.
AE, D, MC, V. BP.*

Outdoor Activities and Sports

Like an adventure camp for adults, **Dreamsport USA** dangles the op-
portunity for you to live a "week on the edge" in Florida with pack-
ages including two days of wakeboarding, barefooting, or waterskiing,
a day of ocean scuba diving with preliminary training in the pool, and
time for offshore boating racing and tandem parachute jumping, all
with expert instruction. Lodging is in a private lakeside villa with
most meals served family style, and airport transfers are available. Rates,
including equipment, are $1,700 per person from January to June. ☒
1732 S. Congress Ave., ☎ *561/585–7902.*

The **Gulfstream Polo Club,** the oldest such club along the Palm Beaches,
began in the 1920s and plays medium-goal polo (for teams with handi-
caps of 8–16 goals). There are six polo fields. ☒ *4550 Polo Rd.,* ☎
561/965–2057. ☒ *Free.* ☉ *Games Dec.–Apr.*

Nightlife

Some nights you'll encounter free concerts by local and regional artists
and other nights the headliners are nationally known professionals. But
every night, Tuesday through Saturday, there's traditional blues at the
Bamboo Room (☒ 25 S. J St., ☎ 561/585–2583).

The Arts

Lake Worth Playhouse (☒ 713 Lake Ave., 33461, ☎ 561/586–6410)
presents drama and popular musicals on its main stage, including
works by Andrew Lloyd Webber and Tim Rice.

Lantana

㉔   *2 mi south of Lake Worth.*

Lantana—just a bit farther south from Palm Beach than Lake Worth—
also has inexpensive lodging and a bridge connecting the town to its
own beach on Palm Beach's barrier island. Tucked between Lantana
and Boynton Beach is **Manalapan,** a tiny residential community crowned
by a luxury Ritz-Carlton beach resort.

Lantana Public Beach. The beach itself is an ideal spot for sprawling
out to relax, beachcombing, or power-walking. If any of those options
help you work up an appetite, you're in luck. One of the most popu-
lar food concessions around is located here, the **Dune Deck Cafe.**
You'll find fresh fish on weekends and breakfast and lunch specials every
day outdoors under beach umbrellas. ☒ *100 N. Ocean Ave.,* ☎ *no
phone.* ☒ *Parking 25¢ for 15 mins.* ☉ *Daily 9–4:45.*

Dining and Lodging

$$–$$$ ✕ **Old Key Lime House.** Overlooking the Intracoastal Waterway, the
1889 Lyman House has grown in spurts over the years and is now a
patchwork of shedlike spaces, an informal Old Florida seafood house
that serves local seafood and key lime pie—the house specialty. Although

there's air-conditioning, dining is open-air most evenings and in cooler weather. ⊠ *300 E. Ocean Ave.,* ☎ *561/533–5220. AE, MC, V.*

$$$$ ☆ ☷ **Ritz-Carlton, Palm Beach.** Despite its name, this hotel is actually in Manalapan, halfway between Palm Beach and Delray. The bisque-color, triple-tower landmark looks as though it was built by Addison Mizner. A huge double-sided marble fireplace dominates the elegant lobby and foreshadows the luxury of the guest rooms, which have rich upholstered furnishings and marble tubs. Most rooms have ocean views, and all have balconies. Apart from a fabulous beach, there's a large pool and courtyard shaded by coconut palms—all of which are served by attendants who can fulfill whims from iced drinks to cool face towels. ⊠ *100 S. Ocean Blvd., Manalapan 33462,* ☎ *561/533–6000 or 800/ 241–3333,* ᴵᴬˣ *561/588–4555,* ᵂᴱᴮ *www.ritz-carlton.com. 257 rooms, 13 suites. 4 restaurants, room service, in-room data ports, minibars, 5 tennis courts, pool, hair salon, massage, sauna, spa, steam room, beach, snorkeling, bicycles, basketball, 2 bars, baby-sitting, children's programs (ages 5–12), laundry service, concierge, business services; no-smoking rooms. AE, D, DC, MC, V.*

$ ☷ **Super 8 Motel.** What's special about this sprawling one-story motel is the price—a bargain, considering its proximity to Palm Beach. Efficiencies and rooms (some with refrigerators) are clean but basic. ⊠ *1255 Hypoluxo Rd., 33462,* ☎ *561/585–3970,* ᴵᴬˣ *561/586–3028. 129 rooms, 8 efficiencies. Pool, laundry facilities. AE, DC, MC, V.*

Outdoor Activities and Sports

B-Love Fleet (⊠ 314 E. Ocean Ave., ☎ 561/588–7612) offers three deep-sea fishing excursions daily: 8–noon, 1–5, and 7–11. No reservations are needed; just show up 30 minutes before the boat is scheduled to leave. The cost is $24 per person.

Boynton Beach

㉕ *3 mi south of Lantana.*

In 1884 when fewer than 50 settlers lived in the area, Nathan Boynton, a Civil War veteran from Michigan, paid $25 for 500 acres with a mile-long stretch of beachfront thrown in. How things have changed, with today's population at about 118,000 and property values still on an upswing. Far enough from Palm Beach to remain low-key, Boynton Beach has two parts, the mainland and the barrier island, connected by a causeway.

Knollwood Groves. The groves date from the 1930s, when it was planted by the partners of the *Amos & Andy* radio show. You can take a 30-minute, 30-acre tram tour through the orange groves and a processing plant and visit the **Hallpatee Seminole Indian Village,** with an alligator exhibit and crafts shop. During the high season, Native American educator Martin Twofeathers conducts a weekly one-hour alligator-handling show. ⊠ *8053 Lawrence Rd.,* ☎ *561/734–4800,* ᵂᴱᴮ *www. knollwoodgroves.com.* ☛ *Tour $1, show $6.* ☉ *Daily 8:30–5:30, show Sat. 2. Closed Sun. June–Oct.*

☾ **Puppetry Arts Center.** Shows and educational programs are on tap here at the home of the Gold Coast Puppet Guild. ⊠ *3633 S. Federal Hwy.,* ☎ *561/737–3334.* ☛ *Shows $2.50.* ☉ *Call for schedule.*

Oceanbeach Park. There's an inviting beach, boardwalk, concessions, grills, a jogging trail, and playground here. Parking costs more if you're not a Boynton resident. ⊠ *Ocean Ave. at Rte. A1A,* ☎ *no phone.* ☛ *Parking $10 per day in winter, $5 per day rest of year.* ☉ *Daily 9 AM–midnight.*

OFF THE
BEATEN PATH

ARTHUR R. MARSHALL–LOXAHATCHEE NATIONAL WILDLIFE REFUGE – The most robust part of the Everglades, this 221-square-mi refuge is one of three huge water-retention areas accounting for much of the Everglades outside the national park. These areas are managed less to protect natural resources, however, than to prevent flooding to the south. Start from the visitor center, where there are two walking trails: a boardwalk through a dense cypress swamp and a marsh trail to a 20-ft-high observation tower overlooking a pond. There is also a 5½-mi canoe trail, best for more experienced canoeists since it's overgrown. Wildlife viewing is good year-round, and you can fish for bass and panfish. ⊠ *10119 Lee Rd., off U.S. 441 between Boynton Beach Blvd. (Rte. 804) and Atlantic Ave. (Rte. 806), west of Boynton Beach,* ☎ *561/734–8303.* ⊟ *$5 per vehicle, $1 per pedestrian.* ⊙ *Daily 6 am–sunset; visitor center weekdays 9–4, weekends 9–4:30.*

Dining and Lodging

$–$$ ✕ **Mama Jennie's.** Tucked in a strip mall, this inviting, casual Italian restaurant attracts families hungry for big pizzas topped with mozzarella, mushrooms, and anchovies. Spaghetti with meatballs, eggplant parmigiana, and stuffed shells are also fine choices, and all dishes are homemade. ⊠ *706 W. Boynton Beach Blvd.,* ☎ *561/737–2407. AE, MC, V. No lunch.*

$$ ▥ **Holiday Inn Express.** Conveniently located off Interstate 95, this four-story hotel has large rooms with purple and green fabrics, blond-wood furniture, and a small sitting area. A large sundeck surrounds the heated pool. Complimentary breakfast is served, and complimentary beverages are on tap at the end of the day. ⊠ *480 W. Boynton Beach Blvd., 33435,* ☎ *561/734–9100,* FAX *561/738–7193. 105 rooms, 6 suites. Pool, laundry facilities. AE, DC, MC, V. BP.*

Outdoor Activities and Sports

FISHING

You can fish the canal at the **Arthur R. Marshall–Loxahatchee National Wildlife Refuge** (☎ 561/734–8303). There's a boat ramp, and the waters are decently productive, but bring your own equipment.

GOLF

Boynton Beach Municipal Golf Course (⊠ 8020 Jog Rd., ☎ 561/742–6500) has 27 holes.

Gulf Stream

㉖ *2 mi south of Boynton Beach.*

This small beachfront community also was influenced by Mizner. As you pass the bougainvillea-topped walls of the Gulf Stream Club, don't be surprised if a private security officer stops traffic for a golfer to cross.

Lodging

$ ▥ **Riviera Palms Motel.** Hans and Herter Grannemann have owned this quaint two-story motel dating from the 1950s since 1978. It's clean and well located, across Route A1A from midrise apartment houses on the ocean. Three wings with green awnings surround a grassy front yard and heated pool. Rooms are done in Danish modern and a blue, brown, and tan color scheme; all have at least a refrigerator but no phone. ⊠ *3960 N. Ocean Blvd., 33483,* ☎ *561/276–3032. 17 rooms, suites, and efficiencies. Refrigerators, pool; no room phones. No credit cards.*

Delray Beach

27 *2 mi south of Gulf Stream.*

This onetime artists' retreat with a small settlement of Japanese farmers has grown into an increasingly sophisticated beach town. Thanks to an energetic historic preservation movement, Atlantic Avenue, the once dilapidated main drag, has evolved into a 1-mi stretch of palm-dotted brick sidewalks, almost entirely lined with stores, art galleries, and dining establishments. Running east–west and ending at the beach, it's a pleasant place for a stroll, day or night. Another active pedestrian way begins at the edge of town, across Northeast 8th Street (George Bush Boulevard), along the big broad swimming beach that extends north and south of Atlantic Avenue.

Cason Cottage. A restored Victorian-style home that dates from about 1915, it now serves as the Delray Beach Historical Society's offices. It's filled with Victorian-era relics, including a pipe organ donated by descendants of a Delray Beach pioneer family. Periodic displays celebrate the town's architectural evolution. The cottage is a block north of the cultural center. ⊠ *5 N.E. 1st St.,* ☎ *561/243–0223.* 🎟 *Free.* ☉ *Tues.–Fri. 11–4.*

Colony Hotel. The chief landmark along Atlantic Avenue is this Mediterranean revival hotel, still open only for the winter season as it has been almost every year since 1926. ⊠ *525 E. Atlantic Ave.,* ☎ *561/276–4123.*

★ **Morikami Museum and Japanese Gardens.** Out in the boonies west of Delray Beach seems an odd place to encounter the inscrutable east, but there awaits this cultural and recreational facility heralding the Yamato Colony of Japanese farmers. The on-site Cornell Café serves light Asian fare. ⊠ *4000 Morikami Park Rd.,* ☎ *561/495–0233,* 𝕎𝔼𝔹 *www.morikami.org.* 🎟 *Park and museum $8, free Sun. 10–noon.* ☉ *Park daily sunrise–sunset; museum and café Tues.–Sun. 10–5.*

Municipal Beach. A boat ramp and volleyball court are on this stretch of beach. ⊠ *Atlantic Ave. at Rte. A1A.*

Old School Square Cultural Arts Center. Just off Atlantic Avenue, the arts center houses several museums in restored school buildings dating from 1913 and 1926. The **Cornell Museum of Art & History** offers an ever-changing array of art exhibits. ⊠ *51 N. Swinton Ave.,* ☎ *561/243–7922,* 𝕎𝔼𝔹 *www.oldschool.org.* 🎟 *$6.* ☉ *Tues.–Sat. 11–4, Sun. 1–4.*

Dining and Lodging

$$–$$$ ✕ **Peter's Stone Crabs.** There's no mystery to the main attraction here, but apart from stone crabs at market price served for dinner every day, you can order from a diverse menu with pastas, several kinds of fish, veal, beef, and sometimes Alaskan king crab. ⊠ *411 E. Atlantic Ave.,* ☎ *561/278–0036. No lunch. AE, DC, MC, V.*

$$–$$$ ✕ **Safari Steakhouse.** Carnivores revel in this African-theme outpost with items such as Serengeti ostrich fillet in a peppercorn sauce. There's a small bar up front and the overall mood is convivial. Appetizers include escargot and crab cakes, and patrons rave over the center-cut filet mignon with Boursin cheese and wild mushroom demi-glace. ⊠ *4 E. Atlantic Ave.,* ☎ *561/272–3739. AE, DC, MC, V.*

$$–$$$ ✕ **Splendid Blendeds Café.** Dine on the sidewalk terrace or in the dining room decorated with original primitive art. The café is popular day and night, and cuisine is a blend of savory Italian, Mexican, Asian, and contemporary. Tasty starters include roasted corn chowder and grilled Thai duck satay. Entrées range from pasta dishes to grilled yellowfin

THE MORIKAMI: ESSENCE OF JAPAN IN FLORIDA

A **MAGICAL PATCH OF LAND** where the Far East meets the South lies just beyond Palm Beach's allure of sun and sea and glittering resorts. It's called the Morikami Museum and Japanese Gardens, and it's a testament to one man's perseverance against agricultural angst. It's also a soothing destination for reflection, an oasis of culture, pine forest, trails, and lakes.

In 1904, Jo Sakai, a New York University graduate, returned to his homeland of Miyazu, Japan, to recruit hands for farming what is now northern Boca Raton. With help from Henry Flagler's East Coast Railroad subsidiary they colonized as Yamato, an ancient name for Japan. When crops fell short, everyone left except for George Sukeji Morikami, who carried on cultivating local crops, eventually donating his land to memorialize the Yamato Colony. His dream took on new dimension with the 1977 opening of The Morikami, a living monument bridging cultural understanding between Morikami's two homelands.

The original Yamato-Kan building chronicles the Yamato Colony, and a main museum has rotating exhibits along with 5,000 art objects and artifacts, including a 500-piece collection of tea ceremony items. You can enjoy a demonstration of *sado*, the Japanese tea ceremony, in the Seishin-an tea house, or learn about Japanese history in the 5,000-book library. There are also expansive Japanese gardens with strolling paths, a tropical bonsai collection, small lakes teeming with koi, plus picnic areas, a shop, and a café.

— Lynne Helm

tuna, filet mignon stuffed with roasted garlic, or jerk chicken. ⊠ 432 E. Atlantic Ave., ☎ 561/265–1035. AE, MC, V. Closed Sun.

$–$$$ ✕ **Pineapple Grille.** This tropical enclave is a magnet for regulars intent on the Caribbean fare served in an informal atmosphere. An extensive menu includes items such as macadamia nut–crusted crab cakes and mango goat cheese chicken along with imaginative pizzas. There's also a good wine list at affordable prices and live music on weekends. ⊠ 800 Palm Trail in the Palm Trail Plaza, ☎ 561/265–1368. AE, MC, V.

$–$$ ✕ **Blue Anchor.** Yes, this pub was actually shipped from England, ★ where it stood for 150 years as the Blue Anchor Pub in London's historic Chancery Lane. There it was a watering hole for famed Englishmen, including Winston Churchill. The Delray Beach incarnation has stuck to authentic British pub fare. Chow down on a ploughman's lunch (a chunk of Stilton cheese, a hunk of bread, and pickled onions), shepherd's pie, fish-and-chips, and bangers and mash (sausages with mashed potatoes). English beers and ales are on tap and by the bottle. ⊠ 804 E. Atlantic Ave., ☎ 561/272–7272. AE, MC, V.

$–$$ ✕ **Boston's on the Beach.** Restaurants overlooking a beach often rely ★ on location alone to keep tables filled, but at Boston's you'll also find good fare, from New England clam chowder and several lobster dishes to fresh fish grilled, fried, or just about any other way. Wooden tables are old, and walls are laden with conversation starters, heavy on paraphernalia from the Boston Bruins, New England Patriots, and Boston Red Sox, including a veritable shrine to Ted Williams. Catch ocean breezes from an outdoor deck upstairs. ⊠ *40 S. Ocean Blvd. (Rte. A1A),* ☎ *561/278–3364. AE, MC, V.*

$$$–$$$$ 🏨 **Delray Beach Marriott.** A bright pink five-story hotel, it's by far the largest property in Delray, with a stellar location at Atlantic Avenue's east end, across the road from the beach and within walking distance of restaurants, shops, and galleries. Rooms and suites are spacious and many have stunning ocean views. The giant, free-form pool surrounded by a comfortable deck for sunning looks across the street to the ocean. ⊠ *10 N. Ocean Blvd., 33483,* ☎ *561/274–3200,* FAX *561/274–3202,* WEB *www.marriotthotels.com. 244 rooms, 68 suites. 3 restaurants, room service, in-room data ports, in-room safes, minibars, pool, health club, hot tub, beach, 2 bars, laundry facilities, business services. AE, DC, MC, V.*

$$$–$$$$ 🏨 **Seagate Hotel & Beach Club.** You'll find value, comfort, style, and ★ personal attention at this lovely garden enclave. All units have at least kitchenettes. Less-expensive studios have compact facilities behind foldaway doors, and others have a separate living room and larger kitchen. The one- and two-bedroom suites are chintz and rattan, with many upholstered pieces. Dress up and dine in a smart little mahogany- and lattice-trimmed beachfront salon or have the same Continental fare in casual attire in the equally stylish bar. As a guest, you'll have access to the private beach club. ⊠ *400 S. Ocean Blvd., 33483,* ☎ *561/276– 2421 or 800/233–3581. 70 suites. Restaurant, in-room data ports, kitch- enettes, saltwater pool, beach, bar. AE, DC, MC, V.*

Nightlife and the Arts

THE ARTS

The **Crest Theater** (⊠ 51 N. Swinton Ave., ☎ 561/243–7922), in the Old School Square Cultural Arts Center, presents productions in dance, music, and theater.

NIGHTLIFE

The **Back Room Blues Lounge** (⊠ 909 W. Atlantic Ave., ☎ 561/243– 9110), behind Westside Liquors, has a DJ Wednesday through Satur- day. **Boston's on the Beach** (⊠ 40 S. Ocean Blvd., ☎ 561/278–3364) presents live reggae music Monday and rock 'n' roll Tuesday through Sunday. The **Colony Hotel** (⊠ 525 E. Atlantic Ave., ☎ 561/276–4123) has a convivial bar and live music most nights.

Outdoor Activities and Sports

BIKING

There is a bicycle path in Barwick Park and a special oceanfront lane along Route A1A. **Rich Wagen's Cycles** (⊠ 217 E. Atlantic Ave., ☎ 561/276–4234) rents bikes by the hour or day, providing maps of nearby bicycle routes.

SCUBA DIVING AND SNORKELING

Scuba and snorkeling equipment can be rented from longtime family- owned **Force E** (⊠ 660 Linton Blvd., ☎ 561/276–0666). It has PADI affiliation, provides instruction at all levels, and offers charters.

TENNIS

Each winter the **Delray Beach Tennis Center** (⊠ 201 W. Atlantic Ave., ☎ 561/243–7380) hosts a professional women's tournament attract- ing top-ranked players. The center is also a great place year-round to practice or learn on 14 clay courts and five hard courts. You can book individual lessons and clinics.

WATERSKIING

Lake Ida Park (⊠ 2929 Lake Ida Rd., ☎ 561/964–4420) is a great place to water-ski, whether you're a beginner or a veteran. The park has a boat ramp, a slalom course, and a trick ski course.

Shopping

Street-scaped **Atlantic Avenue** is a showcase for art galleries, shops, and restaurants. This charming area, from Swinton Avenue east to the ocean, has maintained much of its small-town integrity. Large name retailers have not taken over the retail spaces yet, and locals like it this way. **Snappy Turtle** (⊠ 1038 Atlantic Ave., ☎ 561/276–8088) is a multiroom extravaganza where Mackenzie Childs and Lily Pulitzer mingle with other fun fashions for the home and family. A store in the historic Colony Hotel, **Escentials Apothecaries** (⊠ 533 Atlantic Ave., ☎ 561/276–7070) is packed with all things good smelling for your bath, body, and home. Just off Atlantic is **Mermaid's Purse** (⊠ 6 S.E. 5th Ave., ☎ 561/276–5937), where vintage bags, handpicked from local estate sales and European flea markets, are tucked into every corner and hanging from the ceiling.

Boca Raton

28 *6 mi south of Delray Beach.*

Less than an hour south of Palm Beach and anchoring the county's south end, upscale Boca Raton has much in common with its fabled cousin. Both reflect the unmistakable architectural influence of Addison Mizner, their principal developer in the mid-1920s. The meaning of the name Boca Raton (pronounced Boca Rah-tone) often arouses curiosity, with many folks mistakenly assuming it means "rat's mouth." Historians say the probable origin is "Boca Ratones," an ancient Spanish geographical term for an inlet filled with jagged rocks or coral. Miami's Biscayne Bay had such an inlet, and in 1823, a map maker copying Miami terrain confused the more northern inlet, thus mistakenly labeling this area "Boca Ratones." No matter what, you'll know you've arrived in the heart of downtown when spotting the town hall's gold dome on the main drag, Federal Highway.

2 East El Camino Real. Built in 1925 as the headquarters of the Mizner Development Corporation, this structure is an example of Mizner's characteristic Spanish revival architectural style, with its wrought-iron grilles and handmade tiles. As for Mizner's grandiose vision of El Camino Real, the architect/promoter once prepared brochures promising a sweeping wide boulevard with Venetian canals and arching bridges. Camino Real is pretty, heading east to the Boca Raton Resort & Club, but don't count on feeling you're in Venice.

Town Hall Museum. This building with its shimmering golden dome houses a vital repository of archival material and special exhibits on the area's development. ⊠ *71 N. Federal Hwy.,* ☎ *561/395–6766.* ⊡ *Free.* ☉ *Weekdays 10–4.*

Boca Raton Museum of Art. In a spectacular building in Mizner Park, the museum has an interactive children's gallery and changing exhibition galleries showcasing internationally known artists. Upstairs galleries house a permanent collection including works by Picasso, Degas, Matisse, Klee, and Modigliani as well as notable pre-Columbian art. ⊠ *501 Plaza Real,* ☎ *561/392–2500,* WEB *www.bocamuseum.org.* ⊡ *$8.* ☉ *Tues., Thurs., Sat., 10–5, Wed. and Fri. 10–9, Sun. noon–5.*

Old Floresta. The residential area behind the Boca Raton Museum of Art was developed by Addison Mizner starting in 1925 and landscaped with varieties of palms and cycads. It includes houses that are mainly in a Mediterranean style, many with upper balconies supported by exposed wood columns.

☺ **Children's Science Explorium.** Hands-on interactive exhibits make this a kid pleaser. Children can create their own laser-light shows, explore a 3-D kiosk that illustrates wave motion, and try assorted electrifying experiments. There are also wind tunnels, microscopes, and microwave and radiation experiment stations. ⊠ *300 S. Military Trail,* ☎ *561/347–3913.* ☞ *Free.* ☉ *Weekdays 8 AM–10:30 PM, Sat. 8–5, Sun. 10–5.*

☺ **Gumbo Limbo Nature Center.** A big draw for kids, the center has four huge saltwater tanks brimming with sea life—from coral to stingrays—and a boardwalk through dense forest with a 50-ft tower you can climb to overlook the tree canopy. In spring and early summer, staffers lead nocturnal turtle walks for watching nesting females come ashore and lay eggs. ⊠ *1801 N. Ocean Blvd.,* ☎ *561/338–1473,* WEB *www.fau.edu/ gumbo.* ☞ *Free; turtle tours $4; tickets must be obtained in advance.* ☉ *Mon.–Sat. 9–4, Sun. noon–4; turtle tours late May–mid-July, Mon.– Thurs. 9 PM–midnight.*

Dining and Lodging

$$–$$$$ ✕ **La Finestra.** Belle Epoque lithographs decorate the walls, and although
★ the formal interior is just this side of austere, the cuisine itself is an extravaganza of taste treats. Veal chops, tuna, and anything with mushrooms draw raves, but count on hearty fare rather than a light touch. Start with the Portobello mushroom with garlic or the Corsican baby sardines in olive oil. For a main course, try a pasta dish, such as ricotta ravioli, scallopini of veal stuffed with crabmeat, lobster, and Gorgonzola, or the Tuscan fish stew. Be sure to make reservations for weekend nights. ⊠ *171 E. Palmetto Rd.,* ☎ *561/392–1838. AE, DC, MC, V. No lunch.*

$$–$$$$ ✕ **La Vieille Maison.** Considered one of the Gold Coast's temples of haute
★ cuisine, this restaurant—set in a 1920s-era dwelling believed to be an Addison Mizner design—is pricey and worth it. Intimate private dining rooms set the stage for seasonal prix-fixe and à la carte menus showcasing Provençal dishes with tropical overtones. Don't miss the *soupe au pistou* (vegetable soup with basil and Parmesan), venison chop with red currant–pepper sauce and roasted chestnuts, and French apple tarte, if they're available. The wine list is one of Florida's most extensive and service is impeccable. ⊠ *770 E. Palmetto Park Rd.,* ☎ *561/391–6701 or 561/737–5677. AE, D, DC, MC, V. Closed early July–Aug.*

$$–$$$$ ✕ **Mark's at the Park.** Exotic cars pour into valet parking at this Mark
★ Militello creation, where the decor—a whimsical interpretation of retro and art deco—competes with the masterful seasonal menu for your attention. The dazzling food includes starters of scallops with foie gras–infused mashed potatoes and spicy steamed mussels, and main courses range from crab-crusted mahimahi to roast duck with sweet potatoes. Desserts are deliciously old-fashioned. You'll need to make reservations for weekend nights. ⊠ *344 Plaza Real, Mizner Park,* ☎ *561/395–0770. AE, D, MC, V.*

$$–$$$ ✕ **Crab House Seafood Restaurant.** Crowds come here day and night for fresh Florida seafood and the restaurant's well-known crab specials along with chicken, steaks, and salads. Decor has a nautical theme, and there's a wide deck for outside dining, a raw bar, and a cocktail lounge. ⊠ *6909 S.W. 18th St.,* ☎ *561/750–0498. AE, D, MC, V.*

$$–$$$ ✕ **Uncle Tai's.** The draw at Boca's most upscale Chinese restaurant is some of the best Szechuan cuisine on Florida's east coast. House specialties include sliced duck with snow peas and water chestnuts in a tangy plum sauce and Orange Beef Delight—flank steak stir-fried until crispy and then sautéed with pepper sauce, garlic, and orange peel. Szechuan-style cooking is hot and spicy, but Uncle Tai's will go easy on the heat on request. Service is quietly efficient. ⊠ *5250 Town Center Circle,* ☎ *561/368–8806. AE, MC, V.*

$–$$ ✕ **Draft House.** Sports aficionados love this place. It's decorated with sports equipment, memorabilia, and photos of famed coaches, players, and moments in sports, plus a dozen televisions for can't-miss events. Apart from inexpensive draft beer, regulars order homemade chili wings, fried chicken tenders, and juicy burgers. For the ravenous, there are char-grilled New York strips or racks of baby-back ribs. ✉ *22191 Powerline Rd.,* ☎ *561/394–6699. AE, MC, V.*

$–$$ ✕ **Tom's Place.** "This place is a blessing from God," says the sign over
★   the fireplace, and after sampling Tom's sauce-slathered ribs that are nothing short of heaven, you may add, "Amen!" Baby-backs or St. Louis–style ribs can be ordered in half racks or full racks. Also rating raves are fried catfish, collard greens, and corn bread. Pick up a bottle of Tom's barbecue sauce to go, just as have a rush of entertainers and NFL players. ✉ *7251 N. Federal Hwy.,* ☎ *561/997–0920. MC, V. Closed Sun., Mon.*

$ ✕ **TooJay's.** There are more than a dozen TooJay's delicatessens in Florida, all worthy of giving New York favorites a run for your money, and definitely the place to come for huge sandwiches piled high, from corned beef on rye and roast beef and onion on pumpernickel to the tuna melt. Boca Raton has a couple of locations and you will find others in Lake Worth, Vero Beach, Palm Beach, and Wellington. All menus are identical, although daily specials and soups of the day can vary. TooJay's is the place to go when you're overwhelmed by the urge for chicken soup, meat loaf, lox and bagels, or killer desserts. ✉ *5030 Champion Blvd.,* ☎ *561/241–5903;* ✉ *3013 Yamato Rd.,* ☎ *561/997–9911. AE, DC, MC, V.*

$$$–$$$$ ▥ **Boca Raton Resort & Club.** Addison Mizner built the Mediterranean-
★   style Cloister Inn here in 1926, and additions over time have created this sparkling, sprawling resort with a beach accessible by shuttle. There's an amazing selection of recreational activities here as well as a full range of lodging options: traditional Cloister rooms are small, but warmly decorated; accommodations in the 27-story Tower are more spacious; Beach Club rooms are light, airy, and contemporary; golf villas are large and attractive and, naturally, near the golf course. In addition to a redesigned golf course, there's a two-story golf clubhouse, and a deluxe Tennis & Fitness Center. ✉ *501 E. Camino Real, 33431-0825,* ☎ *561/395–3000 or 800/327–0101,* ℻ *561/447–5888,* 🕸 *www.bocaresort.com. 840 rooms, 63 suites, 60 golf villas. 7 restaurants, room service, in-room safes, some kitchens, 36-hole golf course, 40 tennis courts, 5 pools, 3 health clubs, hair salon, beach, snorkeling, windsurfing, boating, marina, fishing, basketball, racquetball, 3 bars, nightclub, shops, children's programs (ages 2–17), laundry service, concierge, business services, convention center, meeting rooms. AE, DC, MC, V.*

$$ ▥ **Inn at Boca Teeca.** If golf is your game, this is an excellent choice. Inn guests can play the outstanding course at the adjoining Boca Teeca Country Club, otherwise available only to club members. Rooms are in a three-story building, and most have a patio or balcony. Although the inn is nearly 30 years old, refurbished small rooms are comfortable and contemporary. ✉ *5800 N.W. 2nd Ave., 33487,* ☎ *561/994–0400,* ℻ *561/998–8279. 46 rooms. Restaurant, 27-hole golf course, 6 tennis courts. AE, DC, MC, V.*

$$ ▥ **Ocean Lodge.** The price is right at this small motel because, instead of being on the beach, it's across the street. Rooms are in a simple two-story building, and all have refrigerators. Eleven rooms also have small kitchenettes with a two-burner stove top. Restaurants are within walking distance. ✉ *531 N. Ocean Blvd., 33432,* ☎ *561/395–7772,* ℻ *561/395–0554. 18 rooms. Pool, laundry facilities. AE, DC, MC, V.*

Nightlife and the Arts

THE ARTS

Caldwell Theatre Company (⊠ 7873 N. Federal Hwy., ☎ 561/241–7432) hosts the multimedia Mizner Festival each April and May and stages four productions each winter.

NIGHTLIFE

Drop by the **Ambience Bar & Bistro** (⊠ 5500 N. Federal Hwy., ☎ 561/988–8820) any night of the week for live bands. Sounds range from new wave and alternative to 1970s through '90s.

Outdoor Activities and Sports

BEACHES

Red Reef Park (⊠ 1400 N. Rte. A1A) has a beach and playground plus picnic tables and grills. In addition to its beach, **Spanish River Park** (⊠ 3001 N. Rte. A1A) has picnic tables, grills, and a large playground. Popular **South Beach Park** (⊠ 400 N. Rte. A1A) has a concession stand along with its sand and ocean.

BIKING

Plenty of bike trails and quiet streets make for pleasant pedaling; for current information, contact the city of Boca Raton's **Bicycle Coordinator** (☎ 561/346–3410). You can rent bikes and Rollerblades at **International Bicycle** (⊠ 17 E. Palmetto Park Rd., ☎ 561/394–0404) by the hour or the day. Free bike maps show off the trails in the area.

BOATING

For the thrill of blasting across the water at up to 80 mph, check out **Air and Sea Charters** (⊠ 107 E. Palmetto Park Rd., Suite 330, ☎ 561/368–3566). For $80 per person (three-person minimum), you can spend a wild-eyed half hour gripping your life vest aboard a 1,000-horsepower offshore racing boat. For a more leisurely trip go for Air and Sea's two 55-ft catamarans or 45-ft sailboat; rates start at $35 per person for 2½ hours.

GOLF

Two championship courses and golf programs run by Dave Pelz and Nicklaus/Flick are available at **Boca Raton Resort & Club** (⊠ 501 E. Camino Real, ☎ 561/395–3000).

POLO

Royal Palm Polo Sports Club (⊠ 6300 Old Clint Moore Rd., ☎ 561/994–1876), founded in 1959 by Oklahoma oilman John T. Oxley and now home to the $100,000 International Gold Cup Tournament, has seven polo fields within two stadiums. Games take place January through April, Sunday at 1 and 3. Admission is $8 to $15 for seats, $15 per car.

SCUBA DIVING AND SNORKELING

Force E (⊠ 877 E. Palmetto Park Rd., ☎ 561/368–0555) has information on dive trips and also rents scuba and snorkeling equipment.

Shopping

Mizner Park (⊠ Federal Hwy., one block north of Palmetto Park Rd., ☎ 561/447–8105) is a distinctive 30-acre shopping center with apartments and town houses among its gardenlike retail and restaurant spaces. Some three dozen stores, including a Jacobson's specialty department store, mingle with fine restaurants, sidewalk cafés, galleries, a movie theater, and two museums. **Town Center Mall** (⊠ 6000 W. Glades Rd., ☎ 561/368–6000) is an upscale shopping mall in a business park setting. Major retailers include Nordstrom, Bloomingdale's, Burdines, Lord & Taylor, Saks Fifth Avenue, and Sears. The mall's specialty may be women's fashion, but there is something for everyone here, with more than 200 stores and restaurants.

Locals know that Boca "strip malls" contain great shops. While stopping by for essentials at Publix, be sure to check out that unassuming consignment, shoe, or fashion boutique next door and you may discover one of Boca's better finds.

THE TREASURE COAST

From south to north, the Treasure Coast encompasses the top of Palm Beach County plus Martin, St. Lucie, and Indian River counties. Although dotted with destinations, this coastal section is one of Florida's quietest. Most towns are small with lots of undeveloped land in between. Vero Beach, the region's most sophisticated area, is the one place you'll find fine-dining establishments and upscale shops. Nesting sea turtles lay their eggs in the sand along the coast here between late April and August. You can join locally organized watches to view them, but it's illegal to touch or disturb turtles or their nests.

Palm Beach Shores

29 *7 mi north of Palm Beach.*

This residential town rimmed by mom-and-pop motels is at the southern tip of Singer Island, across Lake Worth Inlet from Palm Beach. To travel between the two, however, you must cross over to the mainland before returning to the beach. This unpretentious community's main attraction is affordable beachfront lodging and proximity to several nature parks.

Peanut Island. A 79-acre island in the Intracoastal Waterway between Palm Beach Shores and Riviera Beach, the island was opened in 1999 as a recreational park. There are a 20-ft-wide walking path surrounding the entire island, a 19-slip boat dock, a 170-ft T-shape fishing pier, six picnic pavilions, a visitor center, and 20 overnight campsites. The small **Palm Beach Maritime Museum** (☎ 561/842–8202) is open Friday and Saturday and showcases the "Kennedy Bunker," a bomb shelter prepared for President John F. Kennedy (call for exact visiting hours.) To get to the island, you'll need your own boat or a water taxi (call for schedules and pickup locations). ⊠ *6500 Peanut Island Rd., Riviera Beach,* ☎ *561/845–4445,* WEB *www.pbmm.org.* 🎟 *Free.* ☉ *Sunrise–sunset for noncampers.*

OFF THE BEATEN PATH

JOHN D. MACARTHUR BEACH STATE PARK – Almost 2 mi of beach, good fishing and shelling, and one of the finest examples of subtropical coastal habitat remaining in southeast Florida are among treasures here. To learn about what you see, take an interpretive walk to a mangrove estuary along the upper reaches of Lake Worth. Or visit the **William T. Kirby Nature Center** (☎ 561/624–6952), open Wednesday to Monday from 9 to 5, which has exhibits on the coastal environment. ⊠ *10900 Rte. A1A, North Palm Beach,* ☎ *561/624–6950.* 🎟 *$3.25 per vehicle with up to 8 people.* ☉ *8–5:30.*

LOGGERHEAD PARK MARINE LIFE CENTER OF JUNO BEACH – Established by Eleanor N. Fletcher, the "turtle lady of Juno Beach," the center focuses on sea turtle history, including loggerheads and leatherbacks, with displays of coastal natural history, sharks, whales, and shells. ⊠ *1200 U.S. 1 (entrance on west side of park), Juno Beach,* ☎ *561/627–8280,* WEB *www.marinelife.org.* 🎟 *Free.* ☉ *Tues.–Sat. 10–4, Sun. noon–3.*

FLORIDA'S SEA TURTLES: THE NESTING SEASON

FROM MAY TO OCTOBER it's turtle nesting season all along the Florida coast. Female loggerhead, Kemp's ridley, and other species living in the Atlantic Ocean or Gulf of Mexico swim up to 2,000 mi to the Florida shore. By night, they drag their 100- to 400-pound bodies onto the beach to the dune line. Then each digs a hole with her flippers, drops in 100 or so eggs, covers them up, and returns to sea.

The babies hatch about 60 days later, typically at night, sometimes taking days to surface. Once they burst out of the sand, the hatchlings must get to sea rapidly or risk dehydration from the sun, or being caught by crabs, birds, or other predators.

Instinctively baby turtles head toward bright light, probably because for millions of years starlight or moonlight reflected on the waves was the brightest light around, serving to guide hatchlings to water. But now light from beach development can lead the babies in the wrong direction, and many hatchlings are crushed by vehicles after running to the street rather than the water. To help, many coastal towns enforce light restrictions during nesting months, and more than one Florida home owner has been surprised by a police officer at the door requesting that lights be dimmed on behalf of baby sea turtles.

At night, volunteers walk the beaches, searching for signs of turtle nests. Upon finding telltale scratches in the sand,

they cordon off the sites, so beachgoers will leave the spots undisturbed. Volunteers also keep watch over nests when babies are about to hatch and assist if the hatchlings do get disoriented.

It's a hazardous world for baby turtles. They can die after eating tar balls or plastic debris, or they can be gobbled by sharks or circling birds. Only about one in 1,000 survives to adulthood. Once reaching the water, the babies make their way to warm currents. East coast hatchlings drift into the Gulf Stream, spending years floating around the Atlantic.

Males never, ever return to land, but when females attain maturity, taking 15–20 years, they return to shore to lay eggs. Remarkably, even though migrating hundreds and even thousands of miles out at sea, most return to the very beach where they were born to deposit their eggs. Sea turtles nest at least twice a season—sometimes as many as 10 times—and then skip a year or two. Each time they nest, they come back to the same stretch of beach. In fact, the more they nest, the more accurate they get, until eventually they return time and again to within a few feet of where they last laid their eggs. These incredible navigation skills remain for the most part a mystery despite intense scientific study. To learn more, check out the Sea Turtle Survival League's and Caribbean Conservation Corporation's Web site at www.cccturtle.org.

— Pam Acheson

Dining and Lodging

$$–$$$ ✕ **Sailfish Marina Restaurant.** Once known as The Galley, this waterfront restaurant looking out to Peanut Island remains a great place to chill out after a hot day of mansion gawking or beach bumming. Sit inside or outdoors to order tropical drinks or mainstays from conch chowder or grouper to meat loaf. More upscale entrées—this, after all, is still Palm Beach County—include lobster tail or baby sea scallops sautéed in garlic and lemon butter. Breakfast is a winner here, too. ✉ *98 Lake Dr.,* ☎ *561/842–8449. MC, V. No dinner Mon.*

$$$–$$$$ ▥ **Radisson Palm Beach Shores Resort.** At the edge of a long stretch
★   of golden beach is this pink, six-story resort with a red tile roof that's a superb family destination. All rooms are suites with a separate bedroom, living room with a sofa bed, plus refrigerator, microwave, and dining area. Suites are furnished in natural rattan and tropical prints. The oceanfront pool is surrounded by a brick courtyard. The Beach Buddies Kids Club has an array of programs that include field trips, arts and crafts, seashell hunts, and water sports. ✉ *181 Ocean Ave., 33404,* ☎ *561/863–4000,* FAX *561/863–9502,* WEB *www.radisson.com. 257 suites. Restaurant, pool, health club, spa, beach, bar, children's programs (ages 2–12). AE, D, DC, MC, V.*

$$ ▥ **Sailfish Marina and Sportfishing Resort.** This long-established one-
★   story motel has a marina with 94 deepwater slips and 30 rooms and efficiencies that open to landscaped grounds. None are directly on the water, but Units 9–11 have ocean views across the blacktop drive. Rooms have peaked ceilings, carpeting, king-size or twin beds, and stall showers; all have ceiling fans. From the seawall you can see fish through the clear inlet water. The motel's staff is informed and helpful. ✉ *98 Lake Dr., 33404,* ☎ *561/844–1724 or 800/446–4577,* FAX *561/848–9684,* WEB *www.sailfishmarina.com. 30 units. Restaurant, grocery, pool, dock, bar. AE, MC, V.*

Outdoor Activities and Sports

BIKING

To rent bikes by the hour or the day, head for the **Sailfish Marina and Resort** (✉ 98 Lake Dr., ☎ 561/844–1724). Ask for a free map of the bike trails.

FISHING

The **Sailfish Marina and Resort** (✉ 98 Lake Dr., ☎ 561/844–1724) has a large sportfishing fleet, with 28-ft to 60-ft boats and seasoned captains. You can book a full- or half-day of deep-sea fishing for a maximum of six people.

Palm Beach Gardens

③⓪   *5 mi north of West Palm Beach.*

About 15 minutes northwest of Palm Beach is this relaxed, upscale residential community known for its high-profile golf complex, the PGA National Resort & Spa. Although not on the beach, the town is less than a 30-minute drive away from the ocean.

Dining and Lodging

$$–$$$ ✕ **Arezzo.** The aroma of fresh garlic will draw you into this out-
★   standing Tuscan grill at the PGA National Resort & Spa. Families are attracted by affordable prices (as well as the food), so romantics might be tempted to pass on by, but that would be a mistake. Dishes include chicken, veal, fish, steaks, a dozen pastas, and almost as many pizzas. Decor includes an herb garden in the center of the room and upholstered banquettes. Thanks to the unusually relaxed atmosphere of this upscale resort, you'll be equally comfortable in shorts or in jacket and

tie. ✉ *400 Ave. of the Champions,* ☎ *561/627–2000. AE, MC, V. No lunch.*

$$ ✕ **River House.** Patrons keep returning to this waterfront restaurant for large portions of straightforward American fare; the large salad bar and fresh, slice-it-yourself breads; and the competent service. Choices include seafood (with a daily catch), steaks, chops, and seafood-steak combo platters. Booths and freestanding tables are surrounded by light wood, high ceilings, and nautical art. Expect a wait on Saturday night in season; however, you can make reservations for the 20 upstairs tables, available weekends only, where it's slightly more formal and there's no salad bar. ✉ *2373 PGA Blvd.,* ☎ *561/694–1188. AE, MC, V. No lunch.*

$$$$ 🏨 **PGA National Resort & Spa.** The entire resort is richly detailed, from
★ the outstanding mission-style rooms decorated in deep-toned florals to the lavish landscaping to the extensive sports facilities to the excellent dining options. The spa is in a building styled after a Mediterranean fishing village, and six outdoor therapy pools, dubbed "Waters of the World," are joined by a collection of imported mineral salt pools. Flowering plants adorn golf courses and croquet courts amid a 240-acre nature preserve. Lodging options also include two-bedroom, two-bath cottages with kitchens. Among the dining options is a Don Shula's Steakhouse. ✉ *400 Ave. of the Champions, 33418,* ☎ *561/627–2000 or 800/633–9150,* 🖷 *561/622–0261,* 🕸 *www.pga-resorts.com. 279 rooms, 60 suites, 80 cottages. 5 restaurants, room service, in-room safes, some kitchens, 90-hole golf course, 19 tennis courts, 9 pools, lake, health club, hot tub, massage, sauna, spa, boating, croquet, 4 bars, baby-sitting, children's programs (ages 3–12), business services, meeting rooms. AE, D, DC, MC, V.*

Nightlife

For DJ'd Top 40s, try the **Club Safari** (✉ 4000 RCA Blvd., ☎ 561/622–8888), except on Thursday, when the focus is on oldies.

Outdoor Activities and Sports

AUTO RACING

Weekly ¼-mi drag racing; monthly 2¼-mi, 10-turn road racing; and monthly AMA motorcycle road racing take place year-round at the **Moroso Motorsports Park** (✉ 17047 Beeline Hwy., ☎ 561/622–1400).

GOLF

PGA National Resort & Spa (✉ 1000 Ave. of the Champions, ☎ 561/627–1800) has a reputedly tough 90 holes.

Shopping

The Gardens Mall (✉ 3101 PGA Blvd., ☎ 561/775–7750) could be the most civilized mall in South Florida. It offers an above-par shopping mall experience—a calm, spacious, airy, and well-lit environment. Anchors Bloomingdale's, Burdines, Macy's, Saks Fifth Avenue, and Sears support more than 160 specialty retailers including Swarovski, Godiva, Tommy Hilfiger, Laura Ashley, and Charles David.

Jupiter

③ *12 mi north of Palm Beach Shores.*

This little town is one of the few in the region without an island in front. Beaches here are part of the mainland, and Route A1A runs for almost 4 mi along the beachfront dunes.

Carlin Park. This recreational area has beachfront picnic pavilions, hiking trails, a baseball diamond, playground, six tennis courts, fishing sites, and, naturally, a beach. The Park Galley, serving snacks and burgers, is open daily 9–5. ⊠ *400 Rte. A1A,* ☎ *no phone.* ☉ *Daily sunrise–sunset.*

Dubois Home. Take a look at how life once was in this modest pioneer outpost dating from 1898. Sitting atop an ancient Jeaga Indian mound 20 ft high and looking onto Jupiter Inlet, it features Cape Cod as well as Cracker (old Florida) design. Even if you arrive when the house is closed, surrounding **Dubois Park** is worth the visit for its lovely beaches and swimming lagoons. ⊠ *Dubois Rd.,* ☎ *no phone.* ⊡ *Free.* ☉ *Wed. 1–4.*

Florida History Center and Museum. Permanent exhibits here review not only modern-day development along the Loxahatchee River but also shipwrecks, railroads, and steamboat-era, Seminole, and pioneer history. ⊠ *805 N. U.S. 1, Burt Reynolds Park,* ☎ *561/747–6639.* ⊡ *$5.* ☉ *Tues.–Fri. 10–5, weekends noon–5.*

Jupiter Inlet Lighthouse. Designed by Civil War hero Gen. George Meade, this redbrick Coast Guard navigational beacon has operated here since 1860. Tours of the 105-ft-tall landmark unfold every half hour, and there is a small museum. The lighthouse has undergone significant change, courtesy of an $858,000 federal grant, transforming it from bright red to natural brick, the way it looked from 1860 to 1918. ⊠ *Off U.S. 1,* ☎ *561/747–8380,* WEB *www.jupiterinletlighthouse.com.* ⊡ *Tour $6.* ☉ *Sun.–Wed. 10–4, last tour 3:15.*

Dining and Lodging

$$–$$$$ ✕ **Charley's Crab.** The grand view across the Jupiter River complements
★   the soaring ceilings and striking interior architecture of this marineside restaurant. Come here for expertly prepared seafood, such as grouper, pompano, red snapper, or yellowfin tuna. There are also great pasta choices such as the *pagliara* with scallops, fish, shrimp, mussels, spinach, garlic, and olive oil. Other Charley's Crab locations are in Boca Raton, Deerfield Beach, Fort Lauderdale, Palm Beach, and Stuart. ⊠ *1000 N. U.S. 1,* ☎ *561/744–4710. AE, D, DC, MC, V.*

$$–$$$ ✕ **Sinclairs Ocean Grill & Rotisserie.** This popular spot in the Jupiter Beach Resort has French doors looking out to the pool, and a menu with a daily selection of fresh fish, such as cashew-encrusted grouper, Cajun-spiced tuna, and mahimahi with pistachio sauce. There are also thick juicy steaks—filet mignon is the house specialty—or chicken and veal dishes. Sunday brunch is a big draw. ⊠ *5 N. Rte. A1A,* ☎ *561/745–7120. AE, MC, V.*

$–$$ ✕ **Lighthouse Restaurant.** Low prices match the plain decor in this coffee shop–style building, but the menu and cuisine are a tasty surprise. You can order chicken breast stuffed with sausage and fresh vegetables, burgundy beef stew, king-crab cakes, and great pastries. The same people-pleasing formula has been employed since 1936: round-the-clock service (except 10 PM Sunday–6 AM Monday) and a menu that changes daily to take advantage of best seasonal market buys. ⊠ *1510 U.S. 1,* ☎ *561/746–4811. D, DC, MC, V.*

$$$–$$$$ ▥ **Jupiter Beach Resort.** This unpretentious resort has undergone a multimillion-dollar refurbishment and it shows. Rooms, in pastels with floral prints and rattan, are within an eight-story tower, most with balconies. Those on higher floors have great ocean views. Plentiful activities and a casual atmosphere draw families here, and the resort offers turtle watches in season, May through October. Snorkeling and scuba equipment and jet skis are for rent, and there's a restaurant worth staying on the premises for in the evening. ⊠ *5 N. Rte. A1A, 33477,* ☎ *561/746–2511 or 800/228–8810,* FAX *561/747–3304,* WEB *www.jupiterbeachresort.com. 187 rooms, 28 suites. 2 restaurants, tennis court, pool, beach, dive shop, 2 bars, recreation room, laundry facilities, business services. AE, D, MC, V.*

Outdoor Activities and Sports

BASEBALL

Both the **St. Louis Cardinals and Montreal Expos** (⊠ 4751 Main St., ☎ 561/684–6801) train at the $28 million Roger Dean Stadium that seats 7,000 and has 12 practice fields.

CANOEING

Canoe Outfitters of Florida (⊠ 4100 W. Indiantown Rd., ☎ 561/746–7053) runs trips along 8 mi of the Loxahatchee River, Florida's only government-designated Wild and Scenic River. Canoe rental for two, with drop-off and pickup, costs $35 for the first two hours (two-hour minimum) and then $4 per additional hour plus tax.

GOLF

The **Golf Club of Jupiter at Indian Creek** (⊠ 1800 Central Blvd., ☎ 561/747–6262) offers 18 holes of varying difficulty. **Jupiter Dunes Golf Club** (⊠ 401 Rte. A1A, ☎ 561/746–6654) has 18 holes and a putting green.

Jupiter Island and Hobe Sound

32 *5 mi north of Jupiter.*

Northeast across the Jupiter Inlet from Jupiter is the southern tip of Jupiter Island, including a planned community of the same name. Here expansive and expensive estates often retreat from the road behind screens of vegetation, and at the north end of the island, turtles come to nest in a wildlife refuge. To the west, on the mainland, is the little community of Hobe Sound.

Blowing Rocks Preserve. Within the 73-acre Nature Conservancy holding, you'll find plant communities native to beachfront dune, coastal strand (the landward side of the dunes), mangrove, and hammock (tropical hardwood forests). The best time to visit is when high tides and strong offshore winds coincide, causing the sea to blow spectacularly through holes in the eroded outcropping. Park in the lot; police ticket cars parked along the road. ⊠ *Rte. 707, Jupiter Island,* ☎ *561/744–6668.* ⊡ *$4.* ☉ *Daily 9–4:30.*

Hobe Sound National Wildlife Refuge. The refuge actually consists of two tracts: 232 acres of sand-pine and scrub-oak forest in Hobe Sound and 735 acres of coastal sand dune and mangrove swamp on Jupiter Island. Trails are open to the public in both places. Turtles nest and shells wash ashore on the 3½-mi beach, which has been severely eroded by winter high tides and strong winds. ⊠ *13640 S.E. Federal Hwy., Hobe Sound,* ☎ *561/546–6141;* ⊠ *Beach Rd. off Rte. 707, Jupiter Island.* ⊡ *$5 per vehicle.* ☉ *Daily sunrise–sunset.*

Hobe Sound Nature Center. Although on the Hobe Sound National Wildlife Refuge, the appealing nature center is an independent organization. Its museum, which has baby alligators and crocodiles, and a scary-looking tarantula, is a child's delight. Interpretive exhibits focus on the environment, and a ½-mi trail winds through a forest of sand pine and scrub oak—one of Florida's most unusual and endangered plant communities. A classroom program on environmental issues is for preschool-age children to adults. ⊠ *13640 S.E. Federal Hwy., Hobe Sound,* ☎ *561/546–2067.* ⊡ *Free.* ☉ *Trail daily sunrise–sunset; nature center weekdays 9–11 and 1–3, call for Sat. hrs.*

Jonathan Dickinson State Park. Once you've gotten to the park, follow signs to Hobe Mountain. An ancient dune topped with a tower, it yields a panoramic view across the park's 10,285 acres of varied terrain, as well as the Intracoastal Waterway. The Loxahatchee River, part of the federal government's Wild and Scenic Rivers program, cuts through the park and harbors manatees in winter and alligators year-round. Two-hour boat tours of the river leave four times daily. Among amenities here are bicycle and hiking trails, a campground, and a snack bar. ⊠ *16450 S.E. Federal Hwy., Hobe Sound,* ☎ *561/546–2771 or 561/746–5804.* ⊡ *$3.25 per vehicle with up to 8 people, boat tours $12.* ⊘ *Daily 8–sunset.*

Outdoor Activities and Sports

Jonathan Dickinson's River Tours (⊠ Jonathan Dickinson State Park, ☎ 561/746–1466) rents canoes for use around the park.

Stuart

㉝ *7 mi north of Hobe Sound.*

This compact little town on a peninsula that juts out into the St. Lucie River has a remarkable amount of river shoreline for its size as well as a charming historic district. The ocean is about 5 mi east.

★ **Historic Downtown Stuart.** Strict architectural and zoning standards guide civic renewal projects in this area that has a delightful assortment of antiques shops, restaurants, and more than 50 specialty shops within a two-block area. A self-guided walking tour pamphlet is available at assorted locations downtown to clue you in on this once small fishing village's early days. The old courthouse has become the **Cultural Court House Center** (⊠ 80 E. Ocean Blvd., ☎ 561/288–2542) and presents art exhibits. The George W. Parks General Store is now the **Stuart Heritage Museum** (⊠ 101 S.W. Flagler Ave., ☎ 561/220–4600). On the National Register of Historic Places, the **Lyric Theatre** (⊠ 59 S.W. Flagler Ave., ☎ 561/220–1942) has been revived for performing and community events; a gazebo has free music performances. For information on the historic downtown, contact the **Stuart Main Street Office** (⊠ 151 S.W. Flagler Ave., 34994, ☎ 561/286–2848).

Dining and Lodging

$$ ✕ **Jolly Sailor Pub.** In an old historic-district bank building, this eatery is owned by a British Merchant Navy veteran, which accounts for all the ship paraphernalia in the pub. A veritable Cunard museum, it has a model of the *Britannia,* prints of 19th-century side-wheelers, and a big bar painting of the *QE2*. There is a wonderful brass-railed wood bar, a dartboard, and pub grub such as fish-and-chips, cottage pie, and bangers and mash, with Guinness and Double Diamond ales on tap. You also can get hamburgers and salads. ⊠ *1 S.W. Osceola St.,* ☎ *561/221–1111. AE, MC, V.*

$–$$ ✕ **The Ashley.** Despite the hanging plants and artwork, this restaurant still has elements of the old bank that was robbed three times early in the 20th century by the Ashley Gang (hence the name). The big outdoor mural in the French impressionist style was paid for by downtown revivalists, whose names are duly inscribed on wall plaques inside. The Continental menu has lots of salads, fresh fish, and pastas. Crowds head to the lounge for a popular happy hour. ⊠ *61 S.W. Osceola St.,* ☎ *561/221–9476. AE, MC, V. Closed Mon. in off-season.*

$–$$ ✕ **No Anchovies.** Sharing is half the fun, so don't be shy about asking to at this casual neighborhood trattoria. Sandwiches come on your choice of Italian loaf, semolina, whole wheat, or a spinach tortilla wrap with fillings such as oven-roasted turkey breast with sun-dried tomatoes or chicken salad. Entrées range from pastas to chicken or shrimp, and you can create your own savory pizza, perhaps starting with fresh goat cheese from the Turtle Creek dairy. There are two other equally good

No Anchovies locations in the area. ⊠ *150 S.W. Monterey Rd.,* ☎ *561/ 287–6699;* ⊠ *2650 PGA Blvd., Palm Beach Gardens,* ☎ *561/622–7855;* ⊠ *711 Village Blvd., West Palm Beach,* ☎ *561/684–0040. AE, MC, V.*

$–$$$ ☒ **Harborfront Inn B&B.** On the quiet banks of the St. Lucie River, this
★ cozy enclave provides imaginative extras, including picnic baskets and conciergelike custom planning. Units are eclectic, ranging from a spacious chintz-covered suite to an apartment with full kitchen, from rooms that are tweedy and dark to those that are airy and bright with a private deck. Furnishings mix wicker and antiques. You can relax in hammocks in the yard or in the hot tub, or take a full- or half-day sail on the 33-ft sailboat tied to the dock. ⊠ *310 Atlanta Ave., 34994,* ☎ *561/288–7289. 6 rooms, 2 suites, 1 cottage, 2 apartments. Hot tub, dock, boating. MC, V.*

Outdoor Activities and Sports
Deep-sea charters are available at the **Sailfish Marina** (⊠ 3565 S.E. St. Lucie Blvd., ☎ 561/283–1122).

Shopping
More than 60 restaurants and shops containing antiques, art, and fashions have opened along **Osceola Street** in the restored downtown area. Operating for more than two decades, the **B&B Flea Market,** the oldest and largest such enterprise on the Treasure Coast, has a street bazaar feel with shoppers happily scouting for the practical and unusual. ⊠ *2885 S.E. Federal Hwy.,* ☎ *561/288–4915,* 🖳 *Free.* ☉ *Sat.– Sun. 8–3.*

Hutchinson Island (Jensen Beach)

㉞ *5 mi northeast of Stuart.*

Area residents have payed unusual care here to curb the runaway development that has created the commercial crowding found to the north and south, although some high-rises have popped up along the shore. The small town of Jensen Beach, occupying the core of the island, actually stretches across both sides of the Indian River. Citrus farmers and fishermen still play a big community role, anchoring the area's down-to-earth feel. Between late April and August more than 600 turtles come here to nest along the town's Atlantic beach.

Coastal Science Center. Run by the Florida Oceanographic Society, the center consists of a coastal hardwood hammock and mangrove forest. Expansion has yielded a visitor center, a science center with interpretive exhibits on coastal science and environmental issues, and a ½-mi interpretive boardwalk. Guided nature walks are offered. ⊠ *890 N.E. Ocean Blvd.,* ☎ *561/225–0505,* 🆆🅴🅱 *www.fosusa.org.* 🖳 *$6.* ☉ *Mon.– Sat. 10–5, nature walks Mon.–Sat. 10:30 and by request.*

Elliott Museum. The pastel-pink building was erected in 1961 in honor of Sterling Elliott, inventor of an early automated addressing machine and a four-wheel cycle. The museum displays antique automobiles, dolls and toys, and fixtures from an early general store, blacksmith shop, and apothecary shop. ⊠ *825 N.E. Ocean Blvd.,* ☎ *561/225–1961,* 🆆🅴🅱 *www.goodnature.org.* 🖳 *$6.* ☉ *Daily 1–5.*

House of Refuge Museum. Built in 1875, this is the only remaining building of nine such structures erected by the U.S. Life Saving Service (a predecessor of the Coast Guard) to aid stranded sailors. Exhibits include antique lifesaving equipment, maps, artifacts from nearby wrecks, and boatmaking tools. ⊠ *301 S.E. Mac Blvd.,* ☎ *561/225–1875,* 🆆🅴🅱 *www.goodnature.org.* 🖳 *$4.* ☉ *Tues.–Sun. 11–4.*

🐾 **Maritime & Yachting Museum.** Linking the watery past with a permanent record of maritime and yachting events contributing to Treasure Coast lore, this museum has programs for children, historic exhibits, restoration of vessels, ship modelers, and more. Call for events and activities schedule. ⊠ *3551 N.W. Federal Hwy., Square One Mall,* ☎ *561/ 692–1234,* ⌑ *$4.* ⊘ *Call for hrs.*

Dining and Lodging

$$–$$$ ✕ **11 Maple Street.** This 16-table restaurant is as good as it gets on
★   the Treasure Coast, with a Continental menu that changes nightly. Soft recorded jazz and friendly staff satisfy along with food served in ample portions. Appetizers run from panfried conch and crispy calamari to spinach salad, and entrées include pan-seared rainbow trout, wood-grilled venison with onion potato hash, and beef tenderloin with white truffle and chive butter. Desserts such as a white-chocolate custard with blackberry sauce are seductive, too. ⊠ *3224 Maple Ave.,* ☎ *561/334– 7714. Reservations essential. MC, V. Closed Mon.–Tues. No lunch.*

$$–$$$ ✕ **Scalawags.** The look is plantation tropical—coach lanterns, gingerbread molding, wicker, slow-motion paddle fans—but the top-notch buffets are aimed at today's resort guests. Standouts are the prime rib buffet on Friday night and the all-you-can-eat Wednesday evening seafood extravaganza with jumbo shrimp, Alaskan crab legs, clams on the half shell, marinated salmon, and fresh catch. There's also a regular menu with a big selection of fish. The main dining room in this second-floor restaurant overlooks the Indian River. ⊠ *Marriott Beach Resort, 555 N.E. Ocean Blvd.,* ☎ *561/225–6818. AE, DC, MC, V.*

$$ ✕ **Conchy Joe's.** This classic Florida stilt house full of antique fish mounts, gator hides, and snakeskins dates from the 1920s, although Conchy Joe's, like a hermit crab sliding into a new shell, moved up from West Palm Beach in 1983. Under a huge Seminole-built *chickee* (palm frond–roofed) platform, you'll find a supercasual atmosphere and fresh seafood from a menu changing daily. Staples are grouper marsala, broiled sea scallops, and fried cracked conch. There's live music Thursday, Friday, and Saturday nights; heady rum drinks; and a happy hour daily 3 to 6 and during NFL games. ⊠ *3945 N. Indian River Dr.,* ☎ *561/334–1130. AE, D, MC, V.*

$ ✕ **The Emporium.** Hutchinson Island Beach Resort & Marina's coffee shop is an old-fashioned soda fountain and grill that also serves hearty breakfasts. Specialties include eggs Benedict, omelets, deli sandwiches, and salads. ⊠ *555 N.E. Ocean Blvd.,* ☎ *561/225–3700. AE, DC, MC, V.*

$$$–$$$$ 🏨 **Hutchinson Island Marriott Beach Resort & Marina.** With golf, tennis, a 77-slip marina, and a full water-sports program, plus many restaurants and bars, this 200-acre self-contained resort is excellent for families. Reception, some restaurants, and many rooms are in a trio of yellow four-story buildings that form an open courtyard with a large pool. Additional rooms and apartments with kitchens are spread over the property, some overlooking the Intracoastal Waterway and marina, others looking onto the ocean or tropical gardens. ⊠ *555 N.E. Ocean Blvd., Hutchinson Island, Stuart 34996,* ☎ *561/225–3700 or 800/775– 5936,* ⅀ᴬˣ *561/225–0033,* ᵂᴱᴮ *www.marriotthotels.com. 290 rooms, 27 suites, 150 condominiums. 5 restaurants, golf privileges, 13 tennis courts, 4 pools, spa, beach, dock, boating, 4 bars, business services, meeting rooms. AE, DC, MC, V.*

$$–$$$ 🏨 **Hutchinson Inn.** Sandwiched among the high-rises, this modest two-story motel from the mid-1970s has the feel of a B&B thanks to the management's friendly attitude. An expanded Continental breakfast is served in the lobby or on tables outside, and you can borrow books or magazines to take to your room, where homemade cookies are

delivered nightly. On Saturday there's a noon barbecue. Motel-style rooms range from small but comfortable to fully equipped efficiencies and two seafront suites with private balconies. ⊠ *9750 S. Ocean Dr., 34957,* ☎ *561/229–2000,* FAX *561/229–8875,* WEB *www.hutchinsoninn. com. 21 rooms, 2 suites. Tennis court, pool, beach. MC, V. CP.*

Outdoor Activities and Sports

BASEBALL
The **New York Mets** (⊠ 525 N.W. Peacock Blvd., Port St. Lucie, ☎ 561/871–2115) train at the St. Lucie County Sport Complex.

BEACHES
Bathtub Beach (⊠ MacArthur Blvd. off Rte. A1A), at the north end of the Indian River Plantation, is ideal for children because the waters are shallow for about 300 ft offshore and usually calm. At low tide bathers can walk to the reef. Facilities include rest rooms and showers.

GOLF
Hutchinson Island Marriott Beach Resort & Marina (⊠ 555 N.E. Ocean Blvd., ☎ 561/225–7131 or 800/775–5936) has 18 holes. The PGA-operated **PGA Golf Club at the Reserve** (⊠ 1916 Perfect Dr., Port St. Lucie, ☎ 561/467–1300 or 800/800–4653) is a public facility with three courses.

Fort Pierce

③⑤ *11 mi north of Stuart.*

About an hour north of Palm Beach, this community has a distinctive rural feel, focusing on ranching and citrus farming. There are several worthwhile stops, including those easily seen while following Route 707.

A. E. "Bean" Backus Gallery. As the home of the Treasure Coast Art Association, the gallery displays works of one of Florida's foremost landscape artists. The gallery mounts changing exhibits and offers exceptional buys on work by local artists. ⊠ *500 N. Indian River Dr.,* ☎ *561/465–0630.* ☞ *Donation welcome.* ⊙ *Tues.–Sun. 1–5.*

Fort Pierce Inlet State Recreation Area. The 340 acres here contain sand dunes and a coastal hammock. The park offers swimming, surfing, picnic facilities, hiking, and a self-guided nature trail. ⊠ *905 Shorewinds Dr.,* ☎ *561/468–3985.* ☞ *$3.25 per vehicle with up to 8 people.* ⊙ *Daily 8–sunset.*

Harbor Branch Oceanographic Institution. You can explore the world of underwater science at this diversified research and teaching facility. Its research fleet—particularly two submersibles—operates globally for NASA and NATO, among other contractors. A 90-minute tour of the 500-acre facility includes aquariums of sea life indigenous to the Indian River Lagoon and marine technology exhibits. Look for lifelike, whimsical bronze sculptures created by founder J. Seward Johnson Jr. and a gift shop with imaginative sea-related items. ⊠ *5600 Old Dixie Hwy.,* ☎ *561/465–2400 or 800/333–4264,* WEB *www.hboi.com.* ☞ *$12.* ⊙ *Lagoon boat tours at $19 are Mon.–Sat. at 1 and 3 PM.*

Heathcote Botanical Gardens. A self-guided tour of the gardens takes in a palm walk, a Japanese garden, and subtropical foliage. ⊠ *210 Savannah Rd.,* ☎ *561/464–4672.* ☞ *$3.* ⊙ *Tues.–Sat. 9–5, also Sun. 1–5 Nov.–Apr.*

Jack Island Wildlife Refuge. Accessible only by footbridge, the refuge contains 4⅓ mi of trails. The 1½-mi Marsh Rabbit Trail across the island traverses a mangrove swamp to a 30-ft observation tower overlooking the Indian River. ⊠ *Rte. A1A,* ☎ *561/468–3985.* ⌨ *Free.* ☉ *Daily 8–sunset.*

St. Lucie County Historical Museum. Highlights here include early 20th-century memorabilia, photos, vintage farm tools, a restored 1919 American La France fire engine, replicas of a general store and the old Fort Pierce railroad station, and the restored 1905 Gardner House. ⊠ *414 Seaway Dr.,* ☎ *561/462–1795.* ⌨ *$3.* ☉ *Tues.–Sat. 10–4, Sun. noon–4.*

☾ **Savannahs Recreation Area.** Once a reservoir, the 550-acre recreation area has been returned to its natural state. Today the semiwilderness area has campsites, a petting zoo, botanical garden, boat ramps, and trails. ⊠ *1400 E. Midway Rd.,* ☎ *561/464–7855.* ⌨ *$1 per vehicle.* ☉ *Daily 8–6.*

UDT Navy Seals Museum. Commemorating more than 3,000 navy frogmen training along Treasure Coast shoreline during World War II, the museum has weapons and equipment on view and exhibits depicting the history of the UDTs (Underwater Demolition Teams). Patrol boats and vehicles are displayed outdoors. ⊠ *3300 N. Rte. A1A,* ☎ *561/595–5845.* ⌨ *$4.* ☉ *Tues.–Sat. 10–4, Sun. noon–4.*

Dining and Lodging

$$–$$$ ✕ **Mangrove Mattie's.** Since opening in the 1980s, this upscale but rustic spot on Fort Pierce Inlet has provided dazzling waterfront views and imaginative nautical decor with delicious seafood. Dine on the terrace or within the dining room, and try the coconut-fried shrimp or the chicken and scampi. Or come by during happy hour (weekdays 5–8) for a free buffet of snacks. ⊠ *1640 Seaway Dr.,* ☎ *561/466–1044. AE, D, DC, MC, V.*

$$ ✕ **Theo Thudpucker's Raw Bar.** People dressed for work mingle here with folks fresh from the beach wearing shorts. On squally days everyone piles in off the jetty. Specialties include oyster stew, smoked fish spread, conch salad and conch fritters, fresh catfish, and alligator tail. ⊠ *2025 Seaway Dr. (South Jetty),* ☎ *561/465–1078. MC, V.*

$–$$ ▥ **Dockside Harbor Light Resort.** Formerly two adjacent motels, this expanded resort is the pick of the pack of lodgings lining the Fort Pierce Inlet along Seaway Drive. Spacious units on two floors have a kitchen or wet bar and routine but well-cared-for furnishings. Some rooms have a waterfront porch or balcony. In addition to the motel units a set of four apartments is across the street (off the water), where in-season weekly rates are $360. ⊠ *1156–1160 Seaway Dr., 34949,* ☎ *561/468–3555,* ⓦⓔⓑ *www.docksideinn.com. 60 rooms, 4 apartments. Pool, fishing, laundry facilities. AE, D, DC, MC, V.*

$–$$ ▥ **Mellon Patch Inn.** This appealing B&B has a prime location—across the shore road from a beach park, at the end of a canal leading to the Indian River Lagoon. One side of the canal has attractive new homes; the other has the Jack Island Wildlife Refuge. Andrea and Arthur Mellon built this B&B in 1994, and images of split-open melons (note the pun) permeate the house—on pillows, crafts, and candies on night tables. All guest rooms face the finger canal behind the inn and each themed room has imaginative accessories and art. The cathedral-ceiling living room has a fireplace. ⊠ *3601 N. Rte. A1A, North Hutchinson Island 34949,* ☎ *561/461–5231 or 800/656–7824,* ⓦⓔⓑ *www.mellonpatchinn.com. 4 rooms. Hot tub, dock, boating, fishing. AE, MC, V. BP.*

Outdoor Activities and Sports

For charter boats and fishing guides, try the **Dockside Harbor Light Resort** (⊠ 1152 Seaway Dr., ☎ 561/461–4824).

Fort Pierce Jai Alai (⊠ 1750 S. Kings Hwy., off Okeechobee Rd., ☎ 561/464–7500 or 800/524–2524) operates seasonally for live jai alai and year-round for off-track betting on horse-racing simulcasts. Admission is $1, with live games January through April, Wednesday and Saturday at noon and 7, Friday at 7, and Sunday at 1. Call to confirm schedule.

Some 200 yards from shore and ¼ mi north of the UDT-Seal Museum on North Hutchinson Island, the **Urca de Lima Underwater Archaeological Preserve** contains remains of a flat-bottom, round-bellied storeship. Once part of a treasure fleet bound for Spain, it was destroyed by a hurricane. Dive boats can be chartered through the **Dockside Harbor Light Resort** (⊠ 1152 Seaway Dr., ☎ 561/461–4824).

En Route   To reach Vero Beach, you have two options—Route A1A, along the coast, or Route 605 (also called Old Dixie Highway), on the mainland. As you approach Vero on the latter, you'll pass through an ungussied landscape of small farms and residential areas. On the beach route, part of the drive is through an unusually undeveloped section of the Florida coast. Both trips are relaxing.

Vero Beach

㊱ *12 mi north of Fort Pierce.*

Tranquil and chic, this affluent Indian River County seat has a strong commitment to the environment and the arts. You'll find plenty to do here, even though many visitors gravitating to this training ground for the L.A. Dodgers opt to do little at all. In the town's exclusive Riomar Bay area, roads are shaded by massive live oaks, and a popular cluster of restaurants and shops is just off the beach.

Environmental Learning Center. In addition to aquariums filled with Indian River Lagoon life, the outstanding 51 acres here have a 600-ft boardwalk through mangrove shoreline and a 1-mi canoe trail. The center is on the north edge of Vero Beach, on Wabasso Island, and the pretty drive is worth the trip. ⊠ *255 Live Oak Dr.,* ☎ *561/589–5050,* WEB *www. elcweb.org.* ⊠ *Free.* ☉ *Tues.–Fri. 10–4, Sat. 9–noon, Sun. 1–4.*

Indian River Citrus Museum. More grapefruit is shipped from the Indian River area than anywhere else in the world, as you'll learn at this museum where historic memorabilia harks back to when families washed and wrapped the luscious fruit to sell at roadside stands, and oxen hauled citrus-filled crates with distinctive Indian River labels to the rail station. A video shows current harvesting and shipping methods, and you can book free guided grove tours. ⊠ *2140 14th Ave.,* ☎ *561/770–2263.* ⊠ *Free.* ☉ *Tues.–Sat. 10–4, Sun. 1–4.*

McKee Botanical Garden. On the National Register of Historic Places, the gardens are an 18-acre subtropical paradise with a hammock supporting a diverse collection and several restored architectural treasures. ⊠ *350 U.S. Highway 1,* ☎ *561/794–0601,* WEB *www.mckeegarden.org.* ⊠ *$6.* ☉ *Tues.–Sat. 10–5, Sun. noon–5.*

Dining and Lodging

$$–$$$ ✕ **Black Pearl Riverfront.** One of Vero's trendiest dining options, this intimate, sophisticated restaurant has a stunning riverfront location accompanying superb Continental cuisine. Fresh fish offerings are a specialty and there's a martini bar. Choose from appetizers such as the house-specialty fish chowder or chilled leek and asparagus soup and from entrées that include onion-crusted grouper and beef Wellington. Desserts include a hot chocolate lava cake, similar to a chocolate soufflé. You'll need reservations from October through April. ⊠ *4455 N. Rte. A1A,* ☎ *561/234–4426. AE, MC, V. No lunch weekends.*

$$–$$$ ✕ **Ocean Grill.** Opened by Waldo Sexton as a hamburger shack in 1938,
★ the Ocean Grill with its ocean view now has Tiffany-style lamps, wrought-iron chandeliers, and paintings of pirates and Seminoles. Count on at least three kinds of seafood any day on the menu, along with tasty soups and salads. The house drink, the Leaping Limey, a curious blend of vodka, blue curaçao, and lemon, commemorates the 1894 wreck of the *Breconshire,* that occurred just offshore and from which 34 British sailors escaped. ⊠ *1050 Sexton Plaza (Beachland Blvd. east of Ocean Dr.),* ☎ *561/231–5409. AE, D, DC, MC, V. Closed 2 wks following Labor Day. Dinner nightly, but lunch weekdays only.*

$$ ✕ **Pearl's Bistro.** Caribbean-style cuisine is the draw at this less-expensive sister restaurant to the Black Pearl. For starters try the Bahamian conch fritters or the Jamaican jerk shrimp. Or try the baby-back barbecued pork ribs, grouper pepper pot, or blackened New York strip with peppery rum sauce. ⊠ *56 Royal Palm Blvd.,* ☎ *561/778–2950. AE, MC, V. No lunch weekends.*

$$$–$$$$ ⊡ **Disney's Vero Beach Resort.** On 71 pristine oceanfront acres, this
★ sprawling family-oriented retreat, operating both as a time-share and a hotel, is Vero's top resort. The main four-story building, three freestanding villas, and six beach cottages, all painted in pastels with gabled roofing in an approximation of turn-of-the-19th-century old Florida style, are nestled among tropical greenery. Units, some with kitchens and many with balconies, have bright interiors with rattan furniture and tile floors. Shutters, one of two restaurants, has American cuisine in an oceanfront setting. ⊠ *9235 Rte. A1A, 32963,* ☎ *561/ 234–2000,* WEB *dvc.disney.go.com. 161 rooms, 14 suites, 6 cottages. 2 restaurants, room service, in-room safes, some kitchens, some refrigerators, in-room VCRs, miniature golf, 6 tennis courts, pool, wading pool, hot tub, massage, sauna, beach, boating, bicycles, basketball, bar, video game room, baby-sitting, children's programs (ages 4–12), laundry facilities; no-smoking rooms. AE, D, DC, MC, V.*

$$$–$$$$ ⊡ **Ocean Suites Vero Beach.** A five-story rose-color stucco hotel, formerly flagged as a DoubleTree property, it's right on the beach and near restaurants, specialty shops, and boutiques. One- and two-bedroom suites have patios opening onto a pool or balconies and excellent ocean views. ⊠ *3500 Ocean Dr., 32963,* ☎ *561/231–5666. 54 suites. 2 pools, wading pool, hot tub, bar. AE, D, DC, MC, V.*

$$–$$$ ⊡ **Palm Court Resort.** This white, five-story building with outstanding views is tucked among palm trees on the beach. Oceanfront units look out to the water across private balconies. Most other units have partial ocean views. Rattan furnishings and pastels provide a comfortable, tropical sense of well-being. The rectangular pool looks out over the water, and pink shade umbrellas and blue-and-white stripe cabanas line the beach. Efficiencies and suites have kitchens. ⊠ *3244 Ocean Dr., 32963,* ☎ *561/231–2800 or 800/245–3297,* WEB *www.palmcourtvero. com. 110 rooms, 4 efficiencies, 2 suites. Restaurant, pool, exercise equipment, beach. AE, DC, MC, V.*

$$ 🏨 **Captain Hiram's Key West Inn.** A pale aqua inn trimmed in white with a lobby embellished with a classic surfboard collection brings a Key West look to Sebastian's Riverfront, about 17 mi north of Vero at marker 66 on the Intracoastal. All rooms have private balconies and most have oak furnishings. A heated pool has a tropical sundeck, shaded by tables with umbrellas. A complimentary deluxe Continental breakfast is included. ⊠ *1580 U.S. 1, 32958,* ☎ *561/589–4345 or 800/833–0555. 56 rooms. Pool. AE, DC, MC, V. CP.*

The Arts

The **Civic Arts Center** (⊠ Riverside Park), a cluster of cultural facilities, includes the **Riverside Theatre** (⊠ 3250 Riverside Park Dr., ☎ 561/231–6990), staging six productions each season in its 633-seat performance hall; the **Agnes Wahlstrom Youth Playhouse** (⊠ 3280 Riverside Park Dr., ☎ 561/234–8052), mounting children's productions; and the **Center for the Arts** (⊠ 3001 Riverside Park Dr., ☎ 561/231–0707), which presents exhibitions, art movies, lectures, workshops, and other events, with a focus on Florida artists.

Riverside Children's Theatre (⊠ 3280 Riverside Park Dr., ☎ 561/234–8052) offers a series of professional touring and local productions, as well as acting workshops at the Agnes Wahlstrom Youth Playhouse.

Outdoor Activities and Sports

BASEBALL

The **Los Angeles Dodgers** (⊠ 4101 26th St., ☎ 561/569–4900) train at Dodgertown, actually in Vero Beach.

BEACHES

Humiston Park is one of the beach-access parks along the east edge of town that have boardwalks and steps bridging the foredune. There are picnic tables and a children's play area, and shops are across the street. ⊠ *Ocean Dr. below Beachland Blvd.,* ☎ *561/231–5790.* ⛱ *Free.* ☉ *Daily 7 AM–10 PM.*

Full-service **Round Island Park** (⊠ A1A near the Indian River/St. Lucie county line, ☎ 561/231–0578) is a good bet for relaxation. There is a full range of services at **Treasure Shores Park** (⊠ A1A, 3 mi north of County Road 510 at the Wabasso Bridge, ☎ 561/589–6441). **Wabasso Beach Park** (⊠ County Road 510, east of the A1A intersection, north of Disney Resort, ☎ 561/589–8291) is a good option for a day in the sun.

Shopping

Along **Ocean Drive** near Beachland Boulevard, a specialty shopping area includes art galleries, antiques shops, and upscale clothing stores. Just west of Interstate 95, **Prime Outlets at Vero Beach** (⊠ 1824 94th Dr., ☎ 561/770–6171) is a discount shopping destination with brand name stores including Anne Klein, Bose, Levi's, Lenox, Reebok, and Versace.

Sebastian

③⑦ *14 mi north of Vero Beach.*

One of few sparsely populated areas on Florida's east coast, this fishing village has as remote a feeling as you're likely to find between Jacksonville and Miami Beach. That adds to the appeal of the recreation area around Sebastian Inlet, where you can walk for miles along quiet beaches.

McLarty Treasure Museum. A National Historical Landmark, it underscores the credo of "wherever gold glitters or silver beckons, man will move mountains," and has displays dedicated to the 1715 storm sinking a fleet of Spanish treasure ships, leaving some 1,500 survivors struggling to shore between Sebastian and Fort Pierce. ⊠ *13180 N. Rte. A1A,* ☎ *561/589–2147.* ⌑ *$1.* ☉ *Daily 10–4:30.*

Mel Fisher's Treasure Museum. You've really come upon hidden loot when stepping into this museum, where you can view some of what was recovered in 1985 from the Spanish treasure ship *Atocha* and its sister ships of the 1715 fleet. A similar museum in Key West is also operated by the late Mel Fisher's family. ⊠ *1322 U.S. 1,* ☎ *561/589–9875,* WEB *www.melfisher.com.* ⌑ *$5.* ☉ *Mon.–Sat. 10–5, Sun. noon–5.*

Sebastian Inlet State Recreation Area. Because of the highly productive fishing waters of Sebastian Inlet, at the north end of Orchid Island, this 578-acre area is one of the Florida park system's biggest draws. Both sides of the high bridge spanning the inlet—views are spectacular—attract plenty of anglers as well as those eager to enjoy the fine sandy shores, known for having some of the best waves in the state. A concession stand on the inlet's north side sells short-order food, rents various craft, and has an apparel and surf shop. There's a boat ramp, and not far away is a dune area that's part of the **Archie Carr National Wildlife Refuge,** a haven for sea turtles and other protected Florida wildlife. ⊠ *9700 S. Rte. A1A, Melbourne Beach,* ☎ *407/984–4852;* ⊠ *1300 Rte. A1A, Melbourne Beach,* ☎ *561/589–9659;* WEB *www.dep. state.fl.us/parks.* ⌑ *$3.25.* ☉ *Daily 24 hrs, bait and tackle shop daily 7:30–6, concession stand daily 8–5.*

Dining and Lodging

$$–$$$ ✕ **Hurricane Harbor.** Built in 1927 as a garage and used during Prohibition as a smugglers' den, this restaurant draws a year-round crowd for lunch and dinner. Waterfront window seats are especially coveted on stormy nights, when waves break outside in the Indian River Lagoon. Count on seafood, steaks, and grills, along with lighter fare. There's live music nightly, and on-premises docking. Peek into the Antique Dining Room, with a huge breakfront, used only for special occasions. ⊠ *1540 Indian River Dr.,* ☎ *561/589–1773. AE, D, MC, V. Closed Mon.*

$–$$ ✕ **Capt. Hiram's Restaurant & Bars.** This family-friendly outpost on the Indian River Lagoon is easygoing, fanciful, and fun—as the sign says, NECKTIES ARE PROHIBITED. Don't miss Capt. Hiram's Sandbar, where kids can play while parents enjoy drinks at stools set in an outdoor shower or a beached boat. Order the fresh catch, crab cakes, stuffed shrimp, raw-bar items, or a juicy steak. There's a weekday happy hour and nightly entertainment in season. ⊠ *1606 N. Indian River Dr.,* ☎ *561/589–4345. AE, D, MC, V.*

$ ⊡ **Davis House Inn.** Owner Steve Wild, a Vero native, modeled his two-story inn after the clubhouse at Augusta National, yet it fits right in with Sebastian's fishing-town look. Overhung roofs shade wraparound porches. In a companion house that Steve calls the Gathering Room, a complimentary expanded Continental breakfast is served. Rooms are expansive—virtual suites, with large sitting areas—although sparsely furnished. You can grill or chill out at the self-serve Tiki Bar. Overall, it's a terrific value. ⊠ *607 Davis St., 32958,* ☎ *561/589–4114,* WEB *www.davishouseinn.com. 12 rooms. Kitchenettes, microwaves, bicycles. MC, V. CP.*

Outdoor Activities and Sports

CANOEING AND KAYAKING

The concession stand at **Sebastian Inlet State Recreation Area** (⊠ *9700 S. Rte. A1A, Melbourne Beach,* ☎ *321/984–4852*) rents canoes, kayaks, and paddleboats.

FISHING

The region's best inlet fishing is at **Sebastian Inlet State Recreation Area** (⊠ 9700 S. Rte. A1A, Melbourne Beach), where the catch includes bluefish, flounder, jack, redfish, sea trout, snapper, snook, and Spanish mackerel. For deep-sea fishing, try *Miss Sebastian* (⊠ Sembler Dock, ½ block north of Capt. Hiram's restaurant, ☎ 561/589–3275); $25 for a half day covers rod, reel, and bait. **Sebastian Inlet Marina at Capt. Hiram's** (⊠ 1606 Indian River Dr., ☎ 561/589–4345) offers half- and full-day fishing charters.

PALM BEACH AND THE TREASURE COAST A TO Z

To research prices, get advice from other travelers, and book travel arrangements, visit www.fodors.com.

AIR TRAVEL

CARRIERS

Palm Beach International Airport (PBIA) is served by Air Canada, American/American Eagle, American TransAir, Bahamasair, Comair, Continental, Delta, JetBlue, Metrojet, Midway, Northwest, Southwest Airlines, Spirit Airlines, United, and US Airways/US Airways Express.

➤ AIRLINES AND CONTACTS: **Air Canada** (☎ 800/247–2262). **American/American Eagle** (☎ 800/433–7300). **American TransAir** (☎ 800/225–2995). **Bahamasair** (☎ 800/222–4262). **Comair** (☎ 800/354–9822). **Continental** (☎ 800/525–0280). **Delta** (☎ 800/221–1212). **JetBlue** (☎ 800/538–2583). **MetroJet** (☎ 800/638–7653). **Midway** (☎ 800/446–4392). **Northwest** (☎ 800/225–2525). **Southwest Airlines** (☎ 800/435–9792). **Spirit Airlines** (☎ 800/772–7117). **United** (☎ 800/241–6522). **US Airways/US Airways Express** (☎ 800/428–4322).

AIRPORT INFORMATION

Route 10 of Tri-Rail Commuter Bus Service runs from the airport to Tri-Rail's nearby Palm Beach airport station daily.

Palm Beach Transportation provides taxi and limousine service from PBIA. Reserve at least a day in advance for a limo. The lowest fares are $1.75 per mile, with the meter starting at $1.25. Depending on your destination, a flat rate (from PBIA only) may save money. Wheelchair-accessible vehicles are available.

➤ AIRPORT INFORMATION: **Palm Beach International Airport (PBIA)** (⊠ Congress Ave. and Belvedere Rd., West Palm Beach, ☎ 561/471–7400). **Palm Beach Transportation** (☎ 561/689–4222). **Tri-Rail Commuter Bus Service** (☎ 800/874–7245).

BUS TRAVEL

Greyhound Lines buses arrive at the station in West Palm Beach.

Palmtran buses, running between Worth Avenue and Royal Palm Way in Palm Beach and major areas of West Palm Beach, require exact change. Fares are $1.25, or 50¢ for students, senior citizens, and people with disabilities (with reduced-fare I.D.). Service operates from 5:25 AM to 8:55 PM. Call for schedules, routes, and rates for multiple-ride punch cards.

➤ BUS INFORMATION: **Greyhound Lines** (☎ 800/231–2222); West Palm Beach (⊠ 100 Banyan Blvd., ☎ 561/833–8534). **Palmtran** (☎ 561/233–4287).

CAR TRAVEL

Interstate 95 runs north–south, linking West Palm Beach with Fort Lauderdale and Miami to the south and with Daytona, Jacksonville, and the rest of the Atlantic coast to the north. To access Palm Beach, exit east at Belvedere Road or Okeechobee Boulevard. Florida's Turnpike runs from Miami north through West Palm Beach before angling northwest to reach Orlando.

U.S. 1 threads north–south along the coast, connecting most coastal communities, whereas the more scenic Route A1A ventures out onto the barrier islands. Interstate 95 runs parallel to U.S. 1 but a few miles inland.

A nonstop four-lane route, Okeechobee Boulevard carries traffic from west of downtown West Palm Beach, near the Amtrak station in the airport district, directly to the Flagler Memorial Bridge and into Palm Beach. Plans are afoot to eventually turn Flagler Drive over to pedestrian use.

The best way to access Lake Okeechobee from West Palm is to drive west on Southern Boulevard from Interstate 95 past the cutoff road to Lion Country Safari. From there, the boulevard is designated U.S. 98/441.

EMERGENCIES

Dial 911 for police or ambulance.

➤ LATE-NIGHT PHARMACIES: **Eckerd Drug** (⊠ 3343 S. Congress Ave., Palm Springs, ☎ 561/965–3367). **Walgreens** (⊠ 1688 S. Congress Ave., Palm Springs, ☎ 561/968–8211; ⊠ 7561 N. Federal Hwy., Boca Raton, ☎ 561/241–9802; ⊠ 1634 S. Federal Hwy., Boynton Beach, ☎ 561/737–1260; ⊠ 1208 Royal Palm Beach Blvd., Royal Palm Beach, ☎ 561/798–9048; ⊠ 6370 Indiantown Rd., Jupiter, ☎ 561/744–6822; ⊠ 20 E. 30th St., Riviera Beach, ☎ 561/848–6464).

ENGLISH-LANGUAGE MEDIA

NEWSPAPERS AND MAGAZINES

To keep abreast of local issues and find what's new in entertainment options, pick up copies of the *Palm Beach Post*, *Palm Beach Daily News*, *Vero Press Journal*, or *Boca Raton* magazine.

RADIO

LOVE 93.9 FM easy listening, WDBF 1420 AM jazz, WDDO 93.1 FM classical.

GETTING AROUND

The **Downtown Transfer Facility** (⊠ Banyan Blvd. and Clearlake Dr., West Palm Beach), off Australian Avenue at the west entrance to downtown, links the downtown shuttle, Amtrak, Tri-Rail (the commuter line of Miami-Dade, Broward, and Palm Beach counties), county bus systems, Greyhound, and taxis.

TAXIS

Palm Beach Transportation has a single number serving several cab companies. Meters start at $1.25, and the charge is $1.75 per mile within West Palm Beach city limits; if the trip at any point leaves the city limits, the fare is $2 per mile. Some cabs may charge more. Waiting time is 50¢ per minute.

➤ TAXI INFORMATION: **Palm Beach Transportation** (☎ 561/689–4222).

TOURS

Capt. Doug's offers three-hour lunch and dinner cruises along the Indian River on a 35-ft sloop. Cost is $100 per couple, including meal, beer, wine, and tips. J-Mark Fish Camp has 45- to 60-minute airboat rides for $30 per person, with a minimum of two people and a maximum of six. Jonathan Dickinson's River Tours runs two-hour guided riverboat cruises daily at 9, 11, 1, and 3. The cost is $12. Loxahatchee Everglades Tours operates airboat tours year-round from west of Boca Raton through the marshes between the built-up coast and Lake Okeechobee. The *Manatee Queen,* a 49-passenger catamaran, offers day and evening cruises November–May on the Intracoastal Waterway and into the park's cypress swamps.

Ramblin' Rose Riverboat operates luncheon, dinner-dance, and Sunday brunch cruises along the Intracoastal Waterway. Water Taxi Scenic Cruises has several different daily sightseeing tours in a 16-person launch. Two are designed to let you get a close-up look at the mansions of the rich and famous. The southern tour passes Peanut, Singer, and Munyan islands and many mansions of Palm Beach. A second tour runs solely along the shore of Palm Beach mansions. A third tour takes you past the Craig Norman estate and goes into Lake Worth and Sawgrass Creek.

Contact the Audubon Society of the Everglades for field trips and nature walks.

The Boca Raton Historical Society offers afternoon tours of the Boca Raton Resort & Club on Tuesdays year-round and to other South Florida sites. Main Street Fort Pierce gives walking tours of the town's historic section, past buildings erected by early settlers. The Indian River County Historical Society conducts walking tours of downtown Vero on Wednesday at 11 and 1 (by reservation). Old Northwood Historic District Tours leads two-hour walking tours that include visits to historic home interiors. They leave Sunday at 2, and a $5 donation is requested. Tours for groups of six or more can be scheduled almost any day.

➤ Tours Information: **Audubon Society of the Everglades** (⊠ Box 16914, West Palm Beach 33461, ☎ 561/588–6908). **Boca Raton Historical Society** (⊠ 71 N. Federal Hwy., Boca Raton, ☎ 561/395–6766). **Capt. Doug's** (⊠ Sebastian Marina, Sebastian, ☎ 561/589–2329). The **Indian River County Historical Society** (⊠ 2336 14th Ave., Vero Beach, ☎ 561/778–3435). **J-Mark Fish Camp** (⊠ Torry Island, ☎ 561/996–5357). **Jonathan Dickinson's River Tours** (⊠ Jonathan Dickinson State Park, 16450 S.E. Federal Hwy., Hobe Sound, ☎ 561/746–1466). **Loxahatchee Everglades Tours** (⊠ 10400 Loxahatchee Rd., ☎ 561/482–6107). **Main Street Fort Pierce** (⊠ 131 Main St., Fort Pierce, ☎ 561/466–3880). *Manatee Queen* (⊠ Jonathan Dickinson State Park, 16450 S.E. Federal Hwy., Hobe Sound, ☎ 561/744–2191). **Old Northwood Historic District Tours** (⊠ 501 30th St., West Palm Beach, ☎ 561/863–5633). *Ramblin' Rose Riverboat* (⊠ 1 N.E. 1st St., Delray Beach, ☎ 561/243–0686). **Water Taxi Scenic Cruises** (⊠ Sailfish Marina and Riviera Beach Marina, Palm Beach, ☎ 561/775–2628).

TRAIN TRAVEL

Amtrak connects West Palm Beach with cities along Florida's east coast and the Northeast daily and via the *Sunset Limited* to New Orleans and Los Angeles three times weekly. Included in Amtrak's service is transport from West Palm Beach to Okeechobee; the station is unmanned.

Tri-Rail, the commuter rail system, has six stations in Palm Beach County (13 stops altogether between West Palm Beach and Miami). The round-trip fare is $5, $2.50 for students and senior citizens.

➤ Train Information: **Amtrak** (☎ 800/872–7245; West Palm Beach: ⊠ 201 S. Tamarind Ave., ☎ 561/832–6169; Okeechobee: ⊠ 801 N. Parrott Ave.). **Tri-Rail** (☎ 800/874–7245).

VISITOR INFORMATION

➤ TOURIST INFORMATION: **Belle Glade Chamber of Commerce** (✉ 540 S. Main St., Belle Glade 33430, ☎ 561/996–2745). **Chamber of Commerce of the Palm Beaches** (✉ 401 N. Flagler Dr., West Palm Beach 33401, ☎ 561/833–3711). **Clewiston Chamber of Commerce** (✉ 544 W. Sugarland Hwy., Clewiston 33440, ☎ 863/983–7979). **Glades County Chamber of Commerce** (✉ U.S. 27 and 10th St., Moore Haven 33471, ☎ 863/946–0440). **Indian River County Tourist Council** (✉ 1216 21st St., Box 2947, Vero Beach 32961, ☎ 561/567–3491). **Indiantown and Western Martin County Chamber of Commerce** (✉ 15518 S.W. Osceola St., Indiantown 34956, ☎ 561/597–2184). **Okeechobee County Chamber of Commerce** (✉ 55 S. Parrott Ave., Okeechobee 34974, ☎ 863/763–6464). **Pahokee Chamber of Commerce** (✉ 115 E. Main St., Pahokee 33476, ☎ 561/924–5579). **Palm Beach County Convention & Visitors Bureau** (✉ 1555 Palm Beach Lakes Blvd., Suite 204, West Palm Beach 33401, ☎ 561/471–3995). **St. Lucie County Tourist Development Council** (✉ 2300 Virginia Ave., Fort Pierce 34982, ☎ 561/462–1535). **Stuart/Martin County Chamber of Commerce** (✉ 1650 S. Kanner Hwy., Stuart 34994, ☎ 561/287–1088). **Town of Palm Beach Chamber of Commerce** (✉ 45 Cocoanut Row, Palm Beach 33480, ☎ 561/655–3282). **U.S. Army Corps of Engineers (Okeechobee area information)** (✉ South Florida Operations Office, 525 Ridgelawn Rd., Clewiston 33440-5399, ☎ 863/983–8101).

6 THE FLORIDA KEYS

The Keys are one of America's last
frontiers. Here both humans and nature
seek refuge in a verdant island chain that
stretches raggedly west-southwest across
a deep blue-green seascape at the base
of the Florida peninsula.

A **WILDERNESS OF FLOWERING JUNGLES** and shimmering seas, a jade necklace of mangrove-fringed islands dangling toward the tropics, the Florida Keys are also, at the same time and in direct contrast to this, a string of narrow islands overburdened by a growing population and booming tourism that have created sewage contamination at beaches and a 110-mi traffic jam lined with garish billboards, hamburger stands, shopping centers, motels, and trailer courts. Unfortunately, in the Keys you can't have one without the other.

Revised by
Diane P.
Marshall

The river of visitor traffic gushes along U.S. 1 (also called the Overseas Highway), the main artery linking the inhabited islands. Residents of Monroe County live by diverting the river's flow of green dollars to their own pockets. In the process, the fragile beauty of the Keys—or at least the 45 that are inhabited and linked to the mainland by 43 bridges—is paying an environmental price. At the top, nearest the mainland, is Key Largo, becoming more and more congested as it evolves into a bedroom community and weekend hideaway for escaping residents of Miami and Fort Lauderdale. At the bottom, 106 mi southwest, is Key West, where for several years now the effluent of the overburdened island has washed into the near-shore waters and closed the island's major beaches for months.

Despite designation as "an area of critical state concern" in 1975 and a subsequent state-mandated development slowdown, growth has continued, and the Keys' natural resources remain imperiled. In 1990, Congress established the Florida Keys National Marine Sanctuary, covering 2,800 square nautical mi of coastal waters. Adjacent to the Keys landmass are spectacular, unique, and nationally significant marine environments, including sea-grass meadows, mangrove islands, and extensive living coral reefs. These fragile environments support rich and diverse biological communities possessing extensive conservation, recreational, commercial, ecological, historical, research, educational, and aesthetic values.

The sanctuary protects the coral reefs and water quality, but problems continue. Increased salinity in Florida Bay causes large areas of sea grass to die and drift in mats out of the bay. These mats then block sunlight from reaching the reefs, stifling their growth and threatening both the Keys' recreational diving economy and tourism in general.

Other threats to the Keys' charm also loom. Debate continues on the expansion of U.S. 1 to the mainland to four lanes, opening the floodgates to increased traffic, population, and tourism. Observers wonder if the four-laning of the rest of U.S. 1 throughout the Keys can be far away and if a trip to paradise will then be worth it.

The solutions are not easy. Keys residents struggle with the issues at home, in social settings and in the voting booths. In 1998, 1999, and 2000 local communities dissatisfied with the county's handling of the impacts of tourism and development went to the polls to determine their own destinies as independent municipalities.

For now, however, take pleasure as you drive down U.S. 1 along the islands. Gaze over the silvery blue and green Atlantic and its still-living reef, with Florida Bay, the Gulf of Mexico, and the backcountry on your right (the Keys extend east–west from the mainland). At a few points the ocean and gulf are as much as 10 mi apart. In most places, however, they are from 1 to 4 mi apart, and on the narrowest landfill islands, they are separated only by the road. First, remind yourself to get off the highway. Once you do, rent a boat, anchor, and then fish, swim, or marvel at the sun, sea, and sky. In the Atlantic you can dive spectacular coral reefs or pursue grouper, blue marlin, and other deep-water game fish. Along Florida Bay's coastline you can kayak and canoe to secluded islands and bays or seek out the bonefish, snapper, snook, and tarpon that lurk in the grass flats and in the shallow, winding channels of the backcountry.

More than 600 kinds of fish populate the reefs and islands. Diminutive deer and pale raccoons, related to but distinct from their mainland cousins, inhabit the Lower Keys. And throughout the islands you'll find such exotic West Indian plants as Jamaican dogwood, pigeon plum, poisonwood, satin leaf, and silver and thatch palms, as well as tropical birds, including the great white heron, mangrove cuckoo, roseate spoonbill, and white-crowned pigeon. Mangroves, with their gracefully bowed prop roots, appear to march out to sea. Day by day they busily add more keys to the archipelago.

With virtually no distracting air pollution or obstructive high-rises, sunsets are a pure, unadulterated spectacle that each evening attracts thousands to waterfront parks, piers, restaurants, bars, and resorts throughout the Keys.

Weather is another attraction: winter is typically 10°F warmer than on the mainland; summer is usually 10°F cooler. The Keys also get substantially less rain, around 30 inches annually, compared with an average 55–60 inches in Miami and the Everglades. Most rain falls in quick downpours on summer afternoons, except in June, September, and October, when tropical storms can dump rain for two to four days. Winter continental cold fronts occasionally stall over the Keys, dragging overnight temperatures down to the high 40s.

The Keys were only sparsely populated until the early 20th century. In 1905, however, railroad magnate Henry Flagler began building the extension of his Florida railroad south from Homestead to Key West. His goal was to establish a Miami to Key West rail link to his steamships that sailed between Key West and Havana, just 90 mi across the Straits of Florida. The railroad arrived at Key West in 1912 and remained a lifeline of commerce until the Labor Day hurricane of 1935 washed out much of its roadbed. The Overseas Highway, built over the railroad's old roadbeds and bridges, was completed in 1938.

Pleasures and Pastimes

Biking

Cyclists are able to ride all but a tiny portion of the bike path that runs along the Overseas Highway from MM 106 south to the Seven Mile Bridge. The state plans to extend the route throughout the Keys. Some areas have lots of cross-traffic, however, so ride with care.

Boating

If it floats, local marinas rent it. For up-close exploration of the mangroves and near-shore islands in Florida Bay, nothing beats a kayak or canoe. You can paddle within a few feet of a flock of birds without disturbing them, and on days when the ocean is too rough for diving or fishing, the rivers that course through the bay-side mangroves are tranquil. Visiting the backcountry islands and inlets of Everglades National Park requires a shallow-draft boat: a 14- to 17-ft skiff with a 40- to 50-horsepower outboard is sufficient. For diving the reef or fishing on the open ocean, you'll need a larger boat with greater horsepower. Houseboats are ideal for cruising the Keys.

Only experienced sailors should attempt to navigate the shallow waters surrounding the Keys with deep-keeled sailboats. On the other hand, small shallow-draft, single-hull sailboats and catamarans are ideal. Personal water vehicles, such as Wave Runners and Jet Skis, can be rented by the half hour or hour but are banned in many areas. Flat, stable pontoon boats are a good choice for anyone with seasickness. Those interested in experiencing the reef without getting wet can take a glass-bottom boat trip.

Dining

A number of talented young chefs have settled in the Keys—especially Key West—contributing to the area's image as one of the nation's points of culinary interest. Restaurants' menus, rum-based fruit beverages, and music reflect the Keys' tropical climate and their proximity to Cuba and other Caribbean islands. Better restaurants serve imaginative and tantalizing fusion cuisine that draws on traditions from all over the world.

Florida citrus, seafood, and tropical fruits figure prominently, and Florida lobster and stone crab should be local and fresh from August to March. Also keep an eye out for authentic key lime pie. The real McCoy has a yellow custard in a graham-cracker crust and tastes like nothing else.

Restaurants may close for a two- to four-week vacation during the slow season—between mid-September and mid-November. Check local newspapers or call ahead, especially if driving any distance.

CATEGORY	COST*
$$$$	over $30
$$$	$20–$30
$$	$10–$20
$	under $10

*per person for a main course at dinner

Fishing

These sun-bathed waters are home to 100 species of game fish as well as to lobster, shrimp, and crabs. Flats fishing and backcountry fishing are Keys specialties. In flats fishing, a guide poles a shallow-draft outboard boat through the shallow, sandy-bottom waters while sighting for bonefish and snook to be caught on light tackle, spin, and fly. Backcountry fishing may include flats fishing or fishing in the channels and basins around islands in Florida Bay. Charter boats fish the reef and Gulf Stream for deep-sea fish. Party boats, which can be crowded, carry up to 50 people to fish the reefs for grouper, kingfish, and snapper. Some operators boast a guarantee, or "no fish, no pay" policy.

Lodging

All prices are for a standard double room, excluding 6% sales tax (more in some counties) and 1%–4% tourist tax.

CATEGORY	COST
$$$$	over $220
$$$	$140–$220
$$	$80–$140
$	under $80

Scuba Diving and Snorkeling

Diving in the Keys is spectacular. In shallow and deep water with visibility up to 120 ft, you can explore sea canyons and mountains covered with waving sea plumes, brain and star coral, historic shipwrecks, and sunken submarines. The colors of the coral are surpassed only by the brilliance of the fish that live around it. There's no best season for diving, but occasional storms in June, September, and October cloud the waters and make seas rough.

You can dive the reefs with scuba, snuba (a cross between scuba and snorkeling), or snorkeling gear, using your own boat, a rented boat, or by booking a tour with a dive shop. Tours depart two or three times a day, stopping at two sites on each trip. The first trip of the day is usually the best. It's less crowded—vacationers like to sleep in—and visibility is better before the wind picks up in the afternoon. There's also night diving.

If you want to scuba dive but are not certified, take an introductory resort course. Although it doesn't result in certification, it allows you to dive with an instructor in the afternoon following morning classroom and pool instruction.

Nearly all the waters surrounding the Keys are part of the Florida Keys National Marine Sanctuary and thus are protected. Signs, brochures, tour guides, and marine enforcement agents remind visitors that the reef is fragile and shouldn't be touched.

Exploring the Florida Keys

Finding your way around the Keys isn't hard once you understand the unique address system. Many addresses are simply given as a mile marker (MM) number. The markers themselves are small, green rectangular signs along the side of the Overseas Highway (U.S. 1). They begin with MM 126, a mile south of Florida City, and end with MM 0, in Key West. Keys residents use the abbreviation BS for the bay side of U.S. 1 and OS for the ocean side. From Marathon to Key West, residents may refer to the bay side as the gulf side.

The Keys are divided into four areas: the Upper Keys, from Key Largo to the Long Key Channel (MM 106–65) and Ocean Reef and North Key Largo, off Card Sound Road and Route 905, respectively; the Middle Keys, from Conch (pronounced *konk*) Key through Marathon to the south side of the Seven Mile Bridge, including Pigeon Key (MM 65–40); the Lower Keys, from Little Duck Key south through Big Coppitt Key (MM 40–9); and Key West, from Stock Island through Key West (MM 9–0). The Keys don't end with the highway, however; they stretch another 70 mi west of Key West to the Dry Tortugas.

Numbers in the text correspond to numbers in the margin and on the Florida Keys and Key West maps.

Great Itineraries

IF YOU HAVE 3 DAYS

You can fly and then dive; but if you dive, you can't fly for 24 hours, so spend your first morning diving or snorkeling at John Pennekamp Coral Reef State Park in ⊞ **Key Largo** ②. If you aren't certified, take a resort course, and you'll be exploring the reefs by afternoon. Afterward, breeze through the park's visitor center. The rest of the afternoon can be whiled away either lounging around a pool or beach or visiting the Maritime Museum of the Florida Keys. Dinner or cocktails at a bay-side restaurant or bar will give you your first look at a fabulous Keys sunset. On day two, get an early start to savor the breathtaking views on the two-hour drive to Key West. Along the way make stops at the natural-history museum that's part of the Museums and Nature Center of Crane Point Hammock, in **Marathon** ⑧, and Bahia Honda State Park, on **Bahia Honda Key** ⑨, where you can stretch your legs on a forest trail or snorkel on an offshore reef. Once in ⊞ **Key West** ⑫–㉞, you can watch the sunset before dining at one of the island's first-class restaurants. Spend the next morning exploring beaches, visiting any of the myriad museums, or taking a walking or trolley tour of Old Town before driving back to the mainland.

IF YOU HAVE 4 DAYS

Spend the first day as you would above, overnighting in 🏨 **Key Largo** ②. Start the second day by renting a kayak and exploring the mangroves and small islands of Florida Bay or take an ecotour of the islands in Everglades National Park. In the afternoon stop by the Florida Keys Wild Bird Rehabilitation Center before driving down to 🏨 **Islamorada** ④. Pause to read the inscription on the Hurricane Monument, and before day's end, make plans for the next day's fishing. After a late lunch on day three—perhaps at one of the many restaurants that will prepare your catch for you—set off for 🏨 **Key West** ⑫–㉞. Catch the sunset celebration at Mallory Square, and spend the last day as you would above.

IF YOU HAVE 7 DAYS

Spend your first three days as you would in the four-day itinerary, but stay the third night in 🏨 **Islamorada** ④. In the morning catch a boat, or rent a kayak to paddle, to Lignumvitae Key State Botanical Site, before making the one-hour drive to 🏨 **Marathon** ⑧, where you can visit the natural-history museum that's part of the Museums and Nature Center of Crane Point Hammock and walk or take a train across the Old Seven Mile Bridge to Pigeon Key. The next stop is just 10 mi away at Bahia Honda State Park, on 🏨 **Bahia Honda Key** ⑨. Take a walk on a wilderness trail, go snorkeling on an offshore reef, wriggle your toes in the beach's soft sand, and spend the night in a waterfront cabin, letting the waves lull you to sleep. Your sixth day starts with either a half day of fabulous snorkeling or diving at Looe Key Reef or a visit to the National Key Deer Refuge, on **Big Pine Key** ⑩. Then continue on to 🏨 **Key West** ⑫–㉞, and get in a little sightseeing before watching the sunset. The next morning take a walking, bicycling, or trolley tour of town or catch a ferry or seaplane to Dry Tortugas National Park before heading home.

When to Tour the Florida Keys

High season in the Keys is mid-December through March, and traffic on the Overseas Highway is inevitably heavy. From November to the middle of December, crowds are thinner, the weather is superlative, and hotels and shops drastically reduce their prices. Summer, which is hot and humid, is becoming a second high season, especially among families and Europeans. Key West's annual Fantasy Fest is the last week in October; if you plan to attend this popular event, reserve at least six months in advance. Rooms are also scarce the first few weekends of lobster season, which starts in August.

THE UPPER KEYS

The tropical coral reef tract that runs a few miles off the seaward coast accounts for most of the Upper Keys' reputation. This is a diving heaven, thanks to scores of diving options, accessible islands and dive sites, and an established tourism infrastructure.

But even though diving is king here, fishing, kayaking, and nature touring draw an enviable number of tourists. Within 1½ mi of the bay coast lie the islands of Everglades National Park; here naturalists lead ecotours to see one of the world's few saltwater forests, endangered manatees, dolphins, roseate spoonbills, and tropical-bird rookeries. Although the number of birds has dwindled since John James Audubon captured their beauty on a visit to the Keys, bird-watchers won't be disappointed. At sunset flocks take to the skies, and in spring and autumn

The Florida Keys

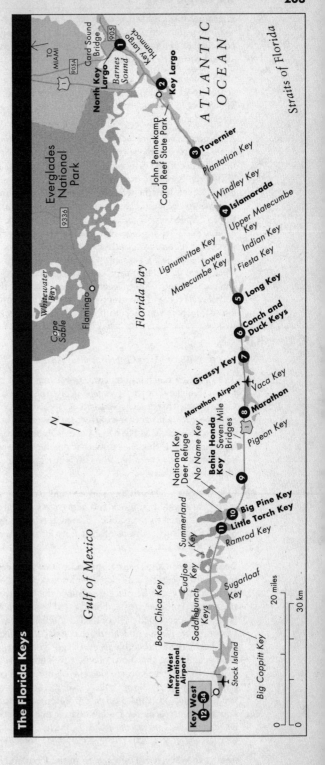

TO MIAMI

905A

Card Sound Bridge

905

North Key Largo

Key Largo Hammock

Barnes Sound

1

Everglades National Park

1

2 **Key Largo**

John Pennekamp Coral Reef State Park

3 **Tavernier**

Plantation Key

Windley Key

4 **Islamorada**

Upper Matecumbe Key

Lignumvitae Key

Lower Matecumbe Key

Indian Key

Fiesta Key

5 **Long Key**

6 **Conch and Duck Keys**

7

Grassy Key

Vaca Key

Marathon Airport

8 **Marathon**

Pigeon Key

Seven Mile Bridges

Bahia Honda Key

National Key Deer Refuge

No Name Key

9

10 **Big Pine Key**

11 **Little Torch Key**

Ramrod Key

Summerland Key

Cudjoe Key

Boca Chica Key

Saddlebunch Keys

Sugarloaf Key

Big Coppitt Key

Stock Island

Key West International Airport

Key West 12-34

9336

Whitewater Bay

Cape Sable

Flamingo

Florida Bay

Gulf of Mexico

ATLANTIC OCEAN

Straits of Florida

N

20 miles

30 km

0

migrating birds add their numbers. Tarpon and bonefish teem in the shallow waters surrounding the islands, providing food for birds and a challenge to light-tackle fishermen. These same crystal-clear waters attract windsurfers, sailors, and powerboaters.

With few exceptions, dining in the Upper Keys tends toward the casual in food, service, and dress. Wherever you go, you'll find a pleasant mix of locals, visitors, snowbirds (in season), and South Floridian weekenders.

Accommodations are as varied as they are plentiful. The majority are in small waterfront resorts, whose efficiency and one- or two-bedroom units are decorated in tropical colors. They offer dockage and either provide or will arrange boating, diving, and fishing excursions. Depending on which way the wind blows and how close the property is to the highway, noise from U.S. 1 can be bothersome. In high season, expect to pay $85–$165 for an efficiency (in low season, $65–$145). Campground and RV park rates with electricity and water run $25–$55. Some properties require two- or three-day minimum stays during holidays and on weekends in high season. Conversely, discounts are given for midweek, weekly, and monthly stays, and rates can drop 20%–40% April–June and October–mid-December. Keep in mind that salty winds and soil play havoc with anything man-made, and constant maintenance is a must; inspect your accommodations before checking in.

Key Largo

56 mi south of Miami International Airport.

The first Key reachable by car, 30-mi-long Key Largo—named Cayo Largo (long key) by the Spanish—is also the largest island in the chain. Comprising three areas—North Key Largo, Key Largo, and Tavernier—it runs northeast–southwest between Lake Surprise and Tavernier Creek, at MM 95. Most businesses are on the four-lane divided highway (U.S. 1) that runs down the middle, but away from the overdevelopment and generally suburban landscape you can find many areas of pristine wilderness.

① One such area is **North Key Largo,** which still contains a wide tract of virgin hardwood hammock and mangroves as well as a crocodile sanctuary (not open to the public). To reach North Key Largo, take Card Sound Road just south of Florida City, or from within the Keys, take Route 905 north.

Dagny Johnson Key Largo Hammocks State Botanical Site. Rest rooms, information kiosks, and picnic tables make the 2,400-acre park user-friendly and a terrific place to explore the largest remaining stand of the vast West Indian tropical hardwood hammock and mangrove wetland that once covered most of the Keys' upland areas. Nearly 100 species of protected plants and animals coexist here, including the endangered American crocodile, Key Largo wood rat, Key Largo cotton mouse, and Schaus swallowtail butterfly. Interpretive signs describe many of the tropical tree species along a 1¼-mi paved road (2½ mi round-trip) that invites walking, rollerblading, and biking. On guided tours, rangers point out rare species, tell humorous nature stories, and encourage you to taste the fruits of native plants. Pets are welcome if on a 6-ft leash. ⊠ *1 mi north of U.S. 1 on Rte. 905, OS, North Key Largo,* ☎ *305/451–1202.* ⌑ *Free.* ☉ *Daily 8–5. Tours Thurs. and Sun. 10.*

Taking the Overseas Highway from the mainland lands you closer to **②** **Key Largo** proper, abounding with shopping centers, chain restaurants, and, of course, dive shops.

★ **John Pennekamp Coral Reef State Park.** Whenever people talk about the best diving sites in the world, this park is on the short list. The park encompasses 78 square mi of coral reefs, sea-grass beds, and mangrove swamps. Its reefs contain 40 of the 52 species of coral in the Atlantic Reef System and more than 650 varieties of fish. Its revamped visitor center/aquarium features a large center floor-to-ceiling aquarium surrounded by numerous smaller tanks, a video room, and exhibits. A concessionaire rents canoes and powerboats and offers snorkel, dive, and glass-bottom boat trips to the reef. The park also includes short nature trails, two man-made beaches, picnic shelters, a snack bar, and a campground. No pets are allowed for visitors who are camping or going out on a boat trip. ⊠ *MM 102.5, OS, Box 487, 33037,* ☎ *305/451–1202,* WEB *www.dep.state.fl.us/parks.* 🖘 *$4 per vehicle plus 50¢ per person, $1.50 per pedestrian or bicyclist.* ☉ *Daily 8–sunset.*

Key Largo Harbor Marina. Few images conjure up more romance than the *African Queen*—the steam-powered boat on which Katharine Hepburn and Humphrey Bogart rode in the movie of the same name. This 20th-century icon is moored at the marina from which you depart on an hour-long ride. ⊠ *MM 99.7, OS, next to the Holiday Inn Key Largo Resort,* ☎ *305/451–4655.* 🖘 *Boat ride $15.* ☉ *Boat ride by appointment.*

❸ **Florida Keys Wild Bird Rehabilitation Center.** In Tavernier, the southernmost part of Key Largo, injured and recovering ospreys, hawks, pelicans, cormorants, terns, and herons of various types rest undisturbed in large, screened enclosures lining a winding boardwalk on some of the best waterfront real estate in the Keys. Wood-carver and teacher Laura Quinn opened the center in 1991. Rehabilitated birds are set free; others become permanent residents. A short nature trail runs into the mangrove forest (bring bug spray May–October), and a video explains the center's mission. ⊠ *MM 93.6, BS, Tavernier,* ☎ *305/852–4486.* 🖘 *Free.* ☉ *Daily sunrise–sunset.*

Harry Harris County Park. Weekends are crowded at this park that has play equipment, a small swimming lagoon, a boat ramp, ball fields, barbecue grills, and rest rooms. Although the turnoff is clearly marked on the Overseas Highway, the road to the ocean is circuitous. ⊠ *MM 93, OS, Burton Dr., Tavernier,* ☎ *305/852–7161 or 888/227–8136.* 🖘 *Weekdays free, weekends $5.* ☉ *Daily 7:30 AM–sunset.*

Dining and Lodging

$$–$$$ ✕ **The Fish House.** A nautical, Keys-y casual decor and friendly, dili-
★ gent servers at this perennial favorite create the feeling of dining in the home of a friend, albeit a friend who knows how to prepare fresh seafood like a superchef. Fish is prepared any way you like—from charbroiled or fried to Jamaican jerked or pan-sautéed. Nightly specials like shrimp and lobster creole in a spicy tomato sauce keep happy diners coming back. The key lime pie is homemade. The next-door annex, the Gift House, has coffees, fabulous desserts, and souvenirs. ⊠ *MM 102.4, OS,* ☎ *305/451–4665. AE, D, MC, V. Closed early Sept.–early Oct.*

$–$$$ ✕ **Frank Keys Café.** Hundreds of little white twinkling lights visible
★ from the porch and windows of the wooden Victorian-style house create a romantic setting for dinner. Equally enticing is the skillfully prepared cuisine that includes fresh-fish dishes like yellowtail *tropicale* (a pan-sautéed yellowtail snapper topped with fresh tropical fruit in a Malibu rum sauce). There's a different dessert soufflé each night. The downside to this otherwise lovely restaurant is that smoking is allowed in the small indoor space. ⊠ *MM 100, OS,* ☎ *305/453–0310. AE, MC, V. Closed Tues. year-round, Tues.–Wed. Easter–Christmas.*

$–$$ ✕ **Café Largo.** You're on vacation and someone in your group wants
★ Italian, and someone else craves seafood. This bistro-style eatery prepares both quite well. The penne with shrimp and broccoli has tender
shrimp, al dente broccoli, and a hint of garlic. There's lobster and shrimp
scampi, too. A more than ample wine list, international beers, Italian
bottled waters, focaccia, garlic rolls, and, of course, espresso and cappuccino are offered, and the dessert list is short but sweet. For lunch
with a view, try the sister restaurant, the Bayside Grille, behind the café.
⊠ *MM 99.5, BS,* ☎ *305/451–4885. AE, MC, V. No lunch.*

$–$$ ✕ **Calypso's.** Much of what you find on the menu here was created
by self-taught chef Todd Lollis, such as his special Nuts for Snapper,
a local yellowtail snapper encrusted in macadamia nuts and served in
an orange Frangelica coulis. A select wine list shows he knows his wines,
too. The dockfront setting is Keys casual; plastic outdoor furniture is
complemented by paper napkins and plastic cutlery. ⊠ *MM 99.5, OS,
1 Seagate Blvd.,* ☎ *305/451–0600. D, MC, V. Closed Tues.*

$–$$ ✕ **Mrs. Mac's Kitchen.** Fortunately, some things never change. The ar-
chitecture, atmosphere, and decor of this rustic wood-paneled, screened,
open-air restaurant harken back to the 1950s, when the Keys had more
fishermen than well-heeled visitors. The cooks still serve up traditional American sandwiches, burgers, barbecue, and seafood like the
popular TJ Dolphin, a mahimahi fillet with a spicy tomato salsa served
with black beans and rice. At breakfast and lunch, the counter and booths
fill up early with locals. Regular nightly specials are worth the stop.
The chili is always good. ⊠ *MM 99.4, BS,* ☎ *305/451–3722. No credit
cards. Closed Sun.*

$ ✕ **Alabama Jack's.** This weathered open-air seafood restaurant floats
on two roadside barges in an old fishing community 13 mi southeast
of Homestead. Regular customers include Keys characters, Sunday cyclists, local retirees, and boaters, all of whom come to admire tropical
birds in the nearby mangroves, the occasional crocodile in the canal,
or the live band on weekends. The menu has traditional Keys dishes
like cracked and fried conch, fish sandwiches, burgers, fries, salads, and
lots of beer. Jack's closes by 7 or 7:30, when the skeeters come out. ⊠
58000 Card Sound Rd., Card Sound, ☎ *305/248–8741. MC, V.*

$ ✕ **Chad's Deli & Bakery.** "This sandwich is huge," is the frequent cry
of first-timers to this small four-table establishment that specializes in
attractively priced ($5.25–$6.25) sandwiches made on a choice of
eight kinds of fresh-baked bread. If you're not in the mood for one of
the regular sandwiches, ranging from certified Angus roast beef to veg-
gie, try the daily special. The menu also includes salads, sides, soft drinks,
and white-chocolate macadamia nut and chocolate chip cookies—
with a whopping 8″ diameter. Most orders are takeout. ⊠ *MM 92.3,
BS,* ☎ *305/853–5566. No credit cards. No dinner.*

$ ✕ **Harriette's Restaurant.** If you're looking for comfort food in a cozy
Keys setting, come to this refreshing throwback. Little has changed here
over the years in this bright-yellow-and-turquoise roadside eatery.
Owner Harriette Mattson still personally welcomes her guests, and the
regulars—many of whom have been coming here since it opened—still
come for breakfast: steak and eggs with hash browns or grits and toast
and jelly for $7.95 or old-fashioned hot cakes with butter and syrup
and sausage or bacon for $4.75. ⊠ *MM 95.7, BS,* ☎ *305/852–8689.
No credit cards. No dinner.*

$$$$ ▥ **Jules' Undersea Lodge.** Had he been a time traveler to this century,
the 19th-century namesake French writer might have enjoyed staying
in this hotel, a former underwater research lab, at 5 fathoms (30 ft) below
the surface. The only way to gain access to the lodge is by diving, and
guests must either be certified divers or take the hotel's three-hour introductory course (an additional $75). Rates include breakfast, dinner,

snacks, beverages, and unlimited dives and diving gear. Because of the length of stay underwater, once back on terra firma, you can't fly for 24 hours. ⊠ *MM 103.2, OS, 51 Shoreland Dr., 33037,* ☎ *305/451–2353,* FAX *305/451–4789,* WEB *www.jul.com. 2 rooms. Kitchens, room TVs with VCR, saltwater pool, dive shop; no kids under 10, no smoking. AE, D, MC, V.*

$$$$ ⚏ **Marriott's Key Largo Bay Beach Resort.** The Upper Keys are best known for small, mom-and-pop-style accommodations. One of the exceptions is this 17-acre bay-side resort whose five lemon-yellow, grill-balconied, and spire-topped stories slice between highway and bay and exude an air of warm, indolent days. There are diversions galore. You can while away the days on the sandy beach or poolside or take an adventurous parasail or personal watercraft ride. Rooms and suites have rattan tropical-style furnishings and balconies. From some you can watch the sunset sweep across the bay. ⊠ *MM 103.8, BS, 103800 Overseas Hwy., 33037,* ☎ *305/453–0000 or 800/932–9332,* FAX *305/453–0093,* WEB *www.marriotthotels.com. 153 rooms, 20 3-bedroom suites, 6 3-bedroom suites, 1 penthouse suite. 3 restaurants, room service, fans, in-room data ports, in-room safes, some kitchens, minibars, cable TV with movies, miniature golf, tennis court, pool, health club, hot tub, spa, beach, dive shop, snorkeling, jet skiing, marina, parasailing, fishing, bicycles, volleyball, 3 bars, shop, dry cleaning, laundry facilities, concierge, business services, meeting rooms; no-smoking rooms. AE, D, DC, MC, V.*

$$$–$$$$ ⚏ **Kona Kai Resort.** These beautifully landscaped cottages offer an es-
★ cape from everyday stress. That probably explains its repeat business. Amenities include CD players with CDs by local artists, tropical furnishings, fruit-scented toiletries, and Noritake china. Studios and one- and two-bedroom suites—with full kitchens and original art—are spacious and light filled. Beachfront hammocks and a heated pool make it easy to laze away the day, or you could try a paddleboat or kayak or visit the art gallery or orchid house. Maid service is every third day to assure your privacy; however, fresh linens and towels are available at any time. ⊠ *MM 97.8, BS, 97802 Overseas Hwy., 33037,* ☎ *305/852–7200 or 800/365–7829,* WEB *www.konakairesort.com. 11 units. Fans, some kitchens, cable TV, some in-room VCRs, tennis court, pool, hot tub, beach, dock, boating, basketball, shuffleboard, volleyball, concierge, Internet; no room phones, no kids, no smoking. AE, D, MC, V.*

$$$–$$$$ ⚏ **Westin Beach Resort, Key Largo.** Rather than destroy the vegetation
★ and clutter the roadside landscape with yet another building, the original owners ensconced this compact resort off the road in a bay-front hardwood hammock. Most rooms overlook the water or woods; others face the lushly landscaped parking lot. The spacious, comfortable rooms have tropical furnishings. Rate includes buffet breakfast and two drink coupons. Lighted nature trails and boardwalks wind through the woods to a small beach. Two small pools are separated by a coral rock wall and waterfall. Both restaurants, one very casual, overlook the water. ⊠ *MM 96.9, BS, 97000 Overseas Hwy., 33037,* ☎ *305/852–5553 or 800/826–1006,* FAX *305/852–8669,* WEB *www.keylargoresort.com. 190 rooms, 10 suites. 2 restaurants, 2 grills, tapas bar, room service, in-room data ports, in-room safes, minibars, some microwaves, some refrigerators, cable TV with movies and video games, 2 tennis courts, 2 pools, health club, hot tub, sauna, spa, beach, dive shop, dock, snorkeling, boating, jet skiing, marina, parasailing, fishing, piano bar, shop, business services, airport shuttle; no-smoking rooms. AE, D, DC, MC, V. BP.*

$$–$$$ ⚏ **Coconut Palm Inn.** Formerly Frank's Key Haven Resort, this has the same casual ambience as before, but the small waterfront lodge has been spruced up with new carpets and furniture on the inside, more palm trees and sand on the outside. Towering gumbo-limbo and button-wood trees shelter the lodge, which was built in the 1930s to withstand hurricanes. For years it was almost exclusively a dive resort, but today, the owners help arrange fishing, diving, kayaking, and ecotours and attract guests with many interests, including those who just want to read on the screened porch. Rooms vary from one-room efficiencies, with refrigerators, to one- and two-bedroom apartments, with kitchens. ⊠ *MM 92, BS, 198 Harborview Dr., Tavernier 33070,* ☏ *305/852–3017 or 800/765–5397,* FAX *305/852–3880,* WEB *www.fkeyhaven.com. 16 units. Fans, some kitchens, refrigerators, cable TV, pool, beach, dock, snorkeling, boating, fishing, laundry facilities; no smoking. MC, V.*

$$ ⊡ **Largo Lodge.** A palpable calm hangs over the 1950s-vintage adults-
★ only one-bedroom guest cottages hidden in a tropical garden of palms, sea grapes, and orchids. Accommodations are cozy and fully equipped with small kitchens, rattan furniture, and screened porches. There's 200 ft of bay frontage for swimming, sitting, or contemplating. Late in the day, wild ducks, pelicans, herons, and other birds come looking for a handout from longtime owner Harriet "Hat" Stokes, who sets the tone at this laid-back, top-value tropical hideaway not too far down the Keys. ⊠ *MM 101.5, BS, 101740 Overseas Hwy., 33037,* ☏ *305/451–0424 or 800/468–4378,* WEB *www.largolodge.com. 6 apartments, 1 efficiency. Fans, kitchenettes, cable TV, beach, dock; no room phones. MC, V.*

$$ ⊡ **Popp's Motel.** A high wall with stylized metal white herons marks the entrance to this 50-year-old family-run motel. It's roomy, homey, breezy, and ideal for families whose kids can safely play on swings and a sandy beach just yards from their rooms. Clean, well-maintained bed-room units and efficiencies have a kitchen, dark wood paneling, and terrazzo floors. It's simple, but a gem of a resort. A weekly stay is required during busy periods. ⊠ *MM 95.5, BS, 95500 Overseas Hwy., 33037,* ☏ *305/852–5201,* FAX *305/852–5200,* WEB *www.popps.com. 9 units. Picnic area, fans, kitchens, cable TV, beach, dock, snorkeling, boating, waterskiing, fishing, shuffleboard, playground. AE, MC, V.*

$ △ **America Outdoors.** This friendly waterfront campground nestled in a heavily wooded strip along Florida Bay fills up with repeat campers, especially snowbirds from January to mid-March, and South Floridi-ans, who crowd the place on weekends and holidays. Security is tight and it has the best camping amenities in the Keys, including satellite TV, a recreation center, shuffleboard, horseshoes, two tidy air-conditioned bathhouses, a marina, fishing pier, bait shop, boat ramp and rentals, windsurfing, and Internet access. It's family oriented, pet friendly, clean, orderly, and well managed. Sites, some on the beach, are on the smallish side, but afford privacy. ⊠ *MM 97.5, BS, 97450 Overseas Hwy., 33037,* ☏ *305/852–8054,* WEB *www.aokl.com. 155 sites. Restaurant, beach, boating, marina, fishing, horseshoes, shuffleboard, shop, laundry facilities, some pets allowed. AE, D, MC, V.*

Nightlife

The semiweekly *Keynoter* (Wednesday and Saturday), weekly *Reporter* (Thursday), and Friday to Sunday editions of the *Miami Herald* are the best sources of information on entertainment and nightlife.

Local movers and shakers mingle with visitors over cocktails and sun-sets at **Breezers Tiki Bar** (⊠ MM 103.8, BS, ☏ 305/453–0000), in Mar-riott's Key Largo Bay Beach Resort. Walls plastered with Bogart memorabilia remind customers that the classic 1948 Bogart-Bacall flick *Key Largo* was shot in the **Caribbean Club** (⊠ MM 104, BS, ☏ 305/451–9970). An archetype of a laid-back Keys bar, it draws a hairy-faced, down-home group to shoot the breeze while shooting pool, but is friendlier than you might imagine. It also has postcard-perfect sunsets and live entertainment that's good enough to draw late-night crowds on Friday and Saturday and at 6 on Sunday evenings. **Coconuts** (✉ MM 100, OS, 528 Caribbean Dr., ☎ 305/453–9794), in Marina Del Mar Resort, has nightly entertainment year-round, except Sunday and Monday during football season. The crowd is primarily thirty- and fortysomething, sprinkled with a few grizzled locals.

Outdoor Activities and Sports

BIKING

Tavernier Bicycle & Hobbies (✉ 91958 Overseas Hwy, MM 91.9, BS, Tavernier, ☎ 305/852–2859) rents single-speed adult and children's bikes. Cruisers go for $8 a day, $40 a week. Helmets and locks are free with rental.

FISHING

Sailors Choice (✉ MM 99.7, OS, ☎ 305/451–1802 or 305/451–0041) runs a party boat twice daily plus a night trip on Friday and Saturday. The ultramodern 60-ft, 49-passenger boat with air-conditioned cabin costs $30 and leaves from the Holiday Inn docks.

SCUBA DIVING AND SNORKELING

American Diving Headquarters (✉ MM 105.5, BS, ☎ 305/451–0037 or 877/451–0037), a PADI five-star facility in business since 1962, is a good choice if you want to roll out of your condo, step onto the boat, and get to the reef fast on roomy 50-ft dive boats. The cost is $65 for a two-tank reef dive with tank and weight rental, $100 if you need everything; $106–$112 includes a wet suit, suggested in winter. Ask about dive accommodations/dive packages.

Amy Slate's Amoray Dive Resort (✉ MM 104.2, BS, ☎ 305/451–3595 or 800/426–6729) makes diving easy. You get out of bed, walk out your room and into a full-service dive shop (NAUI, PADI, TDI, and British BSAC certified), then onto a 45-ft catamaran. They provide multidive discounts and accommodations packages and perform underwater weddings.

Coral Reef Park Co. (✉ John Pennekamp Coral Reef State Park, MM 102.5, OS, ☎ 305/451–6322) offers scuba and snorkeling tours of the park aboard sailing and motorized boats.

Divers City, USA (✉ MM 104, OS, ☎ 305/451–4554 or 800/649–4659) keeps convenient hours—daily 8 to 6—for divers who need to purchase or have their equipment repaired. It also offers some of the best prices on equipment in town and runs two-tank, two-location dives for $49.95, tanks and weights included.

Quiescence Diving Service, Inc. (✉ MM 103.5, BS, ☎ 305/451–2440) sets itself apart in two ways: it limits groups to six to ensure personal attention and offers day, night, and twilight (in summer) dives an hour before sundown, the time when sea creatures are most active.

WATER SPORTS

Coral Reef Park Co. (✉ John Pennekamp Coral Reef State Park, MM 102.5, OS, ☎ 305/451–1621) frequently renews its fleet of canoes, kayaks, and Spyaks(personal glass-bottom boats) for scooting around the mangrove trails or the sea. You can rent a canoe, a one- or two-person sea kayak, or even camping equipment from **Florida Bay Outfitters** (✉ MM 104, BS, ☎ 305/451–3018). Real pros, they help with trip planning and match the equipment to the skill level, so even novices feel confident paddling off. Rentals are by the half day or full day. They also run myriad tours and sell camping and outdoor accessories, kayaks, and canoes.

Shopping

Original works by major international artists—including American photographer Clyde Butcher, French painter Jalinepol W, and French sculptor Polles—are shown at **The Gallery at Kona Kai** (✉ MM 97.8, BS, 97802 Overseas Hwy., ☎ 305/852–7200). It's in the Kona Kai Resort. There are lots of shops in the Keys that carry fun souvenirs. The **Gift House** (✉ MM 102.3, OS, 102341 Overseas Hwy., ☎ 305/451–0650) stands out because, along with the usual kitschy magnets, wind chimes, and shell flowers, it also carries handcrafted gift items and home furnishings by Caribbean and local artists. There's also a dessert and coffee bar with wonderfully decadent desserts. It's adjacent to the Fish House restaurant.

Islamorada

④ *MM 90.5–70.*

Early settlers named Islamorada after their schooner, the *Island Home,* but to make the name more romantic, they translated it into Spanish—*isla morada.* The local chamber of commerce prefers to say it means "the purple isles." Early maps show Islamorada as only Upper Matecumbe Key, but the incorporated "Village of Islands" comprises the islands between Tavernier Creek at MM 90 and Fiesta Key at MM 70, including Plantation Key, Windley Key, Upper Matecumbe Key, Lower Matecumbe Key, Craig Key, and Fiesta Key. In addition, two islands—Indian Key, in the Atlantic Ocean, and Lignumvitae Key, in Florida Bay—belong to the group.

Islamorada is one of the world's most renowned sportfishing areas. For nearly 100 years, seasoned anglers have recognized these clear, warm waters as home to a huge variety of game fish as well as lobster, shrimp, and crabs. The rich, the famous, and the powerful have all fished here, including Lou Gehrig, Ted Williams, Zane Grey, and presidents Hoover, Truman, Carter, and Bush Sr. More than 150 backcountry guides and 400 offshore captains operate out of this 20-mi stretch.

Activities range from fishing tournaments to historic reenactments. During September and October, Heritage Days highlights include free lectures on Islamorada history, a golf tournament, and the Indian Key Festival. Holiday Isle Resort sponsors boating, fishing, car, and golf tournaments, as well as bikini and body-building contests.

Plantation Key. Between 1885 and 1915, settlers earned good livings growing pineapples here, using black Bahamian workers to plant and harvest their crops. The plantations are gone, replaced by a dense concentration of homes, businesses, and a public park. ✉ *MM 90.5–86.*

Windley Key. At 16 ft above sea level, Windley is the highest point in the Keys. Originally two islets, the area was first inhabited by Native Americans, who left middens and other remains, and then by settlers, who farmed and fished in the mid-1800s and called the islets the Umbrella Keys. The Florida East Coast Railway bought the land from homesteaders in 1908, filled in the inlet between the two islands, and changed the name. They quarried rock for the rail bed and bridge approaches in the Keys—the same rock used in many historic South Florida structures, including Miami's Vizcaya and the Hurricane Monument on Upper Matecumbe. Although the Quarry Station stop was destroyed by the 1935 hurricane, quarrying continued until the 1960s. Today a few resorts and attractions occupy the island. ✉ *MM 86–84.*

Windley Key Fossil Reef State Geologic Park. The once-living fossilized coral reef that was laid down about 125,000 years ago shows that the Florida Keys were at some time underwater. When the Florida East Coast Railway excavated Windley Key's limestone bed, it exposed the petrified reef. The park contains the **Alison Fahrer Environmental Education Center,** which contains historic, biological, and geological displays about the area. There also are guided and self-guided tours along trails that lead to the railway's old quarrying equipment and cutting pits, where you can take rubbings of beautifully fossilized brain coral and sea ferns from the quarry walls. There's an annual festival in February. ⊠ *MM 85.5, BS,* ☎ *305/664–2540.* ⊡ *Education center free, quarry trails $1.50.* ◔ *Education center Thurs.–Mon. 8–5; inquire about quarry tour schedule.*

ⓒ **Theater of the Sea.** The lush, tropical 17-acre facility is the second-oldest marine mammal center in the world. Entertaining and educational shows provide insight into conservation issues, natural history, and mammal anatomy, physiology, and husbandry. Shows run continuously. You can ride a glass-bottom boat and take a four-hour Dolphin Adventure Snorkel Cruise or guided tours to view marine life, raptors, and reptiles. You can visit dolphins and sea lions and participate in animal interaction programs such as Swim with the Dolphins ($125), Swim with Sea Lions ($85), Stingray Reef Swim ($35), and Trainer for a Day ($75). Reservations are recommended for interaction programs. Program fees include general admission. You can also have lunch at the grill, shop, and sunbathe at a lagoon-side beach. ⊠ *MM 84.5, OS, 84721 Overseas Hwy., 33036,* ☎ *305/664–2431,* ᴡᴇʙ *www.theaterofthesea. com.* ⊡ *$17.25.* ◔ *Daily 9:30–4.*

Upper Matecumbe Key. This was one of the earliest of the Upper Keys to be permanently settled, and homesteaders were so successful at growing pineapples as well as limes in the rocky soil here that at one time the island had the largest U.S. pineapple crop. However, Cuban pineapples and the hurricane of 1935 killed the industry. Today life centers on fishing and tourism, and the island is lively with homes, charter fishing boats, bait shops, restaurants, stores, nightclubs, marinas, nurseries, and offices. ⊠ *MM 84–79.*

Home to the local chamber of commerce, a **red train caboose** sits at the site where the Florida East Coast Railway had a station and living quarters, before they washed away with the hurricane of 1935. ⊠ *MM 82.5, BS.* ⊡ *Free.* ◔ *Weekdays 9–5, Sat. 9–4.*

Hurricane Monument. Although the possibility of a hurricane is something Keys residents live with, few hurricanes actually make landfall here. One major exception was the 1935 Labor Day hurricane, in which 423 people died. Beside the highway, the 65-ft-by-20-ft art deco–style monument commemorates their deaths. Many of those who perished were World War I veterans who had been working on the Overseas Highway. The monument, built of Keys coral limestone with a ceramic map of the Keys, depicts wind-driven waves and palms bowing before the storm's fury. ⊠ *MM 81.6, OS.*

Islamorada County Park. Tucked away behind the Islamorada library is this park with a small beach on a creek. The water isn't very deep, but it is crystal clear. Currents are swift, making swimming unsuitable for young children, but they can enjoy the playground, and there are picnic tables, grassy areas, and rest rooms. ⊠ *MM 81.5, BS.*

Islamorada Founder's Park. Formerly part of a commercial resort, this is now a public village park with a beach, marina, dog park, skate park, water-sports equipment rentals, an Olympic-size pool, and clean restroom and shower facilities. If you're staying in Islamorada hotels, you can enter the park free and pay the village rate of $2/$3 weekdays/

weekends for the pool. Otherwise, it's $6/$10 to enter the park and $8/$12 to use the pool. ⊠ *MM 87, BS*, ☎ *305/853–1685.*

OFF THE
BEATEN PATH

INDIAN KEY STATE HISTORIC SITE – Murder, mystery, and misfortune surround 10½-acre Indian Key on the ocean side of the Matecumbe islands. Before it became one of the first European settlements outside of Key West, it was inhabited by Native Americans for several thousand years. The islet served as a county seat and base for 19th-century shipwreck salvagers until an Indian attack wiped out the settlement in 1840. Dr. Henry Perrine, a noted botanist, was killed in the raid. Today his plants overgrow the town's ruins. In October the Indian Key Festival celebrates the key's heritage. Guided tours were suspended because of damage to the docks from recent hurricanes, but you can roam among the marked trails and sites. The island is reachable by boat—your own, a rental, or a ferry. Robbie's Marina, the official concessioner, rents kayaks and boats and operates twice-daily ferry service daily except Tuesday and Wednesday. For information, contact Long Key State Recreation Area. Locals kayak out from **Indian Key Fill** (⊠ MM 78.5, BS). Rentals are available from Florida Keys Kayak and Sail. ⊠ *MM 78.5, OS*, ☎ *305/664–9814 for ferry service; 305/664–4815 for Long Key State Recreation Area.* ⊟ *Ferry (includes tour) $15, $25 with Lignumvitae Key.* ☉ *Daily sunrise–sunset.*

LIGNUMVITAE KEY STATE BOTANICAL SITE – On the National Register of Historic Places, this 280-acre bay-side island is the site of a virgin hardwood forest and home and gardens that chemical magnate William Matheson built as a private retreat in 1919. Access is by boat—your own, a rental, or a ferry operated by the official concessionaire, Robbie's Marina, which also rents kayaks and boats. (Kayaking out from Indian Key Fill, at MM 78.5, is a popular pastime.) On the key you can take a tour with the resident ranger and request a list of native and well-naturalized plants. As a courtesy, you should arrange for a tour in advance with Long Key State Recreation Area if you're using your own or a rental boat. On the first weekend in December, the Park Service holds an annual Lignumvitae Christmas Celebration. ⊠ *MM 78.5, BS*, ☎ *305/664–9814 for ferry service; 305/664–4815 for Long Key State Recreation Area.* ⊟ *Free; tour $1; ferry (includes tour) $15, $25 with Indian Key.* ☉ *Tours Thurs.–Mon. 10 and 2.*

☃ **Robbie's Marina.** Tarpon, large prehistoric-looking denizens of the not-so-deep, congregate around the docks here on Lower Matecumbe Key, where children—and lots of adults—buy a $2 bucket of bait fish to feed them. ⊠ *MM 77.5, BS*, ☎ *305/664–9814 or 877/664–8498.* ⊟ *Dock access $1.* ☉ *Daily 8–5:30.*

Anne's Beach. On Lower Matecumbe Key, this is a popular village park whose beach is best enjoyed at low tide. It also has a ½-mi elevated wooden boardwalk that meanders through a natural wetland hammock. Covered picnic areas along the boardwalk provide a place to rest and enjoy the view. Rest rooms are at the north end. Weekends are packed with Miami day-trippers. ⊠ *MM 73.5, OS*, ☎ *305/852–2381.*

Dining and Lodging

$$–$$$$ ✕ **Morada Bay.** This bay-front restaurant is wildly popular. First,
★ there's the spectacular water view. Then, there's the traditional wooden Conch architecture decorated with Clyde Butcher's black-and-white Everglades photos. Best of all is the contemporary menu with tapas and original small dishes, mostly from the sea. Meals start with a basket of fresh rolls and a plate of tapenade, white-bean dip, and garlic-infused olive oil. You can dine indoors (noisy) or outdoors overlooking

a beach dotted with Adirondack chairs. There's frequently live entertainment, especially on weekends, and a monthly full-moon party. ✉ *MM 81, BS,* ☎ *305/664–0604. AE, MC, V.*

$$–$$$$ ✕ **Pierre's.** Morada Bay restaurant, the tony Moorings resort, and this
★ restaurant and lounge were started by French windsurfer-turned-Keys-entrepreneur Hubert Baudoin. This two-story showpiece marries British colonial decadence with South Florida trendiness. The place is loaded with dark wood, rattan, French doors, Indian and Asian architectural artifacts, and a wide, wicker-chair–strewn veranda that overlooks the bay. Dishes, heavily inspired by those same Asian, Indian, and Floridian accents, are complex: layered, colorful, and beautifully presented. Weather permitting, dine outside. The sophisticated downstairs bar provides a perfect vantage point for sunset watching. Reservations are recommended. ✉ *MM 81.5, BS,* ☎ *305/664–3225. AE, MC, V.*

$$–$$$ ✕ **Squid Row.** The food is so fresh and good at this seafood eatery that
★ no gimmicks are needed to lure customers. That doesn't prevent the affable staff from offering a playful challenge. Along with local fish—grilled and divinely flaky or breaded and sautéed—they offer a nightly special bouillabaisse ($27.95), thick with fish and shellfish—even stone crab claws—that is wonderful. If you can eat it all by yourself, they'll give you a free slice of key lime pie. Instead of rolls, meals start with a slice of warm banana bread; it's also great with coffee as dessert. ✉ *MM 81.9, OS,* ☎ *305/664–9865. AE, D, DC, MC, V.*

$–$$ ✕ **Manny & Isa's.** A Keys institution, there are no frills, fancy decor, or pretense here. Instead, it has friendly waitresses who serve consistently delicious Cuban and Spanish dishes and local seafood in a simple, crowded room. There are daily fish, chicken, and pork-chop specials and a paella that's loaded with fresh seafood. Order it the day before for at least two people ($19.95 each). Manny's sweet-tart key lime pies are legendary. Order them by the slice or by the pie. There's always a wait for dinner on weekends and during the winter high season. Avoid the line by calling for takeout. ✉ *MM 81.6, OS, 81610 Old Hwy.,* ☎ *305/664–5019. Reservations not accepted. AE, D, MC, V. Closed Tues. and mid-Oct.–mid-Nov.*

$$$$ 🏨 **Cheeca Lodge.** This classy, classic resort combines a sense of luxury with a sense of familiarity. A complex of buildings, gardens, beach, and fish-filled lagoons stretch across 27 oceanfront acres. Tropically decorated units and screened balconies (on suites) encourage you to linger, but the beach, sports, and massages, facials, and body treatments at the Avanyu Spa beckon. Suites have kitchens; fourth-floor rooms in the main lodge have ocean or bay views. The resort is the local leader in green activism with everything from recycling programs to ecotours. Camp Cheeca for kids is both fun and educational. ✉ *MM 82, OS, Box 527, 33036,* ☎ *305/664–4651 or 800/327–2888,* 📠 *305/664–2893,* 🌐 *www.cheeca.com. 139 rooms, 64 suites. 2 restaurants, room service, in-room data ports, some minibars, some refrigerators, cable TV with movies, in-room VCRs, 9-hole golf course, 6 tennis courts, 2 pools, saltwater pool, health club, 5 outdoor hot tubs, spa, beach, dive shop, dock, snorkeling, boating, parasailing, fishing, bicycles, bar, lobby lounge, shops, laundry service, baby-sitting, children's programs (ages 6–12), playground, business services, meeting rooms; no-smoking rooms. AE, D, DC, MC, V.*

$$$–$$$$ 🏨 **Casa Morada.** This resort resembles something you'd find on the Mexican Riviera. Clean, cool tile and terrazzo floors invite you to kick off your shoes and step out to your private patio overlooking the gardens and bay. The furnishings—mahogany and wrought-iron mixed with European artifacts and lamps—are made to order in Mexico for the resort and you can buy the pieces as well. The pool's built on a small concrete island in the bay. Nearby restaurants abound, or use the spotless communal kitchen to cook yourself and then eat on the terrace. ✉ *MM 82, BS, 136 Madeira Rd., 33036,* ☎ *305/664–0044 or 888/881–3030,* FAX *305/664–0674,* WEB *www.casamorada.com. 16 suites. Fans, in-room data ports, in-room safes, refrigerators, cable TV, pool, massage, dock, boating, marina, boccie; no smoking. AE, MC, V.*

$$$–$$$$ ★ 🖾 **The Moorings.** When you think of a tropical retreat, visions of palm trees, beaches, and wooden houses with porches and wicker furniture come to mind. That's what you'll find here at one of the Keys' finest hostelries. Tucked in a beachfront tropical forest are one-, two-, and three-bedroom cottages and two-story houses outfitted with wicker and artistic African fabrics and pristine kitchens. There are exquisite touches, from thick towels to cushy bedcovers. The beach has Adirondack chairs and hammocks and a swimming dock. There's a two-night minimum on one-bedrooms and a one-week minimum on other lodgings. ✉ *MM 81.6, OS, 123 Beach Rd., 33036,* ☎ *305/664–4708,* FAX *305/664–4242,* WEB *www.themooringsvillage.com. 18 cottages and houses. Fans, in-room data ports, some kitchens, some kitchenettes, cable TV, tennis court, pool, beach, windsurfing, boating, laundry facilities. MC, V.*

$$–$$$ ★ 🖾 **Sea Isle Resort and Marina.** This picturesque resort on 8½ acres has a beautiful sandy beach, two docks, and two types of accommodations. Old concrete duplex "villas" were modernized with very tasteful island furnishings, tile floors, and a private deck or patio. You can smell the sea from all of them. Next door are the gilded lilies: Caribbean-style one- and two-bedroom houses with open-beam ceilings, wraparound porches and light, breezy, oh-so-tropical decor. Public areas are equally appealing. The large walk-in, beach-entry-style pool is surrounded by palm trees and lounge chairs. ✉ *MM 82, OS, 109 E. Carroll St., Box 1298, 33036,* ☎ *305/664–2235 or 800/799–9175,* FAX *305/664–2093,* WEB *www.seaisleres.com. 21 units, 9 villas, 12 houses. Fans, some kitchens, cable TV, some in-room VCRs, pool, outdoor hot tub, beach, dock, snorkeling, marina, fishing. AE, MC, V.*

$$ 🖾 **White Gate Court.** This well-run inn on the edge of Florida Bay comprises five restored wooden 1940s cottages laid out on three pretty landscaped acres along 200 ft of white-sand beach. Resident owner Susanne Orias de Cargnelli created this intimate escape, where everyone in the family, including the dog, is welcome. All the units, which sleep either two or four, are as well equipped as your own home, except your backyard probably doesn't have the barbecue grill and umbrella-shaded table under big old palm trees swaying with the sea breeze. ✉ *MM 76, BS, 76010 Overseas Hwy., 33036,* ☎ *305/664–4136 or 800/645–4283,* WEB *www.whitegatecourt.com. 7 units. Picnic area, fans, in-room data ports, kitchens, cable TV, beach, dock, snorkeling, boating, bicycles, laundry facilities, some pets allowed (fee). MC, V.*

$ 🖾 **Ragged Edge Resort.** Smack on the water's edge, this no-frills, laid-back getaway has simple, clean rooms with pine paneling, chintz, and a tile bath suite, and most have kitchens with irons. Many downstairs units have screened porches, although upper units have large decks, more windows, and beam ceilings. It's affordable because of a lack of staff and things like no in-room phones. It's a warm, homey kind of place where guests congregate under the thatch-roof observation tower by day and the barbecue pits, where they grill up their catch by night. There's not much of a beach, but you can swim off the dock. ✉ *MM 86.5, OS, 243 Treasure Harbor Rd., 33036,* ☎ *305/852–5389 or 800/436–2023,* WEB *www.ragged-edge.com. 10 units. Picnic area, fans, some kitchens, some kitchenettes, some refrigerators, pool, dock, marina, fishing, bicycles, shuffleboard; no room phones, no TV in some rooms. MC, V.*

Nightlife

Holiday Isle Beach Resorts & Marina (✉ MM 84, OS, ☎ 305/664–2321) is the liveliest spot in the Upper Keys. On weekends, especially during spring break and holidays, the resort's three entertainment areas are mobbed, primarily with the under-30 set. Live bands play everything from reggae to heavy metal. Behind the larger-than-life mermaid is the Keys-easy, over-the-water cabana bar the **Lorelei** (✉ MM 82, BS, ☎ 305/664–4656). Live nightly sounds are mostly reggae and light rock. **Zane Grey Long Key Lounge** (✉ MM 81.5, BS, ☎ 305/664–4244) above the World Wide Sportsman was created to honor Zane Grey, one of South Florida's greatest legends in fishing and writing and one of the most famous members of the Long Key Fishing Club. The lounge features the author's photographs, books, and memorabilia, as well as live music on weekends, and a wide veranda that invites sunset watching.

Outdoor Activities and Sports

BOATING

Wildlife in the Keys is most active at sunrise and sunset. Be there comfortably at both times with **Houseboat Vacations of the Florida Keys** (✉ MM 85.9, BS, 85944 Overseas Hwy., 33036, ☎ 305/664–4009, WEB www.thefloridakeys.com/houseboats), which rents a fleet of 42- to 44-ft boats that accommodate from six to eight people and come fully outfitted with safety equipment and necessities—except food. The three-day minimum starts at $847; a week costs $1,408. Kayaks, canoes, and 16-ft skiffs are also for hire.

Robbie's Boat Rentals & Charters (✉ MM 77.5, BS, 77520 Overseas Hwy., 33036, ☎ 305/664–9814) rents a 15-ft skiff with a 25-horsepower outboard (the smallest you can charter) for $25 an hour, $70 for four hours, and $90 for the day. Boats up to 27 ft are also available, but there's a two-hour minimum; pontoon boats, with a half-day minimum.

When you're in the Keys, do as the locals do. Get out on the water, preferably for a few days. Captains Pam and Pete Anderson of **Treasure Harbor Marine** (✉ MM 86.5, OS, 200 Treasure Harbor Dr., 33036, ☎ 305/852–2458 or 800/352–2628, WEB www.treasureharbor.com) provide everything you'll need for a vacation at sea: linens, safety gear, and, best of all, advice on where to find the best beaches, marinas, and lobster sites. You can rent a vessel bareboat or crewed, with sail or with power. Boats range from a 19-ft Cape Dory to a 51-ft Morgan Out Island. Rates start at $95 a day, $395 a week. Marina facilities are basic—water, electric, ice machine, laundry, picnic tables, and shower/rest rooms—and dockage is only $1.25 a foot.

FISHING

Long before fly-fishing became a trendy sport, Sandy Moret was fishing the Keys for bonefish, tarpon, and redfish. Now he operates **Florida Keys Outfitters** (✉ MM 82, BS, ☎ 305/664–5423), home to a store and the Florida Keys Fly Fishing School, which attracts anglers from around the world. Two-day weekend fly-fishing classes, which include classroom instruction, equipment, arrival cocktails, and daily breakfast and lunch, cost $895. Add another $900 for two days of fishing. Guided fishing trips cost $310 for a half day, $450 for a full day. Fishing and accommodations packages (at Cheeca Lodge) are available.

The 65-ft party boat *Gulf Lady* (✉ Whale Harbor Marina, MM 83.5, OS, ☎ 305/664–2461) has full-day ($55 includes everything) and night trips. Bring your lunch or buy one from the dockside deli. The boat can be crowded, so call about loads in advance.

Captain Ken Knudsen of the **Hubba Hubba** (✉ MM 79.8, OS, ☎ 305/ 664–9281) quietly poles his flats boat through the shallow water, barely making a ripple. Then he points and his client casts. Five seconds later there's a zing, and the excitement of bringing in a snook, redfish, trout, or tarpon begins. Knudsen has fished Keys waters since he was 12. Now a licensed backcountry guide, he's ranked among the top 10 guides in Florida by national fishing magazines. He offers four-hour sunset trips for tarpon ($325) and two-hour sunset trips for bonefish ($175), as well as half- ($275) and full-day ($400) outings. Prices are for one or two anglers. Tackle and bait are included.

SCUBA DIVING AND SNORKELING

Florida Keys Dive Center (✉ MM 90.5, OS, Box 391, Tavernier 33070, ☎ 305/852–4599 or 800/433–8946) organizes dives from John Pennekamp Coral Reef State Park to Alligator Light. The center has two Coast Guard–approved dive boats, offers scuba training, and is one of the few Keys dive centers to offer Nitrox (mixed gas) diving. Since 1980, **Lady Cyana Divers** (✉ MM 85.9, BS, Box 1157, Islamorada 33036, ☎ 305/664–8717 or 800/221–8717), a PADI five-star training resort, has operated dives on deep and shallow wrecks and reefs between Molasses and Alligator reefs. The 40- and 55-ft boats provide everything a diver needs, including full bathrooms.

TENNIS

Not all Keys' recreation is on the water. You can play tennis year-round at the **Islamorada Tennis Club** (✉ MM 76.8, BS, ☎ 305/664–5340). It's a well-run facility with four clay and two hard courts, same-day racket stringing, ball machines, private lessons, a full-service pro shop, night games, and partner pairing. Rates are from $14 an hour.

WATER SPORTS

Florida Keys Kayak and Sail (✉ MM 77.5, BS, 77522 Overseas Hwy., ☎ 305/664–4878) rents kayaks within a 20- to 30-minute paddle of Indian and Lignumvitae keys, two favorite destinations for kayakers. Rates are $15 per hour, $30 per half day.

Shopping

Whether you're looking to learn more about Keys history, flora and fauna, or fishing, you'll find it in a large selection of books, cards, and maps on Florida and the region at **Cover to Cover Books** (✉ Tavernier Towne Shopping Center, MM 91.2, BS, 91272 Overseas Hwy., ☎ 305/ 852–1415). At **Down to Earth** (✉ MM 82.2, OS, 82229 Overseas Hwy., ☎ 305/664–9828), you can indulge your passion for *objets* that are at once practical and fanciful such as salad tongs carved from polished coconut shells or Italian dishes painted with palm trees. Prices are reasonable, too. When locals need a one-of-a-kind gift, they head for the **Gallery at Morada Bay** (✉ MM 81.6, BS, ☎ 305/664–3650), stocked with blown glass and glassware, and home furnishings, original paintings and lithographs, sculptures, and hand-painted scarves and earrings by top South Florida artists. Among the best buys in town are the used best-sellers and hardbacks that sell for less than $5 after locals trade them in for store credit at **Hooked on Books** (✉ MM 82.6, OS, 82681 Overseas Hwy., ☎ 305/517–2602). They also carry new titles, audio books, cards, and CDs. **Island Silver & Spice** (✉ MM 82, OS, ☎ 305/ 664–2714) bills itself as a "tropical department store." To that end, it sells women's and men's resort wear, a large jewelry selection with high-end Swiss watches and marine-theme jewelry, tropical housewares, cards, toys and games, bedding, and bath goods.

Former U.S. presidents, celebs, and record holders beam alongside their catches in black-and-white photos on the walls at **World Wide Sports-**

man (✉ MM 81.5, BS, ☎ 305/664–4615), a two-level attraction and retail center that sells upscale fishing equipment, art, resort clothing, and gifts. There's also a marina and the Zane Grey Long Key Lounge.

ART GALLERIES

Art Lovers Gallery (✉ MM 82.2, OS, ☎ 305/664–3675) showcases the work of almost 100 primarily South Florida artists, including Kendall Van Sant (bronze sculptures) and Jim Lewk (copper creations). It's an unlikely setting for an art gallery. That said, **The Carpet Gallery** (✉ MM 88.6, OS, 88665 Overseas Hwy., ☎ 305/852–6101), which derives its name from the carved carpets created by resident rug artisan Thomas Gallagher as well as the carpets, tiles, and wood flooring that it sells, is attracting crowds to its one-artist exhibitions. A new show opens with a meet-the-artist reception on the first Friday of each month. Each Sunday the gallery hosts an open-house brunch. The **Rain Barrel** (✉ MM 86.7, BS, ☎ 305/852–3084) is a natural and unhurried shopping showplace. Set in a tropical garden of shady trees, native shrubs, and orchids, the 1977 crafts village comprises shops with works by local and national artists and eight resident artists in studios, including John Hawver, noted for Florida landscapes and seascapes. In March it hosts the largest arts show in the Keys; some 20,000 visitors, 100 artists, and live jazz. The Garden Café is a beautiful respite and has a primarily vegetarian menu of sandwiches and salads. The **Redbone Gallery** (✉ MM 81, OS, 200 Industrial Dr., ☎ 305/664–2002), the largest sporting-art gallery in Florida, has hand-stitched clothing and giftware in addition to works by wood and bronze sculptors such as Kendall Van Sant; watercolorists Chet Reneson, Jeanne Dobie, and Kathleen Denis; and painters C. D. Clarke and Tim Borski. One of the most-photographed subjects in the Upper Keys is the enormous fabricated lobster by artist Richard Blaes that stands in front of **Treasure Village** (✉ MM 86.7, OS, 86729 Old Hwy., ☎ 305/852–0511), a former 1950s treasure museum that houses a dozen crafts and specialty shops and a small restaurant.

Long Key

 MM 70–65.5.

Long Key is steeped in cultural and ecological history. Among its attributes is **Long Key State Recreation Area.** On the ocean side, the Golden Orb Trail leads onto a boardwalk through a mangrove swamp alongside a lagoon, where waterbirds congregate. The park has a campground, picnic area, rest rooms and showers, a canoe trail through a tidal lagoon, and a not-very-sandy beach fronting a broad expanse of shallow grass flats. Bring a mask and snorkel to observe the marine life in this rich nursery area. Repairs and replantings following hurricanes have left the park with improved facilities, but with a lot less shade. Replanting efforts continue. Across the road, near a historical marker partially obscured by foliage, is the **Layton Nature Trail** (✉ MM 67.7, BS), which takes 20–30 minutes to walk and leads through tropical hardwood forest to a rocky Florida Bay shoreline overlooking shallow grass flats. A marker relates the history of the Long Key Viaduct, the first major bridge on the rail line, and the exclusive Long Key Fishing Camp, which Henry Flagler established nearby in 1906 and that attracted sportsman Zane Grey, the noted Western novelist and conservationist, who served as its first president. The camp was washed away in the 1935 hurricane and never rebuilt. For Grey's efforts, the creek running near the recreation area was named for him. ✉ *MM 67.5, OS, Box 776, 33001,* ☎ *305/664–4815,* WEB *www.dep.state.fl.us/parks.* ✉ *$3.75 for 1 person, plus 50¢ each additional person; canoe rental $4 per hr, $10 per day; Layton Nature Trail free.* ☉ *Daily 8–sunset.*

Dining and Lodging

$–$$ ✕ **Little Italy.** Good food. Good value. It doesn't say it on the menu, but ask locals about this traditional family-style Italian and seafood restaurant and that is often the answer. Lunch favorites include Caesar salad, chicken marsala, stone crabs, and stuffed snapper for $4.25–$8.50. Dinner selections are equally tasty and well priced—pasta, chicken, seafood, veal, and steak. Don't miss the rich, dreamy hot chocolate-pecan pie. Breakfast, too, is served, and a light-bites menu has smaller portions for kids and calorie-watchers. ⊠ *MM 68.5, BS,* ☎ *305/664–4472. AE, MC, V.*

$$ 🏨 **Lime Tree Bay Resort.** This popular 2½-acre resort is on Florida Bay and far from the hubbub of other hotels and businesses. An on-site watersports concession encourages activity. However, if you would rather do nothing more energetic than turn the pages of a book, head for the beach or settle into a hammock in the pleasantly landscaped garden. Rooms are decorated with breezy wicker- and rattan furnishings. The best units are the cottages out back (no bay views) and four deluxe rooms upstairs that have cathedral ceilings and skylights. The best bet for two couples traveling together is the upstairs Tree House. ⊠ *MM 68.5, BS, Box 839, Layton 33001,* ☎ *305/664–4740 or 800/723–4519,* FAX *305/664–0750,* WEB *www.limetreebayresort.com. 30 rooms. Picnic area, fans, some kitchens, cable TV with movies, tennis court, pool, outdoor hot tub, beach, dive shop, dock, snorkeling, windsurfing, boating, jet skiing, fishing, bicycles, horseshoes, shuffleboard; nosmoking rooms. AE, D, DC, MC, V.*

$ ⚠ **Long Key State Recreation Area.** Trees and shrubs are filling in nicely around tent and RV sites following damage by two hurricanes. Fishing for bonefish, permit (bigger than bonefish), and tarpon remains good in the near-shore flats. All sites have water and electricity. You can reserve up to 11 months in advance by phone or in person. Sites cost $19, plus $2 for electricity. ⊠ *MM 67.5, OS, Box 776, 33001,* ☎ *305/664–4815. 60 sites. Picnic area, beach, fishing, hiking. AE, D, MC, V.*

Outdoor Activities and Sports

At **Lime Tree Water Sports** (⊠ MM 68.5, BS, Lime Tree Bay Resort Motel, ☎ 305/664–0052) you can sign up for sunset cruises, backcountry fishing trips, and snorkeling and scuba excursions or rent a sailboat, powerboat, kayak, sailboard, or Wave Runner. They also offer PADI diving certification and windsurfing and sailing lessons.

En Route   As you cross Long Key Channel, look beside you at the old **Long Key Viaduct.** The second-longest bridge on the former rail line, this 2-mi-long structure has 222 reinforced-concrete arches.

THE MIDDLE KEYS

Stretching from Conch Key to the far side of the Seven Mile Bridge, the Middle Keys contain U.S. 1's most impressive stretch, MM 65–40, bracketed by the Keys' two longest bridges—Long Key Viaduct and Seven Mile Bridge, both historic landmarks. Activity centers on the town of Marathon, the Keys' third-largest metropolitan area.

Fishing and diving are the main attractions. In both bay and ocean, the deepwater fishing is superb at places like the Marathon West Hump, whose depth ranges from 500 to more than 1,000 ft. Anglers successfully fish from a half dozen bridges, including Long Key Bridge, the Old Seven Mile Bridge, and both ends of Toms Harbor. There are also many beaches and natural areas to enjoy in the Middle Keys.

Conch and Duck Keys

6 MM 63–61.

This stretch of islands is rustic. Fishing dominates the economy, and many residents are descendants of immigrants from the mainland South. Across a causeway from Conch Key, a tiny fishing and retirement village, lies Duck Key, an upscale community and resort.

Dining and Lodging

$$–$$$$ ✕ **Waters Edge.** This plush, yet relaxed restaurant at the Hawk's Cay Resort gathers flavors and techniques from the Caribbean, Florida, and Europe. Favorites include St. Thomas, a land-and-sea combo of jumbo shrimp and tournedos of beef, chicken Key West (stuffed with crab, shrimp, and scallops), and Florida stone crab claws (in season), and for dessert mud pie and coconut ice cream. Soup and a 40-item salad bar are included with dinners. You can dine indoors or outdoors. A collection of historic photos on the walls recalls the regional history and the notable visitors. ⊠ *MM 61, OS, Duck Key,* ☎ *305/743–7000. AE, D, DC, MC, V. No lunch mid-Dec.–mid-Apr.*

$$$$ ⊡ **Hawk's Cay Resort.** This rambling Caribbean-style retreat, which
★ opened in 1959, is popular with vacationing families and people looking for a little piece of a tropical paradise. Two-bedroom villas and upgrades improved the tony resort, which has spacious rooms decorated in a light, casual style of wicker and earthy colors. Sports and recreational facilities are extensive, as are supervised programs for kids and teens. The Dolphin Connection provides three educational experiences with dolphins, including the in-the-water Dolphin Discovery program that lets you get up-close and personal with the intelligent mammals. ⊠ *MM 61, OS, 33050,* ☎ *305/743–7000 or 800/432–2242,* ℻ *305/743–5215,* 🖳 *www.hawkscay.com. 160 rooms, 16 suites, 170 2-bedroom villas. 4 restaurants, room service, fans, in-room data ports, some kitchens, refrigerators, cable TV with movies, golf privileges, 8 tennis courts, 5 pools, health club, outdoor hot tub, dive shop, snorkeling, boating, jet skiing, parasailing, waterskiing, fishing, basketball, volleyball, 2 bars, shop, children's programs (ages 5–12), laundry facilities, laundry service, concierge, business services, meeting rooms, airport shuttle, car rental; no-smoking rooms. AE, D, DC, MC, V.*

$$ ⊡ **Conch Key Cottages.** Shrubs covered with brightly colored flowers, palm trees, hammocks, a beach, and ocean breezes evoke the spirit of the tropics at this small, secluded resort comprising a four-plex motel efficiency and lattice-trimmed pastel-color cottages furnished in reed, rattan, and wicker. One- and two-bedroom cottages have kitchens. Three cottages face the beach. Although not on the water, the small honeymoon cottage is very charming. On rare days when the wind shifts, highway noise can be distracting. Complimentary use of a double kayak is included. ⊠ *MM 62.3, OS, R.R. 1, Box 424, Marathon 33050,* ☎ *305/289–1377 or 800/330–1577,* ℻ *305/743–8207,* 🖳 *www.conchkeycottages.com. 12 units. Fans, some kitchenettes, some kitchens, cable TV, some in-room VCRs, pool, beach, dock, snorkeling, laundry facilities; no room phones, no-smoking rooms. D, MC, V.*

Grassy Key

7 MM 60–57.

Local lore has it that this sleepy little key was named not for its vegetation—mostly native trees and shrubs—but for an early settler with the name Grassy. It's primarily inhabited by a few families who operate small fishing camps and motels.

CLOSE ENCOUNTERS OF THE FLIPPER KIND

HERE IN THE FLORIDA KEYS, where Milton Santini created the original 1963 *Flipper* movie, close encounters of the Flipper kind are an everyday occurrence at a handful of facilities that allow you to commune with trained dolphins.

There are in-water and waterside programs. The former are the most sought-after and require advance reservations. All of the programs emphasize education and consist of three parts: first, you learn about dolphin physiology and behavior from a marine biologist or researcher; then you go waterside for an orientation on do's and don'ts (for example, don't talk with your hands—you might, literally, send the wrong signal); finally, you interact with the dolphins—into the water you go.

For the in-water programs, the dolphins swim around you and cuddle up next to you. If you lie on your back with your feet out, they use their snouts to push you around; or you can grab onto a dorsal fin and hang on for an exciting ride. The in-water encounter lasts about 10 to 25 minutes, depending on the program.

On waterside-interaction programs, participants feed, shake hands, kiss, and do tricks with the dolphins from a submerged platform. The programs vary from facility to facility, but share a few rules, and the entire program, from registration to departure, takes about two hours. The best time to go is when it's warm, from March through December. You spend a lot of time near or in and out of the water, and even with a wet suit on you can get cold on a chilly day.

Call ahead to get information on restrictions (there are often age or height requirements) and other relevant details. Also, be wary of programs not listed below. Some industrious types have made a business of chartering boats, chumming the waters, and then letting wild dolphins swim with you—this is very dangerous and can lead to serious injury.

Dolphin Connection at Hawk's Cay Resort. Marine biologists at the Dolphin Connection inspire awareness and promote conservation through programs at this stylish mid-Keys resort. Dolphin Discovery is an in-water, nonswim program that lasts about 45 minutes and lets you kiss, touch, and feed the dolphins. ⊠ *MM 61 OS, 61 Hawks Cay Blvd., Duck Key,* ☎ *888/814–9174.* ⊠ *Cost: $90 resort guests/$100 nonguests.*

Dolphin Cove. The educational part of the Dolphin Encounter program takes place on a 30-minute boat ride on adjoining Florida Bay. Then it's back to the facilities lagoon for a get-acquainted session from a platform. Then you slip into the water for the program's highlight: swimming and playing with your new dolphin pals. ⊠ *101900 Overseas Hwy., MM 101.9, BS, Key Largo,* ☎ *305/ 451–4060,* ⊠ *Cost: $150.*

Dolphin Research Center. This not-for-profit organization is home to a colony of Atlantic bottlenose dolphins and California sea lions. Dolphin Encounter is a swim-interaction program, and in Dolphin Splash you stand on a submerged platform rather than swim. ⊠ *MM 59, Marathon Shores,* ☎ *305/289–1121 or 305/ 289–0002.* ⊠ *Cost: Dolphin Encounter $135, Dolphin Splash $75.*

Dolphins Plus, Inc. Programs here emphasize education and therapy. Natural Swim begins with a one-hour briefing, and then you don snorkel gear and enter the water to become totally immersed in the dolphins' world. ⊠ *31 Corrine Pl., MM 99, Key Largo,* ☎ *305/451–1993 or 866/860–7946.* ⊠ *Cost: $150.*

Theater of the Sea. The Dolphin Swim program at this marine park starts with a 30-minute classroom session and orientation. Then, through a variety of trained behaviors, including kisses, dorsal tows, and jumps, dolphins interact with swimmers in a 15-ft-deep saltwater lagoon. ⊠ *84721 Overseas Hwy., MM 84.7, Islamorada,* ☎ *305/664–2431.* ⊠ *Cost: $125.*

— Diane Marshall

Dolphin Research Center. The original *Flipper* movie popularized the notion of dolphins interacting with humans. The film's creator, Milton Santini, also created this center, now home to a colony of dolphins and sea lions. This not-for-profit organization offers tours, narrated programs every 30 minutes, and several programs that allow you to interact with dolphins in the water (Dolphin Encounter) or from a submerged platform (Dolphin Splash). Some programs have age or height restrictions and some require 30-day advance reservations. ⊠ *MM 59, BS, Box 522875, Marathon Shores 33052,* ☎ *305/289–1121 general information; 305/289–0002 interactive program information,* WEB *www.dolphins. org.* 🎫 *Tours $15, Dolphin Splash $75, Dolphin Encounter $125.* ☉ *Daily 9–4, walking tours daily 10, 11, 12:30, 2, and 3:30.*

OFF THE
BEATEN PATH

CURRY HAMMOCK STATE PARK – This littoral park covers 260 acres of upland hammock, wetlands, and mangroves on the ocean and bay sides of U.S. 1. On the bay side, there's a trail through thick hardwoods to a rocky shoreline. The ocean side is more developed, with a sandy beach, a clean bathhouse, picnic tables, and a parking lot. Brown park signs mark the entrance. Plans for a campground and entrance fees are still undecided. Locals consider the trails that meander under canopies of arching mangroves one of the best areas for kayaking in the Keys. Manatees frequent the area, and it's a birding paradise. Information is provided by Long Key State Recreation Area. ⊠ *MM 57, OS, Crawl Key,* ☎ *305/664–4815.* 🎫 *Free.* ☉ *Daily 8–sunset.*

Dining and Lodging

$–$$ ✕ **Grassy Key DB Seafood Grille.** A casual island menu that's strong on seafood has earned this friendly, family-owned, 1959 restaurant a loyal following of locals and returning visitors. The DB stands for Dairy Bar. Despite the name, the only ice cream served is a yummy ice cream pie. The popular broiled dolphinfish with black beans and rice and cheese sauce is recommended. There are also broiled or grilled fish with wasabi, homemade bread, and fresh-cut beef. On Tuesday night they add Mexican dishes to the menu, and in fall there's OctoberFest with German foods, beers, and music. ⊠ *MM 58.5 OS, 58152 Overseas Hwy.,* ☎ *305/743–3816. MC, V. Closed Sun.–Mon.*

$ ⌂ **Valhalla Beach Motel.** Just steps from the water, this simple motel has clean rooms, efficiencies, and a suite. You can lounge on the beach or read in the Adirondack chairs, grill dinner on a barbecue, or paddle a canoe through mangrove trails in the neighboring state park. It's quiet here, and the views of the undisturbed outdoors are awesome. ⊠ *MM 56.3, OS, 56243 Ocean Dr., Crawl Key 33050,* ☎ *305/289– 0616. 4 rooms, 1 suite, 5 efficiencies. Fans, some kitchens, some refrigerators, cable TV, beach, dock, boating; no room phones. No credit cards.*

$ ⌂ **Valhalla Point.** This unpretentious Crawl Key motel with a to-die-for waterfront location has the feel of a friend's simple beach house. It includes a very good beach with hammocks and chaises, a dock from which manatees are frequently sighted, picnic tables, barbecue grills, and kayaks and canoes, a nice touch since the property borders Curry Hammock State Park. Family-oriented snorkeling trips to the reefs are offered. ⊠ *MM 56.2, OS, 56223 Ocean Dr., Crawl Key 33050,* ☎ *305/289–0614,* WEB *www.keysresort.com. 1 room, 4 efficiencies. Picnic area, some kitchens, cable TV, beach, dock, snorkeling, boating; no room phones. MC, V.*

Marathon

❽ *MM 53–47.5.*

Marathon became an independent municipality in 1999, and now this commercial hub in the Middle Keys is carving out a more visible piece of the local tourist pie. Commercial fishing—still a big local industry—began here in the early 1800s. Pirates, salvagers, fishermen, spongers, and, later, farmers eked out a living, traveling by boat between islands. About half the population were blacks who stoked charcoal furnaces for a living. According to local lore, Marathon was renamed when a worker commented that it was a marathon task to rebuild the railway across the 6-mi island after a 1906 hurricane.

The railroad brought businesses and a hotel, and today Marathon is a bustling town by Keys standards. Fishing, diving, and boating are the primary attractions.

🌀 **Museums and Nature Center of Crane Point Hammock.** Tucked away from the highway behind a stand of trees, Crane Point—part of a 63-acre tract that includes the last-known undisturbed thatch-palm hammock—is an undeveloped oasis of greenery. The complex comprises the **Museum of Natural History of the Florida Keys,** inside of which are a few dioramas, a shell exhibit, and displays on Keys geology, wildlife, and cultural history. Also here is the **Florida Keys Children's Museum,** which has iguanas, fish, and a replica of a 17th-century Spanish galleon and pirate dress-up room where children can play as swashbucklers. Outside, on the 1-mi indigenous loop trail, you can visit the remnants of a Bahamian village, site of the restored **George Adderly House,** the oldest surviving example of Bahamian tabby (a cement-type material created from sand and seashells) construction outside of Key West. A boardwalk crosses wetlands, a river, and mangroves before ending at Adderly Village. From November to Easter, docent-led tours, included in the price, are available; bring good walking shoes and bug repellent during warm weather months. ✉ *MM 50.5, BS, 5550 Overseas Hwy., Box 536, 33050,* ☎ *305/743–9100.* 💲 *$7.50.* ⊙ *Mon.–Sat. 9–5, Sun. noon–5; call to arrange trail tours.*

Sombrero Beach. Pleasant, shaded picnic kiosks overlook a grassy stretch and the Atlantic Ocean here. Separate areas allow swimmers, jet boats, and windsurfers to share the beach. There are lots of facilities, as well as a grassy park with barbecue grills, picnic kiosks, showers, rest rooms, plus a baseball diamond, a large playground, and a volleyball court. The park is accessible for travelers with disabilities and allows leashed pets. Turn left at the traffic light in Marathon and follow signs to the end. ✉ *MM 50, OS, Sombrero Rd.,* ☎ *305/743–0033.* 💲 *Free.* ⊙ *Daily 8–sunset.*

OFF THE BEATEN PATH

PIGEON KEY – There's a lot to like about this 5-acre island under the Old Seven Mile Bridge. It's reached by walking or riding a tram across a 2⅕-mi section of the old bridge. Once there, you can tour the island on your own with a brochure or join a guided tour. The tour explores the buildings that formed the early 20th-century work camp for the Overseas Railroad, which linked the mainland to Key West. Later, their uses changed as the island became a fish camp, then a park, and then government administration headquarters. Today, the focus is on Florida Keys culture, environmental education, and marine research. Exhibits in a museum and a video recall the history of the railroad, the Keys, and railroad baron Henry M. Flagler. Pick up the shuttle at the depot on Knight's Key (✉ *MM 47, OS*). ✉ *MM 45, OS, Box 500130, Pigeon Key 33050,* ☎ *305/289–0025 general information,* 🕸 *www.pigeonkey.org.* 💲 *$8.50.* ⊙ *Daily 9–5.*

Dining and Lodging

$$–$$$$ ✕ **Barracuda Grill.** If you pigeonhole Keys food as grilled fish, Barracuda
★ Grill will be a revelation. The sophisticated, eclectic menu capitalizes
on the local bounty—fresh fish—but is equally represented by tender,
aged Angus beef; rack of lamb; and even braised pork shank. Innova-
tion is in everything but not at the expense of good, solid cooking. Local
favorites include Francesca's voodoo stew with scallops, shrimp, and
veggies in a spicy tomato-saffron stock or sashimi of yellowfin tuna
with wasabi and tamari. Decadent desserts include a rich key lime cheese-
cake. The well-thought-out wine list is heavily Californian. ⊠ *MM 49.5,
BS,* ☎ *305/743–3314. AE, MC, V. Closed Sun. No lunch.*

$–$$$ ✕ **Hurricane Grille.** This roadside restaurant has an attractively priced
menu with generous portions of rib-sticking seafood, chicken, and steaks,
as well as shellfish, which comes steamed (clams, crabs, oysters, shrimp,
lobster) or raw (clams only) from the moment the doors open until the
bar closes, as late as 1:30 AM. Nightly blues and rock bands also en-
liven the place. Satellite TV broadcasts sports, keeping the bar, which
takes up half the building, humming. Alas, they have not yet spruced
up the kitschy decor. ⊠ *MM 49.5, BS, 4650 Overseas Hwy.,* ☎ *305/
743–2220. AE, MC, V.*

$–$$$ ✕ **Key Colony Inn.** The inviting aroma of an Italian kitchen pervades
this popular family-owned restaurant. The menu has well-prepared
chicken, steak, pasta, and veal dishes, and the service is friendly and
attentive. For lunch there are fish and steak entrées served with fries,
salad, and bread. At dinner you can't miss with traditional Continen-
tal dishes like veal Oscar and New York strip or such Italian special-
ties as seafood Italiano, a light dish of scallops and shrimp sautéed in
garlic butter over a bed of linguine with a hint of marinara sauce. ⊠
MM 54, OS, 700 W. Ocean Dr., Key Colony Beach, ☎ *305/743–0100.
AE, MC, V.*

$–$$ ✕ **Island City Fish Market and Eatery.** Nothing about this weathered
gray restaurant says "eat here" as you drive past, but business is brisk
thanks to local recommendations. Half the place is glass cases filled
with fresh-from-the-boat seafood that you can buy to take home or
order to be served at one of the few inside tables or outside picnic tables. Try the barbecue shrimp or fish prepared Provençale style, sautéed
with mushrooms, tomatoes, red peppers, and scallions in garlic wine
sauce or stone crab claws in season. There's a kids' menu and takeout
service as well as nationwide overnight shipping. ⊠ *MM 53, OS,
11711 Overseas Hwy.,* ☎ *305/743–9196 or 888/662–4822. AE, MC,
V. Closed Tues.*

$ ✕ **7 Mile Grill.** This nearly 50-year-old, weatherworn open-air restau-
★ rant easily could serve as a movie set for a 1950s-era black-and-white
movie based in the tropics. At the Marathon end of the Seven Mile Bridge,
it serves up friendly service that rivals the casual food at breakfast, lunch,
and dinner. Favorites on the mostly seafood menu include fresh-
squeezed orange juice, creamy shrimp bisque, and fresh grouper and
dolphinfish grilled, broiled, or fried. Don't pass up the authentic key
lime pie, which won the local paper's "Best in the Keys" award three
years in a row. ⊠ *MM 47, BS,* ☎ *305/743–4481. MC, V. Closed
Wed., plus Thurs. mid-Apr.–mid-Nov., and at owner's discretion Aug.–
Sept.*

$$$ ▥ **Seascape Ocean Resort.** The charming lobby filled with soothing
★ sea colors and original artwork gives way to nine pastel-color guest
rooms decorated with more original artwork, hand-painted head-
boards, and fresh flowers and fruit. Transforming the 5-acre ocean-
front property with a large, two-story bay-front house into an exclusive,
yet unsnobbish retreat was the inspiration of painter Sara Stites and
her husband, Bill, a magazine photographer. You can swim, kayak, or

relax around the pool, at the beach, or under a shade tree. Continental breakfast and afternoon cocktails and hors d'oeuvres are complimentary. ⊠ *MM 50.5, OS, 1075 75th St., 33050,* ☎ *305/743–6455 or 800/332–7327,* ℻ *305/743–8469,* 🕸 *www.floridakeys.net/seascape. 9 rooms. Fans, some kitchens, cable TV, pool, beach, dock, boating, Internet; no room phones, no smoking. AE, MC, V. CP.*

$–$$$ 🏠 **Coral Lagoon.** Private sundecks with hammocks have calming views of a deepwater canal and pretty landscaping. Cheerfully painted duplex cottages have king or twin beds, sofa beds, and lots of extras not usually available at this price, including hair dryers, morning coffee, dockage, barbecues, a video library ($1 rental), and lots of sports equipment. For a fee you can use a private beach club and go on scuba and snorkel trips arranged through the Diving Site, a dive shop that also offers certification. ⊠ *MM 53.5, OS, 12399 Overseas Hwy., 33050,* ☎ *305/289–0121,* ℻ *305/289–0195,* 🕸 *www.corallagoonresort.com. 18 units. Fans, kitchens, cable TV, in-room VCRs, tennis, pool, dive shop, dock, snorkeling, fishing, bicycles, laundry facilities; no-smoking rooms. AE, D, MC, V.*

Outdoor Activities and Sports

BIKING

Tooling around on two wheels is a good way to see Marathon. There are paved paths along Aviation Boulevard on the bay side of Marathon Airport, the four-lane section of the Overseas Highway through Marathon, Sadowski Causeway to Key Colony Beach, Sombrero Beach Road to the beach, and the roads on Boot Key (across a bridge on 20th Street, OS). There's easy cycling on a 1-mi off-road path that connects to the 2 mi of the Old Seven Mile Bridge that go to Pigeon Key.

"Have bikes, will deliver" could be the motto of **Bike Marathon Bike Rentals** (⊠ ☎ 305/743–3204), which delivers beach cruisers to your hotel door for $10 per day, $45 per week, including a helmet. It's open Monday to Saturday 9 to 4 and Sunday 9 to 2.

Equipment Locker Sport & Cycle (⊠ MM 53, BS, ☎ 305/289–1670) rents cruisers for $10 per day, $50 per week, and mountain bikes for adults and children (they do not supply helmets). It's open weekdays 9 to 6.

BOATING

Fish 'n' Fun (⊠ MM 53.5, OS, ☎ 305/743–2275), next to the Boat House Marina, lets you get out on the water on 18- to 25-ft boats starting at $95 for a half day, $135–$205 for a full day. You also can pick up bait, tackle, licenses, and snorkel gear.

FISHING

Morning and afternoon, you can fish for dolphinfish, grouper, and other deep-sea game aboard the 75-ft *Marathon Lady* and the 65-ft *Marathon Lady III* (⊠ MM 53.5, OS, at 117th St., 33050, ☎ 305/743–5580), two party boats that depart on half-day ($30, plus $3 equipment) excursions from the Vaca Cut Bridge, north of Marathon. Captain Jim Purcell, a deep-sea specialist for ESPN's *The Outdoorsman,* provides one of the best values in fishing in the Keys. His **Sea Dog Charters** (⊠ MM 47.5, BS, ☎ 305/743–8255), next to the 7 Mile Grill, have personalized half- and full-day offshore, reef and wreck, tarpon, and backcountry fishing trips as well as combination fishing and snorkeling trips on the 32-ft *Bad Dog* for up to six people. The cost is $59.99 per person for a half day, regardless of whether your group fills the boat, and includes bait, light tackle, licensing, ice, and coolers. If you prefer an all-day private charter on a 37-ft boat, he offers those, too, for $550 to $600.

GOLF

Key Colony Golf & Tennis (✉ MM 53.5, OS, 8th St., Key Colony Beach, ☎ 305/289–1533), a 9-hole course near Marathon, charges $7.50 for the course, $2 per person for club rental, and $1 for a pull cart. There are no tee times and there's no rush. Play from 7:30 to dusk. A little golf shop meets basic golf needs. They have two lighted tennis courts open from 7:30 to 10. Rates are $4 for singles, $6 for doubles.

SCUBA DIVING AND SNORKELING

There's more to diving in the Keys than beautiful reefs. So **Hall's Diving Center and Career Institute** (✉ MM 48.5, BS, 1994 Overseas Hwy., 33050, ☎ 305/743–5929 or 800/331–4255), next to Faro Blanco Resort, runs two trips a day to Looe Key, a few other reefs, and several wrecks, including *Thunderbolt* and the *Adolphus Busch*.

En Route   The **Seven Mile Bridge** is one of the most-photographed images in the Keys. Actually measuring 6.79 mi long, it connects the Middle and Lower keys and is believed to be the world's longest segmental bridge. It has 39 expansion joints separating its concrete sections. Each April, runners gather in Marathon for the annual Seven Mile Bridge Run. The expanse running parallel to it is what remains of the **Old Seven Mile Bridge,** an engineering marvel in its day that's now on the National Register of Historic Places. It rested on a record 546 concrete piers. No cars are allowed on the bridge today, but a 2.2-mi segment is open for biking, walking, and rollerblading with a terminus at historic Pigeon Key.

THE LOWER KEYS

In truth, the Lower Keys include Key West, but since it's covered in its own section and is as different from the rest of the Lower Keys as peanut butter is from jelly, this section covers just the limestone keys between MM 37 and MM 9. From Bahia Honda Key south, islands are clustered, smaller, and more numerous, a result of ancient tidal waters flowing between the Florida Straits and the gulf. Here you're likely to see more birds and mangroves than other tourists, and more refuges, beaches, and campgrounds than museums, restaurants, and hotels.

The islands are made up of two types of limestone, both more dense than the highly permeable Key Largo limestone of the Upper Keys. As a result, freshwater forms pools rather than percolating, creating watering holes that support Key deer, alligators, fish, snakes, Lower Keys rabbits, raccoons, migratory ducks, Key cotton and silver rice rats, pines, saw palmettos, silver palms, grasses, and ferns. (Many of these animals and plants can be seen in the National Key Deer Refuge on Big Pine Key.)

Nature was generous with her beauty in the Lower Keys. They're home to both Looe Key Reef, arguably the Keys' most beautiful coral reef tract, and Bahia Honda State Park, considered one of the best beaches in the world for its fine sand dunes, clear warm waters, and panoramic vista of bridges, hammocks, and azure sky and sea.

Bahia Honda Key

🕒 *MM 38–36.*

★ **Bahia Honda State Park.** This 524-acre sun-soaked, state-owned park sprawls across both sides of the highway, giving it beautiful sandy beaches—the best in the Keys—on both the Atlantic Ocean and the Gulf of Mexico. Although swimming, kayaking, fishing, and boating are the main reasons to come, there are many other activities, including walks on the Silver Palm Trail, where you can see rare West Indian plants and several species found nowhere else in the Keys, and seasonal ranger-led nature programs, including illustrated talks on the history of the Overseas Railroad and birding outings. There are rental cabins, a campground, a snack bar, a marina, and a concessioner for snorkeling. You can get a panoramic view of the island from what's left of the railroad—the Bahia Honda Bridge. ⊠ *MM 37, OS, 36850 Overseas Hwy., 33043,* ☎ *305/872–2353,* WEB *www.dep.state.fl.us/parks.* ⌑ *$2.50 for 1 person, $5 per vehicle for 2–8 people plus 50¢ per person county surcharge; $1.50 per pedestrian or bicyclist.* ⊙ *Daily 8–sunset.*

Lodging

$$ ⬚ **Bahia Honda State Park.** You usually have to pay big bucks for the caliber of water views from the cabins here. Each cabin is completely furnished (although there's no television, radio, or phone); has two bedrooms, full kitchen, and bath; and sleeps six. The park also has popular campsites (from $19 per night), suitable for motor homes and tents. Cabins and campsites usually book up early, so reserve up to 11 months before your planned visit. ⊠ *MM 37, OS, 36850 Overseas Hwy., 33043,* ☎ *305/872–2353 or 800/326–3521,* WEB *www.dep.state.fl.us/ parks. 3 duplex cabins, 80 campsites. Picnic area, beach, boating, fishing. AE, D, MC, V.*

Outdoor Activities and Sports

Bahia Honda Dive Shop (⊠ MM 37, OS, ☎ 305/872–3210), the concessionaire at Bahia Honda State Park, manages a 19-slip marina, rents wet suits, snorkel equipment, and corrective masks, and operates twice-a-day offshore-reef snorkel trips ($26 plus $5 for equipment) that run almost three hours (with 90 minutes on the reef). Park visitors looking for other fun can rent kayaks ($10 per hour single, $18 double), bicycles, fishing rods, and beach chairs.

Big Pine Key

🔟 *MM 32–30.*

National Key Deer Refuge. In the Florida Keys, more than 20 animals and plants are endangered or threatened. Among them is the Key deer, which stands about 30 inches at the shoulders and is a subspecies of the Virginia white-tailed deer. The 8,354-acre refuge was established in 1957 to protect the dwindling population of Key deer. Under the refuge's aegis the deer have made a comeback, more than doubling their numbers to around 800. These deer once ranged throughout the Lower and Middle keys, but hunting, habitat destruction, and a growing human population had caused their numbers to decline to fewer than 50. The best place to see Key deer in the refuge is at the end of Key Deer Boulevard (Route 940), off U.S. 1, and on No Name Key, a sparsely populated island just east of Big Pine Key. Deer may turn up along the road at any time of day, so drive slowly. Feeding them is against the law. The **Blue Hole,** a quarry left over from railroad days, is the largest body of freshwater in the Keys. From the observation platform and nearby walking trail, you might see alligators, birds, turtles, Key deer, and other wildlife. There are two well-marked trails: the Jack Watson Nature Trail (⅔ mi), named after an environmentalist and the refuge's first warden; and the Fred Mannillo Nature Trail, one of the most wheelchair-accessible places to see an unspoiled pine rockland forest. The visitor center has exhibits on Keys biology and ecology. The refuge also provides information on the Key West National Wildlife Refuge and the Great White Heron National Wildlife Refuge. Both, accessible only by water, are popular with kayak outfitters. ⊠ *Visitor Center/Headquarters, Big Pine Shopping Center, MM 30.5, BS,* ☎ *305/*

872–0774. ☒ *Free.* ☉ *Daily sunrise–sunset; headquarters weekdays 8–5.*

Dining and Lodging

$ ✕ **No Name Pub.** If you don't like change you'll be delighted by this ramshackle American-casual establishment in existence since 1936. Locals come for the cold beer, excellent pizza, and sometimes questionable companionship. The owners have conceded to the times by introducing a full menu, adding "city food" like pasta and chicken wings. (Real Keys men don't eat chicken wings.) The lighting is poor, the furnishings are rough, and the jukebox doesn't play Ricky Martin. It's hard to find but worth the search if you want to experience the Keys as old-timers say they once were. ☒ *MM 30, BS, N. Watson Blvd., turn north at Big Pine Key traffic light, right at the fork, left at the four-way stop, and then over a humpback bridge; pub is on the left, before the No Name Bridge,* ☎ *305/872–9115. D, MC, V.*

$$–$$$ ⊡ **The Barnacle.** With very little air pollution in the area, the star-flecked
★ moonlit nights seen from this bed-and-breakfast's atrium are as romantic as the sunny days spent lazing on the beach. Owners Tim and Jane Marquis offer two second-floor rooms in the main house; one in a cottage with a kitchen; another, below the house, that opens to the beach; and a smaller fifth room with skylights on the roof. Guest rooms are large. As former owners of a diving business, Tim and Jane offer personalized snorkel and dive charters and fishing excursions. ☒ *MM 33, OS, 1557 Long Beach Dr., 33043,* ☎ *305/872–3298 or 800/465–9100,* ℻ *305/872–3863,* ⬛ *www.thebarnacle.net. 5 rooms. Fans, some kitchens, refrigerators, cable TV, outdoor hot tub, beach, dive shop, snorkeling, boating, bicycles; no kids, no smoking. D, MC, V. BP.*

$$–$$$ ⊡ **Deer Run.** Enjoy Florida wildlife up close at this 2-acre beachfront B&B. A herd of Key deer regularly forages along the beach a few feet from the back door. Innkeeper Sue Abbott also keeps a variety of cats and caged tropical birds. She is caring and informed, well settled and hospitable. Two large oceanfront rooms are furnished with white-washed wicker and king-size beds. An upstairs unit looks out on the sea through trees. Guests share a living room, 52-ft veranda cooled by paddle fans, hammocks, a barbecue grill, and water toys. ☒ *MM 33, OS, 1985 Long Beach Dr., Box 430431, 33043,* ☎ *305/872–2015,* ℻ *305/872–2842,* ⬛ *floridakeys.net/deer. 3 room. Fans, cable TV, outdoor hot tub, beach, boating, bicycles; no kids, no smoking. No credit cards. BP.*

$$ ⊡ **Casa Grande.** On a beautiful white-sand beach abutting a rocky shore-
★ line, this adults-only B&B offers a gracious island stay under the proprietorship of Kathleen Threlkeld. Her warm personality pervades the Mediterranean-style house with a massive Spanish door, mainly contemporary furnishings, and high open-beam ceilings. The spacious guest rooms have screened porches and rich Berber carpeting. A screened, second-story waterfront atrium provides you the opportunity to gaze out across the soothing sea. Then on cool nights, you can cozy up to the sitting-room fireplace or watch TV. ☒ *MM 33, OS, 1619 Long Beach Dr., Box 430378, 33043,* ☎ *305/872–2878,* ⬛ *www.floridakeys. net/casagrande. 3 rooms. Picnic area, fans, refrigerator, cable TV, hot tub, beach, dock, snorkeling, windsurfing, boating, bicycles; no kids, no smoking. No credit cards. BP.*

$–$$ ⊡ **Big Pine Key Fishing Lodge.** It's a family affair at this 30-year-old
★ combination lodge and campground. Rooms and sites ($30–$37 per site) are attractively priced and have tile floors, wicker furniture, doors that allow sea breezes to blow through, queen-size beds, a second-bedroom loft, and vaulted ceilings. A skywalk joins them with a pool and deck. Immaculately clean tile lines the spacious bathhouse for campers.

Separate game and recreation rooms house TVs, organized family-oriented activities, and other amusements, and there is dockage along a 735-ft canal. A three-day minimum is required. Discounts on weekly/monthly stays. ⊠ *MM 33, OS, Box 430513, 33043,* ☎ *305/ 872–2351,* FAX *305/872–3868. 16 rooms, 158 campsites, 102 with full hookups, 56 without hookups. Picnic area, some kitchens, cable TV, pool, dock, boating, billiards, Ping-Pong, shuffleboard, recreation room, Internet. D, MC, V.*

Outdoor Activities and Sports

BIKING

A good 10 mi of paved and unpaved roads run from MM 30.3, BS, along Wilder Road, across the bridge to No Name Key, and along Key Deer Boulevard into the National Key Deer Refuge. You might see some Key deer. Stay off the trails that lead into wetlands, where fat tires can do damage to the environment.

Marty Baird, owner of **Big Pine Bicycle Center** (⊠ MM 30.9, BS, ☎ 305/872–0130), is an avid rider and enjoys sharing his knowledge of great places to ride. He's also skilled in repairing and selecting the right bike for customers to rent or purchase. His old-fashioned single-speed, fat-tire cruisers for adults rent for $6 per half day, $9 for a full day, and $34 a week, second week $17; children for $5, $7, $26, and $13. Helmets, baskets, and locks are included. Join him at the shop Sunday mornings at 8 in winter for a free off-road fun ride.

FISHING

You can fish with pros year-round in air-conditioned comfort with **Strike Zone Charters** (⊠ MM 29.6, BS, 29675 Overseas Hwy., 33043, ☎ 305/ 872–9863 or 800/654–9560). Charter rates are $450 for a half day, $595 for a full day.

Little Torch Key

⓫ *MM 28–29.*

With a few exceptions, this key and its neighbor islands are more jumping-off points for divers headed for Looe Key Reef, a few miles offshore, than destinations themselves.

NEED A BREAK? The intoxicating aroma of rich, roasting coffee beans at **Baby's Coffee** (⊠ MM 15, OS, Saddlebunch Keys, ☎ 305/744–9866 or 800/523–2326) arrests you at the door of "the Southernmost Coffee Roaster." Buy it by the pound or by the cup along with fresh-baked goods. While sipping your warm joe, browse through the prints of Olga Manosalvas, whose work appears in tony galleries from Key West to the Hamptons. There's also a gourmet foods section and an arts and crafts fair on the first Saturday of each month.

The undeveloped backcountry is at your door, making this an ideal location for fishing and kayaking, too. Nearby **Ramrod Key**, which also caters to divers bound for Looe Key, derives its name from a ship that wrecked on nearby reefs in the early 1800s.

Dining and Lodging

$$$$ × **Little Palm Restaurant.** The waterfront dining room at the exclusive
★ Little Palm Island resort is one of the most romantic spots in the Keys. Chef Adam Votaw has crafted the contemporary menu to reflect a mix of Caribbean, French, and Asian tastes with dishes such as Gruyere cheese soufflé, barbecued salmon, lobster croissants, and duck in bonito tuna broth. The dining room is open to nonguests on a reservations-only basis. The tropical Sunday brunch buffet is the most

popular time to come. ✉ *MM 28.5, OS, 28500 Overseas Hwy., 33042,* ☎ *305/872–2551. Reservations essential. AE, D, DC, MC, V.*

$–$$ ✕ **Montes Restaurant & Fish Market.** In this gray wood-frame building with screened sides, a canvas roof, wood-plank floors, a tropical mural, and picnic tables, they serve a traditional Keys-style fish sandwich, either grilled dolphinfish or fried grouper, depending on what's fresh, along with a flavorful variation stuffed with crabmeat. Casually clad, experienced waitresses provide good service. The menu also has crabs and shrimp that are steamed, broiled, stuffed, or fried. ✉ *MM 25, BS, Summerland Key,* ☎ *305/745–3731. No credit cards.*

$$$$ 🏨 **Little Palm Island.** *Haute tropical* best describes this luxury retreat ★ on a 5-acre palm-fringed island 3 mi offshore. The decor of the 28 oceanfront one-bedroom, thatch-roof bungalow suites is laid-back luxe, with Mexican-tile baths, mosquito netting–draped king beds, and wicker and rattan furniture. Other comforts include an indoor and outdoor shower, private veranda, a separate living room, and robes and slippers. Two Island Grand Suites are twice the size of the others and offer his and her bathrooms, an outdoor hot tub, and uncompromising ocean views. Cellular phones are *verboten* in public areas. ✉ *MM 28.5, OS, 28500 Overseas Hwy., 33042,* ☎ *305/872–2524 or 800/ 343–8567,* FAX *305/872–4843,* WEB *www.littlepalmisland.com. 30 suites. Restaurant, fans, in-room data ports, in-room safes, some in-room hot tubs, minibars, pool, health club, hair salon, massage, sauna, spa, beach, dive shop, dock, snorkeling, windsurfing, boating, marina, fishing, bar, library, shops, concierge, airport shuttle; no room phones, no room TVs, no kids under 16. AE, D, DC, MC, V.*

$–$$ 🏨 **Parmer's Place.** This is the perfect spot for a family getaway in the ★ Lower Keys. You'll stay in family-style waterfront cottages with a deck or balcony. It's spread out on 5 landscaped acres, so the kids have room to play. And the price is right. Lots of families agree. Many are repeat guests and recommend it. The proprietors treat them all like family, right down to sending out more than 10,000 holiday cards every December. For couples, the motel rooms are comfortable for two people and the best buy. There are water activities galore and a sunny breakfast room. ✉ *MM 29, BS, 565 Barry Ave., 33042,* ☎ *305/872–2157,* FAX *305/872–2014,* WEB *www.parmersplace.com. 45 units, 18 rooms, 12 efficiencies, 13 apartments. Dining room, fans, some kitchens, cable TV, pool, dock, boating, bicycles, laundry facilities, Internet; no room phones, no-smoking rooms. AE, D, MC, V. CP.*

Outdoor Activities and Sports

FISHING

The only thing grouchy about Captain Mark André of **The Grouch Charters** (✉ Summerland Key Cove Marina, MM 24.5, OS, Summerland Key, ☎ 305/745–1172 or 305/304–0039) is his boat's name, derived from his father's nickname. This knowledgeable captain takes up to six passengers on offshore fishing trips ($450 for a half day, $625 for a full day). He also has oceanfront vacation rentals for $725–$850 a week and can package accommodations, fishing, snorkeling, and sightseeing for better deals.

SCUBA DIVING AND SNORKELING

In 1744, the HMS *Looe*, a British warship, ran aground and sank on one of the most beautiful and diverse coral reefs in the Keys. Today, **Looe Key Reef** owes its name to the ill-fated ship. The 5.3-square-nautical-mi reef, part of the **Florida Keys National Marine Sanctuary** (✉ MM 27.5, OS, 216 Ann St., Key West 33040, ☎ 305/292–0311), has stands of elk-horn coral on its eastern margin, purple sea fans, and abundant sponges and sea urchins. On its seaward side, it drops almost vertically 50–90 ft. Snorkelers and divers will find the sanctuary a quiet place to observe reef life, except in July, when the annual Underwater Music Festival pays homage to Looe Key's beauty and promotes reef awareness with six hours of music broadcast via underwater speakers. Dive shops and private charters transport hundreds of divers to hear the spectacle, which includes Caribbean, classical, jazz, New Age, and, of course, Jimmy Buffett.

Rather than the customary morning and afternoon two-tank, two-location trips offered by most dive shops, **Looe Key Reef Resort Dive Center** (⊠ MM 27.5, OS, Box 509, Ramrod Key 33042, ☎ 305/872–2215 Ext. 2 or 800/942–5397), the closest dive shop to Looe Key Reef, runs a single three-tank, three-location dive from 10 AM to 3 PM. The maximum depth is 30 ft, so snorkelers and divers go on the same boat. On Saturday and Wednesday, they run a dive on wrecks and reefs in the area. It's part of the full-service Looe Key Reef Resort, which, not surprisingly, caters to divers. The dive boat, a 45-ft Corinthian catamaran, is docked outside the hotel, whose guests get a 15% discount on tanks, weights, and snorkeling equipment.

Strike Zone Charters (⊠ MM 29.6, BS, 29675 Overseas Hwy., Big Pine Key 33043, ☎ 305/872–9863 or 800/654–9560) offers dive trips to two sites on Looe Key, resort courses, and various certifications. The outfit uses glass-bottom boats, so nondivers can experience the reef, too.

En Route   The huge object that looks like a white whale floating over Cudjoe Key (⊠ MM 23–21) is not a figment of your imagination. It's Fat Albert, a radar balloon that monitors local air and water traffic.

KEY WEST

MM 4–0.

Situated 150 mi from Miami and just 90 mi from Havana, this tropical island city has always maintained a strong sense of detachment, even after it was connected to the rest of the United States—by the railroad in 1912 and by the Overseas Highway in 1938.

The U.S. government acquired Key West from Spain in 1821 along with the rest of Florida. The Spanish had named the island Cayo Hueso (Bone Key) after the Native American skeletons they found on its shores. In 1823 Uncle Sam sent Commodore David S. Porter to chase pirates away.

For three decades, the primary industry in Key West was wrecking— rescuing people and salvaging cargo from ships that foundered on the nearby reefs. According to some reports, when pickings were lean, the wreckers hung out lights to lure ships aground. Their business declined after 1849, when the federal government began building lighthouses.

In 1845 the army started construction of Fort Taylor, which held Key West for the Union during the Civil War. After the war, an influx of Cuban dissidents unhappy with Spain's rule brought the cigar industry here. Fishing, shrimping, and sponge-gathering became important industries, and a pineapple-canning factory opened. Major military installations were established during the Spanish-American War and World War I. Through much of the 19th century and into the second decade of the 20th, Key West was Florida's wealthiest city in percapita terms.

In 1929 the local economy began to unravel. Modern ships no longer needed to provision in Key West, cigar making moved to Tampa, Hawaii dominated the pineapple industry, and the sponges succumbed to a blight. Then the depression hit, and the military moved out. By

1934 half the population was on relief. The city defaulted on its bond payments, and the Federal Emergency Relief Administration took over the city and county governments.

By promoting Key West as a tourist destination, federal officials attracted 40,000 visitors during the 1934–35 winter season, but when the 1935 Labor Day hurricane struck the Middle Keys, it wiped out the railroad and the tourist trade.

An important naval center during World War II and the Korean conflict, the island remains a strategic listening post on the doorstep of Fidel Castro's Cuba. It was during the 1960s that the fringes of society began moving here and in the mid-'70s that gay guest houses began opening in rapid succession.

In April 1982 the U.S. Border Patrol threw a roadblock across the Overseas Highway just south of Florida City to catch drug runners and illegal aliens. Traffic backed up for miles as Border Patrol agents searched vehicles and demanded that the occupants prove U.S. citizenship. City officials in Key West, outraged at being treated like foreigners by the federal government, staged a mock secession and formed their own "nation," the so-called Conch Republic. They hoisted a flag and distributed mock border passes, visas, and Conch currency. The embarrassed Border Patrol dismantled its roadblock, and now an annual festival recalls the secessionists' victory.

Key West reflects a diverse population: native "Conchs" (white Key Westers, many of whom trace their ancestry to the Bahamas), freshwater Conchs (longtime residents who migrated from somewhere else years ago), gays (who now make up at least 20% of Key West's citizenry), black Bahamians (descendants of those who worked the railroads and burned charcoal), Hispanics (primarily Cuban immigrants), recent refugees from the urban sprawl of mainland Florida, navy and air force personnel, and an assortment of vagabonds, drifters, and dropouts in search of refuge.

The island is decidedly gay friendly. It's not unusual to see gay couples holding hands or to see advertisements aimed at gay customers. Although gay men and lesbians will feel welcome in almost all establishments, there are numerous accommodations, restaurants, clubs, businesses, and visitor information services that cater exclusively to a gay clientele.

Although the rest of the Keys are more oriented to nature and the outdoors, Key West has more of a city feel. Few open spaces remain, as promoters continue to foster fine restaurants, galleries, shops, and museums to interpret the city's intriguing past. As a tourist destination, Key West has a lot to sell—an average temperature of 79°F, quaint 19th-century architecture, and a laid-back lifestyle. There's also a growing calendar of festivals and artistic and cultural events—including the Conch Republic Celebration in April and a Halloween Fantasy Fest. Few cities of its size—a mere 2 mi by 4 mi—offer the joie de vivre of this one.

Yet, as elsewhere, when preservation has successfully revived once-tired towns, next have come those unmindful of style and eager for a buck. Duval Street can look like a strip mall of T-shirt shops and tour shills. Mass marketers directing the town's tourism have attracted cruise ships, which dwarf the town's skyline, and Duval Street floods with day-trippers who gawk at the earringed hippies with dogs in their bike baskets, gay couples walking down the street holding hands, and the oddball lot of locals.

Old Town

The heart of Key West, this historic area runs from White Street west to the waterfront. Beginning in 1822, wharves, warehouses, chandleries, ship-repair facilities, and eventually in 1891 the U.S. Custom House sprang up around the deep harbor to accommodate the navy's large ships and other sailing vessels. Wealthy wreckers, merchants, and sea captains built lavish houses near the bustling waterfront. A remarkable number of these fine Victorian and pre-Victorian structures have been restored to their original grandeur and now serve as homes, guest houses, and museums. These, along with the dwellings of famous writers, artists, and politicians who've come to Key West over the past 175 years, are among the area's approximately 3,000 historic structures. Old Town also has the city's finest restaurants and hotels, lively street life, and popular nightspots.

A Good Tour

To cover a lot of sights, take the Old Town Trolley, which lets you get off and reboard a later trolley, or the Conch Tour Train. Old Town is also very manageable on foot, bicycle, or moped, but be warned that the tour below covers a lot of ground. You'll want either to pick and choose from it or break it into two days.

Start on Whitehead Street at the **Hemingway House** ⑫, the author's former home, and then cross the street and climb to the top of the **Lighthouse Museum** ⑬ for a spectacular view. Exit through the museum's parking lot and cross Truman Avenue to the **Lofton B. Sands African-Bahamian Museum** ⑭ to learn about nearly two centuries of black history in Key West. Return to Whitehead Street and follow it north to Angela Street, then turn right. At Margaret Street, the **City Cemetery** ⑮ has above-ground vaults and unusual headstone inscriptions. Head north on Margaret to Southard Street, turn left, then right onto Simonton Street. Halfway up the block, Free School Lane is occupied by **Nancy Forrester's Secret Garden** ⑯. After touring this tropical haven, return west on Southard to Duval Street and turn right, where you can view the lovely tiles and woodwork in the **San Carlos Institute** ⑰. Return again to Southard Street, turn right, and follow it through Truman Annex to **Fort Zachary Taylor State Historic Site** ⑱; after viewing the fort, you can take a dip at the beach.

Go back to Simonton Street and walk north, then turn left on Caroline Street, where you can climb to the widow's walk on top of **Curry Mansion** ⑲. A left on Duval Street puts you in front of the **Duval Street Wreckers Museum** ⑳, Key West's oldest house. Continue west into Truman Annex to see the **Harry S. Truman Little White House Museum** ㉑, President Truman's vacation residence. Return east on Caroline and turn left on Whitehead to visit the **Audubon House and Gardens** ㉒, honoring the artist-naturalist. Follow Whitehead north to Greene Street and turn left to see the salvaged sea treasures of the **Mel Fisher Maritime Heritage Society Museum** ㉓. At Whitehead's north end are the **Key West Aquarium** ㉔ and the **Key West Museum of Art and History** ㉕, the former historic U.S. Custom House.

By late afternoon you should be ready to cool off with a dip or catch a few rays at the beach. (Heed signs about the water's condition.) From the aquarium, head east two blocks to the end of Simonton Street, where you'll find the appropriately named **Simonton Street Beach** ㉖. On the Atlantic side of Old Town is **South Beach** ㉗, named for its location at the southern end of Duval Street. If you've brought your pet, stroll a few blocks east to **Dog Beach** ㉘, at the corner of Vernon and Waddell streets. A little farther east is **Higgs Beach–Astro Park** ㉙, on Atlantic

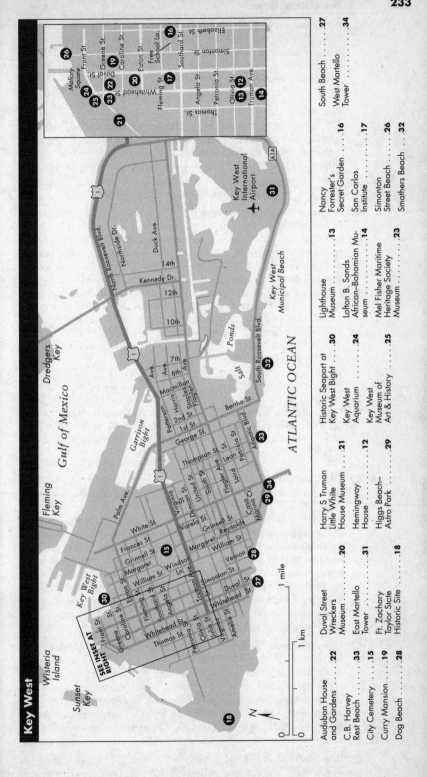

Key West

Wisteria
Island

Sunset
Key

Gulf of Mexico

Fleming
Key

Dredgers
Key

Garrison
Bight

North Roosevelt Blvd.

Northside Dr.

Duck Ave.

14th
Kennedy Dr.
12th
10th

Ponds

Salt

Key West
Municipal Beach

South Roosevelt Blvd.

ATLANTIC OCEAN

Key West
International
Airport

A1A

Key West Bight

Palm Ave.

White St.

Frances St.
Grinnell St.
Margaret
William St.

Windsor Ln.
Simonton St.

Eaton St.
Fleming St.
Southard St.
Angela St.

Front St.
Greene St.
Caroline St.
Whitehead St.
Thomas St.
Petronia St.
Olivia St.
Julia St.
Virginia St.
Amelia St.

Duval St.
Whitehead St.

Truman Ave.

Varela St.
Grinnell St.
Reynolds
William St.
Vernon

Virginia St.
Duncan St.
United St.
South St.
Flagler Ave.
Leon
Patricia St.

Atlantic Blvd.

Bertha St.

George St.

Thompson St.

Ave.
7th
6th Ave.

Macmillan
Flagler
2nd St.
Staples
Harris
Patterson
1st St.

SEE INSET AT
RIGHT

N

1 mile
1 km

Audubon House
and Gardens **22**

C.B. Harvey
Rest Beach **33**

City Cemetery **15**

Curry Mansion ...**19**

Dog Beach **28**

Duval Street
Wreckers
Museum **20**

East Martello
Tower **31**

Ft. Zachary
Taylor State
Historic Site **18**

Harry S Truman
Little White
House Museum ...**21**

Hemingway
House **12**

Higgs Beach–
Astro Park **29**

Historic Seaport at
Key West Bight ...**30**

Key West
Aquarium **24**

Key West
Museum of
Art & History **25**

Lighthouse
Museum **13**

Lofton B. Sands
African–Bahamian Mu-
seum **14**

Mel Fisher Maritime
Heritage Society
Museum **23**

Nancy
Forrester's
Secret Garden **16**

San Carlos
Institute **17**

Simonton
Street Beach **26**

Smathers Beach ...**32**

South Beach **27**

West Martello
Tower **34**

Boulevard between White and Reynolds streets. As the sun starts to sink, return to the north end of Old Town and follow the crowds to Mallory Square, behind the aquarium, to watch Key West's nightly sunset spectacle. For dinner, head east on Caroline Street to **Historic Seaport at Key West Bight** ㉚ (formerly known simply as Key West Bight), a renovated area where there are numerous restaurants and bars.

TIMING

Allow two full days to see all the Old Town museums and homes, especially with a little shopping thrown in. For a narrated trip on the tour train or trolley, budget 1½ hours to ride the loop without getting off, an entire day if you plan to get off and on at some of the sights and restaurants.

Sights to See

㉒ **Audubon House and Gardens.** If you've ever seen an engraving by ornithologist John James Audubon, you'll understand why his name is synonymous with birds. You can see his work in this three-story house, which was built in the 1840s for Captain John Geiger, but now commemorates Audubon's 1832 stop in Key West while he was traveling through Florida to study birds. Several rooms of period antiques and a children's room are also of interest. Admission includes an audiotape (in English, French, German, or Spanish) for a self-guided tour of the house and tropical gardens, complemented by an informational booklet and signs that identify the rare indigenous plants and trees. ⊠ *205 Whitehead St.,* ☎ *305/294–2116,* WEB *audubonhouse.com.* ✆ *$8.50.* ☉ *Daily 9:30–5.*

NEED A
BREAK?

For a partying kind of town, Key West restaurants are oddly unaccommodating for those looking for breakfast at noon, or dinner at midnight. If your appetite is out of sync with most serving schedules, **Iguana Cafe** (⊠ 425C Greene St., ☎ 305/296–6420) will come to the rescue 24 hours a day. Just off Duval Street, the simple shacklike dive puts out tasty recipes from around the globe.

★ ⑮ **City Cemetery.** You can learn almost as much about a town's history through its cemetery as through its historic houses. Key West's celebrated 20-acre burial place is no exception. Among the interesting plots are a memorial to the sailors killed in the sinking of the battleship U.S.S. *Maine,* carved angels and lambs marking graves of children, and grand above-ground crypts. There are separate plots for Catholics, Jews, and martyrs of Cuba. Although you can walk around the cemetery on your own, the best way to take it in is on a 60-minute tour given by the staff and volunteers of the Historic Florida Keys Foundation. Tours leave from the main gate, and reservations are required. ⊠ *Margaret and Angela Sts.,* ☎ *305/292–6718.* ✆ *$10.* ☉ *Sunrise–6, tours Tues. and Thurs. 9:30; call for additional times.*

⑲ **Curry Mansion.** See the opulence enjoyed by Key West's 19th-century millionaires in this well-preserved 22-room house. It was begun by William Curry, a ship salvager and Key West's first millionaire, and completed in 1899 by his son, Milton Curry. The owners have restored most of the house and turned it into a B&B. Take an unhurried self-guided tour; a brochure describes the home's history and contents. ⊠ *511 Caroline St.,* ☎ *305/294–5349,* WEB *currymansion.com.* ✆ *$5.* ☉ *Daily 10–5.*

㉘ **Dog Beach.** Next to Louie's Backyard, this small beach—the only one in Key West where dogs are allowed—has a shore that's a mix of sand and rocks. ⊠ *Vernon and Waddell Sts.,* ☎ *no phone.* ✆ *Free.* ☉ *Daily sunrise–sunset.*

❷⓿ Duval Street Wreckers Museum. Most of Key West's early wealthy residents made their fortunes from the sea. Among them was Francis Watlington, a sea captain and wrecker, who in 1829 built this house, alleged to be the oldest house in South Florida. Six rooms are open, furnished with 18th- and 19th-century antiques and providing exhibits on the island's wrecking industry of the 1800s, which made Key West one of the most affluent towns in the country. ✉ *322 Duval St.,* ☎ *305/294–9502.* ⌦ *$5.* ☾ *Daily 10–4.*

★ **⓲ Ft. Zachary Taylor State Historic Site.** Construction of the fort began in 1845, and in 1861, even though Florida seceded from the Union during the Civil War, Yankee forces used the fort as a base to block Confederate shipping (more than 1,500 Confederate vessels were detained in Key West's harbor). The fort, finally completed in 1866, was also used in the Spanish-American War. You can take a 30-minute tour of this National Historic Landmark. In February, a weekend celebration called Civil War Days includes costumed reenactments and demonstrations. Its uncrowded beach is the best in Key West. There is an adjoining picnic area with barbecue grills and shade trees. ✉ *End of Southard St., through Truman Annex,* ☎ *305/292–6713,* 🕸 *www.forttaylor.com.* ⌦ *$2.50 per person for first 2 people in vehicle plus 50¢ each additional up to $8, then $1 each additional; $1.50 per pedestrian or bicyclist.* ☾ *Daily 8–sunset, tours noon and 2.*

❷⓵ Harry S. Truman Little White House Museum. In a letter to his wife during one of his visits, President Harry S. Truman wrote, "Dear Bess, you should see the house. The place is all redecorated, new furniture and everything." If he visited today, he'd write something similar. The museum includes a photographic review of visiting dignitaries and permanent audiovisual and artifact exhibits on the Florida Keys as a presidential retreat, starting with Ulysses Grant in 1880 and ending with George Bush in the 1990s. Tours begin every 15 minutes. Located on the grounds of **Truman Annex,** a 103-acre former military parade grounds and barracks, the home served as a winter White House for presidents Truman, Eisenhower, and Kennedy. The two-bedroom Presidential Suite with a veranda and sundeck is available for a novelty overnight stay. ✉ *111 Front St.,* ☎ *305/294–9911,* 🕸 *www.trumanlittlewhitehouse.com.* ⌦ *$10.* ☾ *Daily 9–5, grounds 8–sunset.*

★ **⓬ Hemingway House.** Guided tours of Ernest Hemingway's home are full of anecdotes about the author's life in the community and his household quarrels with wife Pauline. While living here between 1931 and 1942, Hemingway wrote about 70% of his life's work, including *For Whom the Bell Tolls.* Few of the family's belongings remain, but photographs help illustrate his life, and scores of descendants of Hemingway's cats have free rein of the property. Literary buffs should be aware that there are no curated exhibits from which to gain much insight into Hemingway's writing career. Tours begin every 10 minutes and take 25–30 minutes; then you're free to explore on your own. ✉ *907 Whitehead St.,* ☎ *305/294–1575,* 🕸 *www.hemingwayhome.com.* ⌦ *$9.* ☾ *Daily 9–5.*

☙ **❷⓽ Higgs Beach–Astro Park.** This Monroe County park is a popular sunbathing spot. A nearby grove of Australian pines provides shade, and the West Martello Tower provides shelter should a storm suddenly sweep in. Across the street, **Astro Park** is a popular children's playground. ✉ *Atlantic Blvd. between White and Reynolds Sts.,* ☎ *no phone.* ⌦ *Free.* ☾ *Daily 6 AM–11 PM.*

❸⓿ Historic Seaport at Key West Bight. What used to be a funky—in some places even seedy—part of town, is now an 8½-acre historic restora-

Close-Up

HEMINGWAY WAS HERE

IN A TOWN WHERE Pulitzer Prize–winning writers are almost as common as coconuts, Ernest Hemingway stands out. Bars and restaurants around the island boast that he ate or drank there, and though he may not have been at all of them, like all legends his larger-than-life image continues to grow.

Hemingway came to Key West in 1928 at the urging of writer John dos Passos and rented a house with wife number two, Pauline Pfeiffer. They spent winters in the Keys and summers in Europe and Wyoming, occasionally taking African safaris. Along the way they had two sons, Patrick and Gregory. In 1931 Pauline's wealthy uncle Gus gave the couple the house at 907 Whitehead Street, now known as Hemingway House and Key West's number one tourist attraction. They renovated the palatial home, added a swimming pool, and put in a tropical garden with peacocks.

In 1935, when the visitor bureau included the house in a tourist brochure, Hemingway promptly built the high brick wall that surrounds it today. He wrote of the visitor bureau's offense in a 1935 essay for *Esquire*, saying, "The house at present occupied by your correspondent is listed as number eighteen in a compilation of the forty-eight things for a tourist to see in Key West. So there will be no difficulty in a tourist finding it or any other of the sights of the city, a map has been prepared by the local F.E.R.A. authorities to be presented to each arriving visitor . . . This is all very flattering to the easily bloated ego of your correspondent but very hard on production."

During his time in Key West, Hemingway penned some of his most important works, including *A Farewell to Arms*, *To Have and Have Not*, *Green Hills of Africa*, and *Death in the Afternoon*. His rigorous schedule consisted of writing almost every morning in his second-story studio above the pool, then promptly descending the stairs at midday. By afternoon and evening he was ready for drinking, fishing, swimming, boxing, and hanging around with the boys.

One close friend was Joe Russell, a craggy fisherman and owner of the rugged bar Sloppy Joe's, originally at 428 Greene Street but now at 201 Duval Street. Russell was the only one in town who would cash Hemingway's $1,000 royalty check. Russell and Charles Thompson introduced him to deep-sea fishing, which became fodder for his writing. Another of Hemingway's loves was boxing. He set up a ring in his yard and paid local fighters to box with him as well as refereeing matches at Blue Heaven, then a saloon but now a restaurant, at 729 Thomas Street.

Feeling at home among Key West's characters, Hemingway honed his macho image dressed in cutoffs and old shirts and took on the name Papa. In turn, he gave his friends new names and used them as characters in his stories. Joe Russell became Freddy, captain of the *Queen Conch* charter boat in *To Have and Have Not*.

Hemingway stayed in Key West for 11 years before leaving Pauline for wife number three. A foreign correspondent, Martha Gellhorn, arrived in town and headed for Sloppy Joe's, intent on meeting him. When the always restless Hemingway packed up to cover the Spanish Civil War, so did she. Though he returned to Pauline occasionally, he finally left her and Key West to be with Martha in 1939. They married a year later and moved to Cuba, and he seldom returned to Key West after that. Pauline and the boys stayed on in the house, which sold in 1951 for $80,000, 10 times its original cost.

— Diane Marshall

tion project of 100 businesses, including waterfront restaurants, open-air people- and dog-friendly bars, museums, clothing stores, bait shops, docks, a marina, a wedding chapel, the Waterfront Market, the Key West Rowing Club, and dive shops. It's all linked by the 2-mi waterfront **Harborwalk**, which runs between Front and Grinnell streets, passing big ships, schooners, sunset cruises, fishing charters, and glass-bottom boats. Additional construction continues on outlying projects.

Ⓒ ㉔ **Key West Aquarium.** Explore the fascinating underwater realm of the Keys without getting wet at this kid-friendly aquarium. Hundreds of brightly colored tropical fish and sea creatures live here. A touch tank enables you to handle starfish, sea cucumbers, horseshoe and hermit crabs, even horse and queen conchs—living totems of the Conch Republic. Built in 1934 by the Works Progress Administration as the world's first open-air aquarium, most of the building has been enclosed for all-weather viewing. Guided tours include shark feedings. ⊠ *1 Whitehead St.,* ☎ *305/296–2051,* ⒲⒠⒝ *www.keywestaquarium.com.* ⌑ *$9.* ☉ *Daily 9–6, tours at 11, 1, 3, and 4:30.*

㉕ **Key West Museum of Art and History.** When Key West was designated a U.S. port of entry in the early 1820s, a customhouse was established. Salvaged cargoes from ships wrecked on the reefs could legally enter here, thus setting the stage for Key West to become the richest city in Florida. Following a $9 million restoration, the imposing redbrick and terra-cotta Richardsonian Romanesque–style U.S. Custom House reopened as a museum in 1999. Its main gallery displays major rotating exhibits. Smaller galleries feature long-term and changing exhibits about the history of Key West, such as *Remember the Maine.* ⊠ *281 Front St.,* ☎ *305/295–6616,* ⒲⒠⒝ *www.kwahs.com.* ⌑ *$6.* ☉ *Daily 9–5.*

⓭ **Lighthouse Museum.** For the best view in town and a history lesson at the same time, climb the 88 steps to the top of this 92-ft lighthouse. It was built in 1847. About 15 years later, a Fresnel lens was installed at a cost of $1 million. The keeper lived in the adjacent 1887 clapboard house, which now exhibits vintage photographs, ship models, nautical charts, and lighthouse artifacts from all along the Key reefs. ⊠ *938 Whitehead St.,* ☎ *305/294–0012.* ⌑ *$8.* ☉ *Daily 9:30–5, last admission 4:30.*

⓮ **Lofton B. Sands African-Bahamian Museum.** Vintage photographs and memorabilia chronicle the nearly 200-year history of Key West's black community in this modest 1928 house on the edge of Bahama Village. The house was built by the namesake owner, a master electrician, in the mid-1920s in what was then called Black Town or Africa Town. There are photographs of graduations and dances at the segregated high school, photos of funeral parades, candids of people at social clubs and balls, and posed wedding pictures. Crafts and demonstrations of traditional Afro-Caribbean arts are scheduled periodically. ⊠ *324 Truman Ave.,* ☎ *305/295–7337 or 305/293–9692.* ⌑ *Free.* ☉ *Daily 10–6. Tours by appointment.*

㉓ **Mel Fisher Maritime Heritage Society Museum.** In 1622, two Spanish galleons loaded with riches from South America foundered in a hurricane 40 mi west of the Keys. In 1985, Mel Fisher recovered the treasures from the lost ships, the *Nuestra Señora de Atocha* and the *Santa Margarita.* In this museum, you can see, touch, and learn about some of the artifacts, including a gold bar weighing 6.3 troy pounds and a 77.76-carat natural emerald crystal worth almost $250,000. Exhibits on the second floor rotate and might cover slave ships or the evolution of Florida maritime history. **Captain's Corner** (⊠ *125 Ann St., 33040,* ☎ *305/296–8865*) can arrange dive expeditions to the *Atocha.*

✉ *200 Greene St.,* ☎ *305/294–2633,* WEB *www.melfisher.org.* ✉ *$6.50.*
🕑 *Daily 9:30–5.*

16 **Nancy Forrester's Secret Garden.** It's hard to believe that this green escape exists in the middle of Old Town Key West. Despite damage by hurricanes and pressures from developers, Nancy Forrester has maintained her naturalized garden for more than 30 years. Growing in harmony are rare palms and cycads, ferns, bromeliads, bright gingers and heliconias, gumbo-limbos strewn with orchids and vines, and a few surprises. The gardens are popular for weddings. There are picnic tables where you can sit and have lunch. An art gallery has botanical prints and environmental art. ✉ *1 Free School La.,* ☎ *305/294–0015.* ✉ *$6.*
🕑 *Daily 10–5.*

17 **San Carlos Institute.** South Florida's Cuban connection began long before Fidel Castro was born. The institute was founded in 1871 by Cuban immigrants. Now it contains a research library and museum rich with the history of Key West and 19th- and 20th-century Cuban exiles. Cuban patriot Jose Martí delivered speeches from the balcony of the auditorium, and opera star Enrico Caruso sang in the Opera House, which reportedly has exceptional acoustics. It's frequently used for concerts, lectures, films, and exhibits. ✉ *516 Duval St.,* ☎ *305/294–3887.* ✉
$3. 🕑 *Tues.–Fri. 11–5, Sat. 11–5, Sun. 11–4.*

26 **Simonton Street Beach.** This small beach facing the gulf is a great place to watch boat traffic in the harbor. Parking, however, is difficult. ✉ *North end of Simonton St.,* ☎ *no phone.* ✉ *Free.* 🕑 *Daily 7 AM–11 PM.*

27 **South Beach.** On the Atlantic, this stretch of sand, also known as City Beach, is popular with travelers staying at nearby motels. It has limited parking and a nearby buffet-type restaurant, the South Beach Seafood and Raw Bar. ✉ *Foot of Duval St.,* ☎ *no phone.* ✉ *Free.* 🕑 *Daily 7 AM–11 PM.*

New Town

The Overseas Highway splits as it enters Key West, the two forks rejoining to encircle New Town, the area east of White Street to Cow Key Channel. The southern fork runs along the shore as South Roosevelt Boulevard (Route A1A), past municipal beaches, salt ponds, and Key West International Airport. Along the north shore, North Roosevelt Boulevard (U.S. 1) passes the Key West Welcome Center, shopping centers, chain hotels, and fast-food eateries. Part of New Town was created with dredged fill. The island would have continued growing this way had the Army Corps of Engineers not determined in the early 1970s that it was detrimental to the nearby reef.

A Good Tour

Attractions are few in New Town. The best way to take in the sights is by car or moped. Take South Roosevelt Boulevard from the island's entrance to the historical museum exhibits at **East Martello Tower** ㉛, near the airport. Continue past the Riggs Wildlife Refuge salt ponds and stop at **Smathers Beach** ㉜ for a dip, or continue west onto Atlantic Boulevard to **C. B. Harvey Rest Beach** ㉝. A little farther along, at the end of White Street, is the **West Martello Tower** ㉞ with its lovely tropical gardens.

TIMING
Allow one to two hours for brief stops at each attraction. If your interests lie in art, gardens, or Civil War history, you'll need three or four hours. Throw in time at the beach, and you can make it a half-day affair.

Sights to See

㉝ C. B. Harvey Rest Beach. This beach and park were named after former Key West mayor and commissioner Cornelius Bradford Harvey. It has half a dozen picnic areas, dunes, and a wheelchair and bike path. ⊠ *Atlantic Blvd., east side of White Street Pier,* ☎ *no phone.* ☜ *Free.* ☉ *Daily 7 AM–11 PM.*

★ **㉛ East Martello Tower.** As a Civil War citadel this spot never saw any action. Today, however, it serves as a museum with historical exhibits of the 19th to 20th century. Among the latter are relics of the U.S.S. *Maine,* a Cuban refugee raft, and books by famous writers—including seven Pulitzer Prize winners—who have lived in Key West. The tower, operated by the Key West Art and Historical Society, also has a collection of Stanley Papio's "junk art" sculptures and Cuban folk artist Mario Sanchez's chiseled and painted wooden carvings of historic Key West street scenes. Hours sometimes fluctuate, so call in advance. ⊠ *3501 S. Roosevelt Blvd.,* ☎ *305/296–3913.* ☜ *$6.* ☉ *Sat.–Sun. 9:30–5, last admission 4.*

㉜ Smathers Beach. This beach has nearly 2 mi of sand, rest rooms, picnic areas, and volleyball courts, all of which make it popular with the Spring Break crowd. Trucks along the road rent rafts, Windsurfers, and other beach "toys." ⊠ *S. Roosevelt Blvd.,* ☎ *no phone.* ☜ *Free.* ☉ *Daily 7 AM–11 PM.*

㉞ West Martello Tower. The ruins of this Civil War–era fort are home to the Key West Garden Club, which maintains lovely gardens of native and tropical plants. It also holds art, orchid, and flower shows in March and November and leads private garden tours in March. ⊠ *Atlantic Blvd. and White St.,* ☎ *305/294–3210.* ☜ *Donation welcome.* ☉ *Tues.–Sat. 9:30–3.*

Dining

American

$–$$ ✕ Pepe's Café and Steak House. Pepe's is a Key West institution. It was established downtown in 1909 (making it the oldest eating house in the Keys) and moved here in 1962. With few exceptions, it's been serving three squares a day with the same nightly specials for years such as meat loaf on Monday, seafood on Tuesday, and traditional Thanksgiving every Thursday. Dine indoors or on the garden patio under the trees. The walls are plastered with local color. Service is fast and friendly. It's worth coming back. ⊠ *806 Caroline St.,* ☎ *305/294–7192.* *D, MC, V.*

Contemporary

$$$–$$$$ ✕ **Café des Artistes.** The food here is superb, reflecting Chef Andrew ★ Berman's French interpretation of tropical cuisine, using fresh local seafood and produce and light sauces. The best choices are the special items of the day such as lobster tango mango, lobster flambéed in cognac and served with a saffron basil butter sauce and sliced mangoes. Wine list choices highlight quality and value with a strong focus on exceptional domestic vintages. Dining is in two indoor rooms or on a rooftop deck beneath a sapodilla tree and the stars. ⊠ *1007 Simonton St.,* ☎ *305/294–7100. AE, MC, V. No lunch.*

$$$–$$$$ ✕ **Louie's Backyard.** Often if a restaurant has a steal-your-breathaway view, it lets its clientele feast their eyes, rather than their palates. Not here. Executive chef Doug Shook consistently offers an enticing menu that changes seasonally. The winter menu might include grilled catch of the day with ginger butter, tomato chutney, and five-spice fried onions. Louie's key lime pie has a pistachio crust and is served with a raspberry coulis. Dine outside under a mahoe tree. Come for lunch if you're on a budget; the menu is less expensive and the view is still just as fantastic. For night owls, the Afterdeck Bar serves cocktails on the water until the wee hours. ⊠ *700 Waddell Ave.,* ☎ *305/294–1061. AE, DC, MC, V.*

$$–$$$$ ✕ **Café Marquesa.** The hospitality machine is well oiled at this refined
★ 50-seat restaurant adjoining the intimate Marquesa Hotel. Chef Susan Ferry, who trained with Norman Van Aken (of Norman's restaurant in Coral Gables), presents 10 or so entrées each night. Although every dish she makes is memorable, frequent guests favor the peppercorn-dusted seared yellowfin tuna. Some low-fat options such as grilled meats are often highlighted, but fresh-baked breads and desserts are quite the dietary contrary. There are also a fine selection of wines and a choice of microbrewery beers. Dinner is served until 11 PM. ⊠ *600 Fleming St.,* ☎ *305/292–1244. AE, DC, MC, V. No lunch.*

$$–$$$ ✕ **Alice's at LaTeDa.** Chef-owner Alice Weingarten, a very popular
★ local chef, serves breakfast, brunch, lunch, and dinner poolside with live evening entertainment. It's right in the middle of LaTeDa Hotel, an in-vogue, very gay-friendly hotel/bar complex. Her talent shows in her exemplary selection of wines that complement the creative mix of seafood, game, beef, pork, and poultry dishes. She's as confident serving Aunt Alice's magic meat loaf as she is whipping up an aromatic pan-roasted Mediterranean chicken served over baby wild greens, kalamata olives, and feta cheese. The bar is as popular as the dining room. ⊠ *1125 Duval St.,* ☎ *305/296–6706. AE, D, MC, V. Closed Mon.*

$$ ✕ **Rick's Blue Heaven.** There's much to like about this historic restaurant where Hemingway once refereed boxing matches and customers watched cockfights. Affordable fresh eats are served in the house and the big leafy yard. Business is booming with thanks to nightly specials such as blackened grouper or lobster with citrus beurre blanc and a good mix of vegetarian options and Caribbean foods. Desserts, breads, tortes, buns, and rolls are baked on-site. Three meals are served six days a week; Sunday there's a to-die-for brunch. The water tower hauled here in the 1920s gave its name to the restaurant's Water Tower Bar. Expect a line—everybody knows how good this is. ⊠ *305 Petronia St.,* ☎ *305/296–8666. Reservations not accepted. D, MC, V.*

Caribbean

$$–$$$ ✕ **Bahama Mama's Kitchen.** At this colorful indoor/outdoor restaurant in the heart of Bahama Village, Cory Sweeting, a fourth-generation Conch from the Bahamas, prepares traditional island foods, from simple, flavorful conch fritters to complex curries. Choose from chicken—curried, gingered, or spiced and jerked—and seafood, including shrimp, red snapper, and grouper, any way you like it. Traditional sides include salads, hush puppies, collard greens, pigeon peas with rice, plaintains, cheese grits, and crab with rice. ⊠ *324 Petronia St.,* ☎ *305/294–3355. MC, V.*

Cuban

$–$$ ✕ **El Siboney.** Dining at this sprawling three-room, family-style restaurant is like going to Mom's for Sunday dinner; that is, if your mother is Cuban. It's noisy—everyone talks as though they're at home—and the food is traditional Cubano. There's a well-seasoned black-bean soup and tasty specials such as beef stew on Monday, chicken fricassee on Wednesday, chicken and rice on Friday, and oxtail stew on Saturday. Always available are roast pork, cassava, paella, and *palomilla* steak (thin, boneless sirloin, breaded and fried). ⊠ *900 Catherine St.,* ☎ *305/ 296–4184. No credit cards. Closed 2 wks in June.*

French

$$–$$$ ✕ **Café Solé.** This little piece of France is concealed behind a high wall
★ and a gate in a residential neighborhood. Inside, chef John Correa shows
his considerable culinary talents. Marrying his French training with local
foods and produce, he creates some delicious takes on classics like rack
of lamb rubbed with *herbes de Provence* and some of the best bouill-
abaisse that you'll find outside of Marseille. From the land, there is
exotic grilled ostrich served with a béarnaise sauce. His salads are lightly
kissed with balsamic vinegar. ⊠ *1029 Southard St.,* ☏ *305/294–0230.
D, MC, V. No lunch.*

Italian

$$–$$$ ✕ **Salute Ristorante Sul Mare.** This funky wooden indoor and open-
★ air restaurant is on Higgs Beach, giving it one of the island's best
lunch views (and a bit of sand and salt spray on a windy day). The
dinner menu is a medley of Italian pastas, antipasto, soups, and delicious dishes such as lobster ravioli with sweet sage butter and baby
greens and grilled black grouper with curry butter and basmati rice.
At lunch there are bruschetta, panini, and mussels and calamari mari-
nara, as well as a fresh local fish sandwich. The wine list shows a knowledgeable palate. Dining here is light and fun. ⊠ *1000 Atlantic Blvd.,
Higgs Beach,* ☏ *305/292–1117. AE, MC, V. Closed Sun.*

$–$$ ✕ **Mangia Mangia.** Elliot and Naomi Baron, ex-Chicago restaura-
★ teurs, serve large, flavorful portions of homemade pasta from the daily
selection that you can match with one of the homemade sauces. Tables are arranged in a twinkly brick garden with specimen palms and
in a nicely dressed-up old-house dining room. It's one of the best
restaurants in Key West—and one of the best values. Everything that
comes out of the open kitchen is outstanding, including the Mississippi
mud pie and key lime pie. The wine list, with more than 350 selections,
the largest in Monroe County, contains a good selection under $20.
⊠ *900 Southard St.,* ☏ *305/294–2469. AE, MC, V. No lunch.*

Steak/Seafood

$$–$$$$ ✕ **Michael's Restaurant.** White tablecloths, subdued lighting, oil paint-
ings, and light music give Michael's the feel of a favorite restaurant in
a comfortable urban neighborhood. Garden seating gives it that Key
West touch. Even the dishes are familiar, but with creative touches.
There's *filet al forno* (tenderloin of beef rubbed with roasted garlic and
Roquefort), as well as grouper Oscar, a fillet stuffed with jumbo lump
crab. If you're a chocolate lover, don't miss the volcano, a hot Ghi-
rardelli chocolate cake with a molten center that erupts when the cake
is broken open. ⊠ *532 Margaret St.,* ☏ *305/295–1300. AE, D, DC,
MC, V. No lunch.*

$$–$$$ ✕ **Seven Fish.** A local favorite, this small, intimate restaurant special-
izes in seafood. You can get it as a main dish such as in yellowtail snap-
per in a Thai curry sauce or as an accompaniment in offerings like penne
pasta with crawfish and scallops or as ravioli stuffed with calamari and
cheese in a lemon chive sauce. Filling out the menu are pasta, vegetable
dishes, and even a meat loaf with real mashed potatoes. ⊠ *6323 Olivia
St.,* ☏ *305/296–2777. AE, D, MC, V. Closed Tues.*

Lodging

Lodging opportunities rival those found in mainland cities. You'll find
historic cottages, restored turn-of-the-last-century Conch houses, and
large resorts. Rates are the highest in the Keys, with a few properties
as low as $75, but the majority from $100 to $300 a night. Most prop-
erties raise prices during October's Fantasy Fest week and other events.
Guest houses and inns often do not welcome children under 16. In

addition, some guest houses and inns do not permit smoking indoors, but provide ashtrays outside. Most include an expanded Continental breakfast and, often, afternoon wine or snack.

Guest Houses

$$$$ **Paradise Inn.** Gloriously chic best describes this romantic palm-shaded
★ inn. Renovated cigar makers' cottages and authentically reproduced Bahamian-style houses with sundecks and balconies stand amid lush gardens with a heated pool, lily pond, and whirlpool, light-years in feeling from the hubbub of Key West. Suites are stylish, spacious, and filled with gracious touches such as French doors, sensuous fabrics, whirlpools in marble bathrooms, plush robes, and polished oak floors. Suite 205 and the Royal Poinciana Cottage are gilded lilies. ⊠ *819 Simonton St., 33040,* ☎ *305/293–8007 or 800/888–9648,* FAX *305/293–0807,* WEB *www.theparadiseinn.com. 3 cottages, 15 suites. Fans, in-room data ports, in-room safes, some in-room hot tubs, minibars, refrigerators, cable TV, pool, outdoor hot tub, laundry service, concierge, business services; no kids under 12; no-smoking rooms. AE, D, DC, MC, V. CP.*

$$$–$$$$ **Heron House.** A high coral fence, brilliantly splashed with spotlights
★ at night, surrounds the compound of four Key West–style buildings with wood siding, railed porches, peaked roofs, and columns centered on a pool. Most units have a complete wall of exquisitely laid wood, entries with French doors, and bathrooms of polished granite. Some have floor-to-ceiling panels of mirrored glass and/or an oversize whirlpool. Complementing the superb interior detailing are daily newspapers, bathrobes, and complimentary breakfast and wine and cheese. ⊠ *512 Simonton St., 33040,* ☎ *305/294–9227,* FAX *305/294–5692 or 888/861–9066,* WEB *www.heronhouse.com. 23 rooms. Fans, in-room data ports, in-room safes, some in-room hot tubs, some minibars, some refrigerators, cable TV with movies, pool, concierge, parking (fee); no kids under 16, no smoking. AE, DC, MC, V. CP.*

$$$–$$$$ **Island City House.** There's a real sense of conviviality at this three-building guest house, each with a unique style (and price). The vintage-1880s Island City House has a widow's walk, antiques, and pine floors. Arch House, a former carriage house, has a dramatic entry that opens into a lush courtyard. Although all suites front on busy Eaton Street, only Nos. 5 and 6 face it. A reconstructed cigar factory has become the Cigar House, with porches, decks, and plantation-style teak and wicker furnishings. Guests share a private tropical garden. Children are welcome—a rarity in Old Town guest houses. ⊠ *411 William St., 33040,* ☎ *305/294–5702 or 800/634–8230,* FAX *305/294–1289,* WEB *www.islandcityhouse.com. 24 suites. Fans, in-room data ports, kitchens, cable TV with movies, in-room VCRs, pool, hot tub, bicycles, concierge; no smoking. AE, D, DC, MC, V. CP.*

$$–$$$$ **Popular House/Key West Bed & Breakfast.** Jody Carlson's B&B is
★ a model of Key West. Local art—large splashy canvases, a mural in the style of Gauguin—hangs on the walls, and tropical gardens and music set the mood. Jody offers both inexpensive rooms with shared bath and luxury rooms, reasoning that budget travelers deserve the same good style (and lavish Continental breakfast) as the rich. Less-expensive rooms burst with colors; the hand-painted dressers will make you laugh. Spacious third-floor rooms are best (and most expensive), decorated with a paler palette and original furniture. Jody also keeps two friendly dogs. ⊠ *415 William St., 33040,* ☎ *305/296–7274 or 800/438–6155,* FAX *305/293–0306,* WEB *www.keywestbandb.com. 8 rooms, 4 with bath. Fans, outdoor hot tub, sauna; no room phones, no room TVs. AE, D, DC, MC, V. CP.*

$$$ ★ ⊞ **Ambrosia House.** If you desire personal attention and a casual atmosphere with a dollop of style, stay at these twin inns comprising pool-view rooms, suites, town houses, and cottages spread out on nearly 2 acres. Ambrosia, Kate Miano's original B&B, has a more intimate setting. She has turned Ambrosia Too, the former Fleming Street Inn, into a delightful art-filled hideaway. Rooms are distinctly decorated with original artwork by Keys artists, wicker or wood furniture, and spacious bathrooms. They all have a private entrance and a deck, patio, or porch. Phones are portable so you can take calls poolside. Poolside Continental breakfast is included and children are welcome. ⊠ *615, 618, 622 Fleming St., 33040,* ☎ *305/296–9838 or 800/535–9838,* FAX *305/296–2425,* WEB *www.ambrosiakeywest.com. 22 rooms, 3 town houses, 1 cottage, 6 suites. Fans, in-room data ports, some in-room hot tubs, some kitchens, refrigerators, cable TV, some in-room VCRs, 3 pools, outdoor hot tub, bicycles, concierge, some pets allowed; no smoking. AE, D, MC, V. BP.*

$$$ ★ ⊞ **Fleur de Key Guesthouse.** You could easily fill a little notebook with design ideas to take home from this charming guest house that caters exclusively to a gay clientele. Conch-style architecture harks back to its origins as a boardinghouse for railroad workers and cigar makers' cottages. Standard rooms in the main house are smallish, so opt for a superior room, which are slightly more expensive but much larger. Rooms have antiques and reproductions and are tastefully decorated in whites and tropical colors. Conveniences are numerous, including robes, and CDs and CD players (in suites). Breakfast is complimentary, as are evening cocktails. ⊠ *412 Frances St., 33040,* ☎ *305/296–4719 or 800/ 932–9119,* WEB *www.fleurdekey.com. 14 suites, 2 rooms. Fans, in-room data ports, some kitchens, refrigerators, cable TV, in-room VCRs, pool, outdoor hot tub; no kids under 16, no-smoking rooms. AE, D, MC, V. CP.*

$$$ ★ ⊞ **Key Lime Inn.** This inn, an 1854 Grand Bahama–style house on the National Register of Historic Places with adjacent cottages and cabanas, succeeds by offering amiable service, good value, and pretty, light-filled rooms with natural wood and white furniture. The tropical ambiance comes from gardens shaded by fruit and palm trees, tin-roof buildings with clapboard siding, classic white picket fences, and breezy porches. The least expensive Cabana rooms, some with a patio, surround the pool. The Garden Cottages have one room; some include a porch. All rooms in the historic Maloney House have a porch or patio. ⊠ *725 Truman Ave., 33040,* ☎ *305/294–5229 or 800/549–4430,* FAX *305/294– 9623,* WEB *www.keylimeinn.com. 30 rooms, 7 cottages. Fans, in-room data ports, in-room safes, some refrigerators, cable TV, some in-room VCRs, pool, concierge; no smoking. AE, D, MC, V.*

$$$ ★ ⊞ **Mermaid & The Alligator.** Rooms in this 1904 Victorian house are uniquely decorated with period furnishings that harken to the colonial Caribbean. Walls are painted in colors so luscious that guests frequently request paint chips. Wood floors, furniture, trim, and French doors complement the color. Some downstairs rooms open onto the deck, pool, and gardens designed by one of the resident owners, a landscape designer. Upstairs room balconies overlook the gardens. The Caribbean Queen honeymoon suite has a large soaking tub, tiny shower, four-poster queen bed, and wraparound veranda, but its street-side location makes it noisy. A full breakfast is served poolside. The owners and their two retrievers make this a delightful place. ⊠ *729 Truman Ave., 33040,* ☎ *305/294–1894 or 800/773–1894,* FAX *305/295– 9925,* WEB *www.kwmermaid.com. 6 rooms. Fans, pool; no kids under 16, no smoking. AE, D, MC, V. BP.*

$$-$$$ ⌂ **Center Court Historic Inn & Cottages.** Duval is half a block away, but when you're here, you're enveloped in calm and quiet. Units range from spacious rooms with a queen bed to efficiency cottages with a deck and spa (sleeping two to eight) to studios and fully equipped three-bedroom, two-bath house-size cottages (they sleep six). There's even a two-bedroom, two-bath house with its own pool. All units are decorated in relaxed tropical style, and both a full breakfast and happy-hour beverages are included. The heated pools are surrounded by lush foliage, whirlpools, and sundecks. ✉ *915 Center St., 33040,* ☎ *305/296–9292 or 800/797–8787,* FAX *305/294–4104,* WEB *www.centercourtkw.com. 4 rooms, 9 suites, 4 efficiencies, 10 cottages, 8 houses. Fans, in-room data ports, in-room safes, some in-room hot tubs, some kitchens, some microwaves, some refrigerators, cable TV, some in-room VCRs, 2 pools, exercise equipment, outdoor hot tub, business services, some pets allowed (fee); no smoking. AE, D, MC, V. BP.*

$$-$$$ ⌂ **Eden House.** This 1920s art deco guest house is one of the best values in town. Two levels of accommodations surround a lush garden courtyard with a pool bordered by lounges and umbrella-covered tables. Rooms range from small, simple spaces with a double or two twin beds with a squeaky-clean bathroom shared by two rooms to large spaces with a queen bed, kitchenette, and private porch. Some rooms even have laundry facilities. No matter the size, they all have pleasant furnishings and tropical colors. Spacious suites come in two sizes and feature paler decors. The genuinely helpful, friendly staff sets up a daily complimentary happy hour. ✉ *1015 Fleming St., 33040,* ☎ *305/296–6868 or 800/533–5397,* FAX *305/294–1221,* WEB *www.edenhouse.com. 4 rooms with shared bath, 17 rooms, 9 suites, 1 2-bedroom unit. Restaurant, fans, some kitchens, some microwaves, some refrigerators, pool, outdoor hot tub, bicycles, library, shop, concierge; no TV in some rooms, no smoking. AE, MC, V.*

$$-$$$ ⌂ **Merlinn Inn.** Key West guest houses don't usually welcome families.
★ The Merlinn Inn is a pleasant exception. Colorful rooms, suites, and cottages are connected by brick walkways that curve through a courtyard, pool area, and tropical plantings. Rooms in the 1930s Simonton House are most suitable for couples. They have queen four-poster beds, and porches. Suites are individually decorated with wooden floors, French doors, area rugs, four-poster beds, sundecks or porches, and queen sleeper sofas. Bright, roomy cottages are equally well appointed. The inn has no parking facilities—a drawback, since it's one block off busy Duval Street. ✉ *811 Simonton St., 33040,* ☎ *305/296–3336 or 800/642–4753,* FAX *305/296–3524,* WEB *www.merlinnkeywest. com. 10 rooms, 6 suites, 4 cottages. Fans, some kitchens, some refrigerators, cable TV, pool, Internet; no room phones, no smoking. AE, D, MC, V.*

$$-$$$ ⌂ **Speakeasy Inn.** This inn's notorious history began during Prohibition, when Raul Vasquez smuggled liquor from Cuba and taxi drivers stopped in to fill suitcases with the bootleg. Today, it's an attractively priced inn. Spacious studios, suites, and two-bedroom units have bright white walls offset by bursts of color in rugs, pillows, and seat cushions; queen-size beds and tables made from salvaged pine; Saltillo tiles in the bathrooms; oak floors; and some claw-foot bathtubs. Maid and concierge service are available. Casa 325 Suites, an upscale all-suites property at the opposite end of Duval, is under the same ownership. ✉ *1117 Duval St., 33040,* ☎ *305/296–2680 or 800/217–4884,* FAX *305/ 296–2680,* WEB *www.keywestcigar.com. 4 suites, 4 studios, 2 2-bedroom units. Fans, some kitchenettes, cable TV, lobby lounge, concierge; no room phones, no smoking. AE, D, MC, V.*

$–$$$ ⊞ **Angelina Guest House.** Two blocks off Duval Street, in the heart of Old Town Key West, this gambling hall and bordello–turned–guest house could command top dollar for its rooms. Instead, it offers simple, clean, attractively priced accommodations. There's a bed, chair, pretty curtains, and shared bath in the plainest rooms; a bed, sleeper sofa, refrigerator, and microwave in others. Built in the 1920s, this charming rambling, white, wooden building has second-floor porches, gabled roofs, and a white picket fence. A pool, fountain, and old bricks accent a lovely garden. Breakfast of homemade baked goods is included. ⊠ *302 Angela St., 33040,* ☎ *305/294–4480,* WEB *www.angelinaguesthouse.com. 14 rooms. Fans, some microwaves, some refrigerators, pool; no room phones, no room TVs. D, MC, V. CP.*

Hostel

$ ⊞ **Hostelling International–Key West.** Yes, you can afford to stay in Key West. This financial refuge in a sea of expensive hotels gets high marks for location, comfort, friendliness, amenities, and good value. It's two blocks from the beach in Old Town, yet costs only $19.50 for members of Hostelling International–American Youth Hostels, $22.50 for nonmembers. There's a communal kitchen. When you're not snorkeling ($28) or scuba diving ($55, gear included), you can rent bicycles, write letters in the outdoor courtyard, or enjoy a barbecue. ⊠ *718 South St., 33040,* ☎ *305/296–5719,* FAX *305/296–0672,* WEB *www. hiayh.org. 96 beds in dorm-style rooms with shared bath, 10 private rooms, 1 suite. Picnic area, fans, some kitchenettes, one in-room hot tub, dive shop, snorkeling, bicycles, billiards, library, recreation room, laundry facilities. MC, V.*

Hotels

$$$$ ⊞ **Ocean Key Resort.** A pool and open-air bar and grill make their home
★ on the Sunset Pier here, which provides the perfect view come sundown. You can also toast the day's end from private balconies that extend from brightly colored rooms that are both stylish and homey. Bring slippers for the white-tile flooring and CDs for the CD-alarm clock. High ceilings, hand-painted furnishings, a wicker sleigh bed, plaid couch, and a wooden chest for a coffee table create a personally designed look. Jet-skis can be rented at the marina, and the early evening hubbub of Mallory Square is right behind the hotel. ⊠ *Zero Duval St., 33040,* ☎ *305/296–7701 or 800/328–9815,* FAX *305/292–7685,* WEB *www.oceankey.com. 100 rooms and suites. 2 restaurants, room service, fans, in-room data ports, in-room safes, some in-room hot tubs, cable TV with movies, pool, health club, spa, dock, marina, bicycles, 2 bars, shops, dry cleaning, concierge, business services, meeting rooms; no-smoking rooms. AE, D, DC, MC, V.*

$$$$ ⊞ **Pier House Resort & Caribbean Spa.** This convivial, sprawling plea-
★ sure complex of weathered gray buildings, including an original Conch house, has a courtyard of tall coconut palms and hibiscus blossoms. Rooms are light filled, cozy, and colorful and have a water, pool, or garden view. Most rooms are smaller than in newer hotels, except in the more expensive Caribbean Spa section, which has hardwood floors, two-poster plantation beds, and CD players. The best lodgings are in the Harbor Front, each with a private balcony. Sunset on the Havana Docks is a special event. Rooms nearest the public areas can be noisy. ⊠ *1 Duval St., 33040,* ☎ *305/296–4600 or 800/327–8340,* FAX *305/ 296–9085,* WEB *www.pierhouse.com. 126 rooms, 16 suites. 3 restaurants, room service, fans, in-room data ports, some in-room hot tubs, some in-room VCRs, pool, health club, spa, beach, 4 bars, shop, laundry service; no-smoking rooms. AE, D, DC, MC, V.*

$$$$ ⚃ **Sunset Key Guest Cottages at Hilton Key West Resort.** It's as if they
★   polled people on their vision of a tropical getaway to create this re-
       sort. You check in at the Hilton Key West Resort, then board a 10-
       minute launch to their two- and three-bedroom cottages on Sunset Key.
       Sandy beaches, swaying palms, flowering gardens, a delicious sense of
       privacy—it's all here. The decor is handsome; the creature comforts
       first-class. Shuttle between the island and Key West around the clock
       at no extra charge or remain at Sunset Key, where you can dine, play,
       and relax at the very civilized beach, complete with attendants and ca-
       banas. ✉ *245 Front St., 33040,* ☎ *305/292–5300,* FAX *305/292–5395,*
       WEB *www.hilton.com. 37 cottages. Restaurant, café, snack bar, room
       service, fans, in-room data ports, in-room safes, kitchens, cable TV with
       movies, in-room VCRs, putting green, 2 tennis courts, pool, gym, spa,
       beach, jet skiing, marina, fishing, basketball, billiards, bar, lounge, li-
       brary, shops, baby-sitting, laundry service, concierge, Internet, busi-
       ness services, meeting rooms; no-smoking rooms. AE, D, DC, MC, V.*

$$$$ ⚃ **Wyndham's Casa Marina Resort.** At any moment, you expect the landed
       gentry to walk across the manicured, oceanfront lawn, just as they did
       during the 1920s when this 13-acre resort was built at the end of the
       Florida East Coast Railway line. It has the same rich, luxurious lobby
       with a beamed ceiling, polished pine floor, and artwork. Guest rooms
       are stylishly decorated, and armoires and wicker chairs with thick cush-
       ions lend a warm touch. The rooms packed with amenities such as fluffy
       bathrobes and designer toiletries are equally luxurious. Two-bedroom
       loft suites with balconies face the ocean, and the main building's ground
       floor lanai rooms open onto the lawn. There are myriad recreational and
       spa facilities. ✉ *1500 Reynolds St., 33040,* ☎ *305/296–3535 or 800/
       626–0777,* FAX *305/296–9960,* WEB *www.casamarinakeywest.com. 311
       rooms, 63 suites. 2 restaurants, room service, in-room data ports, in-
       room safes, minibars, cable TV with movies and video games, 3 tennis
       courts, 2 pools, gym, hair salon, outdoor hot tub, massage, sauna, beach,
       dive shop, snorkeling, windsurfing, boating, jet skiing, fishing, bicycles,
       volleyball, 2 bars, shop, baby-sitting, children's programs (ages 4–12),
       laundry service, concierge, business services, meeting rooms, airport
       shuttle; no-smoking rooms. AE, D, DC, MC, V.*

$$$–$$$$ ⚃ **Marquesa Hotel.** In a town that prides itself on its laid-back luxe,
★   this restored 1884 house stands out. Guests—typically shoeless in
       Marquesa robes—relax among richly landscaped pools and gardens
       against a backdrop of brick steps rising to the villalike suites on the
       property's perimeter. Elegant rooms contain antique and reproduction
       furnishings, Swiss curtains, botanical-print fabrics, and marble baths.
       The lobby resembles a Victorian parlor, with antiques, Audubon prints,
       flowers, and wonderful photos of early Key West, including one of Harry
       Truman in a convertible. Although the clientele is mostly straight, the
       hotel is very gay-friendly. ✉ *600 Fleming St., 33040,* ☎ *305/292–1919
       or 800/869–4631,* FAX *305/294–2121,* WEB *www.marquesa.com. 27
       rooms. Restaurant, room service, fans, in-room data ports, in-room
       safes, minibars, cable TV with movies, 2 pools, spa, bicycles, laundry
       service, concierge, business services. AE, DC, MC, V.*

$$$ ⚃ **Best Western Key Ambassador Inn.** Every room in this well-main-
★   tained 7-acre property has a screened balcony, most with a view of the
       ocean or pool. Accommodations are roomy and cheerful, with
       Caribbean-style light-color furniture and linens in coordinated tropi-
       cal colors. A deck-rimmed, palm-shaded pool that looks over the At-
       lantic and a covered picnic area with barbecue grills encourage
       socializing. The outdoor bar serves lunch, drinks, and light dishes. A
       complimentary Continental breakfast and free weekday newspaper are
       included. ✉ *3755 S. Roosevelt Blvd., New Town 33040,* ☎ *305/296–
       3500 or 800/432–4315,* FAX *305/296–9961,* WEB *www.keyambassador.*

com. 100 rooms. Picnic area, refrigerators, cable TV with movies, pool, shuffleboard, bar, laundry facilities, airport shuttle. AE, D, DC, MC, V. CP.

Motels

$$ ⊞ **Harborside Motel & Marina.** This simple little motel neatly packages three appealing characteristics—affordability, safety, and a pleasant location between a quiet street and Garrison Bight (the charter-boat harbor), at the border of Old Town and New Town. Units are boxy, clean, and basic, with little patios, ceramic-tile floors, phones, and lots of peace and quiet. Four stationary houseboats each sleep four. Barbecue grills are available for cookouts. Spring breakers need not apply: the motel likes to maintain a relative calm. ⊠ *903 Eisenhower Dr., 33040,* ☎ *305/294–2780 or 800/501–7823,* FAX *305/292–1473,* WEB *www.keywestharborside.com. 14 efficiencies. Fans, kitchens, cable TV, pool, dock, marina, laundry facilities. AE, D, DC, MC, V.*

$$ ⊞ **Southwind Motel.** If you're looking for a practical, affordable place to stay that's just a short walk from Old Town, consider this friendly lodging run by the same folks who operate Harborside Motel & Marina. The pastel 1940s-style motel has mature tropical plantings, all nicely set back from the street a block from the beach. Rooms are super clean and have tile floors and basic furnishings. It's as good as you'll find at the price, and although rates have gone up, they drop if demand gets slack. ⊠ *1321 Simonton St., 33040,* ☎ *305/296–2215 or 800/ 501–7826,* WEB *www.keywestsouthwind.com. 13 rooms, 5 efficiencies. Fans, some kitchens, cable TV, pool, laundry facilities. AE, D, DC, MC, V.*

Nightlife and the Arts

The Arts

Catch the classics and the latest art and foreign films shown by the **Key West Film Society** (⊠ 1310 Royal St., ☎ 305/294–5857, WEB www. keywestfilm.org) during the winter season. Sebrina Alfonso directs the **Key West Symphony** (⊠ Florida Keys Community College, 5901 College Rd., ☎ 305/292–1774, WEB www.keywestsymphony.com) during the winter season. Watch for free preconcert lectures at libraries and other venues. With more than 20 years' experience, the **Red Barn Theater** (⊠ 319 Duval St. [rear], ☎ 305/296–9911), a professional small theater, performs dramas, comedies, and musicals, including works by new playwrights. The **Tennessee Williams Fine Arts Center** (⊠ Florida Keys Community College, 5901 College Rd., ☎ 305/296–9081 Ext. 5), on Stock Island, presents chamber music, dance, jazz concerts, and dramatic and musical plays with major stars, as well as other performing arts events, December–April. The **Waterfront Playhouse** (⊠ Mallory Sq., ☎ 305/294–5015), in its 63rd season, is a mid-1850s wrecker's warehouse that was converted into a 180-seat, non-Equity regional theater presenting comedy and drama December–June.

Nightlife

BARS AND LOUNGES

You can pick your entertainment at the **Bourbon Street Complex** (⊠ 724–801 Duval St., ☎ 305/293–9600), a gay-oriented club with five bars and two restaurants. There's a nightly drag show in the 801 Bourbon Bar and 10 video screens along with male dancers grooving to the latest music spun by DJs at the Bourbon Street Pub. In its earliest incarnation, back in 1851, **Capt. Tony's Saloon** (⊠ 428 Greene St., ☎ 305/294–1838) was a morgue and icehouse, then Key West's first telegraph station. It became the original Sloppy Joe's in the mid-1930s, when Hemingway was a regular. Later, a young Jimmy Buffett sang here. Live bands play nightly. Pause for a libation at the open-air **Green Parrot Bar** (⊠ 601 Whitehead St., at Southard St., ☎ 305/294–6133). Built in 1890, the bar is said to be Key West's oldest, a sometimes-rowdy saloon where locals outnumber out-of-towners, especially on weekends when bands play. It opened a smokehouse, Meteor, behind it that serves up smoked shrimp, pork, chicken, and beef. **LaTeDa Hotel and Bar** (⊠ 1125 Duval St., ☎ 305/296–6706) hosts a riotously funny cabaret show nightly in the Crystal Room Cabaret Lounge. There's also live entertainment by popular local singer Lenore Troia in the Terrace Garden Bar. A youngish crowd sprinkled with aging hippies frequents **Margaritaville Café** (⊠ 500 Duval St., ☎ 305/292–1435), owned by former Key West resident and recording star Jimmy Buffett, who has been known to perform here. The drink of choice is, of course, a margarita. There's live music nightly, as well as lunch and dinner.

Nightlife at the **Pier House** (⊠ 1 Duval St., ☎ 305/296–4600) begins with a steel drum band (weekends) to celebrate the sunset on the beach, then moves indoors to the piano bar for live jazz (Thursday to Sunday). The **Schooner Wharf Bar** (⊠ 202 William St., ☎ 305/292–9520), an open-air waterfront bar and grill in the historic seaport district, retains its funky Key West charm. There's live music all day, plus happy hour, and special events. There's more history and good times at **Sloppy Joe's** (⊠ 201 Duval St., ☎ 305/294–5717), the successor to a famous 1937 speakeasy named for its founder, Captain Joe Russell. Ernest Hemingway came here to gamble and tell stories. Decorated with Hemingway memorabilia and marine flags, the bar is popular with travelers and is full and noisy all the time. Live entertainment plays daily, noon–2 AM. The **Top Lounge** (⊠ 430 Duval St., ☎ 305/296–2991) is on the seventh floor of the La Concha Holiday Inn and is one of the best places to view the sunset and enjoy live entertainment on Friday and Saturday. (Celebrities, on the ground floor, has nightly entertainment and serves food.) In the best traditions of a 1950s cocktail lounge, **Virgilio's** (⊠ 524 Duval St., ☎ 305/296–8118) serves up chilled martinis to the soothing tempo of live jazz and blues nightly. It's part of the La Trattoria restaurant complex.

DANCE CLUBS

Originally built as the Monroe Theater in 1912 with a large dance floor, garden bar, and smaller upstairs bars, **Club Epoch** (⊠ 623 Duval St., ☎ 305/296–8521) is a 22,000-square-ft dance club with a garden bar, open-air terrace bar above Duval Street, and a DJ pumping music from the 1970s through today. There's even a teen night, complete with a break-dance competition.

Outdoor Activities and Sports

Biking

Key West is a cycling town, but ride carefully: narrow and one-way streets along with car traffic result in several bike accidents a year. Some hotels rent or lend bikes to guests; others will refer you to a nearby shop and reserve a bike for you.

Keys Moped & Scooter (⊠ 523 Truman Ave., ☎ 305/294–0399) rents beach cruisers with large baskets as well as scooters. Rates start at $12 for three hours. Look for the huge American flag on the roof. **Moped Hospital** (⊠ 601 Truman Ave., ☎ 305/296–3344) supplies balloon-tire bikes with yellow safety baskets for adults and kids, as well as mopeds and double-seater scooters for adults. There's no charge for helmets, but lights cost $4.

Fishing

Captain Steven Impallomeni works as a flats-fishing guide, specializing in ultralight and fly-fishing for tarpon, permit, and bonefish, as well as near-shore and light-tackle fishing. Charters on the **Gallopin' Ghost** leave from Murray's Marina (⊠ MM 5, Stock Island, ☎ 305/292–9837). **Key West Bait and Tackle** (⊠ 241 Margaret St., ☎ 305/292–1961) carries live bait, frozen rigged and unrigged bait, and fishing and rigging equipment. It also has the Live Bait Lounge, where you can unwind and sip ice-cold beer while telling tall tales after fishing. Be sure to ask why the marlin on the roof is red.

Golf

Key West Resort Golf Course (⊠ 6450 E. College Rd., ☎ 305/294–5232) is an 18-hole course on the bay side of Stock Island. Nonresident fees are $140 for 18 holes (cart included) in season, $80 off-season.

Scuba Diving and Snorkeling

Adventure Charters & Tours (⊠ 6810 Front St., Stock Island 33040, ☎ 305/296–0362 or 888/817–0841) offers sail-and-snorkel coral reef adventure tours ($30) aboard the 42-ft trimaran sailboat *Fantasea*, with a maximum of 16 people. There are two daily departures and sometimes one at sunset. In 1999, **Captain's Corner** (⊠ 125 Ann St., 33040, ☎ 305/296–8865), a PADI five star–rated shop, began offering exclusive dives to Mel Fisher's famous *Nuestra Señora de Atocha* wreck, whose treasures are in the Mel Fisher Maritime Heritage Society Museum, and the neighboring reef on which the galleon originally struck. The full-day dive expeditions cost $250, including lunch, and require six people to sign up. Captain's Corner also provides dive classes in several languages. All captains are licensed dive masters and/or instructors. A 60-ft dive boat, *Sea Eagle,* departs twice daily. Reservations are accepted for regular reef and wreck diving.

Shopping

Key West contains dozens of characterless T-shirt shops, as well as art galleries and curiosity shops with lots worth toting home.

Bahama Village is an enclave of new and spruced up shops, restaurants, and vendors leading the way in the restoration of the historic district where black Bahamians settled in the 19th century. The village lies roughly between Whitehead and Fort streets, and Angela and Catherine streets. Hemingway frequented the bars, restaurants, and boxing rings in the village.

Arts and Crafts

The **Gallery on Greene** (⊠ 606 Greene St., ☎ 305/294–1669) showcases politically incorrect art by Jeff McNally and three-dimensional paintings by local artist Mario Sanchez, among others, in the largest gallery exhibition space in Key West. The oldest private art gallery in Key West, **Gingerbread Square Gallery** (⊠ 1207 Duval St., ☎ 305/296–8900), represents mainly Keys artists who have attained national and international prominence in media ranging from graphics to art glass. **Haitian Art Co.** (⊠ 600 Frances St., ☎ 305/296–8932), containing 4,000 paintings and spirit flags, claims the largest collection of Haitian art outside Haiti, representing a range of artists working in wood, stone, metal, and papier-mâché. **Lucky Street Gallery** (⊠ 1120 White St., ☎ 305/294–3973) sells high-end contemporary paintings, watercolors, and jewelry by internationally recognized Key West–based artists. It's part of the White Street Gallery District, where you'll also find Three-Legged Dog Gallery, Harrison Gallery, and The Wave Gallery, the domain of Barbara Grob, the doyenne of outrageous gecko and animal sculptures. **Pelican Poop** (✉ 314 Simonton St., ☎ 305/296–3887) sells Caribbean art in a gorgeous setting around a lush, tropical courtyard garden with a fountain and pool. The owners buy direct from Caribbean artisans every year, so prices are very attractive. (Hemingway wrote *A Farewell to Arms* while living in the complex's apartment.) Potters Charles Pearson and Timothy Roeder *are* **Whitehead St. Pottery** (✉ 322 Julia St., ☎ 305/294–5067), where they display their porcelain stoneware and raku-fired vessels. They also have a photo gallery where they exhibit Polaroid image transfers and black-and-white photos. In the not-to-be-missed category is the **Woodenhead Gallery** (✉ 907 Caroline St., ☎ 305/294–3935), where the artists-owners create avant-garde works from recycled materials and *objets* found in and around Key West. Their coffee bar is a favorite meeting spot for artists, friends, and clients.

Books

Flaming Maggie's (✉ 830 Fleming St., ☎ 305/294–3931) specializes in books, cards, and magazines for and about gays and lesbians and also carries books—and artwork—by or about local authors. It contains a popular coffee bar, too. They expanded the **Key West Island Bookstore** (✉ 513 Fleming St., ☎ 305/294–2904), the literary bookstore of the large Key West writers' community. It carries new, used, and rare titles and specializes in Hemingway, Tennessee Williams, and South Florida mystery writers.

Clothes and Fabrics

Since 1964, **Key West Hand Print Fashions and Fabrics** (✉ 201 Simonton St., ☎ 305/294–9535 or 800/866–0333) has been noted for its vibrant tropical prints, yard goods, and resort wear for men and women. It's in the Curry Warehouse, a brick building erected in 1878 to store tobacco. **Tikal Trading Co.** (✉ 129 Duval St.; 910 Duval St., ☎ 305/296–4463) sells its own line of women's and little girls' clothing of hand-woven Guatemalan cotton and knit tropical prints.

Food and Drink

The air outside **Cole'z Peace Artisan Breads** (✉ 930A Eaton St., ☎ 305/292–6511), an old-world–style bakery, is deliciously redolent of warm breads. Each loaf of hand-kneaded unbleached, unbromated flour, organic flour, or organic grain bread is hand-shaped, then baked in a hearth stone oven. The crusts are hard and thick; the insides light and flavorful. **Fausto's Food Palace** (✉ 522 Fleming St., ☎ 305/296–5663; ✉ 1105 White St., ☎ 305/294–5221) may be under a roof, but it's a market in the traditional town-square sense. Since 1926, Fausto's has been the spot to catch up on the week's gossip and to chill out in summer—it has gourmet groceries, organic foods, marvelous wines, a sushi chef on duty from 8 AM to 6 PM, and box lunches to go. You'll spend the first five minutes at the **Waterfront Market** (✉ 201 William St., ☎ 305/296–0778) wondering how to franchise one of these great markets in your hometown. Along with health and gourmet foods, they sell savory deli items from around the world, produce, salads, cold beer, and wine. Don't miss the fish market, bakery, deli, juice bar, and a new sushi bar fresh from the Origami Restaurant.

Gifts and Souvenirs

Like a parody of Duval Street T-shirt shops, the hole-in-the-wall **Art Attack** (✉ 606 Duval St., ☎ 305/294–7131) throws in every icon and trinket anyone nostalgic for the days of peace and love might fancy: beads, necklaces, harmony bells, and of course Grateful Dead and psychedelic T-shirts. **Fast Buck Freddie's** (✉ 500 Duval St., ☎ 305/294–2007) sells such imaginative items as a noise-activated rat in a trap and a raccoon tail in a bag. There is also crystal, furniture, tropical clothing, and every flamingo item imaginable. The ambiance in **Kindred Spirit** (✉ 1204 Simonton St., ☎ 305/296–1515) is very New Age, but in addition to aromatherapy candles, inspirational music, and scented soaps you'll find jewelry made by Keys artists, delicate picture frames, and tea—tea leaves, tea bags, and formal tea, complete with freshly baked scones, fruitbread, and cake and confections. In a town with a gazillion T-shirt shops, **Last Flight Out** (✉ 503 Greene St., ☎ 305/294–8008) stands out for its selection of classic namesake Ts, specialty clothing, and gifts that appeal to aviation types as well as those reaching for the stars.

Health and Beauty

Key West Aloe (✉ 524 Front St., ☎ 305/294–5592 or 800/445–2563) was founded in a garage in 1971; today it produces some 300 perfume, sunscreen, and skin-care products for men and women. You can also visit the factory store (✉ Greene and Simonton Sts.).

Side Trip

Dry Tortugas National Park

This sanctuary for thousands of birds, 70 mi off the shores of Key West, consists of seven small islands. Its main facility is the long-deactivated Fort Jefferson, where Dr. Samuel Mudd was imprisoned for his alleged role in Lincoln's assassination. You can tour the fort, then lay out your blanket on the sunny beach for a picnic before you head out to snorkel on the protected reef. Many people like to camp here, but note that there's no freshwater supply and you must carry off whatever you bring on to the island. For information and a list of authorized charter boats and water taxis, contact **Everglades National Park** (✉ 40001 Rte. 9336, Homestead 33034-6733, ☎ 305/242–7700).

The fast, sleek 100-ft catamaran, the *Yankee Freedom II*, of the **Yankee Fleet Dry Tortugas National Park Ferry**, cuts the travel time to the Dry Tortugas to 2¼ hours. The time passes quickly on the roomy vessel equipped with three rest rooms, two freshwater showers, and two bars. You can stretch out on two decks; one an air-conditioned salon with cushioned seating, the other an open sundeck with sunny and shaded seating. Breakfast and lunch are included. On arrival, a naturalist leads a 45-minute guided tour, followed by lunch and a free afternoon for swimming, snorkeling (gear included), and exploring. ✉ *Lands End Marina, 240 Margaret St., Key West 33040*, ☎ *305/294–7009 or 800/ 634–0939*, WEB *www.yankeefleet.com.* 🖃 *$109.* ☉ *Trips daily 8 AM.*

THE FLORIDA KEYS A TO Z

To research prices, get advice from other travelers, and book travel arrangements, visit www.fodors.com.

AIR TRAVEL

Service between Key West International Airport and Miami, Fort Lauderdale/Hollywood, Naples, Orlando, and Tampa is provided by American Eagle, Cape Air, Comair/Delta Connection, Discover Air, Gulfstream/Continental Connection, and US Airways/US Airways Express.

The Airporter operates scheduled van and bus pickup service from all Miami International Airport (MIA) baggage areas to wherever you want to go in Key Largo ($35) and Islamorada ($38). A group discount is given for three or more passengers. Reservations are required. The Super Shuttle charges $80 per passenger ($190 for entire van) for trips to the

Upper Keys. To go farther into the Keys, you must book an entire van (up to 11 passengers), which costs $250 to Marathon, $350 to Key West. Super Shuttle requests 24-hour advance notice for transportation back to the airport.

CARRIERS

➤ AIRLINES AND CONTACTS: **American Eagle** (☎ 800/433–7300). **Cape Air** (☎ 800/352–0714). **Comair/Delta Connection** (☎ 800/354–9822). **Discover Air** (☎ 866/359–3247). **Gulfstream/Continental Connection** (☎ 800/525–0280). **US Airways/US Airways Express** (☎ 800/428–4322).

➤ AIRPORT INFORMATION: **Key West International Airport** (✉ S. Roosevelt Blvd., Key West, ☎ 305/296–5439). **Miami International Airport** (☎ 305/876–7000). **Airporter** (☎ 305/852–3413 or 800/830–3413). **Super Shuttle** (☎ 305/871–2000).

BOAT AND FERRY TRAVEL

Boaters can travel to and along the Keys either along the Intracoastal Waterway (5-ft draft limitation) through Card, Barnes, and Blackwater sounds and into Florida Bay or along the deeper Atlantic Ocean route through Hawk Channel, a buoyed passage. Refer to NOAA Nautical Charts Numbers 11451, 11445, and 11441. The Keys are full of marinas that welcome transient visitors, but they don't have enough slips for everyone. Make reservations in advance and ask about channel and dockage depth—many marinas are quite shallow.

For nonemergency information contact Coast Guard Group Key West; VHF-FM Channel 16. Safety and weather information is broadcast at 7 AM and 5 PM Eastern Standard Time on VHF-FM Channels 16 and 22A. There are stations in Islamorada and Marathon.

Key West Shuttle operates a ferry between Key West and Marco Island and Fort Myers, on the mainland's southwest coast. The trip takes four to five hours each way, respectively. Tickets cost $70 one-way, $119 round-trip. Advance reservations are recommended.

Chambers of commerce, marinas, and dive shops offer Teall's Guides, land and nautical charts that pinpoint popular fishing and diving areas. A complete set can also be purchased for $7.95.

➤ BOAT AND FERRY INFORMATION: **Coast Guard Group for the Florida Keys** (✉ Key West, ☎ 305/292–8779; ✉ Islamorada, ☎ 306/664–8077 for information; 305/664–4404 for emergencies; ✉ Marathon, ☎ 305/743–6778 for information; 305/743–6388 for emergencies). **Key West Shuttle** (☎ 888/539–2628). **Teall's Guides** (✉ 111 Saguaro La., Marathon 33050, ☎ 305/743–3942).

BUS TRAVEL

Greyhound Lines runs a special Keys shuttle three or four times a day (depending on the day of the week) between MIA (departing from Concourse E, lower level) and stops throughout the Keys. Fares run from about $13/$26 one-way/round-trip for Key Largo (Howard Johnson, MM 102) to around $31/$60 for Key West (3535 S. Roosevelt, Key West Airport).

The City of Key West Department of Transportation has four color-coded bus routes covering the island from 6:30 AM to 11:30 PM. Stops have signs with the international symbol for bus. Schedules are available on buses and at hotels, visitor centers, and shops. The fare is 75¢ (exact change).

Bone Island Shuttle circles the island from 9 AM to 10 PM, stopping at attractions, hotels, and restaurants. Passengers pay $7 per day for unlimited riding. You can park at the city's Park 'n' Ride 24-hour garage at the corner of Caroline and Grinnell streets and catch a city bus to Old Town at no extra cost. The shuttle runs 7 AM to 7 PM. Parking costs $1.25 an hour/$8 a day.

The Dade–Monroe Express provides daily bus service from the MM 98 in Key Largo to the Florida City Wal-Mart Supercenter. The bus makes several stops in Key Largo, then heads for the islands for daily round-trips on the hour from 6 AM to 9:55 PM. The cost is $1.50 each way.

➤ BUS INFORMATION: **Bone Island Shuttle** (☎ 305/293–8710). **City of Key West Department of Transportation** (☎ 305/292–8160). **Dade–Monroe Express** (☎ 305/770–3131). **Greyhound Lines** (☎ 800/410–5397 or 800/231–2222). **Park 'n' Ride** (✉ 300 Grinnell St., ☎ 305/293–6426).

CAR RENTAL

Two- and four-passenger open-air electric cars that travel about 25 mph are an environmentally friendly way to get around the island. Rent them from Key West Cruisers for $89/$129 a half day for the two-/four-seater or $119/$169 a day.

Avis and Budget serve Marathon Airport. Key West's airport has booths for Alamo, Avis, Budget, Dollar, and Hertz. Tropical Rent-A-Car is based in the city center. Enterprise Rent-A-Car has offices in Key Largo, Marathon, and Key West. Thrifty Car Rental has an office in Tavernier.

CUTTING COSTS

Avoid flying into Key West and driving back to Miami; there are substantial drop-off charges for leaving a Key West car in Miami.
➤ LOCAL AGENCIES: **Alamo** (☎ 305/294–6675 or 800/327–9633). **Avis** (☎ 800/831–2847). **Budget** (☎ 800/527–0700). **Dollar** (☎ 305/296–9921 or 800/800–4000). **Enterprise Rent-A-Car** (☎ 800/325–8007). **Hertz** (☎ 305/294–1039 or 800/654–3131). **Key West Cruisers** (☎ 305/294–4724 or 888/800–8802). **Thrifty Car Rental** (☎ 800/367–2277). **Tropical Rent-A-Car** (☎ 305/294–8136).

CAR TRAVEL

From MIA follow signs to Coral Gables and Key West, which put you on Lejeune Road, then Route 836 west. Take the Homestead Extension of Florida's Turnpike south (toll road), which ends at Florida City and connects to U.S. 1. Tolls from the airport run approximately $1.50. The alternative from Florida City is Card Sound Road (Route 905A), which has a bridge toll of $1. Continue to the only stop sign and turn right on Route 905, which rejoins U.S. 1 31 mi south of Florida City.

In Key West's Old Town, parking is scarce and costly ($1.50 per hour at Mallory Square). It's better to take a taxi, rent a bicycle or moped, walk, or take a shuttle to get around.

Elsewhere in the Keys, a car is crucial. Gas costs more than on the mainland, so fill your tank in Miami and top it off in Florida City.

Most of the Overseas Highway is narrow and crowded (especially weekends and in high season). Expect delays behind RVs, trucks, cars towing boats, and rubbernecking tourists.

The best Keys road map, published by the Homestead/Florida City Chamber of Commerce, can be obtained for $5.50 from the Tropical Everglades Visitor Center.

➤ CONTACTS: **Tropical Everglades Visitor Center** (✉ 160 U.S. 1, Florida City 33034, ☎ 305/245–9180 or 800/388–9669).

EMERGENCIES

Dial 911 for police, fire, or ambulance. Keys Hotline provides information and emergency assistance in six languages. The Florida Marine Patrol maintains a 24-hour telephone service to handle reports of boating emergencies and natural-resource violations. Coast Guard Group Key West responds to local marine emergencies and reports of navigation hazards.

The Keys have no 24-hour pharmacies. Hospital pharmacists will help with emergencies after regular retail business hours.

The following hospitals have 24-hour emergency rooms: Fishermen's Hospital, Lower Florida Keys Health System, and Mariners Hospital.
➤ CONTACTS: **Coast Guard Group Key West** (☎ 305/295–9700). **Fishermen's Hospital** (✉ MM 48.7, OS, Marathon, ☎ 305/743–5533). **Florida Marine Patrol** (✉ MM 48, BS, 2796 Overseas Hwy., Suite 100, State Regional Service Center, Marathon 33050, ☎ 305/289–2320; 800/342–5367 after 5 PM). **Keys Hotline** (☎ 800/771–5397). **Lower Florida Keys Health System** (✉ MM 5, BS, 5900 College Rd., Stock Island, ☎ 305/294–5531). **Mariners Hospital** (✉ MM 88.5, BS, 50 High Point Rd., Plantation Key, ☎ 305/852–4418).

ENGLISH-LANGUAGE MEDIA
NEWSPAPERS AND MAGAZINES

The best of the publications covering Key West is weekly *Solares Hill.* The best weekday source of information on Key West is the *Key West Citizen,* which also publishes a Sunday edition. For the Upper and Middle Keys, turn to the semiweekly *Keynoter.* The *Free Press, Reporter,* and *Upper Keys Independent* cover the same area once a week. The *Miami Herald* publishes a Keys edition with good daily listings of local events. The weekly *Celebrate Key West* and the monthly *Southern Exposure* are good sources of entertainment and information for gay and lesbian travelers.

TELEVISION AND RADIO

WLRN (National Public Radio) is 91.3, 92.1, and 93.5, depending on where you are in the Keys; WKLG 102.1 bilingual (English and Spanish) adult contemporary; WCTH 100.3 country; WFKZ 103.1 adult contemporary; WKEZ 96.9 easy listening; WFFG AM 1300 Keys talk radio, sports, and news; WKYZ 101.3 classic rock.

LODGING

Brenda Donnelly represents more than 60 guest houses, B&Bs, and inns in prices ranging from $60 to $545 a night through Inn Touch in Key West. Key West Vacation Rentals lists historic cottages, homes, and condominiums for rent. Although it prefers to handle reservations for all types of accommodations in advance, the Key West Welcome Center gets a lot of walk-in business because of its location on U.S. 1 at the entrance to Key West. Property Management of Key West, Inc. offers lease and rental service for condominiums, town houses, and private homes. Rent Key West Vacations specializes in renting vacation homes and condos for a week or longer. Vacation Key West lists all kinds of properties throughout Key West.

APARTMENT AND VILLA RENTALS

➤ LOCAL AGENTS: **Inn Touch in Key West** (✉ 1421 Catherine St., Key West 33040, ☎ 305/296–2953 or 800/492–1911, FAX 305/292–1621, WEB www.inntouchkeywest.com). **Key West Vacation Rentals** (✉ 525 Simonton St., Key West 33040, ☎ 305/292–7997 or 800/621–9405,

FAX 305/294–7501). **Key West Welcome Center** (⊠ 3840 N. Roosevelt Blvd., Key West 33040, ☎ 305/296–4444 or 800/284–4482). **Property Management of Key West, Inc.** (⊠ 1213 Truman Ave., Key West 33040, ☎ 305/296–7744). **Rent Key West Vacations** (⊠ 1107 Truman Ave., Key West 33040, ☎ 305/294–0990 or 800/833–7368, WEB www. rentkeywest.com). **Vacation Key West** (⊠ 513 Fleming St., Suite 3, Key West 33040, ☎ 305/295–9500 or 800/595–5397, WEB www.vacationkw. com).

TAXIS

Serving the Keys from Ocean Reef to Key West, Luxury Limousine has luxury sedans and limos that seat up to eight passengers. They'll pick up from any airport in Florida.

In the Upper Keys (MM 94–74), Village Taxi charges $2 per mi for vans that hold six. It also makes airport runs. Florida Keys Taxi Dispatch operates around the clock in Key West. The fare for two or more from the Key West airport to New Town is $5 per person with a cap of $15; to Old Town it's $7 and $30, respectively. Otherwise meters register $1.75 to start, 45¢ for each ⅕ mi, and 45¢ for every 50 seconds of waiting time.

➤ TAXI INFORMATION: **Florida Keys Taxi Dispatch** (☎ 305/296–1800). **Luxury Limousine** (☎ 305/664–0601, 305/367–2329, or 800/664–0124). **Village Taxi** (☎ 305/664–8181).

TOURS

Island Aeroplane Tours flies up to two passengers in a 1941 Waco, an open-cockpit biplane. Tours range from a quick six- to eight-minute overview of Key West ($50 for two) to a 50-minute look at the off-shore reefs ($275 for two). Seaplanes of Key West offers half-day trips to the Dry Tortugas, where you can explore Fort Jefferson, built in 1846, and snorkel on the beautiful protected reef. A cooler of drinks and snorkel equipment is included in the $179 per person fee.

Key West Nature Bike Tour explores the natural, noncommercial side of Key West at a leisurely pace, stopping on back streets and in back-yards of private homes to sample native fruits and view indigenous plants and trees. The tours run 90–120 minutes and cost $20, plus $3 for a bike.

Coral Reef Park Co. runs sailing trips on a 38-ft catamaran as well as glass-bottom boat tours. Captain Sterling's Everglades Eco-Tours operates Everglades and Florida Bay ecology tours ($39 per person), sunset cruises ($29 per person), and a private charter evening crocodile tour ($299 for up to six passengers).

Key Largo Princess offers two-hour glass-bottom boat trips ($18) and sunset cruises on a luxury 70-ft motor yacht with a 280-square-ft glass viewing area, departing from the Holiday Inn docks three times a day. M/V *Discovery* and the 65-ft *Pride of Key West* are glass-bottom boats. Strike Zone Charters offers glass-bottom boat excursions into the backcountry and Atlantic Ocean. The five-hour Island Excursion ($49) emphasizes nature and Keys history. Besides close encounters with birds, sea life, and vegetation, there's a fish cookout on an island. Snorkel and fishing equipment, food, and drinks are included. This is one of the few nature outings in the Keys with wheelchair access.

Victoria Impallomeni, noted wilderness guide and authority on the ecology of Florida Bay, invites nature lovers—and especially children—aboard the *Imp II*, a 24-ft Aquasport, for four-hour half-day ($400) and seven-hour full-day ($600) ecotours that frequently include encounters with wild dolphins. While island-hopping, you visit underwater gardens, natural shoreline, and mangrove habitats. She also offers Dancing Water Spirits retreats, self-transformational retreats with healing therapies and optional live-aboard accommodations on a 36-ft sailboat. All equipment is supplied. Tours leave from Murray's Marina.

The Conch Tour Train is a 90-minute narrated tour of Key West, traveling 14 mi through Old Town and around the island. Board at Mallory Square and Roosevelt Boulevard (just north of the Quality Inn) every half hour (9–4:30 from Mallory Square, later at other stops). The cost is $20. Old Town Trolley operates 12 trackless trolley-style buses, departing from the Mallory Square and Roosevelt Boulevard depots every 30 minutes (9:15–4:30 from Mallory Square, later at other stops), for 90-minute narrated tours of Key West. The smaller trolleys go places the train won't fit. You may disembark at any of nine stops and reboard a later trolley. The cost is $20.

Adventure Charters & Tours loads kayaks onto the 42-ft catamaran *Island Fantasea* and heads out to the Great White Heron National Wildlife Refuge for guided kayak nature tours with a maximum of 14 passengers. Half-day trips ($30) last 2½ hours and depart at 10 and 2. Full-day trips ($100) depart at 9:30 and include snorkeling, fishing, a grilled lunch, drinks, and a sunset.

When captains Emily Graves (outdoor recreational educator) and Bill Keogh (naturalist, educator, and photographer) merged their two well-known kayak nature tour companies to form Big Pine Kayak Adventures, they brought together 50 years of Keys outdoor exploration experience. The new company takes visitors into remote areas of two national wildlife refuges in the Lower Keys to explore mangrove hammocks, islands, creeks, and sponge and grass flats on kayak nature tours, shallow-water skiff ecotours, backcountry catamaran sailing cruises, and shallow-water fishing expeditions. Prices start at $49 per person for a half day.

The folks at Florida Bay Outfitters know Upper Keys and Everglades waters well. You can take a one- to seven-day canoe or kayak tour to the Everglades or Lignumvitae or Indian Key, or a night trip to neighboring islands. Trips run $45–$800. Mosquito Coast Island Outfitters and Kayak Guides runs full-day guided sea-kayak natural-history tours around the mangrove islands just east of Key West. The $55-a-day charge covers transportation, bottled water, a snack, and supplies, including snorkeling gear.

In addition to publishing several good guides on Key West, the Historic Florida Keys Foundation conducts tours of the City Cemetery Tuesday and Thursday at 9:30. As the former state historian in Key West and the current owner of a historic-preservation consulting firm, Sharon Wells of Island City Strolls knows plenty about Key West. She's authored many works, including the "The Walking and Biking Guide to Historic Key West," which features 10 self-guided tours of the historic district. It's available free at guest houses, hotels, and Key West bookstores. If that whets your appetite, sign on for one of her walking tours, including Architectural Strolls, Literary Landmarks, and Historic 1847 Cemetery Stroll, which cost $25.

"Pelican Path" is a free walking guide to Key West published by the Old Island Restoration Foundation. The tour discusses the history and architecture of 43 structures along 25 blocks of 12 Old Town streets. Pick up a copy at the chamber of commerce.

➤ TOURS INFORMATION: **Adventure Charters & Tours** (✉ 6810 Front St., Stock Island 33040, ☎ 305/296–0362, WEB www.keywestadventures. com). **Big Pine Kayak Adventures** (✉ Box 431311, Big Pine Key 33043, ☎ 305/872–2896, 305/395–0930, or 877/595–2925, WEB www. keyskayaktours.com). **Conch Tour Train** (☎ 305/294–5161). **Coral Reef Park Co.** (✉ John Pennekamp Coral Reef State Park, MM 102.5, OS, Key Largo 33037, ☎ 305/451–1621). **Everglades Eco-Tours** (✉ Dolphin's Cove, MM 102, BS, Key Largo 33037, ☎ 305/853–5161 or 888/224–6044, WEB www.captsterling.com). **Florida Bay Outfitters** (✉ MM 104, BS, 104050 Overseas Hwy., Key Largo 33037, ☎ 305/451–3018, WEB www.kayakFloridaKeys.com). **Historic Florida Keys Foundation** (✉ 510 Greene St., Old City Hall, Key West 33040, ☎ 305/292–6718). **Island Aeroplane Tours** (✉ Key West Airport, 3469 S. Roosevelt Blvd., ☎ 305/294–8687, WEB www.seekeywest.com). **Island City Strolls** (☎ 305/294–8380). *Key Largo Princess* (✉ MM 99.7, OS, 99701 Overseas Hwy., Key Largo 33037, ☎ 305/451–4655). **Key West Nature Bike Tour** (✉ Truman Ave. and Simonton St., Key West, ☎ 305/294–1882). **Mosquito Coast Island Outfitters and Kayak Guides** (✉ 310 Duval St., Key West 33040, ☎ 305/294–7178). **Murray's Marina** (✉ MM 5, Stock Island). **M/V** *Discovery* (✉ Land's End Marina, 251 Margaret St., Key West 33040, ☎ 305/293–0099). **Old Town Trolley** (✉ 6631 Maloney Ave., Key West, ☎ 305/296–6688). *Pride of Key West* (✉ 2 Duval St., Key West 33040, ☎ 305/296–6293). **Seaplanes of Key West** (✉ Key West Airport, 3471 S. Roosevelt Blvd., ☎ 305/294–0709, WEB www.seaplanesofkeywest.com). **Strike Zone Charters** (✉ MM 29.6, BS, 29675 Overseas Hwy., Big Pine Key 33043, ☎ 305/872–9863 or 800/654–9560, WEB www.strikezonecharter.com). **Sugarloaf Marina** (✉ MM 17, BS, Sugarloaf Key). **Victoria Impallomeni** (✉ 5710 U.S. 1, Key West 33040, ☎ 305/294–9731 or 888/822–7366, WEB www.captvictoria.com).

VISITOR INFORMATION

➤ TOURIST INFORMATION: **Big Pine and the Lower Keys Chamber of Commerce** (✉ MM 31, OS, Box 430511, Big Pine Key 33043, ☎ 305/872–2411 or 800/872–3722, FAX 305/872–0752). **Florida Keys & Key West Visitors Bureau** (✉ 402 Wall St., Key West 33040, ☎ 800/352–5397, WEB www.fla-keys.com). **Greater Key West Chamber of Commerce (mainstream)** (✉ 402 Wall St., Key West 33040, ☎ 305/294–2587 or 800/527–8539, FAX 305/294–7806). **Greater Marathon Chamber of Commerce & Visitor Center** (✉ MM 53.5, BS, 12222 Overseas Hwy., Marathon 33050, ☎ 305/743–5417 or 800/262–7284). **Islamorada Chamber of Commerce** (✉ MM 82.5, BS, Box 915, Islamorada 33036, ☎ 305/664–4503 or 800/322–5397). **Key Largo Chamber of Commerce** (✉ MM 106, BS, 106000 Overseas Hwy., Key Largo 33037, ☎ 305/451–1414 or 800/822–1088, FAX 305/451–4726). **Key West Business Guild (gay)** (✉ 728 Duval St., Box 1208, Key West 33041, ☎ 305/294–4603 or 800/535–7797, WEB www.gaykeywestfl.com). **Key West Gay and Lesbian Community Center** (✉ 1075 Duval St., Key West 33040, ☎ 305/292–3223, WEB www.glcckeywest.org). **Monroe Council of the Arts** (✉ 5100 College Rd., Box 717, Key West 33040, ☎ 305/294–4406 Key West; 305/743–0079 Middle Keys; 305/852–1469 Upper Keys, WEB www.keysarts.org). **Reef Relief Environmental Center & Store** (✉ 201 William St., Key West 33041, ☎ 305/294–3100).

7 PORTRAITS OF SOUTH FLORIDA

Miami: Magic City

Books and Movies

MIAMI: MAGIC CITY

Magic City. City of the Future. City of Dreams. Gateway to the Caribbean. Capital of South America. The New New York. These names and scores more have been coined for a city that clings to a strip of ancient coral sea bottom heaved up eons ago between the Gulf Stream and the Everglades. Known on the map and in the news as Miami, it was originally an Indian settlement, then an agricultural community purveying some odd root called "coontie," a backwater and a port for pirates and ship-scuttlers. Later, the 1920s boomtown was erased by a scourge called hurricane and entered a period of sleepy tourism. Those "Moon over Miami" days gave rise by the 1950s to an East Coast version of Las Vegas.

Things picked up some more in the 1960s, when Miami became a second home for thousands of Cubans fleeing Fidel Castro, and the city served as the staging area for the ill-fated Bay of Pigs invasion. That stormy decade went out with a bang, with protests in Miami Beach and race riots in Liberty City sparked by the presidential nomination of Richard Nixon at the 1968 Republican National Convention. The 1970s were the glory days of the hometown football team, the Dolphins, and then the 1980s kicked off with the Mariel boat lift of political refugees and purged prisoners from Cuba to South Florida. An explosion of immigration from South America, Latin America, and the Caribbean and, of course, the explosion of *Miami Vice* on television rounded out the decade. Enter the 1990s and more home teams— the Heat and Marlins and Panthers. South Beach was reborn as "SoBe," crammed with more models, more movie and fashion shoots, more art deco hotels, more outdoor cafés, and more retro fashion per square ft than anyplace else on Earth.

In a little more than 100 years of boom and bust, crime and punishment, high times and low, Miami has endured it all. Here, human cycles wax and wane like the tides that have lapped the shores of Biscayne Bay from the days long before time was invented.

Which brings us to the true source of the world's endless fascination with Miami: its natural beauty. Flora and fauna in exotic profusion, and beaches brushed by temperate breezes from an Atlantic riding high outside a sheltering reef, make it a paradise and a wellspring of living poetry: palm, hibiscus, bougainvillea. Anhinga, osprey, gull. Manatee, snapper, bonefish, grouper. Coral reef and hardwood hammock. Mangrove, banyan, and the fabled Dade County pine, so dense, the story goes, it takes two men to carry those two-by-fours. Mango, guava, litchi nut, grapefruit. Alligator and flamingo. Orange, lemon, lime.

Miami is a pleasure dome, but it is also a working city, a place of constant beginnings and renewal, a place where anything can happen—and often does. It is, as it always has been, a city of dreams. The late poet Richard Hugo once told a gathering of students that he had always lived on the edge in his profession and lifestyle, just as he had always lived on the edge of the continent, on one coast or another. "It's the perfect place for the writer," he said. "Out there on the edge, looking in, where you're able to observe things more clearly."

Hugo would have loved Miami, city on the edge, on the frontier; gateway between North and South, portal to the Caribbean, entry point for seekers of the American Dream. Contemporary commentators as diverse as Joan Didion (*Miami*), David Rieff (*Going to Miami*), and T. D. Allman (*Miami: City of the Future*) have agreed that the very future of the nation can be glimpsed from the vantage point of this city. As New York served as bellwether for a changing America at the beginning of the 20th century and Los Angeles did at midcentury, so Miami serves at the end of one century and the beginning of the next. Hugo would have loved the intellectual energy of it all, as wave after wave of new, revitalizing culture sweeps ashore. Miami is not a melting pot, but rather a rich stew, dizzying in its complexity.

A Miami commuter, stalled in an unaccountable traffic jam, stares in wonder as a young, bare-chested man races down the center line of a busy multilane boulevard, holding aloft a Nicaraguan flag the size of a small billboard. Buoyant strains of music trail in the young man's wake. There's a flatbed truck stopped in the intersection ahead, a troupe of musicians up there, blaring Latin rhythms at maximum volume, a cheering crowd gathered around. Nicaragua has just defeated Colombia in soccer, someone explains to the stalled commuter. Just an exhibition match in the Orange Bowl, a few miles away, but it's a big victory anyway, and normal life will have to wait a few minutes here in Miami. The stalled commuter reflects that, as reasons for being stuck in traffic go, this one is, at the very least, remarkable.

There's a certain chaos to life in a city of some 2 million that contains a full-blown colony of so many Latin American and Caribbean expatriates. But what a panoply of variety comes with the chaos: shops, markets, restaurants, consulates, and even ethnic driving schools devoted to serving a newly arrived populace. Within a 20-minute driving radius, places like these offer the old-timer (someone who's lived in Miami for more than a decade) a taste of another, and then another, culture. Some people might pick a place to live or to visit because it's all of a piece—no surprises, every warp and weave of the cultural fabric an indistinguishable part of the whole. Comfortable perhaps, and reassuring, but they won't find it in Miami.

Hugo would have treasured Miami's everyday poetry: the sights, sounds, smells, and tastes—and the touch of the Gulf Stream breeze. There might be millions of bodies milling about the metropolis, but there's always an avenue of escape. Live a lifetime in Miami, and the possibilities only multiply. Calm bay waters for sailing or for puttering about the shallows in a johnboat with a pole and some bait shrimp, prospecting for mangrove snapper. Find a friend or a willing captain for a high-powered cruise to Hemingway's beloved great blue Gulf Stream, where the fins and the swords of the great game fish still cross—all just a half hour out.

Say you're a country kid at heart, yearning for a fix of rustic—if that's the case, you head south. Fortify yourself with a breakfast of *huevos rancheros* at a modest South Miami-Dade storefront run by a Mexican family that came over to work the sprawling vegetable fields covering that part of Miami-Dade County. Another few miles south, you find yourself covering terrain as vast, unspoiled, and awesome as the African veldt. No lions lurking in the unpopulated "river of grass" that is Everglades National Park, of course, but don't tell your imagination that. Besides, once you get to Flamingo—the end of the road—and stare out over those boundless tidal flats at the thousands of meandering pink creatures that give the place its name, you'll forget about the lions anyway.

Locals like to make this trip in winter. For one thing, the mosquitoes are in hibernation. For another, you can stop off on the way home for a fresh-picked-strawberry shake and some home-baked goods at the stand an enterprising Amish family maintains every season, a place tucked alongside a country road as remote and Rockwellian as a Pennsylvania lane.

Another mood might send a person into Miami's heart, say, for lunch on bustling Calle Ocho—Southwest 8th Street—the main thoroughfare of Little Havana. Although Little Havana might now be more properly called Little Latin America, there are still any number of Cuban restaurants where veteran waitresses will guide the uninitiated toward *ropa vieja,* fried pork or grouper chunks, a chicken breast braised in lime juice, and some black beans and rice and diced onion to go with that, of course. To wash it down, maybe have a Hautey cerveza or two, now that the once-celebrated Cuban beer is again being produced, now stateside. Come to Little Havana in the evening and you can combine dinner with a visit to a club for a Rio-style revue or a knockout solo performance. Whether you watch Cuban chanteuse Albita belting out a tune or high-kicking beauties in Carmen Miranda getups, you'll swear you've slipped through a warp into another life and time. But it's really Miami, and there are still another three dozen cuisines and cultures to go.

No misunderstanding why Miami has been called America's Casablanca. In the same way bits of every Mediterranean culture found their way to that North African port, so has every Latin and Caribbean culture left its mark on modern-day Miami. Much as Casablanca did, Miami mixes the elegant and the raffish, the sophisticated and the casual. At one of the scores of sidewalk cafés on South Beach sidewalks, a pair of leggy models in bikini tops and cutoffs rollerblade up to a table, chatting in German. They plop down next to a group of suited businessmen hammering out the possibilities—in rapid-fire Spanish—of a convention hotel on the vacant property just over there, at the end of Ocean Drive, where barely a decade ago one might have snapped up a run-down pensioner's hostel for the price of an upscale automobile.

A T THE EDGE, there is always action, and there is the heat that comes with it. Where a decade ago there was only one professional sports team in South Florida, suddenly there are four, and it's no accident that the basketball club is named for that amalgam of climatological factors and plain old frictional force known as heat.

Of course, to some, being "on the edge" leads to edginess, what with all those cultures colliding and sometimes sending off sparks. Nothing like a session of the Miami-Dade County government for a lesson in pluralism, for example. This friction has captured the attention of a certain group of artists.

In the 1920s, the writers went off to Paris. In the late 1950s, the poets hung out in North Beach and Berkeley, the novelists took New York, and the most interesting among them were known as the Beats. Now, as a new century begins—apparently these things cycle every 40 years or so—there's another literary center and another group of writers scribbling away there: genus, *Miami*; species, *mystery writer*.

There's little doubt that Miami supports more crime, thriller, and mystery writers per capita than just about any other city in the country. There's Carl Hiaasen, James W. Hall, Edna Buchanan, Paul Levine, Barbara Parker, James Grippando, Carolina Garcia Aguilera, Vicki Hendricks, and Cherokee Paul MacDonald, not to mention yours truly. Elmore Leonard spends half the year down this way and sets about the same amount of his work in these parts. Although, sadly, John D. MacDonald, who gave us Travis McGee, and Charley Willeford, who gave us Hoke Moseley, have left us, and Doug Fairbairn (*Shoot, Street Eight*) is no longer writing, their work is still in print and swells the oeuvre significantly.

Not too long ago, *Tropic* magazine commissioned a spoof, a serialized mystery novel jestingly titled *Naked Came the Manatee*, to be penned in weekly installments by members of the Miami mystery crew. Within days, and long before the first word saw newsprint, three major publishing houses heard of the venture and entered into a bidding war that escalated well into the six figures, this for the rights to reprint within hard covers what is essentially an extended joke.

How to explain it? As James W. Hall likes to say, Miami history can be divided into three periods: 1) before *Miami Vice,* 2) during *Miami Vice,* and 3) after *Miami Vice.* It's not only a good joke, it is incisive commentary on what is going on here. The 1980s television series ("*Saturday Night Fever* on a Donzi ," as one wag dubbed it) not only revolutionized American television, but ingrained in our consciousness, worldwide and forevermore, the idea that danger, double-dealing, and flash flourish in Miami. The impact of *Miami Vice* is more than an accident of television programming. Viewers and readers are captivated by the beauty here, to be sure, as they are by the irony and the tragedy of violence in such paradise. And the attraction of Miami crime fiction, whether in print, on film, or on television, goes deeper.

Miami has become the American city of the future, the focal frontier town where immigrants stream in to settle, clash, and clamor up against all the interests that have been established before them. It is, above all, a city on the edge, where everything is up for grabs, where nothing has yet been decided, where the conflicts and the comminglings presage that which is to come for America as a whole.

South Florida's beauty represents paradise. Its open portals signify promise. The attendant and seemingly inescapable violence portends the difficulties faced by a nation that has been living on the quick since the first days of the republic. But the flip side is the sense of possibility that's palpable in the Miami air. There's a freshness here, a sense that no group's firmly in charge, that one person's dreams are as good as anyone else's, and just as likely to come true. In Miami. On the edge.

—*Les Standiford*

Les Standiford, one of Miami's crew of crime novelists, is the author of nine books, including Presidential Deal, Black Mountain, and Miami: City of Dreams.

BOOKS AND MOVIES

Books

Suspense novels that are rich in details about South Florida include Pulitzer Prize–winner Edna Buchanan's *Miami, It's Murder* and *Contents Under Pressure*; Les Standiford's *Done Deal,* about violence in the Miami construction business; former prosecuting attorney Barbara Parker's *Suspicion of Innocence*; Clifford Irving's *Final Argument*; Elmore Leonard's *La Brava*; John D. MacDonald's *The Empty Copper Sea*; Joan Higgins's *A Little Death Music*; and Charles Willeford's *Miami Blues.* James W. Hall features South Florida in many of his big sellers, such as *Mean High Tide,* the chilling *Bones of Coral,* and *Hard Aground.*

Peter Matthiessen's *Killing Mister Watson* re-creates turn-of-the-last-century lower southwest Florida. Look for *Princess of the Everglades,* a novel about the 1926 hurricane, by Charles Mink, and Carl Hiaasen's Florida-based books, including *Double Whammy, Lucky You,* and, most recently, *Sick Puppy.*

Other recommended titles include Roxanne Pulitzer's *Facade,* set against a backdrop of Palm Beach; Pat Booth's *Miami*; Sam Harrison's *Bones of Blue Coral* and *Birdsong Ascending*; T. D. Allman's *Miami*; Joan Didion's *Miami*; David Rieff's *Going to Miami*; *To Have and Have Not,* by Ernest Hemingway; *The Day of the Dolphin,* by Robert Merle; and *Their Eyes Were Watching God,* by Zora Neale Hurston.

Among recommended nonfiction books are *The Commodore's Story,* by Ralph Munroe and Vincent Gilpin, a luminous reminiscence about the golden years (prerailroad) of Coconut Grove; *Key West Writers and Their Homes,* by Lynn Kaufelt; *The Everglades: River of Grass,* by Marjory S. Douglas; and *Florida's Sandy Beaches,* University Press of Florida. Mark Derr's *Some Kind of Paradise* is an excellent review of the Florida's environmental follies; John Rothchild's *Up for Grabs: A Trip Through Time and Space in the Sunshine State,* equally good, is about Florida's commercial lunacy. Good anthologies include *The Florida Reader: Visions of Paradise* (Maurice O'Sullivan and Jack Lane, editors), *The Rivers of Florida* (Del and Marty Marth, editors), and *Subtropical Speculations: An Anthology of Florida Science Fiction* (Richard Mathews and Rick Wilber, editors).

A good companion to this guide, Fodor's *Compass American Guides: Florida* has handsome photos and historical, cultural, and topical essays.

Books that are also available on audiotape include Peter Dexter's *The Paperboy,* as well as several by Carl Hiaasen: *Native Tongue, Skin Tight, Stormy Weather, Strip Tease, Basket Case,* and *The Tourist Season,* his immensely funny declaration of war against the state's environment-despoiling hordes. For more on Miami's questionable politics and weird culture, pick up *Kick Ass,* a collection of Hiaasen's newspaper columns.

Movies

Greater Miami's ever-growing film business is visible as movie, fashion, and music video shoots take over the streets of South Beach, locations such as the Venetian Pool, or lush lots in Coconut Grove. Locals have come to take the street closings and detours in stride, but celebrity sightings are duly reported the next day in the *Miami Herald.*

Certainly Greater Miami's moviemaking industry has increased in stature since 1967, when Elvis Presley's *Clambake* was shot here (despite the appearance of mountains in some of the Miami scenes), and 1972, when Linda Lovelace's infamous *Deep Throat* gained notoriety. Recent movies at least partially filmed in South Florida include *Random Hearts,* with Harrison Ford; *Primary Colors,* with John Travolta and Emma Thompson; *Donnie Brasco,* with Johnny Depp and Anne Heche; *The Birdcage,* with Robin Williams and Nathan Lane; *Up Close and Personal,* with Robert Redford and Michelle Pfeiffer; and *Wrestling Ernest Hemingway,* with Robert Duvall and Shirley MacLaine.

The blockbuster gross-out comedy *There's Something About Mary,* with Cameron Diaz and Ben Stiller, was filmed at several South Florida locations. So was Jim Carrey's popular *Ace Ventura: Pet Detective. True Lies,* one of James Cameron's pre-*Titanic* megaeffects extravaganzas, captivated downtown Miami for days during filming of a helicopter mounted on a high-rise. Key scenes for critical dud *The Specialist,* with sometime Miami resident Sylvester Stallone and Sharon Stone, were shot at the Biltmore in Coral Gables.

Other films—panned by critics but sometimes providing escapist fun—include *Wild Things,* with Kevin Bacon and Neve Campbell; *Big City Blues,* with Burt Reynolds and Vivian Wu; *Fair Game,* with William Baldwin and Cindy Crawford; *Blood and Wine,* with Jack Nicholson and Jennifer Lopez; and the unfortunate film version of Carl Hiaasen's very funny novel *Strip Tease,* starring Demi Moore and Burt Reynolds.

For an in-depth study on Florida's role in the movies, check out *Hollywood East* (1992), by James Ponti.

INDEX

Fodor's Key to the Guides

America's guidebook leader publishes guides for every kind of traveler.
Check out our many series and find your perfect match.

Fodor's Gold Guides
America's favorite travel-guide series offers the most detailed insider reviews of hotels, restaurants, and attractions in all price ranges, plus great background information, smart tips, and useful maps.

Fodor's Road Guide USA
Big guides for a big country—the most comprehensive guides to America's roads, packed with places to stay, eat, and play across the U.S.A. Just right for road warriors, family vacationers, and cross-country trekkers.

COMPASS AMERICAN GUIDES
Stunning guides from top local writers and photographers, with gorgeous photos, literary excerpts, and colorful anecdotes. A must-have for culture mavens, history buffs, and new residents.

Fodor's CITYPACKS
Concise city coverage with a foldout map. The right choice for urban travelers who want everything under one cover.

Fodor's EXPLORING GUIDES
Hundreds of color photos bring your destination to life. Lively stories lend insight into the culture, history, and people.

Fodor's POCKET GUIDES
For travelers who need only the essentials. The best of Fodor's in pocket-size packages for just $9.95.

Fodor's To Go
Credit-card–size, magnetized color microguides that fit in the palm of your hand—perfect for "stealth" travelers or as gifts.

Fodor's FLASHMAPS
Every resident's map guide. 60 easy-to-follow maps of public transit, parks, museums, zip codes, and more.

Fodor's CITYGUIDES
Sourcebooks for living in the city: Thousands of in-the-know listings for restaurants, shops, sports, nightlife, and other city resources.

Fodor's AROUND THE CITY WITH KIDS
68 great ideas for family days, recommended by resident parents. Perfect for exploring in your own backyard or on the road.

Fodor's ESCAPES
Fill your trip with once-in-a-lifetime experiences, from ballooning in Chianti to overnighting in the Moroccan desert. These full-color dream books point the way.

Fodor's FYI
Get tips from the pros on planning the perfect trip. Learn how to pack, fly hassle-free, plan a honeymoon or cruise, stay healthy on the road, and travel with your baby.

Fodor's Languages for Travelers
Practice the local language before hitting the road. Available in phrase books, cassette sets, and CD sets.

Karen Brown's Guides
Engaging guides to the most charming inns and B&Bs in the U.S.A. and Europe, with easy-to-follow inn-to-inn itineraries.

Baedeker's Guides
Comprehensive guides, trusted since 1829, packed with A–Z reviews and star ratings.

At bookstores everywhere.   www.fodors.com/books